The 1619 Project

A NEW ORIGIN STORY

The 1619 Project

Edited by *NIKOLE HANNAH-JONES, CAITLIN ROPER,
ILENA SILVERMAN, and JAKE SILVERSTEIN*

ONE WORLD
New York

Published in the United States by One World, an imprint of Random House, a division of Penguin
Random House LLC, New York.

ONE WORLD and colophon are registered trademarks of Penguin Random House LLC.

Contains some material previously published in THE NEW YORK TIMES MAGAZINE in August 2019,
sometimes in different form.
Image credits and permissions are located on page 560.

LIBRARY OF CONGRESS CATALOGING-IN-PUBLICATION DATA
Names: Hannah-Jones, Nikole. | New York Times Company.
Title: The 1619 Project : a new origin story / created by Nikole Hannah-Jones and
The New York Times Magazine.
Description: First edition. | New York : One World, [2021] | Includes index. Identifiers: LCCN
2021019866 (print) | LCCN 2021019867 (ebook) | ISBN 9780593230572 (hardcover) | ISBN 9780593230589
(ebook)
Subjects: LCSH: Slavery—Political aspects—United States—History. | African-Americans—United
States—History. | United States—Race relations. | United States—Civilization. | 1619 Project.
Classification: LCC E441 .A15 2021 (print) | LCC E441 (ebook) | DDC 973—dc23
LC record available at https://lccn.loc.gov/2021019866
LC ebook record available at https://lccn.loc.gov/2021019867

Printed in the United States of America on acid-free paper

oneworldlit.com
randomhousebooks.com

2 4 6 8 9 7 5 3 1

FIRST EDITION

Design by Bobby Martin, Champions Design

To the more than thirty million descendants of American slavery

The poetry and fiction that appears on gray pages between the nonfiction chapters of this book occurs on a timeline that runs chronologically from 1619 to the present.

While the nonfiction chapters are not strictly chronological, they have been arranged with the historical narrative in mind.

Preceding each chapter is a photograph that relates to the topic of the essay. The individuals pictured are not well known; in some cases, their names have been lost to history.

CONTENTS

CONTENTS

CONTENTS

CONTENTS

CONTENTS

A NOTE ABOUT THIS BOOK

This book uses a variety of terms to describe aspects of the era of slavery. In almost every case, the editors have avoided the word "slave" to describe persons held in bondage; the alternate term "enslaved person" accurately conveys the condition without stripping the individual of his or her humanity. In some instances where it does not refer to a person (e.g., "slave state") and in some of the historical poetry and fiction, "slave" does appear.

The editors have also attempted to limit the use of terms that are sometimes used euphemistically, such as "plantation" or "master," or to substitute when possible other terms that more accurately convey the historical situation of enslavement. As this book contains the work of many different authors, some of them representing different scholarly fields, there remains some heterogeneity in how these terms are deployed.

—The Editors

I am the American heartbreak—
The rock on which Freedom
Stumped its toe
The great mistake
That Jamestown made
Long ago.

—Langston Hughes,
"American Heartbreak: 1619"

Origins

Nikole Hannah-Jones

I was maybe fifteen or sixteen when I first came across the date 1619. Whenever I think about that moment, my mind conjures an image of glowing three-dimensional numbers rising from the page. Of course, in reality, they were printed in plain black text on the cheap page of a paperback. Still, while the numbers did not literally glow, I remember sitting back in my chair and staring at the date, a bit confused, thrown off-kilter by an exhilarating revelation starting to sink in.

For as long as I can remember, I have been fascinated with the past. Even as a young girl, I loved watching documentaries and feature films about events that took place in a bygone era. As a middle school student, I read all of my dad's Louis L'Amour westerns and the entire *Little House* series because they transported me to the mythic American frontier. I loved sitting in my grandparents' basement, leafing through aged photo albums filled with square black-and-white images and asking questions about the long-dead relatives frozen in the frame. My favorite subjects in school were English and social studies, and I peppered my teachers with questions. History revealed the building blocks of the world I now inhabited, explaining how communities, institutions, relationships came to be. Learning history made the world make sense. It provided the key to decode all that I saw around me.

Black people, however, were largely absent from the histories I read. The vision of the past I absorbed from school textbooks, television, and the local history museum depicted a world, perhaps a wishful one, where Black people did not really exist. This history rendered Black Americans, Black people on all the earth, inconsequential at best, invisible at worst. We appeared only where unavoidable: slavery was mentioned briefly in the chapter on this nation's most deadly war, and then Black people disappeared again for a full century, until magically reappearing as Martin Luther King, Jr., gave a speech about a dream. This quantum leap served to wrap the Black experience up in a few paragraphs and a tidy bow, never really explaining *why*, one hundred years after the abolition of slavery, King had to lead the March on Washington in the first place.

We were not actors but acted upon. We were not contributors, just recipients. White people enslaved us, and white people freed us. Black people could choose either to take advantage of that freedom or to squander it, as our depictions in the media seemed to suggest so many of us were doing.

The world revealed to me through my education was a white one. And yet my intimate world—my neighborhood, the friends I rode the bus with for two hours each day to and from the schools on the white side of town, the boisterous bevy of aunts, uncles, and cousins who crowded our home for barbecues and card games—was largely Black. At school, I searched desperately to find myself in the American story we were taught, to see my humanity—our humanity—reflected back to me. I snatched *Roll of Thunder, Hear My Cry* from our elementary school library shelf because it was the one book with a Black girl on the cover. In high school, when my advanced placement English teacher assigned us a final project on a famous American literary figure, I wrote about the only Black poet I had been exposed to: Langston Hughes.

My public high school in Waterloo, Iowa, offered a one-semester elective called "The African American Experience," which I took my sophomore year. Only other Black kids filled the seats each day, and the only Black male teacher I'd ever have taught the course. Rail-thin and mahogany-skinned, with a booming laugh that revealed the wide gap between his front teeth, Mr. Ray Dial deftly navigated our class through the ancient Mali, Songhai, Nubian, and Ghana empires (it was he who taught me that "from here to Timbuktu" referred to an African center of learning), surveying the cultures and knowledge and civilizations that existed among African peoples long before Europeans decided that millions of human beings could be forced across the ocean in the hulls of ships and then redefined as property. He taught us about Richard Allen founding the first independent Black denomination on this soil, and how hard enslaved people fought for the legal right to do things every other race took for granted, such as reading or marrying or keeping your own children. He taught us about Black resistance and Black writers. He taught us about Martin but also Marcus and Malcolm and Mamie and Fannie.

Sitting in that class each day, I felt as if I had spent my entire life struggling to breathe and someone had finally provided me with oxygen. I feel a pang of embarrassment now when I recall my surprise that so many books existed about Black people and by Black people, that Black people had so much history that *could* be learned. I felt at once angry and empowered, and these dueling emotions drove an appetite for learning Black American history that has never left me. I began asking Mr. Dial for books to read beyond the assigned texts, devouring them, then asking for others.

"Dr. Hannah!" he exclaimed one day, flashing his trademark toothy grin as he put a book in my hands: *Before the Mayflower,* by the historian and journalist Lerone Bennett, Jr. As soon as I got home that afternoon, I sat down at our dining room table and pulled it from my book bag. A few dozen pages in, I read these words:

> She came out of a violent storm with a story no one believed. . . . A year before the arrival of the celebrated *Mayflower,* 113 years before the birth of George Washington, 244 years before the signing of the Emancipation Proclamation, this ship sailed into the harbor at Jamestown, Virginia, and dropped anchor into the muddy waters of history. It was clear to the men who received this "Dutch man of War" that she was no ordinary vessel. What seems unusual today is that no one sensed how extraordinary she really was. For few ships, before or since, have unloaded a more momentous cargo.[1]

Wait.

I had assumed that *Before the Mayflower* referred to Black people's history in Africa before they were enslaved on this land. Tracing my fingers across the words, I realized that the title evoked not a remote African history but an *American* one. African people had lived here, on the land that in 1776 would form the United States, since the *White Lion* dropped anchor in the year 1619. They'd arrived one year before the iconic ship carrying the English people who got the credit for building it all.

Why hadn't any teacher or textbook, in telling the story of Jamestown, taught us the story of 1619? No history can ever be complete, of course. Millions of moments, thousands of dates weave the tapestry of a country's past. But I knew immediately, viscerally, that this was not an innocuous omission. The year white Virginians first purchased enslaved Africans, the start of American slavery, an institution so influential and corrosive that it both helped create the nation and nearly led to its demise, is indisputably a foundational historical date. And yet I'd never heard of it before.

Even as a teenager, I understood that the absence of 1619 from mainstream history was intentional. People had made the choice not to teach us the significance of the year. And it followed that many other facts of history had been ignored or suppressed as well. What else hadn't we been taught? I was starting to figure out that the histories we learn in school or, more casually, through popular culture, monuments, and political speeches rarely teach us *the* facts but only *certain* facts.

In the United States, few examples better reveal this than how we're taught about the foundational American institution of slavery. A 2018 report by the Southern Poverty Law Center (SPLC) called *Teaching Hard History* found that in 2017 just 8 percent of U.S. high school seniors named slavery as the central cause of the Civil War, and less than one-third knew that it had taken a constitutional amendment to abolish it. The majority of high school students can't tell you that the famous abolitionist Frederick Douglass had once been enslaved; nor can they define the Middle Passage, which led to the forced migration of nearly 13 million people across the Atlantic and transformed—or, arguably, enabled—the existence of the United States.[2]

Considering the confusing and obfuscatory way school curricula tend to address the institution of slavery, this is unsurprising. Myriad examples exist. As recently as six years ago, a McGraw-Hill world geography textbook referred to African people brought to the Americas in the bowels of slave ships not as the victims of a forced migration who were violently coerced into labor but as "workers," a word that implies consensual and paid labor.[3] Within the last decade, Alabama social studies courses for second graders listed Harriet Tubman, the woman who became famous for escaping slavery and then helping others do the same, as an "exemplary" American without ever mentioning the words "slave" or "slavery."[4] In Texas, which, because of its large population, plays an outsized role in shaping the content of national textbooks, the Republican-led state board of education approved curriculum standards that equated the Confederate general Thomas "Stonewall" Jackson, who fought against the United States government, with Douglass as examples of "the importance of effective leadership in a constitutional republic."[5]

School curricula generally treat slavery as an aberration in a free society, and textbooks largely ignore the way that many prominent men, women, industries, and institutions profited from and protected slavery.[6] Individual enslaved people, as full humans, with feelings, thoughts, and agency, remain largely invisible, but for the occasional brief mention of Douglass or Tubman or George Washington Carver.

One of the reasons American children so poorly understand the history and legacy of slavery is because the adults charged with teaching them don't know it very well, either. A 2019 *Washington Post*–SSRS poll found that only about half of American adults realize that all thirteen colonies engaged in slavery.[7] Even educators struggle with basic facts of history, the SPLC report found: only about half of U.S. teachers understand that enslavers dominated the presidency in the decades after the founding and would dominate the U.S. Supreme Court and the U.S. Senate until the Civil War.[8] Of more than seventeen hundred social studies teachers surveyed in the SPLC study, "a bare majority say they feel competent to teach about slavery. Most say that the available resources and preparation programs have failed them."[9] As the renowned slavery historian Ira Berlin wrote in an essay in *Slavery and Public History: The Tough Stuff of American Memory,* "The simple truth is that most Americans know little about the three-hundred-year history of slavery in mainland North America with respect to peoples of African descent and almost nothing of its effect on the majority of white Americans."[10]

Berlin, who was white and who died in 2018, contributed to a wave of important research and scholarship in the past fifty years, much of it by Black historians, that challenged those prevailing views about American history. The work of these scholars, who were often inspired to ask new questions about our past by focusing on primary source material inaccessible to or ignored by previous generations, has made clear the central role that slavery and anti-Blackness played in the development of our society and its institutions. To argue otherwise, among professional historians, is now widely understood to be anachronistic and ahistorical.

But this scholarship, so uncontroversial among historians, has often struggled to permeate mainstream understanding of American history, which is still wedded to a mythology of our founders as unimpeachable heroes and our founding as divine event. There is, as the historian Jelani Cobb told me, a "gap between the academy and the world. So while scholars of color and progressive white scholars have spent decades fighting and, for the most part, winning these battles in the academy and in the profession, they've remained isolated from the rest of the world."[11] As a result, the American public has an outdated and vague sense of the past. And yet the 2019 *Washington Post* poll found that despite their meager knowledge of slavery, two-thirds of Americans believe that the legacy of slavery still affects our society today. They can see and feel the truth of this fact—they just haven't learned a history that helps them understand how and why.[12]

"We are committing educational malpractice," says Hasan Kwame Jeffries, a historian at Ohio State University.[13] Jeffries served as chair of the advisory board that produced the Southern Poverty Law Center's *Teaching Hard History* report. "Our preference for nostalgia and for a history that never happened is not without consequence," Jeffries writes. "Although we teach [students] that slavery happened . . . in some cases, we minimize slavery's significance so much that we render its impact—on people and on the nation—inconsequential." This, Jeffries continues, "is profoundly troubling" because it leaves Americans ill-equipped to understand racial inequality today, and that, in turn, leads to intolerance, opposition to efforts to address racial injustice, and the enacting of laws and policies detrimental to Black communities and America writ large. "Our narrow understanding of the institution . . . prevents us from seeing this long legacy and leads policymakers to try to fix people instead of addressing the historically rooted causes of their problems," he notes.[14]

In other words, we all suffer for the poor history we've been taught.

At the start of 2019, two and a half decades after I first learned of the year 1619 in the pages of a book my teacher gave me, most Americans still did not know that date. As the four-hundred-year anniversary approached that August, I understood that, like so much of the uncomfortable history of our country, this momentous date would likely come and go with little acknowledgment of its significance. But by 2019, I was no longer a curious teenager attending a public high school in a small Midwestern town. I now worked at one of the most powerful media institutions in the world. I wanted to try to use that global platform to help force a confrontation with our past and the foundations upon which this country was built.

I made a simple pitch to my editors: *The New York Times Magazine* should create a special issue that would mark the four-hundredth anniversary by exploring the unparalleled impact of African slavery on the development of our country and its continuing impact on our society. The issue would bring slavery and the contributions of Black Americans from the margins of the American story to the center, where they belong, by arguing that slavery and its legacy have profoundly shaped modern American life, even as that influence had been shrouded or discounted. The issue would pose and answer these questions: What would it mean to reframe our understanding of U.S. history by considering 1619 as our country's origin point, the birth of our defining contradictions, the seed of so much of what has made us unique? How might that reframing change how we understand the unique problems of the nation *today*—its stark economic inequality, its violence, its world-leading incarceration rates, its shocking segregation, its political divisions, its stingy social safety net? How might it help us understand the country's best qualities, developed over a centuries-long struggle for freedom, equality, and pluralism, a struggle whose DNA could also be traced to 1619? How would looking at contemporary American life through this lens help us better appreciate the contributions of Black Americans—not only to our culture but also to our democracy itself? I wanted to do for other Americans what reading Lerone Bennett's book, and absorbing decades of scholarship on Black American history, had done for me. I wanted people to know the date 1619 and to contemplate what it means that slavery predates nearly every other institution in the United States. I wanted them to be transformed by this understanding, as I have been.

As soon as I received the green light, I reached out to nearly two dozen scholars covering the fields of history, economics, law, sociology, and the arts who specialize in slavery and its legacy and convened a brainstorming session at *The New York Times*. I asked them to help us produce a list of modern American institutions and phenomena that could be traced back to slavery. We filled a whiteboard with ideas, and then over the next six months, the magazine worked to create a project that would try to unflinchingly tell a four-hundred-year story that connected the past to the present.

Every day, I felt the weight of this responsibility and the height of the stakes. I immersed myself in the sorrow of the suffering of millions of Black people and the depravity of those who visited that suffering upon them, but also in the audacious resistance and resilience of Black Americans. I read every word of the project, I looked at every image. On the day when we printed the pages of the magazine and tacked them to the wall to review before publishing the issue, I turned to my dear friend Wesley Morris, who had written an essay about music for the project. We wrapped our arms around each other and sobbed.

The night before publication, sleep taunted, refusing to grant me grace. As I lay in bed, my mind flicked back to that teenage girl in high school, the daughter and granddaughter of people born onto a repurposed slave-labor camp in the deepest South, people who could not have imagined their progeny would one day rise to a position to bring forth such a project. I also worried: What if we told a story that centered slavery and Black Americans and, well, no one read it? What if despite all of our work, no one actually cared?

On Sunday, August 18, the day we published the magazine in print, tweets and Instagram posts and videos began popping up all over the country. People were telling stories of going to store after store in search of it only to find all the copies of the Sunday *New York Times* sold out. A man in North Carolina posted a video of himself looking giddy, his fingers wrapped around the magazine, saying he'd driven miles but he'd finally snagged a copy. Parents stashed copies away to pass on to their children. Incarcerated people wrote to me, seeking the issue. Over the coming weeks, readers started holding 1619 reading clubs, and the #1619 hashtag on Instagram showed teachers decorating their classrooms with 1619 Project art and families baking 1619 Project cookies. Across the country, at libraries, museums, cultural centers, and schools, people gathered to talk about the 1619 Project and slavery's impact on America. Then–U.S. Senate minority leader Chuck Schumer spoke about the project in the Capitol Visitor Center's Emancipation Hall. He related a story I told in my opening essay about my father and the American flag. In the run-up to the 2020 presidential election, Democrats seeking the nomination mentioned the project in their speeches.

Educators in all fifty states began teaching a curriculum based on the project, and I met hundreds of high school students who, somewhat breathlessly, recounted the same off-kilter sense of exhilaration while reading the 1619 Project that I had felt reading *Before the Mayflower*. Black students, especially, told me that for the first time in their lives, they'd experienced a feeling usually reserved for white Americans: a sense of ownership of, belonging in, and influence over the American story. Arterah Griggs, who attended a public high school in Chicago, the first district in the country to make the project part of its curriculum, told a reporter from the *Chicago Sun-Times* what the project helped her realize: "We were the founding fathers. We put so much into the U.S. and we made the foundation." Another student, Brenton Sykes, said, "Now that I'm aware of the full history of America without it being whitewashed or anything, it kind of makes me see things in a different light. I feel like I have to carry myself better because I have what my ancestors went through."[15]

I will never forget the woman I met after giving a talk in New Orleans, one of the most brutal slave-trading cities in our country. Almost ninety years old, she came up and hugged me, wiping her eyes as she thanked me for helping birth a project that had allowed her to release the shame that comes with being told that the only thing Black people have contributed to this country is our brute labor. "I always knew the truth," she told me. "But I didn't have the facts of what happened."

On one of my last trips before the pandemic, I brought my nine-year-old daughter, Najya, with me to a talk I gave at the university that Thomas Jefferson founded in Charlottesville, Virginia, a university built largely by enslaved people to educate the sons of the men who owned them. Before the lecture, we took a walk through the town square, where we saw the site of a slave auction block, and we marveled, her hand in mine, at some numbers recently scrawled on the lamppost by the placard marking the spot: 1619.

As the reach of the 1619 Project grew, so did the backlash. A small group of historians publicly attempted to discredit the project by challenging its historical interpretations and pointing to what they said were historical errors. They did not agree with our framing, which treated slavery and anti-Blackness as foundational to America. They did not like our assertion that Black Americans have served as this nation's most ardent freedom fighters and have waged their battles mostly alone, or the idea that so much of modern American life has been shaped not by the majestic ideals of our founding but by its grave hypocrisy. And they especially did not like a paragraph I wrote about the motivations of the colonists who declared independence from Britain.

"Conveniently left out of our founding mythology," that paragraph began, "is the fact that one of the primary reasons the colonists decided to declare their independence from Britain was because they wanted to protect the institution of slavery." Later, in response to other scholars who believed we hadn't been specific enough and to clarify that this sentence had never been meant to imply that every single colonist shared this motivation, we changed the sentence to read "some of the colonists." But that mattered little to some of our critics. The linking of slavery and the American Revolution directly challenged the cornerstone of national identity embedded in our public history, the narratives taught to us in elementary schools, museums and memorials, Hollywood movies, and in many scholarly works as well.[16]

The assertions about the role slavery played in the American Revolution shocked many of our readers. But these assertions came directly from academic historians who had been making this argument for decades. Plainly, the historical ideas and arguments in the 1619 Project were not new.[17] We based them on the wealth of scholarship that has redefined the field of American history since at least the 1960s, including Benjamin Quarles's landmark book *The Negro in the American Revolution*, first published in 1961; Eric Foner's *Reconstruction: America's Unfinished Revolution, 1863–1877*; Annette Gordon-Reed's *The Hemingses of Monticello: An American Family*; and Alan Taylor's *The Internal Enemy: Slavery and War in Virginia, 1772–1832*. What seemed to provoke so much ire was that we had breached the wall between academic history and popular understanding, and we had done so in *The New York Times,* the paper of record, in a major multimedia project led by a Black woman.

The project came under intense scrutiny, as should any major work that seeks to disrupt conventional narratives. Those outside the academy tend to think of history as settled, as a simple recounting of what events happened on what date and who was involved in those incidents. But while history *is* what happened, it is also, just as important, how we *think* about what happened and what we unearth and choose to remember about what happened. Historians gather at conferences, present research, and argue, debate, and quibble over interpretations of fact and emphasis all the time. Scholars regularly publish articles that analyze, question, or disagree with the respected and peer-reviewed work of their colleagues. As Mary Ellen Hicks, a historian and Black studies scholar, wrote in a Twitter thread, "The discussions about the 1619 project . . . have made me realize that historians may have missed an opportunity to demystify the production of scholarly knowledge for the public. The unsexy answer is that we produce constantly evolving interpretations, not facts." Hicks explained that historians can look at the same set of facts—President Lincoln's public remarks on colonization, for example—and come to different conclusions about whether his speeches reflected his personal views on repatriating Black Americans outside the United States or that he was simply engaging in a political strategy to avoid scaring away white moderates who opposed both slavery *and* Black citizenship. "The reality is," she wrote, "a valid interpretation could come down on both sides of the issue."[18]

But some who opposed the 1619 Project treated a few scholars' disagreements with certain claims and arguments as justification to dismiss the entire work as factually inaccurate, even as other equally prominent scholars defended and confirmed our facts and interpretations.

In truth, most of the fights over the 1619 Project were never really about the facts. The Princeton historian Allen C. Guelzo, a particularly acerbic critic, published several articles that denounced the 1619 Project for treating "slavery not as a blemish that the Founders grudgingly tolerated . . . not as a regrettable chapter in the distant past, but as a living, breathing pattern upon which all American social life is based." Guelzo then made clear that the source of his antipathy was not just *what* the project was saying but *who* was saying it: "It is the bitterest of ironies that the 1619 Project dispenses this malediction from the chair of ultimate cultural privilege in America, because in no human society has an enslaved people suddenly found itself vaulted into positions of such privilege, and with the consent—even the approbation—of those who were once the enslavers."[19]

In the months after the project was published, the opposition went from broadsides from critics to government attempts to prevent the project from being taught in schools and universities. In July 2020, a prominent U.S. senator, Tom Cotton, introduced a bill called the "Saving American History Act," which sought to strip federal funding from public schools teaching the 1619 Project.[20] More than a dozen Republican legislatures have introduced similar bills, including in my home state of Iowa and my dad's home state of Mississippi. (Both of those bills failed; the Cotton bill went nowhere.)

In September 2020, after a summer that saw the largest protest movement for racial justice in our country's history, President Trump, who'd railed against the 1619 Project, used an executive order to hastily convene what he called the 1776 Commission. This group spent weeks assembling its report, which Trump released as one of the last acts of his presidency, on Martin Luther King Day. Written without input from any scholars who specialize in American history, it sought to reinforce the exceptional nature of our country, and to put forth a "patriotic" narrative that downplays racism and inequality and emphasizes a unity predicated on seeing slavery, segregation, and ongoing racial injustice as aberrations in a fundamentally just and exceptionally free nation.[21]

The commission faced wide condemnation, with forty-seven groups representing academic historians signing a statement drawn up by the American Historical Association that accused the commission of issuing a report "written hastily in one month after two desultory and tendentious 'hearings,' without any consultation with professional historians of the United States" and failing "to engage a rich and vibrant body of scholarship that has evolved over the last seven decades."[22] President Joe Biden rescinded the executive order in one of his first acts in office.[23] But by July 2021, regulations enforcing the ideology of the 1776 Commission and/or seeking to ban the teaching of the 1619 Project and teaching about racism had either been enacted or were being considered in eighteen states.[24] But Republican legislators in Texas introduced the 1836 Project, named after the year Texas declared independence from Mexico in order to found a slaveholding republic.[25] That project seeks to establish a "patriotic education" in public schools. In other words, many people want laws passed that would ensure that students continue to learn the version of American history that American children have always been taught.

What these bills make clear is that the fights over the 1619 Project, like most fights over history, at their essence are about power. "Why would we expect the nation's power structure even to acknowledge, much less come to terms with, such a dark and formative chapter in our collective family history?" the renowned historian Peter H. Wood wrote in a 1999 paper on slavery and denial. "After all, as several eminent academics have recently reminded us, 'nations need to control national memory, because nations keep their shape by shaping their citizens' understanding of the past.' "[26]

As Frederick Douglass wrote in his 1892 autobiography, "The story of the master never wanted for narrators. The masters, to tell their story, had at call all the talent and genius that wealth and influence could command. They have had their full day in court. Literature, theology, philosophy, law and learning have come willingly to their service, and if condemned, they have not been condemned unheard."

Our part, as Douglass said, "has been to tell the story of the slave."[27]

After the special issue's publication, as people across the political spectrum debated the 1619 Project, we began to think about turning it into a book. With more time, we knew, we could create a more fully realized version of the project, with additional contributors exploring a broader range of subjects. We wanted to learn from the discussions that surfaced after the project's publication and address the criticisms some historians offered in good faith, using them as road maps for further study. For example, we expanded the essay on slavery and American capitalism to include important material on the constitutional bases of property rights. We added more nuance to a section on the evolution of President Lincoln's racial views in my opening essay, and we included more information in other chapters about slavery elsewhere in the Americas that predated 1619. We also added seven new essays written by historians, on subjects ranging from slavery and the Second Amendment to settler colonialism and the expansion of slavery to how the Haitian Revolution helped to deeply embed fear of Black Americans in the national psyche.[28] And we substantially expanded, revised, and refined the project's original ten essays and added a final essay, written by me, on the subject of economic justice, which brings the book to a close with a look to future solutions. The literary timeline that imagines moments in the history of slavery, anti-Blackness, resistance, and struggle has also been expanded. It now consists of thirty-six original works of fiction and poetry by some of this nation's most profound Black writers, which through a chorus of voices try to tell a story of the past four hundred years. The book opens with a poem by Claudia Rankine on the arrival of the *White Lion* in 1619 and closes with a poem by Sonia Sanchez on the murder of George Floyd and the 2020 protest movement it spawned. We also added a series of photographic portraits, some from the distant past, some contemporary, of regular Black Americans, the descendants of American slavery, who have lived through all this history with resilience, beauty, pride, and a humanity that is too often unrecognized.

Just like the original project, the book relies heavily on historical scholarship, but is not a conventional history. Instead, it combines history with journalism, criticism, and imaginative literature to show how history molds, influences, and haunts us in the *present*. This essential feature of American life, the way our unreconciled past continues to affect our present, has been made starkly apparent in the two years since we first published the 1619 Project. During that time, the nation witnessed the police killings of George Floyd, Breonna Taylor, and many others, highlighting the long legacy of state violence against Black Americans. When the Covid-19 pandemic broke out, Black people suffered disproportionately severe health outcomes, mirroring an enduring legacy of racially driven medical and health disparities: in 2020, Covid-19 slashed the life expectancy of Black men by three years and eliminated ten years of progress toward narrowing the life-expectancy gap between Black and white Americans. And there were the efforts by President Donald Trump and his followers to undermine a free and fair 2020 presidential election—one where high Black turnout in key heavily Black cities would largely determine the results. That, along with the introduction of hundreds of voter suppression laws by Republican lawmakers, demonstrated once again the belief among some white people that Black and other non-white Americans are illegitimate voters, a racist and undemocratic position that has plagued the country since the end of the Civil War. Another echo of the past: in the face of this attempted disenfranchisement, Black voters organized and overcame efforts to suppress their votes in an election where many feared that the nation was careening toward authoritarianism, showing yet again the vital and unparalleled role of Black people in preserving our democracy.

The legacy of 1619 surrounds us, whether we acknowledge it or not. This is why, in assembling this book, we have described the history it offers as an origin story. Like all origin stories, this one seeks to explain our society to itself, to give some order to the series of dates, actions, and individuals that created a nation and a people. In doing so, we argue that much about American identity, so many of our nation's most vexing problems, our basest inclinations, and its celebrated and unique cultural contributions spring not from the ideals of 1776 but from the realities of 1619, from the contradictions and the ideological struggles of a nation founded on both slavery and freedom.

The story of Black America cannot be disentangled from the story of America, and our attempts to do so have forced us to tell ourselves a tale full of absences, evasions, and lies, one that fails to satisfactorily explain the society we live in and leaves us unable to become the society we want to be.

The typical origin story of the United States begins with scrappy colonists inspired by noble ideals declaring independence and launching the American Revolution. In this version, "the American Revolution is a timeless story of the defense of freedom and the rights of all humankind," write the editors of the anthology *Remembering the Revolution: Memory, History, and Nation Making from Independence to the Civil War.* For centuries, this story has worked as a powerful source of national cohesion for white Americans. "Today Americans most often recall tales of a Revolution led by a group of 'demigods' who towered above their fellow colonists, led them into a war against tyranny, and established a democratic nation dedicated to the proposition that all men were endowed by their creator with equal rights," the editors continue. "Above all, it is the story of the founding of a nation."[29]

Many historians have been seduced by the desire to manage the story of our founding, protecting our identity as an exceptional, fundamentally just nation, the freest in the history of the world. "Our memory of the past is often managed and manipulated," according to the historian Gary B. Nash.[30] The revolutionary period remains "a sacred relic."[31] "Even for many white liberal historians, the Revolution is the last thing that people let go of," says Woody Holton, a scholar whose work centers on the role of slavery in the American Revolution.[32]

But for Black Americans, the traditional origin story has never rung true. Black Americans understand that we have been taught the history of a country that does not exist. What I have heard again and again since the original project was published is that the 1619 Project, for many people, finally made America make sense.

As the Howard University historian Ana Lucia Araujo writes in *Slavery in the Age of Memory,* "despite its ambitions of objectivity," public history is molded by the perspectives of the most powerful members of society. And in the United States, public history has often been "racialized, gendered and interwoven in the fabric of white supremacy."[33] Yet it is still posed as objective. "History is the fruit of power," writes Michel-Rolph Trouillot in *Silencing the Past: Power and the Production of History,* and "the ultimate mark of power may be its invisibility; the ultimate challenge, the exposition of its roots."[34] In exposing our nation's troubled roots, the 1619 Project challenges us to think about a country whose exceptionalism we treat as the unquestioned truth. It asks us to consider who sets and shapes our shared national memory and what and who gets left out. As the Pulitzer Prize–winning historian David W. Blight writes in *Race and Reunion: The Civil War in American Memory*, our nation's "glorious remembrance" is "all but overwhelmed by an even more glorious forgetting."[35]

Not all Americans have been so willing to forget. Black Americans, because of our particular experience in this land, because we have borne the brunt of this forgetting, are less given to mythologizing America's past than white Americans. How do you romanticize a revolution made possible by the forced labor of your ancestors, one that built white freedom on a Black slavery that would persist for another century after Jefferson wrote "We hold these truths to be self-evident, that all men are created equal"? I put it something like this a few years ago, while reporting on school resegregation in Alabama: white Americans desire to be free of a past they do not want to remember, while Black Americans remain bound to a past they can never forget.[36]

This is why the memories and perspectives of Black Americans have so often been marginalized and erased from the larger narrative of this nation: we are the stark reminders of some of its most damning truths. Eight in ten Black people would not be in the United States were it not for the institution of slavery in a society founded on ideals of freedom. Our nation obscures and diminishes this history because it shames us. During the Revolution and in the decades after, Black Americans such as Sojourner Truth, John Brown Russwurm, and Ida B. Wells used the rhetoric of freedom and universal rights espoused by white colonists and enshrined in our founding documents to reveal this nation's grave hypocrisies. In 1852, as white Americans commemorated this nation's founding, Frederick Douglass reminded them that millions of their countrymen and -women suffered in absolute bondage:

What, to the American slave, is your 4th of July? I answer: a day that reveals to him, more than all other days in the year, the gross injustice and cruelty to which he is the constant victim. To him, your celebration is a sham; your boasted liberty, an unholy license; your national greatness, swelling vanity; your sounds of rejoicing are empty and heartless; your denunciation of tyrants brass fronted impudence; your shouts of liberty and equality, hollow mockery; your prayers and hymns, your sermons and thanksgivings, with all your religious parade, and solemnity, are, to him, mere bombast, fraud, deception, impiety, and hypocrisy—

a thin veil to cover up crimes which would disgrace a nation of savages. There is not a nation on the earth guilty of practices, more shocking and bloody, than are the people of the United States, at this very hour.[37]

During World War II, as white Americans prided themselves on the fight to liberate Europe, Black Americans launched the Double V for Victory campaign to remind this nation that Black soldiers who were fighting abroad in a Jim Crow military also sought victory against the fascism they experienced at home. And more recently, when millions of white Americans expressed shock that violent insurrectionists would try to overturn an election in the "world's oldest democracy," Black Americans reminded them that violent efforts to subvert U.S. democracy were not novel nor unprecedented and that true democracy has been attempted in this country only since 1965, when after a bloody and deadly decades-long Black freedom struggle, Congress passed the Voting Rights Act.

Our myths have not served us well. We are the most unequal of the Western democracies. We incarcerate our citizens at the highest rates. We suffer the greatest income inequality. Americans' life spans are shorter than those of the people in the nations we compare ourselves to. The 1619 Project seeks to explain this present-day reality and challenge these myths not to tear down or further divide this country, as some critics suggest, but so that we can truly become the country we already claim to be. Whether we grapple with these ugly truths or not, they affect us still. The 1619 Project is not the only origin story of this country—there must be many—but it is one that helps us fundamentally understand the nation's persistent inequalities in ways the more familiar origin story cannot. With this project, we work toward a country that, in the words of Douglass, "shall not brand the Declaration of Independence as a lie."[38] If we are a truly great nation, the truth cannot destroy us.

On the contrary, facing the truth liberates us to build the society we wish to be. One of the criticisms of the project is that we focus too much on the brutality of slavery and our nation's legacy of anti-Blackness. But just as central to the history we are highlighting is the way that Black Americans have managed, out of the most inhumane circumstances, to make an indelible impact on the United States, serving as its most ardent freedom fighters and forgers of culture. The enslaved and their descendants played a central role in shaping our institutions, our intellectual traditions, our music, art, and literature, our very democracy. The struggle of Black Americans to force this country to live up to its professed ideals has served as inspiration to oppressed people across the globe. Too long have we shrouded and overlooked these singular contributions. They form a legacy of which *every* American should be proud.

I am reminded of a story that the famed sociologist, civil rights activist, and writer W.E.B. Du Bois related in his 1939 sociological study *Black Folk Then and Now*. He recounted watching a talk to the graduating class of Atlanta University in which the scholar Franz Boas regaled the students with stories of the Black kingdoms of Africa. Du Bois had by then earned a PhD from Harvard University, the first Black person to ever do so, and was teaching at historically Black Atlanta University at the time. "I was too astonished to speak," he recalled. "All of this I had never heard and I came then and afterwards to realize how the silence and neglect of science can let truth utterly disappear or even be unconsciously distorted."[39]

Du Bois had described the same experience I would endure some five decades later in high school. But perhaps new generations will tell a different story. Last year, after many years without any courses dedicated to Black history, my old high school began once again offering "The African American Experience." Our history is still optional: it remains an elective. But in that class, students now study the work of a girl from Waterloo who took that course all those years ago and would remain forever changed by the date 1619.

The 1619 Project

August 1619

A ship arrives near Point Comfort, a coastal port in the English colony of Virginia, which was founded twelve years earlier. The *White Lion* carries some twenty to thirty captive Africans, who are traded to the Virginia colonists for provisions, making them the first enslaved Africans in the English colonies that will become the United States. Among them are a man named Anthony and a woman named Isabella, who gives birth several years later to a child named William.

The White Lion

Claudia Rankine

Even dawn begins before its beginning
and still, in the tale of the beginning
that forestalls an end, let's agree—
a long way from the Kingdom of Ndongo,
two English ships pirate a third,
the Portuguese *São João Bautista*,
and split up its human cargo. The first
vessel to land at Point Comfort
on the James River enters history,
and thus history enters Virginia
as *twenty and odd Negroes*
are *off-loaded* from the *White Lion*,
the man-of-war carrying movables,
Blacks stripped to Christian names.
The *White Lion*, carrying
a man-made fate, makes landfall,
while Virginia, beginning
its system of land grants, whitens
white indentured servants
by bestowing on them property,
whitens whites who, through
the act of trading victuals
for the stolen renamed unfree
transatlantic labor (*their griefs
transient, in reason much inferior*),

are inaugurated master as if
any Black would, as if
anyone could, surrender
their value, human,
to tobacco, sugar, and cotton,
the yield of Powhatan lands;
while Virginia writes itself colonial,
filling its first property
ledger with *twenty and odd*
of the uprooted twelve million,
including Anthony and Isabella,
who, out of the *White Lion*'s hold,
step into the whole of history
to give birth to the first child
to take the first steps, provisionally,
toward African American
in Virginia—William, so called,
born free, they say, though
all the while Virginia's wiles
still sail across centuries,
leaving a wake with each
recurring swell, drowning out
what Anthony and Isabella said
to William about love, in love,
in Kimbundu or Kikongo, as if
we could stop knowing
how to know what we know.

Milton Hannah, Nikole Hannah-Jones's father, Germany, 1960s

CHAPTER 1

Democracy

NIKOLE HANNAH-JONES

My dad always flew an American flag in our front yard. The blue paint on our two-story house was sometimes chipped; the fence, or the rail by the stairs, or the front door might occasionally fall into disrepair, but that flag always flew pristine. Our corner lot, which had been redlined by the federal government, was along the river that divided the Black side from the white side of our Iowa town. At the edge of our lawn, high on an aluminum pole, soared the flag, which my dad would replace with a new one as soon as it showed the slightest tatter.

My dad was born into a family of sharecroppers on a white plantation in Greenwood, Mississippi, where Black people bent over cotton from can't-see-in-the-morning to can't-see-at-night, just as their enslaved ancestors had done not long before. The Mississippi of my dad's youth was an apartheid state that subjugated its Black residents—almost half of the population[1]—through breathtaking acts of violence. White residents in Mississippi lynched more Black people than those in any other state in the country,[2] and the white people in my dad's home county lynched more Black residents than those in any other county in Mississippi, for such "crimes" as entering a room occupied by white women, bumping into a white girl, or trying to start a sharecroppers union.[3] My dad's mother, like all the Black people in Greenwood, could not vote, use the public library, or find work other than toiling in the cotton fields or toiling in white people's houses. In the 1940s, she packed up her few belongings and her three small children and joined the flood of Black Southerners fleeing to the North. She got off the Illinois Central Railroad in Waterloo, Iowa, only to have her hopes of the mythical Promised Land shattered when she learned that Jim Crow did not end at the Mason-Dixon Line.

Grandmama, as we called her, found a Victorian house in a segregated Black neighborhood on the city's east side and then found the work that was considered Black women's work no matter where Black women lived: cleaning white people's homes. Dad, too, struggled to find promise in this land. In 1962, at age seventeen, he signed up for the army. Like many young men, he joined in hopes of escaping poverty. But he went into the military for another reason as well, a reason common to Black men: Dad hoped that if he served his country, his country might finally treat him as an American.

The army did not end up being his way out. He was passed over for opportunities, his ambition stunted. He would be discharged under murky circumstances and then labor in a series of service jobs for the rest of his life. Like all the Black men and women in my family, he believed in hard work, but like all the Black men and women in my family, no matter how hard he worked, he never got ahead.

So when I was young, that flag outside our home never made sense to me. How could this Black man, having seen firsthand the way his country abused Black Americans, the way it refused to treat us as full citizens, proudly fly its banner? My father had endured segregation in housing and school, discrimination in employment, and harassment by the police. He was one of the smartest people I knew, and yet by the time I was a work-study student in college, I was earning more an hour than he did. I didn't understand his patriotism. It deeply embarrassed me.

I had been taught, in school, through cultural osmosis, that the flag wasn't really ours, that our history as a people began with enslavement, and that we had contributed little to this great nation. It seemed that the closest thing Black Americans could have to cultural pride was to be found in our vague connection to Africa, a place we had never been. That my dad felt so much honor in being an American struck me as a marker of his degradation, of his acceptance of our subordination.

Like most young people, I thought I understood so much, when in fact I understood so little. My father knew exactly what he was doing when he raised that flag. He knew that our people's contributions to building the richest and most powerful nation in the world were indelible, that the United States simply would not exist without us.

In August 1619, just twelve years after the English settled Jamestown, Virginia, one year before the Puritans landed at Plymouth, and some 157 years before English colonists here decided they wanted to form their own country, the Jamestown colonists bought twenty to thirty enslaved Africans from English pirates.[4] The pirates had stolen them from a Portuguese slave ship whose crew had forcibly taken them from what is now the country of Angola. Those men and women who came ashore on that August day mark the beginning of slavery in the thirteen colonies that would become the United States of America. They were among the more than 12.5 million Africans who would be kidnapped from their homes and brought in chains across the Atlantic Ocean in the largest forced migration in human history until the Second World War.[5] Almost two million did not survive the grueling journey, known as the Middle Passage.[6]

Before the abolition of the international slave trade, more than four hundred thousand of those 12 million enslaved Africans transported to the Americas would be sold into this land.[7] Those individuals and their descendants transformed the North American colonies into some of the most successful in the British Empire. Through backbreaking labor, they cleared territory across the Southeast. They taught the colonists to grow rice and to inoculate themselves against smallpox.[8] After the American Revolution, they grew and picked the cotton that, at the height of slavery, became the nation's most valuable export, accounting for half of American goods sold abroad and more than two-thirds of the world's supply.[9] They helped build the forced labor camps, otherwise known as plantations, of George Washington, Thomas Jefferson, and James Madison, sprawling properties that today attract tens of thousands of visitors from across the globe captivated by the history of the world's greatest democracy.[10] They laid the foundations of the White House and the Capitol, even cast with their unfree hands the *Statue of Freedom* atop the Capitol dome.[11] They lugged the heavy wooden ties of the railroads that crisscrossed the South and carried the cotton picked by enslaved laborers to textile mills in the North, fueling this country's Industrial Revolution. They built vast fortunes for white people in both the North and the South—at one time, the second-richest man in the nation was a Rhode Island "slave trader."[12] Profits from Black people's stolen labor helped the young nation pay off its war debts and financed some of our most prestigious universities. The relentless buying, selling, insuring, and financing of their bodies and the products of their forced labor would help make Wall Street a thriving banking, insurance, and trading sector, and New York City a financial capital of the world.[13]

But it would be historically inaccurate to reduce the contributions of Black people to the vast material wealth created by our bondage. Black Americans have also been, and continue to be, foundational to the idea of American freedom. More than any other group in this country's history, we have served, generation after generation, in an overlooked but vital role: it is we who have been the perfecters of this democracy.

The United States is a nation founded on both an ideal and a lie. Our Declaration of Independence, approved on July 4, 1776, proclaims that "all men are created equal" and "endowed by their Creator with certain unalienable rights." But the white men who drafted those words did not believe them to be true for the hundreds of thousands of Black people in their midst. A right to "Life, Liberty and the pursuit of Happiness" did not include fully one-fifth of the new country. Yet despite being violently denied the freedom and justice promised to all, Black Americans believed fervently in the American creed. Through centuries of Black resistance and protest, we have helped the country live up to its founding ideals. And not only for ourselves—Black rights struggles paved the way for every other rights struggle, including women's and gay rights, immigrant and disability rights.

Without the idealistic, strenuous, and patriotic efforts of Black Americans, our democracy today would look very different; in fact, our country might not be a democracy at all.

One of the very first to die in the American Revolution was a Black and Indigenous man named Crispus Attucks who himself was not free. In 1770, Attucks lived as a fugitive from slavery, yet he became a martyr for liberty in a land where his own people would remain enslaved for almost another century.[14] In every war this nation has waged since that first one, Black Americans have fought—today we are the most likely of all racial groups to serve in the United States military.

My father, one of those many Black Americans who answered the call, knew what it would take me years to understand: that the year 1619 is as important to the American story as 1776. That Black Americans, as much as those men cast in alabaster in the nation's capital, are this nation's true founding fathers. And that no people has a greater claim to that flag than we do.

In June 1776, Thomas Jefferson sat at his portable writing desk in a rented room in Philadelphia and penned those famous words:[15] "We hold these truths to be self-evident, that all men are created equal, that they are endowed by their Creator with certain unalienable Rights, that among these are Life, Liberty and the pursuit of Happiness." For the last two and a half centuries, this fierce assertion of the fundamental and natural rights of humankind to freedom and self-governance has defined our global reputation as a land of liberty. As Jefferson composed his inspiring words, however, a teenage boy who would enjoy none of those rights and liberties waited nearby to serve at his master's beck and call. His name was Robert Hemings, and he was the half-

Black brother of Jefferson's wife, Martha, born to her father and a woman he enslaved.[16] It was common and profitable for white enslavers to keep their half-Black children in slavery. Jefferson, who would later hold in slavery his own children by Hemings's sister Sally, had chosen Robert Hemings, from among about 130 enslaved people who worked on the forced-labor camp he called Monticello, to accompany him to Philadelphia and ensure his every comfort as he drafted the text making the case for a new republican union based on the individual rights of men.[17]

At the time, one-fifth of the population within the thirteen colonies struggled under a brutal system of racial slavery that through the decades would be transformed into an institution unlike anything that had existed in the world before.[18] Chattel slavery was not conditional but racial. It was heritable and permanent, not temporary, meaning generations of Black people were born into it and passed their enslaved status on to their children. Enslaved people were not recognized as human beings but were considered property that could be mortgaged, traded, bought, sold, used as collateral, given as a gift, and disposed of violently. Jefferson's fellow white colonists knew that Black people were human beings, but over time the enslavers created a network of laws and customs, astounding in both their precision and their cruelty, designed to strip the enslaved of every aspect of their humanity. As the abolitionist William Goodell would write, "If any thing founded on falsehood might be called a science, we might add the system of American slavery to the list of the strict sciences."[19]

The laws, known as slave codes, varied from colony to colony, state to state, and over time. Some prohibited enslaved people from legally marrying; others prevented them from learning to read or from meeting privately in groups. Enslaved people had no claim to their own children, who could be bought, sold, or traded away from them on auction blocks alongside furniture and cattle, or behind storefronts that advertised NEGROES FOR SALE. Enslavers and the courts did not honor kinship ties to mothers, siblings, cousins. In most courts, the enslaved held no legal standing. Enslavers could rape or murder their "property" without legal consequence. In the eyes of the law, enslaved people could own nothing, will nothing, and inherit nothing. They were legally tortured, including those working for Jefferson. They could be worked to death, and often were, to produce exorbitant profits for the white people who owned them.

Yet in making the argument against Britain's tyranny, one of the colonists' favorite rhetorical devices was to claim that *they* were the slaves—to Britain. "One need not delve far into the literature of the Revolution to find out that, of all words, the one that persistently, most contentiously, and most flexibly drove the era's rhetorical engine was slavery," writes Peter A. Dorsey, a scholar of literature of the American Revolution, in *Common Bondage*.[20] George Washington, in 1774, argued of the British that "those from whom we have a right to seek protection are endeavouring by every piece of Art and despotism to fix the Shackles of Slavery upon us."[21] At the time he wrote those words, Washington derived his wealth and influence from the forced slave labor of more than 120 human beings, in addition to the men, women, and children that had been passed on to his wife after the death of her first husband.

It's useful to remember the situation in the colonies at the time in order to understand why evoking slavery proved so powerful. The colonies had not yet united to form a new nation. They remained thirteen distinct jurisdictions with their own leadership and individual charters and relationships with Britain. They had differing economic, agricultural, and social practices—a white Bostonian did not naturally feel an alliance with a white South Carolinian. Yet in the period leading up to the Revolution, burdened by rising debt to the motherland, higher taxes, and an intermittent recession, many white colonists felt their status deteriorating.[22] The wealthy, educated men who led the revolt against Britain needed to unify the disparate colonists across social class and region. For those leaders, the comparison to slavery constituted a powerful rhetorical tool. "The Crisis is arrivd when we must assert our Rights, or Submit to every Imposition that can be heap'd upon us; till custom and use, will make us as tame, & abject Slaves, as the Blacks we Rule over with such arbitrary Sway," Washington warned in an August 1774 letter to his friend and neighbor Bryan Fairfax.[23]

It was precisely because white colonists so well understood the degradations of actual slavery that the metaphor of slavery held so much power to consolidate their disparate interests: no matter a colonist's politics, background, or class, by being white, he could never fall as low as the Black people who were held in bondage. As the scholar Patricia Bradley puts it in *Slavery, Propaganda, and the American Revolution*, "Once transposed into metaphor, slavery could serve to unite white colonists of whatever region under a banner of white exclusivity."[24] The decision to deploy slavery as a metaphor for white grievances had devastating consequences for those who were actually enslaved: it helped ensure that abolition would *not* become a revolutionary cause, Bradley argues. Instead, the true institution of slavery would endure for nearly a century after the Revolution.

But Black people held their own ideas about freedom and independence and would become their own force in fomenting the Revolution. No one voluntarily submits to slavery. Enslaved people had always resisted. They broke tools, slowed down their work, and self-emancipated by stealing themselves away. They also did what the white colonists themselves advocated: they took up arms against their oppressors to secure their freedom. White colonists lived in constant fear of insurrections by the enslaved living among them, and with reason: the years leading up to the Revolution were defined by the frequent plotting and carrying out of revolts by enslaved people in the mainland and across the Caribbean. As tensions rose between the Crown and the colonists, the British exploited colonists' concerns about their "internal enemy," and the enslaved shrewdly exploited the fight between white colonists and their British rulers. The enslaved had but one loyalty: their freedom. And they used the conflict to organize and conspire against the colonists as early as 1774, running away to join British troops and presenting themselves at British forts.[25] Over the course of the war, thousands of enslaved people would join the British—far outnumbering those who joined the Patriot cause.

One act in particular would alter the course of the Revolution. The fighting had not yet reached the Southern colonies when, in April 1775, seeking to suppress the rebellion, Virginia's royal governor, John Murray, the Earl of Dunmore, warned the colonists that if they took up arms there, he would "declare Freedom to the Slaves, and reduce the City of Williamsburg to Ashes."[26] Enslaved people did not wait for Dunmore to make good on that threat. By the hundreds they liberated themselves and ran to the British troops. One man, Joseph Harris, escaped in July and joined Dunmore, who had fled to a Royal Navy ship after his efforts to suppress the rebellious colonists put him in danger of being captured. Harris, prized by his enslaver as a pilot with considerable seafaring knowledge of the Chesapeake Bay, aided the British in their attack that fall in Hampton. It was there, directly across the water from the place where the first twenty to thirty Angolans had been sold into slavery in 1619, that enslaved fugitives joined the British in the first Southern battle of the American Revolution.[27] That next month, Dunmore issued a proclamation offering freedom to any enslaved person belonging to a Patriot if he fled his enslaver and joined Dunmore's "Ethiopian Regiment."[28]

An enslaver himself, Dunmore was no abolitionist. He issued his proclamation as a war tactic, an approach Abraham Lincoln used again nearly ninety years later. Just as enslaved people during the Civil War fled to the side they thought offered the best chance of freedom and inspired the Emancipation Proclamation, enslaved people running away to the British during the Ameri-

can Revolution inspired Dunmore's proclamation, which, in turn, further provoked the actions of enslaved people in Virginia and elsewhere. Rumors of
rebellions spread across the colony, many of them true as enslaved people
plotted and sought their freedom.

Dunmore's proclamation infuriated white Virginians, making revolutionaries out of them. "All over Virginia, observers noted, the governor's freedom
offer turned neutrals and even loyalists into patriots," writes the historian
Woody Holton in *Forced Founders*.[29] Grievances against the British had already
been stacking up for white Virginians. They'd opposed the Stamp Act and
were angry at the Crown's efforts to restrict their taking of Indian lands and
to tamp down on molasses smuggling intended to subvert a royal edict that
forced the colonists to purchase the molasses they needed to make rum from
Britain's Caribbean colonies. And their resentment had already been stoked
by a British high court ruling about slavery three years earlier. In 1772, the
court decided the case of James Somerset, an enslaved man from Virginia,
who claimed freedom when his owner brought him to Britain. The British
judge decided in Somerset's favor, proclaiming that British common law did
not allow slavery on the soil of the mother country—even as Britain was investing in it and profiting from it in her Caribbean and North American colonies.

Though limited, the Somerset ruling sent reverberations through the colonies, where newspapers reported it widely. "Although the ruling did not apply
there, colonial masters felt shocked by the implication that their property
system defied English traditions of liberty," the historian Alan Taylor writes in
his Pulitzer Prize–winning book *The Internal Enemy: Slavery and War in Virginia, 1772–1832*.[30] The colonists took the ruling as an insult, as signaling that
they were of inferior status, and feared that it would encourage their most
valuable property to slow away to Britain seeking freedom.

In early 1775, James Madison, who operated a slave-labor camp in Orange
County, Virginia, reported hearing a rumor that British Parliament had introduced a bill to emancipate the colonies' enslaved. In addition, a report from
the Virginia House of Burgesses accused British officials of contemplating a
"most diabolical" scheme to "offer Freedom to our Slaves, and turn them
against their Masters."[31] Both further enflamed colonists already worried
about the British encroaching on their "property" rights.

At first, founders such as Jefferson, Washington, John Hancock, and John
Adams had constituted "restorers and not reformers," Holton told me. "There
is a huge difference between being angry and joining a protest and wanting to
declare independence. Two events in 1775 turn the rebellion into a revolution.

For men like John Adams, it was the battles of Lexington and Concord. For men like Washington, Jefferson, and Madison, the Dunmore Proclamation ignited the turn to independence."[32]

Virginia's slaveholding elite had grown paranoid. Fears of enslaved people plotting and executing revolts ran rampant, and an alliance between the British and the enslaved men and women who the white colonists already feared would seek every opportunity to slit their throats proved too much. White Virginians morphed from "restorers" to revolutionaries. "If we never had slavery, that takes away many of the things that push the South to independence," Holton told me. "I think they would have done what other British colonies did, which was stay in the empire." The specter of their most valuable property absconding to take up arms against them "did more than any other British measure to spur uncommitted white Americans into the camp of rebellion," wrote the historian Gerald Horne in *The Counter-Revolution of 1776*.[33]

And yet none of this is part of our founding mythology, which conveniently omits the fact that one of the primary reasons some of the colonists decided to declare their independence from Britain was because they wanted to protect the institution of slavery. They feared that liberation would enable an abused people to seek vengeance on their oppressors. In many parts of the South, Black people far outnumbered white people. The wealth and prominence that allowed Jefferson, at just thirty-three, and the other founding fathers to believe they could successfully break off from one of the mightiest empires in the world came in part from the dizzying profits generated by chattel slavery. So they also understood that abolition would have upended the economies of both the North and the South.

The truth is that we might never have revolted against Britain if some of the founders had not understood that slavery empowered them to do so; nor if they had not believed that independence was required in order to ensure that the institution would continue unmolested. For this duplicity—claiming they were fighting for freedom while enslaving a fifth of the people—the Patriots faced burning criticism both at home and abroad. As Samuel Johnson, an English writer opposed to American independence, quipped, "How is it that we hear the loudest yelps for liberty among the drivers of Negroes?"[34]

The founders recognized this hypocrisy. As Jefferson sat down in that rented room in Philadelphia in 1776 to draft our founding document, he initially tried to argue that slavery wasn't the colonists' fault. Instead, he blamed the king of England for forcing the vile institution on the unwilling colonists, called trafficking in human beings a crime, and, in a reference to Lord Dunmore's proclamation, railed against the Crown for stoking insurrections by the enslaved. In the end, the other congressmen struck the passage, which many understood called unwanted attention to an unjust system that was already a source of division among the colonies.

Congress retained only one reference to slavery in the final version of the Declaration, which directly addressed the rebellions by enslaved people that the British, including Dunmore, were fomenting. It came at the very end of the long list of grievances against the king, insisting: "He has excited domestic insurrections amongst us."[35] As several historians have pointed out, unlike modern writing, which often places the most important information toward the top, during the colonial period, listing this grievance last in the document indicated its importance.

"Thomas Jefferson spoke for other white Americans when he stated, in the largest and angriest complaint in the Declaration of Independence, that Dunmore's emancipation proclamation was a major cause of the American Revolution," Holton writes.[36] Or as the historian Michael Groth put it, "In one sense, slaveholding Patriots went to war in 1775 and declared independence in 1776 to defend their rights to own slaves."[37]

"Having justified a bloody revolution on the grounds of a national belief in human freedom, Americans call their history a freedom story," the historian James Oliver Horton writes in *Slavery and Public History*. "For a nation steeped in this self-image, it is embarrassing, guilt-producing, and disillusioning to consider the role that race and slavery played in shaping the national narrative."[38] To address these discomfiting facts, we have created a founding mythology that teaches us to think of the "free" and "abolitionist" North as the heart of the American Revolution. Schoolchildren learn that the Boston Tea Party sparked the Revolution and that Philadelphia was home to the Continental Congress, the place where intrepid men penned the Declaration and Constitution. But while our nation's founding documents were written *in* Philadelphia, they were mainly written *by* Virginians.

White sons of Virginia initiated the drafting of the Declaration of Independence, the Constitution, and the Bill of Rights. The primary authors were all enslavers. For the first fifty years of our nation, Southerners served as president for all but twelve years, and most of them were Virginians. No place shaped the Revolution and the country it birthed more than Virginia. And no place in the thirteen colonies was as strongly shaped by slavery. At the time of the Revolution, Virginia stood as the oldest, largest, wealthiest, and most influential of the colonies. It was Virginia that introduced African slavery into

British North America, just twelve years after the first English settlers arrived. It was Virginia that first enshrined racialized chattel slavery into law, excluding Black people from all civic life and setting a precedent followed throughout the colonies. And it was Virginia tobacco, cultivated and harvested by enslaved workers, that was exported to help finance the Revolution.

Following Bacon's Rebellion in 1676, where an alliance of white and Black indentured servants and enslaved Africans rose up against Virginia's white elite, the colony passed slave codes to permanently enshrine legal and social distinctions between Black and white residents that ensured that all white people, no matter their status, permanently existed in a status above all Black people. These laws divided exploited white workers from exploited Black workers by designating people of African descent as "hereditary slaves" who would serve in bondage for life. "We normally say that slavery and freedom are opposite things—that they are diametrically opposed," the historian Ira Berlin said. "But what we see here in Virginia in the late seventeenth century, around Bacon's Rebellion, is that freedom and slavery are created at the same moment."[39]

Virginia and the rest of the American South constituted one of just five "great slave societies" in the *history of the world,* according to the historian David W. Blight.[40] This meant that the colony did not simply engage in slavery as many nations had for centuries before; it created a culture where, as Blight puts it, "slavery affected everything about society," its social relationships, laws, customs, and politics.[41] And that is why we simultaneously deify Virginians such as Washington, Madison, and Jefferson as champions of freedom while marginalizing the slaveholding region they came from as exceptionally backward, as not reflective of the real America.

By the period of the Revolution, white Virginian elites had traded their reliance on white laborers for the more economically profitable and less politically troublesome enslaved African labor. In 1776, Virginia held 40 percent of all enslaved people in the mainland colonies. As a result, white free laborers and tenant farmers numbered too few in Virginia to challenge the white men in power. The historian Edmund S. Morgan argues in his classic book *American Slavery, American Freedom* that well-off white Virginians, most of whom enslaved people, could champion a form of republican representative government defined by the absence of a formal ruling class or monarchy without threatening their own status as elites for one simple reason: they knew that the system of slavery meant that most of the poor in Virginia were enslaved, so they had no legal rights and could never participate in politics.

The slave codes helped to ensure that poorer white Virginians felt relatively empowered. "Many of the European-descended poor whites began to identify themselves, if not directly with the rich whites, certainly with being white," the historian Robin D. G. Kelley said. "And here you get the emergence of this idea of a white race as a way to distinguish themselves from those dark-skinned people who they associate with perpetual slavery."[42] Whiteness proved a powerful unifying elixir for the burgeoning nation. Whether laborer or elite planter, "neither was a slave. And both were equal in not being slaves."[43] And so it served the interests of both groups to defend slavery.

Slavery was not a *necessary* ingredient for the founders' belief in Republican equality, Morgan writes, but in Virginia and the other Southern colonies, it proved *the* ingredient. It is, therefore, not incidental that ten of this nation's first twelve presidents were enslavers. In fact, some might argue that this nation was founded not as a democracy but as a slavocracy.

Even so, the founders were deeply conflicted over slavery. So when it came time to draft the Constitution, the framers carefully constructed a document that preserved and protected slavery without ever using the word. In the key texts for framing our republic, the founders did not want to explicitly acknowledge their hypocrisy. They sought instead to shroud it. The Constitution contains eighty-four clauses. Six deal directly with the enslaved and their enslavement, as the historian David Waldstreicher demonstrates, and five more hold implications for slavery. The Constitution protected the "property" of those who enslaved Black people, prohibited the federal government from intervening to end the importation of enslaved people from Africa for a term of twenty years, allowed Congress to mobilize the militia to put down insurrections by the enslaved, and forced states that had outlawed slavery to turn over enslaved people who had escaped and sought refuge there.[44]

During the Constitution's ratification in the 1780s, a few bold Americans of both races sustained a new abolitionist movement. They considered the Constitution deceitful. "The words [are] dark and ambiguous; such as no plain man of common sense would have used," wrote the abolitionist Samuel Bryan. They "are evidently chosen to conceal from Europe, that in this enlightened country, the practice of slavery has its advocates among men in the highest stations."[45]

This ambivalence about slavery would haunt the nation, as those both for and against slavery would seize on the hallowed document to justify their views. As Frederick Douglass would explain in 1849, the Constitution bound the nation "to do the bidding of the slave holder, to bring out the whole naval and military power of the country, to crush the refractory slaves into obedience to their cruel masters."[46] The nation's most ardent and prominent abolitionist, Douglass had escaped slavery in 1838 and then spent the next three decades fighting to free the rest of his people. He characterized the Constitution as so "cunningly" framed that "no one would have imagined that it recognized or sanctioned slavery. But having a terrestrial, and not a celestial origin, we find no difficulty in ascertaining its meaning in all the parts which we allege relate to slavery. Slavery existed before the Constitution. . . . Slaveholders took a large share in making it." Two years later, Douglass announced a "change in opinion," believing that a stronger political argument could be made not by condemning our founding document for supporting slavery but by claiming that slavery was antithetical to the Constitution and that the Constitution was, in fact, as he would go on to argue, a "glorious liberty document."[47]

Indeed, when the South seceded from the Union, white Confederates believed *they* were the inheritors of the founders' revolutionary legacy and upholders of the true Constitution. Jefferson Davis gave his second inaugural address as president of the Confederate States of America on George Washington's birthday, vowing that the Confederacy would "perpetuate the principles of our Revolutionary fathers. The day, the memory, and the purpose seem fitly associated. . . . We are in arms to renew such sacrifices as our fathers made to the holy cause of Constitutional liberty."[48]

Even the fact that the Constitution allowed for Congress to prohibit the external slave trade after a twenty-year period, beginning in 1808, which is often held up as proof of the anti-slavery sentiment of the framers, can be seen in some respects as self-serving. At the time the Constitution was written, enslaved Black people accounted for about 40 percent of the population in Virginia, and in many places in the colony, the enslaved outnumbered white people. Many white Virginians fretted that continuing to import Africans would produce a frighteningly dangerous ratio for a white population well aware of the possibility of deadly insurrections.

These fears were borne out just a few years later in the Caribbean. In the 1790s, another successful revolution occurred, one that terrified rather than inspired the nation's leaders: enslaved people in the colony of Saint-Domingue—which was the most lucrative colony in the world at the time and later became known as Haiti—rose up and overthrew their French enslavers in the largest and most successful rebellion of enslaved people in the history of the Western Hemisphere.[49] What would become known as the Haitian Revolution financially devastated Napoleon and, amid a sea of slave colonies, established the first free Black republic in the Americas.[50]

Further, years of tobacco growing had depleted the soil, and landowners like Jefferson were turning to crops that required less labor, such as wheat. That meant they needed fewer enslaved people to turn a profit. White Virginians, therefore, stood to make money by cutting off the supply of new people from Africa and instead filling the demand in the Deep South for enslaved labor by selling their surplus laborers to the cotton and sugar forced-labor camps in Georgia and South Carolina.

Jefferson himself considered the people he enslaved in the coldest economic terms, saying he calculated that a "woman who brings a child every two years as more profitable than the best man of the farm. What she produces is an addition to capital, while his labors disappear in mere consumption."[51]

So, in 1808, during Jefferson's presidency, when the Constitution's prohibition on banning the international slave trade expired, Congress had already voted to outlaw the trade and the new law took effect immediately. But cutting off the importation of Africans created a horrific second Middle Passage in which hundreds of thousands of enslaved people were sold from the Upper South to the Lower. The domestic human trade tore apart about one-third of all first marriages between the enslaved and, over time, ripped millions of children from their parents. Between the 1830s and the Civil War, Virginia alone sold between 300,000 and 350,000 enslaved people south, nearly as many as all of the Africans sold into the United States over the course of slavery.[52]

With independence, the founding fathers could no longer blame slavery on Britain. The sin became this nation's own, and so, too, the need to cleanse it.[53] The shameful paradox of continuing chattel slavery in a nation founded on individual freedom, scholars today assert, led to a further consolidation of whiteness across class, religious, and ethnic lines, and a hardening of the racial caste system. American democracy had been created on the backs of unfree Black labor.[54] Blackness came to define whiteness—and whiteness defined American democracy prior to the Civil War.

This ideology, reinforced not just by laws but increasingly by racist science and literature, maintained that Black people came from an inferior race, a belief that allowed white Americans to live with their betrayal. By the early 1800s, according to the legal historians Robert J. Cottrol, Raymond T. Diamond, and Leland B. Ware, white Americans, whether they engaged in slavery or not, "had a considerable psychological as well as economic investment in the doctrine of Black inferiority."[55] While liberty was the unalienable right of the people who would be considered white, enslavement and subjugation became the natural station of people who had any discernible drop of "Black" blood.

Racist justifications for slavery gained ground during the mid-nineteenth century. The majority of the Supreme Court enshrined this thinking in the law in its 1857 Dred Scott decision, declaring that Black people, whether enslaved or free, came from a "slave" race. This made them permanently inferior to white people and, therefore, incompatible with American democracy. Democracy existed for citizens, and the "Negro race," the court ruled, was "a separate class of persons," one the founders had "not regarded as a portion of the people or citizens of the Government" and who had "no rights which the white man was bound to respect."[56] This belief, that Black people were not merely enslaved but a slave race, is the root of the endemic racism we cannot purge from this nation to this day. If Black people could not ever be citizens, if they were a caste apart from all other humans, then they did not require the rights bestowed by the Constitution, and the "we" in the "We the People" was not a lie.

On August 14, 1862, a mere five years after the nation's highest court declared that no Black person could be an American citizen, President Abraham Lincoln met with a group of five esteemed free Black men at the White House. It was one of the few times that Black people had ever been invited to the White House as guests. The men, part of Washington's small Black elite, had been selected by their religious and civic organizations to represent Black Americans.[57] The Civil War had been raging for more than a year, and Black abolitionists had been pressuring Lincoln to end slavery. Entering the White House, these men must have felt a sense of great anticipation and pride.

The war was not going well for Lincoln. Britain was weighing whether to intervene on the side of the Confederacy, and the Union struggled to recruit enough new white volunteers. Meanwhile, enslaved people were fleeing their forced-labor camps, serving as spies, sabotaging Confederate installations, and pleading to take up arms for the Union cause as well as their own. Inspired by Black Americans' self-emancipation, the president decided he was going to issue a proclamation to emancipate all enslaved people in the Confederate states as a tactic to deprive the Confederacy of its labor force.

But Lincoln worried about the consequences of the radical step toward abolition. Like many white Americans, he opposed slavery as a cruel system at odds with American ideals, but he also opposed Black equality. And he feared that a proclamation calling for the emancipation of enslaved people in the rebel states would alienate white moderates who supported a war to maintain the Union but were not willing to fight over slavery. His political career had shown him the limits of what white American voters would tolerate. During the 1850s, Lincoln never could have won election in Illinois, a virulently racist state, had he embraced racial equality. Prior to becoming president, as a lawyer and politician in Illinois, Lincoln himself had believed that free Black people amounted to a "troublesome presence" incompatible with a democracy intended only for white people. "Free them, and make them politically and socially our equals?" he had asked just a few years before the Civil War. "My own feelings will not admit of this; and if mine would, we well know that those of the great mass of white people will not."[58]

And so, Lincoln decided that the same document that would emancipate millions of enslaved people in rebel territory would also call for them, once free, to voluntarily leave their country and resettle elsewhere. This idea, known as "colonization," had been circulating since the 1790s, and counted among its proponents presidents such as Jefferson and James Monroe. In 1816, a group of white enslavers and politicians in Washington, D.C., created the American Colonization Society (ACS) to promote the removal of free Black people, who would be encouraged to leave the United States and resettle in West Africa. The ACS soon had chapters in much of the country, alongside other local colonization organizations. It drew many adherents who were fearful of the growing population of free Black people following the American Revolution. They believed colonization could rid the nation of free Black people while protecting the institution of slavery. But some who opposed slavery embraced colonization, too. Many white Americans across the political spectrum believed Black people held no place in American society as free citizens, and some abolitionists—Black and white—did not think free Black people would ever know real freedom here.

Lincoln had first publicly voiced support for colonization in 1852, and as president, in 1861, he'd asked his secretary of the interior to research a plan to colonize Black people on the western coast of what would become Panama.[59] By 1862, as the Union struggled, he'd begun to worry that he would lose support for emancipation, a necessary war strategy, if he did not pair it with a colonization scheme. That day in August, as the five Black men arrived at the White House, they were greeted by the towering Lincoln and a man named James Mitchell, who eight days before had been installed in the newly created post of commissioner of emigration. One of Mitchell's first tasks in that role had been to call the meeting with a delegation of Black leaders, some of whom supported colonization, to sell the idea. After exchanging a few niceties, Lincoln informed his guests that Congress had appropriated funds—some $600,000—to ship Black people, once freed, to another country.

"Why should they leave this country? This is, perhaps, the first question for proper consideration," Lincoln told his visitors. "You and we are different races. . . . Your race suffers very greatly, many of them, by living among us, while ours suffer from your presence. In a word, we suffer on each side."[60]

You can imagine the heavy silence in that room as the weight of what the president had said settled upon these Black men. It was 243 years to the month since the first of their ancestors had arrived on these shores—before Lincoln's family, long before most of the white people insisting that this was not their country. The Union had entered the war not to end slavery but to keep the South from splitting off, yet Black men wanted to fight to restore the Union and liberate their people. And now Lincoln was blaming them for the war, and urging them to persuade the Black population to leave their native land. "Although many men engaged on either side do not care for you one way or the other . . . without the institution of slavery and the colored race as a basis, the war could not have an existence," the president told them. "It is better for us both, therefore, to be separated."[61]

As Lincoln closed the remarks, Edward Thomas, the delegation's chairman, informed the president that they would consult on his proposition.[62] "Take your full time," Lincoln said. "No hurry at all."[63]

Black Americans denounced the meeting. Frederick Douglass, perhaps the greatest American this country has ever produced, called Lincoln's colonization scheme "a safety valve . . . for white racism" and said that the meeting "expresses merely a desire to get rid of" Black Americans. That August meeting was the only time Lincoln took his colonization proposal directly to Black Americans. The next month, in September 1862, he issued a preliminary Emancipation Proclamation that advocated colonization, and in his annual address to Congress in December, he called for a constitutional amendment to aid colonization, which became Lincoln's last known public call to colonize Black Americans.

On January 1, 1863, Lincoln issued the final version of the Emancipation Proclamation. It no longer included the mention of colonization, and it also provided for something Black leaders had long advocated for: the ability for Black men to enlist in the Union and fight for their freedom. Eventually, some two hundred thousand Black Americans would serve in the Union, accounting for one in ten Union soldiers. An astounding 78 percent of free Black military-age men living in free states would serve in the Union army, even as they faced greater risk than white soldiers. Confederate troops often killed Black soldiers rather than capture them and also enslaved Black war captives.[64] Thousands of Black women also contributed to the war effort, serving as cooks and nurses and spies, and withdrawing their valuable labor from

Confederates by escaping to Union lines. About one in five Black soldiers died in the war, mirroring the percentage of white soldiers, and Lincoln acknowledged that Black contributions helped turn the tide in favor of the Union.[65]

That's because enslaved people knew something about resistance and revolution. The cost to Black soldiers who fought in the war, like the cost to white ones, proved great. But for the former, this cost has often been unrecognized. "They expected to have to fight for their freedom. They expected that the brutality that accompanied the making of slavery would accompany its undoing. They knew many would suffer and die before any of them experienced freedom, that their families, despite their best efforts, would again be torn apart," says the historian Thavolia Glymph. "As they fled alone to Union lines, in family units, or as communities to Union lines or resisted from within Confederate lines, they knew they were in 'for harder times,' one Union officer wrote." Glymph adds, "The American Civil War was not exceptional in these regards but the history of the slaves' war within the Civil War remains to be fully told."[66]

In our national story, we crown Lincoln the Great Emancipator, the president who ended slavery, demolished the racist South, and ushered in the free nation our founders set forth. But this narrative, like so many others, requires more nuance. Douglass would never forget that the president initially suggested that the only solution, after abolishing an enslavement that had lasted for centuries, was for Black Americans to leave the country they helped to build. More than a decade later, organizers asked Douglass to eulogize the assassinated president at the unveiling of a new memorial for Lincoln and the freedmen in Washington, D.C. The abolitionist, whose mother had been sold away from him when he was a young child, had met with Lincoln a few times during his presidency and had repeatedly prodded Lincoln in his writings and speeches to emancipate the enslaved.[67]

Early in his speech in D.C., Douglass called the president "a great public man whose example is likely to be commended for honor and imitation long after his departure to the solemn shades, the silent continents of eternity." But he soon made clear that he hadn't come to simply promote the narrative of Lincoln as the Great Emancipator who set his people free. "Abraham Lincoln was not, in the fullest sense of the word, either our man or our model. . . . He was preeminently the white man's president, entirely devoted to the welfare of white men. He was ready and willing at any time during the first years of his administration to deny, postpone, and sacrifice the rights of humanity in the colored people to promote the welfare of the white people of this country. . . .

You are the children of Abraham Lincoln. We are at best only his step-children; children by adoption, children by forces of circumstances and necessity."

Douglass then launched into a breathtaking litany of Lincoln's shortcomings, referring in part to that White House meeting with Black leaders in 1862: "Our faith in him was often taxed and strained to the uttermost . . . when he strangely told us that we were the cause of the war; when he still more strangely told us that we were to leave the land in which we were born." However, though the Union was worth more to Lincoln than enslaved people's freedom, Douglass said, "under his wise and beneficent rule we saw ourselves gradually lifted from the depths of slavery to the heights of liberty and manhood."[68]

Douglass understood that Lincoln existed as both an "astute politician and a man of principle," according to Christopher Bonner, a historian and the author of *Remaking the Republic: Black Politics and the Creation of American Citizenship.* Bonner says that Douglass's perspective is vital for understanding Lincoln. "We would do well to listen to Douglass," he told me. "Douglass knew Lincoln, Douglass knew slavery, and Douglass knew the nineteenth-century United States, and so he is a great source for us to understand Lincoln's complexity." Douglass understood that Lincoln's ideas about Black people changed over the course of the war. The president had been deeply moved by the valor of the Black men who'd helped save the Union and had been influenced by Black men such as Douglass, whom he held in high esteem. Though the first version of his Emancipation Proclamation advocated colonization, by the end of the Civil War, Lincoln had abandoned these efforts and advocated for the Thirteenth Amendment, abolishing slavery. In his final speech before his assassination, Lincoln expressed an openness to enfranchising a limited number of Black men—particularly educated men and those who'd fought in the war.

"That last speech calling for partial inclusion of Black Americans, that's an evolution, and among the many tragedies of Lincoln's death is that he did change so much in such a short period of time," Bonner said. "Still, the final stage of Lincoln is still a person who only believes in partial Black inclusion and who is only advocating for inclusion of certain Black people on certain terms. It's valid to expect that he would have continued to evolve, but what we do know is that in the unfortunately short period of his presidency, Lincoln wasn't an advocate for full equality."[69]

Nearly three years after Lincoln met with those men in the White House, General Robert E. Lee surrendered at Appomattox, effectively ending the Civil War and suddenly freeing four million Black Americans. Few were interested in leaving the country. Instead, most would have fervently supported the sentiment of a resolution against Black colonization put forward at a convention of Black leaders in New York some decades before: "This is our home, and this our country. Beneath its sod lie the bones of our fathers. . . . Here we were born, and here we will die."[70]

That the formerly enslaved did not take up Lincoln's offer to abandon these lands is an astounding testament to their belief in this nation's founding ideals. As W.E.B. Du Bois wrote, "Few men ever worshiped Freedom with half such unquestioning faith as did the American Negro for two centuries."[71] Black Americans had long called for universal equality and believed, as the abolitionist Martin Delany said, "that God has made of one blood all the nations that dwell on the face of the earth."[72] Liberated by war, then, they did not seek vengeance on their oppressors, as so many white Americans feared. Rather they did the opposite.

During this nation's brief period of Reconstruction, from 1865 to 1877, formerly enslaved people zealously engaged with the democratic process. The role Black Americans played in bringing about Reconstruction has often been overlooked, because until 1870 and the passage of the Fifteenth Amendment, which finally granted Black men the right to vote, no Black people had ever been allowed to serve in any elected office in the U.S. Congress or in most states and so their names do not often appear in the political histories.

But that absence can be misleading. Through speeches, pamphlets, conferences, direct lobbying, and newspaper editorials, Black Americans pushed an all-white Congress to enshrine equality into the Constitution, powerfully shaping what the country would be like after its second founding. Once the Constitution had been "shorn of its proslavery features" with the passage of the Thirteenth Amendment, the historian Eric Foner writes, Black people moved to recast it to reflect the liberatory assertions of the Declaration of Independence, a document they had long admired and looked to for inspiration.

Within months of slavery's end, in fall of 1865, a Black newspaper called the *New Orleans Tribune* put forth a radical plan for an America that had been purged by fire. The paper called for suffrage for Black men, equality before the law, the redistribution of land from the former labor camps to the formerly enslaved, and equal access to schools and transportation. The plan advocated that the Constitution be amended to prohibit states from making "any distinction in civil rights and privileges" based on race.[73]

Black activists like Frances Ellen Watkins Harper, Martin Delany, Douglass, and Mary Ann Shadd Cary, as well as a small group called the Radical Republicans—rare white men such as Thaddeus Stevens and Charles Sumner who truly believed in Black equality—viewed Reconstruction as "a once-in-a-lifetime opportunity to purge the republic of the legacy of slavery."[74] Thanks to their efforts, the years directly after slavery saw the greatest expansion of human and civil rights ever witnessed in this nation. A year after Congress passed the Thirteenth Amendment, outlawing slavery, Black Americans, exerting their new political power, lobbied white legislators to pass the Civil Rights Act of 1866, the nation's first such law and one of the greatest pieces of civil rights legislation in American history. The law codified Black American citizenship for the first time, prohibited housing discrimination, and provided all Americans the legal right to buy and inherit property, make and enforce contracts, and seek redress from courts.[75]

In 1868, Congress ratified the Fourteenth Amendment, ensuring citizenship to Black Americans and all people born in the United States. Foner has written that "no change in the Constitution since the Bill of Rights has had a more profound impact on American life."[76] Today, thanks to this amendment, every child born here, and all their progeny thereafter, gains automatic citizenship. The Fourteenth Amendment also, for the first time, constitutionally guaranteed equal protection and codified equality in the law. Ever since, nearly all other marginalized groups have used the Fourteenth Amendment in their fights for equality (including the 2015 successful arguments before the Supreme Court on behalf of same-sex marriage). Finally, in 1870, Congress passed the Fifteenth Amendment, establishing the most critical aspect of democracy and citizenship—the right to vote—to all men regardless of "race, color, or previous condition of servitude."

With federal troops tempering widespread white violence, Black Southerners started branches of the National Equal Rights League—one of the nation's first human rights organizations—to fight discrimination and organize voters. They headed in droves to the polls, where they placed other formerly enslaved people into seats their enslavers had once held. The South, for the first time in the history of this country, began to resemble a democracy, with Black Americans elected to local, state, and federal offices. Some sixteen Black men served in Congress—including Hiram Revels of Mississippi, who became the first Black man elected to the U.S. Senate in 1870. (Demonstrating just how brief this period would be, Revels and Blanche Bruce, who was elected four years later, would go from being the first Black men elected to the last for nearly a hundred years, until Edward Brooke of Massachusetts took office in 1967.) More than six hundred Black men served in Southern state legislatures, and hundreds more in local positions.[77]

These Black officials joined with white Republicans, some of whom came down from the North and believed that abolition would also expand the rights of white Americans, to write the most egalitarian state constitutions the South had ever seen. They helped pass more equitable tax legislation and laws that prohibited discrimination in public transportation, accommodations, and housing. Perhaps their biggest achievement was the establishment of that most democratic of American institutions: the public school.[78]

Public education effectively did not exist in the South before Reconstruction. The white elite sent their children to private schools, while poor white children went without an education. But newly freed Black people, who had been prohibited from learning to read and write during slavery, were desperate for an education, which they saw as integral to true liberty. So Black legislators successfully pushed for a universal, state-funded system of schools—not just for their own children but for white children, too. Black legislators also helped pass the first compulsory education laws in the region. Southern children, Black and white, were now required to attend schools, the way their Northern counterparts did. Just five years into Reconstruction, every Southern state had enshrined the right to a public education for all children into its constitution.[79] In some states, like Louisiana and South Carolina, small numbers of Black and white children, briefly, attended schools together. Remarkably, in 1873 the University of South Carolina became the only state-sponsored college in the South to fully integrate, becoming majority Black—just like the state itself—by 1876. (When white former Confederates regained power a year later, they closed the university. After three years, they reopened it as an all-white institution; it would remain that way for nearly a century, until a court-ordered desegregation in 1963.)[80]

For the fleeting moment known as Reconstruction, the majority in Congress, and the nation, seemed to embrace the idea that out of the ashes of the Civil War, we could birth the multiracial democracy that Black Americans envisioned, even if our founding fathers had not.

But it would not last.

"Tyranny is a central theme of American history," the historian David Brion Davis writes in his 2006 book, *Inhuman Bondage: The Rise and Fall of Slavery in the New World,* and "racial exploitation and racial conflict have been part of the DNA of American culture."[81] So, too, is the belief, articulated by Lincoln, that Black people constitute the obstacle to national unity. The many gains of Reconstruction were met with widespread and coordinated white resistance, including unthinkable violence against the formerly enslaved, wide-scale voter suppression, electoral fraud, and even, in extreme cases, the violent overthrow of democratically elected biracial governments. Faced with this violent recalcitrance, the federal government once again settled on Black people as the problem and decided that for unity's sake, it would leave the white South to its own devices. In 1877, President Rutherford B. Hayes, in order to secure a compromise with Southern Democrats that would grant him the presidency in a contested election, agreed to pull the remaining federal troops from the South. With the troops gone, white Southerners quickly went about eradicating the gains of Reconstruction. The systemic white suppression of Black life proved so severe that this period between the 1880s and the early twentieth century became known as the second slavery or the Great Nadir, a phrase taken from the work of the historian and public intellectual Rayford W. Logan.

Democracy would not return to the South for nearly a century.

White Southerners of all economic classes, on the other hand, thanks in significant part to the progressive policies and laws Black people had championed, experienced substantial improvement in their lives even as they forced Black people back into quasi-slavery. As Waters McIntosh, who had been enslaved in South Carolina, lamented, "It was the poor white man who was freed by the war, not the Negroes."[82]

Georgia pines flew past the windows of the Greyhound bus carrying Isaac Woodard home to Winnsboro, South Carolina. After serving four years in the army in World War II, where he had earned a battle star, he had received an honorable discharge earlier that day at Camp Gordon and was headed home to meet his wife. When the bus stopped at a small drugstore an hour outside Atlanta, Woodard asked the white driver if he could go to the restroom and a brief argument ensued. About half an hour later, the driver stopped again and told Woodard to get off the bus. Crisp in his uniform, Woodard stepped from the stairs and saw white police waiting for him. Before he could speak, one of the officers struck him in the head with a billy club, then continued to beat him so badly that he fell unconscious. The blows to Woodard's head were so severe that when he woke in a jail cell the next day, he could not see. The beating occurred just four and a half hours after the soldier's military discharge. At twenty-six, Woodard would never see again.[83]

There was nothing unusual about Woodard's horrific maiming. It was part of a wave of systemic violence that had been deployed continuously against Black Americans for decades since the end of Reconstruction, in both the

North and the South. As the racially egalitarian spirit of post–Civil War America evaporated under the desire for national reunification, Black Americans, simply by existing, served as a problematic reminder of this nation's failings. White America dealt with this inconvenience by constructing a savagely enforced system of racial apartheid that excluded Black people almost entirely from mainstream American life—a system so grotesque that Nazi Germany would later take inspiration from it for its own racist policies.[84]

Despite the guarantees of equality in the Fourteenth Amendment, the Supreme Court's landmark *Plessy v. Ferguson* decision in 1896 declared the racial segregation of Black Americans constitutional. With the blessing of the nation's highest court and no federal will to vindicate Black rights, Southern states passed a series of laws and codes starting in the late 1800s meant to make slavery's racial caste system permanent by denying Black people political power, social equality, economic independence, and basic dignity. They enacted literacy tests to keep Black people from voting and created all-white primaries for elections. Black people were prohibited from serving on juries or testifying in court against a white person. South Carolina prohibited white and Black textile workers from using the same doors. Oklahoma forced phone companies to segregate phone booths. Memphis had separate parking spaces for Black and white drivers. Baltimore passed an ordinance outlawing Black people from moving onto a block more than half white and white people from moving onto a block more than half Black. Georgia made it illegal for Black and white people to be buried next to each other in the same cemetery. Alabama barred Black people from using public libraries that their own tax dollars were paying for. In the North, white politicians implemented policies that segregated Black people into slum neighborhoods and into inferior all-Black schools, operated white-only public pools, and held white and "colored" days at the county fair. White businesses regularly denied Black people service, placing WHITES ONLY signs in their windows. States like California joined Southern states in barring Black people from marrying white people, while local school boards in Illinois and New Jersey mandated segregated schools for Black and white children.[85]

White Americans maintained this caste system through wanton racial terrorism. And Black veterans like Woodard, especially those with the audacity to wear their uniform, had since the Civil War been the target of a particularly gruesome violence. This intensified during the two world wars because many white people understood that once Black men had gone abroad and experienced life outside the suffocating racial oppression of America, they were unlikely to quietly return to their subjugation at home. As Senator James K.

Vardaman of Mississippi said on the Senate floor during World War I, Black servicemen returning to the South would "inevitably lead to disaster." Giving a Black man "military airs" and sending him to defend the flag would bring him "to the conclusion that his political rights must be respected."[86]

Many white Americans saw Black men in the uniforms of America's armed services not as patriotic but as exhibiting a dangerous pride. Hundreds of Black veterans were beaten, maimed, shot, and lynched. We like to call those who lived during World War II the Greatest Generation, but that allows us to ignore the fact that many of this generation fought for democracy overseas while brutally suppressing democracy for millions of American citizens. During the height of racial terror in this country, Black Americans were not merely killed in mob attacks and lynchings but castrated, burned alive, and dismembered, with their body parts displayed in storefronts and strewn across lawns in Black communities. This violence was meant to terrify and control Black people, but perhaps just as importantly, it served as a psychological balm for white supremacy: you would not treat human beings this way. The extremity of the violence was a symptom of the psychological mechanism necessary to absolve white Americans of their country's original sin. To answer the question of how they could prize liberty abroad while simultaneously denying liberty to an entire race back home, white Americans resorted to the same racist ideology that Jefferson and the framers had used at the nation's founding: that Black people were an inferior race whose degraded status justified their treatment.

This ideology did not simply disappear once slavery ended. If the formerly enslaved and their descendants became educated, if we thrived in the jobs white people did, if we excelled in the sciences and arts, then the entire rationale for how this nation had allowed slavery would collapse. Free Black people posed a danger to the country's idea of itself as exceptional in its creed of freedom and equality; they held up a mirror into which the nation preferred not to peer. And so the inhumanity visited on Black people by every generation of white America justified the inhumanity of the past and the inequality of the present.

Just as white Americans feared, World War II ignited what became Black Americans' second sustained effort to democratize this nation. As the editorial board of the Black newspaper *The Pittsburgh Courier* wrote, "We wage a two-pronged attack against our enslavers at home and those abroad who will enslave us."[87] Woodard's blinding is largely seen as one of the catalysts for the decades-long rebellion we have come to call the civil rights movement. But it is useful to pause and remember that this was the second mass movement for

Black civil rights, after Reconstruction. As the centennial of slavery's end neared, Black people were still seeking the rights they had fought for and won after the Civil War: the right to be treated as full citizens before the law, which was guaranteed in 1868 by the Fourteenth Amendment; the right to vote, which was guaranteed in 1870 by the Fifteenth Amendment; and the right to be treated equally in public accommodations, which was guaranteed by the Civil Rights Act of 1875.[88] In response to Black demands for these rights, white Americans strung them from trees, beat them and dumped their bodies in muddy rivers, assassinated them in their front yards, firebombed them on buses, mauled them with dogs, peeled back their skin with fire hoses, and murdered their children with explosives set off inside a church.

For the most part, Black Americans fought back alone, never getting a majority of white Americans to join and support their freedom struggles. Yet we never fought only for ourselves. The bloody freedom struggles of the civil rights movement laid the foundation for every other modern rights struggle. This nation's white founders set up a decidedly undemocratic Constitution that excluded Black people and did not provide the vote or equality for most Americans. But the laws born out of Black resistance guarantee the franchise for all and ban discrimination based not just on race but on gender, nationality, religion, and ability. It was the civil rights movement that led to the passage of the Immigration and Nationality Act of 1965, which upended the racist immigration quota system intended to keep this country white. Because of Black Americans, Black and brown immigrants from across the globe are able to come to the United States and live in a country in which legal discrimination is no longer allowed. It is a truly American irony that some Asian Americans, among the groups able to immigrate to the United States in large numbers because of the Black civil rights struggle, have sued universities to end programs designed to help the descendants of the enslaved.

No one cherishes freedom more than those who have not had it. And to this day, Black Americans, more than any other group, embrace the democratic ideals of a common good. We are the most likely to support programs like universal healthcare and a higher minimum wage and to oppose programs that harm the most vulnerable. For instance, Black Americans suffer the most from violent crime, yet we are the group most strongly opposed to capital punishment. Our unemployment rate is nearly twice that of white Americans, yet we are still the most likely of all groups to say that this nation should take in refugees who others claim will be a drain on American institutions.[89]

The truth is that as much democracy as this nation has today, it has been borne on the backs of Black resistance and visions for equality. Our founding fathers may not have actually believed in the ideals they espoused, but Black people did. As the scholar Joe R. Feagin put it, "Enslaved African-Americans have been among the foremost freedom-fighters this country has produced."[90] For generations, we have believed in this country with a faith it did not deserve. Black people have seen the worst of America, yet, somehow, we still believe in its best.

They say our people were born on the water.

When it occurred, no one can say for certain. Perhaps it was in the second week, or the third, but surely by the fourth, when they had not seen their land or any land for so many days that they had lost count. It was after fear had turned to despair, and despair to resignation, and resignation to an abiding understanding. The teal eternity of the Atlantic Ocean had severed them so completely from what had once been their home that it was as if nothing had ever existed before, as if everything and everyone they cherished had simply vanished from the earth. They were no longer Mbundu or Akan or Fulani. These men and women from many different nations, all shackled together in the suffocating hull of the ship, they were one people now.

Just a few months earlier, they'd had families, and farms, and lives, and dreams. They'd been free. They had names, of course, but their enslavers had not bothered to record them. They had been made Black by those people who believed that they themselves were white, and where they were heading, Black equaled "slave," and slavery in America required turning human beings into property by stripping them of every element that made them individuals. This process was called seasoning, in which people stolen from western and central Africa were forced, often through torture, to stop speaking their native tongues and practicing their native religions.

But as the sociologist Glenn Bracey writes, "Out of the ashes of white denigration, we gave birth to ourselves."[91] For as much as white people tried to pretend, Black people were not chattel. And so the process of seasoning, instead of erasing identity, served an opposite purpose: in the void, we forged a new culture all our own.

Today, our very manner of speaking recalls the Creole languages that enslaved people innovated to communicate with both Africans who used various dialects and the English-speaking people who enslaved them.[92] Our style of dress, the defining flair, stems from the desires of enslaved people—shorn of all individuality—to assert their own identity. Enslaved people would wear a hat in a jaunty manner or knot a head scarf intricately. Today's avant-garde nature of Black hairstyles and fashion displays a vibrant reflection of enslaved people's determination to feel fully human through self-expression.[93] The improvisational quality of Black art and music comes from a culture that rejected convention in order to cope with constant disruption. Black naming practices, so often impugned by mainstream society, are themselves an act of resistance. Our last names often derive from the white people who once owned us. That is why the insistence of many Black Americans, particularly those most marginalized, to give our children names that we create, that are neither European nor from Africa, a place we have never been, is an act of self-determination. When the world listens to quintessentially American music, it is our voice they hear. The sorrow songs we sang in the fields to soothe our physical pain and find hope in a freedom we did not expect to know until we died became American gospel. Amid the devastating violence and poverty of the Mississippi delta, we birthed jazz and the blues. And it was in the deeply impoverished and segregated neighborhoods where white Americans forced the descendants of the enslaved to live that teenagers too poor to buy instruments used old records to create a new music known as hip-hop.

Our speech and fashion and the drum of our music echo Africa but are more than African. Out of our unique isolation, both from our native cultures and from white America, we forged this nation's most significant original culture. In turn, "mainstream" society has coveted our style, our slang, and our song, seeking to appropriate the one truly American culture as its own. As Langston Hughes wrote in 1926, "They'll see how beautiful I am / And be ashamed— / I, too, am America."[94]

For centuries, white Americans have been trying to solve the "Negro problem." They have dedicated thousands of pages to this endeavor. It is common, still, to point to rates of Black poverty, out-of-wedlock births, crime, and college attendance as if these conditions in a country built on a racial caste system are not utterly predictable. But crucially, you cannot view those statistics while ignoring another: that Black people were enslaved here longer than we have been free.

As a woman in my forties, I am part of the first generation of Black Americans in the history of the United States to be born into a society in which Black people had full rights of citizenship. Black people suffered under slavery for 250 years; we have been legally "free" for just fifty. Yet in that briefest of spans, despite continuing to face rampant discrimination, and despite there never having been a genuine effort to redress the wrongs of slavery and the century of racial apartheid that followed, Black Americans have made astounding progress, not only for ourselves but also for all Americans.

What if America understood, finally, now, at the dawn of its fifth century, that we have never been the problem, but the solution?

When I was a child—I must have been in fifth or sixth grade—a teacher gave our class an assignment intended to celebrate the diversity of the great American melting pot. She instructed each of us to write a short report on our ancestral land and then draw that nation's flag. As she turned to write the assignment on the board, the other Black girl in class locked eyes with me. Slavery had erased any connection we had to an African country, and even if we tried to claim the whole continent, there was no "African" flag. It was hard enough being one of two Black kids in the class, and this assignment would be just another reminder of the distance between the white kids and us. In the end, I walked over to the globe near my teacher's desk, picked a random African country, and claimed it as my own.

I wish now that I could go back to the younger me and tell her that her people's ancestry started here, on these lands, and to boldly, proudly, draw the stars and those stripes of the American flag.

We were told once, by virtue of our bondage, that we could never be American. But it was by virtue of our bondage that we became the most American of all.

December 1662

Virginia's House of Burgesses passes a new law holding that "all children borne in this country shalbe held bond or free only according to the condition of the mother." This doctrine, known as *partus sequitur ventrem* ("that which is brought forth follows the belly"), is a departure from English tradition, in which a child's status followed that of the father. The law incentivizes the rape of enslaved Black women by their white enslavers.

Daughters of Azimuth

Nikky Finney

I lead my sisters into the woods on Sundays when Missus goes to town.
We don't have long but have long enough. I am Mintu from the world

before, not Mindy, from now. My womb has been made ready. All that
remains is the long math of my feet guiding my swollen eyes to look

beyond their iron codes and paper declarations. There are five of us
who have stopped our line. Barren of them and un-ownable. We afford

no one a swollen belly to weigh or follow, work as hard as men but that
is not what pounds their empty chambers. The vertical ones with gold

coin eyes care only of the Increase. Their new laws fatten our children
into a tableau tapestry of fatted calves, height and weight their only worth.

The mercantile window to seed us has been shut by our own hands.
Without the whole truth in plain sight they sell Azimuths fast. We look

the part but can never join the Increase. Their spewing vertical rods have
poked us raw, back and front, behind the barn. Mornings, we are tied,

hanging from oak trees by our lion arms while they spread their vertical
seed inside our hearths. We refuse the birth of any new world, blue-eyed,

enslaved Other. Before we are sold again we pass on, to the girls coming,
how not to barren themselves from each other, how to angle far enough

away, as far as any un-ownable woman can, become a kernel of late August
corn inside of this dark cave, as far away as any un-free woman might be

able to live, above the vertical death they have now inked into their country
with our defying blood. Yesterday, seven new girls in a wagon. Bent, shaking,

wailing for *Mama*. What's that? Long dead village of women whose legs we
all fell from, but who were not allowed entrance into this bloodthirsty plane.

Each girl has dropped her first seed so we move fast. The gray-headed
women, rolling their hands like the head of an owl to the moon have given

their nod. We made enough blue paste to fortify and camouflage. Once in
the woods we pair, squat, hold our legs open to each other. One Azimuth

for every new girl. Our long tender hands coat each blooming womb.
Ever careful around their buttons, riding shotgun near their pleasure,

in order to remember *the point at which the vertical circle passes through the
object in order to intersect the endless horizon*. The blue paste is sealed inside.

They will cramp and swell, float about like a pod of baby whales, for
seven days until they get their bearings. In Arabic, I will recite the old

poetry ending with *altitude is never the same as azimuth*.

*

She is Euka from the world before, not Emily, from now, stooping on the
bank, soon to instruct the final things if the dirt and ankles are willing,

two long right angles, north and south, in pugnacious eastern alignment.
Euka, our tall surveyor, instructing where to put our valuables, swing our

thick waists, telescope every parrot eye in search of one motion. Head-
wrapped doula of return, leading back to the land of mother wit, after

40

the mother has been gagged, bound, and pushed overboard again. How
to turn ourselves away from their shiny human franchise, their gold portrait

coins, interfering with the purlieu of our bearings, who we are and how
it is possible, here, even in their savage world, to visit ourselves, levitate

our world of before. All this and more can horizontally and without sound
still belong to us. We are one line of women, foot and eye-hitched to the

celestial zenith, slinking together along the lone rim of the horizon, free
of their feral seed, knowing full well they would slaughter us like hogs,

had they half a notion that beyond their animal husbandry fuckery,
we kept loving each other.

1682

Virginia's House of Burgesses makes interracial marriage punishable by imprisonment. Over the next decade, Virginia and other colonies continue to pass laws restricting or prohibiting marriage between white and Black people. No such laws exist in England at the time. They are unique to the North American colonies and help create a racial caste system that strictly forbids interracial relationships of all kinds.

Loving Me

Vievee Francis

It was simple. So immediate we didn't note a change.
The birds flew in that moment as they did
anywhere else. Lifting their wings over the waters.
And the sun that had risen in the morning would fall
to its knees in the evening, like any other living thing.
I am not of a mind to prove what is plain as God's speech
through the white pines. The trees that day, amassed
in their strange configurations, gave rest to the snake
and crying insect alike. We couldn't have been expected to
know. Weren't we taught to fear knowledge? But
the ruddy apple of your face made me reach out—
And I know the power of my own gaze.
Why else would those who seek to own me want me
                    to cast my eyes down?

Two young women holding hands, c. 1890   BEINECKE LIBRARY, YALE UNIVERSITY

CHAPTER 2

Race

DOROTHY ROBERTS

On a summer day in 2019, Ashley Ramkishun and Samuel Sarfo thought they were making a routine trip to the clerk's office in Arlington County, Virginia, to apply for a marriage license. They didn't expect that the computerized Marriage Register form they were directed to fill out would include a box titled "Race," with an asterisk indicating it was required information. Under "Race" was the instruction to "Select One," with a drop-down list of seven categories to choose from—American Indian/Alaskan Native, African American/Black, Asian, Caucasian, Hispanic/Latino, Pacific Islander, and Other.[1] Sarfo, who was thirty-two years old at the time and working at a bank, is a Black man who grew up in Ghana and immigrated to the United States as a teenager. Ramkishun was twenty-six years old and had recently graduated from law school. Her parents are of Indian descent and came to the United States from Guyana, a nation on the Caribbean coast of South America.

When the couple asked if there was a way to apply without identifying a race, they were told that their only option was to select "Other." "I didn't want to pick 'Other,'" Ramkishun would recall. "I've been having to pick 'Other' all my life. None of it defines who I am."[2] Because she and her fiancé refused to click on a race category, the computer system couldn't process their license application. They could not get married without specifying their race.

This would have been true in any of Virginia's ninety-five counties, all of which required applicants to identify their race in order to obtain a marriage license. In Rockbridge County, for example, applicants were required to choose a racial identification from a list of 230 terms that includes "Mulatto," "Quadroon," "Nubian," and "Aryan."[3] And Virginia was not alone. Soon after they'd attempted to wed in Arlington County, Ramkishun landed a job in the state attorney's office in Miami and the pair moved to Florida. Once there, they again applied for a marriage license. To their surprise, the application in Miami-Dade County also included the race question. After Ramkishun called county officials to complain, however, the couple was able to print out the form and complete it without identifying themselves by race. Ramkishun and Sarfo wed in December 2019.

By that time, they had also decided to join two other couples in Virginia who had been denied marriage licenses for refusing to racially identify and filed a lawsuit challenging the state's requirement in federal court. In late 2019, Judge Rossie D. Alston, Jr., handed down a decision: there was no compelling reason to maintain the racial-identification law, which burdened the plaintiffs' fundamental right to marry and therefore violated the Due Process Clause of the Fourteenth Amendment of the U.S. Constitution.[4]

In deciding for the plaintiffs, Judge Alston traced the racial-classifications requirement to a Virginia law passed in 1924 entitled "An Act to Preserve Racial Integrity." This law required local and state registrars to keep certificates of "racial composition" for everyone born in the state and to require accurate "statements as to color of both man and woman" on applications for marriage licenses.[5] It also strictly prohibited interracial marriages.

In 1967, the U.S. Supreme Court struck down the act's interracial marriage ban in its celebrated *Loving v. Virginia* decision, but it left intact the racial-classification system itself. According to the Court's reasoning, the prohibition on interracial marriage violated the Fourteenth Amendment's Equal Protection Clause not because it employed racial classifications but because it used them to enforce racial separation.[6] The opinion failed to overturn the racial-identification scheme—including the marriage license requirement, which is why Sarfo and Ramkishun encountered it in the Arlington County clerk's office in 2019.

Despite the decision in favor of Sarfo and Ramkishun, the practice of dividing people into racial categories permeates our society. It has become so routine to identify people by race that most of us don't think twice about it. We check off racial boxes on the U.S. Census form, college applications, public school records, mortgage applications, and medical charts. It's common for people to say they know race exists because they can "see" it. Research by social psychologists who study how people racially categorize others has suggested that paying attention to race is an automatic process that occurs almost instantaneously when a person encounters a face.[7] Social psychologist Destiny Peery uses computer-generated faces deliberately made to appear "racially ambiguous" to investigate the multiple types of information people compute to arrive at a racial determination.[8] Even people who are born blind have reported that they were taught how to "see" race—by touching other people's hair, smelling them, or listening to their speech.[9] Race seems to be natural and inherited.

Where does this thinking come from? As the justices unanimously found in their *Loving* decision, the 1924 Racial Integrity Act originated as "an incident to slavery" and its racial classifications served as nothing more than "measures designed to maintain White Supremacy." The chief promoter of that act, Walter Ashby Plecker, Virginia's state registrar of vital statistics from 1912 to 1946, was a doctor with deep ties to both eugenicists and white supremacists. Plecker turned his office into the state's most powerful tool for implementing the belief in an innate racial hierarchy.[10] Plecker wrote in his preface to the Racial Integrity Act that the state must use "radical measures" to prevent the "intermarriage of the white race with mixed stock."

He was especially worried that growing numbers of "near white people" were surreptitiously gaining white privileges despite their "intermixture of colored blood." Plecker's administrative apparatus, composed of midwives and doctors who reported births, undertakers who reported deaths, and marriage license clerks, ensured that the racial identities of all Virginians were accurately recorded, and that the prohibition against intermarriage was strictly enforced. The Racial Integrity Act made it a crime for a "white person" to marry anyone other than another "white person," defined as having "no trace whatsoever of any blood other than Caucasian," and prevented officials from issuing marriage licenses until they were satisfied that the applicants' statements as to their race were correct. A misstatement on the license application was punishable as a felony. The goal was, according to the U.S. Supreme Court in the 1967 *Loving* decision, a "comprehensive statutory scheme aimed at prohibiting and punishing interracial marriages."[11]

The bedrock of this statutory scheme was a network of laws passed in the colonial era governing sex and race. These laws, which created the racial-classification systems we still live with today, were primarily concerned with policing interracial sex. They maintained a clear line between who was Black and who was white, who was enslaved and who was free, by banning interracial intercourse and enforcing a rule of matrilineal descent: if a mother was Black and enslaved, so was her child. Though these laws were partly aimed at preventing miscegenation, they also incentivized the rape of Black women by their white enslavers, who could profit from their sexual assaults by enslaving any resulting children.

Over the next two hundred years, white authorities intent on maintaining and justifying slavery solidified a racial-classification system backed by sexual regulation. The founders of the new nation incorporated the colonial categorization of races and made exclusion of Africans and Native tribes from the democracy foundational to the U.S. Constitution. Even after slavery ended and into the twentieth century, laws like the Racial Integrity Act continued to define and enforce racial lines, sometimes even more meticulously than during the slavery era. But this system, which grew partly out of colonial anxiety about interracial sex, did and still does more than maintain racial categories. The laws that invented race also created a regime intent on policing Black women's sexuality and controlling Black women's bodies. Many generations later, we are still living with its legacy of entangled racial injustice and sexual violence.

In the early days of colonial America, the vast majority of people compelled to work for landowners were vagrant children, convicts, and indentured laborers imported from Europe. The wealthy settlers who benefited from their unfree labor did not at first distinguish between the status of European, African, and Indigenous servants.[12] But as the slave trade mushroomed, Africans began to be subjected to a distinct kind of servitude: they alone were considered the actual property of their enslavers.[13] Colonial legislatures enforced the distinction between Black and white people through a series of new laws passed in the mid-1600s that established a legal regime that differentiated the political status of Europeans and Africans. It was particularly concerned with sex because sex between Black and white people produced children who confounded the strict distinctions between those two categories.

The first officially recorded condemnation of interracial sex was the public whipping of Hugh Davis, a white man, ordered by the Virginia General Assembly in 1630 for "abusing himself to the dishonor of God and shame of Christians, by defiling his body in lying with a Negress."[14] A decade later, when another white man, Robert Sweet, impregnated a Black woman, the Black woman was flogged, while Sweet was ordered to do penance in church.[15] There was also the question of how to regard the children of these sexual interactions. It was critical to the emerging racial order to identify their status. Should they be classified as white and free, like their fathers, or Black and enslaved, like their mothers? Today, most Americans would quickly identify these children born to Black women as Black—as if they were applying a universal rule of biological inheritance. But in the 1600s, the racial-classification rules had not yet been established.

The Virginia House of Burgesses—the first elected legislature in the colonies—met to debate the question. According to the patriarchal mandates of British inheritance and kinship law, the children should have had the status of their white fathers. Yet the colonists could see the political and economic disadvantages of classifying children born to Black women as white: such a decision would expand the pool of human beings who were entitled to the privileges of whiteness, and it would decrease the pool of human beings who could be enslaved. In the end, in 1662, the colonists passed a statute that maintained the racial hierarchy:

> Whereas some doubts have arrisen whether children got by any Englishman upon a negro woman should be slave or free, *Be it therefore enacted and declared by this present grand assembly,* that all children borne in this country shalbe held bond or free only according to the condition of the mother.[16]

Enslaved Black women gave birth to enslaveable children even if the fathers were white. In discarding English legal tradition, the colonists adopted the Roman principle of *partus sequitur ventrem*—"the offspring follows the belly"—used to determine the ownership of animals. As a litter of pigs belonged to the owner of the sow, the children born to Black women were the property of the mother's enslaver.

The law allowed white men to profit from their sexual assaults on Black women. Freed from the worry that their mixed-race offspring had any legal claim to freedom, white men could rape enslaved women with total impunity, maintaining their domination while increasing their wealth. Their control over Black women's bodies was key to creating a permanent labor supply.[17] The white enslaver crafted a "convenient game," wrote Lydia Maria Child, a Massachusetts abolitionist, that "enables him to fill his purse by means of his own vices."[18]

The law also helped to invent the meaning of race. Although they clearly determined the status of Black women's children for political and economic reasons, the Virginia legislators pretended slave status was a natural identity passed down through procreation. They constructed a racial-classification scheme but made it seem like an inherited condition. Though they imposed slavery by power, they cast Black women's wombs as the producers of their children's subjugated condition.

In 1663, a year after Virginia passed the law enslaving the children of enslaved women, the Maryland Colony enacted a similar statute. Enslavement soon became a heritable condition across colonial America.[19] This stark distinction in political status necessitated stricter enforcement of the boundaries between racial categories.

Virginia's racialized legal regime also included a 1691 criminal law prohibiting Negro, mulatto, and Indian men from marrying or "accompanying" a white woman.[20] By requiring that white women gave birth only to white children, the law preserved white men's exclusive sexual access to white women, as well as white racial purity. Mulatto children born to white women were not subject to the 1662 statute, which applied only to enslaved Black women, and therefore were born free—posing a threat to white male dominance. In 1705, the colony reinforced its disdain for interracial relationships by making it a crime for a white person to marry a Black person, punishable by six months in prison.[21]

This anti-miscegenation law was accompanied by a set of measures designed to codify the superior status of white people and the subordination of Black people.[22] The law gave white indentured laborers "freedom dues"— a payment in cash, land, or supplies received when they completed their contract term—while enslaved Black people were entitled to no freedom at all.[23] The legislature enacted a set of "slave codes," which declared that an enslaver who killed a person he enslaved while "correcting" the victim would not be prosecuted for a felony.[24] The same statute, by contrast, prohibited masters from inflicting "immoderate correction" on white indentured laborers and allowed those laborers to file complaints against masters who violated this restriction.[25] The codes also prohibited Black or mulatto individuals from holding public office, testifying in court, or otherwise swearing under oath.[26] This legal distinction in status based on race alone turned racial classification into a caste system. Through these laws, colonial landowners constructed race as a system of power in which anyone categorized as Black could be dominated by anyone categorized as white.

By the turn of the eighteenth century, the British North American colonies were governed by a complex and rigid racial-classification system that determined whether a person was entitled to freedom or subjected to enslavement. To reinforce the power and purity of people identified as white, it was necessary to regulate sex, which was often done through violence. Black men accused of even attempting to have sex with a white woman were subjected to barbaric punishments. And Black women, because they were considered human chattel, had no legal right to bodily autonomy. Courts did not recognize the rape of enslaved women and girls by *any* man as a crime. The very notion of rape didn't apply to Black women and girls, because they were considered incapable of consenting or not consenting to sex.[27]

None of this changed with the founding of the nation, whose framers preserved the slavery regime in the new Constitution and state laws. Sally Hemings, born in 1773, was the daughter of her mother's enslaver—John Wayles, the father of Thomas Jefferson's wife, Martha. Jefferson acquired Hemings when she was a child as part of his inheritance from Wayles. While Hemings and Jefferson were living in Paris, where Jefferson was serving as the foreign minister to France and Hemings as a lady's maid to Jefferson's daughters, Jefferson made Hemings his concubine. According to historian Annette Gordon-Reed, it is likely that by the time Hemings was sixteen, she was either pregnant or about to become pregnant with Jefferson's child. Hemings lived with Jefferson at Monticello for more than thirty years, giving birth to seven children. Because Hemings was enslaved, her children were deemed Jefferson's property. Four of Hemings's children lived to be adults, and Jefferson then arranged to free them.[28]

The law continued to regard Black women and their children this way for many decades. In the 1850s, a Mississippi jury convicted an enslaved man named George for raping an enslaved girl under the age of ten. Judge E. G. Henry of Madison County sentenced George to death by hanging. George's enslaver appealed the decision to the state's High Court of Errors and Appeals. John D. Freeman, the lawyer representing George, argued that because the victim was enslaved, George had committed no legally recognizable offense. "The crime of rape does not exist in this State between African slaves," Freeman noted. "Our laws recognize no marital rights as between slaves; their sexual intercourse is left to be regulated by their owners. The regulations of law, as to the white race, on the subject of sexual intercourse, do not and cannot, for obvious reasons, apply to slaves."[29] The high court agreed and threw out the indictment. "Masters and slaves cannot be governed by the same system of laws; so different are their positions, rights and duties," the court reasoned.

Husbands were legally entitled to force sex on their wives, and the marital rape exemption lasted in all fifty states until the 1970s.[30] White women who claimed they were assaulted by white men who were not their husbands had to clear a host of evidentiary hurdles, such as proving that they had resisted, had reported the attack quickly, were severely injured, were not having sex outside of marriage, and had corroborating evidence. These legal impediments were insurmountable for Black women. The vast majority of enslaved women had no right to testify in court at all against white men charged with felonies. The only legal recourse existed when an enslaved woman was raped by a man other than her enslaver. In that case, the enslaver could sue the abuser for trespass to chattel, a civil violation of the enslaver's property rights.[31] White men settled disputes between them arising from sexual abuse of enslaved women by enslaved men outside of court.[32]

We don't know exactly how frequently white enslavers raped enslaved women and girls. An analysis by historian Thelma Jennings of 514 narratives of formerly enslaved people found that 12 percent of the female authors referred to experiences of coerced sex by white men. Of those women, 35 percent had fathers who were white men or had given birth to children fathered by white men.[33] Jennings noted that the numbers were likely far larger, given the reluctance of recently freed Black women to discuss such private matters with their white interviewers. Census records show that in 1850, roughly 11 percent of the enslaved population was classified as mulatto.[34]

New evidence of white men's sexual violence against enslaved women is emerging from the genome. A 2020 study sampling the DNA of fifty thousand people—thirty thousand with African ancestry—reinforced the historical record. Spurred by Joanna Mountain, the senior director of research at 23andMe, scientists used DNA in the company's direct-to-consumer database to trace the ancestry of customers whose grandparents were born in one of the regions touched by the transatlantic slave trade. The researchers found that although a majority of the more than 12 million enslaved people who arrived in the Americas were men, enslaved women contributed more to the current gene pool. The genetic contribution of European men to the ancestry of African Americans is three times greater than that of European women. This means that enslaved men were more likely to die before they were able to have children and that enslaved women were often raped by white men and forced to bear their children.[35]

Since Black women had no right to deny sex to their enslavers, they had no right to defend themselves against forced sex. Enslaved women who successfully fought off enslavers who tried to assault them were sold away from their families, gruesomely maimed, or executed.[36] In 1850, within a year of his wife's death, a white Missouri farmer named Robert Newsom purchased a fourteen-year-old girl named Celia for the purpose of having sex with her.[37] He raped Celia for the first time on the journey home from the sale. Newsom put Celia up in a tiny cabin on his farm and there continued to rape her repeatedly over the course of five years. Celia gave birth to at least one child resulting from Newsom's assaults. In the summer of 1855, Celia begged Newsom to stop because she was sick and pregnant and warned him that she would resist his advances. She began to keep a large stick in the corner of her cabin to protect herself. When Newsom ignored her pleas and came to her cabin on the night of June 23, 1855, Celia clubbed him twice over the head with the stick, killing him.

Celia confessed to Jefferson Jones, who was sent by white citizens to interview her in her prison cell to find out if she had any accomplices. She was tried for first-degree murder before a jury composed entirely of white men, and Jones testified for the prosecution. Celia argued that she should be found not guilty under the state law of self-defense. An 1854 Missouri statute provided that women could defend themselves against "every person who shall take *any woman*, unlawfully, against her will, with intent to compel her by force, menace or duress . . . to be defiled" (emphasis added). But the presiding judge instructed the jury that the law didn't apply to Celia, for Celia didn't fall within the category of "any woman." Instead, the judge considered Celia the chattel property of Newsom and therefore without any legal right to protect herself against him.[38] The jury found Celia guilty of murdering Newsom. The judge delayed her execution so she could give birth to her third child, which would become the property of the Newsom family. But the baby was stillborn; Celia's other two children were sold. Celia was hanged on December 21, 1855.

With the end of slavery, racial classification no longer determined whether people were enslaved or free, but the ideas that denied Black women's bodily autonomy for nearly 250 years still held great force. The legal system that countenanced sexual violence against Black women and girls had required a moral excuse for its barbarism—especially in a nation that espoused ideals of female chastity and male civility. That justification came in the form of a particular kind of mythology that developed during the slavery period that disparaged Black women's sexuality. Whether free or enslaved, Black women were portrayed as sexually licentious, always consenting, and therefore unrapeable.

This thinking had been in place even before the African slave trade began. During the 1600s, English travelers to West and Central Africa sometimes praised African women's beauty, but they also explained the need to control Africans by mythologizing the voracious sexual appetites of African people.[39] White writers constructed the image of a Black woman governed by her sexual desires, identified by historian Deborah Gray White as the "Jezebel" after the biblical wife of King Ahab. As early as 1736, the *South-Carolina Gazette* described "African Ladies" as women "of 'strong robust constitution' who were 'not easily jaded out' but able to serve their lovers 'by Night as well as Day.' "[40] The lascivious Black temptress was a convenient icon: if Black women were inherently promiscuous, they could not be violated. In his 1835 pamphlet *The Morals of Slavery,* the celebrated South Carolina intellectual William Gilmore Simms wrote that Black women lacked the "consciousness of degradation" possessed by even the most disreputable white prostitutes in the North. Contributing to the Jezebel stereotype was the practice of selling mulatto women for the purpose of forcing them into sex work and concubinage for the sexual gratification of white men.[41] Some white Southerners saw the sexual availability of enslaved women as one of slavery's bonuses, because it protected the honor of white women from white male exploitation.[42]

This caricature of the hypersexual Black woman persisted even after slavery was abolished. White scholars and politicians linked sexual stereotypes of Black women to claims that Black mothers procreated recklessly, passing socially damaging traits to their children. In *The Plantation Negro as a Freeman,* published after the Civil War in 1889, prominent historian Philip A. Bruce set the stage by presenting Black women's sexual impurity as evidence that free Black people were regressing to a naturally immoral state. Bruce argued that Black women raised their daughters to follow their own licentious lifestyle, failing to "teach them, systematically, those moral lessons that they peculiarly need as members of the female sex."[43]

These ideas persisted into the twentieth century and drove government programs that attempted to regulate Black women's reproductive lives. State and federally funded family-planning programs engaged in massive campaigns to sterilize Black women. For example, between 1933 and 1976, the Eugenics Board of North Carolina approved the involuntary sterilizations of more than 7,500 people—affecting Black people at a disproportionate rate—on the grounds that they were "mentally defective."[44] In 1973, a federal district judge presided over a case of two Black sisters from Montgomery, Alabama, who were sterilized at ages twelve and fourteen when government-paid nurses pushed their illiterate mother into signing a consent form with an X.[45] The judge, Gerhard Gesell, in ruling against this practice, noted that "over the last few years, an estimated 100,000 to 150,000 low-income persons have been sterilized annually under federally funded programs."[46]

In addition to coercive family-planning programs, major social policies implemented throughout the second half the twentieth century were fueled by notions of Black women's dangerous maternity resulting from an unbridled sexuality. Daniel Patrick Moynihan's 1965 report *The Negro Family: The*

Case for National Action furthered the theory that Black mothers were responsible for the disintegration of the Black family and the consequent failure of Black people to succeed in America. But hundreds of years of state-imposed hardship and unequal treatment made such success nearly impossible for most Black people: in addition to monumental losses inflicted by enslavement, Black families had been severely disadvantaged by racist housing policies, employment discrimination, inferior schools, exclusionary banking practices, and unjust law enforcement. They were also deliberately prevented from benefiting from the radical government-assistance programs of the New Deal that promoted the well-being of white families. Yet many white sociologists blamed unwed Black mothers for creating a dysfunctional family structure by displacing Black men as the heads of households and transmitting a depraved lifestyle to their children.

By attributing this urban crisis to Black family pathology instead of structural racism, Moynihan's analysis promoted policies that tied poverty-relief programs to harsh crime-control interventions in Black neighborhoods. The 1968 crime act, for example, dramatically expanded federal funding for local police operations and led to a policy shift toward massive incarceration and surveillance.[47] During the Reagan era, the media and politicians promoted the image of the Black welfare queen—a woman who had babies just to get a government check. Now that a white elite no longer profited from the children Black women bore, they painted Black women's procreation as stealing money from white taxpayers. This mythology was powerful enough to successfully fuel a bipartisan campaign in the 1990s to abolish the federal entitlement to welfare.

During the crack epidemic, the media reported stories of Black women who traded sex for crack cocaine. They were described as lacking maternal instincts and incapable of caring for their babies. This caricature reinforced the idea that Black women were innately dissolute when it came to sexuality and mothering. Numerous Black women were arrested for drug use during pregnancy on the grounds they would give birth to "crack babies," who were predicted to cause major social problems—in sharp contrast to the largely empathetic response to the toll the opioid epidemic is currently taking on white families.[48] Medical research has since definitively discredited the "crack baby" myth. A study that tracked more than one hundred babies born between 1989 and 1992 for two decades found that children exposed to crack cocaine in utero fared no worse than children with the same socioeconomic background whose mothers didn't use drugs.[49] The hardships these Black children faced were caused primarily by the structural legacies of slavery, poverty, and other social inequities, not their mothers' stigmatized behavior.

Today, the idea of Black female hypersexuality still circulates in our society, often extending even to children. On a Saturday evening in April 2008, an eleven-year-old Black girl named Danielle Hicks-Best sneaked out of her house in the Columbia Heights neighborhood of Washington, D.C., after her parents put her in a time-out for coming home late from the playground.[50] After she encountered a group of young men from the neighborhood, she walked with one of them to a basement apartment a few blocks away. Two other young men who were already there locked the door and raped her repeatedly throughout the night. Several weeks later, Danielle was sexually assaulted again by some of the same men. After both assaults, Danielle was questioned for hours by D.C. police officers. Medical exams after each incident confirmed that she had been raped.

Yet none of the men involved in raping Danielle was charged. Instead, in June 2008, a prosecutor charged Danielle with filing a false police report and issued a warrant for her arrest. Danielle was declared a ward of the state and spent two years confined to residential mental-health facilities. The prosecutor argued that details of the stories Danielle told the police during questioning were inconsistent. An email exchange between police officers told more: "All sex was consexual [sic]. Parents are unable to accept the fact of this child's promiscuous behavior caused this situation."

How could police blame an eleven-year-old girl for being sexually abused by adult men? Why would state officials respond to a traumatized child by tearing her from her family and criminalizing her? A study by the Georgetown Law Center on Poverty and Inequality showed that adults tend to view Black girls between ages five and fourteen as less innocent and more adult-like than their white peers and treat them as if they are grown-ups. This phenomenon is so common that the term "adultification" is used to describe it.[51] Black girls are perceived as needing less protection and nurturing than white girls, and as having advanced knowledge about adult topics like sex.[52]

More than a century after slavery ended, the legal system that refused to protect a young enslaved girl who was raped by a man named George still fails to protect Black women and girls from sexual violence. With wide discretion to pursue criminal cases, prosecutors are far less likely to bring charges against men accused of raping Black women than men accused of raping white women.[53] A review of prosecutorial decisions in sexual-assault cases in Kansas City and Philadelphia discovered that prosecutors were 4.5 times more likely to file charges in rapes by strangers involving white victims than Black victims.[54] For cases that go before a jury, if the plaintiff is Black, the accused has a better chance of being acquitted and, if convicted, receiving a lighter sentence. It is not surprising then that according to Blackburn Center, which provides services to survivors of sexual violence in Westmoreland County, Pennsylvania, for every fifteen Black women who are raped, only one reports the assault.[55] Many Black women and girls see the criminal legal system as offering little recourse for the sexual violence they experience.

Indeed, the police themselves often inflict violence on Black women. As Andrea J. Ritchie, an attorney and organizer, notes in her book *Invisible No More*, she has found during twenty-five years of research that "police violence against women of color takes place disproportionately, and with alarming frequency, in the context of responses to domestic and sexual violence."[56] In other cases, police have preyed on vulnerable Black women.[57] In one notorious case, in December 2013, an Oklahoma City police officer named Daniel Holtzclaw began stopping Black women in low-income neighborhoods and sexually assaulting them. He forced one woman he arrested to perform oral sex on him while she was handcuffed to a hospital bed. He assaulted others in his patrol car, their homes, and deserted locations. Holtzclaw deliberately targeted women he thought would not report him—sex workers or women with a substance-use problem.[58] He often threatened to arrest women with outstanding tickets or warrants if they didn't perform sex acts on him.[59]

Holtzclaw went undetected until the early morning of June 18, 2014, when he pulled over Jannie Ligons, a fifty-seven-year-old Black grandmother on her way home from a friend's house.[60] After ordering her to sit in the backseat of his patrol car, Holtzclaw, his gun in sight, forced her to expose her breasts, pull down her pants, and perform oral sex on him. Ligons immediately reported the assault to the police, launching the internal investigation that exposed Holtzclaw's criminal behavior. Thirteen Black women eventually agreed to testify at the trial for felony sexual battery and rape the following year. Although he was convicted of eighteen of thirty-six counts and sentenced to 263 years in prison, we are left to wonder how many similar assaults of Black women and girls go unaccounted for. An Associated Press state-by-state review prompted by the Holtzclaw case turned up nearly one thousand officers across the country who lost their badges between 2009 and 2014 for sexual misconduct.[61]

———

Like Jannie Ligons, who reported Holtzclaw's assault to the police in the twenty-first century, and Celia, who fought back against her enslaver's sexual assaults in the nineteenth, Black women have long resisted domination of their bodies. Despite the law's denial of their humanity, enslaved women devised numerous ways to claim some control over their lives. They escaped from enslavers, endured severe punishments, pretended to be sick, used abortifacients, and cared for their children in order to hold on to as much sexual and reproductive autonomy as possible.[62] Today, Black women continue to work collectively to imagine and build ways to liberate their sexuality.

One of those women is Loretta J. Ross, the co-founder of SisterSong Women of Color Reproductive Justice Collective, an Atlanta-based organization established in 1997 as a network of sixteen organizations representing women of color. Ross's activism emerged from personal experiences of sexual and reproductive violence. A survivor of rape by a stranger at age eleven, Ross was sexually abused by a distant relative when she was fourteen and gave birth to a son. She nevertheless graduated from high school as an honors student and was admitted to Radcliffe College. But she lost her scholarship because she had a child. Ross went to Howard University instead and, as a first-year student in 1970, became involved in anti-apartheid activism and anti-gentrification organizing. Then, at age twenty-three, Ross endured another shattering violation. A white doctor failed to treat an infection caused by the Dalkon Shield, the dangerous intrauterine device marketed in the early 1970s. Ross had to be hospitalized and ended up unconscious for a day. While she was still comatose, doctors performed an emergency hysterectomy, sterilizing her.[63] "I've been working in the women's movement pretty much ever since then," Ross says. "It sounds like a horror, but it opened up the rest of my life."[64]

The 1970s was a period of foment for Black women activists addressing sexual violence. Among the most influential was a group of Black lesbian writers and activists who came together in Boston in 1974 to develop a feminism that reflected the distinctive experiences of Black women. In 1977, the group released a pioneering statement, quoting Angela Y. Davis: "Black women have always embodied, if only in their physical manifestation, an adversary stance to white male rule and have actively resisted its inroads upon them and their communities in both dramatic and subtle ways." This political activism embraced the view that "interlocking" systems of oppression determine "the conditions of our lives."[65]

In 1972, Ross started working as a volunteer at a rape crisis center in Washington, D.C., the first in the country; she became executive director in 1979.

She joined Black feminists like Davis in thinking about a radical approach to sexual violence that started from the premise that policies to protect Black women and girls must address intimate and institutional violence simultaneously and can't rely on police officers and prisons, which themselves unjustly target Black women. She also, in 1989, joined the National Black Women's Health Project, the first national organization that paid specific attention to Black women's health issues.

In June 1994, Ross was among twelve Black feminist activists attending a pro-choice conference in Chicago who felt that the healthcare agenda presented by representatives from the Clinton administration was too concerned with avoiding Republican opposition and did not adequately address concerns of Black women around sexual and reproductive autonomy. These issues included maternal mortality, evidence-based sex education, and whether women could afford abortions or preventative reproductive healthcare.

Black women not only were less likely to be able to afford an abortion but also were more likely to be deemed sexually reckless, to undergo coerced sterilizations, and to die from pregnancy-related causes. These Black feminists decided to caucus separately and came up with the term "reproductive justice" to describe a new framework that included the human right to have children and to raise them with dignity in a safe, healthy, and supportive environment, along with the right *not* to have a child, which dominated pro-choice advocacy.[66]

Ross believes it is possible to contest sexual violence against Black women while also celebrating Black women's sexuality. When she was the coordinator of SisterSong, she planned large public gatherings, held strategy summits for leaders of organizations, and offered training sessions to activists around the country. She also created "Let's Talk About Sex" conferences where more than a thousand Black women and other women of color come together. "You can't keep people safe from sexual abuse, from STDs and HIV, from sexual domination—from all the things that can go wrong with sex—if you can't talk about sex," Ross explains.[67] Topics at the conferences also include ending the stigmas around sexual pleasure, queer sex, and abortion, and differing visions of sexual and reproductive freedom.[68]

Black women were crucial to the racial-classification system established by white colonists to maintain and manage slavery. The colonial legal apparatus treated them as innately unrapeable and their children as innately enslaveable, while the culture justified that barbarity by slandering them as lascivious Jezebels. This destructive thinking has been reinforced by laws, policies, and myths that, to this day, monitor racial boundaries and Black women's sexuality and childbearing. These ideas circulate in police departments, child welfare agencies, county clerks' offices, medical clinics, and the ubiquitous racial boxes we are required to check. The creative work of Black women activists can help lead us toward liberation from this damaging heritage.

June 24, 1731

An enslaved man named Samba who works as an interpreter for the Superior Council in the French colony of Louisiana is charged with planning an uprising. Two years earlier, enslaved people and Native Americans joined forces in the Natchez rebellion, which killed more than two hundred French settlers in Louisiana. In its aftermath, rumors of new plots abounded. One concerned Samba, a Bambara man who had been a boatman on the Senegal River and was sold into slavery after attempting to lead an uprising against the French in Africa. For his alleged conspiracy in Louisiana, Samba and other plotters are either burned alive or broken on the wheel.

Conjured

Honorée Fanonne Jeffers

The Officer & I reported [the conspiracy to revolt] to the Governor who was very satisfied with my conduct, to have stopped these eight Conjured [Africans] without anyone noticing.

—Antoine-Simon Le Page du Pratz, *Histoire de la Louisiane*

How old? How tall? How kind?
We won't ever know, but Samba kept plotting
the demise of the French until his end.
   And all right, that's a tragedy for him—
the one whose name means "second son"
in the Fulbe language—
as well as those other conspiring
   Africans who died alongside him.
Were they *conjured* as that Frenchman claimed,
his excuse for scoring their flesh with fire,
these men who dared to want freedom?
   Or did those brothers simply love Samba,
a man who'd revolted once before, back in Africa
in some fort that was constantly tugged
between the French and the Portuguese.
   Samba had refused to accept
slavery: perhaps he knew that death
is a blink, a pain before crossing
to a place of no bondage.

And aren't you reading
Samba's story right now?
Aren't you curling your
lips around his people's language
                    and tasting the blood of struggle?
And what of that colonizer who resorted
to the cowardly wheel, recording what he believed
to be victory over Samba—
                    Be honest with me.
Will you even remember
that Frenchman's name?

May 10, 1740

The South Carolina Commons House of Assembly passes the Negro Act, making it illegal for enslaved Africans to move freely, assemble in groups, grow food, earn money, or learn to read and write. These restrictions come in response to the Stono Rebellion, the largest uprising of enslaved people in the colonies to date. It was spearheaded the previous year by a man named Jemmy, who was most likely Kongolese. Jemmy led a band of roughly twenty men southward from the Stono River, killing white people, burning plantations, and recruiting new fighters along the way. Their goal was to reach Spanish Florida, which offered freedom to fugitives, but before they could escape South Carolina, they were defeated by a white militia.

A Ghazalled Sentence After "My People . . . Hold On" by Eddie Kendricks and the Negro Act of 1740

Terrance Hayes

WHEREIN, a particular people
are allowed to make slaves of people

after the 1739 revolt where people convinced
tools useful in implementing their people's

freedom had been stolen from them pursued
people to a river shallow enough for people

to cross on horseback & some of the people leapt
into the river kicking their legs like people

on the riverbank kicking the legs of the horses
& the people on the horses while some people

managed to briefly evade retrieval
by people who could not see the people

they pursued could not be retrieved,
People,

because your body belongs to you,
& certainly not to the kind of people

who devised laws to make properties
of people after the people

at the river were captured, their heads
put on stakes along the road & people

who briefly eluded pursuit before
being recouped or returned to people

so afraid of working for themselves
they made it illegal for other people

to work for themselves, grow their own food,
congregate & educate their own people,

without say-so of the kind of people who come
after people pursuing freedom for their people

while pursuing freedom for the people
who come after their people.

A child during Mardi Gras, New Orleans, 2005 MARIO TAMA

CHAPTER 3

Sugar

KHALIL GIBRAN MUHAMMAD

On the banks of the Mississippi River, a few dozen miles west of New Orleans, rusted sugar mills dot the fertile landscape of southern Louisiana. Rising high above country roads bordered on two sides by dense foliage, the mill smokestacks stand tall like rounded obelisks, monuments to Queen Sugar's regal history. Most of the plantation houses and fields that once fed these mills are less visible. They are concealed down long driveways, hidden behind thick underbrush, and trapped in a false memory of the past.

The Whitney Plantation is different. It sits on the northern edge of St. John the Baptist Parish, once home to dozens of thriving sugar plantations. But unlike the others, it beckons to passersby. When you approach the place at the edge of a gravelly entrance, a bright white sign with red lettering announces, THE STORY OF SLAVERY. Framed by lush trees in need of trimming, the Whitney Plantation's main residence, where generations of owners once lived, is a French colonial structure, built for the tropical climate. Its wide-hipped roof overhangs a two-level wraparound porch that offers maximal shade. Louvered doors and window shutters abound, a means of managing the insufferably hot, sticky air. Nine columns stand squat across the front of the house, seeming to reach deep down into the soil, like anchors to keep the Atlantic hurricanes from washing it into the waters from whence its enslaved workers originally came.

The rear of the house opens to a green expanse where all is visible. The first structure you see is the main kitchen, a detached building two hundred feet to the right of the house. Down a bit farther are a mule barn, a blacksmith's shop, the machinery of sugar making, and a half dozen slave quarters that resemble the dilapidated shotgun homes of New Orleans's Lower Ninth Ward, except without paint. From the enslavers' bedroom windows, the Whitney's cane fields stretch out to the horizon.

Before the Europeans arrived, all of this land was home to Taensa Indians. German farmers began showing up in 1719, after which the area was called the German Coast, because unlike most of the earliest colonial settlers to Louisiana, these particular newcomers were not French.[1] The Whitney Plantation was built in 1752. From its rich soil, enslaved Africans, many of whom were from Senegambia, cultivated corn, indigo, and rice until sugar took over at the turn of the nineteenth century. The Whitney operated continuously until 1975. Today it is a museum. But unlike many plantation museums in the South, this one is designed not to glorify a past of putatively genteel masters and mistresses but to educate visitors and offer them a chance to bear witness to the exploitation and extraction that are the foundation of our modern world.

What little Americans are taught or think they know about the slavery-based economy is largely a success story of how cotton became the nation's leading export in the nineteenth century. Some people might also think of tobacco as a cash crop worked by enslaved people in places like Virginia in earlier eras. But even though cotton and tobacco dominated the colonial American economy, it was sugar that anchored the economy of the larger Atlantic world from the sixteenth century onward. Sugar slavery, which was uniquely destructive and deadly, made Brazil the focal point in the triangular trade in the century before twenty to thirty Africans landed in Point Comfort, Virginia, in 1619. Until then, European colonists had considered North America little more than an afterthought.

"White gold," as sugar was called, drove trade in goods and people, fueled the wealth of European nations, and, for the British in particular, shored up the financing of the North American colonies. Over the span of nearly three hundred years, from the mid-sixteenth century on, a succession of European nations—Portugal, Spain, the Netherlands, France, and Britain—plied an international slave trade, with African elites and dealers on one side of the ocean and an insatiable demand by white colonists for enslaved labor on the other.

It is not an overstatement to say that the crop they produced changed the world. Cane stalks still grow at the Whitney Plantation Museum, as they do on nearly every speck of fertile ground as far as the eye can see, a lush green testament to the unquenchable taste for the plant's sweet juice. The Whitney's tiny annual crop, which helps pay the museum's bills, is an infinitesimal portion of U.S. domestic sugar production, which itself is but a portion of a global sugar industry that produces some two hundred million tons per year. The world's leading sugar producer is Brazil; the United States ranks fifth in global production, with about nine million tons annually. Domestically, the sugar produced from sugarcane and sugar beets remains one of the country's most important agricultural products. Louisiana's sugarcane industry is by itself worth $3 billion, generating an estimated 16,400 jobs.

As important as sugar has become to American agriculture, it's had an even bigger impact on the American diet—some 73 pounds of sugar and related sweeteners, such as high-fructose corn syrup, are consumed per person per year, according to United States Department of Agriculture data.[2] That makes us the biggest per capita consumers of sugar in the world. Those nine million tons we grow each year aren't nearly enough to meet our demand, so we import an additional three million tons annually.

And sugar is no average foodstuff. What was once a luxury to adorn the lavish banquets of elites has become a toxic foodstuff for the masses. America's high rate of sugar consumption is a major factor in our poor national health. The average American's sugar consumption is nearly twice the limit the USDA recommends, based on a two-thousand-calorie diet, and sugar has been linked in the United States to diabetes, obesity, and cancer. Over the last thirty years, the group of Americans who are obese or overweight grew 30 percent among all adults, to 73 percent from 56 percent, according to the Centers for Disease Control and Prevention.[3] During the same period, diabetes rates overall nearly tripled.

But if sugar is killing all of us, it is killing Black people faster. In the food deserts of many redlined Black communities, where supermarkets are scarce, cheap, sugary processed foods fill the shelves of convenience stores and the bellies of Black shoppers. African Americans are overrepresented in the national figures on obesity; diabetes rates among Black men and women are nearly one and a half times those of white men and women.[4] One of the great ironies of sugar's history in the United States is that the brutal work of the enslaved created an industry whose success in producing unhealthy food for mass consumption has taken its greatest toll on Black communities today.

None of this was in any way foreordained, or even predictable. For thousands of years, sugarcane was a heavy and unwieldy crop that had to be cut by hand and immediately ground to release the juice inside; otherwise it would spoil within a day or two. Even before harvesttime, rows had to be dug, stalks planted, and plentiful wood chopped as fuel for boiling the liquid and reducing it to crystals and molasses. From the earliest traces of cane domestication on the Pacific island of New Guinea ten thousand years ago to its island-hopping advance to ancient India in 350 B.C., sugar was locally consumed and remained little more than an exotic spice, medicinal glaze, or sweetener for elite palates.

This was in part because it was incredibly labor-intensive to produce. To achieve scale for export and trade, cane required tremendous coerced and coordinated human labor in warm climates and on fertile land. Arab enslavers from as far back as the eighth century are credited with spreading sugar plantations throughout the Mediterranean basin of southern Europe and North Africa—Sicily, Cyprus, Malta, Spain, and Morocco—as Muslim rulers conquered parts of the region over the next two centuries. "Sugar, we are told, followed the Koran," wrote the late anthropologist Sidney Mintz.[5]

As sugar spread in Europe in the Renaissance period, its high price marked it as a luxury good and a symbol of wealth—often in the form of sugar replicas of monumental castles, animals, and other self-aggrandizing objects fancied by nobles. It was after Christopher Columbus's second voyage across the Atlantic Ocean, in 1493, bringing sugarcane stalks with him from the Spanish Canary Islands, that everything changed. By then, Spain and Portugal had already begun to put enslaved Africans to work growing sugarcane on the Atlantic islands off the coast of North Africa, and the potential for an industry based on forced labor, fertile land, and a dawning era of global trade had reached an inflection point. "The true Age of Sugar had begun," Marc Aronson and Marina Budhos write in their book *Sugar Changed the World*. "And it was doing more to reshape the world than any ruler, empire or war had ever done."[6] Over the next two centuries, on the sugar islands of the Greater Antilles—Saint-Domingue, Cuba, and Puerto Rico, among others—and the mainlands of Mexico and Brazil, European powers destroyed countless Indigenous lives as colonists staked out vast agricultural operations on their land and enslaved millions of Africans to work the fields.

By the mid-seventeenth century, in this already-established Atlantic world, the British would stake a claim to the sugar islands of Barbados and Jamaica and the North American colonies. Soon, they came to dominate the international slave trade, too. Although England first established trading posts for acquiring gold and ivory along a span of five thousand coastal Atlantic miles from present-day Morocco to South Africa, by 1672, King Charles II had conferred a monopoly on the Royal African Company specifically for the slave trade.[7] The company used military personnel, government agents, and private investment capital garnered by selling stock to merchants to build the single most successful transatlantic slave-trading institution in history.

Ships traveled a sea route that in its simplest form resembled an isosceles triangle. The voyage typically started with Royal African ships departing from Bristol, Liverpool, or London, heading to Africa carrying rum, guns, iron bars, fetters, glass beads, clothes, and copper pots to trade for people. Those ships would arrive, for example, in Cape Coast Castle, in present-day Ghana—Britain's West African slaving capital—where they would load African captives. With their human cargo, they would sail across the Atlantic. This became known as the Middle Passage, since it was the middle leg of the triangular route. Arriving in Barbados or Jamaica, the ships would exchange people for sugar, molasses, and lumber. From there they would return home to England, completing the last part of the triangle.

Other forms of this triangular route existed, with stops in the North American colonies to load rice, tobacco, flour, and rum, but the crucial leg of the journey was the Middle Passage. Without African lives as the human raw materials in the making of sugar, along with other wealth-producing plantation commodities—tobacco, rice, indigo, and cotton—the distribution of Atlantic peoples and the wealth of the world would likely be very different today. From finance to finished goods, the transatlantic trade spawned a dizzying array of British businesses, manufacturing ships and armaments, glass and iron, linens and pottery, and distilling rum and beer, which would be sold in Africa, the West Indies, and North America, as well as at home in the British Isles.[8]

"Are we not indebted to that valuable People, the Africans, for our Sugars, Tobaccoes, Rice, Rum, and all other Plantation Produce?" asked Malachy Postlethwayt, a London merchant, member of the Royal African Company, and author of *The African Trade: The Great Pillar and Support of the British Plantation Trade in America,* published in 1745. The more "Negroes imported," he wrote, the more British goods were made and exported for trade. "The Negro-trade," he emphasized, was the foundation of "an inexhaustible Fund of Wealth and Naval Power to this Nation."[9]

Postlethwayt's bullish report was backed by solid evidence. In its first decade, the Royal African Company of England rapidly increased its share of the trade from one-third to three-quarters of the market. During the 1750s, England became the "supreme slaving nation in the Atlantic world," write historians James Rawley and Stephen D. Behrendt.[10] In Bristol, England, a local annalist writing about the eighteenth century noted, "There is not a brick in the city but what is cemented with the blood of a slave."[11]

And that blood was spilled, more than anywhere else, in the production of sugar. As production grew and the market increased, the craze for the sweetener gradually trickled down from elites to the laboring poor. By 1850, sweetened tea, the combination of East and West Indian imports of tea and sugar, was a stimulant, calorie boost, and hot meal substitute for English men, who were working more and more in city factories than on country farms. The increasing supply from sugar plantations lowered the cost and made cheap sugar "the single most important addition to the British working-class diet during the nineteenth century," according to Sidney Mintz.[12]

The voracious appetite for wealth creation and the unyielding desire for sugar combined to create the foundation of the modern world. From the first time Royal African Company slavers set sail for North America, through the years of the American Revolution, until the abolition of the international slave trade in 1808, roughly three million souls, many of them forever branded with the company's initials, RAC, on their bodies, would be forcibly removed from their homes, their kin, and their way of life, the majority of them to feed demand for a sweetener. Countless fortunes were made. In Liverpool, the Martins Bank Building, opened in 1932, and the former home of Barclays, memorialized the role of banks in financing the trade with a relief sculpture of two African boys fettered about the neck and ankles and holding bags of money.[13]

The slave trade was complex and evolved out of existing networks of exchange indigenous to Africa. Before European slavers arrived, African chiefs and merchants were already trading among themselves, along well-established routes from West to East, from the Saharan north to the sub-Saharan south, and all points in between. In addition to trading palm cloth, copper jewelry, ivory ornaments, cutlery, wood, and musical instruments, merchants would exchange enslaved people, captured in wars or village raids. Like elsewhere in the world, "a ready system of servitude" already existed, writes historian Sowande' Mustakeem, the author of *Slavery at Sea*. European traders "came as business partners" in what she calls "the human manufacturing process," which consisted of three violent stages of preconditioning—capture, transport, and delivery—for the brutalities of work awaiting them on faraway sugar plantations.[14]

African elites did not typically sell their own kin. Captives tended to be "culturally and ethnically alien to those who enslaved them," writes the historian James Campbell, the author of *Middle Passages: African American Journeys to Africa, 1787-2005*.[15] About half the captives were prisoners of war, according to Rawley and Behrendt. Another third were people labeled as criminals, undesirables, or outcasts and treated with disdain (similar to how the English regarded indentured servants forcibly shipped to their North American colonies and Australia in the seventeenth and eighteenth centuries). The 20 percent remaining, Rawley and Behrendt estimate, were victims of kidnapping.[16]

But some historians think that the kidnapping number is much higher. Mustakeem cites 70 percent for the proportion of "purchased slaves" who, by the eighteenth century, had been "snatched from their homes and communities" before being removed by sea.[17] Certainly from the perspective of many of the men, women, and children who were put in the holds of slave vessels, the technical definition of kidnapping was a difference without distinction. Few non-elites were spared. One example, recorded in the testimony given to the British Parliament's House of Commons in the late 1700s, gives a sense of the violence of the enterprise. Off the coast of Bonny Point, in present-day Nigeria, a young woman was grabbed by two men, who "secured her hands behind her back, beat her, and ill-used her, on account of the resistance she made," according to testimony given by John Douglas, a slave trader.[18] Traders routinely tore families asunder as they captured and stole people away from mothers, fathers, sons, and daughters. Even some African traders ended up in fetters because of the treachery of it all. One measure of the horrors of kidnapping captives is evidenced by the British Parliament outlawing it in 1750.[19]

After being captured or sold, individuals were dragged to barracks, where they often lived for months—some of them died there—before slavers loaded them onto ships, one batch of bodies at a time. The transport phase of the human manufacturing process lasted anywhere from three to five weeks, depending on whether a ship was traveling to Barbados, Jamaica, or New England. Slavers who had originated in Bristol or Liverpool carried, during the peak years, an average of 356 captives on board.[20] Strong, healthy African men in their prime, between fifteen and twenty-five years old, made up the bulk of the enslaved at sea. "Planters preferred adult males for work in sugar cultivation," Rawley and Behrendt write, and particularly favored men from Guinea, who were perceived to be "docile and agreeable." Ship captains aimed for a two-to-one ratio of men to women, with a small percentage of boys and girls.[21] Traders judged women's fitness by their reproductive potential, just as horse breeders might judge the qualities of a broodmare. In the House of Lords' Records of Certificate of Slaves Taken on Board Ships, one merchant recorded: "the Women in general having good Breasts were strong and well."[22]

Slavery at sea, as historians have long written, brought terrors to the captives beyond our worst nightmares. The extreme challenges of food preservation and water rationing made the transoceanic journey itself treacherous.[23] The economics of the trade and financial incentives for captains and ship surgeons conspired to keep alive as many captives as possible. But there were limits. Starting with space. The surgeon Alexander Falconbridge described conditions aboard his ship where captives "had not so much room as a man in his coffin, neither in length or breadth, and it was impossible for them to turn or shift with any degree of ease."[24] Captain John Ashley testified before the members of the House of Commons that he "frequently heard them crying out when below for the want of air."[25] Suffocating as if buried alive, with human waste uncontainable, men were shackled side by side as metal and iron tore into flesh with every jolt of the ocean. Mustakeem found a report in the archives of several men on the *Venus* who died from "Part of the Scrotum torn off w'th their Irons."[26]

Slave crews typically separated men from women, leaving women in their own quarters, unchained and unprotected. All the easier for sailors to rape them. John Newton, a slave trader turned abolitionist who wrote the hymn "Amazing Grace," described this in his memoir: "they are often exposed to the wanton rudeness of white savages." Another ship's crew referred to the area where women were held as the "whore hole." Instances of sexual violation on these voyages are impossible to count definitively. But from ship logs, journals, and testimonies it is evident that they were numerous. On the British vessel *African* in 1753, William Cooney raped a pregnant woman; she was listed in the log as "number 83," following a common practice for a kind of deadnaming of captives. He took her "into the room and lay with her brute like in view of the whole quarter deck."[27]

In these moments, slave traders were conditioning Africans for plantation slavery. But the captives were also forming a new identity, a diasporic Blackness, forged out of their collective fate, as they found strength in one another with every miserable day that passed. Uprisings of captives at sea were rare but were the most spectacular instances of collective resistance. A 1731 insurrection involved 140 Africans; they killed most of the crew and escaped with the ship.[28] Much more frequent acts of resistance took the form of recalcitrance, a refusal by captives to eat or to exercise. They plotted conspiracies to poison the crew's food and beverage. And they also took complete control of their individual bodies and minds when they sought freedom in another realm. The surgeon Isaac Wilson recalled a man who threw himself into the sea and seemed to relish his own drowning. He "went down as if exulting that he got away," the physician remembered.[29]

On the Middle Passage, mortality rates ranged from 5 to 20 percent, lowering as the centuries passed. Africans died most often from diseases, including scurvy (an acute vitamin C deficiency), smallpox, pneumonia, and tapeworms. The flux, or dysentery, the most common cause of death, produced its own slow torture of blood-soaked diarrhea and incessant vomiting, triggered by a bacterial infection from contaminated food or water.[30] By the time captives became enslaved on the other side, they had experienced "layered cycles of violence, deprivation, and death," Mustakeem writes, seasoned "by the terrorizing dynamics of shipboard captivity."[31]

American slavers were the last to enter the trade. But from the ports of Rhode Island, beginning in 1709 and lasting officially to 1807, Rhode Islanders managed to make nearly a thousand voyages to Africa, procuring 106,544 enslaved people.[32] Illegal trafficking continued for decades. Alongside the triangular trade, American colonists opened direct lines of trade that didn't resemble a triangle at all. They traded directly with England, delivering mainland commodities produced by enslaved labor, such as rice, tobacco, and cotton, as well as flour and lumber, and returned home with manufactured goods and luxury items. On separate voyages, American colonists also exported North Atlantic dried cod, flour, and pine wood to plantations in the British West Indies, in exchange for sugar and molasses.

Molasses was a key part of the sugar trade.[33] It is made during the boiling stage of sugar production, when the cane juice is heated in huge kettles until sugar crystals begin to form as a result of evaporation. This granulation process is repeated several times, producing more crystals, which are filtered out or collected by a strainer. What is left behind is a thicker and thicker concentrate of liquid residue, which becomes molasses. Sugar was incredibly profitable, but molasses became an indispensable exchange commodity, too. It was crucial to the manufacturing of desserts, sweet rolls and buns, and other processed foods. It was also the key ingredient in the making of rum. And rum was the lubricant that helped make the international slave trade run like a well-oiled machine.[34]

Americans excelled at fermenting and distilling molasses to make millions of gallons of rum, which American-built slave ships, often called "rum vessels," brought to West Africa, among other places, to trade for African captives.[35] Aside from being an essential "naval ration" in the Age of Sail, rum was "an essential part of the cargo of the slave ship, particularly the colonial American slave ship," writes the historian Eric Williams in *Capitalism and Slavery*. "It was profitable to spread a taste for liquor on the coast. The Negro dealers were plied with it, were induced to drink till they lost their reason, and then the bargain was struck."[36]

The New England colonies, led by Rhode Island, operated several distilleries, which produced millions of gallons of rum and brought huge fortunes to white Americans.[37] Eight years before the Boston Tea Party, colonists took part in a lesser-known Rhode Island revolt against the Sugar Act of 1764, which dramatically increased enforcement of duties collected on imported sugar and molasses. Rhode Islanders had avoided paying these taxes by illegally smuggling in molasses for their lucrative rum business from cheaper French West Indian suppliers, bypassing the British West Indies. On April 7, 1765, a group of men blackened their faces to disguise themselves as Native Americans and seized the cargo of the *Polly,* which included "barrel after barrel of molasses from the sugar islands," write Aronson and Budhos.[38] John Adams observed that the British Parliament had gone too far with its revenue scheme. "Molasses was an essential ingredient of American independence," Adams would later write.[39]

Though Britain's North American colonies participated extensively in the sugar trade, the climate of these regions favored other crops, such as tobacco, indigo, rice, and cotton. Americans today tend not to think of sugar as the primary crop of slavery, in part because production was mostly limited to the West Indies, colonies held by Spain, Britain, and France that did not ultimately become part of the United States. The main exception to this is Louisiana, which was occupied by the French until 1803. In New Orleans in 1751, French Jesuit priests planted the first cane stalks in the area, near Baronne Street. In the Gulf region of southern Louisiana, weather conditions were more like those in the Caribbean, a geographic space the historian Matthew Guterl called the American Mediterranean.[40] Given the city's tropical climate, the plant thrived, which it had failed to do in the British colonies of Georgia and South Carolina.

Within a few decades sugarcane production in Louisiana took root. In 1795, Étienne de Boré, a New Orleans sugar planter, granulated the first sugar crystals in the Louisiana Territory. With the advent of local sugar processing, sugar plantations exploded up and down both banks of the Mississippi River.

All of this was possible because of the abundantly rich alluvial soil, combined with the technical mastery of seasoned French and Spanish planters who had come to Louisiana from around the cane-growing basin of the Gulf and the Caribbean—and because of the toil of thousands of enslaved people. Estimates suggest that twenty to twenty-two thousand Africans were captured and brought to Louisiana between 1763 and 1812.[41] Most of them, according to the Louisiana Slave Database, built in the 1990s by the historian

Gwendolyn Midlo Hall, had been born in Africa on the coasts of Senegambia, the Bight of Benin, the Bight of Biafra, and West-Central Africa. The most common ethnicities were Congo, Mandinga, Mina, Bambara, and Wolof.[42]

One of the major contributors to the booming Louisiana sugar industry was the Haitian Revolution. More French planters and their enslaved expert sugar workers poured into Louisiana as Toussaint Louverture and Jean-Jacques Dessalines led a successful revolt in Saint-Domingue to secure independence from France in 1804. For decades, Saint-Domingue had been a top producer of sugar, and an especially brutal one, so perhaps it is no surprise that the African-descended inhabitants of that colony became the first enslaved sugar workers to stage a successful insurrection.

It was just one year before, in 1803, that the Whitney Plantation had become a prosperous sugar operation, under the leadership of Jean Jacques Haydel, Sr., who had inherited the property from his father, Ambroise Heidel. In 1820, Haydel, Sr., passed the plantation on to his two sons and eventually to a widowed daughter-in-law, Marie Azélie Haydel, in 1840.[43] Marie, in turn, became one of Louisiana's most successful planters. In the 1840s and '50s, the plantation produced hundreds of thousands of pounds of sugar, peaking in the 1854–55 season with 407,000 pounds. According to the Whitney museum's director of research, Ibrahima Seck, the Whitney's sugar output made it "one of the most important plantations in Louisiana."[44]

The Whitney's economic success contributed to Louisiana's rapid growth in the global sugar trade. By the 1850s, Louisiana planters were producing a quarter of the world's cane-sugar supply. During her antebellum reign, Queen Sugar bested King Cotton locally, making Louisiana the second-richest state in per capita wealth. According to the historian Richard Follett, in 1840 the state ranked third in banking capital, behind New York and Massachusetts. The value of enslaved people alone represented tens of millions of dollars in capital that financed investments, loans, and businesses. Much of that investment funneled back into the sugar mills, the "most industrialized sector of Southern agriculture," Follett writes.[45] No other agricultural region came close to the amount of capital investment in farming by the eve of the Civil War. In 1853, Representative Miles Taylor of Louisiana bragged that his state's success was "without parallel in the United States, or indeed in the world in any branch of industry."[46]

None of this growth was possible without trafficking in human lives. Or to put it in the words of the U.S. commissioner of agriculture in 1867: "Land without labor [was] worthless."[47] After the official end of the international slave trade as of January 1, 1808, the domestic trade from the Upper South to the

Lower South exploded, while traffic continued on the Atlantic. As a result, Louisiana's enslaved population soared, quadrupling over a twenty-year period to 125,000 souls in the mid-nineteenth century. New Orleans became the Walmart of people-selling. The number of enslaved labor crews on its sugar plantations doubled. And in every sugar parish, Black people outnumbered white.

These were some of the most skilled laborers, doing some of the most dangerous agricultural and industrial work in the United States. Some enslaved workers mastered the technical skills of distillation, turning cane juice into raw sugar and molasses under intense time pressure, to ensure no spoilage and maximum yields. In the mills, alongside adults, children toiled like factory workers with assembly-line precision and discipline under the constant threat of boiling-hot kettles, open furnaces, and grinding rollers. "All along the endless carrier are ranged slave children, whose business it is to place the cane upon it, when it is conveyed through the shed into the main building," wrote the free-born upstate New Yorker Solomon Northup in *Twelve Years a Slave*, his 1853 memoir of being kidnapped while visiting Washington, D.C., and forced into slavery on Louisiana plantations.[48]

To achieve the highest efficiency, sugar houses operated night and day. "On cane plantations in sugar time, there is no distinction as to the days of the week," Northup wrote.[49] Fatigue might mean losing an arm to the grinding rollers or being flayed for failing to keep up. Enslavers often met resistance with sadistic cruelty.

A formerly enslaved Black woman named Mrs. Webb described a torture chamber used by her enslaver, Valsin Marmillion. "One of his cruelties was to place a disobedient slave, standing in a box, in which there were nails placed in such a manner that the poor creature was unable to move," she told a WPA interviewer in 1940. "He was powerless even to chase the flies, or sometimes ants crawling on some parts of his body."[50]

Louisiana led the nation in destroying the lives of Black people in the name of economic efficiency. The historian Michael Tadman found that Louisiana sugar parishes had a pattern of "deaths greatly exceed[ing] births."[51] Backbreaking labor and "inadequate net nutrition meant that enslaved people working on sugar plantations were, compared with other working-age enslaved people in the United States, far less able to resist the common and life-threatening diseases of dirt and poverty," wrote Tadman in a 2000 study published in *The American Historical Review*.[52] Life expectancy was lower than on a cotton plantation and closer to that of a Jamaican cane field, where the most overworked and abused could drop dead after seven years of labor.

Nevertheless, some enslaved sugar workers managed to fight back. In 1811, in the German Coast area, near the Whitney Plantation, as many as five hundred sugar rebels joined a liberation army heading toward New Orleans, one of the largest revolts of enslaved people in United States history. They were soon cut down by federal troops and local militia; no record of their actual plan survives. About a hundred were killed in battle or executed later; many of their heads were severed and placed on pikes throughout the region. There were nearly twice as many executions as there were during Nat Turner's more well-known 1831 rebellion, according to historians' estimates.

There are no oral histories from the Whitney Plantation to preserve the firsthand testimonies of those who experienced the harsh brutalities of life there. The museum's archived inventory records of enslaved people at the time of Marie Azélie Haydel's passing in 1860, on the eve of the Civil War, suggest that the enslavers systematically sold children for profit, severing offspring from parents. According to Ashley Rogers, the Whitney's executive director, of the 101 people counted, most were adult men, several were Creole-identified women, and 32 were young children, who could not be sold under Louisiana law unless accompanied by their mothers. "There were no children older than ten years," she told me. "None."[53]

America's sugar slavery ended in 1865, but by that time sugar was a staple product everywhere in the world. After the Civil War, Black people sought to build lives on their own terms, and in the decades that followed, U.S. sugar plantations reorganized themselves around the labor of free Black workers. Though many Black Louisianans found that the crushing work with sugarcane remained mostly the same, during the early days of Reconstruction, Black political organizing in the form of Union Leagues swept the sugar region, along with the rest of the South.

Given the large Black populations in these areas, freedmen made significant gains overnight, electing Black state officials and inspiring economic changes and labor organizing on sugar plantations. Agents from the Freedmen's Bureau, the federal agency responsible for ensuring Black people's safety and welfare following the war, often noted in their reports that planters frequently complained that when they dismissed one worker, the others "would immediately quit work & threaten to leave the place."[54] As new wage earners, Black sugar workers acting in solidarity negotiated the best terms they could, signed labor contracts for up to a year, and moved from one plantation to another in search of a life whose daily rhythms beat differently than before.

But the gains of Reconstruction were short-lived. As W.E.B. Du Bois so eloquently wrote in his 1935 book *Black Reconstruction in America, 1860–1880:* "The slave went free; stood a brief moment in the sun; then moved back again toward slavery."[55] The domestic terrorism that ended Reconstruction and destroyed so many Black lives was particularly vicious in the sugar region. Striking sugar workers were often met with swift and violent reprisals. In November 1887, a decade after former Confederates had regained political control of the South and had terrorized and purged much of Louisiana's Black political leadership from office, a national union attempted to organize sugar workers. In three parishes during harvest season, workers had "downed their tools, walked off the job," and insisted on higher wages paid in cash rather than plantation credit, writes Follett. Strikebreakers and state militiamen responded with a show of force. Shots rang out, and at least thirty Black people—some sources estimated hundreds—were killed in their homes and on the streets of Thibodaux, Louisiana. "I think this will settle the question of who is to rule[,] the nigger or the White man? for the next 50 years," a local white planter's widow, Mary Pugh, wrote, rejoicing, to her son.[56]

Sugar enslavers never lost their grip on the land. Compared with Black sharecropping on cotton plantations, where African Americans gained a small measure of physical independence as individual family units living and working on white-owned land, Black cane workers had little choice but to live in somebody's old slave quarters. As had been the case for centuries, making cane into sugar required access to huge swaths of land, large amounts of capital, and gang labor to plant, harvest, and mill the crop.

In spite of the substantial barriers of capital and racism, African Americans nevertheless aspired to own sugarcane farms or rent them from white owners. A small number of Black sugar farmers inherited land from their antebellum free Black ancestors or accumulated property on their own. But they faced discrimination at every turn and the threat of violence if their success challenged the Jim Crow racial order. The historian Rebecca Scott found that although "black farmers were occasionally able to buy plots of cane land from bankrupt estates, or otherwise establish themselves as suppliers, the trend was for planters to seek to establish relations with white tenants or sharecroppers who could provide cane for the mill."[57] And if Black sugarcane farmers succeeded in the face of all these obstacles, they still had to face racist actions by government agencies, banks, and real estate developers who conspired to take their land.

Mechanization made matters worse, by rewarding large-scale farming and shrinking the number of jobs. Increasingly, only poorly paid seasonal work remained. By World War II, many Black people in the sugar-growing regions sought opportunity and autonomy elsewhere, moving from the cane fields in Louisiana to car factories in the North. Today, the number of Black sugar farmers in Louisiana is likely in the single digits.

The Mississippi River is and always has been the lifeblood of the region, nurturing the southern Louisiana soil and linking this place to a many-centuries-old Atlantic market in sugar and the enslaved. It bears witness to all that has happened here—the human beings stolen, shipped, and sold on plantations, the harsh realities of lives cut short by sugar. The road that leaves the Whitney Plantation follows the river, which snakes along just beyond the grass-covered levees. On most days there's not much traffic. The land is quiet and sun-drenched, with round hay bales that lie like small animals resting peacefully atop the grass. There is something idyllic about the landscape, but there is nothing innocent about the history of this place, where human beings corrupted nature to do great harm to humanity.

Though Black labor no longer plays a big role in producing sugar, sugar still plays a big role in the lives of Black people. Among all Americans, added sugar has been linked to growing rates of certain chronic illnesses, including those from which Black people suffer the most. African Americans are more likely to eat poorer-quality, processed foods with high amounts of added sugars. In 2013, public-health researchers at Johns Hopkins University used the U.S. Census and InfoUSA food-store data to analyze supermarket availability by census tract. As poverty increased, the number of supermarkets decreased, but the prevalence of junk-food-stocked convenience stores increased. And when poverty was held constant, the researchers found, Black communities still had the "fewest supermarkets."[58]

In a 2015 study of healthful food availability in Topeka, Kansas, researchers at Kansas State University found that even low-income white neighborhoods were twice as likely to have a food store as Black ones. "Food deserts and food insecurity," they concluded, "are perhaps the most important deleterious consequence of residential segregation in the United States."[59] The scarcity of healthful food options in Black neighborhoods is offset by the abundance of bad ones. Recent nutritional surveys by the National Center for Health Statistics found that among children, adolescents, and adults, Black people consume a higher percentage of their daily calories from fast food than do Hispanic and white people.[60]

In addition, certain food companies have targeted Black youths with advertising. A marketing analysis of television advertising dollars found a 50 percent increase, between 2013 and 2017, in ads for sweetened food and beverages, and snacks aimed at Black households. Shiriki Kumanyika, a co-author of the study and the chair of Drexel University's Council on Black Health, said of the findings: "At best, these advertising patterns imply that food companies view Black consumers as interested in candy, sugary drinks, fast food and snacks with a lot of salt, fat or sugar, but not in healthier foods."[61]

Since sugar came to these shores, there hasn't been a time when Black people weren't getting the short end of the cane stalk. From plantation to farm to table, African Americans have always paid the highest costs for sugar cultivation.

March 5, 1770

A confrontation between colonists and British soldiers erupts outside the Boston Custom House. In the ensuing melee, Crispus Attucks, a fugitive from slavery now employed as a dockworker, becomes the first colonist to die for the cause of independence. The event, which comes to be known as the Boston Massacre, is one of the factors that turns the colonies against British rule and leads to the American Revolution.

First to Rise

Yusef Komunyakaa

African & Natick blood-born
known along paths up & down
Boston Harbor, escaped slave,

harpooner & ropemaker,
he never dreamt a pursuit of happiness
or destiny, yet rallied

beside patriots who hurled a fury
of snowballs, craggy dirt-frozen
chunks of ice, & oyster shells

at the stout flank of redcoats,
as the 29th Regiment of Foot
aimed muskets, waiting for fire!

How often had he walked, gazing
down at gray timbers of the wharf,
as if to find a lost copper coin?

Wind deviled cold air as he stood
leaning on his hardwood stick,
& then two lead bullets

tore his chest, blood reddening snow
on King Street, March 5, 1770,
first to fall on captain's command.

Five colonists lay for calling hours
in Faneuil Hall before sharing a grave
at the Granary Burying Ground.

They had laid a foundering stone
for the Minutemen at Lexington
& Concord, first to defy & die,

& an echo of the future rose over
the courtroom as John Adams
defended the Brits, calling the dead

a "motley rabble of saucy boys,
negroes & mulattoes, Irish
teagues & outlandish jacktars,"

who made soldiers fear for their lives,
& at day's end only two would pay
with the branding of their thumbs.

1773

A publishing house in London releases *Poems on Various Subjects, Religious and Moral,* by Phillis Wheatley, a twenty-year-old enslaved woman in Boston, making her the first African American to publish a book of poetry. Wheatley was captured in West Africa when she was seven years old. Her first name was derived from the ship that took her across the Atlantic Ocean. Her last name belonged to the prominent Boston family who purchased her. After her book is published, Wheatley is freed. The remainder of her life is marked by poverty and illness.

proof [dear Phillis]

Eve L. Ewing

Among the blacks is misery enough, God knows, but no poetry. . . . Religion
indeed has produced a Phyllis Wheatley; but it could not produce a poet. The
compositions published under her name are below the dignity of criticism.

—Thomas Jefferson, *Notes on the State of Virginia*

Pretend I wrote this at your grave.
Pretend the grave is marked. Pretend we know where it is.
Copp's Hill, say. I have been there and you might be.
Foremother, your name is the boat that brought you.
Pretend I see it in the stone, with a gruesome cherub.
Children come with thin paper and charcoal to touch you.
Pretend it drizzles and a man in an ugly plastic poncho
circles the Mathers, all but sniffing the air warily.
We don't need to pretend for this part.
There is a plaque in the grass for Increase, and Cotton.
And Samuel, dead at 78, final son, who was there
on the day when they came looking for proof.
Eighteen of them watched you and they signed to say:
>   *the Poems specified in the following Page, were (as we verily believe)*
>   *written by Phillis, a young Negro Girl, who was but a few Years since,*
>   *brought an uncultivated Barbarian from Africa*
and the abolitionists cheered at the blow to Kant
>   *the Negroes of Africa have by nature no feeling that rises above the trifling*

and the enlightened ones bellowed at the strike against Hume
no ingenious manufacturers amongst them, no arts, no sciences

Pretend I was there with you, Phillis, when you asked in a letter to no one:
How many iambs to be a real human girl?
Which turn of phrase evidences a righteous heart?
If I know of Ovid, may I keep my children?

Pretend that on your grave there is a date
and it is so long before my heroes came along to call you a coon
for the praises you sang of your captors
who took you on discount because they assumed you would die
that it never ever hurt your feelings.
Or pretend you did not love America.
Phillis, I would like to think that after you were released unto the world,
when they jailed your husband for his debts
and you lay in the maid's quarters at night,
a free and poor woman with your last living boy,
that you thought of the Metamorphoses,
making the sign of Arachne in the tangle of your fingers.
And here, after all, lay the proof:
The man in the plastic runs a thumb over stone. The gray is slick and tough.
Phillis Wheatley: thirty-one. Had misery enough.

Trini and Halim, Lower East Side, 2000 *OLD SCHOOL LOVE*, BY JAMEL SHABAZZ

CHAPTER 4

Fear

LESLIE ALEXANDER AND MICHELLE ALEXANDER

On May 25, 2020, a Black man named George Floyd was forced to the ground by several Minneapolis police officers; he remained there, pinned for more than nine minutes, as Officer Derek Chauvin pressed his knee into Floyd's neck, killing him slowly even as he begged for his life and called out to his dead mother.[1] Just a short time before, a clerk at a convenience store had called 911, claiming that Floyd had purchased cigarettes with a counterfeit twenty-dollar bill. Minutes after police arrived on the scene, Floyd was dead.

In the days after the killing, a viral video of the murder sparked widespread outrage, and yet none of the officers responsible for Floyd's death were arrested or faced criminal charges—a pattern that felt, to many in Minneapolis and beyond, painfully familiar. Nationwide, police officers are rarely arrested or charged when they kill, and Black people are significantly more likely to be killed by the police than white people. Public attention to this issue had been growing since 2014, when Officer Darren Wilson shot and killed an unarmed Black teenager named Michael Brown in Ferguson, Missouri, igniting a major uprising in Ferguson and protests from coast to coast. Wilson was never criminally charged for that killing. Two years later, in Falcon Heights, less than ten miles from where Floyd was killed, a thirty-two-year-old Black man named Philando Castile was shot and killed during a traffic stop. No officers were found guilty of any wrongdoing, even though that tragedy was livestreamed on social media and provoked a national outcry. And just two months before Floyd's death, a twenty-six-year-old Black woman named Breonna Taylor was killed in her Louisville, Kentucky, apartment when white plainclothes officers, searching for evidence against a suspected drug dealer, broke into her apartment in the middle of the night with a battering ram and sprayed her home with bullets. Again, no officers were held accountable for the killing. All of these killings were officially justified, according to law enforcement and public officials, by fear—fear of Black people who were viewed as threats by the police.

When it appeared that—yet again—the police would be allowed to kill a Black person with impunity, the rage and grief in the streets of Minneapolis became combustible. Two days after Floyd's death, Derek Chauvin, the officer who killed him, was still free despite the video circulating around the globe revealing beyond any reasonable doubt that Chauvin had murdered a defenseless Black man whom he was sworn to serve and protect. Peaceful protests evolved into outright rebellion, as residents began throwing bricks, bottles, rocks, and Molotov cocktails at police precincts and cruisers, looting retail stores, and burning buildings to the ground. By the time Officer Chauvin was arrested, on May 29—four days after Floyd was killed—it was too late; the uprisings had already spread, and multiple cities were aflame. Fresh kindling had been laid in the months and years prior. Decades of false political promises, desperate living conditions, simmering racial tensions, mass criminalization in Black communities, and failed efforts at police reform fueled a brief wave of political violence in cities across the country in the days that followed. Protesters recognized that white fear of the racial "other" is not limited to the police or even to our criminal injustice system, but is endemic to our society as a whole.

In fact, just weeks before Floyd was murdered, another viral video had revealed to the nation—and much of the world—that white fear is easily and routinely weaponized by ordinary people with potentially deadly consequences. In this case, the video showed how Ahmaud Arbery, a twenty-five-year-old Black man, was chased by three white vigilantes as he jogged in a predominantly white neighborhood near Brunswick, Georgia, and was then shot and killed by one of them. The men claimed they suspected that Arbery had robbed homes in the area, but he had merely been jogging in a place where white men believed that he didn't belong.

For many, that tragedy was reminiscent of yet another killing, the 2012 shooting of Trayvon Martin, a seventeen-year-old Black high school student in Sanford, Florida. Martin had been walking through a gated community carrying nothing more than a package of Skittles and a cold drink when he was stalked and killed by George Zimmerman, a volunteer neighborhood watchman who found Martin's presence in the neighborhood suspicious. His death prompted waves of protests and racial-justice organizing, as well as a slew of viral videos showing police killings, vigilante threats, and attacks upon Black people who were doing nothing more than living their lives, trying to be free. Yet the threats and violence continued unabated. Just hours before George

Floyd took his last breath, yet another video had gone viral, this one showing a white woman in New York City dialing 911, falsely claiming that a Black man named Christian Cooper was endangering her. The incident began when Cooper, who was bird-watching in Central Park, asked the woman to put a leash on her dog, in accordance with park rules. When she became hostile, Cooper recorded the encounter, which shows him calmly speaking to the woman as she threatens to tell the police that "there's an African American man threatening my life."[2]

By the time Floyd was murdered, pervasive police violence and the tragic consequences of white fear of Black people had become undeniable in the eyes of many Americans. In the weeks and months that followed, thousands upon thousands of protesters took to the streets in all fifty states, in large cities like Los Angeles, Chicago, Detroit, Atlanta, and New York, as well as in suburbs, small and medium-sized towns, and rural areas. Protests erupted even in places as far away as Hong Kong, South Africa, Germany, South Korea, and New Zealand. Never before had a Black rebellion been met with such widespread support by people of all colors, classes, and walks of life. After an initial wave of violence, these protests were overwhelmingly peaceful. The demonstrators were determined to make their voices heard and to show a united front against racism and police violence. People gathered by the dozens, the hundreds, or the thousands in parks and city centers or marched to municipal buildings like police departments and city halls while chanting slogans, carrying signs, and demanding justice. Of the more than 7,750 demonstrations that took place in the United States between May 26 and August 22, nearly 95 percent were nonviolent, according to the Armed Conflict Location & Event Data Project. Fewer than 220 locations reported any form of "violent demonstrations"; in the tally, that term was defined to include any acts of vandalism (including graffiti and toppling of statues), property destruction, or violence of any kind against individuals.[3]

But the response by police was brutal, encouraged by President Donald Trump, who condemned the protests; blasted the "Black Lives Matter" slogan, calling it a "symbol of hate"; and pledged his allegiance to "law and order." Images filled television screens and social-media feeds of police officers and federal agents, at times joined by white nationalist organizations like the Proud Boys, attacking peaceful protesters, beating them with batons, using pepper spray and pellets, chasing them down streets and alleys, driving cars into crowds, and forcing people into unmarked vehicles.[4] During mass protests in Wisconsin, a white seventeen-year-old from Illinois named Kyle Rittenhouse, who considered himself a militia member, traveled to the city of

Kenosha to assist the police. In a video, he was seen carrying a military-style rifle and chatting with police officers, who thanked him for his service and gave him water not long before he shot three people, killing two.[5] Ultimately, the federal government sent more than seventeen thousand members of the National Guard to patrol the streets in twenty-three states and Washington, D.C.[6] When protesters gathered at the Lincoln Memorial, dozens of National Guard officers lined up in rows to defend federal property. They were among the hundreds stationed throughout the city at other sites.

Those same troops were nowhere in sight months later when an overwhelmingly white mob, composed of white nationalists and Trump supporters, stormed the United States Capitol, smashing windows and ransacking offices while lawmakers were in the process of certifying president-elect Joseph Biden's electoral victory. For months, President Trump had falsely claimed that the 2020 presidential election had been rigged against him, ultimately leading his supporters to converge on the Capitol in an effort to overturn the results. More than a hundred police officers were assaulted during the mayhem; five people died, including one officer. But despite many warnings that the crowd on January 6 could turn violent, the National Guard was not deployed until after the rioting had already begun. Police presence at the Capitol was light, too. Some officers were even seen letting the insurrectionists approach the building and standing aside as the mob poured inside.

The glaring double standard reflects a centuries-old pattern in which Black strivings for liberation have been demonized, criminalized, and subjected to persecution, while white people's demands for liberty are deemed rational, legitimate, and largely unthreatening. As James Baldwin explained a half century earlier, when "any white man in the world says, 'Give me liberty or give me death,' the entire white world applauds. When a Black man says exactly the same thing—word for word—he is judged a criminal and treated like one, and everything possible is done to make an example of this bad [n—] so there won't be any more like him."[7]

There has never been a time in United States history when Black rebellions did not spark existential fear among white people, often leading to violent response. Even when resistance has been peaceful or purely symbolic—such as Black fists raised during the medal ceremony at the 1968 Olympics or a knee taken on the football field during the national anthem nearly fifty years later—any sign of rebellion has frequently resulted in threats or acts of violence perpetrated by white vigilantes, militia groups, and the police, often culminating in the creation or strengthening of systems of racial and social control.

The reflexive impulse to respond to Black people with severe punitiveness is traceable to the eighteenth and nineteenth centuries, when white people desperately sought to control a large unfree population who refused to submit to their enslavement. The deep-seated, gnawing terror that Black people might, one day, rise up and demand for themselves the same freedoms and inalienable rights that led white colonists to declare the American Revolution has shaped our nation's politics, culture, and systems of justice ever since. The specific forms of repression and control may have changed over time, but the underlying pattern established during slavery has remained the same. Modern-day policing, surveillance, and mass criminalization, as well as white vigilante violence and "know-your-place aggression," have histories rooted in white fear—not merely of Black crime or Black people but of Black liberation. Nothing has proved more threatening to our democracy, or more devastating to Black communities, than white fear of Black freedom dreams.

Most schoolchildren are taught the Declaration of Independence's most famous lines: "We hold these truths to be self-evident, that all men are created equal, that they are endowed by their Creator with certain unalienable Rights, that among these are Life, Liberty and the pursuit of Happiness." But relatively few children or adults today are as familiar with the right to revolt that follows: "Whenever any Form of Government becomes destructive of these ends, it is the Right of the People to alter or to abolish it. . . . When a long train of abuses and usurpations, pursuing invariably the same Object evinces a design to reduce them under absolute Despotism, it is their right, it is their duty, to throw off such Government, and to provide new Guards for their future security."[8]

When Thomas Jefferson penned those words, he owned hundreds of enslaved people. Yet he was acutely aware that Black people yearned for freedom no less than the white colonists who had waged the American Revolution and that no principle of justice could defend slavery. Even God, he later claimed, would likely side with enslaved people if they organized a successful revolt against their enslavers. In *Notes on the State of Virginia*, published in 1785, Jefferson admitted that rebellions were a legitimate, rational response to an immoral and inhumane system: "I tremble for my country when I reflect that God is just; that his justice cannot sleep forever; that considering numbers, nature and natural means only, a revolution of the wheel of fortune, an exchange of situation, is among possible events; that it may become probable by supernatural interference!"[9]

Jefferson's anxious reflections were a kind of inheritance, something passed down from generation to generation among uneasy white enslavers. At the heart of slavery lay a terrifying conundrum—an epic struggle between the enslavers who sought to extract labor, loyalty, and submission from their human property and the enslaved people who longed for freedom and were willing to obtain their liberation by any means necessary. Jefferson, whose ancestors had been enslaving Africans on large Virginia plantations since the seventeenth century, understood this dilemma well. Slavery, he once quipped, was akin to having a "wolf by the ear"—white people could not release their grip on it, but they also knew that beneath the surface boiled a formidable Black rage that could not be fully contained.[10]

From the founding of the original thirteen colonies, white people in the North and South lived in constant fear that the men and women they whipped, raped, and forced to work without pay would, if given the chance, rise up and take revenge on their white enslavers. This is why governmental surveillance and severe punishment of Black people began almost concurrently with the introduction of slavery itself. In 1669, the Carolina colony granted every free white man "absolute Power and Authority over his Negro Slaves." Within decades, Carolina law drastically bolstered white authority, mandating that *all* white people ought to be responsible for policing all Black people's activities. Any white person who failed to properly monitor suspicious Black activity would be fined forty shillings.[11] This notion—that Black people were inherently devious and criminal, and that white people were required to monitor and police them—ultimately defined the nature of race relations in the United States.

Convinced that the prevailing social and economic order could be preserved only if Black people were objects of perpetual surveillance and control, authorities across the colonies enacted slave codes, laws that governed Black people's lives and denied them basic human rights, including the rights to move freely, to "resist" any white person, and to carry weapons of any kind.[12] Failure to adhere to these restrictions resulted in brutal punishment. Early slave codes also legally empowered enslavers to beat, maim, assault, or even kill an enslaved person without penalty.[13] And if found guilty of participating in insurrectionary activity, an enslaved person would automatically receive the death penalty.[14] In many colonies, such as Virginia, the public treasury was even required to compensate enslavers if an enslaved person was killed while resisting or running away.[15]

Even so, these efforts proved insufficient. In the colonial era alone, fifty documented conspiracies against slavery were identified in the mainland British colonies and nearly fifty more in the British Caribbean.[16] On April 6,

1712, for example, approximately two dozen enslaved men and women gathered in New York City in the early morning hours. Armed with guns, axes, clubs, and knives, they set a building ablaze, hoping to inspire panic. When unsuspecting white people arrived to douse the flames, the rebels ambushed them, killing nine and wounding seven others. The rebellion was quickly quashed. Twenty-one people were executed: some were burned at the stake, while others were hanged in chains or had their necks snapped. One rebel was strapped to a large stone wheel, each of his bones broken with a wooden mallet while he screamed in agony, and then he was left to die painfully.[17]

Fearful of just these sorts of rebellions, colonists at the turn of the eighteenth century created civilian-based systems of law enforcement. Initially, these patrols were reminiscent of the *posse comitatus* in England, in which bands of men were called out to chase down and arrest people suspected of felony crimes.[18] It soon became clear, however, that an ad hoc voluntary system was wholly inadequate for the challenge of controlling thousands of enslaved people, especially in places like the Carolina colony, where enslaved people outnumbered white people.[19] Eventually, white colonists devised a new law enforcement institution, one that would serve, to a significant degree, as the foundation for modern policing: the slave patrol.[20]

The first official slave patrol was created in South Carolina in 1704, following rumors of a planned rebellion. As the historian Sally Hadden writes in her comprehensive study *Slave Patrols,* colonists already fearful of attack by the Spanish in Florida concluded that they needed two military forces: "a militia to repel foreign enemies, and a patrol to leave behind as a deterrent against slave revolts."[21] Every militia captain would select a group of men under his command to serve as patrollers, a separate unit that was responsible for enforcing slave codes. Patrollers were required to hunt fugitives and rebellious enslaved people and to visit every plantation at least once a month; there they invaded slave cabins, confiscating any items they believed to be stolen, as well as anything they judged could be used as a weapon.[22]

By the late 1720s, slave patrolling in the Carolina colony had become a fundamental part of the militia's regular duties.[23] Virginia and North Carolina soon created their own slave patrols, and by the mid-eighteenth century, colonial authorities there had transformed groups of white settlers, who were recruited and handsomely rewarded, into a militarized law enforcement organization that, as Hadden notes, was primarily engaged in "watching, catching, or beating black slaves." Patrollers enforced slave codes and routinely broke into the homes of enslaved people, aggressively searching them and their quarters and subjecting women to sexual violence.[24]

Everywhere the pattern was the same: white people enslaved, raped, ter-rorized, and murdered Black people, mostly for profit and also to enforce a rigid racial hierarchy in which they maintained both status and power. Black people resisted and rebelled, often violently. White fear of Black rebellions soared after each rumored or attempted revolt, leading to heightened surveil-lance, brutal patrolling, and new waves of laws or policies that aimed to per-manently subdue the enslaved population.

The Stono Rebellion offers a dramatic example. On September 9, 1739, in South Carolina, twenty enslaved Africans gathered near the Stono River some ten miles southwest of Charleston, where they plotted their revolt. Led by a man named Jemmy, they raided a local store, grabbing weapons and ammu-nition, and then marched from plantation to plantation, killing nearly thirty enslavers as they burned and raided their properties. Using drums and other musical instruments, the rebels attracted supporters, and soon the uprising blossomed to more than a hundred persons. When the local militia caught wind of the attacks, they hunted down the rebels and successfully quelled the revolt; dozens of enslaved people lay dead. Heads were displayed on massive wooden poles at every milepost leading to Charleston as a ghoulish warning that the cost of resistance would be death. Over the next few months, South Carolina officials arrested more than 150 Black people, publicly hanging ten per day.[25]

South Carolina legislators, enraged and horrified by the Black insurrection, passed the Negro Act of 1740, which was designed to force enslaved people into "due subjection and obedience" and to save the "public peace and order." The legislation aimed to go further than any previous form of racial control by authorizing the policing of nearly every aspect of Black people's lives. The act prohibited enslaved people from moving beyond the boundaries of their plantations, assembling in groups on roads, growing their own food, or earn-ing money, and it imposed harsh penalties on enslaved people who learned to read. It also empowered constables to deputize any white person to "disperse any assembly or meeting of slaves which may disturb the peace or endanger the safety of his Majesty's subjects" and to "search all suspected places for arms, ammunition or stolen goods, and to apprehend and secure all such slaves as they shall suspect to be guilty of any crimes or offences whatsoever." In an effort to reinforce universal white authority over Black people, lawmak-ers also empowered all white people to "pursue, apprehend, and moderately correct" any Black person who refused to submit to their authority. If any enslaved persons tried to defend themselves, they could be "lawfully killed."[26]

In the years that followed, South Carolina's Negro Act became a model for slave codes throughout the colonies, governing Black lives for more than a century. Such laws existed in the Northern colonies as well, even though the enslaved population was comparatively small. In New York, for example, authorities banned enslaved people from gathering in groups larger than three, holding funerals at night, being out after sunset without a lantern, selling food in the streets, playing musical instruments, or associating with free Black people. Enslaved Black people weren't even allowed to simply ride a horse, for fear they would use the horse to escape.[27] Northerners also implemented strict curfew laws, which targeted all Black people, enslaved and free. Legislation in Connecticut and Rhode Island, for example, explicitly encouraged anti-Black vigilantism by authorizing *any white person* to capture an enslaved person who appeared to be out after nine without specified permission.[28]

These oppressive laws did not cease after the collapse of British rule. Instead, government policing of Black communities, free and enslaved, persisted throughout the American Revolution, and became state law once the United States gained its independence. However, no amount of brutal repression could prevent enslaved people from dreaming of—and fighting for—freedom. And no quest for liberation would terrify white Americans more than the one that would take place on a small island in the Caribbean, about fifteen years after the United States was founded.

In 1791, just seven hundred miles from U.S. shores, enslaved men and women in France's most profitable colony, Saint-Domingue, unleashed a rebellion. The revolt should have surprised no one. Like many other colonies in the Americas, Saint-Domingue's main cash crop was sugar. Planting, growing, and harvesting it required intense labor performed in sweltering heat under the constant pain of the lash. Processing sugar was equally grueling, often pushing enslaved people to exhaustion, injury, and dismemberment as they labored throughout the night to feed the cane stalks through the mills.[29] More than half of the men and women imported into Saint-Domingue directly from the African continent died within a few years, and those who survived were typically subjected to harsh punishments and outright torture. Following a whipping, enslaved people in Saint-Domingue were often burned with an open flame, while others were subjected to burning wax, hot coals, or boiling cane juice; some were even buried alive. The conditions for rebellion were especially ripe on the island, since the enslaved people there—the largest enslaved population in the Caribbean—far outnumbered the white enslavers and colonizers.[30]

Gathering nightly over several days in mid-August in the northern region of Saint-Domingue, enslaved people painstakingly planned an insurrection—a revolutionary war against their white enslavers that they intended to fight to the death in order to reclaim their human right to freedom. Dutty Boukman, an enslaved man and a highly respected spiritual leader, assembled hundreds of enslaved people in the woods at Bois Caïman and led them in a religious ceremony, calling upon their God to guide them and sealing their revolutionary pact with oaths and ritual sacrifices. On the night of August 21, 1791, rebels began seizing their freedom. Spreading rapidly across the northern region over the next two days, nearly two thousand rebels marched from plantation to plantation, armed with machetes, burning and destroying workhouses and other buildings, and killing their oppressors. Within a week, French authorities believed, nearly ten thousand enslaved people had joined the revolt, and it seemed unstoppable. "We were attacked by a horde of assassins," one plantation manager later wrote, "and could offer only meager resistance." By the end of September, more than one thousand plantations had been burned and hundreds of white people lay dead. Eventually expanding to an estimated eighty thousand rebels, the revolt erupted into the largest, bloodiest, and most successful rebellion of enslaved people in history.[31]

White enslavers throughout the world recoiled in shock and horror. Enslaved people were rising up and asserting their determination to be free at any cost. In the United States—the world's newest slaveholding republic—President George Washington and the other "founding fathers" openly panicked, nervously speculating about whether the spirit of rebellion would be infectious enough to afflict their fledgling nation. Politicians throughout the country expressed outrage and horror as Black people in a neighboring nation sought their own liberty, even as they basked in the glow of their own revolution, during which they had sought to free themselves from tyranny and oppression.

Just weeks after the rebellion in Saint-Domingue began, Charles Pinckney, the governor of South Carolina, warned President Washington that similar uprisings would soon spread to the Southern United States and devastate the economy. "I am afraid," Pinckney wrote to Washington, that if the insurrection is "not checked in time it is a flame which will extend to all the neighbouring islands, & may eventually prove not a very pleasing or agreeable example to the Southern States . . . [and be] particularly unpleasant to us who live in Countries where Slaves abound."[32] By the end of 1791, Washington had finally succumbed to the growing panic. "Lamentable! to see such a spirit of revolt among the Blacks," Washington exclaimed. "Where it will stop, is difficult to say."[33] Thomas Jefferson also fretted about the "formidable insurrection" in Saint-Domingue, as did Alexander Hamilton, who expressed regret about "the calamitous event" taking place just a short distance away.[34]

As the uprising unfolded in Haiti, rumors of potential revolts in the United States spread like wildfire, prompting desperate new measures to prevent and thwart rebellions by the enslaved.[35] Authorities in Charleston, South Carolina, for example, tried to protect themselves by banning the importation of French enslaved people.[36] In Richmond, Virginia, the mayor mandated a search of all enslaved people in the city and enlisted extra patrols throughout the remainder of the state.[37] On the federal level, in 1793 lawmakers passed a fugitive slave law, clearly warning enslaved people that rebellion or flight was useless, as they would find no paths to freedom in the United States. The new legislation empowered enslavers to cross state lines to pursue and recapture enslaved people "escaping from the service of their masters." It also imposed a fine on anyone who prevented the capture and return of a fugitive from slavery.[38]

Meanwhile, the flames of insurrection continued to burn brightly in Saint-Domingue. Toussaint Louverture, who had assumed leadership of the rebellion, and his army successfully held off military invasions from the French, Spanish, and British—the greatest military powers on earth at the time. In 1794, the French National Convention agreed to abolish slavery throughout Saint-Domingue, hoping it would quell the resistance. But peace did not return. Saint-Domingue remained under French control, formerly enslaved people still labored under oppressive plantation systems, and rebels persisted in their demand for full freedom, equality, and sovereignty for all Black people.[39] Emboldened by the uprisings in Saint-Domingue, free and enslaved Black people in Martinique, Curaçao, Jamaica, Grenada, and many other slaveholding colonies, including Spanish Louisiana, demanded their freedom and proved that they, too, were willing to sacrifice their lives to obtain it.[40]

By the late 1790s, it had become clear that the rebellion in Saint-Domingue could not be contained. White politicians in the United States grew increasingly alarmed. In a letter to Thomas Jefferson, one prominent Virginian, Arthur Campbell, expressed his concern that the Saint-Domingue rebellion would lead to similar "calamities" in Virginia.[41] If that happened, he warned, the United States would "rapidly decline." Henry Tazewell, a U.S. senator from Virginia, apparently agreed, anxiously urging Jefferson to recognize that people from Saint-Domingue gave the Southern states "much to dread."[42] Fear permeated the highest levels of government, and in 1799, Secretary of State

Timothy Pickering urgently wrote to President John Adams, arguing that in the interest of national security, the United States must use all necessary measures to prevent Black revolt: "Our southern states . . . are yet in much danger from attempts to excite the blacks to insurrection." It is essential, he urged, "to guard against the danger to be apprehended from St. Domingo."[43]

The fear was well founded. Enslaved people in the United States and across the Americas saw themselves as part of a joint struggle for freedom, as news of insurrections traveled across the water. The following year, an enslaved man in Virginia named Gabriel was inspired by the uprising in Saint-Domingue to hatch an insurrection of his own, which reportedly grew to several hundred conspirators.[44] As Virginia governor (and future president) James Monroe, himself an enslaver, wrote in a letter to Vice President Thomas Jefferson, "It is unquestionably the most serious and formidable conspiracy we have ever known of the kind."[45] Although traitors betrayed Gabriel's plot before the rebellion could fully materialize, Virginia responded by further restricting Black people's lives. Governor Monroe ordered the state militia to patrol the capitol, sweep the region, and arrest any enslaved person they deemed suspicious.[46] White Virginians also strengthened the slave codes, hoping that strict surveillance and control over gatherings would stymie the ability of Black people to plot and execute rebellions. They further circumscribed the movements of enslaved people, explicitly preventing gatherings on Sundays or in the evenings and banning education and literacy among the enslaved. The new law also required Black people freed by their owners to leave the state within twelve months or face reenslavement.[47] In Virginia, then, to be Black was to be enslaved. To be free and Black was to be a threat.

Nevertheless, the Black sovereignty that white Americans feared most eventually came to pass. On November 29, 1803, Jean-Jacques Dessalines, the new leader of the rebel army in Saint-Domingue, declared victory in the revolution against French authority. Weeks later, he publicly unveiled l'Acte de l'Indépendance d'Haïti (the Act of Independence of Haiti), officially introducing Haiti to the world as a sovereign nation.[48] In a speech delivered in the port city of Gonaïves, Dessalines called upon his people to pledge themselves to liberty at any cost. "Let us swear before the whole universe, to posterity, to ourselves," he urged, "to renounce France forever, and to die rather than live under its dominion. To fight until our last breath for the independence of our country."[49]

The announcement sent shockwaves around the world. Slavery in Saint-Domingue had provided France with nearly half of its global trade profit on an annual basis, and by 1791 Saint-Domingue was the world's largest producer of coffee and sugar.[50] Although France had fought desperately to maintain its power to exploit and control the Black population, the rebels had managed to defeat Napoleon's army—reportedly the greatest military power on earth—and declare their independence less than three decades after American colonists declared their own.

In establishing their own nation, Black rebels had accomplished what the scholar Michel-Rolph Trouillot has described as the "unthinkable."[51] After all, Haiti became the first and only country in the Americas where enslaved Africans threw off their shackles, fought for their freedom, defeated European powers, established their own nation, and pledged to defend their freedom and independence until their "last breath." The Haitian act of independence radically upended the basic premise of white supremacy upon which slavery rested, and asserted Black people's fundamental human rights to liberty and self-governance.

The emergence of a sovereign Black nation, rising from the ashes of France's most profitable slave colony, represented the culmination of white people's deepest fears and Black people's deepest hopes. After all, if the enslaved in Haiti could have a successful rebellion, defeat multiple armies, and establish a sovereign country, couldn't the same thing happen elsewhere? Perhaps in their very midst?

White people in the United States did not have to wait long for answers to these questions. Embracing sovereign Haiti as a symbol for global Black freedom, enslaved people in the United States waged their own battles for liberation. Multiple revolts erupted in the early nineteenth century, nearly all of them inspired in some way by the Haitian Revolution. In 1811, Black people rose up in Louisiana and were brutally suppressed in what became known as the German Coast rebellion.[52] About a decade later, in 1822, political officials in Charleston, South Carolina, reported that Denmark Vesey, a free Black abolitionist, had developed a plot with other rebels to undermine slavery and escape to Haiti. Although that revolt never fully came to fruition, and some historians have contested its existence, the rumors of insurrection terrified white Americans and led to the bloody executions of thirty-five alleged conspirators, including Vesey.[53] As a correspondent to President Thomas Jefferson noted, "Who can reflect on the Scenes of St Domingo, & of often occurrences among you, of now one, & then another, murdered by his Slaves, Houses fired," and not wonder when the next uprising would come?[54]

And then, about a decade later, on August 21, 1831, Nat Turner, an enslaved man in Virginia who believed that slavery violated God's law and that God had selected him to lead his people to freedom, unleashed a bloody rebellion.[55] Over the next two days, he and his followers, which included several free Black people, attacked farms and killed some sixty white enslavers throughout Southampton County.[56] The local militia, joined by troops from the United States Navy, which was anchored nearby, murdered at least a hundred Black rebels in an effort to suppress the uprising.[57] Turner himself remained at large for six weeks, but he was eventually captured, hung, skinned, and brutally dismembered.[58]

While Turner was still free, however, roving gangs of white men attacked Black people in Southampton and nearby counties, killing as many as two hundred to ensure that Black rebels would not dare to attempt another revolt. One observer wrote that white vigilantes "formed themselves into patrol bands, and went wherever they chose among the colored people, acting out their brutal will." Virginia lawmakers also surrendered to fear. Although, in the aftermath of Turner's rebellion, they briefly considered abolishing slavery, they ultimately elected, once again, to pass draconian laws severely restricting Black people's lives. Aware that literacy inspired Black people's strivings for freedom, and that religious gatherings were used as opportunities to plot rebellions, lawmakers augmented punishments for enslaved people who learned to read, held unsupervised religious gatherings, or interacted with free Black people.[59]

In the decade following Nat Turner's rebellion, as rural areas struggled to suppress the enslaved population, Southern cities concluded that the only way to protect their residents from uprisings in surrounding areas was to invest in armed patrols.[60] In most urban areas, after establishing a city patrol, officials would also build a town jail and a punishment site, often referred to as "the cage," where suspicious enslaved people could be incarcerated and tortured.[61] By 1837, the patrol in Charleston, South Carolina, comprised one hundred armed officers, who policed free and enslaved Black communities, captured fugitives, prevented rebellions, and enforced the slave codes.[62]

Legally free Black people, in both the North and the South, were subjected to similar forms of surveillance and terrorism. Lawmakers across the nation enacted legislation to ensure that free Black people would remain firmly in their place, at the bottom of the social order. Foreshadowing the "know your place" aggression that would dominate race relations in the twentieth and twenty-first centuries, white politicians outlawed any Black behavior that was not immediately recognizable as labor or subservience. In Louisiana, for example, it was illegal for free people of color to "conceive themselves equal to the whites." As the law explicitly stated, Black people should "yield" to white people "on every occasion, and never speak or answer them but with respect." If legally free Black people failed to submit to white authority, they were subject to imprisonment.[63]

By the time the Civil War began, in 1861, Southern states had established an elaborate governing framework for race relations. Through trial and error, as well as careful planning, white authorities had created oppressive laws and systems of patrolling, surveillance, and punishment, all of which were designed to protect enslavers and the white citizenry from the consequences of their own unmitigated violence and to ensure centuries of prosperity for the planter elite. If the Confederacy had been a separate nation when the Civil War began, it would have ranked among the richest in the world. As the historian Steven Deyle writes in *Carry Me Back: The Domestic Slave Trade in American Life*, the monetary value of the enslaved population in 1860 was "equal to about seven times the total value of all currency in circulation in the country, three times the value of the entire livestock population, . . . twelve times the value of the entire U.S. cotton crop, and forty-eight times the total expenditures of the U.S. federal government that year."[64]

Ultimately, the war ended the South's economic power, but it did not reduce white fear of Black liberation or the perpetual quest for racial control. To the contrary, white fear and paranoia grew as Southern white people lost control over the Black population in their midst. Formerly enslaved people literally walked away from their plantations, causing panic and outrage among plantation owners. Large numbers took to the streets and highways in the early years after the war, looking for work and missing family members. Some converged on towns and cities; others joined and formed militias.[65] Many white people feared violent reprisals or a "turning of the tables" now that Black people had access to arms and ammunition and were no longer subject to perpetual surveillance and control by white plantation owners.

Violent insurrection, however, was not the only fear seizing the minds of many white Southerners in the aftermath of the Civil War. White people of all classes and backgrounds feared permanent economic ruin, a disordered social system, and the loss of white privilege. Without the stolen labor of formerly enslaved people, the region's economy swiftly collapsed, and without the institution of slavery, there was no longer a formal mechanism for maintaining racial hierarchy and preventing "amalgamation" with a group of people considered intrinsically inferior and vile. Plantation owners had benefited the most from the institution of slavery, yet the collapse of the racial order was a bitter pill for poor white people as well. In the antebellum South, the lowliest white person at least possessed his or her white skin—a badge of superiority over the most skilled enslaved or prosperous free Black person. Poor white people feared that the abolition of slavery would erase the line that separated them from the most abused and despised people on earth.

Any stride toward freedom by Black people provoked alarm throughout the South, as any perceived increase in Black political and economic power triggered white fears of losing power and status.[66] Although many white Northerners supported voting rights and other basic civil rights for Black people, at least initially, white Southerners overwhelmingly opposed any move toward greater freedom or equality for the Black people in their midst. In the years that followed the Civil War, white Southerners employed a wide range of weapons—legal and extralegal—to restore their control over rebellious Black people and return them to "their place." Southern states swiftly reinvented their tools for racial control and enacted "Black Codes" that were akin to the old slave codes. As expressed by one Alabama planter: "We have the power to pass stringent police laws to govern the negroes—This is a blessing—For they must be controlled in some way or white people cannot live amongst them."[67]

Some of the Black Codes foreshadowed Jim Crow laws by policing the movement of Black people, whose recent emancipation had become a perpetual source of fear and resentment. These codes segregated schools and prohibited, for example, interracial seating in the first-class sections of railroad cars. Other codes were intended to establish systems of peonage resembling slavery to ensure a cheap labor force. Vagrancy laws were adopted and selectively enforced against Black people; these essentially made it a criminal offense not to work, often forcing formerly enslaved people to sign labor contracts with the same people who had once enslaved them. Simply being Black and standing on a street corner could be interpreted as idleness or vagrancy by the police and result in arrest. In several states, convict leasing laws allowed the hiring out of people in county prisons to plantation owners and private companies in an unsubtle effort to establish another system of forced labor. In the words of W.E.B. Du Bois, "The Codes spoke for themselves. . . . No open-minded student can read them without being convinced they meant nothing more nor less than slavery in daily toil."[68]

Perhaps most disconcerting for white Southerners was the prospect of Black people holding political power over white people, and thus gaining the opportunity to rewrite the rules, overturn exploitative economic arrangements, and redesign the social and political order. With the passage of the Reconstruction Act in 1867, followed by the Fifteenth Amendment, guaranteeing that the right to vote "shall not be denied or abridged" on the basis of race, an era of rising Black power began. For nearly a decade, Black people voted in huge numbers across the South, electing a total of sixteen Black men to serve in the U.S. Congress, including two in the Senate. Literacy rates climbed, and educated Black people began to populate state legislatures, open schools, and initiate successful businesses.

Tragically, the Black freedom dreams that propelled swift progress toward equality were arrested by the late 1870s, as a fierce white backlash against Black freedom succeeded in turning back the clock on racial progress.[69] Southern white people effectively nullified the post–Civil War amendments that were intended to dismantle the racial caste system in the South, including the Fourteenth Amendment, guaranteeing "equal protection of the laws," and the Fifteenth Amendment. The Freedmen's Bureau—an agency created by Congress in 1865 and charged with the responsibility of providing food, clothing, and other forms of assistance to destitute former enslaved people— was dismantled, and a plethora of discriminatory practices, such as poll taxes and literacy tests, were employed to prevent Black people from exercising their right to vote and gaining political power. When those efforts proved insufficient to maintain complete control, white Southerners wielded their most effective weapon: vigilante violence and terrorism.

In 1898, for example, a group of white residents orchestrated a successful coup to overthrow the city government in Wilmington, North Carolina, home to a thriving majority-Black population. Four years earlier, the Populist movement had joined with the Republican Party to form the "Fusion Party," a political organization that managed to unite poor and working-class white people, formerly enslaved people and their descendants, and liberal Republicans in a movement for economic justice. This racially diverse party defeated old-guard politicians (many of whom were white supremacists and former Confederates) in a series of state and local elections, including in places like Wilmington. In response, the disgruntled white establishment plotted a coup to regain power and reinstate white-only rule that culminated in the murder of Black residents, burning of Black neighborhoods, and the unveiling of a "White Declaration of Independence" at a mass meeting led by a former congressman.[70]

Throughout the South, local police forces were often made up of former slave patrollers and members of the Ku Klux Klan, and they adopted many of the same strategies that patrollers had employed, using the excuse of nightly curfews and vagrancy laws to control, harass, detain, and punish Black citizens for daring to behave as though they were free.[71] The Klan, operating extralegally, openly murdered Black people who violated the written and unwritten rules of white supremacy.

Often the precise causes and triggers of white fear and rage were mixed or unclear, but the consequences were always devastating. Between 1877 and 1950, more than four thousand Black men, women, and children lost their lives to lynching.[72] Fleeing violence, harsh segregation laws, and exploitative economic conditions, many Black Americans headed north, in what would become known as the Great Migration, to take advantage of the need for industrial workers that arose during the First World War and to achieve some modicum of safety. Unfortunately, many soon realized that white mob violence reigned there as well. One of the bloodiest race massacres in the twentieth century occurred in East St. Louis, Illinois, in 1917. That tragedy involved a spree of lynchings, mayhem, and brutal burnings of people and buildings that left an official death toll of at least thirty-nine Black and eight white Americans, though historians estimate that more than a hundred Black people were actually killed.[73]

White fear of the disruption of the racial order meant that almost any act by a Black person, especially anything that signaled Black progress or the willingness of a Black person to step out of their place in the racial hierarchy, could spark a conflagration. Simply declaring your patriotism by wearing a military uniform while Black could be enough. Between 1877 and 1950, thousands of Black veterans suffered brutal abuse at the hands of white vigilante mobs who viewed Black military service as an offensive and threatening assertion of equal citizenship. Many of those assaults resulted in lynchings. Black economic success could prove deadly too, such as in Tulsa, Oklahoma, in 1921, when a mob composed of more than two thousand white men and women commenced a devastating pogrom in the city's thriving Greenwood District, known as Black Wall Street, killing as many as three hundred people and burning more than thirty-five blocks of Black homes and businesses to the ground. The attack rendered ten thousand Black people homeless and caused more than $2 million in damage.[74] Simply daring to smile at a white woman could get you killed as well. Emmett Till, a fourteen-year-old Black boy, was murdered in Mississippi in 1955 because he allegedly flirted with a white woman. As historian Carol Anderson observes in *White Rage,* the mere presence of Black people was not the problem; the problem was "blackness with ambition, with drive, with purpose, with aspirations, and with demands for full and equal citizenship."[75] Just as in the days of the Haitian Revolution and before, nothing frightened and enraged white people more than Black people who were determined to be free.

After the civil rights movement began, a fresh wave of white terrorism washed over those who had the audacity to organize for freedom and equality. Between the 1940s and 1970s, white vigilantes and mobs—frequently with the support or direct involvement of the police—attacked civil rights activists in Selma, Little Rock, Boston, Chicago, New Orleans, and scores of other cities and towns across the country as they protested legalized segregation in housing and schools, on buses and trains, and at lunch counters and beyond. Protesters were killed, beaten, attacked by police dogs, and arrested en masse for desegregating buses and trains, marching peacefully for voting rights, and demonstrating against the Jim Crow regime. State and federal authorities were complicit, defining their mission to include the monitoring and sabotage of Black leaders, activists, and organizations.

Most famously, the FBI's notorious counterintelligence program (CO-INTELPRO) targeted Reverend Martin Luther King, Jr., Malcolm X, Stokely Carmichael (later known as Kwame Ture), and others, subjecting them to tactics adopted from military counterintelligence that, a Senate intelligence committee later found, "would be intolerable in a democratic society even if all of the targets had been involved in violent activity."[76] As explained in that committee's report, published in 1976, COINTELPRO functioned as "a sophisticated vigilante operation aimed squarely at preventing the exercise of First Amendment rights of speech and association, on the theory that preventing the growth of dangerous groups and the propagation of dangerous ideas would protect the national security." The unstated premise of COINTELPRO operations was that activism challenging racial, social, and economic injustice was dangerous and "that a law enforcement agency has the duty to do whatever is necessary to combat perceived threats to the existing social and political order."[77] Over the course of fifteen years, under the leadership of FBI director J. Edgar Hoover, COINTELPRO infiltrated numerous organizations devoted to Black freedom, such as the Black Panther Party, harassing, imprisoning, torturing, and even murdering its members, including Fred Hampton.[78]

By the late 1960s, many Black activists and young people had reached their breaking point, no longer willing to tolerate abusive law enforcement and white vigilante violence, and no longer willing to subscribe to nonviolence as a social philosophy or political strategy, as preached by Reverend Martin Luther King, Jr., and others. Although the federal government passed historic civil rights legislation in 1964 and 1965, formally banning race discrimination in voting, employment, and public accommodations—including lunch counters and train stations, which had been sites of protracted nonviolent civil rights protest and struggle—economic conditions in many Black communities were dire and worsening. Many gains achieved through the civil rights movement seemed largely symbolic to Black people who were subject to pervasive police violence and trapped in segregated, impoverished ghettos that had been created by white racism and government action.[79] King himself acknowledged this dilemma, wondering aloud shortly before his death, "What good is having the right to sit at a lunch counter if you can't afford to buy a hamburger?"[80]

When King was assassinated on April 4, 1968, profound despair and grief swept Black communities nationwide, and violent rebellions erupted in more than two hundred cities. In what came to be known as the Holy Week Uprising, thousands of people were injured, scores killed, and hundreds of buildings looted or burned, marking the nation's greatest wave of social unrest since the Civil War.[81] While many civil rights leaders pleaded for peace in the streets, insisting that any form of violent rebellion would dishonor King's memory and legacy, others refused to condemn the violence. Floyd McKissick, the national director of the Congress of Racial Equality (CORE), told *The New York Times* on the night of King's murder that his death meant the end of nonviolence as a political strategy. "Nonviolence is a dead philosophy, and it was not the black people that killed it. It was the white people that killed nonviolence and white racists at that."[82] That sentiment was echoed by other Black activists and leaders, such as Julius Hobson, who headed a civil rights group called ACT: "The next black man who comes into the Black community preaching nonviolence should be violently dealt with by the Black people who hear him. The Martin Luther King concept of nonviolence died with him. It was a foreign ideology anyway—as foreign to this violent country as speaking Russian."[83]

A wave of Black rebellion rocked the United States in the months and years that followed. Roughly two thousand uprisings occurred between May 1968 and December 1972, nearly all of which were sparked by routine police violence.[84] As the historian Elizabeth Hinton explains in *America on Fire*, virtually every major urban center burned during those four years: "Violence flared up not only in archetypal ghettoes including Harlem and Watts, and in majority-Black cities such as Detroit and Washington, D.C.; it appeared in Greensboro, North Carolina, in Gary, Indiana, in Seattle, Washington, and countless places in between—every city, small or large, where Black residents lived in segregated, unequal conditions."[85]

This was not a surge of purposeless criminality, as many white observers claimed; it was a sustained revolt. Throughout American history, white mob violence had been understood as thoroughly political in nature. It was obvious to everyone concerned that white people frequently became enraged when their status or power was threatened, and that they were willing to maintain the racial order through violence—including burning buildings, looting homes, and attacking or lynching Black people. But when Black rebellions swept our nation, they were cast as deviant, criminal, and irrational. Hinton observes, "It was only when white people no longer appeared to be the driving force behind rioting in the nation's cities, and when Black collective violence against exploitative and repressive institutions surfaced, that 'riots' came to be seen as purely criminal, and completely senseless, acts."[86]

Some experts and politicians during that period did acknowledge that the desperate and unjust conditions in which millions of Black people lived were at least partly to blame for the uprisings, most notably the members of the Kerner Commission, which had been created by President Lyndon Johnson to investigate the causes of highly destructive and deadly rioting that had occurred in Detroit and Newark in 1967. The commission's initial report, released just weeks before King was killed, concluded that severe segregation, poverty, joblessness, lack of access to housing, lack of access to economic opportunities, and discrimination in the job market, combined with pervasive police violence and harassment, had created a tinderbox of rage and despair that would certainly result in more uprisings if drastic action was not taken. The report found that many white people were in denial about the true causes of Black uprisings, but Black people were not: "What white Americans have never fully understood but what the Negro can never forget—is that white society is deeply implicated in the ghetto. White institutions created it, white institutions maintain it, and white society condones it."[87]

Conservative white people mostly rejected the Kerner Commission's report, preferring to place responsibility for the widespread political violence directly and solely on the Black community and an imagined culture of lawlessness that had been encouraged by civil rights protests. Throughout the civil rights movement, conservative politicians like Richard Nixon argued that the increasing crime rate was not caused by poverty or joblessness but, instead, "can be traced directly to the spread of the corrosive doctrine that every citizen possesses an inherent right to decide for himself which laws to obey and when to disobey them."[88]

Others went further, insisting that integration causes crime.[89] That type of fearmongering failed to prevent the passage of major civil rights legislation in 1964 and 1965, but the imagery associated with the rebellions, as well as the scale and scope of the destruction, helped fuel the racist argument that civil rights for Black people led to rampant crime and disorder. Many white people pointed to the images on their television screens, as Black people burned buildings or looted stores, and claimed that white people had good reason to fear the changes that were being forced upon them, and that Black people must be controlled at any cost. What was happening in the streets was criminal, they argued. Nothing more and nothing less.

President Johnson was not among those who denied that legitimate reasons existed for the rebellions. Echoing Thomas Jefferson more than a century after he'd warned of the dangers of holding a "wolf by the ear," Johnson said of the uprisings that followed the assassination of Martin Luther King, Jr.: "What did you expect? I don't know why we're so surprised. When you put your foot on a man's neck and hold him down for three hundred years, and then you let him up, what's he going to do? He's going to knock your block off."[90] In a July 1967 speech about Black rebellions in Detroit and Newark, he condemned the violence as criminal but also admitted that "the only genuine, long-range solution for what has happened lies in an attack—mounted at every level—upon the conditions that breed despair and violence."[91]

Like many liberals, Johnson's rhetoric indicated that he favored social programs to address "root causes" of Black despair, but in practice he—as well as both political parties—increasingly looked to law enforcement as the best strategy to achieve and maintain law and order. The Kerner Commission, in its final report, which became a bestselling book in 1968, warned against this lopsided approach, saying that absent a massive investment in poor Black communities, rebellion and "white retaliation" would render racial inequality a permanent feature of American life.[92]

That warning was largely ignored. White fears of losing political, economic, and social dominance—combined with fears of unruly, rebellious Black people—led to massive investments in punitive control over Black people, rather than massive investments that might have repaired the harm caused by centuries of racial oppression. For more than four decades, our nation has declared wars on drugs and crime, invested billions of dollars in highly militarized police forces, and embarked on a race to incarcerate in Black communities, while slashing funding from education, drug treatment, public housing, and welfare.[93] The result has been disastrous. The United States now has the highest rate of incarceration in the world—the number of people behind bars has quintupled in the past four decades—while the Black-white economic divide is as wide as it was in 1968.[94]

In recent years, politicians have defended mass incarceration on the grounds that "getting tough" on crime was what Black people wanted—in other words, that Black fear, not white fear, drove the phenomenon. This is a partial truth. Desperate to address rising crime rates largely caused by the disappearance of work in segregated, ghettoized communities, some Black people have, over the years, supported and advocated for mandatory minimum sentences and other harsh policies. Other Black people—including civil rights activists and organizations—have strenuously opposed crime legislation that propels mass incarceration. The NAACP called the draconian crime bill championed by President Bill Clinton in 1994 "a crime against the American people." Yet Black voices challenging the prison-building boom and demanding investments in education, full employment, drug treatment, and affordable housing were ignored. As Elizabeth Hinton wrote with the historian Julilly Kohler-Hausmann and the political scientist Vesla M. Weaver in a *New York Times* opinion piece in 2016: "It's not just that those demands were ignored completely. It's that some elements were elevated and others were diminished—what we call selective hearing. Policy makers pointed to black support for greater punishment and surveillance, without recognizing accompanying demands to redirect power and economic resources to low-income minority communities."[95]

Rather than focus on "root causes" of crime and violence, and the systems and structures that create and maintain inequality, politicians across the political spectrum capitulated to a narrative that segregationists had been selling decades earlier—and that enslavers had embraced before them: namely, that Black people were lazy, had to be forced to work, were inherently or culturally criminal, and thus must be subject to perpetual control.

This narrative made it easy to rationalize draconian punishments as well as stop-and-frisk and surveillance tactics not unlike those employed by slave patrollers more than a century ago. In choosing this path, liberal and conservative politicians proved that they could hear, loud and clear, reactionary white voices—belonging to what some media pundits and politicians dubbed the "angry white men," people who viewed racial and social justice as a zero-sum game they were afraid to lose—even as they claimed not to hear Black people pleading with their representatives to take the road less traveled and to end the cycle of racial oppression, rebellion, and punitive control once and for all.[96]

This problem of "selective hearing" of Black voices might be dismissed as a profound misunderstanding if it did not fit so neatly into a recurring pattern dating back to our nation's founding. The impulse to resist efforts by Black people to gain freedom and equality and to respond with punishment or violence, no matter whether demands are made through peaceful protest, lobbying, or outright rebellion, has been the defining feature of Black-white race relations since the first slave ships arrived on American shores. This habitual impulse has been driven by chronic fear not just of Black people—because similar responses can be found in post-colonial dealings with other racial groups and Indigenous communities—but, more deeply, of what true justice might require.

Considering this history, it should have come as no surprise that the election of the first Black president and anxiety over shifting racial demographics due to immigration—including a widely publicized projection that white people will be a racial minority by the mid-twenty-first century—would be followed by a rise in white nationalism, hate crimes, and vigilante violence, as well as the election of politicians like Donald Trump, a man who rose to power by exploiting racial fears and divisions and sought to maintain power by thwarting democracy.[97]

In the same vein, it should have been obvious that rebellions in Black communities would sweep our nation again and again, given that police officers and vigilantes continue to kill unarmed Black people like Breonna Taylor, Ahmaud Arbery, and George Floyd, and given that the deplorable conditions documented in the Kerner Commission's report remain mostly unaddressed. While some Black people have benefited from the social and policy changes brought by the civil rights movement, in many respects, things have gotten worse for Black communities since that report was published, with so many more Black people in prison, on probation or parole, and subject to legal discrimination due to criminal records.

What does come as a surprise, a welcome one, is that in 2020, the predictable cycle—white fear and violence followed by uprisings and rebellions that lead to white reprisals, retaliation, and strengthening of systems of control—didn't play out exactly as usual. Instead, the largest racial-justice protests in history—including people of all colors and ages and from all walks of life—occurred during the Trump presidency, after a major Black rebellion, and in the midst of a global pandemic. Protesters carried aloft signs saying, BLACK LIVES MATTER and DEFUND THE POLICE, reflecting the understanding that so long as we continue to invest in the types of punitive systems of organized violence that have oppressed and controlled Black people for centuries— rather than in the programs, policies, and forms of structural change that Black communities need to thrive—we will never achieve a truly inclusive, egalitarian democracy that honors the dignity and value of Black lives.

James Baldwin famously said, "Not everything that is faced can be changed, but nothing can be changed unless it is faced." Perhaps our nation is finally beginning to face our history, as a new generation of activists challenges us to choose a radically different path forward. The future of Black communities, and our democracy as a whole, depends on us finally getting it right this time.

November 7, 1775

In the face of a growing Patriot insurgency, Lord Dunmore, the royal governor of Virginia, issues a proclamation offering freedom to all enslaved people held by colonists sympathetic to the Patriot cause in return for their joining the British Army. More than eight hundred enslaved men escape to Dunmore's lines and enlist, wearing uniforms with the motto "Liberty to Slaves." Dunmore's regiment sees action in one major battle and several skirmishes, but smallpox soon decimates its ranks.

Freedom Is Not for Myself Alone

Robert Jones, Jr.

If you remember the ship, if it didn't take your mind from you, then you understand.

When we get to the place where the paper tell us to go, first thing I ask the toubab, one of Lord Dunmore's soldiers, is what about my woman and my little boy, and he say that my freedom is for me and me alone. But how could it be that? What use is being forever unchained if my love still bound up? These toubab, no matter where they from, no matter how they sound, they share a strange way of thinking about freedom. They don't know what's free unless they line it up against what ain't. And for them, what "ain't" always got to be you.

"Give me liberty or give me death!" We heard that a slave owner named Patrick Henry said that in a speech he give to the other toubab. I laugh for two reasons. For one, he don't know what he say to be invitation for his own slaves to rise up against him. They feel yoked by they Mother England like we yoked by her colonies. If they break the chains, they showing how we can break our own. And there is at least as many of us as there is them. Only guns make it uneven.

For two, for people who have everything, they seem to know not a thing. The only way to have what's yours—and for no other reason than because you here, because you alive—is to kill yourself to keep it? But if you remember the ship, the bellowing, rocking ship, you reckon they make it such that something so foolish makes all the sense in the world.

I didn't even say goodbye to Catherine and William because what use is there in remembering faces I ain't never gwine see again? I just run off in the night with Right John and Left Julius and me in the middle of them, stumbling in the woods, looking for the spot where Left Julius, the only one of us who can read, which cost him his left eye, told us the paper said we was supposed to go. When we finally arrive, the first thing I ask about is Catherine and William and I know I was right to leave in silence instead of remembering their faces.

When they put the rifle in my hand and dress me up in soldier's uniform—with a bunch of other people by my side, some happy, some, like me, leaving everything behind so happiness won't ever be their fortune— I don't want to admit it, but holding that metal, cold until my grip warms it, makes me almost feel like a man. What I mean is, I almost feel like one of them, the toubab, and the feeling ain't as repulsive as I thought it'd be.

They gwine put us on the front line, I know. This man ain't call for us out of the goodness of his graces. I knew that the minute they left me no choice but to abandon flesh and blood. I know I ain't nothing but one of many to be used as cannon fodder, a body to fill out his shrinking and stunted ranks. To help deny liberty to the men who denied me liberty, proving that toubab have no idea what that word mean. Never did. And never will.

Might be all worth it, though, to see the massas, overseers, and catchers running like cowards at the sight of *us* with the guns for once. To have *us* hooting and howling like *we* on the hunt. Holding torches high in the night so the shadows don't hide *their* trembling bodies. Shot down in the back. Have their families weep over their bodies. And those of us who make it rejoice for our own selves and our own selves alone, which ain't hardly enough.

I hope I ain't one of those who make it. I can't sail over those waters again. That's what they tell us gwine happen. Those of us who fight for the Crown and live to tell about it will be put on a boat and shipped off to England—whether we be triumphant or defeated. Crossing that same dreadful ocean that split us from our first families, with no promise that this trip will bring us anything different from what we got before except having hearts broke twice instead of once. Who to say Dunmore is a man of his word? Never safe to trust toubab.

If you remember the ship, if it didn't take your mind from you, then you understand.

August 19, 1791

Benjamin Banneker, a mathematician, inventor, philosopher, almanac compiler, and free Black man from Baltimore, sends then—secretary of state Thomas Jefferson a letter protesting the treatment and condition of "those of my complexion" in the new nation. Two years earlier the U.S. Constitution went into effect, enshrining both the Three-fifths Compromise and the Fugitive Slave Clause. In his letter, Banneker tells Jefferson that the institution of slavery contradicts the ideals in the Declaration of Independence.

Other Persons

Reginald Dwayne Betts

I.

Always in the center of things,
even with the flimflam; they say,
    Race doesn't exist

in the Constitution: four thousand
five hundred & forty-three words, another
word for Black is Crispus Attucks,

his eyes as vacant as a dead Confederate
soldier's. Another word for Black is John Brown
at Harpers Ferry; another word for race is

slavery, another word for slavery is a fraction.
    Article I, Section 2, now unconstitutional (maybe):

    Three fifths. Respective Numbers, apportioned.
    Three fifths: the whole number,
    Adding taxes, service, not adding Indians,
    Not adding all other persons,
    Not included within this Union; three fifths: not
    Persons. This Union, this Union.

II.

My father went to a school named
after Paul Laurence Dunbar,
& in the parking lot of a school

christened after Francis Scott Key,
drugs turned some people into
three-fifths of what they were before

a crack pipe. Lost in that story
is a cemetery of people enslaved
by George Washington. To be counted

is a euphemism for freedom:
A man who claims to own a man
& talks about democracy is

a euphemism for a gun.
The blood at the end of his whip
is a story about tomorrow.

> *Taxed for a term of years by*
> *Excluding. Indians, Three fifths,*
> *Apportioned among the free*
> *Persons, adding all and all and all*
> *And all bound. Three fifths of all*
> *Other persons. Bound. Within this Union*

What of the man who once
held a woman in the dirt, owned
his children; my children call me Daddy.

Does an enslaved man call
any white man Father? What care of what
happened next? My ancestors

have no name for what would
come with dawn.

Three fifths: the whole person.
Three fifths and Indians, may be
Excluded. From this Union. Excluded.
Respective of numbers, apportioned;
All Three fifths, Indians, all but other
Persons excluded, taxed.

III.

Benjamin Banneker wrote Thomas Jefferson
a letter; one thousand four hundred & ninety something
words—

  I am fully sensible of the greatness of that freedom
  Which I take with you . . .

There is a school in a city
filled with Black people named after Banneker,

  Three fifths not free persons,
  Indians, not free—bound
  To service; Three fifths bound to free
  persons, apportioned within this Union:

& nine miles away, along a highway where even
the Lord must endure traffic,
is a middle school named after Jefferson.

  Suffer me to recall to your mind that time in which the Arms
  and tyranny of the British Crown were exerted with every powerful
  effort in order to reduce you to a State of Servitude

Between Banneker & Jefferson lie sixteen thousand Civil War
soldiers at Arlington National Cemetery;
Lord, how can those children read in a city where freedom
is adjacent to war & the cemetery is adjacent to
reconstruction & Black is everything,
including the memory of *Cruickshank* & Jim Crow,

including Juvie who died six months after parole,
whatever disease coursing through his bones as much
the memory of a cell as anything else, who
dies after surviving twenty-six years in prison?

> *Not Persons, three fifths. Indians, not*
> *Persons. Indians and three fifths,*
> *Excluded, not apportioned among*
> *The whole. Number the bound,*
> *Number the three fifths, the Indians.*

Two hundred–odd years is not so long.
All I know of the Constitution is Article I, Section 2,
the fourth paragraph of Banneker's letter
has more restraint than a slaver.

> *I apprehend you will readily embrace every opportunity to eradicate*
> *that train of absurd and false ideas and opinions which so generally*
> *prevails with respect to us*

I cannot imagine desiring a bullet &
settling for a pen. This is America.

> *For years, for several years, for this Union,*
> *For this whole Union. Indians and three*
> *fifths not persons, not free: shall be*
> *Bound by this Union. Several states.*
> *Representatives. A term determined*
> *By adding, by excluding, by which.*
> *Apportioned free. This union of*
> *Three fifths and Indians.*

I cannot imagine wanting all this death.

> *Wean yourselves from those narrow prejudices.*

IV.

Every letter is a kind of confession:

> *I freely and Chearfully acknowledge, that I am of the African race, and in
> that colour which is natural to them of the deepest dye.*

& every confession, a kind nod toward history:

> *Wean yourselves from these narrow prejudices.*

Toward what happens to the memory of men who die.

> *Your knowledge of the situation of my brethren is too extensive to need a
> recital here*

A way to say, Jefferson, I know you know
About the suffering at the end of your whip.

Two young Ho-Chunk women, Carrie Elk (ENooKah), left, and her cousin Annie Lowe Lincoln (Red Bird), c. 1904   WISCONSIN HISTORICAL SOCIETY

CHAPTER 5

Dispossession

TIYA MILES

On November 18, 1785, a contingent of Cherokee people arrived at Hopewell Plantation, on the bucolic banks of a South Carolina river, for a meeting that would help set the structure of the American racial hierarchy for centuries to come. It was the first in a set of negotiations between the United States and the Cherokee, Choctaw, and Chickasaw Nations. In the aftermath of the American Revolution, these negotiations would begin to lay the groundwork for the relationship between the United States and Native governments. If the United States was to consolidate and grow as a country, it had to contend with all of the Indigenous people, who, though devastated by over a century of imperial and colonial battles, were still populous and powerful, and who controlled most of the American continent.

Native people were critical to the American economy as the procurers of skins for the profitable fur trade, and they also posed a threat to American settler communities. In the years before the American Revolution, Cherokees and English colonists in South Carolina had carried out attacks against one another amid trade disputes and cultural misunderstandings, and in retribution for prior killings. These altercations led to the deaths of nearly two hundred Carolinians at Cherokee hands in the year 1760 alone and disrupted the racial power structure by giving some enslaved Black people the opportunity to flee their English captors. A year later, following what is known as the Anglo-Cherokee War, English troops crushed nearby Cherokee towns, pushing the Cherokees into a defensive posture that lasted through the cataclysmic war that broke out between the Patriots and the English in the 1770s.[1]

At the time of that war, the largest Indigenous societies south of the Ohio River in the eighteenth century—the Cherokees, Choctaws, Chickasaws,

Creeks, and Seminoles—resided in hundreds of towns linked by kinship, language, religion, cultural practices, economic exchange, and governing structures across the present-day states of North Carolina, South Carolina, Georgia, Florida, Tennessee, Alabama, and Mississippi. When the colonists resisted the British and mounted an armed defense that evolved into full-scale war, Native people, squeezed by both sides, had to choose alliances. As the conflict intensified, many large and influential Native nations leaned toward Great Britain.[2] Once it was over, the Indigenous people knew that if they were to survive the encroachment of their land, the taking of natural resources, and the local violence that an ambitious new nation in their midst portended, they had to come to terms with the victor in that contest. And so the Cherokee contingent traveled to Hopewell.

The land on which discussions would unfold was a plantation—a place where enslaved people would be forced to labor against their will—owned by General Andrew Pickens, a formidable South Carolina militia leader during the American Revolution. Pickens had been a man of modest means from a South Carolina interior Scots-Irish family who gradually rose to prominence during the war years. By 1773, Pickens had managed to obtain two enslaved Black people, an essential first step in his climb up the Southern social and economic ladder. In July 1784, in recognition of his service in America's Revolutionary War, General George Washington awarded Pickens 573 acres on the Keowee River. This fertile land had previously belonged to the Cherokees, who had generally sided with the British in the conflict and had been badly beaten by Washington's army. For a low price, Pickens quickly acquired adjacent parcels totaling over a thousand acres, which he registered in the names of his children, including a future governor of the state, Andrew Pickens, Jr.[3] With his newfound wealth and status secured, Andrew Pickens, Sr., had a sizable house built near a majestic oak tree and began his career as a country gentleman.

Pickens was joined by three men from elite families who also enslaved people and whom Congress had appointed as treaty commissioners. Colonel Benjamin Hawkins, the son of a wealthy tobacco agriculturalist from North Carolina, would conduct the bulk of the negotiations. Joseph Martin, who hailed from a wealthy Virginia clan, and General Lachlan McIntosh, a Georgia rice agriculturalist, would participate as well.[4]

The commissioners had expected a small cadre of Indigenous representatives to appear when they invited the head men of the Cherokee nation to convene at Hopewell. They were shocked when five hundred Cherokees arrived, including women, and soon after several hundred more. These congregants may have expected the distribution of diplomatic gifts from their hosts, which was an Indigenous custom, picked up by the French and, to a lesser extent, the British. In addition, at the time, Native peoples of the South were deeply democratic and arrived at decisions by consensus. Ultimately, two individuals, Corn Tassel and the Beloved Woman Nanye-hi (or Nancy Ward), both of Chota town, emerged as chief spokespeople.[5] Under the branches of the large oak tree, in the shadow of a plantation house, the Cherokee leaders and the commissioners met to formalize a settlement.

Corn Tassel and the Beloved Woman Nanye-hi attempted to defend their claim to the Southern soil. These leaders complained about the thousands of white people who had encroached on their lands and made homes there, urging the treaty commissioners to remove them as a condition of the peace. The American officials asserted that they had no power to act, because the squatters were so numerous. There was nothing they could do.

The Cherokee negotiators suspected that Hawkins and the rest were being disingenuous. In many ways, these settlers were the advance guard of U.S. expansion into Indigenous territory. Corn Tassel responded with more than a hint of sarcasm. "Are Congress, who conquered the King of Great Britain, unable to remove the people?" he asked.[6]

But the commissioners made it clear that the Cherokees must sign agreements with the Americans in order to avoid the devastation of further conflict, and it would have been apparent to the Cherokee leaders that they had little choice. A grand cotton plantation owned by a military leader made the ideal setting to demonstrate American presence, authority, and expectations. Pickens was also known by Native leaders for his brutality; he had personally led violent incursions into the villages of the Cherokees during the war, and as Colin Calloway, a colonial historian, put it, his militia "hacked to death the defenseless occupants as they fled on foot."[7]

On November 28, 1785, ten days after the Cherokees had arrived, American and Cherokee negotiators agreed to the terms of the first Treaty of Hopewell. The Cherokees would accept the "protection of the United States of America, and of no other sovereign." They would return all U.S. prisoners as well as "restore all the Negroes, and all other property taken during the late war from the citizens." Some of these Black former captives were being held in unfree status among the Cherokees, and others had married into Native families. The treaty also stipulated that the Cherokees were to abide by a set of geographical boundary lines drawn between themselves and white Americans.[8]

In return, the United States agreed to prohibit its citizens from "settl[ing] on any of the lands westward or southward of the said boundary," excluding lands inside those boundaries that Corn Tassel had explicitly highlighted as an area where many white people were already illegally living. The United States also promised to regulate trade between Cherokee people and white people and to treat the Cherokees justly. If the Cherokees handed over the Black people and other "property" and respected the new boundaries and U.S. law, "the hatchet," the commissioners attested, "shall be forever buried."[9]

This first Treaty of Hopewell was followed by two others that winter, with the Choctaws and the Chickasaws, with nearly identical stipulations.[10] Hawkins, the principal negotiator, effectively hemmed in large populations of Native people with the establishment of explicit official borders. The American insistence on crafting treaties at the national level recognized Native political and territorial sovereignty, but the terms of the treaties subordinated Native nations to the American nation.

They also underscored a meaningful difference between Native and Black people.[11] Just as the colonies had formerly been under the "protection" of the British, Native nations would now be under the "protection" of the Americans. And while that protected status was arguably a less independent one than had previously existed, it was nevertheless a privileged one in relation to African Americans. Whereas members of the Native nations were citizens of their own countries, deserving, at least on paper, human and political rights, African Americans were citizens of nowhere and undeserving even of the rights of personhood.

During these three visits to Hopewell, the Native participants learned important lessons from the plantation scene splayed before them and from the language of the treaties: white people were citizens, Black people were possessions, and Indigenous people were now subject to national interference. In order to maintain the "protection" of the United States from its own citizens, Native leaders were being indirectly encouraged to participate in a form of racial hierarchy that was considered part and parcel of civilized American society—one that has distorted Native and Black relations ever since.

Today, African Americans and Native Americans share the highest incarceration and poverty rates in the country, as well as the lowest high school graduation numbers. Both groups appear at the bottom of a range of health and well-being indicators, and both have suffered high rates of serious illness during the Covid-19 pandemic.[12] And yet the two groups have often struggled to find solidarity, a painful legacy of the way they learned to regard each other in the nation's formative years.

––––––––––

The leaders of the tribal nations, and subgroups within them, that supported Great Britain were choosing the devil they knew. Although English settlers had often taken advantage of Native people with dire effect, the British government exercised greater control over the actions of its subjects than American statesmen seemed inclined to do. This was in large part an economic, not a humanitarian, calculation. During the colonial era, the colonists' constant westward settlement financially strained the Crown, which was called upon to protect these incursions into Native territory with troops and forts. In 1763, King George III issued a royal proclamation asserting authority to oversee trade with Native Americans and forbidding the expansion of white settlement west of the Appalachian Mountains. Although there was no enforcement arm for this provision, its existence created a legal barrier that colonists resented, and Native leaders lauded.

In fact, this tension was a contributing factor to the American Revolution. The colonies were growing rapidly in population and running out of fertile Southern plantation ground that would support the sons of landholders, as well as open territory that would satisfy the desire for upward mobility among the swelling yeoman farmer ranks, whose contentment was necessary for political stability. In addition, as the historian Jeffrey Ostler has elucidated, eastern elites such as George Washington held financial interests in these westerly lands that could not be exploited while the Proclamation of 1763 prevented freewheeling land sales.[13] As Calloway succinctly put it in *The Indian World of George Washington:* "The Revolution was not only a war for independence and a new political order; it was also a war for the North American continent."[14]

It is little wonder, then, that Native people tended to side with the British. During the war American soldiers attacked hundreds of Native towns and British loyalist strongholds. Native soldiers also raided Patriot settlements. In 1777, a group of intransigent Cherokees called the Chickamauga warriors, led by Dragging Canoe, Doublehead, the Glass, Bloody Fellow, and others, began a series of guerrilla attacks on settlements. Sometimes Black people were taken captive, enslaved, or given to other Cherokees.

After the war, as American political leaders prepared to form a new national government, they knew that they had a significant problem. The British did not control most of the lands signed over in the 1783 Treaty of Paris, which ended the American Revolution—Native people did, and some of the aggrieved Cherokee men continued to fight against the Americans in the interior. The road map for living alongside unpredictable Native American nations and, furthermore, for accessing those coveted lands that Native peoples claimed and actively defended, was not clear-cut for the leaders of the infant republic.

The new American politicians and their British forebears believed that Native people should be treated simultaneously as citizens of nations and as members of lower-order societies. The Americans inherited a grab bag of strategies for dealing with Indigenous peoples from the English, who had generally viewed Native nations as separate political bodies with prior occupancy of the soil. But the British also saw Native people as unchristian "heathens" and as "savages" who had not actually developed the land in a civilized manner that would qualify them as rightful owners. The Doctrine of Discovery, a longstanding belief that Christian nations had the right to rule over non-Christian nations and their property, helped justify English imperialism despite prior Native presence. English officials as well as private buyers purchased Indigenous land by contract while also grabbing land through manipulation, coercion, and outright seizure in the aftermath of war. Because the English subscribed to the principles of the rule of law and the primacy of property rights, they used isolated crimes by Native men as rationalizations for large-scale attacks on Native communities.

Following the Revolution, American statesmen carried on with this mixed approach. They recognized Native nations, politically and geographically, as sovereign entities with the authority to govern themselves, define their citizenry, and occupy their territory. The United States made treaties with tribal nations as with foreign governments, even if these nations were not seen as fully equivalent to European states.[15] And among the most important treaties was the one set in place at Hopewell with the Cherokee Nation. This agreement was negotiated when the United States was just being shaped and it established the first geographical border to the west. But that was not the only reason it was so influential. It also established slavery as part of the American way.

Slavery was not unknown to Native Southerners when they met with the American commissioners at Hopewell. Before the formation of the modern Cherokee, Choctaw, Chickasaw, and Creek Nations in the sixteenth and seventeenth centuries, ancient Indigenous civilizations had organized life around hierarchical governing structures now called Mississippian chiefdoms. A man or woman with inherited rank, the town chief or paramount chief with influence over multiple towns, customarily enjoyed privileged status and decision-making authority. Chiefdoms practiced a form of slavery in which people of a lower caste (seized from other Native societies) were forced to labor for the chiefs they served and were sometimes ritually killed and buried with them.

With the arrival of European explorers and conquistadors in the 1500s, chiefdoms encountered deadly foreign diseases as well as another threat: European slavery. They would certainly have noticed that conquistadors often arrived with captive people of darker-hued skin.

When Hernando de Soto came ashore in present-day Tampa, Florida, in 1539, intent on finding riches for the Spanish Crown, in addition to a contingent of 625 soldiers and 250 horses, he brought enslaved people. He also carried iron restraints for locking up Indigenous people he hoped to seize. De Soto and his men marched from coastal Florida through the inner reaches of Georgia and Carolina, attacking Native villages, raiding their food supplies, ransacking their dwellings in search of gold and silver, and capturing some of the inhabitants. During their ruthless trek, de Soto and his men encountered sophisticated societies with intricate political and cultural systems and ample natural resources. In present-day South Carolina, de Soto's party met a woman chieftain of the domain of Cofitachequi. Struck by her stately appearance—she was borne aloft in a sedan chair carried by several men—de Soto seized two hundred pounds of pearls and deerskins from her temple and then kidnapped her. Just beyond the borders of her domain, this captive, known in the historical record as the Lady of Cofitachequi, escaped with a cache of her precious pearls. Later, Spanish deserters reported that they had seen the Lady of Cofitachequi living as a spouse with a "Spanish slave" who had also escaped. This person was almost certainly of African descent.[16]

In this dramatic instance, it seems that an Indigenous leader and an African captive found common cause and forged new lives together in a dangerous and changing political environment, but the space in which mutual support was possible would shrink in the coming decades. By 1680, the Cofitachequi chiefdom had disappeared. Disease, political instability, and slaving had ravaged Mississippian chiefdoms in the century and a half after Europeans arrived and led to a widespread societal collapse that left behind what the anthropologist Robbie Ethridge has termed a "shatter zone."[17]

Europeans in the Southeast established towns that thrived, in large part, on a virulent slave trade. These colonists, who possessed deadly weapons, traded manufactured English goods to Native hunters for deerskins. They also demanded to enslave Indigenous people in exchange for goods and as payment for debts that Native hunters had accrued in past transactions. As they sought to survive in a maelstrom of change set in motion by modern European capitalism, colonialism, and racial slavery, Native Americans began actively raiding and seizing people from other tribes in order to establish strong trade relations with the English, to service debts, and to avoid being hunted themselves. As the historian Alan Gallay has documented, at least thirty to fifty thousand Indigenous Southerners were enslaved by Anglo colonists before the year 1715. Many of these Native people were traded to enslavers in the Caribbean and Europe; a large number were transported to New England; and some were sold to operations in the Upper South, particularly Virginia. Even as an African diaspora was taking shape, as Africans were tracked down in their own regions and brought to others through the Middle Passage, an "American diaspora," writes the anthropologist Jack Forbes, was developing as Indigenous Americans were also violently relocated.[18]

Thrown together by European invasion, colonization, and slavery in the sixteenth, seventeenth, and early eighteenth centuries, Indigenous and African people came into intimate contact and forged relationships that changed their lives and bound their fates. In the colonial period, Charles Towne (now Charleston, South Carolina) was a major site for the sale of both African and Native people, as was New Amsterdam (New York City). These captives stood on the same auction blocks, traversed the Atlantic on the same ships, and finally ended up in the same Northern households or Southern or Caribbean plantations, where they lived, labored, suffered, and surely dreamed together.[19]

These shared circumstances of enslavement led to the merger of families, cultures, and fates. Indigenous American people intermarried with Africans and their American-born descendants.[20] Corn-based and leafy green–intensive Indigenous diets fused with African American cooking that relied on sweet potatoes, black-eyed peas, and pork to form a fundamental part of Southern regional culinary culture. Black women became expert basket weavers, most notably along the Carolina and Georgia coasts, using Native American plant preferences, even as Black men likely learned to build dugout canoes from Indigenous men. Enslaved Black people used local plants as herbal medicines in accordance with Indigenous knowledge, and both groups developed a rich and perhaps mutually informed folklore centering on trickster rabbit stories. Enslaved Black and Native Americans produced a distinctive pottery style known by archaeologists as colonoware. Many of these earthen vessels, which have been discovered on Virginia, South Carolina, and Georgia estates, are marked with hybrid circle and cross symbols believed to be reflective of West African, Native American, and Christian religious beliefs.[21]

Black and Native people also ran away together and had families. Their mixed-race and bicultural children were both African and Indigenous American but were often recorded simply as "Negro" in private and colonial ledgers, rendering them virtually invisible to historical researchers. Black and Native people also enacted small-scale rebellions, such that British agents and colonial leaders expressed great concern about the probability of organized and effective political alliances between these groups. This fear continued, and when Seminole, Creek, and Black people waged a prolonged defensive war against American soldiers in the Seminole country of Florida in the early 1800s, American military commanders expressed particular consternation because of its interracial character.[22]

Yet all along free Indigenous Southerners could not have failed to notice that imported captive foreigners with dark skin were outnumbering Native people among the unfree population. They surely would have been alarmed, too, at how English colonial law deemed these African captives unfree for life, a status passed through the womb. While there were opportunities for some Native people, who were considered potentially redeemable and assimilable, to be converted to Christianity in regions like New England and the Great Lakes, the rules were different for African captives in the South. Even if they embraced Christianity, they would retain their unfree status, due to new English laws crafted to disallow an escape hatch from slavery by way of Christian conversion. Unlike older forms of Indigenous American slavery in the Southeast that involved the capture of people from different tribes whose status was often transitory, English captivity had become both racial and heritable.[23]

Native Southerners soon recognized the difference that race made and saw that Black people were being defined as a distinct and inferior group with no hope of incorporation into the new American nation as free and respected people. By 1793, some Native Americans in the South were making racial distinctions and displaying prejudices. That year, a Cherokee leader named Little Turkey was recorded as using the term "mulattoes" as a slur against the Spanish in a letter to the American governor of Tennessee, and by 1811 a Cherokee chief named Richard Brown, who disputed a white man's possession of a horse, protested the dismissal of his demands by asking the U.S. agent, "Are we considered as negroes who cannot support our claims?"[24] Slavery was no longer a bridge between Indigenous and African people struggling to survive in similar straits but a wall of division. As a color line hardened and Native people struggled to keep to the free side of it, they were able to leverage political standing as members of nations and economic players that Africans, stolen from their tribes and homelands, could not.

Even so, in the years after the treaties were signed at Hopewell, the situation deteriorated for the tribal nations. Almost immediately, in clear violation of the agreements, American citizens expanded their footprint on Southern soil by crossing tribal borders and establishing homesteads and businesses that evolved into settlements and towns. The flood of settlers—many of them men with weapons—washed through the forests and mountains, threatening the safety, hunting grounds, and livelihood of Native peoples.[25] Furious about the injustice of white encroachment and the failure of the states and the national government to uphold the terms of the treaties, resistant Chickamauga Cherokees relocated to a Tennessee River stronghold and from there launched a series of guerrilla attacks.

Dealing with this grave situation was one of the most pressing matters during George Washington's first term as president. Together with his secretary of war Henry Knox, Washington devised a federal policy that would avoid "exterminating" Native people and focus instead on civilizing them, as this seemed the most humanitarian and effective way to bring them under U.S. authority and foster their eventual assimilation. The architects of the early American state were Age of Enlightenment thinkers who believed that Indigenous people had the intelligence and ability to assimilate into proper society, unlike Africans, whom they viewed as innately insufficient.

In an address to Congress in 1791, Washington outlined six principles for federal relations with Native people; these included delivering "impartial" justice, regulated methods of land sales and trade, the right of the government to distribute diplomatic presents, penalties for those who violated Natives' rights, and "rational experiments . . . for imparting to them the blessings of civilization." The following year, Washington urged Congress to create a plan for "promoting civilization among the friendly tribes."[26]

This view was reflected in the Treaty of Holston, signed in 1791, an update of the Hopewell Treaties, which compelled Cherokees to "be led to a greater degree of civilization, and to become herdsmen and cultivators, instead of remaining in a state of hunters."[27] Native people's ways of life necessitated broad swaths of land for growing corn, squash, and beans; for plants collected from diverse locations; for extensive hunting; and for ceremonial travel to far-off towns with spiritual significance. But the "civilization" program assumed that Indians would recognize the superiority of Western culture and be willing to change without being coerced by force. As civilized tribes, Washington reasoned, the Native people would neither need nor claim so much land. And in exchange for the Cherokees' consent to "civilizing" practices, the United States promised to prevent Americans from pushing past the new boundaries.

George Washington appointed Benjamin Hawkins superintendent to the Southern tribes in 1796 to translate this plan on the ground. When offering the post to Hawkins, Washington reportedly entreated him to conduct "the experiment which you have suggested, and try the effects of civilization among them," implying that Hawkins had influenced Washington's own ideas.[28]

The federal civilization plan was spare on specifics but transformative in practice. American officials intended to drive what the historians Theda Perdue and Michael Green have termed "comprehensive cultural change," converting a communal lifestyle rooted in sustainable farming and hunting into an individualistic lifestyle punctuated by private property and male authority. The policy demanded that Native men give up the bow for the plow, and that Native women cease farming corn and turn their attention to the domestic work of spinning thread, weaving cloth, and other "properly" feminine activities. Native people were advised to adopt Christianity and begin producing "civilized crops" like cotton.[29] And Native tribes, which held lands in common, were expected to embrace, as Henry Knox put it, "a love for exclusive property."[30] To aid in this reinvention of Indigenous society, the United States would provide tools, fund the establishment of Christian missions and schools, and commission blacksmiths. If Native people did not prove that they could rise above savagery and assimilate, Hawkins and others believed, they would be crowded out or killed.[31]

And there was yet one more thing. Native communities were encouraged to adopt what had emerged as a defining characteristic of civilized Euro-American society in the South: the enslavement of Black people.

Because the federal civilization policy was conceived, developed, and enforced by enslavers who felt their way of life was advanced and ideal, it included the tacit expectation that the most progressive among Native Americans, those who would lead their people into the future, should also enslave Black people. Although this was not explicitly written into the plan, Natives who enslaved people found favor with the U.S. government, garnering positive reviews in the federal agents' reports and earning government contracts and military honors.

This lesson was also clear on Benjamin Hawkins's model farm in the Creek Nation, where he resided and had relocated many of his enslaved Black people from North Carolina. Here he provided not only an agricultural demonstration for Native people he viewed as pupils but also what the colonial historian James Merrell has called a "racial education." Well-positioned mixed-race Native families of Indigenous and European ancestry began to follow Hawkins's example first, and soon their large farms became models for others in how to maintain a racial order with the Black population at the bottom.[32]

Over the next two decades, until his death in 1816, Hawkins was the chief civilian enforcer of this plan, a role that saw him traveling frequently to the nations under his charge to survey their progress toward cultural change. His notes on these visits indicate that while Native people were experimenting with Black slavery, many were not yet doing so precisely as he had intended. The agent recorded these failings, including Native women who were marrying Black captives and Native men who were working in fields alongside the people they were enslaving.[33] While Hawkins found a number of Creek and Cherokee people exhibiting "no economy or management" during his visits, he did find one person deemed "industrious" as early as 1796. That man, Hawkins recorded, was worthy of such praise for having sixty-one enslaved people, more than two hundred horses, four hundred cattle, and three hundred hogs.[34]

Even so, within the nations that had signed treaties at Hopewell Plantation, slavery gradually took root. Among the Indigenous nations, Cherokees enslaved the largest number of people, but Creeks, Choctaws, and Chickasaws also developed entrenched systems of Black enslavement tethered to racial prejudice.[35] And although it is the case that enslavers in Native nations were always a small minority of their populations (approximately 2.3 percent by the 1860s, in comparison with approximately 20 percent in the white South), they were also elite members of their rapidly changing societies. These were the men who formed new centralized governing bodies, wrote the laws, and negotiated treaties.[36]

One such individual was James Vann, the son of a Scottish trader and Cherokee woman. Vann had defended collective Cherokee landholdings in negotiations with American officials. But by the early 1800s, he had established a large wheat, corn, and cotton estate in Cherokee territory, becoming the Cherokee Nation's best example of a Native proponent of American-style race slavery. Vann controlled nearly eight hundred acres of rich agricultural land bordered by a prominent waterway. A wily strategist and smart entrepreneur, he did business with the federal government, invited Christian missionaries to his grounds, lobbied for a federal road to pass by his home, and then established a string of hospitality and transport businesses.[37]

He also owned nearly seventy women, men, and children of African descent; they cleared land, farmed crops, constructed buildings, prepared meals, cleaned and maintained his living quarters, wove textiles, watched

147

over the cattle, delivered goods, and tended to the physical and emotional needs of his family. Vann employed a violent overseer, had once burned down enslaved people's cabins in a fit of rage, and personally carried out or oversaw the chaining and hanging of enslaved men. By the time of his death in 1809, James Vann lived in an impressive home with his Cherokee wife (also of mixed European and Cherokee parentage) and had enslaved more than one hundred Black people.[38]

James's son "Rich Joe" Vann inherited the estate and many of the enslaved Black residents. The younger Vann replaced the existing family home with an imposing brick manor house festooned with white columns and intricate hand-carved wooden interiors, as well as an architecturally noteworthy "floating" staircase. Joe Vann's Georgia mansion, in which his Cherokee family ate off imported European china and drank from expensive glassware, was meant to symbolize civilizational progress and to showcase his affluence to the planners, like Benjamin Hawkins, of the new American nation-state.[39]

But adopting a republican form of government and operating plantations worked by slave labor would not be enough to protect Native Southerners. White citizens craved more land, and they would have it.

In 1828, Andrew Jackson surged to the presidency on a wave of populist enthusiasm. In his inaugural address, he expressed his understanding that Native nations were subject to U.S. authority and referred to "Indian tribes within our limits," instead of using the language of sovereign nationhood.[40] Jackson's second State of the Union address, in December 1830, advocated for the expulsion of Native people from their homes, towns, houses of worship, and seats of government. He urged Congress to effect Native "removal" through legislation. This would be a national policy of expulsion with limited financial support, affecting not only the Cherokees and other Southeastern nations but also nations in the Midwest. Arguing that American progress was to be commended, not lamented, Jackson insisted: "Philanthropy could not wish to see this continent restored to the condition in which it was found by our forefathers. What good man would prefer a country covered with forests and ranged by a few thousand savages to our extensive Republic?"[41]

In Jackson's view, the removal of Native people in the East to a region west of the Mississippi River was "not only liberal, but generous."[42] There they would be isolated and protected from the white man's influence, and their cultures better preserved. In the end, Jackson reasoned, this relocation would benefit Native Americans. Using the excuse of the government's inability to control white settlers, as had been claimed in the Hopewell Treaty negotiations nearly forty-five years prior, Jackson asked, "Can it be cruel in this Government when, by events which it cannot control, the Indian is made discontented in his ancient home to purchase his lands, to give him a new and extensive territory, to pay the expense of his removal, and support him a year in his new abode? How many thousands of our own people would gladly embrace the opportunity of removing West on such conditions!"[43]

Jackson's rhetoric emboldened state leaders who already felt that Indigenous lands of the South should be occupied by their citizens instead of by Native Americans. Some advocates for white occupation and Native expulsion used explicit racial arguments, challenging the unique status of Native people as citizens of tribal nations. The editor of one Georgia newspaper, for instance, insisted that Cherokees were "a *colored* people" and therefore not due the respect of legal protections accorded to sovereign tribes. When it came to differentiating between Native Americans and people of color, he contended, "Abstractly, there is no difference."[44] Despite vociferous protest by Native leaders and white allies, the U.S. Congress passed the Indian Removal Act, which authorized the president to remove tribes from their homes and lands east of the Mississippi and relocate them on land west of the river. On May 28, 1830, Jackson signed the bill into law.[45]

Shortly afterward, in June 1830, Georgia put into effect a law the state had passed two years earlier, asserting jurisdiction over Cherokee territory; the idea of taking over that land had become even more enticing after gold was discovered. The Georgia Guard, an armed force created to patrol the Cherokee Nation, violated Cherokee borders, destroyed the nation's printing press, harassed Native women, and arrested national leaders. In 1832, Georgia established a lottery for the redistribution of all Cherokee land to white Georgians. Cherokees had no say as their homes, outbuildings, and fields were surveyed and assigned to white owners. Mayhem followed.[46]

The Vann family was not spared. In 1833, Rich Joe and more than a dozen family members were powerless as they huddled together in a single room of their brick manor house while two white men who both claimed ownership of the estate through the lottery fought over who would get it. One of the men was a Georgia Guard commander, accompanied by soldiers. He ordered them to fire on his rival for the property. Gunshots ignited the wood of the showstopper stairway, which burst into flames.[47] The Vann family escaped the fire, relinquishing their land and house but not the enslaved people, whom they brought along when they took refuge in their second home in Tennessee. This respite for the Vanns would be short-lived, however, as they and other Cherokees, rich and poor, would be expelled again within five years.

———

With Andrew Jackson in the presidency, federal and state proponents of Native expulsion worked in tandem to pressure the Cherokees into leaving the South for Indian Territory, western lands acquired through the Louisiana Purchase in 1803. Convinced that exile was inevitable, a small cohort of elite Cherokee men (mostly enslavers) signed the Treaty of New Echota in 1835, relinquishing the people's claim to their remaining land in the Southeast. The treaty was deemed fraudulent by the Cherokees' elected principal chief, John Ross (also an enslaver), who had not authorized these men to represent the nation. Cherokees organized a campaign of legal and political resistance as hundreds of white Northerners flooded Congress with petitions rejecting the idea of removing Native people from their lands. Nevertheless, the Senate ratified the treaty. The first Cherokees to move in accordance with the Treaty of New Echota were the elite men who had signed the agreement. Other wealthy families, including the Vanns, also emigrated early, selecting the most fertile locations on which to rebuild their homes and enterprises. Upon arrival in Indian Territory, the Vanns ordered their enslaved workforce to clear land, plant crops, and construct a replica of the family's stately manor house back in Georgia.[48]

For those Cherokees who had not quickly accepted removal, the federal government made the consequences clear. On May 10, 1838, General Winfield Scott, the officer in charge of the removal campaign, threatened Cherokees in unveiled language:

> My troops already occupy many positions . . . and thousands and thousands are approaching from every quarter to render assistance and escape alike hopeless. . . . Will you, then by resistance compel us to resort to arms . . . or will you by flight seek to hide yourself in the mountains and forests and thus oblige us to hunt you down?[49]

Scott and his men and the local Georgia militia followed through on this ultimatum, ordering women, men, children, and the elderly from their homes and fields at gunpoint and bayonet tip and setting in motion the Trail of Tears. Forced to abandon most of their possessions, the Cherokees witnessed white Georgians taking ownership of their cabins and all within them. Daniel Butrick, a missionary to the Cherokees, described what he witnessed: "Women absent from their families on visits, or for other purposes, were seized, and men far from their wives and children were not allowed to return, and also children being forced from home, were dragged off among strangers. Cattle, horses, hogs, household furniture, clothing and money not with them were taken and left."[50] In the words of one Georgia militiaman who was also present: "I fought through the civil war and have seen men shot to pieces and slaughtered by thousands, but the Cherokee removal was the cruelest work I ever knew."[51]

After being ousted from their homes that spring and summer, Cherokee people were placed in temporary shelters. Crowded close together in the stifling heat, many fell ill.[52] In the fall, those who remained traveled in groups across Tennessee, Kentucky, Illinois, Missouri, and Arkansas with insufficient supplies. Among these groups were African Americans and Cherokees of African descent, both enslaved and free. They all walked through the fall and into the harsh winter months, many dying from cold, disease, and accident.[53]

In addition to bearing the physical and emotional hardships of the journey, enslaved Black people in the nation hunted game, nursed the sick, prepared meals, guarded the camps, and removed obstructions from roads.[54] Daniel Butrick, who accompanied the Cherokees to whom he evangelized, recorded details about the work and deaths of a handful of Black people in his detachment. One elderly Black woman whose children had recently purchased her freedom "died in the camps," Butrick wrote. Her son and daughter-in-law were then sold to speculators. One Black man "cut some wood for the night," and a woman Butrick referred to as "our kind Nancy" was "employed . . . to wash and [dry] our clothes in the evening by the fire."[55] Approximately one thousand Cherokees died during the eviction, and the decline in the birthrate meant a total population loss of more than thirty-four hundred people.[56] The death toll of Black people on the trail has yet to be determined.

The historian Mary Hershberger has observed that slavery played a role in the successful passage of the Indian Removal Act, since the Three-fifths Clause of the U.S. Constitution (which apportioned additional representation in Congress for numbers of enslaved people owned) increased the voting power of Southern white residents who sought Native land.[57] And after the Indian Removal Act had been enforced, white Southerners benefited yet again. The expulsion of Cherokees and other tribal nations cleared the way for Southerners to move with the people they enslaved onto former Native lands, an expansion of a kind of slavery that far surpassed Cherokee slavery in intensity and extent. As the historians David and Jeanne Heidler have put it in their book *Indian Removal*, the institution of American slavery and the event of Indian Removal were, in both cause and effect, "twin evils."[58]

Brought together and then ripped apart by slavery and racism, the futures of Native and Black people would be again entwined in the exodus of the tribes from their lands. Some eighty thousand Indigenous people were driven out of the South and the Midwest in the mid-nineteenth century. As the historian Claudio Saunt has poignantly pointed out in *Unworthy Republic,* the movement of Indian removal followed the same routes as the domestic trade of Black people into the Cotton Belt, which had "served to make plausible the forced migration of other nonwhite peoples." Native expulsion was, he writes, "the war the slaveholders won."[59]

Nearly two hundred years later, around ninety registrants attended a virtual conference organized by the Descendants of Freedmen of the Five Civilized Tribes Association, a group that most Americans have never heard of. The association is composed of members whose ancestors were enslaved by five nations—Cherokees, Creeks, Choctaws, Chickasaws, and Seminoles—prior to the American Civil War. The members had inherited a legacy of Blackness in the United States, of Indigeneity on the North American continent, and of marginalization within their own tribes.

The intention of the organizers of this gathering, held in the midst of the Covid-19 pandemic in November 2020, was to offer education about the "history and culture" of the "African-Indian freedmen and their descendants" and to fight "against ongoing racial discrimination against the freedmen descendants."[60]

The concerns of the Descendants of Freedmen of the Five Civilized Tribes Association relate to the outcome of the Civil War in Indian Territory. After the expulsion of the slaveholding Native nations from the South, the wealthiest among them reestablished estates in present-day Oklahoma and used enslaved Black people to rebuild their homes, towns, and fortunes. When the Civil War erupted in South Carolina, it had an impact far beyond the American Southeast. Native leaders to the West in Indian Territory faced a dire decision. Their governments and towns stood within a unique territory on the margins of the United States and the Confederate states. Like the slave states in the South, they might choose to secede and ally with the Confederacy, which would include political representation in the Confederate Congress, or they could elect to remain "loyal" to the Union. Would these Native nations support the United States, with which they had forged many (violated) treaties in the past and by whom they had been abandoned at the start of the war as violence broke out in Indian Territory, or would they join with the Southern Confederacy, the government with which they shared certain principles of custom and racial ideology but had no history of treaty relations?[61] After decades of participation in Southern plantation culture, Native leaders in Indian Territory identified as slaveholders and referred to their people as slaveholding nations. Though the political picture was complex, in many of these nations significant factions chose to support the Confederate states.[62]

In the aftermath of the war, the United States initiated a new set of treaty negotiations with the slaveholding Native nations, which collectively held captive approximately eight thousand Black people.[63] The series of Reconstruction agreements that resulted, known as the 1866 treaties, compelled these nations to free the enslaved among them, to accept freedpeople as citizens with political rights in these nations, and to allow railroad development in their territories. Not every nation agreed, and even those who did promise equal rights to the formerly enslaved and their descendants did not fully live up to that vow.

In 1907, Oklahoma became a state, subsuming the majority of the former Indian Territory within it, even as tribal nations retained discrete borders and governments. A celebration of statehood held in Guthrie before twenty-five thousand people included a staged ceremony that dramatized how the new Oklahoma citizenry would be configured. In it, a woman of Cherokee descent, "Miss Indian Territory," mock-wed a white man, "Mr. Oklahoma Territory," symbolizing the union of the two peoples and places and excluding the African American and Afro-Native presence altogether. Among the first acts taken up by the new state legislature in Senate Bill No. 1 was the passage of Jim Crow laws that categorized Native Americans with white people and segregated Black people based on a one-drop racial rule.[64] As in the United States, where the rights and protections of citizenship came slowly, haltingly, or not at all, in the Indigenous nations of Oklahoma, Black and mixed-race Afro-Native people would strive for decades to achieve full inclusion.

It is this struggle that the Descendants of Freedmen of the Five Civilized Tribes Association was founded to advance. And it is an indication of this complicated racial and political history that the association's founder and current president is Marilyn Vann, a descendent of the extended family of "Rich Joe" and James Vann. Marilyn Vann is Cherokee "by blood" as well as the descendant of Black people owned by Cherokees. She and others among the conference organizers and speakers bear the surnames of influential plantation-owning nineteenth-century Native American families. Some of these families had been formed, in part, through sexual intimacies across the color line, both freely chosen and forced. Other Native Americans in these tribal nations did not share blood ties with Africans but did share a history of cultural exchange.[65]

A retired engineer, Vann has been organizing freedmen and freedwomen descendants for decades. When I first attended a descendants' conference, a couple of decades ago, the event was held in a post office and had the informal mood of a warm family reunion with a few scholars mixed in. In 2020, the conference had major sponsors and influential Native speakers, including the principal chief of the Cherokee Nation, a sitting tribal court judge, and attorneys with expertise in federal Indian law. In her opening remarks, Vann asserted, "We fight for enforcement of 1866 treaty rights to freedom descendants" before she introduced "a word of prayer."

Vann's words about the political fight reflected a long history. Descendants of freedpeople in the Five Tribes have been organizing for political inclusion, for cultural recognition, and for economic parity with tribal citizens since the late 1800s. Decades of meeting, fundraising, political campaigning, and vocal speech are now yielding major results, at least in one of the nations in question. Members of the Descendants of Freedmen of the Five Civilized Tribes Association were party to a decisive legal suit that ended in a 2017 federal court ruling requiring the Cherokee Nation to extend civil rights to descendants of formerly enslaved people after decades of resistance on the part of the tribe.[66]

At the 2020 virtual gathering, African-descended attendees spoke passionately about their family histories, about ties to the land, about racial violence, and about the need to remember the past.[67] Vanessa Adams Harris, the host and emcee, set the tone by openly acknowledging the reality of the racial rift. She made a pointed remark about the ways in which tribal nations had resisted bestowing equal rights upon Black people descended from the formerly enslaved and about the pain of color prejudice. "Part of claiming your history is claiming your citizenship," she said. "And when you are a sovereign nation like we have here, [a] sovereign nation within sovereign nations, then citizenship is really important. . . . These descendants have every right."[68]

But there was also talk of connection. Joe Deere, a non-Black member of the Cherokee Nation Tribal Council, titled his presentation "From Reconciliation to Solidarity: A Discussion of Common Ground," and highlighted the shared history of dispossession and oppression. As the Chicana feminist theorist Cherríe Moraga once poetically observed, Native and Black people were "the first and the forced" Americans.[69] These populations share a distinctive history, but at the same time they have faced each other across what has often been a deep divide.

In the last decade, though, Indigenous, Black, and Afro-Native activists have joined forces in notable ways. In 2015–16, when thousands of Indigenous people and allies from around the world gathered in South Dakota to protest the construction of the Dakota Access Pipeline through Sioux homelands, Black Lives Matter activists joined them there and staged a rally in Chicago. In the Black Lives Matter wave of national protests in the pandemic summer of 2020, Native activists and tribal leaders marched, painted murals, and issued statements of solidarity.[70]

When Deere spoke, he emphasized this spirit of allegiance and showed photographs of Native people marching, holding eye-catching signs, and packaging supplies during those protests. His remarks and those of his copanelists garnered thanks in the conference chat, expressed in both English and Cherokee. "Spoken very well," one audience member typed, adding a thank-you in Cherokee: *"Wado."* Deere concluded his presentation with a slide that showed a drawing of two brown arms, one dark, one light, grasping hands against a vivid blue background. The tan arm had written across it, in artful lettering reminiscent of a tattoo, INDIGENOUS SOVEREIGNTY; the dark arm, a near–mirror image, answered with the inscription BLACK LIBERATION.[71]

August 30, 1800

Gabriel, a twenty-four-year-old enslaved blacksmith held captive on a forced labor camp run by Thomas Prosser in Henrico County, Virginia, organizes an extensively planned rebellion. After other enslaved people share details of his plot, Gabriel's Rebellion is thwarted. He is later tried, found guilty, and hanged.

Trouble the Water

Barry Jenkins

As he approached the Brook Swamp beneath the city of Richmond, Virginia, Gabriel Prosser looked to the sky. Up above, the clouds coalesced into an impenetrable black, bringing on darkness and a storm the ferocity of which the region had scarcely seen. He may have cried and he may have prayed but the thing Gabriel did not do was turn back. He was expecting fire on this night and would make no concessions for the coming rain.

And he was not alone. A hundred men, five hundred men, *a thousand men* had gathered from all over the state on this thirtieth day of August 1800. Black men, African men—men from the fields and men from the house, men from the church and the smithy—men who could be called many things but after this night would not be called slaves gathered in the flooding basin armed with scythes, swords, bayonets, and smuggled guns.

One of the men tested the rising water, citing the Gospel of John: "For an angel went down at a certain season into the pool, and troubled the water: whosoever then first after the troubling of the water stepped in was made whole of whatsoever disease he had." But the water would not abate. As the night wore on and the storm persisted, Gabriel was overcome by a dawning truth: The Gospel would not save him. His army could not pass.

Governor James Monroe was expecting them. Having returned from his appointment to France and built his sweeping Highland plantation on the periphery of Charlottesville, Monroe wrote to his mentor Thomas Jefferson seeking advice on his "fears of a negro insurrection." When the Negroes Tom and Pharoah of the Sheppard plantation betrayed Gabriel's plot on a Saturday morning, Monroe was not surprised. By virtue of the privilege bestowed upon him as his birthright, he had been expecting them.

Gabriel ~~Prosser~~ was executed on October 10, 1800. Eighteen hundred: the year of John Brown's and Nat Turner's births, the first year of Denmark Vesey's life as a freedman. As he awaited the gallows near the foot of the James River, Gabriel could see all that was not to be: the first wave of men tasked to set fire to the city perimeter, the second to fell a city weakened by the diversion; the governor's mansion, James Monroe brought to heel and served a lash for every man, woman, and child enslaved on his Highland plantation; the Quakers, Methodists, Frenchmen, and poor whites who would take up with his army and create a more perfect Union from which they would spread the infection of freedom. Gabriel saw it all.

He even saw Tom and Pharoah, manumitted by the government of Virginia, a thousand dollars to their master as recompense; a thousand dollars for the sabotage of Gabriel's thousand men. He did not see the other twenty-five men in his party executed. Instead, he saw Monroe in an audience he wanted no part of and paid little notice to. For Gabriel ~~Prosser~~ the blacksmith, leader of men and accepting no master's name, had stepped into the troubled water. To the very last, he was whole. He was free.

January 1, 1808

The Act Prohibiting Importation of Slaves goes into effect, ending the legal trade in enslaved people from outside the United States. But the law does not end slavery, nor restrict the buying and selling of the more than one million enslaved people who are already in the country. As the domestic trade increases rapidly, more and more Black families are broken apart on the auction block.

Sold South

Jesmyn Ward

The whisper run through the quarters like a river swelling to flood. We passed the story to each other in the night in our pallets, in the day over the well, in the fields as we pulled at the fallow earth. They ain't stealing us from over the water no more. We dreamed of those we was stolen from: our mothers who oiled and braided our hair to our scalps, our fathers who cut our first staffs, our sisters and brothers who we pinched for tattling on us, and we felt a cool light wind move through us for one breath. Felt like ease to imagine they remained, had not been stolen, would never be.

That be a foolish thing. We thought this later when the first Georgia Man come and roped us. Grabbed a girl on her way for morning water. Snatched a boy running to the stables. A woman after she left her babies blinking awake in their sack blankets. A man sharpening a hoe. They always came before dawn for us chosen to be sold south.

We didn't understand what it would be like, couldn't think beyond the panic, the prying, the crying, the begging, and the screaming, the endless screaming from the mouth and beyond. Sounding through the whole body, breaking the heart with its volume. A blood keen. But the ones that owned and sold us was deaf to it. Was unfeeling of the tugging the children did on their fathers' arms or the glance of a sister's palm over her sold sister's face for the last time. But we was all feeling, all seeing, all hearing, all smelling: We felt it for the terrible dying it was. Knowed we was walking out of one life and into another. An afterlife in a burning place.

The farther we marched, the hotter it got. Our skin grew around the rope. Our muscles melted to nothing. Our fat to bone. The land rolled to a flat bog, and in the middle of it, a city called New Orleans. When we shuffled into that town of the dead, they put us in pens. Fattened us. Tried to disguise our limps, oiled the pallor of sickness out of our skins, raped us to assess our soft parts, then told us lies about ourselves to make us into easier sells. Was told to answer yes when they asked us if we were master seamstresses, blacksmiths, or lady's maids. Was told to disavow the wives we thought we heard calling our names when we first woke in the morning, the husbands we imagined lying with us, chest to back, while the night's torches burned, the children whose eyelashes we thought we could still feel on our cheeks when the rain turned to a fine mist while we stood in lines outside the pens waiting for our next hell to take legs and seek us out.

Trade our past lives for new deaths.

Bill Hurley, Charlottesville, 1909   RUFUS HOLSINGER STUDIO, UNIVERSITY OF VIRGINIA LIBRARY

CHAPTER 6

Capitalism

MATTHEW DESMOND

A couple of years before he was convicted of securities fraud in 2017, Martin Shkreli was the chief executive of a pharmaceutical company that acquired the rights to Daraprim, a lifesaving antiparasitic drug. Previously the drug had cost $13.50 a pill, but in Shkreli's hands, the price quickly increased by a factor of 56, to $750 a pill. At a healthcare conference, Shkreli told the audience that he should have raised the price even higher. "No one wants to say it, no one's proud of it," he explained. "But this is a capitalist society, a capitalist system, and capitalist rules."[1]

This is a capitalist society. It's a fatalistic mantra that seems to get repeated to anyone who questions why America can't be more fair or equal. But around the world, there are many types of capitalist societies. Some are more equitable, and some are more exploitative; some more restrained, and some more unregulated. When Americans declare that "we live in a capitalist society"—as a real estate mogul told the *Miami Herald* in 2018 when explaining his feelings about small-business owners being evicted from their Little Haiti storefronts—what they're often defending is our nation's peculiarly brutal version of capitalism: "low-road capitalism," the University of Wisconsin–Madison sociologist Joel Rogers has called it.[2] In a capitalist society like ours, wages are depressed as businesses compete over the price, not the quality, of goods, and so-called unskilled workers are typically incentivized through punishments, not promotions. Inequality reigns and poverty spreads.

The United States stands today as one of the most unequal societies in the history of the world. The richest 1 percent of Americans owns 40 percent of the country's wealth, while a larger share of working-age people (those eighteen to sixty-five) live in poverty than in any other nation belonging to the

Organisation for Economic Co-operation and Development (OECD).[3] The OECD, an international consortium of democratic countries with market-based economies, scores nations along a number of economic indicators, such as how countries regulate temporary work arrangements and how easy it is to terminate employees. Scores in these categories run from 5 ("very strict") to 1 ("very loose"). When it comes to regulations on temporary workers, Brazil scores 4.1 and Thailand 3.7, signaling that in those countries, workers enjoy a range of toothy protections; farther down the list are Norway (3.4), India (2.5), and Japan (1.3). The United States scores 0.3, tied for second-to-last place with Malaysia. What about how easy it is to fire workers? Countries like Indonesia (4.1) and Portugal (3) have strong rules about severance pay and reasons for dismissal. Those rules relax somewhat in places like Denmark (2.1) and Mexico (1.9). They virtually disappear in the United States, ranked dead last out of seventy-one nations, with a score of 0.5.[4]

Those searching for reasons the American economy is uniquely severe and unbridled have found answers in many places (religion, politics, culture). But recently, historians have pointed persuasively to the gnatty fields of Georgia and Alabama, to the cotton houses and auction blocks, as an early example of America's low-road approach to capitalism.

As a source of the fledgling nation's financial might, slavery shaped our political institutions and founding documents, our laws governing private property and financial regulation, our management techniques and accounting systems, and our economic systems and labor unions. By the eve of the Civil War, the Mississippi Valley was home to more millionaires per capita than anywhere else in the United States.[5] Cotton grown and picked by enslaved workers was the nation's most valuable export. The combined value of enslaved people exceeded that of all the railroads and factories in the nation. In the mid-1830s, New Orleans boasted a denser concentration of banking capital than New York City.[6] Small wonder, then, that "American slavery is necessarily imprinted on the DNA of American capitalism," as the historians Sven Beckert and Seth Rockman have written. The task now, they argue, is "cataloging the dominant and recessive traits" that have been passed down to us, tracing the unsettling and often unrecognized lines of descent by which America's national sin is even now being visited upon the third and fourth generations.[7]

Colonial America was a relatively prosperous society. The Southern colonies were the wealthiest, as white planters reaped high returns on staple crops like rice and tobacco.[8] But the Revolution left the colonies broke and vulnerable. Incomes plummeted in the final decades of the eighteenth century, and if the states could not come together to form a national government, they would be susceptible to foreign invasion and economic collapse. In the spring and summer of 1787, representatives of each state met in Philadelphia to draft a constitution and found a new nation.[9]

The delegates were deeply polarized over a host of issues, none more contentious than slavery. When the Revolution began, slavery was legal in all thirteen colonies, but during the 1770s, voices condemning human bondage had grown louder throughout New England and Britain. By the time the framers began writing the Constitution, states that did not rely heavily on enslaved labor within their borders, like Massachusetts and New Hampshire, had already outlawed it. On the other hand, states like Virginia and Georgia vehemently defended the right to own and sell Black people.

At several points, the issue of slavery ground the Constitutional Convention to a halt, and both Northern and Southern representatives threatened to dissolve the Union altogether. As James Madison, the "father of the Constitution," observed on June 30, 1787: "The States were divided into different interests not by their difference of size, but by other circumstances; the most material of which resulted partly from climate, but principally from their having or not having slaves."[10] What pro-slavery advocates feared most was democracy itself: that Northern majorities would use the power of the federal government to dismantle slavery. This fear shaped our political institutions in ways still felt today.

To protect slavery, Southerners fought for and won several provisions that all but ensured that majoritarian rule over the South would be impossible. On May 29, 1787, Governor Edmund Randolph of Virginia rose and proposed that congressional representation be based on population and not the one-vote-per-state rule that had governed the Articles of Confederation. Northern and Southern delegates debated whether Black enslaved people should count toward a state's population, until the so-called Great Compromise was proposed in July. Congress would be divided into two houses, a lower house based on population—with each enslaved Black person counting as three-fifths of a citizen—and an upper house that gave all states an equal number of votes. The Southern advantage conferred by the Three-fifths Clause was extended to the executive branch through the Electoral College, proposed by Madison, which provided each state a number of electors that aligned with its representation in the lower house of Congress. Slaveholding states secured outsized political power in both Congress and the presidency, which was controlled by pro-slavery advocates until the election of Lincoln in 1860.[11]

The Constitution empowered all states with "a practical veto on national policy," according to historian Mark Graber, which made it effectively impossible for the federal government to regulate slavery without the South's consent. To this day, the fifteen states where slavery remained legal as of 1861 still hold the power to block a constitutional amendment supported by the other thirty-five.[12]

So if Washington often feels broken, that's because it was built that way. A 2011 study of twenty-three long-standing democracies identified the United States as the only country in the group that had four "veto points" empowered to block legislative action: the president, both houses of Congress, and the Supreme Court. Most other democracies in the study had just a single veto point.[13] In those nations, parties govern, pass policies, and get voted in or out. Things *happen* at the federal level. But the United States government is characterized by political inaction—and that was by design. By creating political structures that weakened the role of the federal government's ability to regulate slavery, the framers hobbled Washington's ability to pass legislation on a host of other matters.

Chief among these was taxation. If they wished to raise an army and fund the government, the framers also had to devise a way to levy taxes on the citizenry. But delegates couldn't agree on the best way to do this because slavery kept getting in the way. It was impossible to debate taxes without also debating how to tax the enslaved. Should enslaved Black workers be taxed as people or property or not at all? The three-fifths clause provided a potential solution—treat enslaved Black workers as partial citizens for the purposes of taxation—but Southern enslavers quickly realized that that would require them to pay more than Northerners who didn't enslave people. For example, if the federal government established a poll tax levied on every person, in 1790 the three-fifths apportionment would have mandated that a Virginian be taxed $1.39 and a South Carolinian $1.45 for every $1 charged to a free Northerner. Predictably, Southerners rejected this plan. "Our Slaves being our Property," argued South Carolina representative Thomas Lynch, "why should they be taxed more than the Land, Sheep, Cattle, Horses?" Lynch and other Southerners wanted their human property to count *toward* their congressional representation but not *against* their tax bill.[14]

The delegates finally decided that imports should be taxed. It was a tax everyone could agree on. A tariff could be levied without reference to slavery because it didn't require counting enslaved workers or estimating the value of their products exported to other countries. Merchants would foot the bill and pass the cost on to consumers. In this way, the tax was invisible and often optional, in the sense that you could decide to purchase an imported good or not.[15]

Though politically palatable, the import tax stunted the bureaucratic infrastructure of the nation, allowing the United States to neglect developing the administrative systems necessary for progressive taxation and government services. The result was the creation of a financially and bureaucratically weak federal government. It was not until 1861, when the bill for the Civil War came due, that the nation was finally forced to establish an income tax and an Internal Revenue Service to collect it (originally called the Bureau of Internal Revenue). The American public, which had never been made to pay income tax, reacted unkindly to this fledgling agency, calling it inefficient and corrupt. After the war ended, so too did the national income tax. Congress passed a modest income tax almost thirty years later, in 1894, but in a 5-to-4 decision, the Supreme Court ruled it unconstitutional. The federal government didn't acquire the power to "lay and collect taxes on incomes" until 1913, when the Sixteenth Amendment was ratified.

By 1900, an income tax supplied roughly 12 percent of government revenue in Italy and the United Kingdom and about 20 percent in Germany and the Netherlands.[16] Imagine if the United States had followed a similar path, establishing the Internal Revenue Service not in a moment of crisis but at the nation's founding. In this alternative universe, the IRS could have been given adequate financial backing and administrative support, enabling it to function efficiently and fairly. Taxes would not have been hidden in American consumerism (as was the import tax); rather, they could have been transparently collected as a portion of each person's income and seen as a patriotic duty, an investment in the nation. But, of course, this is not our history.

Progressive taxation remains among the best ways to limit economic inequality, funding public services like schools and healthcare and incentivizing business to work for the common good. America's present-day tax system, however, is regressive and insipid in part because it was born out of political compromise steered by debates over slavery. This generates inequality and enables large corporations to avoid paying their fair share—or *any* share. In 2018, sixty Fortune 500 companies, including Amazon, Chevron, Delta Air Lines, and Netflix, paid no federal income taxes.[17]

Slavery shaped the Constitution in profound and lasting ways. "One consequence," writes the historian Robin Einhorn, "may well be the exceptionally powerful devotion to individual property rights that made American business stronger, American labor weaker, and the American welfare state a comparative 'laggard.' "[18]

Private property is the cornerstone of capitalism. It is what allows someone to own a factory or a corporation, a piece of land or an apartment building, and to secure profit from the workers or tenants who do not own such assets. It is what allows the luxuries purchased from those profits to be protected by the full weight of the state. It is what enables a private landowner to fence off natural resources and forests and rivers, assets that originally belonged to no one and were stewarded by the surrounding community, transforming common goods into commodities controlled by a single person or business entity. Capitalism depends on private property, and private property depends on the law.

When private property extends to human beings, however, a particularly strong and expansive set of protections is required. Human beings, after all, can run away or revolt. The founders recognized this, and in the Constitution they safeguarded the human property of those who owned enslaved people through a number of provisions. Article I, Section 8 granted Congress the power to summon the militia to "suppress insurrections," understood to mean rebellions of the enslaved.[19] Article I, Section 9 forbade Congress from ending the slave trade until 1808. Article V, Section 2 prohibited free states from emancipating runaways: human property in the South would remain human property in the North. The framers helped create a doctrine of private property strong enough to justify and enforce human trafficking, so much so that abolitionists publicly burned copies of the Constitution.

The importance of this specific kind of private property—enslaved people—was both enshrined in the Constitution itself and affirmed by the Supreme Court's interpretations of the highest law of the land. After the Constitution was ratified in 1788, in case after case the Court protected private property in general, and slavery in particular, sometimes going to extraordinary lengths to deny Black freedom in the name of ownership rights. The 1812 case *Hezekiah Wood v. John Davis and Others* concerned the situation of John Davis, a Black man born to a mother who had never been enslaved. According to the law of matrilineal descent, this should have established Davis's own freedom, but Wood, an enslaver who claimed Davis as his property, argued that he had purchased Davis before his mother had proven her freedom. The Court sided with Wood. The following year, the Court's decision in the case of *Mima Queen and Child v. Hepburn* denied Black people the right to provide hearsay evidence that supported their freedom claims, prioritizing the propertied interests of enslavers over the lives of people those enslavers claimed belonged to them.[20]

The Court's vigorous defense of human bondage, encased in property law, continued as amendments were added to the Constitution. The Fifth Amendment, which prohibited Congress from depriving anyone of "life, liberty, or property, without due process," informed the Supreme Court's decision to uphold slavery in its infamous 1857 *Dred Scott v. Sandford* case. Born into slavery, Dred Scott was moved to Alabama and Missouri, then to Illinois, before once more returning to Missouri. Having relocated from a free state (Illinois) to a slave state (Missouri), Scott sued his putative "owner" for his freedom, citing the state court doctrine of "once free, always free." The case pitted Scott's liberty against his enslaver's property, and when the Supreme Court heard the case, the justices ruled in favor of bondage. The Court decided that manumitting Scott would infringe on the property rights of his enslaver.[21]

Slavery, then, required "the magic of property." As historian Stephanie Jones-Rogers documents in her book *They Were Her Property*, elite white women were particularly invested in securing a jurisprudence that valued (white) property over (Black) freedom because their economic independence and influence depended on it. (Southern parents tended to give their daughters more enslaved hands than land.) Slavery demanded a legal defense of ownership rights much more far-reaching and severe than would have been necessary to secure, say, a house or a herd of cattle. Houses do not attempt to become non-property by running away. Cattle do not stage armed revolts. But humans treated as property were constantly doing both.[22]

After the Civil War, legal provisions originally developed to protect slavery were extended to strengthen corporate interests and promote laissez-faire capitalism. The Fifth Amendment's language protecting private property resurfaced in the Fourteenth Amendment, ratified during Reconstruction, which established legal and civil rights for Black Americans by mandating "equal protection of the laws" and prohibiting states from denying people "life, liberty, or property, without due process." It didn't take long for corporate attorneys to realize that the Fourteenth Amendment could help strengthen business interests too. This was affirmed in 1886 by Chief Justice Morrison Waite, who plainly stated before oral arguments for *Santa Clara County v. Southern Pacific Railroad Co.* that the Supreme Court believed that the Fourteenth Amendment applied to corporations as well as to people.[23]

The Fourteenth Amendment became the most cited amendment in Supreme Court cases, leaving a profound impact on private law. A 1912 study found that of the 604 Fourteenth Amendment cases decided by the Supreme Court, more than half involved corporations and largely protected their power, including by striking down attempts to end child labor and establish a minimum wage. Less than 5 percent of those cases concerned the rights of African Americans, who lost nearly all of the cases they brought. Once again, white ownership interests took precedence over Black freedom and safety. One of the most consequential Fourteenth Amendment cases was *Lochner v. New York* (1905). Joseph Lochner, the owner of a bakery in Utica, was fined by New York State for violating a labor statute that prevented bakers from working more than sixty hours a week or ten hours a day. Lochner appealed his case, and when it was heard in front of the Supreme Court, the justices ruled in his favor, finding that extending protections to bakery workers would infringe on the property rights of bakery owners.[24]

Today's law students are taught that *Dred Scott* and *Lochner* were wrong. But the Court's defense of corporate personhood has continued to the present day. In 2010, the Court ruled in *Citizens United v. Federal Election Commission* that corporations' political speech, including "independent expenditures"—spending in support of a candidate for office without making a direct contribution—was protected by the Constitution. The 2012 presidential election that followed *Citizens United* received nearly 600 percent more independent expenditures than the previous presidential election, in 2008, had.[25] Of course, the founders could not see this far ahead—how the political concessions made to protect the human property in the Constitution would fundamentally shape the nation's economy and the political institutions that governed it.

Just a few years after all thirteen states ratified the Constitution, American life changed utterly and invariably. The cotton gin was invented. Before the gin, enslaved workers grew more cotton than they could clean. The gin broke the bottleneck, making it possible to clean as much cotton as you could grow. This helped to ignite the cotton trade, which had a profound impact on America's economic development. A key factor that made the cotton economy boom in the United States, and not in all the other far-flung parts of the world with climates and soil suitable to the crop, was our nation's unflinching willingness to use violence on nonwhite people and to exert its will on seemingly endless supplies of land and labor.

Enslaved Black workers picked in long rows, bent bodies shuffling through cotton fields white in bloom. Men, women, and children picked, using both hands to hurry the work but careful not to snap a branch.[26] Some picked in Negro cloth, their raw product having returned to them by way of New England mills. Some picked completely naked.[27] Young children ran water across the humped rows, while overseers peered down from horses. "Hands are required to be in the cotton field as soon as it is light in the morning," wrote Solomon Northup in his 1853 memoir, *Twelve Years a Slave*, "and, with the exception of ten or fifteen minutes, which is given them at noon to swallow their allowance of cold bacon, they are not permitted to be a moment idle until it is too dark to see, and when the moon is full, they often times labor till the middle of the night."[28]

Before the industrialization of cotton, people wore expensive clothes made of wool or linen and dressed their beds in furs or straw. Whoever mastered cotton could master textiles and make a killing. But cotton needed land. A field could tolerate only a few straight years of the crop before its soil became depleted. Planters watched as acres that had initially produced a thousand pounds of cotton yielded only four hundred a few seasons later. The thirst for new farmland grew even more intense after the invention of the cotton gin.[29]

The United States solved its land shortage by expropriating millions of acres from Native Americans, often with military force, acquiring Georgia, Alabama, Tennessee, and Florida. It then sold that land on the cheap—just $1.25 an acre in the early 1830s ($38 in today's dollars)—to white settlers.[30] Naturally, the first to cash in were the land speculators. Companies operating in Mississippi flipped land, selling it soon after purchase, commonly for double the price. Enslaved workers felled trees by ax, burned the underbrush, and leveled the earth for planting. "Whole forests were literally dragged out by the roots," John Parker, an enslaved worker, remembered.[31] A lush, twisted mass of vegetation was replaced by a single crop as American money exerted its will on the earth, bringing floods and erosion, erasing natural habitats, and otherwise spoiling the environment for profit.[32]

Cotton was to the nineteenth century what oil was to the twentieth: one of the most valuable and widely traded commodities in the world. It gave rise to factories, vast manufacturing enterprises, and large industrial proletariat workforces, forming whole industries around itself.[33] Unlike other staple crops grown by enslaved Black workers—rice in coastal South Carolina and Georgia, sugar in Louisiana—cotton could be cultivated throughout the South, relied heavily on industrial production, and was sought by consumers across the developed world.[34] Together, cotton planters, enslaved workers in the South, wage laborers in the North, and millers and consumers from across the ocean helped fashion a new economy, one that was global in scope and required the movement of capital, labor, and products across long distances. In other words, one that was capitalist. "The beating heart of this new system," Beckert notes, "was slavery."[35]

During this period, "Americans built a culture of speculation unique in its abandon," writes the historian Joshua Rothman in his book *Flush Times and Fever Dreams*. That culture would drive cotton production up to the Civil War, and it has been a defining characteristic of American capitalism ever since. It is the culture of acquiring wealth without work, growing at all costs, and abusing the powerless. It is the culture that brought us catastrophic downturns, like the Panic of 1837, the stock market crash of 1929, and the recession of 2008. It is the culture that has produced staggering inequality and undignified working conditions.[36]

As slave-labor camps spread throughout the South, cotton production surged. By 1831, the country was delivering nearly half the world's raw cotton crop, with 350 million pounds picked that year. Just four years later, it harvested 500 million pounds. Southern white elites grew rich, as did their counterparts in the North, who erected textile mills to form, in the words of Massachusetts senator Charles Sumner, an "unhallowed alliance between the lords of the lash and the lords of the loom."[37]

As America's cotton sector expanded, the value of enslaved workers soared. In New Orleans between 1804 and 1860, the average price of a male field hand aged twenty-one to thirty-eight grew from roughly $500 to over $1,500 (in 1830 dollars).[38] Because they believed they couldn't grow their cotton empires without more enslaved workers, ambitious planters needed to find a way to raise enough capital to purchase more hands. Enter the banks. People could be sold much more easily than land, and in multiple Southern states, more than eight in ten mortgage-secured loans used enslaved people as full or partial collateral. As the historian Bonnie Martin has written, "slave owners worked their slaves financially, as well as physically," by mortgaging people to buy more people.[39] Access to credit grew faster than Mississippi kudzu would after being imported at the end of the century, leading one 1836 observer to remark that in cotton country "money, or what passed for money, was the only cheap thing to be had."[40] Centuries before the home mortgage became the defining characteristic of Middle America, Southerners decided to use the people they owned as collateral for mortgages and took on immense amounts of debt to finance their operations.

The math worked out. The owner of a cotton plantation in the first decade of the nineteenth century could leverage his enslaved workers at 8 percent interest and record a return three times that. So leverage they did, sometimes volunteering the same enslaved workers for multiple mortgages. Banks lent with little restraint. By 1833, Mississippi banks had issued twenty times as much paper money as they had gold in their coffers.[41] In several Southern counties, mortgages taken out on enslaved workers injected more capital into the economy than sales from the crops harvested by workers themselves.

Global financial markets had powered the slave economy for years. When Thomas Jefferson mortgaged his enslaved workers in 1796 to build Monticello, it was a Dutch firm that put up most of the money.[42] The Louisiana Purchase, which opened millions of acres to cotton production, was financed by Baring Brothers, the well-heeled British commercial bank.[43] Most of the credit that powered the sectors of the American economy based on the labor of enslaved Black people came from the London money market. Years after abolishing the African slave trade in 1807, Britain, and much of Europe along with it, was bankrolling slavery in the United States. To raise capital, state-chartered banks pooled debt generated by mortgages on enslaved workers and repackaged it as bonds promising investors annual interest. During slavery's boom time, banks did swift business in bonds, finding buyers in Hamburg and Amsterdam, in Boston and Philadelphia.

Banks issued tens of millions of dollars in loans on the assumption that rising cotton prices would go on forever. Speculation reached a fever pitch in the 1830s, as businessmen, planters, and lawyers convinced themselves that they could amass real treasure by joining a risky game that everyone seemed to be playing.[44] If planters thought themselves invincible, able to bend the laws of finance to their will, it was most likely because they had been granted authority to bend the laws of nature to their will, to do with the land and the people who worked it as they pleased. As the historical sociologist Orlando Patterson once remarked, "The slave variant of capitalism is merely capitalism with its clothes off."[45]

We know how these stories end. The American South rashly overproduced cotton, thanks to an abundance of cheap land, enslaved labor, and fast credit; consumer demand didn't keep up with supply; and prices fell. The value of cotton started to drop as early as 1834 before plunging like a bird winged in mid-flight, setting off the Panic of 1837.[46] Investors and creditors called in their debts, and enslaved workers were taken from planters and sold by courts on behalf of creditors in an attempt to right the balance sheets.[47]

It wasn't enough. Mississippi planters owed the banks in New Orleans $33 million in a year their crops yielded only $10 million in revenue. They couldn't simply liquidate their assets to raise the money. When the price of cotton tumbled, it pulled down the value of enslaved workers and land along with it. Because enslavers couldn't repay their loans, the state-chartered banks couldn't make interest payments on their bonds. Shouts went up around the Western world, as investors began demanding that states raise taxes to keep their promises. After all, the bonds were backed by taxpayers, leaving states on the hook for the enslavers' debt. Facing a swell of populist outrage, states decided not to squeeze the money out of every Southern family, coin by coin. Furious bondholders mounted lawsuits, but the bankrupt states refused to pay. The South chose to cut itself out of the global credit market, the hand that had fed cotton expansion, rather than hold planters and their banks accountable for their negligence and avarice.[48]

Some planters lost their shirts. Others absconded to Texas (an independent republic at the time) with their treasure and their enslaved workforce.[49] But many large-scale planters stayed put, drew on their reserves, and weathered the Panic just fine. They knew that cotton prices wouldn't stay down for long; global demand was simply too robust. The biggest planters owned not only more land but better land. They could afford a recession and could even profit from one, turning short-term loss into long-term gain by storing their crop and selling as much as possible when prices climbed in bumper years. Planters and their banks took the risk, but others paid the price. Enslaved Black workers paid for it, sold away from their families to settle debts. Small farmers unable to borrow money and commit to the high-risk/high-reward business of cotton farming paid for it, losing their land and livelihoods. Bank clerks and cashiers paid for it, committing suicide as debts went unpaid and their jobs dissolved.[50]

If slavery's economy sparked a "culture of speculation unique in its abandon," as Rothman put it, it was in part because enslavers realized they could enrich themselves by breaking the rules with little consequence.[51] Such side effects of capitalism—"externalities," the economists call them—are routinely felt today. The Great Recession of 2008 caused the average Black family to lose a third of its wealth, and most Black businesses did not survive the downturn. Almost all of the major financial institutions responsible for that downturn, however, did survive.[52]

Slavery not only shaped America's political institutions, laws, and financial culture; it also helped mold modern management techniques. Historians have tended to connect the development of modern business practices to the nineteenth-century railroad industry, viewing plantation slavery as precapitalistic, even primitive. It's a more comforting origin story, one that protects the idea that America's economic ascendancy developed not because of, but in spite of, millions of Black people toiling on plantations. But management techniques used by nineteenth-century corporations were very similar to those implemented during the previous century by plantation owners.[53]

Planters aggressively expanded their operations to capitalize on economies of scale inherent to cotton growing, buying more enslaved workers, investing in large gins and presses, and experimenting with different seed varieties. To do so, they developed complicated workplace hierarchies that combined a central office, made up of owners and lawyers in charge of capital allocation and long-term strategy, with several divisional units, responsible for different operations. In her book *Accounting for Slavery,* the historian Caitlin Rosenthal writes of one Jamaican plantation where, in 1779, the owner supervised a top attorney (a kind of financial manager), who supervised another attorney, who supervised an overseer, who supervised three bookkeepers, who supervised sixteen enslaved head drivers and specialists (like bricklayers), who supervised hundreds of enslaved workers. This organizational form was very advanced for its time, displaying a level of hierarchal complexity equaled only by large government structures, like that of Britain's Royal Navy.[54]

Like today's titans of industry, planters understood that their profits climbed when they extracted maximum effort out of each worker. So they paid close attention to inputs and outputs by developing precise systems of record-keeping. Plantation entrepreneurs developed spreadsheets, like Thomas Affleck's *Plantation Record and Account Book,* which was first published around 1850 and ran into eight editions; it circulated until the Civil War.[55] Affleck's book was a one-stop-shop accounting manual, complete with rows and columns that tracked per-worker productivity. This book "was really at the cutting edge of the informational technologies available to businesses during this period," Rosenthal told me. "I have never found anything remotely as complex as Affleck's book for free labor."[56]

Enslavers used the book to determine end-of-the-year balances, tallying expenses and revenues and noting the causes of their biggest gains and losses. They quantified capital costs on their land, tools, and enslaved workforces, applying Affleck's recommended interest rate. Perhaps most remarkably, they also developed ways to calculate depreciation, a breakthrough in modern management procedures, by assessing the market value of enslaved workers over their life spans. Values generally peaked between the prime ages of twenty and forty but were individually adjusted up or down based on sex, strength, and temperament: people reduced to data points. In her book *The Price for Their Pound of Flesh,* the historian Daina Ramey Berry shows that enslaved workers even had monetary value in death, their bodies sold as cadavers to medical schools and physicians.[57]

Detailed data analysis also allowed planters to anticipate rebellion. Tools were accounted for on a regular basis, to make sure that a large number of axes or other potential weapons didn't suddenly go missing. "Never allow any slave to lock or unlock any door," advised a Virginia enslaver in 1847.[58] In this way, new bookkeeping techniques developed to maximize returns also helped ensure a monopoly on the tools of violence, allowing a minority of white people to control a much larger group of enslaved Black people. American planters never forgot what had happened in Saint-Domingue in 1791, when enslaved workers took up arms and revolted. In fact, many white enslavers overthrown during the Haitian Revolution had relocated to the United States and started over.

Overseers recorded each enslaved worker's yield. Accountings took place not only after nightfall, when cotton baskets were weighed, but throughout the workday. In the words of a North Carolina planter, enslaved workers were to be "followed up from day break until dark."[59] Having hands line-pick in rows sometimes longer than five football fields allowed overseers to spot anyone lagging behind. The uniform layout of the land had a logic, one designed to dominate. Faster workers were placed at the head of the line, which encouraged those who followed to match the captain's pace. When enslaved workers grew ill or old or became pregnant, they were assigned to lighter tasks. One enslaver established a "sucklers gang" for nursing mothers, as well as a "measles gang," which at once quarantined those struck by the virus and ensured that they did their part to contribute to the productivity machine.[60]

Bodies and tasks were optimized with rigorous exactitude. In trade magazines, owners swapped advice about the minutiae of planting, including diets and clothing for those they enslaved, as well as the kind of tone of voice an enslaver should use. In 1846, one Alabama planter advised his fellow enslavers to always give orders "in a mild tone and try to leave the impression on the mind of the negro that what you say is the result of reflection."[61] The devil (and his profits) were in the details.

The uncompromising pursuit of measurement and scientific accounting displayed in slave-labor camps predates industrialism. Northern factories would not begin adopting these techniques until decades after the Emancipation Proclamation. As the large slave-labor camps grew increasingly efficient, the productivity of enslaved Black workers increased at an astonishing pace.

During the sixty years leading up to the Civil War, the daily amount of cotton picked per enslaved worker increased 2.3 percent a year. That means that in 1862, the average enslaved fieldworker picked not 25 percent or 50 percent more but 400 percent more cotton than his or her counterpart did in 1801. Historians and economists have attributed this surge in productivity to several factors—for example, Alan Olmstead and Paul Rhode found that improved cotton varieties enabled hands to pick more cotton per day—but advanced techniques that improved upon ways to manage land and labor surely played their part as well.[62]

The cotton plantation was America's first big business, and the overseer was the nation's first corporate Big Brother. And behind every cold calculation, every rational fine-tuning of the system, violence lurked. Plantation owners used a combination of incentives and punishments to squeeze as much as possible out of enslaved workers.[63] Some beaten workers passed out from the pain and woke up vomiting. Some "danced" or "trembled" with every hit. An 1829 first-person account from Alabama recorded how an overseer shoved the faces of women he thought had picked too slowly into their cotton baskets, then opened up their backs.[64]

There is some comfort, I think, in attributing the sheer brutality of slavery to dumb racism. We imagine pain being inflicted somewhat at random, doled out by a stereotypical poor white overseer, full of racist hate. But many overseers weren't allowed to whip enslaved workers at will. Such punishments had to be authorized by the higher-ups. It was not so much the rage of the poor white Southerner as the greed of the rich white planter that drove the lash. The violence was neither arbitrary nor gratuitous. It was a rational part of the plantation's design. "Each individual having a stated number of pounds of cotton to pick," a formerly enslaved worker, Henry Watson, wrote in 1848, "the deficit of which was made up by as many lashes being applied to the poor slave's back."[65] Overseers closely monitored enslaved workers' picking abilities. Falling short could get you beaten, but overshooting your target could bring misery the next day, because an overseer might raise your picking rate.[66]

Planters' profits were harnessed through the anguish of the enslaved. Punishments rose and fell with global market fluctuations. Speaking of cotton in 1854, John Brown, a fugitive from slavery, remembered, "When the price rises in the English market, the poor slaves immediately feel the effects, for they are harder driven, and the whip is kept more constantly going."[67] In making possible the pursuit of nearly limitless personal fortunes at someone else's expense, slavery put a cash value on our moral commitments.

Slavery, and the racism it nourished, also played a decisive role in weakening the American labor movement. Capitalists leveraged slavery and its racial legacy to divide workers—free from unfree, white from Black—diluting their collective power. Instead of resisting this strategy, white-led unions embraced it until it was too late, undercutting their movement and creating conditions for worker exploitation and inequality that exist to this day.

The large-scale cultivation of cotton by enslaved people hastened the development of the factory, an institution that propelled the Industrial Revolution and changed the course of history.[68] In 1810, there were eighty-seven thousand cotton spindles in America. Fifty years later, there were five million. Slavery, wrote one of its defenders in *De Bow's Review,* a widely read agricultural magazine, was the "nursing mother of the prosperity of the North."[69] The Northern textile mills that spun cotton grown and harvested in slave-labor camps helped usher in a new economic arrangement, one that required workers to sell not crops or goods but bits of their life: their labor. Cotton manufacturing required people to give up their old lives and join the "newly emerging factory proletariat."[70]

What should have followed, Karl Marx and a long list of other political theorists predicted, was a large-scale labor movement. Factory workers made to log long hours under harsh conditions should have locked arms and risen up against their bosses, gaining political power in the formation of a Labor Party or even ushering in a socialist revolution. Britain experienced a militant working-class movement throughout the 1830s and 1840s, while France veered close to the wholesale adoption of socialism during the Second Republic (1848–51).[71] An American labor movement did emerge in the nineteenth century, but it failed to bring about the kinds of sweeping reforms and political transformations that remade Western Europe.[72]

Had socialism taken root in America, perhaps the country would have adopted a kind of "social democratic capitalism" that combined a market-based economy with big state investments in public education and social-welfare programs.[73] Perhaps workers' wages would be considerably higher and CEO compensation considerably lower. Income inequality decreases when unionization increases, as a result of organized labor fighting for better pay for the rank and file and keeping employer power in check.[74]

But socialism never flourished here, and a defining feature of American capitalism is the country's relatively low level of labor power. In Iceland,

90 percent of wage and salaried workers belong to trade unions authorized to fight for living wages and fair working conditions. In Italy, 34 percent of workers are unionized, as are 26 percent of Canadian workers. But only 10 percent of American wage and salaried workers carry union cards. The United States remains the sole advanced democracy missing a Labor Party, one dedicated, at least in original conception, to representing the interests of the working classes.

Initially, American workers resisted the concept of wage labor, finding it antithetical to freedom and self-sufficiency. But as industrialization forged ahead while white indentured servitude declined, paying workers' wages became, according to historian Erica Armstrong Dunbar, "the preferred labor system."[75] As some of the world's first white industrial proletarians searched for a language to voice their grievances, they found traction in analogies to chattel slavery. Mill hands worked hours similar to those imposed on enslaved field hands, from dawn to dusk, and were dependent on factory owners for sustenance. In 1845, a labor newspaper referred to mill workers as "white slaves of capital." An immigrant from Germany, a shoemaker, put it this way: "We are free, but not free enough."[76] At inception, the American labor movement defined itself as a movement of and for white workers, a bulwark against their downward slide into "wage slavery," Blackness, and un-freedom. "Do not let them make niggers out of you," a machine stitcher told a crowd of mill workers in 1860, encouraging them to strike and demand a higher wage.[77] Whiteness colored the American labor movement's initial identity and governed its boundaries of solidarity, ultimately limiting its power.

White workers viewed Black workers, both free and enslaved, as a threat to their livelihood. According to the pro-slavery *New York Herald,* if four million enslaved Black workers were emancipated, they would flock to Northern cities and "the labor of the white man will be depreciated."[78] As documented by historian Joe Trotter, Jr., white mobs throughout the first half of the nineteenth century attacked free Black workers in Cincinnati, Philadelphia, New York City, and elsewhere because they were motivated by the hope that running Black people out of town would drive up white wages.[79]

Slavery pulled down all workers' wages. Labor power had little chance when the bosses could instead choose to buy people, rent them, contract indentured servants, take on apprentices, or hire children or prisoners. Within this environment, white workers formed labor unions and advocated for better pay, improved conditions, and shorter work days. Yet nearly all those unions withheld membership from free Black workers.[80] White workers viewed Black people not only as rate busters but also as political adversaries, since Black constituencies were generally aligned with the Republican Party—the party of Lincoln and emancipation, but also the party of big business—while white union members sided with the Democratic Party, seen as more sympathetic to labor and immigrants.[81]

By upholding racial segregation within their unions, white workers made their fears of being undercut by Black labor a foregone conclusion. Closing the door on Black people created a pool of available and desperate men and women who could be used to break strikes and quell unrest. Companies hired Black workers to put down labor militancy in a number of industries, replacing steelworkers, meatpackers, longshoremen, railroad hands, and garment workers. To Black workers, strikebreaking was a means to gain a foothold in the growing industrial economy and to secure opportunities long denied them. Black leaders even encouraged strikebreaking and began promoting Black workers as safe investments for industrialists. Booker T. Washington, among the leading spokesmen for the Black community during the late nineteenth and early twentieth centuries, plainly said that Black workers were "very willing strikebreakers," noting on another occasion that they were "almost a stranger to strife, lock outs, and labor wars."[82]

Given the choice between parity with Black people—by inviting them into unified unions—and poverty, white workers chose poverty, spoiling the development of a multiracial mass labor movement in America. That decision, wrote W.E.B. Du Bois, "drove such a wedge between white and black workers that there probably are not today in the world two groups of workers with practically identical interests who hate and fear each other so deeply and persistently and who are kept so far apart that neither sees anything of common interest."[83]

As Northern elites were forging an industrial proletariat of factory workers who would replace independent craftsmen, Southern elites, through the legislative and judicial branches they controlled, began creating an agrarian proletariat. In the mid-nineteenth century, planters denied farmers animal grazing rights on common lands, undermining the ability of poor white people to subsist on their own and making them dependent on large plantation owners.[84] They could quit, but quit and do what? During the decade leading up to the Civil War, Southern planters buoyed by the tide of rising cotton prices squeezed white yeomen off their farms to expand their landholdings and plant more of the lucrative crop. The former freeholders often found work as overseers on the planters' ever-expanding estates, driving enslaved Black hands. In

Houston County, Georgia, for example, between 1850 and 1860, the number of households headed by overseers doubled, but the share of overseers who owned land declined dramatically, from 26 to 8 percent.[85]

The yeomen lost their farms but retained their whiteness as consolation. If liberty could not be materially secured through landholding, at least it could be somewhat felt. Witnessing the horrors of slavery drilled into poor white workers that things could be worse, and American freedom became broadly defined as the opposite of bondage. This had the effect of making "all nonslavery appear as freedom," as the economic historian Stanley Engerman has written.[86] It was a freedom that understood what it was against but not what it was for, a malnourished and mean kind of freedom that kept you out of chains but did not provide bread or shelter or a means to get ahead. It was a definition of freedom far too easily satisfied, a freedom ready with justifications and rationalizations as to why some were allowed to live like gods while others were cast into misery and poverty, a freedom ready with the quick answer: *"Hey, this is a capitalist society, a capitalist system, and capitalist rules."*

The staggering inequality that warps today's America characterized life here in the nineteenth century as well. By 1860, the top 5 percent of income earners had grabbed over a quarter of the nation's income, while the bottom 40 percent took home only 10.7 percent. Before the Civil War, inequality increased most dramatically in the South Atlantic states, where among free households the share of income going to the top 1 percent almost doubled between 1774 and 1860, while the share going to the poorest 40 percent was cut in half. In 1860, two in three men with estates valued at $100,000 or more lived in the South, and three-fifths of the country's wealthiest men were enslavers.[87]

In the aftermath of the Civil War, America established twinned economic and political systems that pushed capitalists and workers further apart, creating winners and losers, the rich and the rest. Many formerly enslaved Black workers were pushed into indentured servitude or imprisoned and leased out to companies as convict laborers, dual systems that "replicated the antebellum cycles of racial subordination and exploitation," writes the historian Talitha LeFlouria.[88] Meanwhile, Northern white elites became the most powerful in the world, shrugging off the Puritan frugality and modesty of their forbears, who had been rich but not spectacularly so and had maintained an egalitarian affect. When Alexis de Tocqueville visited the United States in the early nineteenth century, he remarked on how wealthy Americans "keep on easy terms with the lower classes" and "speak to them every day." In fact, he remarked, "The most opulent members of a democracy will not display tastes very different from those of the people."[89]

But the new elite, who had amassed significantly more money and power than the old guard, flourished their wealth, distanced themselves from "the people," and became suspicious of—even antagonistic toward—democracy, just as several of the founders had been. It was easier to be restrained, it seems, when the money was. In 1935 Du Bois described the spirit of this new ruling class: "Profit, income, uncontrolled power in My Business for My Property and for Me—this was the aim and method of the new monarchial dictatorship that displaced democracy in the United States."[90]

Throughout the twentieth century, labor made attempts to check the bosses' power, but time and again these efforts were curtailed by the same racism that had divided workers both during and after slavery. In the years following World War I, racism pitted Black workers against white veterans, who felt entitled to the jobs Black people had filled during the war. At mid-century, Black factory hands, long shunned by unions, resisted white-led strike efforts, even coming to blows with picketers.[91] Rare and muscular moments of multiracial solidarity—wildcat strikes that brought Black and white workers shoulder to shoulder; biracial coalitions that sprang up spontaneously during walkouts so massive they humbled whole cities—provide a glimpse of what might have been. These were exceptions, however. More common was a labor movement prevented from realizing its full potential, hobbled by white workers too often persuaded that their whiteness was advantage enough.

America has evolved into one of the world's most inequitable societies. Today, the richest 10 percent of Americans own over 75 percent of the country's wealth, with the top 1 percent owning well over a third.[92] Many of the political systems, legal arrangements, cultural beliefs, and economic structures that uphold and promote this level of inequality trace their roots back to slavery and its aftermath. If today America promotes a particular kind of low-road capitalism—a union-busting capitalism of poverty wages, gig jobs, and normalized insecurity; a winner-take-all capitalism of stunning disparities not only permitting but rewarding financial rule-bending; a racist capitalism that ignores the fact that slavery didn't just deny Black freedom but built white fortunes, originating the Black-white wealth gap that annually grows wider—one reason is that American capitalism was founded on the lowest road there is.

July 27, 1816

U.S. troops attack a Black military installation, known as Negro Fort, in Spanish Florida, killing nearly all the soldiers, women, and children. The fort was established by the British during the American Revolution and left at the war's end to a unit of free Black people and fugitives from slavery. The presence of this fort struck fear in the hearts of white Southerners, in part because of the long history of Spanish Florida as a haven for fugitives, dating back to Fort Mose, a legendary Black stockade that inspired rebellions, escape, and white reprisals during the colonial era. The Battle of Negro Fort begins the Seminole Wars, which lead to Andrew Jackson's conquest of Florida and the end of the region as a destination for those escaping slavery.

Fort Mose

Tyehimba Jess

They weren't headed north to freedom—
they fled away from the North Star,
turned their back on the Mason-Dixon Line,
put their feet to freedom by fleeing
farther south to Florida.
Ran to where 'gator and viper roamed
free in the mosquito swarm of Suwannee.
They slipped out deep after sunset,
shadow to shadow, shoulder to shoulder,
stealthing southward, stealing themselves,
steeling their souls to run steel
through any slave catcher who'd dare
try stealing them back north.
They billeted in swamp mud,
sawgrass, and cypress—
they waded through waves
of water lily and duckweed.
They thinned themselves in thickets
and thornbush hiding their young
from thieves of black skin marauding
under moonlight and cloud cover.
Many once knew another shore
an ocean away, whose language,
songs, stories were outlawed
on plantation ground. In swampland,

they raised flags of their native tongues
above whisper smoke
into billowing bonfires
of chant, drum, and chatter.
They remembered themselves
with their own words
bleeding into English,
bonding into Spanish,
singing in Creek and Creole.
With their sweat
forging farms in
unforgiving heat,
never forgetting scars
of the lash, fighting
battle after battle
for generations.
Creeks called them Seminole
when they bonded with renegade Creeks.
Spaniards called them cimarrones,
runaways—escapees from Carolina
plantation death-prisons.
English simply called them Maroons,
flattening the Spanish to make them
seem alone, abandoned, adrift—
but they were bonded,
side by side,
Black and Red,
in a blood-red hue—
maroon.
Sovereignty soldiers,
Black refugees,
self-abolitionists, fighting
through America's history,
marooned in a land
they made their own,
acre after acre,
plot after plot,
war after war,
life after life.

They fought only
for America to let them be
marooned—left alone—
in their own unchained,
singing,
worthy
blood.

July 2, 1822

White authorities in Charleston execute Denmark Vesey, a free Black man and A.M.E. Church member, and five others, who were captured and put on trial for planning a rebellion. Vesey, who had been inspired by the successful uprising in Saint-Domingue that led to the Haitian Revolution, intended to burn much of Charleston and set sail for Haiti. His plan attracted many dozens of followers, both free and enslaved, which eventually led to word of the plot reaching local authorities.

Before His Execution

Tim Seibles

This chiming light, like God's voice
has found me most mornings

and so many days I treated the dawn
as if it were common like milkweed

or moss. This is the curse
of too much trouble:

too much thinking and watching
my thoughts—couldn't see
past the chance for freedom

and plans for revenge
that I savored and believed
would have worked.

Though this be my last sunrise
and what continues will continue
beyond my reach, I am afraid—

not of the noose, nor of white men
and their ease with brutality but
of *willful ignorance:* that famous

stupidity that gives its adherents
comfort and many companions.

Ever since I came to know
how and why my life was
disfigured, it's been fury

that woke me, fury
that took my weary body to bed.
I go to bed forever soon:

my heart blacker yet
for all we might have done.

The ones who betrayed us
got a few coins, some
new shoes, maybe two days rest

from the fields—
and because they've known
the cutting snap of the lash,

maybe God
can somehow forgive them.

A washerwoman for the Union army, mid-1800s

CHAPTER 7

Politics

JAMELLE BOUIE

Early on the morning of November 4, 2020, with millions of votes still out-standing in the states that would determine the election, President Donald Trump declared victory. "I want to thank the American people for their tre-mendous support," he began. "Millions and millions of people voted for us tonight. And a very sad group of people is trying to disenfranchise that group of people and we won't stand for it. We will not stand for it."[1] Over the follow-ing weeks and months, Trump's legal team mounted dozens of lawsuits aimed at throwing out votes that had been cast for his opponent, Joe Biden, and overturning the election in Trump's favor. "If you count the legal votes, I easily win," he said in a White House speech. "If you count the illegal votes, they can try to steal the election from us."[2]

Even before the election, the president and his allies had tried to suppress so-called illegal votes. In September, his attorney general, William Barr, falsely alleged that mail-in voting—which for many Americans was a necessity in the face of the Covid-19 pandemic—was "fraught with the risk of fraud and coer-cion," incorrectly citing a 2005 commission report on voting from James Baker and former president Jimmy Carter. Robocalls from unidentified groups in Michigan warned residents that mail-in voting could leave their personal information in the hands of the police. In Georgia, voting officials slashed the number of polling places in majority-Black precincts even as the number of voters surged.[3] After Trump lost, with the majority of mail-in bal-lots going to his opponent, his campaign argued that illegal voting had been particularly rampant in a few cities within the states that had determined the election: Atlanta, Detroit, Philadelphia, and Milwaukee.

No one has ever accused Donald Trump of being subtle, but even for him, this was blatant. Atlanta is 51 percent Black; Detroit, 78 percent. Philadelphia is 42 percent Black, and Milwaukee has a Black population of just under 39 percent. So-called illegal votes were, in actuality, just Black votes. This wasn't about election integrity; it was about casting Black voters as politically illegitimate. As the NAACP Legal Defense Fund said in its lawsuit representing a group of Michigan voters against the Trump campaign, "Defendants' tactics repeat the worst abuses in our nation's history."[4]

The president's effort to overturn the election culminated in an attack on the United States Capitol as Congress began to certify the Electoral College results. Trump's allies called the mob to Washington for a rally to "stop the steal," and then Trump sent the mob after the legislature with the most inflammatory speech of his career. "We want to go back and we want to get this right because we're going to have somebody in there that should not be in there and our country will be destroyed and we're not going to stand for that," he said.[5] A multiracial coalition of Black, brown, and white Americans had defeated Trump and put Biden and Kamala Harris, the first woman and first woman of color to become vice president, in the White House, and the president's supporters, with his direct encouragement, stormed the national legislature to try to nullify the result.

The iconography of the mob was striking. The men and women who invaded the Capitol carried Gadsden flags ("DON'T TREAD ON ME"), "TRUMP 2020" flags, and "BLUE LIVES MATTER" flags. In one frequently reproduced photograph, a rioter was seen holding a Confederate flag while walking through the Capitol Rotunda adjacent to a portrait of South Carolina senator John C. Calhoun, chief statesman of the planter class, committed advocate for slavery, and intellectual forefather of the Confederacy.

That image, more than any other taken that day, captured the meaning of not just the mob but the Trump movement itself. It was never about "populism" or "nationalism" or the interests of working Americans. It was never about restoring the country to any kind of "greatness." It was always about the contours of our national community: who belongs and who doesn't; who counts and who shouldn't; who can wield power and who must be subject to it.

And Trumpism, as the iconography of his movement demonstrates, has race at its core. Trump began his march to the White House as the chief proponent of the "birther" conspiracy, arguing relentlessly that the country's first Black president was foreign-born and therefore illegitimate. His appeal as a presidential candidate was to white Americans who believed that their racial identity and the country's national identity were one and the same. Many of those supporters saw a political victory such as Biden's, propelled by Black votes, as suspect. What began with the "birther" crusade ended with the charge that Barack Obama's America itself was illegitimate and could not hold power.

None of this was an innovation of the Trump era. Obama's election reignited a centuries-old fight over democratic legitimacy—about who can claim the country as their own and who has the right to act as a citizen. Ever since our founding, an exclusive, hierarchical, and racist view of political legitimacy has been a persistent strain in our politics. Adherents of this view—who seek to narrow the scope of participation and wield power through minority rule—are the direct heirs to a tradition of American reactionary belief with its own peculiar history, not just in the ideological battles of the founding but in the institution that shaped and defined the early republic as much as any other.

The plantations that dotted the landscape of the antebellum South produced the commodities that fueled the nation's early growth.[6] But plantations didn't just produce goods; they produced ideas, too. Enslaved laborers developed an understanding of the society in which they lived. The people who enslaved them, likewise, constructed elaborate sets of beliefs, customs, and ideologies meant to justify their positions in this economic and social hierarchy. Those ideas permeated the entire South, taking deepest root in places where slavery was most entrenched.

In many respects, South Carolina was a paradigmatic slave state. Although the largest enslavers resided in the Lowcountry region, with its large rice and cotton plantations, nearly the entire state participated in plantation agriculture and the economy built on slavery. By 1820 most South Carolinians were enslaved Africans. By midcentury, the historian Manisha Sinha notes in *The Counterrevolution of Slavery,* it was the first Southern state where a majority of the white population held enslaved people.[7]

Not surprisingly, enslavers dominated the state's political class. "Carolinian rice aristocrats and the cotton planters from the hinterland," Sinha writes, "formed an intersectional ruling class, bound together by kinship, economic, political and cultural ties."[8] The government they built was the most undemocratic in the Union. The coastal districts, with their large numbers of enslaved people, enjoyed nearly as much representation in the legislature as more populous regions in the interior of the state. Statewide office was restricted to wealthy property owners. To even qualify for the governorship, you needed a large, debt-free estate. Rich enslavers were essentially the only people who could participate in the highest levels of government. To the extent that there were popular elections, they were for the lowest levels of government, because the state legislature tended to appoint most high-level offices.

But immense power at home could not compensate for declining power in national politics. Despite the Three-Fifths Clause in Article I of the Constitution, which gave enslavers an almost uninterrupted hold on the presidency from 1789 to 1850, there were clear signs in the first decades of the nineteenth century that the South's influence was coming to an end. Immigration to the North and the growth of the North's white population in general, as well as the growth of the free Northwest, threatened Southern dominance in Congress. Major rebellions of enslaved people in Louisiana and Virginia, as well as the rise of Haiti as an independent Black nation, left the owners of enslaved people paranoid to the point of hysteria. A steady stream of escaped enslaved men and women threatened the defense of chattel slavery, as the formerly enslaved unsettled the ideological foundations of the South with their own lives and testimony. And the movement to end slavery, once a small fringe, had gained strength and numbers, as well as new arguments and new advocates. By the 1840s, political abolition had come into its own as a movement with real weight on the stage of American politics.

Out of this atmosphere of fear and insecurity came a number of thinkers and politicians who set their minds to defending the slavery-dependent South from a North they perceived as hostile. Arguably the most prominent and accomplished of these planter-politicians was Calhoun, who in addition to his career in the Senate was vice president under John Quincy Adams and Andrew Jackson and secretary of state under John Tyler and James Polk. The son of Scots-Irish Presbyterian transplants to Great Britain's North America colonies, John Caldwell Calhoun had been born in 1782 in the backcountry of South Carolina to Patrick Calhoun, a successful enslaver with thousands of acres and dozens of enslaved people to his name. Educated in New England, Calhoun was elected to the House of Representatives in 1810; he arrived there the following year as a pro-war nationalist, a modernizer who wanted to extend America's influence across the entire continent.

In Calhoun's view, there was no moral difference between slavery and other forms of labor in the modern world. "Let those who are interested remember that labor is the only source of wealth, and how small a portion of it, in all old and civilized countries, even the best governed, is left to those by whose labor wealth is created," he would later write in a congressional committee report. He continued:

Let them also reflect how little volition or agency the operatives in any country have in the question of its distribution—as little, with a few exceptions, as the African of the slaveholding States. . . . Nor is it the less oppressive, that, in one case, it is effected by the stern and powerful will of the Government, and in the other by the more feeble and flexible will of a master. If one be an evil, so is the other.[9]

It was because of this commitment to slavery that Calhoun feared outsized federal power over commerce, taxation, and trade. At a time when Northern manufacturers sought to protect their industries from foreign competition with tariffs and other restrictions on free trade, Calhoun worried that a growing and assertive federal government would extend that authority to slavery and the trade in enslaved people. This, in turn, led him to "nullification": the theory that any state subject to federal law was entitled to invalidate it. He first advanced the idea in an anonymous letter, written when he was Jackson's vice president, protesting the Tariff of 1828, which sought to protect Northern industry and agriculture from outside competitors. Passed under the "general welfare" clause of the Constitution, the tariff, for its opponents, raised the specter of an overly powerful federal government. If Congress had the authority to pass tariffs for the "general welfare," what was there to stop it from limiting or even abolishing slavery? "Let us say distinctly to Congress, 'HANDS OFF,'" wrote one South Carolina polemicist.[10]

Calhoun agreed. The tariff went beyond the power of the federal government, and its passage was a sign that the South was under threat by an overbearing North. "To the reflecting mind," he wrote to Virginia senator Littleton Waller Tazewell a year before the tariff was passed, "[the tariff issue] clearly indicates the weak part of our system. . . . The freedom of debate, the freedom of the press, the division of power into three branches . . . afford, in the main, efficient security to the *constituents against rulers,* but in an extensive country with diversified and opposing interests, another and not less important remedy is required, *the protection of one portion of the people against another.*"[11]

There was one specific portion with whose protection Calhoun was chiefly concerned. "Our geographical position, our industry, pursuits and institutions are all peculiar," he later wrote, referring to the slavery-dependent South.[12] Against a domineering North, he argued, "representation affords not the slightest protection."[13]

Calhoun was driven by a sense of approaching doom. "It is, indeed, high time for the people of the South to be roused to a sense of impending calamities—on an early and full knowledge of which their safety depends," he wrote in an 1831 report to the South Carolina legislature. "It is time that they should see and feel that . . . they are in a permanent and hopeless minority on the great and vital connected questions."[14]

On this defense of the prerogatives of the Southern section of the nation, Calhoun built an entire theory of government. Seeing the threat democracy posed to slavery, he set out to limit democracy. To do so he employed a novel conception of the Constitution. For Calhoun there was no "Union" per se. Instead, the United States was simply a compact among sovereigns with distinct, and often competing, sectional interests. This compact could survive only if all sides had equal say about the meaning of the Constitution and the shape and structure of the law. Individual states, Calhoun thought, should be able to veto federal laws if they believed the federal government had favored one state or section over another. The Union could act only with the assent of the entire whole—what Calhoun called "the concurrent majority." This was in opposition to the Madisonian idea of rule by numerical majority, albeit mediated by compromise and consensus.

Calhoun initially lost the tariff fight, which pitted him against an obstinate Andrew Jackson, but he did not give up on nullification. He expanded on the theory at the end of his life, proposing an alternative system of government that gave political minorities a final say over majority action. In this "concurrent government," each "interest or portion of the community" would have an equal say in approving the actions of the state. Full agreement would be necessary to "put the government in motion." This was the only way, Calhoun argued, that the "different interests, orders, classes, or portions, into which the community may be divided, can be protected."[15]

To Calhoun, this wasn't just compatible with the Constitution, it was the realization of the founding vision for the American republic. In his view, and against the arguments of James Madison and other key framers, the Constitution did not establish the principle of majority rule. Instead, as the historian Robert Elder noted in the biography *Calhoun: American Heretic*, Calhoun believed that it established a system in which power was vested in "the whole— the entire people– to make it in truth and reality the Government of the people, instead of a Government of a dominant over a subject part." Each elected branch—the House, the Senate, the executive—had its part to play in creating this consensus. "Each [department of government] may be imperfect of itself, but if the construction be good, and all the keys skillfully touched, there will be given out in one blended and harmonious whole, the true and perfect voice of the people."[16]

The problem, in Calhoun's eyes, was that the will of the majority, as expressed in the House of Representatives and the election of the president, had too much power. It had to be curbed, lest it overrun this "true and perfect voice of the people." And those "people" whose voices must be heard, of course, were those like him. Those with power. Those with property. Those who enslaved others.

Calhoun would grow more confident and forthright as a defender of slavery. In early 1837, in response to abolitionist calls to end slavery in the District of Columbia, Calhoun gave his signature (and infamous) defense of the institution.

> But let me not be understood as admitting, even by implication, that the existing relations between the two races in the slaveholding States is an evil:—far otherwise; I hold it to be a good, as it has thus far proved itself to be to both, and will continue to prove so if not disturbed by the fell spirit of abolition. I appeal to facts. Never before has the black race of Central Africa, from the dawn of history to the present day, attained a condition so civilized and so improved, not only physically, but morally and intellectually.
>
> In the meantime, the white or European race, has not degenerated. It has kept pace with its brethren in other sections of the Union where slavery does not exist. It is odious to make comparison; but I appeal to all sides whether the South is not equal in virtue, intelligence, patriotism, courage, disinterestedness, and all the high qualities which adorn our nature.
>
> But I take higher ground. I hold that in the present state of civilization, where two races of different origin, and distinguished by color, and other physical differences, as well as intellectual, are brought together, the relation now existing in the slaveholding States between the two, is, instead of an evil, a good—a positive good.[17]

The government Calhoun envisioned would protect this system by defending "liberty": not of the citizen but of the master, the liberty of those who claimed a right to property and a position at the top of a racial and economic hierarchy. This liberty, Calhoun stated, was "a reward to be earned, not a blessing to be gratuitously lavished on all alike—a reward reserved for the intelligent, the patriotic, the virtuous and deserving—and not a boon to be bestowed on a people too ignorant, degraded and vicious, to be capable either of appreciating or of enjoying it."[18]

Calhoun died in 1850. Ten years later, Abraham Lincoln won the White House without a single Southern state and, following the idea of nullification and the concurrent majority to its conclusion, the South seceded from the Union. War came a few months later, and four years of fighting destroyed the system of slavery Calhoun had fought to protect. But parts of his legacy survived. His deep suspicion of majoritarian democracy—his view that government must protect interests, defined by their unique geographic and economic characteristics, more than people—would inform the sectional politics of the South in the twentieth century, as solid blocs of Southern lawmakers would work collectively to stifle any attempt to regulate the region.

Despite insurgencies at home—the Populist Party, for example, swept through Georgia and North Carolina in the 1890s, demanding aid for farmers and a reduction in debts—Southern lawmakers were able to maintain an iron grip on federal offices until the Voting Rights Act of 1965. In their legislative fights the spirit of nullification lived on. Anti-lynching laws and some pro-labor legislation died at the hands of lawmakers from the "Solid South" who took advantage of Senate rules like the filibuster—under which lawmakers could speak indefinitely, tying up the chamber's business—to effectively enact Calhoun's idea of a concurrent majority against legislation that threatened the Southern racial status quo.

Calhoun's idea that states could veto federal laws would return again following the decision in *Brown v. Board of Education,* as segregationists announced "massive resistance" to federal desegregation mandates and sympathizers defended white Southern actions with ideas and arguments that cribbed from Calhoun and recapitulated enslaver ideology for modern American politics.

"The central question that emerges," the *National Review*'s founding editor, William F. Buckley, Jr., wrote in 1957, amid congressional debate over the first Civil Rights Act, "is whether the white community in the South is entitled to take such measures as are necessary to prevail, politically and culturally, in areas which it does not predominate numerically? The sobering answer is *yes*—the white community is so entitled because, for the time being, it is the advanced race." He continued: "It is more important for any community, anywhere in the world, to affirm and live by civilized standards, than to bow to the demands of the numerical majority."[19]

It was a strikingly blunt defense of Jim Crow and affirmation of white supremacy from the father of the conservative movement. Later, when key civil rights questions had been settled by law, Buckley would essentially renounce these views, praising the movement and criticizing race-baiting demagogues like George C. Wallace. Still, his initial impulse—to give white political minorities a veto not just over policy but over democracy itself—reflected a tendency that would express itself again and again in the conservative politics he ushered into the mainstream, emerging when political, cultural, and demographic change threatened a narrow, exclusionary vision of American democracy.

In 1964, Senator Barry Goldwater of Arizona, an opponent of the Civil Rights Act, won the Republican Party's nomination for president. Goldwater allowed that there were "some rights that are clearly protected by valid laws and are therefore 'civil rights.'" But he lamented that "states' rights" were "disappearing under the piling sands of absolutism" and called *Brown v. Board of Education* an "unconstitutional trespass into the legislative sphere of government." "I therefore support all efforts by the States, excluding violence, of course," Goldwater wrote in *The Conscience of a Conservative*, "to preserve their rightful powers over education."[20] Though he lost the general election in a landslide, Goldwater won the Deep South (except for Florida), where white people flocked to the candidate who stood against the constitutional demands of the Black freedom movement.

Writing in the 1980s and '90s, Samuel Francis—a polemicist who would eventually migrate to the very far right of American conservatism—identified this same rejection of democratic processes in the context of David Duke's campaign for governor of Louisiana: "Reagan conservatism, in its innermost meaning, had little to do with supply-side economics and spreading democracy. It had to do with the awakening of a people who face political, cultural and economic dispossession, who are slowly beginning to glimpse the fact of dispossession and what dispossession will mean for them and their descendants, and who also are starting to think about reversing the processes and powers responsible for their dispossession."[21]

There is a homegrown ideology of reaction in the United States, inextricably tied to our system of slavery. And while that ideology no longer carries the explicit racism of the past, the basic framework remains: fear of rival political majorities; of demographic "replacement"; of a government that threatens privilege and hierarchy.

The last decade of Republican extremism is emblematic. In 2008, Barack Obama was elected president. Within months of taking office, he faced a wave of backlash from grassroots conservative activists calling themselves the Tea Party. On paper, and channeling the group's American Revolution–era namesake, this backlash was a revolt against the spending priorities of the new administration and the prospect of higher taxes. Tea Party politicians, like Senator Rand Paul of Kentucky and Representative Michele Bachmann of Minnesota, would come to Washington in 2011 with demands for spending cuts and balanced budgets. But a close examination of the beliefs of Tea Party activists shows a movement consumed with resentment toward an ascendant majority of Black people, Latinos, Asian Americans, and liberal white people. In *Change They Can't Believe In: The Tea Party and Reactionary Politics in America,* their survey-based study of the movement, for example, the political scientists Christopher S. Parker and Matt A. Barreto show that Tea Party Republicans were motivated "by the fear and anxiety associated with the perception that 'real' Americans are losing their country."[22]

The scholars Theda Skocpol and Vanessa Williamson came to a similar conclusion in their contemporaneous book about the movement, based on an ethnographic study of Tea Party activists across the country. "Tea Party resistance to giving more to categories of people deemed undeserving is more than just an argument about taxes and spending," they note in *The Tea Party and the Remaking of Republican Conservatism;* "it is a heartfelt cry about where they fear 'their country' may be headed." And Tea Party adherents' "worries about racial and ethnic minorities and overly entitled young people," Skocpol and Williamson write, "signal a larger fear about generational social change in America."[23]

Convinced of their imminent minority status in American politics, right-wing conservatives embarked on a project to nullify opponents and restrict the scope of democracy. In 2011, Tea Party lawmakers in Congress pushed the entire Republican Party to repeal the Affordable Care Act and make other sharp cuts to the social safety net. Since Democrats controlled the Senate and the White House at the time, and polling showed that the public, overall, was opposed to cutting benefits, there was, however, a limit to what Republicans could accomplish. So they held the government hostage to their demands, using the "debt limit"—a legislative mechanism that sets out the amount of debt the country can take on—to extract concessions. Rather than work within the constraints of ordinary politics, Republicans threatened to throw a wrench into the gears.

"I'm asking you to look at a potential increase in the debt limit as a leverage moment when the White House and President Obama will have to deal with us," said the incoming majority leader, Eric Cantor, at a closed-door retreat days after the 2011 session began, according to *The Washington Post.* Either the White House would agree to harsh austerity measures or Republicans would force the United States to default on its debt obligations, precipitating an economic crisis just as the country, and the world, was climbing out of the Great Recession.[24]

This stand was emblematic of how the Republican Party would approach the rest of Obama's time in office. Either Republicans would succeed in stopping Obama's agenda or they would wreck the system itself. To this end, the Senate Republican leader, Mitch McConnell, embraced and expanded use of the filibuster to nullify the president's ability to nominate federal judges and fill vacancies in the executive branch. And after Republicans took the Senate majority in 2014, he led an extraordinary blockade of the Supreme Court, thereby robbing Obama of a Supreme Court nomination.

But while McConnell's hyper-obstructionist rule in the Senate is arguably the most high-profile example of the nullification strategy, it's far from the most egregious. In state legislatures across the country, Republicans have embraced a view that holds voting majorities—as well as entire constituencies—illegitimate if they don't support Republican candidates for office. In 2012, North Carolina Republicans won legislative and executive power for the first time in more than a century. They used it to gerrymander the electoral map and impose new restrictions on voting, specifically aimed at African Americans. One such restriction, a strict voter-identification law, was designed to target Black North Carolinians with "almost surgical precision," according to the federal judges who struck the law down. When, in 2016, Democrats overcame these obstacles to take back the governor's mansion, the Republican-controlled legislature successfully stripped some power from the office, to prevent Democrats from reversing their efforts to rig the game.[25]

The same happened in Wisconsin. Under Scott Walker, the governor at the time, Wisconsin Republicans gave themselves a structural advantage in the state legislature through aggressive gerrymandering. They redrew the state's maps with such precision that they could continue to win a near supermajority of seats in the legislature even with a minority of the overall vote. After the Democratic candidate toppled Walker in the 2018 governor's race, the Republican majority in the legislature rapidly moved to limit the new governor's power and weaken other statewide offices won by Democrats. They restricted the governor's ability to run public-benefit programs and set rules on the implementation of state laws. And they robbed the governor and the attorney general of the power to either continue or end legal action against the Affordable Care Act.

Michigan Republicans took an almost identical course of action after Democrats in that state managed to win executive office, using their gerrymandered legislative majority to weaken the new Democratic governor and attorney general. One bill shifted oversight of campaign-finance law from the secretary of state to a six-person commission with members nominated by the state Republican and Democratic parties, a move designed to produce deadlock and keep elected Democrats from reversing previous decisions.[26]

The Republican rationale for tilting the field in their permanent favor, or, failing that, nullifying the results and limiting Democrats' power as much as possible, has a familiar ring to it. "Citizens from every corner of Wisconsin deserve a strong legislative branch that stands on equal footing with an incoming administration that is based almost solely in Madison," one Wisconsin Republican said following the party's lame-duck power grab. The speaker of the state assembly, Robin Vos, made his point more explicitly: "If you took Madison and Milwaukee out of the state election formula, we would have a clear majority—we would have all five constitutional officers, and we would probably have many more seats in the Legislature." The argument is straightforward: Their mostly white voters should count. Other voters—Black people and other people of color who live in cities—shouldn't.[27]

Senate Republicans played with similar ideas just before the 2016 election, openly announcing their plans to block Hillary Clinton from nominating anyone to the Supreme Court, should she become president. "I promise you that we will be united against any Supreme Court nominee that Hillary Clinton, if she were president, would put up," declared Senator John McCain of Arizona just weeks before the voting began.[28] And President Trump, of course, has repeatedly and falsely denounced Clinton's popular-vote victory as illegitimate, the product of fraud and illegal voting. "In addition to winning the Electoral College in a landslide," he declared on Twitter weeks after the election, "I won the popular vote if you deduct the millions of people who voted illegally."

The larger implication is clear enough: a majority made up of liberals and nonwhites isn't a real majority. And the solution is clear, too: to write those people out of the polity, to use every available tool to weaken their influence on American politics—whether that means raising barriers to voting and registration or slashing access to the ballot box itself or anything in between. The Trump administration's failed attempt to place a citizenship question on the census was an important part of this effort. By requiring this information, the administration hoped to suppress the number of immigrant respondents, worsening their representation in the House and the Electoral College, reweighting power to the white rural areas that backed Trump and the Republican Party.

————

Donald Trump's false claims of electoral fraud in the wake of the 2020 presidential election were an expression of the idea that only certain majorities are real majorities, that only some Americans deserve to hold power. And while Trump lost and left office, the idea persists. Rather than mobilize new voters or persuade existing ones, Republicans throughout the country have set about restricting access to the forms of voting that helped Democrats win in traditionally Republican states like Georgia and Arizona. In Michigan, likewise, Republican lawmakers want to change the way the state distributes its Electoral College votes to nullify the influence of Detroit on the final result.

You could make the case that none of this has anything to do with slavery and enslavers' ideology. You could argue that it has nothing to do with race at all, that it's simply an aggressive effort to secure conservative victories. But the tenor of an argument, the shape and nature of an opposition movement— these things matter. Republicans stepped onto this path after America elected its first Black president, and they thereafter embraced a racist demagogue and his attacks on the legitimacy of the nation's multiracial character; these actions speak to how the threads of history tie past and present together.

While neutral on their face, these methods—the assaults on the legitimacy of nonwhite political actors, the casting of rival political majorities as unrepresentative, the drive to nullify democratically elected governing coalitions— are downstream of ideas and ideologies that came to fruition in the defense of human bondage and racial segregation. And as long as there are enough Americans who do not trust democracy to protect their privileges—as long as there are those who see in political equality a threat to their power and standing—these ideas and ideologies will have a path to power.

In which case, the price of equality, or at least of the promise of an equal society, is vigilance against those who would make government the tool of hierarchy. And, in turn, we must recognize that this struggle—to secure democracy against privilege on the one hand, and to secure privilege against democracy on the other—is the unresolvable conflict of American life. It is the push and pull that will last for as long as the republic stands.

September 20, 1830

Black leaders convene in Philadelphia at Bishop Richard Allen's Mother Bethel A.M.E. Church for the first gathering of what will come to be known as the Colored Conventions movement, a series of formal meetings of Black Americans dedicated to advancing racial justice and securing Black citizenship. The first convention is called in response to an outbreak of white violence against Black people in Ohio, where a series of laws had been passed to discourage Black settlement. Over the next seven decades, more than two hundred state and national conventions will be held.

We as People

Cornelius Eady

In Ohio,
Black folk can walk free,

But you still have
The rights
Of a mule,
A chicken,
A bloodhound—

Ever see a bloodhound
Cast a vote?
Ever see a piglet
Try to write some law?

We as people
Have to stop waiting,
While the mobs sweep
The Cincinnati streets
Of Black skins, Black thought,

Black laughter, Black prayers,
Black homes, Black children,
Black song, packing our bags
With bruises, skinning our

Breath with knuckles, the tar
Dipped, lit, and torch tossed

On the front porch of your
Consideration. Some of us
Took that hint and flew,

Exit, exile, Exodus.
Others wonder why Jesus
Let the cops chase their fancy
Unpunished,

But we as people have to stop asking
A flood to stop being a flood,
Expecting a hurricane to grow
Some manners.

We've come to Philly to find out
What happens
When we stop running,
And we start talking
Among ourselves.
What better selves
Do we knit?

When you open the doors
To a shelter,
After a bad storm has passed,

Ain't that air sweet? Even if the
Town is in splinters? Ain't
You happy that storm tried its level best
But couldn't stop your heart?

September 18, 1850

Congress passes the Fugitive Slave Act, which requires that fugitives from slavery residing in free states be forcibly returned to their enslavers. This leads to the kidnapping of many Black people in Northern states, regardless of their status, driving some to migrate farther north, into Canada. The new law is resisted by many abolitionists, including Harriet Hayden, herself a fugitive from slavery, who operates the Underground Railroad in Boston and helps hundreds of enslaved people escape.

A Letter to Harriet Hayden

Lynn Nottage

*Restless, a woman gazes out a window coated with winter frost. She absently runs
her fingers across the condensation on the glass, then turns to address a young
reverend seated at a creaky writing desk.*

WOMAN:

I know it's much to ask, Reverend Potter, still, I'd like you to write down
what I say, just as I say it, but more proper-like. I got the words, but not the
learning to place 'em on paper.

A breath.

To My Dear Friend . . . you may wonder what has become of me. I'm living
in a state of disquiet and precarity. I find myself in a land of brutal beauty.
This cold invites a cough that my lungs are unfit to battle, yet it's warmer
company than the dread of being discovered. Please forgive me for leaving
with some haste, I neglected to say goodbye in a manner respectful of our
friendship and your kindness. But I daren't stay for fear of bringing more
trouble to your door, and I daren't tell you that I was leaving, 'cuz I knew
you'd want me to stay, fight this devil's law, but I haven't your courage or . . .
maybe I should say . . . conviction.

I hold tight to the day you welcomed me into your home, my body still
brittle and near broken from travel. You fed me chicken broth that was coal
hot to the tongue, yet I drank it down 'cuz it was an act of graciousness I

couldn't refuse. My throat burned, and I thought maybe freedom hurts just a little bit. I often think back to the excitement of sitting 'round your table, surrounded by much laughter and meals of embarrassing heartiness. I boast to all about your stewed mutton, corn bread, buttered cabbage, milk pudding, and that blackberry pie that tasted like . . . what's the word? . . . bliss. The goodness of your home provided a safety unknown to me, and even now the memory fends off despair. Often, I worried that the burden of my heavy spirit would weigh you down, 'cuz I never knew colored people to live so easy.

By now, you must know that there's a warrant that lays claim to the part of me I no longer recognize. My old master seeks to reunite me with . . .

She turns her gaze to the reverend.

Why'd you stop writing? I'll be all right, Reverend, no harm'll come from recollecting. Keep going.

Another breath.

My old master seeks to reunite me with the intricacies of his cruelty, and I have thus chosen to seek liberty beyond his expanding reach. I passed my life for some twenty-seven years in a state suspended between life and death, wading through the netherworld of bondage. I used to be scolded for carrying too much want and curiosity, 'cuz I dare ask what lie past the knotty swampland. I got switch burns up and down my legs from climbing, mind you without permission, the tallest oak to see if there was a world beyond my mother's fears. And when I found it, I didn't understand that my life would become a collection of goodbyes.

Give my respects to Joseph, Elizabeth, and your dear husband, Lewis. Tell Nelson that I did not take his attention for granted, and think of him with affection. . . . No, best not say that, don't want to give 'em the wrong notion, do I? Put— Think of him with fondness. Yes, fondness. I tucked four dollars beneath the flour jar, I hope you will have found it. I know you wanted a new dress for church. You always say I kept a tidy room, and you'll be pleased to learn that I have found a good situation with the Reverend Potter and his aged mother. They are sympathetic to the anti-slavery movement, and willingly shelter this fugitive.

Know, my sweet friend, that I have not abandoned you or the cause of liberty. My hands, my arms, my feet, my legs, my eyes, my ears, and my heart are all unwitting weapons of resistance.

For now, I'm beyond reach, but cannot say where I reside . . . Most Truly Yours.

A breath.

And . . . Reverend Potter, just sign it . . . A Free Colored Woman . . . she'll know who it is.

Thomas Cobb, Brooklyn, New York, 1990s ELI REED

CHAPTER 8

Citizenship

MARTHA S. JONES

On July 6, 1853, more than one hundred delegates took their seats in Corinthian Hall, the grandest meeting place in Rochester, New York. They had made their way from ten states—Connecticut, Illinois, Indiana, Massachusetts, Michigan, New York, Ohio, Pennsylvania, Rhode Island, and Vermont—for that year's Colored National Convention. Excluded from political parties, statehouses, and Congress, Black activists found, in the convention's three days of deliberation and discussion, a place for developing ideas, honing strategies, and demonstrating a capacity for full citizenship. The proceedings were models of political debate, organized by republican principles of representation and run along parliamentary-style rules of order.[1]

Though closer to Canada than to New York City, Rochester was an apt site for a Black convention. From that city in western New York, one of the leading Black activists of the day, Frederick Douglass, published his independent newspapers, *The North Star* and *Frederick Douglass' Paper.* Papers like these reached the far corners of Black America with news, editorials, lively letters to the editor and reports on the ideas being generated during "colored convention" proceedings.

Since the first convention met in Philadelphia in 1830, delegates had been advancing the cause of slavery's abolition, which grew to be a force of consequence in national culture and politics. Black abolitionists brought together their distinct voices to promote antislavery, along with education, commerce, agriculture, and temperance. In doing so, they defined an African American political agenda, with a focus on establishing their citizenship.

At the 1853 Rochester convention, Frederick Douglass took the floor as chair of the Committee on the Declaration of Sentiments and delivered a lesson on what it meant to belong in the United States. He wove together principles from founding documents like the Declaration of Independence and the Constitution with political history, moral philosophy, and Christian theology. His message was unequivocal: Black Americans were "by birth . . . American citizens; by the principles of the Declaration of Independence, we are American citizens; within the meaning of the United States Constitution, we are American citizens; by the facts of history; and the admission of American statesmen, we are American citizens; by the hardships and trials endured; by the courage and fidelity displayed by our ancestors in defending the liberties and in achieving the independence of our land, we are American citizens."[2]

Citizenship is an old concept, with roots that stretch back to the ancient world. To be a citizen is to be an insider. It is to belong. A citizen may be guaranteed a place within a set of boundaries and entitled to fundamental rights, and bears responsibilities as a member of the polity. Citizenship is a defining feature of democracy in the United States and promises to protect the despised, the unorthodox, and the unwanted from removal, exile, and banishment. However, for most of its first century, the country neglected to define precisely who was a citizen. Its founding texts speak of U.S. citizens but do not address the question directly. Still, the persistent influence of slavery and anti-Black racism on law and politics meant that belonging in the country was determined, in part, by which side of the color line a person was on. No matter what else they might accomplish, most free Black Americans such as the delegates at the colored conventions could not become citizens.

Twenty-first-century Americans become citizens by many routes, including naturalization after marriage and migration. The foremost way to citizenship is, however, the accident of birth. This is due to the first clause of the Fourteenth Amendment, ratified in 1868, which established that: "All persons born or naturalized in the United States, and subject to the jurisdiction thereof, are citizens of the United States and of the state wherein they reside."[3] This birthright principle is now so foundational that many people assume citizenship in the United States has always worked this way. It has not. Convention delegates struggled over decades to establish the birthright principle as a foundation of American democracy, and today's Constitution reflects their vision when it unceremoniously bestows citizenship upon millions of children each year by virtue of their birth on U.S. soil. The birthright principle distinguishes the United States as a democracy and while that rule predominates in the Americas, it is not a standard feature of democracies worldwide. Instead, many nations determine a child's citizenship by a mix of factors in addition to place of birth, including the citizenship status of their parents.

Today, some U.S. lawmakers charge that birthright citizenship is an arbitrary or excessive principle by which to define national belonging. The House of Representatives, in each session since 2007, has introduced the Birthright Citizenship Act, a law that would exclude the U.S.–born children of undocumented immigrants from birthright's protections. In 2018, then-president Donald Trump declared his intent to do away with birthright, though the means by which he would do so were never fully disclosed. Remarkably, figures as highly placed as former U.S. attorney general William Barr and U.S. Supreme Court Associate Justice Amy Coney Barrett, when questioned, have declined to express views about the legal parameters of birthright citizenship despite the principle having been law for more than 150 years.

These dismissals of birthright citizenship's importance overlook the critical history of how this principle has secured the promise of democracy for all, regardless of differences in color, religion, political affiliation, and more. They also erase the decades of work by Black activists, joined at times after 1830 by some white antislavery allies, to clearly define citizenship in the United States. Their efforts are reflected in the first sentence of the Fourteenth Amendment. In twenty-eight words, it made plain that Black Americans were not outsiders; they were citizens.

Black Americans had been exploring citizenship and how to secure it since the eighteenth century. They knew that the Declaration of Independence provided that "all men are created equal" and at one point speaks of "fellow citizens," but did not explain who was and was not a citizen. The Articles of Confederation, drafted in 1777 to govern the new loose assembly of former colonies, told them nothing about who was a citizen and instead promised that "the free inhabitants of each of these states, paupers, vagabonds and fugitives from Justice excepted, shall be entitled to all privileges and immunities of free citizens in the several states."[4] It was not even clear who had the authority to rectify the oversight. The principle of federalism divided governance in the new nation between the states and the federal government, but neither had express authority over citizenship. Ambiguity and confusion followed.

In the years after the American Revolution, Paul and Jonathan Cuffe, men of African and Native descent, lived in Dartmouth, Massachusetts, where they were required to pay taxes but denied the right to vote. This, they argued, was a contradiction. If they were to be taxed like white citizens, they could not then be denied citizenship's political rights. In a series of petitions in 1780 and

1781, the brothers demanded "to know . . . whether all free Negroes & mulattoes Shall have the same Privileges in this Town of Dartmouth as the white People have." If they were equal to white men, the brothers allowed, they should pay their share of local taxes. But without the right to vote—without privileges equal to those of white taxpayers—they would not. The Cuffes eventually settled their dispute by paying a reduced tax. Still, they exposed an ambiguity in the new Massachusetts state constitution, which noted, "All men are born free and equal and have certain natural, essential, and unalienable rights." No one could say for certain whether the Cuffes were included among "All men."[5]

The new U.S. Constitution of 1787 more tightly knit together the states and made express provisions for taxation and national defense. The framers engaged in wide-ranging debates across competing interests—Southern versus Northern; slaveholding versus free-soil; Republican versus Federalist. But they addressed citizenship only indirectly. Article II provided that the president must be a "natural born Citizen." Article I said that members of the House of Representatives must have been U.S. citizens for at least seven years; for senators, the requirement was nine years. Federal courts, the new Constitution provided, could hear disputes between citizens of different states. "Citizens of each state" were entitled to the privileges and immunities of "Citizens in the several states." Still, nowhere did the Constitution define what made one a citizen.[6]

This ambiguity frustrated clergy member Absalom Jones and the men and women of Philadelphia's Free African Society. By the end of the eighteenth century, their city was home to a community of formerly enslaved people and their descendants—free Black Americans—that had burgeoned after 1780, when Pennsylvania began to gradually abolish slavery. They busily built churches, mutual aid societies, and their own political culture even as their lives were plagued by racism. Federal laws, such as the 1790 Naturalization Act, set in place a color line that excluded Black people from citizenship by way of naturalization, further creating an atmosphere of uncertainty about where they stood before the law.[7]

In 1799, seventy-one Black Philadelphians lodged a formal claim and insisted on their entitlement to "Liberties and unalienable Rights" and likened themselves to "every other class of Citizen within the Jurisdiction of the United States."[8] The petition arrived in Congress in January 1800, where representatives managed to do little more than disagree. There was not even a consensus about whether Black Americans had a right to petition Congress in the first place, though the First Amendment guaranteed "the right of the people . . . to petition the Government for a redress of grievances." When it came to the question of whether Black Americans enjoyed the rights of citizens, the House considered the petition only long enough to send it to a committee, where it quietly died.[9]

Dissension—and contradiction—persisted into the 1820s. None among the country's political and legal elite were willing to answer the citizenship question that stalked Black Americans. In 1821, an appeal from customs official William Lindsay, the collector for the Port of Norfolk, Virginia, asked U.S. attorney general William Wirt: Could a free Black man command an American merchant vessel? Federal law, Lindsay understood, barred noncitizens from commanding such ships. Wirt's answer confused as much as it clarified. The attorney general wrote: "I am of the opinion that the constitution, by the description of 'citizens of the United States,' intended those only who enjoyed the full and equal privileges of white citizens in the State of their residence." It followed that because free Black Virginians were not full and equal citizens of their state, they could not be citizens of the United States. They were instead, in Wirt's view, mere residents. But he also left the door open to the idea that if a Black person's home state deemed them a citizen—as did some Northern states, such as Massachusetts and New York—they *might* also be citizens of the United States. Wirt answered the Norfolk official's question, but he did not settle much else.[10]

Congress was similarly muddled in its thinking about Black citizenship. In 1820, the western territory of Missouri was admitted as a new state. In what became known as the Missouri Compromise, Congress decided that slavery would be permitted in Missouri but prohibited in all other parts of the Louisiana Purchase north of the 36°30′ parallel, a surveyor's line that arbitrarily delineated North from South. But soon a second disagreement erupted when lawmakers in Missouri proposed a constitution that flat-out barred "free Negroes and mulattoes" from the state.[11]

Debate on this restriction gave Congress a chance to say whether the Constitution guaranteed to Black Americans, as citizens of the various states, equal rights under the Privileges and Immunities Clause. It was clear that Missouri could not, for example, bar citizens from Ohio from entering. The proposed prohibition against Black migration to Missouri might violate this principle, but only if Black Americans were *citizens*. If Congress found Missouri's proposal to be in violation of the Privileges and Immunities Clause, it would be a roundabout way of affirming Black citizenship.

Members became mired in disagreement and deliberated for many weeks. In 1821, Representative Josiah Butler of New Hampshire and Representative

John Floyd of Virginia faced off on the House floor. Butler argued that in Northern states such as Massachusetts, the "rights of the colored citizens . . . are as sacred as those of the white citizens." In Butler's view, Black Americans were unequivocally citizens of the state and, by implication, entitled to constitutional protection. Floyd deemed such a proposition unthinkable and mocked Butler: "Who is there that believes [Black Americans] ever had any rights but such as the indulgence of the States permitted?" He went so far as to assert that Black Americans' privileges could at any time be rescinded. Free Black people could even be enslaved, without cause or process: "Could not the States now seize their persons, and make them slaves?"[12]

Eventually Congress allowed the ban on Black migration to Missouri to remain but still admonished the new state that it must not pass any law "by which any citizen, of either of the states in this Union, shall be excluded from the enjoyment of any of the privileges and immunities to which such citizen is entitled under the constitution of the United States." Congress self-consciously drew no color line when drafting this provision. Still, life for prospective Black migrants to Missouri was, in the end, no less harrowing than it had been before congressional review.[13]

Lawmakers again and again fumbled when called upon to settle the question of Black citizenship, leaving the country's elite politicians, merchants, lawyers, and philanthropists to devise their own approach. Their most popular "solution" was known as "colonization," a plan to remove Black Americans from the United States. The American Colonization Society (ACS), founded in 1816, committed to preserving the United States as a white man's country by ensuring that Black Americans would not become citizens. The ACS recruited supporters, raised funds, won public appropriations in some places, and built a network that made colonization one of the largest political movements of the time. Some colonizationists encouraged the abolition of slavery, while others agreed with the organization's open espousal of anti-Black racism. Some Southerners opposed colonization, fearing that it might succeed in manumitting enslaved people but then not live up to removing them from the country. Still, the ACS managed to attract supporters across lines of region and party.[14]

In 1822, just one year after Congress allowed a ban on Black migration to Missouri, the ACS established the West African colony of Liberia. Promising migrants economic independence, political autonomy, and citizenship, the society outfitted ships, organized expeditions, and did all it could to encourage Black people to leave the United States. The society worked hand in hand with state lawmakers friendly to its cause; these legislators pressured free

Black Americans into self-exile by enacting local statutes, termed Black laws, that restricted their work, movement, and public gatherings. With life in the United States too onerous, the thinking went, Black Americans might give in to the enticements of Liberia. In some states, lawmakers proposed new laws that would require free people of color to leave by threat of force, or which predicated manumission by owners on an enslaved person's agreement to leave the country once free. Over the next two decades, more than four thousand Black people would go to Liberia.

It fell to Black activists to fight for citizenship and resist colonization, and with that the Colored Convention movement was started. At the inaugural gathering in 1830, Black men came together from New England, the mid-Atlantic, and as far south as Virginia to discuss the rise of Black laws and the prospect of leaving the United States. Among them were delegates from Ohio who were being driven out of their state by discriminatory Black laws. The way forward was not yet clear. Without a way to ensure their equality, some delegates urged resettling in Canada, where Black Americans might be guaranteed that "no invidious distinction of colour is recognised . . . there we shall be entitled to all the rights, privileges, and immunities of other citizens."[15]

Baltimore delegate Hezekiah Grice returned home from the Philadelphia convention determined to fend off exile. He organized the Legal Rights Association, which aimed to prove that Black Americans were citizens. His associate William Watkins, an educator and commentator in the anti-slavery press, summarized the association's argument, one rooted in the Declaration of Independence:

> This imperishable document, whose attributes are truth, justice, and benevolence, has declared to the world that liberty, in the full sense of the word, is the birth-right of "all men"; (consequently, of every colored man in the Union;) that we are not only "born free," but have, by virtue of our existence, "certain rights," which are emphatically termed "inalienable."[16]

Watkins asked whether the Constitution had incorporated the Declaration's ideals: "The Declaration of Independence is our advocate, and we hope it will yet be ascertained, whether or not the Constitution of the U[nited] States secures to us those rights which the Declaration so freely accords." This thinking led Watkins to probe the depths of the nation's morals:

Why, I emphatically ask, should we not enjoy those rights which all must confess have been wrested from us without the shadow of a crime? What evil could possibly accrue from the adoption, by the white people of this nation, of a liberal, just, and humane policy towards three hundred thousand of the home-born citizens of the United States?[17]

While Watkins made his case in newspapers, the same argument animated the deliberations during the second national colored convention, held in 1831.[18] There, a resolution recommended that "the Declaration of Independence and Constitution of the United States, be read in our Conventions; believing, that the truths contained in the former are incontrovertible, and that the latter guarantees in letter and spirit to every freeman born in this country, all the rights and immunities of citizenship."[19] The claim to birthright citizenship had gained traction, and Black activists would grow only more resolute.

But without political clout, even the text of much-revered documents could not carry the debate. Black Americans watched as the ground beneath them shifted again and again, even in Northern free-soil states. Slavery was well on its way to being abolished there, yet lawmakers were still excluding Black men from political rights. In New York, for example, a new 1821 state constitution imposed a hefty $250 property qualification on Black voters while it eliminated property requirements for white voters.[20] Pennsylvania disenfranchised Black men altogether in 1838 by a change to its constitution.[21] While being a citizen did not guarantee the vote—white women were citizens without the franchise in this period—the loss of voting rights was a step backward for men who were building a claim to full belonging.

These shifts were preceded by bitter debates among lawmakers, and the lesson was clear: for Black Americans, full citizenship would not come by the ballot. Nor would it come by way of white lawmakers' benevolence. Instead, the only route to national belonging was through organizing and advocacy. Black activists returned to their own conventions, where the ideal of birthright citizenship galvanized them.[22] They asserted that the Constitution recognized "natural born" and naturalized citizens and that U.S. law recognized citizens and aliens but no in-between rank. Birthright had always been the rule, as the Constitution's requirement that the president be a "natural born" citizen suggested.

The idea was a centerpiece of the 1843 colored convention, held in Buffalo. At that year's meeting, Samuel H. Davis, an Oberlin College graduate, minister, and educator, advocated for the recognition of Black Americans as citizens in his keynote address. The U.S. Constitution guaranteed their "happiness in any part of the country," he said, along with "the elective franchise." Davis insisted that "this is our own native land. . . . We love our country, we love our fellow citizens, but *we love liberty more*." He acknowledged that efforts to secure Black citizenship had not yet succeeded. Still, Davis believed that it was up to Black activists alone to win that recognition: "For ourselves and in ourselves there is a mighty work to be accomplished . . . which can come from no other source."[23]

Ten years later, when Frederick Douglass spoke to the Colored National Convention in Rochester, everyone knew that his claim to be a citizen was tenuous. The seeds of doubt sprouted everywhere. In 1850, the newly adopted Fugitive Slave Act had put at risk the liberty of men like Douglass by authorizing federal officials, in collusion with enslavers, to capture fugitives who had escaped slavery. Free Black Americans, without well-defined rights, risked being branded as fugitives, kidnapped, and enslaved. Moreover, the threat still remained of laws that denied Black children public schooling, barred Black men from the polls and skilled vocations, and encouraged the idea that free Black Americans should be removed or colonized.[24] Douglass and the delegates at the 1853 convention knew that anti-Black racism was on the rise.

Citizenship was seen as a remedy to these ills. But in Douglass's audience that year were Black dissidents who had given up on making a future in the United States. Terming themselves emigrationists, they promoted a movement through which Black Americans could choose alternative lives *and* citizenship in Canada or the Caribbean. Among this movement's most forceful advocates was Douglass's former collaborator at *The North Star,* Martin Delany. The two sharply disagreed: Douglass insisted that Black Americans should remain in the United States to win full citizenship, while Delany urged that it was time to pull up stakes and start anew, in Africa or elsewhere.

Douglass and Delany did agree on one principle: they *were* U.S. citizens by birth. Delany's 1852 book, *The Condition, Elevation, Emigration and Destiny of the Colored People of the United States, Politically Considered,* was likely Douglass's primer as he prepared his convention remarks. In that work, Delany urged that it was time to emigrate from the United States. But he never abandoned his claim to citizenship: "We are Americans, having a birthright citizenship—natural claims upon the country—claims common to all others of our fellow citizens—natural rights, which may, by virtue of unjust laws, be obstructed, but never can be annulled." Even as they disagreed about the way forward, Douglass and Delany pieced together a theory of birthright citizenship.[25]

The colored conventions met on the margins of American politics, but the thinking promoted there was echoed in the deliberations of some of the nation's most elevated institutions—including the U.S. Supreme Court. The chief justice of the United States from 1836 to 1864, Roger Brooke Taney, knew well how the aspirations of free Black Americans had been putting pressure on the question of citizenship for years. Back in 1832, as U.S. attorney general, Taney had penned an opinion that denied that Black people were citizens for the purpose of piloting ships along the nation's coastal waters. In the 1840s, in Supreme Court opinions, Taney asserted that Black Americans had no rights as citizens under the U.S. Constitution.

In an 1849 dispute over whether states had the authority to bar the entry of undesirables into their territory—during what were known as "the Passenger Cases"—Taney scoffed at the notion that any state could be *required* to allow free Black people to enter. He went out of his way to point out in his opinion that white citizens had a right to travel between the states—guaranteed by the part of the Constitution that ensured a right to petition the government. For Black Americans, Taney suggested, the Constitution guaranteed nothing.[26]

For Taney, the debate over Black citizenship came to a head in 1857 in *Dred Scott v. Sandford,* brought by an enslaved man in Missouri who claimed to be free. Dred Scott did not plan on claiming citizenship. His foremost concern was winning freedom for himself and his family. In 1846, Scott and his family had faced a crossroads. As enslaved people, they risked being separated and sold to line an owner's pockets. But Scott argued that he was free because he had, with his owner, resided on free soil in Illinois and the Wisconsin territory, today's Minnesota. The family filed a lawsuit in the Missouri state courts and, after losing there, appealed in federal court. This is where the problem of citizenship reared its head. Only if he was a citizen of Missouri could Scott sue in a federal court. When the case arrived at the U.S. Supreme Court, Taney directed his attention to the question that had long plagued Black Americans: Could Scott—and, by implication, any Black American—sue as a citizen of the United States?[27]

The court's decision dealt a blow to the Black American claim to citizenship: Taney ruled that Scott had no right to sue because as an enslaved person, he was not a citizen. Taney then went a step further. No Black American was intended to be a citizen of the United States by the framers. It was a powerful repudiation of the interpretation of the Constitution long promoted by Black activists. The nation's highest court declared that Blackness rendered them unequivocally noncitizens.[28]

But the decision was not unanimous. Associate Justices Benjamin Curtis and John McLean issued written dissents arguing that free Black Americans could be citizens of the United States. Their reasoning echoed that which had been promoted for decades by Black Americans and endorsed by some white abolitionists and even by Republican lawmakers who did not oppose enslavement but did aim to curb its expansion westward.[29] Justice McLean affirmed that all those born in the United States were citizens by birth: "Being born under our Constitution and laws, no naturalization is required, as one of foreign birth, to make him a citizen."[30] When it came to the Constitution and anti-Blackness, McLean quipped, "This is more a matter of taste than of law."[31]

Justice Curtis offered a more thorough analysis, one that aligned directly with the arguments that had been made in the colored conventions: "The free native-born citizens of each State are citizens of the United States [and] as free colored persons born within some of the States are citizens of those States, such persons are also citizens of the United States."[32] Theoretically then, absent any showing that he was not a citizen of Missouri, Scott should be assumed to be a citizen of the United States with a right to bring suit in its courts. As for men like Frederick Douglass, those deemed citizens of the states in which they resided, as Douglass was in New York, were citizens of the United States by virtue of birth.[33]

Justices Curtis and McLean never acknowledged having been influenced by the deliberations of the colored conventions. Still, the force of Black self-defense—which stretched back to the Cuffe brothers in Massachusetts— had pressed the justices, and many other lawmakers, to confront a question they might otherwise have avoided. Whether they were lonely ship pilots, westward migrants, or enslaved people seeking access to a federal forum in which to claim freedom, Black Americans had been insisting for decades that they were citizens of the United States. Were they surprised when the justices echoed their arguments? It is not likely. The official deliberations over Black citizenship let them know that their ideas were being felt, even when they did not win the day.[34]

In subsequent months, when lower federal courts and state courts alike were asked to enforce Taney's conclusions, they balked and then sided with the views expressed by Justices McLean and Curtis. They set aside Taney's brutal conclusion by parsing the language of his opinion, crafting exceptions to the general rule, and drawing a bright line between the authority of federal versus state judges to say who was a citizen. Despite its intent, Taney's conclusion—that Black Americans were not citizens of the United States— went largely unenforced.[35]

Rather than settling the question, *Scott v. Sandford* further fueled debate;

Black activists skipped no opportunity to condemn the decision and never abandoned their claim to be U.S. citizens. Douglass deemed the ruling "an open, glaring, and scandalous tissue of lies." Taney, Douglass urged, "can do many things, but he cannot perform impossibilities. . . . He cannot change the essential nature of things. . . . Man's right to liberty is self-evident." Douglass urged that a new future was still on the horizon: "The glorious birthright of our common humanity, will become the inheritance of all the inhabitants of this highly favored country."[36] As for Taney, he despaired upon realizing that he had failed to settle the debate over Black citizenship.[37] This confrontation of ideas between Douglass and Taney underscored how the battle over the Constitution's meaning extended beyond the issue of slavery: it was also a battle over citizenship itself.

Even before the Civil War's end in 1865, the tide had begun to shift on Black citizenship. The first sign came in November 1862 when Edward Bates, Abraham Lincoln's attorney general, was asked to render an opinion about a Black seaman who'd been discovered commanding a schooner off the coast of New Jersey. Federal law limited that role to citizens of the United States, and attorneys general as far back as William Wirt in the 1820s and Roger Taney in the 1830s, had tried to settle the question. Bates plainly restated the matter: "Who is a citizen? What constitutes a citizen of the United States?" He scoured court decisions and the "action of the different branches of our political government" and discovered no clear answer: "The subject is now as little understood in its details and elements, and the question as open to argument and to speculative criticism, as it was at the beginning of the government."[38]

Bates then broke with the official past and instead echoed the thinking that had emanated from the deliberations of Black activists in the colored conventions. "Every person born in the country is, at the moment of birth, *prima facie* a citizen; and he who would deny it must take upon himself the burden of proving some great disfranchisement strong enough to override the *'natural born'* right as recognized by the Constitution in terms the most simple and comprehensive, and without any reference to race or color, or any other accidental circumstance."[39] Bates did not go so far as to deem enslaved Black people to be citizens, though he did not close the door on that possibility. But in the case of a free Black gentleman from New Jersey, Bates was unequivocal: he could rightly command the vessel in question as a citizen of the United States.[40]

Two years later, the next National Convention of Colored Men met in Syracuse, New York. It was October 1864, fourteen months *before* the Thirteenth

Amendment would abolish slavery, and yet delegates were already at work on questions of freedom and citizenship. The minutes report how Ohio delegate John Mercer Langston argued that with freedom came citizenship, and he reviewed Attorney General Bates's opinion, lauding it as "a complete answer to the arguments and cavils against us."[41] Freedom—the closing of the door on the long, bloody chapter that had been enslavement—was but a first step for men and women who would now remake their worlds and the nation.

In the years that followed, lawmakers transformed the postwar Congress from an ineffectual and muddled body into a staunch promoter of Black citizenship. It was a struggle. In the wake of the Thirteenth Amendment's formal abolition of slavery in 1865, white Southerners got to work on imposing a slavery-like regime on the newly freed people. Congress responded by promulgating the Civil Rights Act of 1866, which opened with a declaration of citizenship as birthright: "All persons born in the United States and not subject to any foreign power, excluding Indians not taxed, are hereby declared to be citizens of the United States." This phrasing acknowledged that most Native peoples were citizens of their own sovereign nations. For Black Americans, now neither race nor color nor "previous condition of slavery or involuntary servitude" disqualified them from claiming new, affirmative rights: "To make and enforce contracts, to sue, be parties, and give evidence, to inherit, purchase, lease, sell, hold, and convey real and personal property, and to full and equal benefit of all laws and proceedings for the security of persons and property, as is enjoyed by white citizens."[42]

For the act to become law, Congress had to organize the two-thirds majority needed to override a veto from President Andrew Johnson, who had decried the act's challenge to white supremacy: "The distinction of race and color is by the bill made to operate in favor of the colored and against the white race." He did not mask what troubled him: the affirmation as citizens of "the Chinese of the Pacific States, Indians subject to taxation, the people called gypsies, as well as the entire race designated as blacks, people of color, Negroes, mulattoes, and persons of African blood." But for the first time, Congress overrode a president in a dispute over major legislation, and birthright citizenship became federal law.[43]

While Congress and the president battled over the Civil Rights Act, Black activists called for Radical Republican legislators to produce what would become the Fourteenth Amendment to the Constitution. Over many months in the winter and spring of 1866, the Joint Committee on Reconstruction wrangled over how to ensure equal protection, due process, and voting rights for Black men. The final amendment consolidated varied measures. It guaranteed to citizens privileges and immunities and to all persons due process and equal protection of the laws; penalized states that denied any male inhabitants the vote; limited the holding of federal offices to those who could take an ironclad oath to having supported the Constitution in the face of the recent rebellion; and repudiated the Confederate debt and barred compensation to former enslavers for the loss of their property in human beings. Finally, it empowered Congress to enforce the amendment.[44]

Only late in its deliberations did the Senate add birthright citizenship to a new first section of the joint committee's amendment: "All persons born or naturalized in the United States, and subject to the jurisdiction thereof, are citizens of the United States and of the State wherein they reside." The principle was by now familiar, mimicking the terms of the Civil Rights Act of 1866. Still, opponents spun out what they deemed to be the clause's regrettable effects: it would transform people of color into the constitutional equals of white Americans. They could not stop approval of the amendment's new birthright provision, but their objections underscored how consequential a transformation it would bring.[45]

The new Fourteenth Amendment put birthright on secure footing—insulating it from the changing winds of politics and the shifting minds of subsequent sessions of Congress. In June 1866, the proposed amendment was sent on to the states for ratification. Most of the former Confederate states refused to ratify. Congress then passed the Reconstruction Act of 1867, which mandated the establishment of new governments in the South, with Black men now eligible to vote and hold office, and required ratification of the Fourteenth Amendment as a condition of readmission into the Union. In just over two years, in July 1868, the requisite twenty-eight states had approved the amendment, and it was ratified. Notably, however, three of the four slaveholding border states that had remained in the Union—Delaware, Maryland, and Kentucky—did not ratify the amendment until years later, in 1901, 1959, and 1976, respectively. Ambivalence about Black citizenship persisted.[46]

When the 1869 National Convention of the Colored Men of America met in Washington, D.C., it did so under new terms. Over four days, men from twenty-one states and the District of Columbia moved between meetings at the Union League Hall and Israel Bethel Church. Among them were luminaries including Frederick Douglass, who was fifty-one years old but had been recognized as a citizen for only five months by the new Fourteenth Amendment. Or perhaps he'd been a citizen for two years, by the terms of the 1866

Civil Rights Act. Douglass was among the more than five million Black Americans who were finally assured their place in the body politic by way of Congress's grand democratizing act.[47]

The new amendment had finally affirmed the principles for which the colored conventions—dozens of them over nearly four decades—had stood: Black Americans were citizens of the United States by virtue of birthright. That and nothing more made them equals to all other Americans. Those who had instigated the 1869 meeting rooted their urgings in an expansive view of the Fourteenth Amendment: "Surely, citizenship . . . carries with it the rights of citizens." That, they insisted, included the right to vote.[48]

Delegates knew that while a guarantee of citizenship was a milestone, they would need to breathe meaning into their new status. What, they asked, did sweeping phrases such as "equal protection" and "due process" mean? While the Civil War and Reconstruction seemed to establish the unassailable belonging of Black Americans, persistent discrimination and organized violence required that they exercise renewed vigilance. In a short time, convention-goers had already become veterans of struggles over landownership, labor conditions, family autonomy, mobility, public education, and armed self-defense.

The roll call of delegates reflected the new, far-ranging reach of Black politics, with activists from Northern states—Frederick Douglass of New York, John Mercer Langston of Ohio, George Downing of Rhode Island, and George Hackett of Maryland—joined by those from the South: George Mabson of North Carolina, James Simms of Georgia, Hales Ellsworth of Alabama, and P.B.S. Pinchback of Louisiana. But not all delegates were seated easily. Helen Johnson of Allegheny City, Pennsylvania, met with objections from Fields Cook of Virginia, who "understood the call for this Convention to be expressly for colored men." Henry Jerome Brown of Maryland favored seating Johnson, and reportedly argued that "this was a progressive age, and that women would yet have a vote." Johnson was seated and John Willis Menard of Louisiana cautioned the men about what it meant to wield new power as citizens: The "greatest lever in their way was in themselves. . . . They had but one voice in the South, and that was to know no distinctions of color or sex." With citizenship came the grand challenge of showing the way forward on how women fit into the ideals of universal rights.[49]

The deliberations eventually turned to voting rights—this was, delegates agreed, an essential instrument in the ongoing struggle for equal protection and due process. They resolved to demand an additional constitutional amendment, one that would go beyond the Fourteenth Amendment's penalty for states that denied voting rights. Black activists aimed to win a guarantee of access to the ballot box. As the convention discussions wrapped up, members organized into delegations and headed out from the meeting hall, crossing the nation's capital to lobby federal officials about what freedom and citizenship should entail—which, they believed, included access to the polls.[50]

Isaiah Weir from Philadelphia spoke for his committee of men from Rhode Island, Maryland, Georgia, the District of Columbia, Illinois, Mississippi, and Pennsylvania when they appeared before the House Judiciary Committee to "claim, from this nation, protection in the exercise of all political rights belonging to us as American citizens." Weir invoked the Declaration of Independence to suggest that they were men prepared "to assume among the powers of the earth, the separate and equal station to which the Laws of Nature and Nature's God entitle them." He drew upon the Constitution: "We, the people" had delegated to the federal government the obligation to "secure the blessings of liberty" for all Americans. Voting rights, which had long been controlled by the states, must now be a matter of federal concern. Individual states might try to reject Black men as voters, and Congress was obliged to override those race-based barriers. This was, in Weir's view, required by the Thirteenth Amendment's promise of freedom and the Fourteenth Amendment's guarantee of citizenship: "Suffrage cannot be extended as a gratuity." The vote belonged to Black men, and it was Congress's job to ensure that no one kept them from it.[51]

In a matter of weeks, at the end of February 1869, Congress sent the Fifteenth Amendment to the states for ratification: "The right of citizens of the United States to vote shall not be denied or abridged by the United States or by any State on account of race, color, or previous condition of servitude." President Ulysses Grant endorsed the change. States in New England and the Midwest came on board easily. Congress held the key to readmission to the Union for those Confederate states that had not yet been readmitted and, as with the Fourteenth Amendment, made ratification a condition of statehood. Black men were citizens and the Constitution now protected their votes.[52]

Frederick Douglass knew, of course, that no constitutional amendment alone would settle the long struggles over national belonging. He understood that the pernicious tentacles of racism extended beyond his immediate constituency of Black Americans. In an 1867 lecture, composed the year before the Fourteenth Amendment was ratified, he had directed attention to related questions about the belonging of Chinese immigrants and their children. His position was unequivocal: they too must be made citizens. "Would you," he asked, "have them naturalized, and have them invested with all the rights of

American Citizenship? *I would*." Douglass then plunged into a broader debate: "I want a home here not only for the negro, the mulatto and the Latin races, but I want the Asiatic to find a home here in the United States, and feel at home here, both for his sake and for ours."[53]

Douglass was prophetic. In 1870, Congress for the first time opened the possibility of citizenship by naturalization to immigrants of African descent, but it declined to do the same for immigrants from China. In the 1880s, Chinese immigrants and their children found their standing in the United States sharply undercut by a series of exclusion acts that limited their entry and mobility in ways that echoed the Black laws that had decades before restricted free Black Americans. And in 1895 a man of Chinese descent born in the city of San Francisco, Wong Kim Ark, found himself detained in his home city's port, refused entry by federal officials who deemed him a noncitizen. Officials there regarded men like Wong indelibly foreign by virtue of their parents' status as noncitizen Chinese immigrants. It was a devastating deviation from the birthright principle. Only after the 1898 Supreme Court ruling in Wong Kim Ark's case was it clear that Chinese Americans also enjoyed the same birthright protections that Black people had fought for decades to enshrine.[54]

The colored conventions continued their work into the last decade of the nineteenth century. Even with questions about freedom and citizenship settled, giving meaning to these principles required vigilance. And in the years following the defeat of Reconstruction's period of interracial governance, a push for white rule in the South—in politics, business, and everyday life—surged. Onetime federal allies of Black equality—the Supreme Court and Congress included—backed away from their commitments to a democracy led by Black and white men alike.

The last national colored convention on record was held in 1893. There, gathered in Cincinnati, Ohio, some five hundred Black activists upheld a tradition that had begun more than six decades earlier. Delegates stood firm in their belief that they were full and equal citizens before the Constitution. They decried the outrages of the day, including the rise of lynching. They were again among the despised. But now, as citizens, they were more fully equipped to demand that the nation live up to its ideals.[55]

January 1, 1863

Abraham Lincoln issues the Emancipation Proclamation, and Americans gather all over the country to hear it read aloud. One notable gathering is at Camp Saxton, a garrison of Union troops established on a former plantation near Port Royal, South Carolina, two years earlier. Camp Saxton is home to one of the first Black military brigades, the 1st South Carolina Volunteer Infantry Regiment, under the command of Colonel Thomas Wentworth Higginson, a well-known white abolitionist and Unitarian minister. The camp also draws various abolitionists and missionaries to educate and minister to the formerly enslaved people, including Charlotte Forten, a Black abolitionist from Philadelphia, and Seth Rogers, a white doctor and friend of Colonel Higginson's from Boston who was the regiment's surgeon.

The Camp

Darryl Pinckney

Imagine the scene I cannot write. The Colonel steps on to the platform, reciting to himself: "I'll tell you how the sun rose, a ribbon at a time." It is New Year's Day. The President has signed the historic war measure.

The Colonel was not alone in his feeling that after the disgrace of Bull Run, the Union needed to take Port Royal Island, and after the slaughter at Fredericksburg, Port Royal needed this convocation. White women in bonnets and white men in vests crowd the platform. The Colonel studies the 1st South Carolina Volunteers arrayed before him. It is the first black unit.

The men adore campfires, spelling books, and tobacco, but none of them drink. Most have freed themselves. Take a ride on a federal gunboat and join the Cause. A bayonet for a pick, a rifle for a spade. The Colonel told state senators in Rhode Island and newspaper editors in New York City that freedmen in attack on rebel breastworks make the war to save the Union an anti-slavery war. McClellan lost command. The might of Lincoln's arithmetic abides: the Union plus two hundred thousand black warriors will equal liberty. Visitors admire the decoration of the quarters. The wall is covered in variously colored shells. Everywhere, the Colonel sees black women in their Sunday kerchiefs. God's blessings are on dress parade.

The Colonel hands "Final Emancipation Proclamation" to a penitent white man who used to be called Master over in Beaufort. The Colonel said "Oof" when he first got his copy. The orderly's breathing told him that he, too, had read the Proclamation, had felt power naked, actual-armed-rebellion naked, suppressing-said-rebellion naked, shall-be-free naked, maintain-freedom-of-said-persons naked.

The prayer is over. The former Master of cotton is no orator, but the

Colonel is where power and freedom are forging God's naked sword. He
marvels at the Lord's invention, the sheer darkness of his men. Is it not
glorious to be handsome.

The Colonel is ready to receive the regimental colors. Not far away
enough from the parade, ten oxen revolve on spits. It is not the moment for
the Colonel to be reminded by his senses that he has had nothing to eat. He
has been too full of history to dare more than barrel water in his palms.
The Colonel fights to remain in this sacred place where every heart desires
the same thing. He receives the regimental colors and is wrapped again
in the honor of their assault on rebel transports on the St. Marys River
without the loss of a man. Beyond the live oaks another steamer arrives on
the blue water.

Seated nearby are the camp's brilliant Surgeon and its most beautiful
Schoolteacher, the Colonel's friends from home, Boston. It is not that she is
a black woman and he a white man. A free black woman whose family is
richer than either of theirs, the Colonel did not say, thanks to her famous
grandfather, Revolutionary War hero, owner of a big sailmaking company in
Philadelphia. The Surgeon's Quaker beard is shining and the Schoolteacher's
head is uncovered.

The Surgeon reads his wife's letters to the Schoolteacher. How very good
and noble he is, she has merrily cried to the Colonel. The Colonel's wife is
an invalid and the Surgeon's wife is plain. The Schoolteacher is an unfair
quadroon beauty. Her family knows William Lloyd Garrison, and Whittier
writes futile poems to her and her abolitionist sisters. She abandoned her
novels in French and verses in Latin to come south and teach the freed
people of Port Royal. She is so popular some days one hundred pupils of all
ages block the door and two windows of the church that is her schoolroom.
He has heard her call it Calathumpian, the noise members of the 1st South
Carolina Volunteers make when they pull her battered carriage uphill from
the landing as though she were their princess. She and the Surgeon love to
talk of their love for horses, moonlight, and the Cause.

The Colonel is ready to receive the Union flag. He cannot help it. He
regards the Schoolteacher. No one is afraid of her. Whatever she thinks to do
is proper. This is war, the Colonel reflects. The Surgeon knows she writes
poetry. He would have to go back to South America. He was from Vermont.
He was anti-slavery as a child. He came home one day and told his family so.
He'd told both him and the Schoolteacher that story, on the same afternoon,
back in Boston.

The Colonel has the flag in the silence. He slowly waves it, thinking this is the first time it may hold true meaning for them. An elderly black voice begins to sing, *My Country, 'tis of thee . . .* A few black women add their voices. Suddenly, many. The Colonel quiets the white people so that only black people are singing.

The Schoolteacher continues to sing, and so does the Surgeon. *Of thee I sing.*

The camp is always full of music, melancholy tunes in twilight, softer songs in the sentry dark, rising-up songs even before reveille, and sometimes teamster work songs during the day. Unforgettable hymns on a Sunday. But this is different. The difference makes the Colonel close his eyes. The words become long and low. *Let freedom ring.* The Colonel drifts through oxen-scented air and a son of Massachusetts can hear crickets and mockingbirds on New Year's Day.

Male and female voices divide into harmonies. They don't allow the music to trail off. The mass choir raises the last note and then drops it, like that barbershop over on Morris Island where the free black man refused to shave the contraband alongside white men. Black soldiers gathered, many, weary of being contraband. They picked up the free black man's establishment and unhanded it.

Many people are in tears; a ruffian on a tree limb puts his chin down on his knee. The Colonel takes a slow salute. They will to the utmost maintain the freedom of said persons. Tonight there will be rockets. Let everyone be a weapon in the days to come.

Everyone around them has risen. The Schoolteacher and the Surgeon take no note. She is chafing her hands, her gloves are in her lap, on her bonnet. Her hair is coming loose, she is speaking so fast. The Colonel steps down into the wind. He can guess. The Schoolteacher tells the Surgeon about the dreams that have stayed with her, dreams that have changed her ideas, ever after.

It is time. Applause and a cheer say the feast is prepared. These dreams have gone through her and through her, he does, indeed, hear her almost sing to the Surgeon. Like wine through water. She does not look up. One dream has forever altered the color of her mind. She does not look up. The Colonel can see it. The Surgeon is thinking how sweetly she must smile in her sleep.

The Colonel is upon them and pulls the Surgeon up to his true height, bowing to the Schoolteacher as her bonnet returns to such hair. The Colonel escorts them into the crowd.

We of the 1st South Carolina Volunteers have no ill feelings toward you, we have no prejudice against color, and like white people just as well as black, if they behave as well.

The Colonel's men roar in approval at his words. He does not walk between his friends from Boston. She, ravishing, he, tightly buttoned, delightful as always in their love that needs him. The Colonel leads them toward the smoky tree line, his Abelard and his Héloïse and their Cause.

July 30, 1866

A white mob consisting of many Confederate veterans attacks protesters outside a convention in New Orleans, which has been called by Republican leaders in response to the state legislature's passage of a law denying African Americans the right to vote. Among those killed in the ensuing violence is Anthony Paul Dostie, a white abolitionist who led the march on the convention. The mob also kills more than thirty-five other people, mostly Black men. National outrage over the violence helps lead to Republicans gaining control of both houses of Congress in that year's midterm elections.

An Absolute Massacre

ZZ Packer

The bodies all around began to cook and swell in the heat: fingers the size of pickles, forearms rising like loaves until as big and gamy as hams festering in the noontime sun. When the secesh police began their rounds, Lazarus got to crouching, then creeping, until—at last—he had to lie down among the dead, coffining himself between two fallen neighbors, readying himself for the shot to the head.

Just hours earlier, all of colored New Orleans in their finest had come out: veterans from the Louisiana Native Guard had amassed at the procession's front, joined by one or more bands that began to blaze and bray their trumpets and trombones once struck up by some hidden concertmaster. Seamstresses, maids, cooks, bricklayers, and longshoremen: they'd all come out at the behest of Roudanez, owner of the Black folks' paper, as well as Dostie, the Radical Republican dentist Democrats declared a race traitor and nigger lover. The white Republicans could not get votes over the Confederate Democrats without colored men, nor could the colored men get the vote without the whites who fought against the Confederate Redeemer cause.

"Thirty-four niggers dead," Lazarus heard someone say while he played possum. "And that fella Dostie."

Such a pus and rot he'd never smelled before. Needling choruses of gallinippers hiving above yards of bursting flesh. Rodents hurrying forth with their ratchet scratching at wounds. Midges inspecting tonsils on display. Then there was the nearly silent sound of worms at work, underworld missionaries unsewing men from their souls.

It wasn't until three o'clock that the military finally came and gave orders as to what should be done. The wounded were to go to the Freedmen's Hospital, which had once been Marine Hospital; the dead were to lie out in the hundred-degree heat until another wagon became available; and there was to be martial law for the rest of the night, lasting who knew until when.

The ride to the Freedmen's Hospital killed a few who weren't yet dead. A jolting ride over cobblestones, banquettes, undone roads, bricks from the riot left in the middle of the street, while the whole hospital was filled with big moans, the smell of grease and camphor, wet wool and kerosene.

They rolled him onto a flat cot, then put yet another man on top of him and jostled them both through a dark corridor. The blood from the man on top of him seeped into Lazarus's eyes, ran in thin tickling trickles into his ears, clumped in thick waxy clots in his nose, his hair.

It scared him to death to be so in the dark, and try as he might to push the dead man off him, he could not. They carried him into a room, a place that was even more foul-smelling than the stench of bodies swelling in the sun. When his cot passed the threshold, the men who'd been carrying it dropped it, sending the dead man falling to the floor, only the sound didn't sound like Lazarus expected it to, but more like a clank and clatter, as though the heavy doors of an armoire or chifforobe had been banged shut. The men who'd been holding the cot retched, one, then the other.

A young man holding a Colt revolver, c. 1860–70   LIBRARY OF CONGRESS

CHAPTER 9

Self-Defense

CAROL ANDERSON

One night in February 2014, Jessie Murray, Jr., was with his wife at a bar on Old Dixie Highway in Jonesboro, Georgia, just twelve miles from downtown Atlanta. It may have been the twenty-first century, but it felt more like good ol' Dixie to Murray, who is African American and was being harassed by a group of four or five drunken white men. They were loud, obnoxious, and rude and didn't seem to like it that Murray's wife, Tracie, was white. They bumped into the couple, interrupting their conversation. One of the men, Nathan Adams, allegedly told Jessie not to get near him again. Finally, Murray left Tracie at the bar and went to get his gun.[1] He knew he needed to get her out of there, and he figured he might need protection to do so. Returning from his car, he was approaching the door of the bar when suddenly the white men surrounded him and fist after fist after fist pounded his face. It's not entirely clear what happened next, but when the unforgettable sound of gunfire shattered the air, the fighting stopped. Adams, who turned out to be a former police officer, was dead.[2]

Murray, with blood streaming down his black skin, knew that he had responded in self-defense.[3] And he knew that, as an American, he had a right to do so. Like a lot of states, Georgia had adopted a Stand Your Ground law, crafted by the National Rifle Association during the 2000s. The law gave a person the right, when faced with a perceived threat, to be "justified in using force which is intended or likely to cause death or great bodily harm only if he or she reasonably believes that such force is necessary to prevent death or great bodily injury to himself or herself or a third person or to prevent the commission of a forcible felony."[4] It also eliminated the previous requirement to retreat from danger if threatened, which was supposed to make lethal violence the last resort, not the first. Stand Your Ground laws, however, were designed to keep gun owners who shot someone from having to face criminal charges and to ensure that their actions were presumed legally justifiable as the starting point for any investigation.[5] The laws were buttressed in 2008 and 2010, when the U.S. Supreme Court struck down strict gun-control laws in Washington, D.C., and Chicago on the grounds that a *"central component"* of the Second Amendment was "the inherent right of self-defense."[6]

The Court could have gone back even further than that. The United States has long embraced a legal tradition rooted in seventeenth-century English common law, which established the "castle doctrine": if one's home was invaded, the owner had the right to ward off the intruder.[7] The Enlightenment philosopher John Locke laid out what the legal scholar David B. Kopel describes as "the natural right of self-defense . . . the natural right to control and protect one's body and property."[8] But as Jessie Murray would soon find out, this natural right is not universal—and has never been.

In the colonial era, Black people, whether enslaved or free, were explicitly prevented from carrying weapons or defending themselves against white violence.[9] The Second Amendment of the Bill of Rights granted citizens of the new country the right to bear arms in order to provide for a "well regulated militia." But the enslaved were not considered citizens, and in most states, even free Black people struggled to exercise their citizenship rights. The citizenship of free Black people was so contested that a series of laws, judicial decisions, and policies culminated in the 1857 *Dred Scott* U.S. Supreme Court decision, which asserted that Black people had never been citizens of the United States; if they were, Chief Justice Roger Taney wrote, they would have the right "to keep and carry arms wherever they went."[10] Moreover, in the South, which had large enslaved populations, everyone understood that one of the purposes of the Second Amendment's "well regulated militia" was to suppress uprisings of the enslaved. Though it did not explicitly say so, the Second Amendment was motivated in large part by a need for the new federal government to assure white people in the South that they would be able to defend themselves against Black people.

This was codified in a number of state laws in the antebellum period; these were supported by a series of court decisions, such as an 1843 case in Maryland that described free Black people as "a dangerous population" that could not have access to guns even to defend their religious gatherings from attack.[11] The 1846 *Nunn* decision by the Georgia Supreme Court ruled that a law curtailing open carrying of guns for white people violated the Second Amendment's "*natural* right of self defence"[12] but kept in place an 1833 law banning free Black people from carrying any type of gun whatsoever.[13]

In the modern era, gun violence most often occurs within racial groups, and state self-defense laws aren't explicitly racist in the ways those in the colonial and antebellum periods were. But when interracial violence does occur, these laws can end up protecting white people—but leaving Black people vulnerable to white violence. You don't have to look any further than the infamous case of George Zimmerman and Trayvon Martin. In 2012, in Sanford, Florida, Zimmerman, a twenty-eight-year-old white Hispanic man, called 911 as he stalked Martin, a Black teenager, through a gated community. Zimmerman, who was carrying a loaded nine-millimeter pistol, had previously made repeated calls to 911 about Black men in the neighborhood. He ignored the instructions from the 911 operator not to follow the teen, claiming that Martin looked "suspicious," that his type "always get away." He ultimately put a bullet in Martin's chest. Although Zimmerman was the one with the gun and Martin was unarmed, the trial judge framed the jury's instructions around the tenets of Stand Your Ground: Zimmerman could use deadly force if the disparities in the physical capabilities between him and Martin caused the gunman to fear for his life. The jury ruled that the killer had acted in self-defense.[14]

Two years later, as Jessie Murray stood in a Jonesboro parking lot with a dead white man at the end of his gun, Georgia's Stand Your Ground law was some comfort. But that evaporated as soon as the police arrested Murray and charged him with felony murder. At his trial, the very rock of his defense crumbled as the judge, Albert Collier, dismissed the Stand Your Ground defense. He ruled that because the gun had gone off accidentally, it was impossible to claim that Murray had been standing his ground; in other words, one could not accidentally stand one's ground. Second, and equally important, Collier explained, Murray clearly couldn't have felt threatened by the white men who were beating on him. Those men were not doing anything to make Murray "reasonably believe that deadly force was necessary to prevent death or great bodily injury to himself or a third party."[15] Before the trial was over, Murray had pleaded guilty to a weapons charge and been sentenced to five years' probation.

The difference between the Zimmerman and Murray cases exposes the harsh reality that even in the modern era, the enforcement of self-defense laws varies widely according to race. Like many previous such laws, Stand Your Ground depends on the perception of threat, and research shows that

Black people are often linked with danger in the minds of white people. In her 2019 book *Biased*, the Stanford University psychology professor Jennifer Eberhardt shows that African Americans are consistently perceived as a threat.[16] In one 2004 study, she and her colleagues cued subjects with pictures of African American faces, white faces, or no facial images at all, then progressively unblurred images of various objects, including weapons, and asked them to identify what they saw. The results found that subjects more quickly identified the weapons when cued with Black faces than they did when prompted with white faces. Eberhardt summarizes this study, noting "the stereotypic association between blacks and crime influences not only how we see black people but how we see guns."[17] Another set of studies, this one from Phillip Atiba Goff, a psychologist now at Yale, documents how Black boys are perceived as older and less innocent than white boys of the same age.[18] Finally, the research of Anthony Greenwald, a University of Washington psychologist, reveals how in computer simulations, Black people are more likely to be shot than white people who dress and act similarly.[19] This may be why, as shown in study after study, white people are decidedly more successful in invoking Stand Your Ground as a defense than are African Americans.[20]

Stand Your Ground laws are only the latest form of self-defense legislation to be applied unequally. Since the nation's founding, our legal and political architecture has privileged the safety and self-defense of white people over that of Black people. As a consequence, the right to self-defense, so quintessential to American identity, has been experienced unequally by Black and white people. White people continue to use self-defense laws to protect themselves from perceived harm from African Americans; Black people often cannot use self-defense to protect themselves from actual harm by white people.

The results have been devastating.

The War of Independence against Britain revealed the colonies' widespread fear of arming Black people, and the differences between the North and the South in this regard. During the first few years of the war, the colonies banned Black people from joining the Continental Army. The pressure of a series of British victories and the ongoing and worsening reluctance of white men to enlist finally compelled a number of states in the North to offer freedom to their enslaved men in exchange for military service.[21] But the Southern states, with vastly greater populations of enslaved people, were not so moved. Virginia agreed that free Black people could join the army, but the last thing they wanted was to give weapons to all those enslaved Black men they were hold-ing against their will. Even when faced with overwhelming British force, the Southern states resisted arming enslaved people.

After the British occupied Georgia and seized Savannah, they set their sights on South Carolina. In November 1779, the state had only 750 white men available to fend off the attack.[22] George Washington sent an emissary to Charleston to ask the state to arm thousands of the enslaved people who lived there to fight off the British. This request would be one of many. South Carolina resisted. Washington's people kept pressing. Exasperated by years of pressure from Washington's military commanders, in 1782, Edward Rut-ledge, the former governor's brother, reported, "We have had another hard Battle on the Subject of arming the Blacks. . . . I do assure you I was very much alarmed."[23] Despite the pleas, despite the British overrunning Charles-ton, the South Carolina government flat out refused to enlist the enslaved. The state's leaders said they would rather surrender to the British (and take their chances with the king as traitors) than to see those whom they held cap-tive armed.[24]

The Patriots prevailed, but that chasm between the protection of slavery at all costs and the creation of an independent nation predicated on the princi-ple of equality would bedevil the founders. In 1787 in Philadelphia, at what would later be called the Constitutional Convention, James Madison and a group of fifty-four delegates came together to unite a federation of disparate states on the brink of collapse under one Constitution and to create a much stronger central government.

This would not be easy. Madison recognized that though all the delegates were determined to create a viable nation, there were two divergent agendas under the surface. The Deep South was intent on strengthening the slavehold-ers' power and protecting the institution of slavery. Meanwhile, the other del-egates were motivated by a variety of moral, economic, and philosophical reasons. The asymmetry allowed the dream of the United States of America to be held hostage to the tyrannical aims of enslavers.[25]

When, for example, Gouverneur Morris, who represented Pennsylvania, blasted the Atlantic slave trade as "cruel" and "in defiance of the most sacred laws of humanity," John Rutledge of South Carolina issued an extortionist warning about any attempt to curtail it: "If the Convention thinks that North Carolina, South Carolina, and Georgia will ever agree to the plan [for a Con-stitution] unless their right to import slaves [from Africa] be untouched, the expectation is vain."[26] Those threats worked to secure twenty additional years of the Atlantic slave trade, the Three-fifths Clause, and the Fugitive Slave

Clause. And they left a lasting impression on James Madison about how fragile the tendons were that bound the United States of America together.[27]

When it came time to debate federal control of state militias, the issue initially didn't draw much fire. The proposed constitutional language gave Congress the power "to provide for organizing, arming, and disciplining the militia," and deploying the various state militias in service to the United States to deal with invasions and insurrections.[28] After the militia clauses made it into the draft, however, the trouble started with just a few days remaining in the Constitutional Convention. The strongest objection came from the Anti-Federalists—in both the North and the South—who rejected the idea of a stronger central government. They argued against congressional control of the militia, believing that it was the pathway to a standing army, tyranny, and the destruction of democracy.[29]

Initially, the Federalists, like James Madison, prevailed. They had seen the ineffectiveness of the state militias during the War of Independence and believed that strong federal control was necessary. This was codified in Article 1, Section 8, Clauses 15 and 16, which gave Congress the power to summon for battle and organize the state militias.[30] But as Pauline Maier notes in *Ratification,* Madison also explained, as a sop to the South, that the militia clause in the Constitution "gave the states a 'supplementary security' by allowing Congress to enlist the help of other states in suppressing insurrections (including slave uprisings) or resisting invasions."[31]

But Madison's assurances did not mollify the Southern Anti-Federalists as they geared up for the state ratification conventions. For them, the state militias had a very specific purpose. They were key to crushing revolts by enslaved people and buttressing enforcement of the slave codes, laws that maintained the racial hierarchy by banning Black people's access to firearms, literacy, and unfettered movement. Southern delegates worried that placing control of the militias in the hands of Congress was risky because the federal government could decide not to fund or arm the state militias. In this situation, white people would be defenseless against those they enslaved, an unthinkable proposition. This anxiety was driven in part by arguments that had been made during the Constitutional Convention by delegates from the North, such as Gouverneur Morris, who questioned the morality of forcing militias from the North, where numerous states had begun to legally end slavery, to travel south to crush enslaved people's freedom rebellions.[32]

The Southern Anti-Federalists' angst became more apparent as each state brought the document to its ratifying convention. In some, a dangerous movement of resistance to the Constitution began to emerge. By early 1788, the progress toward ratification was grinding to a halt.[33] George Washington raised the alarm and insisted that Madison go to Richmond and use his persuasive powers to bring Virginia into the fold.[34] In June, Madison and 169 others gathered at a convention in Virginia with ratification of the Constitution hanging in the balance.

Madison quickly discovered that the hero of the American Revolution Patrick Henry and George Mason, another prominent enslaver, stood in the way. They strenuously objected that Madison had put control and arming of the militia in the hands of a federal government dominated by Northern states, such as Pennsylvania and Massachusetts, that had already begun to end slavery. Henry and Mason made clear that this equivocation on human bondage meant that the central government could not be trusted with authority over the militia. The question hanging in the air at Virginia's ratifying convention, as the historian David Waldstreicher notes in his book *Slavery's Constitution*, was: "What would keep a Congress dominated by Northerners from refusing to defend the state from a slave rebellion?"[35] Mason predicted that the enslavers would be left "defenseless," according to the legal scholar Michael Waldman.[36] "They'll take your niggers from you," Patrick Henry warned the members of the Virginia legislature.[37] "Slavery is detested" in the North, he fulminated.[38] In the end, Virginia narrowly ratified the Constitution but only with amendments, including the right to "a well regulated militia," based on the 1776 Virginia Declaration of Rights.[39]

Only a few days earlier, New Hampshire had ratified the Constitution, making it the nation's official charter.[40] But three of the thirteen colonies had yet to ratify, and even some of those that did, like Virginia, made clear that they were doing so with reservations. In fact, many were clamoring to rewrite the Constitution in a new national meeting. Henry and his allies were also calling for a Bill of Rights to rein in the power of the federal government and give more authority to the states. They specifically wanted the language about the militia to limit how long state forces would be under national control and to place strict rules on how Congress would use the state militia.[41] In other words, they did not want to be left defenseless.[42]

The intense anger that erupted in Richmond during the ratifying convention would push Madison to take a different tack in future negotiations. Over the next few months, as he ran for Congress, Madison decided that he needed to quell the discontent by crafting a Bill of Rights that would mollify the Anti-Federalists and enslavers, yet still leave the national government's power in place.

After his electoral victory, Madison set out during the First Congress to craft a Bill of Rights. With everything at stake, he was like a man possessed. Congressman Theodore Sedgwick of Massachusetts thought Madison was so fixated on a Bill of Rights because he was "constantly haunted by the ghost of Patrick Henry," who had made it so clear at Virginia's ratifying convention that he could not abide the idea that the federal government would control the militia. Pennsylvania senator Robert Morris was also convinced that whatever had happened at the convention had made Madison "so cursedly frightened . . . that he dreamed of amendments ever since."[43]

The Bill of Rights, which focused on the limits of federal power, shut down the phalanx of opposition to the Constitution. The Second Amendment, in particular, which declared, "A well regulated Militia, being necessary to the security of a free State, the right of the people to keep and bear Arms, shall not be infringed," short-circuited Mason's, Henry's, and other Southerners' worries "that the federal government would, in one way or another, render the militia impotent as a slave control device."[44] The scholar Carl T. Bogus writes in a law review article, "The Hidden History of the Second Amendment":

> As a Virginian, Madison knew that the militia's prime function in his state, and throughout the South, was slave control. His use of the word 'security' [in the Second Amendment] is consistent with his writing the amendment for the specific purpose of assuring the Southern states, and particularly his constituents in Virginia, that the federal government would not undermine their security against slave insurrection by disarming the militia.[45]

The Second Amendment, ratified in 1791, codified for white citizens the right to bear arms and to protect themselves. If there were any doubts about who these rights pertained to, they were put to rest in 1800, when Virginia governor James Monroe called out several regiments of the state's militia to thwart, before it could begin, a widespread revolt planned by an enslaved man named Gabriel, and then to hunt him and the other participants down. As the historian Herbert Aptheker wrote in "American Negro Slave Revolts," as word of Gabriel's revolt spread, the "nation, from Massachusetts to Mississippi, was terror-stricken."[46] The response was to double down and make more explicit through legislation the prohibitions on Black people owning guns.[47] One Virginian wrote in the local newspaper that "we must re-enact all those rigorous laws which experience has proved necessary to keep [slavery] within bounds. In a word, if we will keep a ferocious monster in our country, we must keep him in chains."[48]

———

A little more than a decade before the Constitution was written, John Adams had worried that the colonies were so different, especially the ones with agriculturally based economies dependent on enslaved labor, that "it would be a Miracle, if Such heterogeneous Ingredients did not at first produce violent Fermentations."[49] The uneasy union he had anticipated between the North and the South started to crack not long after it was forged. The slaveholding states demanded greater Northern complicity in maintaining human bondage, threatening secession unless Congress passed laws that made it the responsibility of others to return those who fled enslavement. The Fugitive Slave Act of 1850, in particular, meant that even Black people who were born free, or had managed to buy their freedom or escape slavery, had no legal right to that freedom and limited legal means to defend themselves. But many in the North hated these laws and often refused to comply.[50] It was this tension that led to an unusual situation in the small town of Christiana, Pennsylvania, where for a rare moment Black people were allowed to defend themselves.

Pennsylvania had begun a gradual process of abolition in 1780. Christiana was in Lancaster County, which bordered Maryland, a state that allowed slavery. A small community of Quakers and free Black people, some of whom were fugitives, lived in Christiana. Black people had come together to create a self-defense community to fight off anyone trying to bring them back to bondage.[51] In September 1851, an enslaver from across the state line in Maryland, Edward Gorsuch, went up to Christiana to retrieve his human property, four men who had fled north.[52] He brought along his son, his nephew, and a U.S. marshal, all of whom found themselves in a pitched battle with residents armed with pistols and farm equipment. Surrounded by approximately eighty Black people wielding whatever kinds of weapons they could find, Gorsuch was killed and his son and his nephew wounded. The marshal fled the scene, looking for safety.[53]

After the killing, although some of the Black residents of Christiana escaped to Canada, authorities rounded up a group of others, including a white man, Castner Hanway, and charged them with treason. In the eyes of the state, violating the Fugitive Slave Act of 1850 was the equivalent of waging war against the United States. In his opening statement, the prosecutor did admit that the law was "obnoxious." But he patiently laid out how the group at Christiana, overwhelmingly Black with a smattering of white people, had knowledge of the statute and had refused to aid the U.S. marshal in capturing Gorsuch's runaways.

The judge's instructions to the jury, however, emphasized that those in what would be called the Battle of Christiana were just trying "to protect one another from what they termed kidnappers." Slave catchers, the judge told the jury, had invaded homes and snatched people away, and it didn't matter if they were "a free man or a slave." This "odious" business, spurred by the greed of rewards, had driven Black people to "resist . . . aggressions." This wasn't about treason; this was about self-defense compelled by an unjust law. In fact, after that clear repudiation of the Fugitive Slave Act, no one was ever convicted for Edward Gorsuch's death or the wounding of his son and his nephew.[54] The *Republican and Daily Argus of Baltimore* railed that Gorsuch's murder "remains unatoned for and unavenged."[55]

Shortly after the verdict, a slave catcher, Thomas McCreary from Elkton, Maryland, came across state lines into Chester County, near Christiana, and snatched a ten-year-old free Black girl named Elizabeth Parker. He gagged her and sold her to a slave broker in Baltimore, who shipped her to New Orleans to be enslaved in the Deep South.[56] McCreary then came back and grabbed her sister Rachel, who worked for a white farmer named Joseph Miller. Miller witnessed the kidnapping from afar and took off in hot pursuit. He and a group of his neighbors followed McCreary into Maryland to rescue Rachel. Instead, Miller was taken, tortured, poisoned with arsenic, and hanged. His body was found days later, strung up in a tree.[57] *Frederick Douglass' Paper* stated that the kidnapping scheme was a plot by "blood-thirsty Marylanders" to lure Pennsylvania abolitionists across the state line, where they could "wreak their vengeance upon them without mercy."[58] And without justice. A judge dismissed the kidnapping charge against McCreary, and Miller's killers were never arrested.[59] The judicial proceeding echoed like a tit-for-tat retaliation: Miller for Gorsuch, freedom for slavery.

In the 1860s, the "violent Fermentations" that John Adams had predicted erupted into the Civil War, leading to emancipation and the resulting amendments that ended slavery and codified citizenship for African Americans. This was not freedom given; this was freedom earned. Some 179,000 Black men, 10 percent of the Union army, fought in the war. An additional 19,000 served in the navy.[60] Black women participated too, most notably one well-armed conductor on the Underground Railroad, Harriet Tubman; a Union spy, she led as many as 300 Black soldiers in destroying a Confederate supply depot on the Combahee River on June 2, 1863.[61] The legal status African Americans had fought hard for should have provided the standing to "protect one's body and property" that had not been available to Black people before.[62] But this is not what happened.

Shortly after the war, President Andrew Johnson granted amnesty to many in the Confederate leadership. Free from the threat of the gallows for committing treason, these white men—such as General Benjamin Humphreys, who had fought against the Union at the Battle of Gettysburg and then became governor of Mississippi—assumed positions in the newly formed state governments and passed legislation known as the Black Codes. These laws were designed to reinstall something close to slavery. They required African Americans to sign a yearly labor contract to work for a white employer, blocked their ability to testify in court against a white person, and banned freedpeople's access to and ownership of guns under the threat of a public whipping of thirty-nine lashes.[63]

African Americans pushed back. Many had held on to their wartime firearms and resisted the neo-Confederate government's demand to disarm. They fought back as white state militias and paramilitary organizations worked closely with local governments to seize their weapons.[64] Black people asserted, in publications such as *The Christian Recorder* of the African Methodist Episcopal Church and *The Loyal Georgian,* that they had Second Amendment rights and that stripping them of their guns was denying them the right to self-defense. *The Loyal Georgian* quoted a report by an officer of the Freedmen's Bureau saying that disarming Black people would be "placing them at the mercy of others."[65]

As Black people defied disarmament, they scored some victories, but far too often they were outgunned, and they suffered brutal repercussions as they ran up against the unwillingness of federal officials and local Republican governments to enforce Black citizenship. The slaughter was facilitated by President Johnson's removal from the South of Black troops, which had been a significant part of the occupying army and the line of defense between the freedpeople and white violence. In late 1865 to mid-1866, all the Black troops were removed from the South's interior and sent to coastal fortifications, and by January 1867 they had been expelled altogether.[66]

The result was catastrophic. After the war, President Andrew Johnson had sent a former general, Carl Schurz, to tour the South and report back on conditions there. Schurz unveiled a travelogue of death. He documented hunting parties where Black men were chased down and shot, with dogs left to devour their faces.[67] Near Montgomery, Alabama, he wrote, "negroes leaving the plantations, and found on the roads, were exposed to the savagest treatment." At Selma, he relayed the report from Major J. P. Houston that twelve "negroes were killed by whites."[68] In Choctaw County, Alabama, on separate occasions, Black men were roasted alive; one of them was "chained to a pine tree and *burned to death*."[69] Then there were the "'gallant young men' [who] make a practice of robbing [Black people]. . . . If any resistance is made, death is pretty sure to be the result."[70] Between 1865 and 1868, white people murdered more than one thousand African Americans in one area of Texas. In Pine Bluff, Arkansas, white people "set fire to a black settlement and rounded up the inhabitants. A man who visited the scene the following morning found 'a sight that apald (sic) [him] 24 Negro men woman (sic) and children were hanging to trees all round the Cabbins.'"[71] As Black people tried to defend themselves, white people massacred African Americans in Memphis; New Orleans; Colfax, Louisiana; and Hamburg, South Carolina.

The historian Annette Gordon-Reed called the carnage a "slow-motion genocide."[72] It was clear that anytime a Black person tried to fulfill their right to leave an employer or reunite with their family or demand payment for their labor, they could be violently attacked. The rise of the Ku Klux Klan and similar domestic terrorist organizations like the Knights of the White Camelia and the Red Shirts meant that the precarity of Black life was the defining condition in post–Civil War America. Despite the subsequent repeal of the Black Codes; the rise of Radical Reconstruction, helmed by the U.S. Congress; the advent of the right to vote for African American men in 1867; the ratification of the Fourteenth and Fifteenth Amendments; and the passage of the third Enforcement Act, a law that criminalized white domestic terrorism, the Klan and other vigilante groups were undeterred. The bloodshed was so intense and the lack of justice so evident, despite the fact that Black people were now voting and holding office, that in the mid-1870s President Ulysses S. Grant painfully acknowledged that the slew of murders meant that white people clearly had "the right to Kill negroes . . . without fear of punishment, and without loss of caste or reputation."[73]

Things were no different in the twentieth century. In Atlanta in 1906, white men went on a killing spree against Black people in the city. On trolleys, in barbershops, in hotel lobbies, on street corners, African Americans were hunted down and slaughtered. State militia members, in their own way, were part of the mob. They rampaged through Atlanta, chanting, "We are rough, we are tough, we kill niggers and never get enough!" In the face of this terror, Black people had no stable right of self-defense. In Brownsville, a Black neighborhood, residents took up their guns and prepared to defend themselves from the onslaught. As policemen approached the neighborhood, African American sentries fired, thinking it was the mob attacking. Instead, one police officer died and four others were wounded. The state militia descended upon Brownsville and ransacked homes, terrorized the inhabitants, and confiscated every gun it could find.[74]

White brutality remained a steady fact of life for Black people during this era. But some moments were set apart, such as the orgy of violence known as the Red Summer, which began ramping up as World War I was winding down. The National Association for the Advancement of Colored People and others identified "at least 25 major riots and mob actions . . . and at least 52 black people . . . lynched. Many victims were burned to death" between April and November 1919.[75]

In Arkansas that year, African American sharecroppers in the town of Elaine placed armed sentries outside a church to guard their union-organizing meeting. They knew, as one of the Black men declared, that if their effort to join a labor union was discovered "the whites . . . are going to kill us." Despite the sharecroppers' stealth, as feared, the wealthy landowners had caught wind of the mobilization and sent a local deputy, a detective for the railroad, and a Black prison trusty, Kid Collins, as one participant in the meeting said, "to break up the meeting or to shoot it up." The sentries spotted them. The ensuing gun battle left one white man dead, the other wounded, and Kid Collins running back to town to alert the authorities. The political leaders defined the Black sharecroppers' act of self-defense as the onset of a plot to kill all the white people in the county and, perhaps, the state. The governor called in the U.S. Army, which machine-gunned and shot hundreds of Black residents.[76]

That same year in Knoxville, Tennessee, a white mob gathered in a Black neighborhood to kill as many African Americans as possible after a local sheriff thwarted the lynch mob's plans to hang a Black man arrested for murdering a white woman. In order to hold off the aggressors from laying waste to their neighborhood, Black residents overturned a gravel truck, created makeshift barricades, shot out the streetlights, and fired their rifles and pistols as the white mob attacked. Enraged that Black people had the audacity to defend themselves, white officials called in the 4th Tennessee Infantry Regiment, which then leveled one machine-gun blast after the next into Black homes and businesses.[77]

The next year another incident demonstrated the cost to Black people of exercising their rights to participate in the political process and to protect themselves. When Black residents in Ocoee, Florida, attempted to vote in the 1920 presidential election, white residents there tried to stop them. Poll workers challenged Black voters' registration and payment of the poll tax and required that they get their voting status certified by the town's notary, whom white leaders had deliberately sent out of town on a fishing trip. When one Black man nevertheless tried to cast a ballot and was twice turned away, he began to document the disenfranchisement of African American voters, which enraged a white mob that had been hanging around the polling station intimidating Black voters. The mob threatened to kill him. He fled for refuge to the home of one of the most prominent African Americans in Ocoee, July Perry. The armed mob followed. Perry was warned that they were coming. The men and women in Perry's household had guns, so they set themselves up to defend their home and their lives. But they couldn't repel the onslaught that came their way. A mob of around one hundred white men broke down the door of Perry's home. The residents inside leveled their guns and fired. At least one white man went down. The battle had just begun as white reinforcements poured in from the surrounding counties. Perry's act of self-defense was met with more violence: a white mob lynched him that night, and over the next several days, white people murdered or ran out of town some five hundred Black residents. Ocoee remained an all-white town for five decades.[78]

Nearly a generation later, during the height of the Second World War, Lena Baker, an African American woman in Cuthbert, Georgia, would also experience the lethal consequences of having no right to self-defense. Baker, a forty-four-year-old mother of three children, had been hired to care for a white man, Ernest Knight, who was twenty-three years older than her and had broken his leg. As Lela Bond Phillips writes in *The Lena Baker Story*, Knight would keep the woman captive in his mill house for days and repeatedly rape her. His son was scandalized and almost "beat her half to death" to compel "that bitch to stay away" from his father.[79] But it was Knight, as a white man in rural Jim Crow Georgia, who had the power. Late on the night of April 29, 1944, while her children were already in bed asleep, he went to Lena Baker's house, demanding that she come with him to his grist mill. She didn't want to go, but he took her anyway.[80] The inevitable sexual violence was delayed, however, because he had promised one of his sons that he would go to church with him, so he locked her inside. When he came back a few hours later, on April 30, he insisted on getting what he wanted.[81] What she wanted, however, was to leave. She went for the door, and Knight pulled out a gun. They struggled over it.[82] It went off, and a single bullet struck Knight in the head.

After the shooting, Baker claimed self-defense. The prosecutor charged her with murder. The trial didn't even take a full day. The jury deliberated for less than half an hour and delivered a guilty verdict. The judge sentenced Lena

Baker to death, the first and only woman to die in "Old Sparky," Georgia's electric chair. Lena Baker's last words were "What I done, I did in self-defense, or I would have been killed myself."[83]

Systemic violence against Black people was not just a Southern phenomenon. In California in the 1950s and '60s, the Oakland police force was notorious for brutally beating and killing unarmed African Americans. In one series of episodes, officers harassed and humiliated a young Black married woman by subjecting her to three days of venereal disease tests; beat an African American man severely after they learned his wife was white; killed a Black man they had arrested for loitering; and claimed justifiable homicide for gunning down a man who they insisted had been burglarizing a building that showed no signs of forcible entry.[84] This violence created a demand in the Black community that something be done. In 1966, Huey P. Newton and Bobby Seale answered that call and formed the Black Panther Party for Self-Defense (BPP).

The BPP had a swagger and a militancy that resonated with a besieged community. Dressed in their "uniforms" of leather jackets and berets, the Panthers openly carried rifles and .45s while monitoring Oakland police officers making arrests. As an act of community self-defense, they policed the police. This was unsettling to many white people. A headline to a 1967 article in the *San Francisco Examiner* exclaimed, "Oakland's Black Panthers Wear Guns, Talk Revolution." Even more frightening: "It's All Legal."[85]

The police inveighed upon conservative California assemblyman David Donald "Don" Mulford to change the state's gun laws to make the open carry of firearms illegal and, thus, undermine the Panthers' community self-defense strategy. Mulford readily agreed.[86] He was bolstered in his efforts by the National Rifle Association, the guardians of the Second Amendment. An NRA representative, E. F. "Tod" Sloan, helped draft new gun-control legislation, California Assembly Bill 1591.[87] Mulford adamantly denied that the bill was aimed at African Americans and offered assurances that "there are no racial overtones to this measure."[88] He publicly asserted that AB 1591 was designed to cover the Klan and the Minutemen, covert right-wing groups that, while well-armed, did not openly carry weapons in the state.

Willie Brown, a Black assemblyman from San Francisco, saw through the subterfuge, noting that Mulford had opposed similar legislation "until Negroes showed up in Oakland—his district—with arms."[89] And Mulford's private correspondence demonstrated that the Black Panthers were the target of his bill. He explained to Governor Ronald Reagan that the "Black Panther movement is creating a serious problem." And that AB 1591 had, therefore, been "introduced at the request of the Oakland Police Department."[90] For his part, Reagan, through his legislative secretary, informed Mulford that a prominent district attorney "emphasizes the danger of the carrying of firearms by groups such as the Black Panthers and the need for control in this area."[91]

Many white people in America, in fact, saw the Panthers and the uprisings in Watts, Detroit, and Newark not as protests against police violence but as indications of dangerous Black pathology. A white woman in Joliet, Illinois, remarked, "When I see on TV these demonstrations it makes me think of them as savages."[92] Indeed, 57 percent of white people who lived in large urban areas said that the riots made them feel "unsafe."[93] A woman in New Jersey explained, "People have become afraid of Negroes. When you see them in groups you think they're going to start a riot."[94]

Reagan and other officials quickly realized there was a political gold mine in white fear. Identifying African Americans as criminals, "thugs," and "mad dogs" and as an imminent threat to white communities, white lives, and white prosperity allowed the racialized "public safety" policies of Jim Crow to survive in the post–Civil Rights era.[95] It drove election campaigns steeped in the rhetoric of "law and order" and successfully fueled "soft on crime" charges leveled against opponents.[96] In this political environment, where Black people were *the* threat, the violence that rained down on them seemed justified. Self-defense was not. A machine operator in California actually remarked, "I think there should be more police brutality, more martial law. Then they would have more respect for the law. Martial law is shoot now and ask questions later."[97] As the scholar Susan D. Greenbaum noted in *Blaming the Poor,* the "subtext" of news reports and policy studies was "that African Americans were dangerous, that poverty combined with inept upbringing and untamed rage were all coming to the surface in the successes of the Civil Rights movement."[98] As the perceived threat grew, the focus of self-defense law was to protect white Americans; Black people were left exposed and vulnerable to white violence.[99]

In December 1984, on a subway car in New York City, a thirty-seven-year-old white man, Bernhard Goetz, said he feared that he was going to be mugged by four young African Americans who had asked him for a cigarette and tried to bum five dollars. He pulled out his unlicensed gun and fired five bullets, hitting all his targets, leaving one teen paralyzed and with brain damage, and then left the train. When Goetz turned himself in to the police nine days later and the prosecutor charged him with attempted murder, he became a "hero" to many: the "subway vigilante."[100] He represented the besieged white American who felt threatened by Black people. Indeed, Goetz said he feared for his life, although there was virtually no hard evidence that the teens had tried to attack him before he pulled his gun and fired.[101] Nonetheless, he claimed self-defense. The jury agreed.

Behind the cases of Bernhard Goetz, George Zimmerman, and Jessie Murray, Jr., is a legacy of laws originally created to make it easier for white people to defend themselves against the Black people they enslaved, who were defined as "dangerous" because they wanted desperately to be free. But when they won their freedom, Black people did not also win the right to defend themselves. That has remained elusive to this day. In 2020, the U.S. Commission on Civil Rights reported on the racial implications of Stand Your Ground laws: the criminal justice system is ten times more likely to rule a homicide justifiable if the shooter is white and victim is Black than the other way around.[102] In fact, the report notes that when a white person kills an African American, it is 281 percent more likely to be ruled a "justifiable homicide" than a white-on-white killing.[103] A joint analysis by the Giffords Law Center and the Southern Poverty Law Center, citing the U.S. Commission on Civil Rights Report, summed up the results: "the consequences are predictably deadly and unequal."[104]

March 16, 1870

A month after being sworn in, Mississippi Senator Hiram Rhodes Revels, the first Black member of either house of Congress in U.S. history, gives his first speech on the floor of the Senate. His comments address a debate on whether Congress should force the Georgia state legislature to accept twenty-nine Black state representatives and three Black state senators who had recently been elected but were being denied their seats.

This is a found poem derived from the text of Revels's historic speech.

Like to the Rushing of a Mighty Wind

Tracy K. Smith

I rise. I rise, lifting my voice.
My term is short, fraught,
and I bear about me daily
the keenest sense of the power
of blacks to shed hallowed light,
to welcome the Good News.

Weary of bondage, sorrow,
adjudication delayed, they wait
and they wait. The feelings
which animate them are, by God's
law, natural, logical. Alone,
my own race acts in interrogation:

Would the country believe its
borders wide enough for all truly
loyal men to find within them peace?
And be that loyal man black, will
his pursuit of liberty and happiness
find feuds and contentions, death

and disaster, the very air dark
as an ugly dream? Many of my race
sleep in the countless graves
of the South. If our dead could speak,
what a voice, like to the rushing
of a mighty wind, would come up

from the ground. Her whole people,
white and colored, should race
to each other wholly and with honor,
meet and fit for admission of events
transpired. Now, sir. Sir, now. I wish
my last word upon the bill before us to be:

Now.

September 15, 1883

A conductor on a train traveling from Memphis to Woodstock, Tennessee, insists that Ida B. Wells leave her seat in the first-class rear car and move to the rougher front car, where drinking and smoking are permitted. Wells refuses and is forcibly removed from the train. Afterward, she sues the Chesapeake, Ohio, and Southwestern Railroad Company. She wins and is awarded $500 in damages, but the Tennessee Supreme Court overturns the ruling. Afterward, she writes, "O God, is there no redress, no peace, no justice in this land for us?"

no car for colored [+] ladies
(or, miss wells goes off [on] the rails)

Evie Shockley

—memphis, 1883

she wasn't born a hero, you know. once, she
was twenty: four years an orphan, eighteen years

free. with a passion for brontë & a weakness for
fashion, she might drop a month of her schoolteacher's
salary on clothing at menken's palatial emporium,

to dress as befits a lady. she pays to ride first class
that autumn afternoon, knowing she looks the part: full

skirt, cinched waist, gloves, crown. boarding, she peeps
the drunken white man smoking up the "colored car,"

& no. she's not buying it. her place is in the *ladies'* car.
i know she wasn't born a hero, but once ida b. wells

addresses what befits a lady who pays to ride first class
(*to drift into anywhich seat she selects*), she's becoming one.
outfit be damned, she resists her ouster, till her sleeve's

torn & the conductor's bleeding. she'll pull these threads
until the whole *threadbare lie* of lynching unravels.

William Headly, who escaped from enslavement near Raleigh, North Carolina, c. 1862–65

CHAPTER 10

Punishment

BRYAN STEVENSON

A decade ago, I was in court fighting for the release of a Black man named Matthew who had been condemned to die in prison because of a crime that occurred when he was sixteen. A legal aid organization I'd founded, the Equal Justice Initiative (EJI), was representing Matthew, as well as many others who had been sentenced to life imprisonment without parole when they were children. When EJI was started, in 1989, its purpose was to provide legal representation to people on death row. Over the years, our mission expanded to include providing legal aid to people wrongly convicted or unfairly sentenced. We also began representing condemned children, some as young as thirteen, serving sentences of life without parole. Today, we seek an end to mass incarceration and to the abusive and punitive way our legal system responds to trauma, addiction, and mental illness.

The focus of our work—like the work of so many other individuals and organizations that have arisen throughout the nation's history to fight for and deepen our founding principles of justice and equality before the law—is the particularly punitive nature of the American legal system. The United States has the highest rate of incarceration of any nation on earth: this country contains 4 percent of the planet's population but 20 percent of its prisoners.

This is a relatively recent development. In the early 1970s, our prisons and jails held fewer than 350,000 people; since then, that number has increased to about 2.3 million, with 4.5 million more on probation or parole.[1] In 1980, there were roughly 40,000 people incarcerated for drug offenses; today that number is about 450,000. For more than three decades, our country has spent billions of dollars every year not only on constructing prisons and jails but also on policing and funding a carceral system that has ensnared millions.[2] More than 200,000 Americans are currently condemned to life sentences or virtual life sentences (fifty years or longer).[3]

Disproportionately, those affected by the system are Black. Racial disparities in sentencing are found in almost every crime category. For instance, researchers have repeatedly established that the race of the victim is the greatest predictor of who gets the death penalty in the United States.[4] A study from the 1980s found that in Georgia, Black defendants convicted of killing white people were almost twenty-two times more likely to be sentenced to death than people convicted of crimes against Black victims, a racial disparity that the United States Supreme Court accepted as "inevitable" in a controversial 1987 case, *McCleskey v. Kemp*. And determinations about whether children are prosecuted as juveniles or adults and what kind of punishments are imposed reveal some of the most dramatic racial disparities. In 2008, EJI established that *all* of the thirteen- and fourteen-year-old children in this country sentenced to life in prison without parole for non-homicide offenses were Black, Latino, or Native.[5]

We began representing these children and challenging what we call "death in prison" sentences across the country. Eventually, two of the cases, *Sullivan v. Florida* and *Graham v. Florida,* ended up in the United States Supreme Court. In 2009, I argued to the justices that telling any thirteen-year-old child, "You are fit only to die in prison" is cruel and that these sentences cannot be reconciled with what we know about child development or basic human rights. The Court agreed and declared that life without parole sentences imposed on children convicted of non-homicide offenses are unconstitutional.

The *Graham* decision and a 2012 case we took to the Supreme Court, *Miller v. Alabama,* which banned imposing mandatory sentences of life without parole on children, created the possibility of release for thousands of imprisoned people who had been condemned as minors. However, obtaining parole or release was not guaranteed. Legal appeals would have to be filed, and judges and parole boards would have to be persuaded to grant relief. That's how I met Matthew.

At the time that we represented him, Matthew had been imprisoned for more than forty years. He was one of sixty-two Louisiana prisoners serving life in prison for non-homicide offenses committed when they were children; 89 percent of the condemned were Black. Some had been in prison for nearly fifty years. Almost all had been sent to Angola, a penitentiary that at the time was considered one of America's most violent and abusive.[6] Angola is immense, larger than the island of Manhattan, covering land once occupied by plantations where enslaved Black people were forced to labor. Some of our clients had worked in the fields for years while imprisoned under the supervision of horse-riding, shotgun-toting guards who forced them to pick crops, including cotton.

Even after Supreme Court rulings, securing the release of these men usually required navigating parole review boards, which are highly discretionary. A prisoner's disciplinary record is often one of the most significant factors in parole decisions, and I was worried that some of our clients would be denied release. Some had records documenting that when they had refused to pick cotton or had failed to pick it fast enough, they had been punished with time in "the hole," where food was restricted and inmates were sometimes tear-gassed. Still, some Black prisoners, including Matthew, considered the despair of the hole preferable to the unbearable degradation of being forced to pick cotton at the end of the twentieth century on the site of a former plantation for enslaved people. Because of disciplinary infractions like this, some of our clients were denied parole.

Incarcerated people in most states have no right to counsel for post-conviction appeals, so EJI ended up taking on close to sixty cases in Louisiana. In other states, because of mandatory sentencing and three-strikes laws, I have found myself representing people sentenced to life without parole for stealing a bicycle or for simple possession of marijuana. For a nation that prides itself on being exceptionally committed to freedom, America has produced an endless list of harsh, extreme, and cruel sentences, across the fifty states, for minor and major crimes.

How did it come to this? How did we arrive at a point of so much over-incarceration, abusive policing, and excessive punishment? Why are racial disparities so pronounced throughout this system? We cannot answer these questions without understanding the legacy of slavery and the harsh, racialized instinct for punishment our history has created.

It took only a few decades after the arrival of enslaved Africans in Virginia before white settlers demanded a new world defined by racial caste. The 1664 General Assembly of Maryland decreed that all Negroes shall serve *durante vita,* hard labor "for life."[7] This enslavement would be sustained by the threat of brutal punishment. By 1729, Maryland law had authorized punishments of enslaved people including "to have the right hand cut off . . . the head severed from the body, the body divided into four quarters, and head and quarters set up in the most public places of the county."[8] Enslaved people were punished for learning to read, for questioning their enslavement, or when rumors of escape or rebellion surfaced. In 1740, South Carolina lawmakers restricted some of the most barbaric punishments that had emerged and imposed civil fines on enslavers who "cut out the tongue, put out the eye, castrate, or cruelly scald, burn, or deprive any slave of any limb or member," but it still authorized "whipping or beating with horse whip, cow skin, switch or small stick, or putting irons on, or confining or imprisoning."[9]

Even emancipated and free-born Black people were often considered to be presumptive fugitives to be hunted, captured, and sold into slavery. As one nineteenth-century court ruled, "The presumption arising from the color of a person indicating African descent is, that he is a slave."[10] Some Northern states and territories, including Illinois, Indiana, and Oregon, banned the immigration of free Black people; some Southern states required that enslaved people who obtained freedom from their enslavers leave the state, to avoid any confusion about what Black people represented in American society.

American slavery evolved into a perverse regime that denied the humanity of Black people while criminalizing their actions. Bondage itself was only one part of the system; the myth of racial difference and a belief in white supremacy were another. As the Supreme Court of Alabama explained in an 1861 ruling, enslaved Black people were "capable of committing crimes," and in that capacity were "regarded as persons," but in most every other sense they were "incapable of performing civil acts" and considered "things, not persons."[11]

The Thirteenth Amendment is credited with ending slavery, but it stopped short of that. It made an exception for those convicted of crimes: "Neither slavery nor involuntary servitude, *except as a punishment for crime whereof the party shall have been duly convicted,* shall exist within the United States, or any place subject to their jurisdiction" (emphasis added).[12] And it could not abolish the true evil of American slavery, which was the belief that Black people are less evolved, less human, less capable, less deserving, less trustworthy than white people. Reconstruction may have challenged the existing paradigm, with changes to the Constitution aimed at enforcing equality before the law, but it was short-lived and could not overcome the commitment to white supremacy evident in so many jurisdictions. The existing racial hierarchy was sustained by myths about Black criminality, which led many white people to insist that only the threat of extreme and brutal punishment could preserve order where Black people were concerned. After emancipation, Black people, once seen as less than fully human "slaves," were now seen as less than fully human "criminals."

Formal slavery may have ended in 1865, but the social, legal, economic, and political system built in the South to sustain slavery survived by evolving into new forms. Laws governing slavery were replaced with laws governing free Black people, making the criminal legal system central to new strategies of racial control. As the provisional governor of South Carolina declared in 1865, emancipated Black people had to be "restrained from theft, idleness, vagrancy and crime . . . and taught the absolute necessity of strictly complying with their contracts for labor."[13] An 1866 editorial in the Macon *Daily Telegraph* said: "There is such a radical difference in the mental and moral constitution of the white and black race that it would be impossible to secure order in a mixed community by the same legal sanction."[14] And these beliefs were not limited to the South. The slogan of the 1868 Democratic National Convention, which nominated former New York governor Horatio Seymour as its candidate for president, was: "This Is a White Man's Country; Let White Men Rule."[15]

These strategies intensified whenever Black people asserted their independence or achieved any measure of success. Even before Reconstruction ended, white Americans countered the emergence of Black elected officials and entrepreneurs with mob violence. After Reconstruction, rejection of racial equality intensified with convict leasing, a scheme in which white policy makers invented offenses—congregating after dark, vagrancy, loitering—that could be used to arrest Black people, who were then jailed and "leased" to businesses and farms, where they labored under brutal conditions. An 1887 report in Mississippi found that six months after 204 prisoners were leased to a white man named McDonald, dozens of them were dead or dying, the prison hospital filled with men whose bodies bore "marks of the most inhuman and brutal treatment . . . so poor and emaciated that their bones almost come through the skin."[16] The death rate in some of these prison camps was close to 45 percent. As historian Douglas A. Blackmon's Pulitzer Prize–winning book documents, it was *Slavery by Another Name.*[17] But unlike slavery, in which enslavers at least had a financial interest in keeping enslaved people alive and functional, convict leasing stripped imprisoned people of any protection and made them completely replaceable and easily discarded. In that sense, convict leasing was, as the sociologist David Oshinsky titled his book, *Worse Than Slavery.*[18]

It is not just that this history fostered a view of Black people as presumptively criminal; it also cultivated a tolerance for employing any level of brutality to maintain the racial hierarchy. In 1904 in Mississippi, a Black man was accused of shooting a white landowner who had attacked him. A white mob captured him and the woman with him, cut off their ears and fingers, drilled corkscrews into their flesh, and then burned them alive, while hundreds of white spectators enjoyed deviled eggs and lemonade. The landowner's brother, Woods Eastland, presided over the violence. He was later elected district attorney of Scott County, Mississippi, a position that launched his son James Eastland, an avowed white supremacist, to the U.S. Senate; he served six terms, and was president pro tempore from 1972 to 1978.

In the eyes of white people, Black criminality was broadly defined. Anything Black people did to challenge the racial hierarchy could be seen as a crime, punished either by the law or by lawless lynchings, which were an epidemic in the South but also took place in the West and the North. In 1916, a white mob lynched Anthony Crawford in South Carolina for being successful enough to refuse a low price for his cotton. In 1918, Mary Turner complained about her husband's murder and the mistreatment of sharecroppers in Georgia and a white mob lynched her, too. In 1920, a white mob of up to ten thousand people gathered in Duluth, Minnesota, and lynched three Black men. In 1933, a white mob lynched Elizabeth Lawrence near Birmingham for daring to chastise white children who were throwing rocks at her.

This appetite for harsh punishment has echoed across the decades. Many of the well-dressed Christians and clergy members who took part in the 1955 Montgomery bus boycott were beaten, battered, and bloodied in nonviolent civil rights protests.[19] By the 1960s it was less acceptable to employ the same forms of extralegal racial terrorism that had been used to constrain previous forms of Black protest. But white resistance to racial equality remained strong. A new politics of fear and anger emerged and gave rise to the era of mass incarceration. Richard Nixon's war on drugs, mandatory minimum sentences, three-strikes laws, children tried as adults, "broken windows" policing—these policies were not as expressly racialized as the Black Codes, but their implementation involved many of the same features. Today, it is Black and other nonwhite people who are disproportionately targeted, stopped, suspected, arrested, incarcerated, and shot by the police or prosecuted in courts.

Hundreds of years after the arrival of the first enslaved Africans, a presumption of danger and criminality still follows Black people everywhere. New language has emerged for the non-crimes that have replaced the Black Codes: driving while Black, sleeping while Black, sitting in a coffee shop while Black. All reflect incidents in which African Americans have been mistreated, assaulted, or arrested for conduct that would be ignored if they were white. In schools, Black children are suspended and expelled at rates that vastly exceed the punishment of white children for the same behavior.

———

The smog created by our history of racial injustice is suffocating and toxic. We are too practiced in ignoring the victimization of any Black person tagged as "criminal"; like Woods Eastland's crowd, too many Americans remain willing spectators to horrifying acts of extreme punishment, as long as they are assured that it is in the interest of maintaining order. Today, in courtrooms across America, advocates and lawyers representing Black people cannot effectively assist many of their clients without recognizing that, contrary to the legal doctrine, those clients are presumed guilty and burdened by assumptions of criminality that have been shaped over centuries. The job of the advocate then becomes convincing the court and the jurors of a client's innocence, rather than just defending the client against accusations of guilt, an inversion of the presumption of innocence written into American law. The advocate who fails to understand this reality can actually imperil the life of his or her client.

Recognizing the unbroken links between slavery, Black Codes, lynching, and our current era of mass incarceration is essential. Like generations before, we must struggle for an end to bigotry. We must fight to repair the damage created by centuries of racial injustice. We must commit to a new era of truth and justice, one in which we honestly confront our past so that we can understand what remedies are needed to achieve healthy communities and justice for people who have been unfairly excluded and targeted. Our nation must acknowledge the four hundred years of injustice that haunt us. Truthtelling can be powerful. In many faith traditions, salvation and redemption can come only after confession and repentance. In Germany, there has been a meaningful reckoning with the history of the Holocaust; this sort of reflection and remembrance has been largely absent in America, where many people resist confronting the most disturbing and difficult parts of our past.

With this in mind, in 2018, EJI founded a museum in Montgomery, Alabama, dedicated to the legacy of slavery; the grounds also feature a memorial honoring thousands of Black victims of lynching. Since we've opened, hundreds of thousands of people have visited. I've seen many of them reduced to tears after bearing witness to the traumas of our past; but I've also seen them, before they leave, resolve to make a difference. They understand, perhaps, that we are at one of those critical moments in American history when we will either double down on romanticizing a false narrative about our violent past or accept that there is something better waiting for us, if we can learn to deal honestly with our history.

I sometimes speak with our Angola clients who have now been released, including Matthew. They are grateful to have survived the fields and the hole, to have endured harsh punishment amid an uncertain future. They sometimes talk about what it was like to be told, "You are beyond hope, beyond redemption, and you must stay in prison until you die." We share our convictions that people are wrong when they reduce other human beings to nothing more than their worst act. It is powerful to see individuals I met when they were condemned behind bars living unchained lives that carry the hope and possibility of restoration. But it is also clear to me that for Matthew and others, being outside Angola's haunted plantation gates doesn't mean total freedom. Condemnation frequently leaves a mark, an injury, a trauma that weighs on you. And the conditions that gave rise to unjust condemnation for the people I represent still exist. Black people still bear the burden of presumptive guilt.

A society recovering from a history of horrific human rights violations must make a commitment to truth and justice. As long as we deny the legacy of slavery and avoid this commitment, we will fail to overcome the racially biased, punitive systems of control that have become serious barriers to freedom in this country. It's tempting for some to believe otherwise, but much work remains.

November 10, 1898

A mob of more than one thousand white men overthrows the elected biracial local government in Wilmington, North Carolina, in the only successful coup in American history. Organized by white supremacist politicians virulently opposed to the prospect of elected Black city officials, the mob destroys a thriving Black business district, kills scores of Black people, and drives thousands from their homes; many of them will never return.

Race Riot

Forrest Hamer

We, the undersigned citizens of the City of Wilmington and County of New Hanover, do hereby declare that we will no longer be ruled, and will never again be ruled by men of African origin.

—White Declaration of Independence, 1898

If it will save one white woman, I say lynch a thousand black men.

—Rebecca Latimer Felton, "Woman on the Farm," 1897 speech

If the Wilmington coup of 1898 was even mentioned—

If the Wilmington massacre of 1898 was even mentioned—
(how would the massacred name it?)

If the Campaign for White Supremacy leading up to the 1898 elections
was even mentioned
in the junior-year class on the history of North Carolina,

the events were described as another eruption of Negro dissatisfaction
which, once expressed, quieted.

But in the story of the campaign (for white supremacy), the Negro
had become unruly, needed instead to be ruled
once more out, "Negro rule" ousted into the swampy fantastic

as fear, as specter, as a promise. The phantasm of Negro rule

was what the high school textbook never acknowledged
had rallied the Wilmington race (war) of 1898, the riot

planned and instigated, orderly disorder, the wrong
the Redeemers sought to riot up, right

justifying anything, even murder, the declaration
to "choke the Cape Fear River with the carcasses" of whatever
the Negro populating their fantasies was—threatening

and promising domination, threatening revenge, promising
a North Carolina governed by the many not the few.

A thousand Black rapists (each vote a thousand more) haunted
the campaign the Redeemers rallied to wage. They claimed the fight
to protect their honor. For, if this time they didn't prevail,

who could imagine what they would be subject to?

May 31, 1921

Following the arrest of a young Black man who had ridden in an elevator with a white woman, a confrontation erupts between groups of Black and white citizens at the courthouse in Tulsa, Oklahoma. In response, mobs of white residents, some armed by the city, completely destroy the Greenwood District, then one of the wealthiest Black communities in the country, known as Black Wall Street, and kill hundreds of Black citizens.

Greenwood

Jasmine Mans

The whistle of an unnatural wind
gave word there would be
a lynching,

of a Negro boy
who shined shoes,

not a rapist,
just a boy,
a child boy,
teenage boy,
nineteen-year-old boy
still fresh in his days.

And a wind
that would not know
the enormity of its crime
until morning filled air
with turpentine.

—

An invasion led
by Klansmen,

a hate that would outdo itself
to a menacing ritual of fire,
wood, and blood.

The bombs turned clouds
into shadows of themselves.
Single-engine aircrafts
hovered so low

the bodies under them
thought the world was
ending, and how could
it not be

"Run, Negro!"

Thirty-five(ish) blocks,
and a flame that spent days
burning itself tired,

Three hundred (ish)
Black folks murdered
into anonymity.

Greenwood
has a soggy, muck clay,
a damp inconsistency
of earth, Constitution,
and bone.

Some buried, homeless, in Oaklawn,
some trampled beneath the dirt.

A history tucked away
in attic floorboards
long enough to forget
all it once was.

America has a way of dancing
with its own delusion.

Unable to keep count of its murders
because it, then, would have to keep
count of its murderers,

its good neighbors.

All insurance claims denied
to the residents of Greenwood
and business owners
of Black Wall Street.

And, left, a people
holding their memory
through tongue
folklore,
blood, postcard,
church tale.

A people
chasing a memory
that wasn't
supposed
to become
a memory
at all.

Elmore Bolling and his wife, Bertha Mae Nowden Bolling, in Alabama, c. 1945   COURTESY OF
JOSEPHINE BOLLING MCCALL

CHAPTER 11

Inheritance

TRYMAINE LEE

In Josephine Bolling McCall's living room in Montgomery, Alabama, a black-and-white photograph of her parents, Elmore Bolling and Bertha Mae Nowden Bolling, rests on an easel. Her father is seated with his back straight, wearing a black driver's hat cocked perfectly on his head like a crown. Her mother stands dutifully by his side with a hand on his shoulder. The mounted photograph is large, about two feet wide by three feet tall, but feels even larger. Somehow it seems to fill the whole room. It was taken in the mid-1940s, when things were good for the Bolling family.

Elmore Bolling was a one-man economy in Lowndesboro, where the family lived. He had a large house, a general store, a delivery service, a catering company, and a gas station, all of which were located on a property he leased off Highway 80, one of the most traveled routes between Selma and Montgomery; he grew cotton, corn, and sugarcane and owned a small fleet of trucks.[1] At his peak, Bolling employed as many as forty people, all of them Black like him. And his family estimates that he had as much as $40,000 in the bank and more than $5,000 in physical assets, together worth more than $500,000 in today's dollars.

Bolling came from a long line of Black entrepreneurs that stretched back to the early post-slavery days. From them, he learned how to be successful in the Jim Crow South. In the late 1800s and early 1900s, his father and grandfather had managed to acquire a large plot of land, on which they ran cattle. But just as they were getting ahead, a white man who'd been renting a parcel of land from them claimed that the land was his. Black people had no legal standing when it came to business matters with white folks, so he was able to simply take it from the Bollings. After that, the Bolling men vowed never to buy property again. Instead, they would lease it. On rented land, which could never be stolen from them, they could still set up numerous moneymaking ventures.

That's how Elmore Bolling grew up, thinking a few steps ahead of white people, always weighing the risks of being Black and ambitious against new business opportunities. He leased his farmland and raised his animals and then got into transportation and deliveries, too. He started with a mule and a wagon and eventually upgraded to a Model T, which he converted into a truck. Bolling transported cattle and feed and anything that anyone wanted to move between Lowndes County and Montgomery. Soon, his Model T grew into three tractor-trailer trucks.[2]

But it was the expansion of his little general store that changed his fortunes. Elmore and Bertha Mae started doing Friday night fish fries, serving Sunday dinners, and selling ice cream to the after-church crowd. Ice cream was a delicacy in their little patch of the county, where most folks still didn't have electricity. They used a portable hand-cranked ice cream maker to churn out scoops of the cold stuff for eager customers.[3] The shop became the center of the family's operation, and they grew their business by adding a one-pump gas station out front. Elmore got the idea to sell gas after a white-owned station nearby refused to serve him. At the Bollings' pump, Black drivers would have a safe, reliable place to fill up.

In addition to their successful businesses, Elmore and Bertha Mae had seven children. He sent his two oldest sons to live with their aunt in Montgomery during the week so they could attend school in the city instead of going to the local high school, where the focus was on working the land rather than book learning. "Our father decided that those schools offered a better education," McCall says of her dad, who never learned to read or write. He always preached to his children that getting a good education and achieving financial independence were the only ways Black folks would ever experience any kind of freedom. He had very little of the former but was dead set on grabbing up as much of the latter as he could.

In the portrait in McCall's living room, he almost pops from the frame. His rich brown skin glows against his white shirt and light tie. Bertha Mae leans into him as if he were a boulder. There's a mix of pride and defiance on his face. It took a lot of both to survive and thrive as a Black man. But too much of either could just as easily be one's undoing. And he knew it. They all did.

Not long after that portrait was taken, the Bollings and every Black man, woman, and child in the county would learn the cost of daring to be too successful, too free. On a mild December day in 1947, a deputy sheriff came to Elmore's store while his twelve-year-old son, Willie D, was working and asked where his father was. Willie D told him that his father was away on a trip. A short time later, another white man entered and asked the same question. Willie D knew this meant trouble, but he didn't know what to do. Sensing danger, he told the man that his father wasn't in town. Soon after, Willie D saw the first man's car following his father's truck on the highway about two hundred yards from the store as Elmore, back from Montgomery, attempted to make some deliveries.

As Elmore got out of his truck, two white men confronted him, including one of the men who'd come into the store. It seemed that in buying a pump and selling gas, Elmore had stepped over some invisible line. Suddenly, gunfire rang out. The white men shot Elmore seven times—six times with a pistol and once with a shotgun blast to his back.[4] His wife and three of his children—all under the age of thirteen—heard the terrifying sounds and rushed from the store to find him lying dead in a ditch.

McCall says the shooters didn't bother to cover their faces; they didn't need to. Everyone would know who had killed Elmore and why. "Enraged whites, jealous over the business success of a Negro, are believed to be the lynchers of Elmore Bolling," reported *The Chicago Defender* on December 20, 1947; the story noted that "Bolling has long been a marked man." One local who knew Elmore put it succinctly: he was "too successful to be a Negro."[5]

His murder created a gaping wound in the family, which quickly lost everything he'd built. "Growing up, we never talked much about what happened," McCall says all these years later, sitting on an orange velvet love seat in her meticulously kept living room, not far from the portrait of her parents. "We were all traumatized by it in our own way," she said. The trauma reverberated over the years after her father's lynching, and in addition to the emotional pain, there was the ongoing financial toll. "There was no inheritance," says McCall, "nothing for my father to pass down, because it was all taken away."

The fate suffered by Elmore Bolling and his family was not unique to them, or to Jim Crow Alabama. It was part of a broader social and political campaign to violently safeguard the racial hierarchy that had begun as a reaction to Reconstruction and would stretch over the next century. When legal slavery ended in 1865, the formerly enslaved had great hopes. During the next five years, the Reconstruction amendments established birthright citizenship—making all Black people citizens and granting them equal protection under the law—and gave Black men the right to vote. For the first time in the country's history, Black people had a path to achieving some kind of political power.[6]

But it was a tenuous path that could be pursued only with protection. In the South, where millions of formerly enslaved people were attempting to claim their freedom and begin building their lives, the federal government maintained a military presence; this, alongside Black local and regional self-protection efforts, helped to keep order. These troops were able to briefly hold back some of the most violent and oppressive elements in the South, enabling Black men to exercise their new rights, casting ballots and mounting political campaigns. For the first time, Black men were elected to local and state office.[7]

Reconstruction was an enormous undertaking. To oversee the transition from slavery to freedom, Congress established the Freedmen's Bureau, which provided food, housing, legal assistance, and medical aid to newly emancipated citizens. The agency helped fund the building of thousands of schools for Black children and young people, as biracial Reconstruction governments built the first systems of free public elementary education in the South.[8] These years also saw the founding of a number of historically Black colleges and universities, including Morehouse College and Fisk and Howard Universities.

The Freedmen's Bureau also established a savings bank, chartered by Congress to help four million formerly enslaved people gain financial freedom. The bank's exclusive mission was to offer Black people generally, and Black Civil War veterans specifically, a safe place to deposit and grow their money. Black veterans were among the bank's first depositors, climbing out of the war with back pay and enlistment bonuses.[9]

There was also the promise that after generations of working land they could never own, the formerly enslaved would be compensated. During the war, the Union army had torn through the South and seized a bountiful amount of farmland and property owned by Confederate families. A contingent of so-called Radical Republicans in Congress, led by Thaddeus Stevens, argued that the seized land should be handed over to the formerly enslaved. It would be a form of poetic justice, but also retribution. They figured the redistribution of land would effectively break the back of the traitorous Southern aristocracy.[10]

In January 1865, after meeting with a group of Black ministers, General William Sherman issued an order reallocating hundreds of thousands of acres of white-owned land along the coasts of Florida, Georgia, and South Carolina for settlement by Black families in forty-acre plots. He also said the army would give these families a mule—hence the phrase "forty acres and a mule," which reverberated across the South.[11] But after Lincoln was assassinated, in April 1865, his vice president, Andrew Johnson, a Democrat and a former senator from Tennessee, assumed the presidency, and these policies began to change. The following year, Johnson declared, "This is a country for white men, and by God, as long as I am President, it shall be a government for white men."[12] Over the next decade, the nascent gains of the Reconstruction era would gradually be undone.

From the beginning of his presidency, Johnson insisted that land seized from Confederates must be returned to its former owners, effectively undoing Sherman's order and returning to former enslavers the land that had been seized from them as punishment for taking up arms against the nation. Some forty thousand Black families had settled on confiscated "Sherman land." In some cases, federal troops evicted them by force; in others, Black people fought off returning white people with guns. According to some accounts, about two thousand Black landowners held on to the land they'd been given after the war. But the majority stayed on land they no longer owned and worked as sharecroppers.

Reneging on the land was just one way the federal government betrayed these upstart Americans. The Freedmen's Bureau, always meant to be temporary, was dismantled in 1872. More than sixty thousand Black people had deposited more than $3 million into the savings bank, but its all-white trustees used that money to begin issuing speculative loans to white investors and corporations. When the bank failed in 1874, Black depositors lost much of their savings.[13]

By that time, Reconstruction was nearing its end. White Southerners had staunchly refused to accept the fullness of Black freedom, let alone Black equality, and fought hard to maintain the prewar tenets of white supremacy. They despised the federal troops in their midst and argued for "home rule" to be restored. Following the presidential election of 1876, which came down to disputed returns in Florida, Louisiana, and South Carolina, Southern Democrats agreed to what became known as the Compromise of 1877: Republican Rutherford B. Hayes was installed in the White House, and the federal government pulled out the last Union troops from the South.[14] The results were devastating. Over the course of the next generation, white violence prevented Black people from casting ballots, and Southern state legislatures began to revert to all-white rule. The Black activism of the previous decade would continue only within increasingly violent and narrow strictures.

Starting in the 1870s, in the period of so-called Redemption, lawmakers throughout the South enacted Jim Crow laws that stripped Black people of much of their newfound freedom. Other white people, often aided by law enforcement, waged a campaign of terror against Black people that would go on for decades. In fact, white political violence stretched well into the twentieth and early twenty-first centuries, taking on new and more insidious forms that continue to unsettle Black life in America today.

Some of this historic violence was spurred by what was seen as violations to social codes, including consensual sex between Black and white adults, a lack of proper deference to white people, and Black workers' demanding fair wages or fair treatment. Black political progress was also seen as an affront. But Black people's financial success often seemed to provoke the harshest response, especially from white people who felt threatened by a real or perceived rise in African American prosperity. With limited opportunities to accumulate wealth or even financial stability, Black folks had to work extraordinarily hard and strike just enough luck to cobble together a living. Gathering the means to educate their children and keep their families safe was a full-time mission—a tough one, given that nearly all of them started with nothing. Again and again, when Black people did manage to build any kind of success, they were met with violence.

In 1898, armed white people stormed Wilmington, North Carolina, an affluent majority-Black city. The biracial Fusion Party had managed to win election to a number of city offices, enraging white supremacists in the area, who plotted a violent overthrow of the local government. The mob murdered dozens of Black residents and forced thousands of others to flee their homes in what remains, to this day, the only successful coup in U.S. history.[15] Two decades later, in 1921, in one of the bloodiest racial attacks ever in the United States, a white mob burned and looted another prosperous Black community, the Greenwood neighborhood in Tulsa, Oklahoma. As many as three hundred Black people were killed and some ten thousand were rendered homeless. Thirty-five blocks were destroyed. No one was ever convicted in any of these acts of racist violence.[16]

In the same year as what came to be known as the Tulsa Race Massacre, a case in Georgia captured national attention. Federal officials were investigating a farmer in Jasper County for using peonage, a form of involuntary servitude based on indebtedness that was outlawed in 1867. Through this practice, the farmer had effectively enslaved a number of Black men. To conceal his actions from investigators, the farmer murdered the men working for him.[17]

Governor Hugh M. Dorsey responded to the national outrage over this episode by decrying the vast extent of peonage, lynching, and cruelty in his state. "In some counties the negro is being driven out as though he were a wild beast," Dorsey said in an address in Atlanta that summarized a series of allegations about mistreatment of Black people in Georgia. "In others he is being held as a slave. In others, no Negroes remain. . . . To me it seems that we stand indicted as a people before the world. If the conditions indicated by these charges should continue, both God and man would justly condemn Georgia."[18]

Dorsey told the story of a well-respected Black farmer who managed to save enough money to buy a 140-acre farm, where he lived with his wife and twelve children, three of whom were teachers. The farmer even earned praise in the local paper for raising $12,000 in Liberty bonds to support U.S. war efforts. But after the article was published, his neighbor, an illiterate white man, said, "He's getting too damned prosperous and biggity for a nigger."[19] Not long after, the white neighbor had a property line drawn twenty-five feet into the Black farmer's land and dared him to cross it.

Days later, when the Black man and four of his children went into town, a marshal served him a warrant for trespassing. When the man asked what he'd done, the marshal replied that "he would rather kill the negro than read the warrant."[20] The marshal then attacked the man, pistol-whipping him to the ground. A group of white men jumped in and began to choke and beat him. As his daughters rushed to help their father, a man kicked one of them in the gut. The family was overpowered by the mob and dragged to jail. The man and one of his daughters were badly injured. Three of the man's daughters were charged with resisting arrest, and his son was charged with carrying a pistol, despite the fact that he did not have one. The next day in jail the family learned that their neighbor had told the police that the Black man had been trespassing on his property.[21]

With the man in jail, a mob led by the town marshal went to his house in the middle of the night, while his wife and younger children were sleeping. The mob kicked down the door and then shot up the house. The family fled the next morning. A friend went back the next night and removed the family's livestock and sold it for much less than it was worth. Their crop was a total loss. They never returned—they'd been warned that if they did, they'd be lynched. The father was sentenced to twelve months on a chain gang and fined $250. The daughters were fined $50 each. The son was fined $100.[22]

"The education of his children and the success of his thrift seem to be the sole offense of the negro," Governor Dorsey said.[23] He outlined a series of remedies for these injustices, but strenuous objections from many Georgians prevented any significant reform.

With violence largely sanctioned by state and local governments, Black families, especially in the South, faced poverty coupled with a life in limbo, where safety, stability, access to education, and mental health were always precarious. This was true for many generations. Today, Black Americans far removed from slavery and Jim Crow continue to be handed the economic misfortune of their forebearers. This is why, as of 2017, white households were twice as likely as Black households to receive an inheritance. And when white people inherit money, it's typically three times the amount Black beneficiaries get. Those inheritances help drive the racial wealth gap.[24] Receiving an inheritance boosts the median wealth of white families by $104,000, but for Black families it's just $4,000.[25]

For most Black citizens, passing down a more substantial financial inheritance or a business such as the one Elmore Bolling was building when he was killed has been—and remains—a dream out of reach. Instead of wealth, millions of Black families have passed down something else from one generation to the next: the mental and emotional stress that results from the constant threat of white violence and financial insecurity.

Within a year of Elmore Bolling's murder, nearly all of the family's wealth was gone. White creditors and people posing as creditors took the money the family made from the sale of their trucks and cattle after the killing. Some others, without a shred of proof, claimed that Bolling owed them money. Bertha Mae feared what would happen if she didn't pay them. They even staked claims on what was left of the family's savings. With Bolling gone, there was no one else to run the many arms of the family business. Seemingly overnight the Bollings went from prosperity to poverty.[26]

"My father's murder actually killed aspirations for Black people," says McCall, referring to not just her family but all of the people who worked in their various enterprises. "Everyone had to go back to working for plantation owners. No one wanted to take over the business. My father had brothers, and when someone came in to ask my uncle, 'Are you going to take over Elmore's business?,' he said, 'No, that's what got him killed.'"

Less than two years later, the family fled Lowndes County in the dark of night, fearing for their lives. They found refuge in Montgomery, where Bertha Mae was employed in domestic work. Over the next few decades the family would remain financially and emotionally adrift. Eventually, some of the Bollings were drawn north by the Great Migration, while others joined the military and went overseas. There were marriages and divorces, births and deaths. Yet there was one consistent force connecting their fates: the rippling effects of Elmore's murder. No generation would fully escape.

Of the seven siblings—Louis, Elmore Jr., Willie D, Robert, Mary Magdalene, Morris, and Josephine—only Josephine, the youngest of the Bolling children, managed to earn a college degree. A college education isn't the sole marker of financial or social stability, but for the Bollings, as for most families, those with more education fared better; the men struggled the most, primarily working as low-paid laborers.

"I am the only college graduate," McCall says. "Which is a shame, because my father really emphasized education." She described to me why she thought her path was different from those of her siblings. One day when she was in high school, she told her English teacher that she was interested in a new trade program at the school that allowed students to spend part of the day in class and part on a job site. Her teacher balked: "No, Bolling. You don't want that. You're college material." In that moment, McCall made up her mind to set her sights higher. She eventually enrolled at Alabama State College, one of the state's fifteen historically Black colleges. McCall's mother, who'd left school in the sixth grade, helped pay her tuition with money she earned working at a local dry cleaner. McCall went to class during the week and then spent Friday evening through Sunday evening working for a white family, taking care of the children. After graduating with a degree in physical education and science, she got married and had two children. She worked as a teacher and a school psychologist and later became the first Black president of the Alabama Association of School Psychologists. Both of her children graduated from college.

Unlike some of her older siblings, McCall has very little memory of the day her father was killed. But she has watched its long, slow fallout her entire life. Her oldest brothers, Louis and Elmore Jr., were fifteen and fourteen years old when the men came for their father. Before then, they were being groomed to be the brains of their father's expanding business operation.

Instead, the eldest two Bolling boys dropped out of school not long after their father's murder. Louis married young and worked menial jobs before he was drafted into the army and served a tour in Korea. He eventually divorced, remarried, and started a taxi business. "My father always told them to work for themselves, and they took that literally," McCall said. But Louis's taxi business faltered after a few years, and he took a job at a local bowling alley; he spent the next forty-one years there, before retiring. His second marriage also ended in divorce. He managed to save enough money to buy a plot of land in

Montgomery and have a solid brick house built on it; he still lives there to this day. But he'll never be his own boss again.

Elmore Jr. spent much of his adult life employed in fairly menial jobs, including stints at a chemical plant and a food distributor, sometimes as a manager. He became a minister, in a bit of a spiritual nod to Elmore Sr., who had been a deacon at their childhood church. But he was unable to find the freedom that his father had told him would come with smarts and hustle. He learned that lesson the hard way. Elmore still feels the sting of being passed over for a higher-paying position; instead, it was given to a less-experienced white man he'd trained.

Of all the boys, Willie D, who was twelve when their father died, struggled the most. Elmore had called Willie D his "head man" and had trusted him to get his four younger siblings to school each morning while his older brothers were away in the city. He also ran the family's store part-time, and he was the one who witnessed the most on the day his father was murdered.

Willie D could never shake the sight of his father's brutalized body lying in that ditch. He, too, quit school. As a young man he worked odd jobs, handing over all of his pay to his mother. He eventually got married and found jobs at a Coca-Cola plant, a lumber company, and a wine company. As a young husband he took his pregnant wife to Chicago, looking for better prospects. But he found little in the so-called Promised Land of the North. Before he could lay down roots, he headed back home to Alabama. For a while he worked with his brother Louis, driving taxis. But his life was filled with struggle. He had eight kids and worked multiple jobs to put food on the table.

Then he had a seizure. Around that time, his wife left him, taking their youngest kids to Georgia. Mental illness tightened its grip, and Willie D was diagnosed with bipolar disorder. McCall remembers one especially troubling episode not long after his wife and children moved out, when he barricaded himself in his house with a loaded gun. The family arrived ahead of the police and talked the gun out of his hand. After that, the Bollings made the painful decision to have Willie D committed to a psychiatric facility. He spent the rest of his life in and out of mental institutions, struggling to stay on his meds.

Over a number of days in the early 2000s, he sat with McCall, who at the time was writing a book about their father's lynching, to tell her what he remembered about that day.[27] Details he'd kept locked inside for more than sixty years poured out of him. The white men who came to the store looking for his father. The terror he felt. Helplessly watching the men's car tail his father's truck on the highway near their store. The sounds of gunfire. His father's dead body. He'd even tried to peel the boots off his father's feet because of a saying he'd heard about not being able to get into heaven with them on. McCall says that Willie D's unrealized potential still pains her. He could fix anything mechanical, and he had a sharp mathematical mind and his father's business acumen. She thinks he could have been successful. He died of leukemia in 2007 in Montgomery.

Robert, Mary Magdalene, and Morris all took different paths. McCall says that Robert, who was ten years old when his father died, dropped out of school in the eighth grade and later struggled with alcohol abuse. He got married and headed north to Chicago, hoping to break the curse that had befallen his family. But trouble followed. His marriage failed, he couldn't find work, and one of his three children, a teenage son, was shot and killed in Chicago. Robert returned to Alabama to bury his son and later found work cleaning cars at a local Chevrolet dealership. He remarried, became a Jehovah's Witness, and lived the rest of his life isolated from the rest of the Bollings. He died in 2020.

Mary Magdalene, a year younger than Robert, was the first of the Bollings to graduate from high school. She spent two years at college before getting married and joining the migration north, moving first to Chicago and then to New York City. In New York she worked as live-in help for white families and eventually became a bookkeeper. After twenty-three years in New York, she returned home to Alabama to work at the Montgomery Housing Authority, where she stayed until she retired.

After a rocky academic road that included repeating a grade, Morris, the youngest boy, graduated from high school. For a while he worked for his brother's taxi service, then enlisted in the army. Morris launched a charter bus service in Atlanta, but the business foundered after one of his buses caught fire and his insurance company jacked up his premiums. Today, Morris manages a loading dock for AT&T.

Of Elmore and Bertha Mae's twenty-seven grandchildren, only eight, including McCall's two children, graduated from college. McCall says the rest are unemployed or underemployed. They have never known anything like the prosperity of their grandparents.

How might the family's trajectory have been different if Elmore Bolling had never been murdered? It's impossible to know, of course, but there's no doubt that Elmore's descendants would have enjoyed greater stability if his businesses had been allowed to grow and to be passed down to his children, who might have built on his successes and passed their own on to their own children. "He had established himself as a wealthy man," McCall says. "But I grew up poor.

"Sometimes I've wondered what my life could have been had he lived." Looking back on her family's winding path, she can't help but dwell on her father's strenuous efforts to create prosperity for the family, and how they were undermined. "Every time we take a step up," she said, "there's someone trying to crush it."

1925

Alain Locke publishes *The New Negro: An Interpretation,* an anthology of fiction, poetry, and essays on the art and literature of what will come to be called the Harlem Renaissance. Locke, a philosopher and professor at Howard University, spent much of the decade debating the purpose of art with W.E.B. Du Bois. Du Bois contended that all art was propaganda; Locke believed that it was "a tap root of vigorous, flourishing living," and that the creative explosion of the 1920s represented a new phase of Black life in America.

The New Negro

A. Van Jordan

A Negro voice spoke through a boy's open mouth.
A Negro voice survived through a boy's lynched neck.
A pen's stroke, a brush's sigh across a taut drum
that, under a dark hand, darkens further into song.
To read to write. To see to paint. Life: a deer trot
through cattail tall grass. Death: a figure crossing
against the light. Capture what you see and make
sense of what's out of view of the beholder.
The talented create as much as they think.
Intellect, some call it. Uppity, some call it. Du Bois
enjoys under cover of night what we sing
throughout the day. *The mind has leapt, so to speak,*
upon the parapets of prejudice; the mind has leapt,
so to speak, over the mute of proper into arpeggios of jazz.

And what to make of those shoes—green, anaconda, and shined!
And what to make of the bend in the brim of that hat,
the break of that slack over those shoes' laces. Details grow
in importance when art reaches higher.

Uncle Tom and Sambo have passed on,
and even the "Colonel" and "George" play
barnstorm roles from which they escape
when the public spotlight is off.

Insist on capitalizing the N in the N-word: Negro.
Per letter dated February 18, 1929.

Still, a Negro voice sings to the crowd from the hanged body in the tree.
Maybe he once chewed licorice in his mouth. Maybe an idea
formed before he could recite its lyric, mistaking the secret vowel,
a vowel as round and as warm as the skin of his hand,
keen yet soft as the consonant *N,* which he'll still wield
for his praise song, for his honeyed verse. *But that's cool,*
he'll say, that Negro boy with licorice blithely hanging
from his mouth, a mouth filled too with poems and with curses,
with regrets and gloating, the boy who calls the future to him,
who sees the pattern in the stones set on the path up ahead
and, without a second thought, will speak
and others will lean in a bit closer, hoping to hold some essence
they can neither hold nor fathom without him.

1932

The United States Public Health Service begins the Tuskegee Study of Untreated Syphilis in the Negro Male with more than 600 subjects, approximately two-thirds of whom have syphilis. White doctors tell their subjects only that they are being treated for "bad blood." Ultimately, 128 men die from the disease and related complications; 40 of their wives are also infected and 19 of their children are born with the disease. It is later revealed that for research purposes, the men were denied drugs that could have saved them.

Bad Blood

Yaa Gyasi

Upon closer inspection, the leaf her two-year-old was attempting to put in his mouth in the middle of the playground on that lovely fall day was in fact a used tampon. She snatched it from him and Purelled both of their hands before rushing him back to their apartment on Dean. She put him in the bath and scrubbed, and by the time her husband found them, they were both crying.

"We have to leave New York," she said after he put the baby to bed. "Let's move back home."

"There are tampons in Alabama," he said, and then: "What's the worst that could happen?"

It was the question they'd played out since graduate school, when her hypochondria had been all-consuming. Back then, leaning into her fears, describing them, had given her some comfort, but then they had Booker and suddenly the worst looked so much worse.

"He could get an STD, and then we'd be the Black parents at the hospital with a baby with an STD, and the pediatrician would call social services, and they would take him away, and we'd end up in jail."

"Okay," he said slowly. "That would be bad, but it's statistically very, very unlikely. Would it make you feel better if we called the doctor?"

She shook her head. Her husband only used the word "statistically" when he wanted to avoid using the words "you're crazy." She knew that the doctor would just tell her to trust him, but she also knew that when the worst happens in this country, it often happens to them.

She comes by her hypochondria and iatrophobia honestly. When she was growing up in Alabama, people still talked about their grandfathers, fathers, and brothers who had died of bad blood. That was the catchall term for syphilis, anemia, and just about anything that ailed you. The six hundred men who were enrolled in the Tuskegee Syphilis Study were told they'd get free medical care. Instead, from 1932 to 1972, researchers watched as they developed lesions on their mouths and genitals. Watched as their lymph nodes swelled, as their hair fell out. Watched as the disease moved into its final stage, leaving the men blind and demented, leaving them to die. All this when they knew a simple penicillin shot would cure them. All this because they wanted to see what would happen. For years afterward, her grandmother refused to go to the hospital. Even at eighty-nine, perpetually hunched over in the throes of an endless cough, she'd repeat, "Anything but the doctor." Bad blood begets bad blood.

She's more trusting than her grandmother, but she still has her moments. Like many women, she was nervous about giving birth. All the more so because she was doing it in New York City, where Black women are twelve times as likely to die in childbirth as white women. And in that very statistic, the indelible impression of Tuskegee. The lingering, niggling feeling that she is never fully safe in a country where doctors and researchers had no qualms about watching dozens of Black men die—slowly, brutally—simply because they could. When she held Booker in her arms for the first time and saw her grandmother's nose on his perfect face, love and fear rose up in her. "What's the worst that could happen?" her husband asks, and she can't speak it—the worst. Instead, she tries to turn off the little voice in her head, the one that wants to know: How exactly do you cure bad blood?

Imani Amos and her daughter, Indigo Moon Owusu, Beverly, Illinois, 2018   *MOTHERHOOD*, BY MAYA IMAN

CHAPTER 12

Medicine

LINDA VILLAROSA

In 2002, when Susan Moore received her degree from the University of Michigan Medical School, she joined a small sorority of Black women with the MD credential after their names.[1] That year, fewer than seven hundred Black women graduated from American medical schools—out of a total of nearly sixteen thousand newly minted doctors. Several years later, Moore settled in the Indianapolis area, where she practiced family and geriatric medicine, raised her son, Henry, and cared for her parents. But in 2020, when the Covid-19 pandemic hit, years of medical training and the credentials she'd worked so hard to earn would fail to protect her from the healthcare system itself.[2]

On November 29, Moore tested positive for Covid-19, and soon after, she was checked in to Indiana University Health North Hospital in Carmel, a suburban city near Indianapolis.[3] On December 4, she posted a video on her Facebook page that showed her lying in her hospital bed, a breathing tube inserted in her nose. Her voice halting as she struggled to catch her breath, Moore detailed disrespectful treatment by a white physician, whose name she took the time to spell out. He had rejected her plea for additional doses of an antiviral medication used to treat Covid, she said, adding in the post accompanying the video, "He did not even listen to my lungs, he didn't touch me in any way." And despite what she described as excruciating neck pain, according to her account, he told her he was uncomfortable giving her additional pain medication and tried to send her home. "I was crushed," a tearful Moore said in the video recorded on her cellphone, her eyes wide with a combination of frustration and fear. "He made me feel like I was a drug addict. And he knew I was a physician. I don't take narcotics. I was hurting."

Then, looking directly into the camera, her voice shaking with rage, Moore offered this scathing indictment of the American medical system, which had betrayed her: "I put forth and I maintain if I was white, I wouldn't have to go through that. This is how Black people get killed."[4]

Moore died two weeks later at age fifty-two. In her assessment of the U.S. healthcare system, she was correct on two counts. First, as a Black American, she was more likely to contract Covid-19 than a white American; and second, she was more likely to die from the disease. Around the time of her death, the Centers for Disease Control and Prevention released data showing that Black Americans were 1.4 times more likely than white ones to contract the virus, 3.2 times more likely to be hospitalized, and 2.8 times more likely to die.

Black Americans disproportionately contracted Covid-19 because of the many ways America's history of racial violence and inequality is baked into the institutions and structures of our society.[5] Black Americans are more likely to work in low-wage jobs and to live in segregated, crowded, polluted neighborhoods that lack adequate healthcare facilities and transportation; they are far less likely than white Americans to live near safe outdoor spaces and have access to healthful and affordable food.[6] These factors, the social determinants of health, have long had an outsized influence on health outcomes, and they help explain the racial disparities that were an immediate feature of the pandemic in the United States. The environment itself has been shown to worsen Covid-19 outcomes for Black Americans. In April 2020, as the pandemic surged, researchers from the Harvard T.H. Chan School of Public Health conducted a study that linked long-term exposure to dirty air to higher risk of death from the virus.[7]

This dangerous connection between air pollution and respiratory illness was not lost on those scientists and policy makers who have long known that African Americans shoulder a disproportionate burden of exposure to the nation's polluted environments. These social determinants more commonly impact poor communities. But racial health inequality transcends class, and even well-educated Black people with access to healthcare—like Susan Moore—are more vulnerable to a number of serious diseases. For one, they are affected by the stress of coping with racism embedded in day-to-day life, which can lead to a kind of premature aging. Arline T. Geronimus, a professor at the University of Michigan School of Public Health, does research in this area; she coined the term "weathering" to explain how high-effort coping in the face of continuous racial insults exacts a physical price on the bodies of Black Americans.[8]

What's more, as revealed by Dr. Moore's tragic death, even when Black people go to a medical facility for treatment and care, they can still be subject to racism's dehumanizing effects. The medical establishment has a long history of mistreating Black patients, either by failing to take their suffering seriously or by dismissing their concerns. This often comes up in the context of pain management. The physician who ignored Dr. Moore's distress and denied her pain relief was more than an isolated bad apple; the problem of minimizing Black pain has been well documented in scientific literature. A 2013 review of studies examining racial disparities in pain management published in the *American Medical Association Journal of Ethics* found that Black and Hispanic people—from children with adenoidectomies and tonsillectomies to elders in hospice care—received inadequate treatment for pain, especially as compared with their white counterparts.[9]

Why would this be the case? For centuries, white physicians and scientists went to great lengths to prove that Black bodies were biologically and physiologically different from white bodies.[10] To be clear, "different" almost always meant inferior. These physicians and scientists used their expertise and even empirical data to insist that enslaved Africans were "fit" for slavery and that the institution was not immoral or cruel, as many proclaimed.[11] Over time, their theories became incorporated into and normalized in medical practice, and this racializing of medicine did not end after slavery. Two persistent physiological falsehoods—that Black people were impervious to pain and that they had weak lungs that could be strengthened through hard work—have wormed their way into the scientific consensus, and can still be seen in modern-day medical education and practice. A study of 222 white medical students and residents published in the *Proceedings of the National Academy of Sciences* in 2016 showed that half of the students and residents endorsed at least one false idea about biological differences between Black people and white people, including that Black people's nerve endings are less sensitive than those of white people.[12] When asked to imagine how much pain white or Black patients experienced in hypothetical situations, the medical students and residents who held more false beliefs were more likely to maintain that Black people felt less pain, and thus they were less likely to recommend appropriate treatment.

This is how Black people get killed.

The Covid-19 pandemic has made it clear that by several measures, the health status of Black Americans is on par with that of people living in far poorer nations, and that at every stage of life Black Americans have poorer health outcomes than white Americans and even, in most cases, than other ethnic groups. Racial health disparities show up at the beginning of life and cut lives short at the end. Black babies are more than twice as likely as white babies to die at birth or in the first year of life—a racial gap that adds up to thousands of lost lives every year.[13] African American adults of all ages have elevated rates of conditions such as diabetes and hypertension that among white people are found more commonly at older ages.

In the first half of 2020, owing to the pandemic, the Black-white gap in life expectancy increased to six years, from four in 2019.[14]

This inequality when it comes to the health of Black people's bodies is rooted in false ideas about racial differences, developed and spread during slavery, and long challenged by Black medical practitioners and scholars, that still inform the way medical treatment is administered in America.[15] To understand the racial divide in the health of our nation that was stripped bare by Covid-19, we must examine the roots of these myths.

In the 1787 manual *A Treatise on Tropical Diseases; and on the Climate of the West-Indies,* a British doctor, Benjamin Moseley, claimed that Black people could bear surgical operations much more easily than white people, noting that "what would be the cause of insupportable pain to a white man, a Negro would almost disregard." To drive home his point, in a later edition he added, "I have amputated the legs of many Negroes who have held the upper part of the limb themselves."[16]

Thomas Jefferson, in *Notes on the State of Virginia,* published the same year as Moseley's treatise, listed what he proposed were "distinctions which nature has made."[17] "They secrete less by the kidneys, and more by the glands of the skin, which gives them a very strong and disagreeable odour," he explained, offering no evidence.[18] Jefferson, who both owned and fathered enslaved people, extrapolated that Black people were different emotionally and intellectually. "They seem to require less sleep," he wrote. "A black after hard labour through the day, will be induced by the slightest amusements to sit up till midnight, or later, though knowing he must be out with the first dawn of the morning."[19]

In the years that followed, physicians and scientists embraced some of Jefferson's unproven theories, perhaps none more aggressively than Samuel Cartwright, a physician and professor of "diseases of the Negro" at the University of Louisiana in New Orleans, now Tulane University. His widely circulated paper "Report on the Diseases and Physical Peculiarities of the Negro Race," published in the May 1851 issue of *The New-Orleans Medical and Surgical Journal,* cataloged supposed physical differences between white people and

Black people, including the claim that Black people had lower lung capacity—what he called "vital capacity."[20] To pursue this theory, he became one of the first doctors in the United States to measure pulmonary function with an instrument called a spirometer. According to his subsequent "calculations," "the deficiency in the Negro may be safely estimated at 20 percent." Cartwright, conveniently, saw forced labor as a way to "vitalize" the blood and correct the problem.[21]

Most outrageously, Cartwright maintained that enslaved people were prone to a "disease of the mind" called drapetomania, which caused them to run away from their enslavers. Willfully ignoring the inhumane conditions that drove desperate men and women to attempt escape, he insisted, without irony, that enslaved people could contract this ailment when their enslavers treated them as equals, and he prescribed "whipping the devil out of them" as a preventive measure.[22]

These fallacies had dangerous and terrifying outcomes for Black people. The false theory of higher Black pain tolerance led to the use of Black people as subjects in medical experiments that today we would view as unconscionable torture. The work of physician J. Marion Sims, long celebrated as the father of modern gynecology, offers one of the most infamous examples. Between 1845 and 1849, before anesthesia was widely in use, Sims used enslaved women in Montgomery, Alabama, as the subjects of painful operations so that he could perfect a surgical technique to repair vesicovaginal fistulas, which can be an extreme complication of childbirth. In his autobiography, *The Story of My Life,* Sims described the agony the women suffered as he cut their genitals again and again.[23]

A similar testament of torture, told from the other side of the operating table, is offered in *Slave Life in Georgia: A Narrative of the Life, Sufferings, and Escape of John Brown, a Fugitive Slave, Now in England,* which was published in 1855. Brown, who had been enslaved on a Baldwin County, Georgia, plantation in the 1820s and '30s, was lent by his enslaver to a physician named Dr. Thomas Hamilton. This doctor was obsessed with proving the existence of physiological differences between Black and white people, and Brown wrote about the excruciatingly painful medical experiments Hamilton put him through, until his body was disfigured by a network of scars. Among Hamilton's concerns was determining the thickness of Black skin, which he believed was greater than the thickness of white skin. Brown explains how Hamilton applied "blisters to my hands, legs and feet, which bear the scars to this day. He continued until he drew up the dark skin from between the upper and the under one. He used to blister me at intervals of about two weeks." This went on for nine months, Brown wrote, until "the Doctor's experiments had so reduced me that I was useless in the field."[24]

Hamilton was a courtly Southern gentleman, a wealthy plantation owner, a respected physician, and a trustee of the Medical Academy of Georgia.[25] Like many other Southern doctors of the era, he sought to scientifically prove that Black bodies were composed and functioned differently than white bodies. This was in keeping with the prevailing view of Southern white society at the time: that enslaved people were fit for little besides forced labor. Hamilton and other doctors bolstered this view, arguing that Black people had large sex organs and small skulls, which translated to promiscuity and a lack of intelligence and a higher tolerance for heat. These invented "facts," legitimized in medical journals, justified the barbaric violence of whipping and torture used to maintain slavery.[26]

The abuse of Black people under the guise of advancing medical discovery would continue even after slavery ended. In the early 1930s, scientists recruited Black men to participate in what would become one of the most notorious episodes in American history, the Tuskegee Study of Untreated Syphilis in the Negro Male. Between 1932 and 1972, the U.S. Public Health Service conducted a study on more than 600 Black Alabama day laborers and sharecroppers, including 399 who had syphilis and were not treated, to examine the progression of the disease.

The subjects were told that they would receive treatment for what was described as "bad blood."[27] They never did. Instead, government clinicians, ignoring the pain and suffering these men endured, allowed the illness to advance. Once the men died, doctors autopsied their bodies to compile data on the ravages of the disease.[28]

Today, Cartwright's 1851 paper reads like satire and Hamilton's supposedly scientific experiments appear simply sadistic. In 1997, President Bill Clinton apologized for the Tuskegee Syphilis Study, calling it "shameful" and "deeply, profoundly, morally wrong."[29] And in 2018, a statue commemorating Sims in New York's Central Park was removed after prolonged protest that included women wearing blood-splattered gowns in memory of Anarcha, Betsey, Lucy, and the other enslaved women he brutalized.[30]

Yet fallacies about Black immunity to pain, extra-thick skin, and weakened lung function that were introduced into the scientific literature by these and other racist doctors continue to show up in medical education today. Even Cartwright's footprint remains. Today most commercially available spirometers, used around the world to diagnose and monitor respiratory illness, have a "race correction" built into the software, to control for the assumption that Black people have less lung capacity than white people. In her 2014 book *Breathing Race into the Machine: The Surprising Career of the Spirometer from Plantation to Genetics,* Lundy Braun, a Brown University professor of pathology and laboratory medicine and Africana studies, as well as a professor of medical science at Brown's Warren Alpert Medical School, notes that the "race correction" is conventional practice, treated as fact in textbooks and still taught in many medical schools.[31]

Other unproven theories persist as well. One-third of the medical students surveyed in the 2016 study published by the National Academy of Sciences still believed the lie that Thomas Hamilton tortured John Brown to try to prove nearly two centuries ago: that Black skin is thicker than white skin.[32] Even after many reckonings with its racist past, our medical establishment still has not fully accepted how the distorted beliefs that were born during slavery play a role in creating healthcare inequality today. As a result, scientists, doctors, and other medical providers—and those training to fill such positions in the future—are often unaware of their own complicity in perpetuating the internalized racism and the conscious and unconscious biases that drive them to go against their oath to do no harm.

The hospital system in Indiana where Susan Moore was treated didn't immediately understand the hurt its staff had caused or the impact of lingering false assumptions about Black bodies and Black pain on medical decision-making. After she died, Indiana University Health conducted an external review, which concluded that Moore's caregivers had lacked "awareness of implicit racial bias." Though the report contended that "the medical management and technical care that Moore received did not contribute to her untimely death," it conceded that "there was a lack of empathy and compassion shown in the delivery of her care."[33] An earlier statement from the president and CEO of the organization seemed to blame Moore for her own death. He referred to her as a "complex patient" and said that the nursing staff at the facility might have been intimidated by her medical knowledge as she voiced her concerns and critiqued the care they were delivering.[34]

This is how Black people get killed.

We have long understood the crisis of poor health outcomes for Black Americans as a problem of race. But this implies an inferiority of Black bodies or Black culture. What happened to Dr. Moore speaks to the pervasive, long-running racial bias in the U.S. healthcare system, an erroneous set of deep-seated beliefs formulated during slavery and perpetuated over the decades since by social, political, and economic inequality.

In reality, it's never been race that predicts the disease and disability that disproportionally afflict Black Americans, but racism. Until we come to terms with the discrimination and inequality in American medicine, Black people will continue to be harmed by the very system that's supposed to take care of them.

That is how Black people get killed.

August 28, 1955

Two white men kidnap, beat, torture, and murder Emmett Till after the fourteen-year-old interacts with a white woman in a store in Money, Mississippi. The following month, the men, who will later admit to their crime, are acquitted by an all-white jury. Several months after this, Rosa Parks launches the Montgomery bus boycott.

1955

Danez Smith

two hours west of Egypt, over in Money, that boy.
& his overripe face, river-wrecked, no seed, no amulet.
my grandpa, sixteen & singing, still small, fear-steadied
years from his own violence, pulls the name from the radio
feathered & soaking, stunned blue by the current's silk trample
& keep, what a soft name, you must hum to begin him
mama's massacred lil man made maybe martyr, mural
haunting wallets, a warning tucked between nephews
his face. no face. that face. his. his name wounds time
his face a knife sinking thru centuries, but centuries don't fit
in a year or in a boy's guiltless hands my grandpa before
he was anyone's flinch stood in the kitchen with crows
in his chest he was no sky & yet in his hands a boy
dead enough to be an angel, too drenched to fly, my pa, a sky
stood in wait for the river to drain from wings
where was you someone when the drowned refused flight
& Mamie left his mushy mug to wind & flies, flashes & eyes
that year Rosa utters a coordinated *no* & the world takes off
as my James takes a train north into another white cold kill
& that name still soggy & refused in his hands & all over
all he touches: his daughters, his wife's cheek, the split
hogs, where he is secret & plush, everything, wet with it.

listen—this is true—my grandma met him two summers
before then with his lil quartet, he bought her ice cream
& laid ditties at her flats. summer, evil, bright constant
changes a boy, fills him with a grown terror—i never heard
James's song, not one lonely peep.

February 1, 1960

David Richmond, Franklin McCain, Joseph McNeil, and Ezell Blair, Jr., four freshmen at North Carolina Agricultural and Technical State University, begin a sit-in at a segregated whites-only counter at a Woolworth's in Greensboro. The protest quickly spreads to dozens of other cities around the country. Over the summer, numerous establishments across the South, including the Greensboro Woolworth's, desegregate their dining areas.

From Behind the Counter

Terry McMillan

My cousin who lives out in California told me a long time ago that right
before an earthquake there was a stillness in the air. He said to watch out
because it could mean good news or bad news but it would be something
you can't prepare for. Well, I missed work yesterday because the bus broke
down and by the time I walked to Woolworth's it woulda almost been time
for me to turn around and come on back home so I got a ride to the closest
gas station and they let me use their phone but my boss didn't care what the
reason was I wasn't coming and docked me the seven dollars I woulda made.
It took me almost two hours to walk back home and the whole time I didn't
see one leaf move on any of the trees. Even when I turned the corner and
walked up the hill, I didn't feel a breeze.

I just hoped this wasn't a sign the baby was coming early. Me and my wife
been struggling to get on our feet here in Greensboro after staying with
kinfolks a whole year and now with a baby on the way I need every dime I
can get, which is why I haul trash to the dump on my off days.

The bus ran fine today and this morning was just like most mornings. I
walked out front to clean off the counter. I tried not to watch the parade of
mostly white people carrying bags full of everything I couldn't afford. When
four young colored men in trench coats walked in through the glass doors, I
nodded hello, thinking they must be looking for a job, but before I could
guess again each one stopped right below the giant sign that said WHITES
ONLY and one by one they sat down at the counter and each one set what
looked like a briefcase on the floor next to his legs, which was when I felt all
the air in the diner evaporate.

My heart hurt from beating so hard. I thought maybe they might be confused or lost even though they didn't look it. They looked determined. I made myself breathe.

"Y'all look like you can read," I whispered, glancing up at the sign and then into their eyes.

Just then Mary, a waitress nobody liked because she cursed like a sailor, walked down the counter tapping her pencil, which was when the tooth I needed to see a dentist about started beating like it had a heart and it felt like I was about to have an asthma attack even though I don't have asthma.

"Y'all must can't read. But them suits won't help," she said, looking down at the young men. "Y'all still colored."

My forehead was sweating 'cause I started thinking about the time my cousin got run over by a white woman for smiling at her at a stop sign and she waited for him to step off the curb and take a few steps which was when she pressed on the gas, hit him hard enough we heard his ankle crack. When we told the police and gave them her license plate number, they didn't even bother to write it down.

"Yes, we can read," said the one wearing glasses. He sounded smart. They all looked smart. I wanted to ask them where they worked but they looked too young to have jobs where they would wear what I could see under those trench coats was suits.

"We would like a cup of coffee. Please."

"You know y'all can't sit here."

"We are already sitting here," the one at the end said.

He sounded so proper I wondered if he might be from New York. I was scared. Why'd they have to pick today to do this? I was waiting for my check, and this foolishness might make me lose my job and maybe not get paid. I got a baby just waiting to meet me. Our rent is three days late and my wife had to stop cleaning houses when she couldn't stand the smell of bleach. And nobody can help us because everybody we know is poor.

I heard the cooks talking about how much nerve the niggers had. But they just politely kept asking for a cup of coffee. The waitresses pretended they was deaf.

Finally, one of the young men said, "Our money is just as good as anyone else's."

A different waitress said, "No, it ain't."

But the young men didn't get up. They reached down and pulled out thick books from their satchels and then set them on the counter, opened them right up like they was all studying the same thing. Where did they get this courage from? Was it from those books? I wondered what they was studying and if there was a class they took on bravery and if they knew other brave colored people? One day I wanted to know what courage felt like, too. I was trying to see what they was reading but it was hard to read upside down. I saw numbers. Strange numbers. I saw a black-and-white picture of the world. Another one about science. And history. I wanted to know whose history? But I couldn't ask. I mostly read the Bible.

I prayed all day the police wouldn't walk through the glass doors and try to yank them off those swivel chairs and when them young men resisted— which I could tell they would—that they wouldn't get dragged outside—one by one—then shot and killed for every time they kept on asking for a cup of coffee and didn't get it.

Even when those news people came and turned them bright lights and cameras on, and crowds in all shades came from inside and outside the store, jumping up and down to see what was going on, them young men did not move. They just kept asking for a cup of coffee.

By now, the waitresses was just ignoring them like they weren't even there. I wanted to say something to the young men but I was scared I would get fired. When I picked up the rubber tray full of dirty dishes and walked past them I did push a fork so it would fall on the floor and when I bent down to pick it up I locked eyes with all four of them and they could see I was proud.

I didn't look at any of them again because if something happened to them I didn't want to remember their faces.

I pretended I needed to go to the bathroom and walked through the store into the men's room. I went inside an empty stall, closed the toilet lid, and sat down. I wondered how all this was gon' turn out? I knew it wasn't about coffee, but what would happen if they did get served a cup? Would that mean they could maybe order some eggs and bacon and toast and orange juice and sit there and eat while they read? Me, I never really wanted to sit next to white people to eat. I didn't trust them. But I also never liked that they was the ones who decided it. Just like they was the ones who decided we would be slaves and when we should be free. I always wondered what made them think they was better than us just because they was—I mean *were*—white? I decided that when I got home, I was gon' tell my wife we need to start telling each other how we really feel about how we living. We need to stop being scared of white people and stop acting like we ain't free.

When the store was closing, the police ushered the men out the back door. As the door slammed shut, my boss put his plaid jacket on, headed out toward the front door, and said, "See you tomorrow. And don't be late."

I finished cleaning up the kitchen and went out front and started wiping the counter up and down with a damp rag. The icebox was humming and then it just stopped. Silence can be loud is what I was thinking as I sat down on a stool like I owned the place. I swiveled a few times, staring at the stools where the four young men had sat all day, which was when I threw my damp rag on the floor and poured myself a cup of lukewarm coffee and took a long sip, looking at that empty counter, and at the stools, and up at the WHITES ONLY sign, which was when I felt my body rise up and my arms reached up and I pulled it down.

Two church ladies, Harlem, 1976   *AMEN CORNER SISTERS*, BY MING SMITH

CHAPTER 13

Church

ANTHEA BUTLER

"God damn America."

The words belonged to the Reverend Jeremiah Wright, the leader of Trinity United Church of Christ, and they ripped through the airwaves in 2008, creating a furor for Senator Barack Obama, who was running to be the United States of America's first Black president. Obama had been a member of Wright's congregation for twenty years. He had been married in that Chicago church and had baptized his children there. His relationship to Jesus Christ had solidified in a congregation that, as he later described it, embodied "the black community in its entirety—the doctor and the welfare mom, the model student and the former gang-banger."[1] The title of his 2006 memoir, *The Audacity of Hope,* was taken from one of Wright's sermons.

But the prophetic aspect of Wright's theology, which mounted a direct and forthright critique of American power, would become a problem for Obama. On March 13, 2008, in the middle of his hard-fought Democratic primary with Hilary Clinton, ABC News ran a report called "Obama's Preacher: The Wright Message?" The segment contained a portion of a Palm Sunday sermon Wright gave in 2003 about the Gospel According to Luke and the peril of conflating divine rule with the rule of national governments. Near the end of this sermon, Wright reached a crescendo as he described the plight of Black people in America:

> When it came to treating her citizens of African descent fairly, America failed. She put them in chains. The government put them in slave quarters, put them on auction blocks, put them in cotton fields, put them in inferior schools, put them in substandard housing, put them in scientific

experiments, put them in the lowest paying jobs, put them outside the equal protection of the law, kept them out of their racist bastions of higher education, and locked them into positions of hopelessness and helplessness. The government gives them the drugs, builds bigger prisons, passes a three-strike law, and then wants us to sing "God Bless America." No, no, no. Not God bless America! God damn America! That's in the Bible, for killing innocent people. God damn America for treating her citizens as less than human. God damn America as long as she keeps trying to act like she is God and she is supreme![2]

The news report aired only the final part of this: Obama's pastor shouting, "God damn America" again and again. This critique was unfamiliar to most white Americans, many of whom immediately attacked Wright for being unpatriotic, for sowing seeds of division and hate, and for advocating Black separatism. Within forty-eight hours of the ABC News special, Obama had sent out a statement about Wright's sermon, calling the words of his longtime minister "inflammatory and appalling." "I reject outright the statements by Rev. Wright that are at issue," he wrote.[3] But it quickly became clear to his campaign that he had to respond more fully to the firestorm. He did so by giving a speech in Philadelphia entitled "A More Perfect Union."[4] In that speech, Obama called Wright's sermon "incendiary language" and went on to say that his pastor's message "expressed a profoundly distorted view of this country that sees white racism as endemic and that elevates what is wrong with America above all that we know is right with America."

Obama's response seemed to be designed to save his political career by presenting himself as a measured, reasoned man who loved America and did not believe that all white people were racists. His speech was widely praised, and it succeeded in its aims: three months later he won the Democratic nomination, and that November, the presidency. But it also revealed a painful truth: at the moment the nation was preparing to elect its first Black leader, the role the Black church had played in bringing about that possibility had to be disavowed. The prophetic power of the church had given Obama his soaring speeches and fervor for change, but it was anathema to the political arena of accommodation, especially during an election cycle.

For many Black Christians, however, Wright's adversarial tone, rooted in a centuries-long quest for justice and righteousness, was not out of the ordinary at all. Wright was an adherent of Black liberation theology, a concept developed in the 1960s by James H. Cone, who had been a mentor to Wright. Cone argued that the plight of Black Americans must be a central concern of the church. "Life-giving power for the poor and the oppressed is the primary criterion that we must use to judge the adequacy of our theology," he declared. "Not abstract concepts."[5] Cone criticized white Christians for what he saw as their historical failure to fight against slavery, violence, and racial oppression; that failure, he argued, had proved their tradition to be an unrighteous one, out of step with the essence of the gospel.

Cone's theology grew out of an even older prophetic tradition. Over the centuries, Black preachers in America have used their pulpits just like Wright did, to challenge the hypocrisy of white America's racism, sometimes with harsh language. Black preaching by historical necessity used the jeremiad, a rhetorical mode of denunciation or chastisement about the corruption of people, events, or nations that stretches back to the prophets of the Hebrew Bible. More than two thousand years later, in the antebellum United States, Black preachers castigated the nation for the evils of slavery. Preaching in the Black church was primarily done by men, in part because of religious prohibitions barring women from the pulpit.[6] And while Black preachers generally did not confront the issue of unfairness regarding gender, they repeatedly confronted the moral ills of a society built on chattel slavery.

White Protestant Christianity in early American history also inherited the tradition of the jeremiad, but it was put to different ends, focused on an individual's relationship to God, and personal sin, and legislating morality. "The Puritans gave a special supernatural legitimacy to the Protestant work ethic in the New World," the scholar Sacvan Bercovitch has observed. "They raised the success story to the status of visible sainthood." In his book *The American Jeremiad,* Bercovitch points out that the Puritan jeremiad was a lament about how the colonists had neglected to seize the opportunity presented by land they had been given in New England. "The clergy bewailed," Bercovitch writes, "the 'sloth' of those who failed to take advantage of 'this good land whither the Lord has sent us.'"[7]

By contrast, the style of the Black church that developed following the Great Awakening and in the antebellum period was one of prophetic witness to the moral outrage of racism in America. It was the rhetoric of dissent, according to Bercovitch. David Walker, a nineteenth-century anti-slavery advocate and a member of the A.M.E. Church, embraced this approach in his *Appeal to the Coloured Citizens of the World,* excoriating white Christians for their role in the slave trade: "They cram us into their vessel holds in chains and hand-cuffs—men, women and children all together!! O! save us, we pray thee, thou God of Heaven and of earth, from the devouring hands of the white Christians!!!"[8]

In the twentieth century, Black preachers decried lynching, Jim Crow, segregation, police violence, and other moral ills in America. Martin Luther King, Jr.'s leadership in the civil rights movement and his opposition to the Vietnam War exemplify this tradition as well. In a speech at Riverside Church in 1967, he declared that the government of United States was "the greatest purveyor of violence in the world today." "If we do not act," King thundered, "we shall surely be dragged down the long, dark, and shameful corridors of time reserved for those who possess power without compassion, might without morality, and strength without sight."[9]

But the Black church has not only been a forum for righteous anger. Forged out of slavery, it was also a place of protection and practicality. For many decades it was one of the few places Black people could gather for educational purposes, to arrange mutual aid groups, or to form political organizations. As a result, it has always been a target. As an independent institution operating free of white control and oversight, the Black church had inherent revolutionary potential that often made it an object of white fear and anger. During the widespread violence that followed emancipation, the Ku Klux Klan burned scores of Black churches to the ground, eventually helping to extinguish the promise of Reconstruction. In the buildup to the Wilmington coup in 1898, white "citizens' patrols" harassed Black churches where they suspected leaders were conspiring. During the Tulsa Race Massacre in 1921, white people fired machine guns at the Mount Zion Baptist Church. And on September 15, 1963, members of the Ku Klux Klan bombed the Sixteenth Street Baptist Church in Birmingham, killing four little Black girls and injuring many other people.

This long history of violence against Black churches continues in our own era. After Michael Brown was killed in Ferguson, Missouri, in 2014, the pastor of Flood Christian Church repeatedly called out police brutality.[10] One week after Brown's father was baptized at the church, the building was burned to the ground. The following year, the unthinkable happened: nine members of Emanuel A.M.E. Church in Charleston, South Carolina, one of the country's oldest A.M.E. congregations, were murdered when a white supremacist named Dylann Roof opened fire in a Bible study group that included Reverend Clementa Pinckney, both the pastor of the church and a state legislator.

The murders at Emanuel A.M.E. were devastating. What was also striking to many observers was the speed with which some of the families were willing to forgive Roof. They told him so at his bond hearing just days later. "I forgive you," said Anthony Thompson, whose wife was killed. "My family forgives you." The daughter of Ethel Lance, who was also killed, told Roof, "May

God forgive you. And I forgive you."[11] That Sunday, Reverend Norvel Goff, Sr., told the congregation, "We still believe that prayer changes things . . . prayer not only changes things, it changes us."[12] This spirit of acceptance and forgiveness culminated later in the week when President Obama gave the eulogy for Reverend Pinckney and led the congregation in singing "Amazing Grace."

The controversy over Reverend Wright's sermon and the horrific attack on Emanuel A.M.E. bookended the presidency of the nation's first Black president, offering the country different perspectives on the Black church. Wright's theology, his understanding of the gospel as fundamentally about justice and standing with the oppressed, represented to many white Americans the threat that the Black church has historically posed to the nation's status quo. For others, it was the correct response to the violence and injustice that Black people continue to face in this country, violence exemplified by the shocking murders at Emanuel A.M.E. seven years later. The response of some in the congregation following Roof's massacre represented another dimension of the church: a Christian tradition of forgiveness, nonviolence, love, and suffering. To understand how these tendencies have shaped a unique Black American theology, we need to begin where the Black church began, in slavery.

The African men, women, and children who were captured and transported to the Americas on slave ships brought with them their own religious beliefs and practices.[13] Some were practitioners of African traditional religions like Yoruba and Vodun; others were Muslim or Catholic. But they were all often seen as heathens by the colonists, who found justification for enslaving them in interpretations of biblical scriptures, most notably Genesis 9:25, the "curse of Ham," in which Noah's youngest son, Ham, the father of Canaan, looks upon his father's nakedness and is punished severely: "Cursed be Canaan; a servant of servants shall he be unto his brethren." Theologians of the Reformation period understood Africans to be the descendants of Canaan and, therefore, destined to be slaves.[14]

Still, in the North American colonies, modest numbers of free Black and enslaved people baptized their children and observed other Christian practices. Though this was initially limited by English laws that some colonists interpreted as prohibiting the enslavement of Christians, by the second half of the seventeenth century, new laws had clarified the matter. For instance, one passed in the colony of Virginia in 1667 specified that "the conferring of baptisme doth not alter the condition of the person as to his bondage."[15] This led to further efforts to introduce the enslaved to Christianity. In 1701, the

Church of England founded the Society for the Propagation of the Gospel in Foreign Parts, which evangelized to English colonists and non-Christians, including some enslaved people. Despite the new laws, these missionary efforts alarmed many enslavers, who feared that baptism could lead to freedom.

The First Great Awakening saw the rise of religious fervor not only among white Americans but also in both free and enslaved Black people. This revival period, starting in the 1730s, introduced a more emotional and ecstatic religious practice that would also empower the enslaved. In the decades that followed, they would create what Albert Raboteau describes in his groundbreaking book *Slave Religion* as an "invisible institution." There were few formal Black churches at this point, but the enslaved could gather in outdoor spaces and hear from Black preachers an interpretation of Christianity that diverged from the one offered by white churches, which in most cases amounted to: "slaves ought to be obedient to their masters."[16] The Black preachers and the emerging tradition of Black spirituals contributed to a different understanding of the gospel, one that encouraged and supported a longing for freedom.

In the second half of the eighteenth century, the Methodist Church provided an institutional home for some Black Christians. Though they were segregated from white parishioners, Black Methodists could join congregations, and they soon made up 20 percent of the church's members in North America. It was in this context that the first "visible institutions" for Black religious practice began to emerge.

In April 1787, just one month before the Constitutional Convention gathered in Philadelphia to draft the nation's charter document, two leaders of the city's small community of free Black people, Richard Allen and Absalom Jones, founded an aid organization called the Free African Society to help formerly enslaved people get on their feet. Both had been born into slavery themselves, with Allen purchasing his freedom in his early twenties and Jones being manumitted when he was nearly forty years old. They met at St. George's Methodist Episcopal Church, where Allen, who had been preaching since he was a young man, would sometimes lead services for the small group of Black members. Though the Free African Society was initially a nondenominational organization, it provided services in keeping with the gospel of the church, offering various kinds of aid and support to the many widows, orphans, and sick, injured, or destitute Black people, some of them fugitives from slavery, who were arriving in great numbers in the new nation's capital city during those years.

As the population of free Black people in Philadelphia grew, tensions mounted at St. George's over the increasing number of Black parishioners showing up for services. One Sunday in 1792, a dispute arose over where Allen and Jones would sit and pray. In Allen's memoir, *The Life, Experience, and Gospel Labours of the Rt. Rev. Richard Allen,* he describes the incident:

> Meeting had begun, and they were nearly done singing, and just as we got to the seats, the elder said, "let us pray." We had not been long upon our knees before I heard considerable scuffling and low talking. I raised my head up and saw one of the trustees, H— M—, having hold of the Rev. Absalom Jones, pulling him up off of his knees, and saying, "You must get up—you must not kneel here." Mr. Jones replied, "wait until prayer is over." Mr. H— M— said "no, you must get up now, or I will call for aid and I force you away." Mr. Jones said, "wait until prayer is over, and I will get up and trouble you no more." With that he beckoned to one of the other trustees, Mr. L— S— to come to his assistance. He came, and went to William White to pull him up. By this time prayer was over, and we all went out of the church in a body, and they were no more plagued with us in the church. This raised a great excitement and inquiry among the citizens, insomuch that I believe they were ashamed of their conduct. But my dear Lord was with us, and we were filled with fresh vigor to get a house erected to worship God in.[17]

Both Jones and Allen set about raising funds from Black and white Philadelphians to establish churches. Before they could do so, a yellow fever epidemic struck the city. Many of the city's white residents, including Dr. Benjamin Rush, one of the signers of the Declaration of Independence, erroneously thought that something in the constitution of Black people kept them from catching the virus.[18] So they pressed African Americans into service as nurses, caretakers, and gravediggers. Allen, Jones, and other members of the Free African Society were instrumental in tending to the city's sick, with Allen himself falling ill and recovering. Others were not so lucky. Still, under the leadership of Allen and Jones, the city's Black population performed many noble acts during the crisis. As one Philadelphian wrote in a letter, "I dont know what the people would do, if it was not for the Negroes, as they are the Principal nurses."[19]

Allen preached about the demonstration of Christian charity represented by these selfless acts. Nevertheless, when the virus subsided, Black contributions to the city's survival during the epidemic were contested, erased, and denied, with one white printer going so far as to accuse the city's Black nurses of extorting large fees from their patients and looting their houses. The slander against the city's Black community was so great that Allen and Jones published a response, entitled *A Narrative of the Proceedings of the Black People, During the Late Awful Calamity in Philadelphia, in the Year 1793: And a Refutation of Some Censures Thrown upon Them in Some Late Publications.*[20] Their reputations prevailed, and in 1794, Allen was able to garner enough support to start the Bethel Church in an old blacksmith's shop. That same year, Jones opened the African Episcopal Church of St. Thomas. Both churches had grown out of the Free African Society, the founding of which one A.M.E. pastor would later refer to as "a Liberty Bell for Black folks."[21]

Allen and Jones were not alone in their efforts to establish independent Black churches in some of the nation's Northern cities. In the 1790s, a Second Great Awakening swept through the country, spreading the gospel even farther. By 1816, Black congregations from Baltimore; Attleborough, Pennsylvania; and Salem, New Jersey, had joined together with the Philadelphia churches to incorporate the A.M.E. denomination, with Bethel as its mother church. In 1819, Jarena Lee became the first African American woman licensed to preach, at Richard Allen's invitation. (Lee had approached Allen some years prior, but he had declined her request; she would continue to preach after Allen's death, and would work with the New York Anti-Slavery Society.)[22] Over the next decade, Black people founded other A.M.E. congregations, primarily in the Northeast and the Midwest, and even as far away as Hispaniola, when, in the 1820s, six thousand free Black people emigrated to Haiti from the United States.[23]

From the beginning, these A.M.E. congregations demonstrated the crucial role the Black church would play in resisting slavery and oppression. "God himself was the first pleader of the cause of the slaves," Allen wrote in his autobiography.[24] In 1830, Mother Bethel A.M.E. Church was the site of the inauguration of the Colored Conventions movement, gatherings of free Black leaders who met to discuss and strategize about educational, political, labor, and legal rights. Allen, then seventy years old, was elected president of the convention, combining the roles of spiritual and political leader in a way that would become common for Black clergy.[25] Throughout the nineteenth century, these conventions, which provided a critical foundation for building a political case for abolition, equality, and Black citizenship, were often held in churches.

The gospel clearly contained inspiration for the freedom struggle, and not always through peaceful means. In the first few decades of the nineteenth century, enslaved people, often motivated by religious fervor, regularly joined uprisings led by Black spiritual leaders. Denmark Vesey, a free carpenter and a member of Charleston's A.M.E. church, made plans for a rebellion in the city in 1822. After his capture and execution, local white residents burned the church—the same congregation Dylann Roof attacked in 2015—to the ground. Nat Turner, a preacher who believed he had received prophetic visions of Jesus's apocalyptic return, led a rebellion in 1831 that killed fifty-five white people. After he was captured and executed, along with some two hundred freed and enslaved Black persons, Virginia enacted laws forbidding Black people from attending religious gatherings without white observers present.

After emancipation, some Black religious figures took a new approach to demanding justice: they ran for political office. One of the first was Henry McNeal Turner, a minister in the A.M.E. Church. Born a free man in South Carolina in 1834, Turner joined the church in St. Louis in 1858 and soon after was ordained. In 1863 he played an instrumental role in forming the first Black military regiment in the Union Army (there would ultimately be 175), and he served as the first Black chaplain commissioned to minister to Black troops. At the end of the war, Turner headed south to work for the Freedmen's Bureau and ended up in Georgia, where he planted numerous A.M.E. churches.

But it was as an elected official that he believed he would have the greatest impact during Reconstruction. In 1868, Turner and more than two dozen other Black men in Georgia won races for the state legislature, running as Republicans. In response, white Georgia lawmakers introduced a measure to expel them. Once Turner realized that those white officials had no intention of allowing him or the other newly elected Black lawmakers to be seated, he wrote a defiant speech entitled "I Claim the Rights of a Man." Though it would be voiced from the statehouse floor, it was very much in the tradition of the jeremiad, delivered from the pulpit, that had already begun to define the Black church in America.

In arguing for electoral legitimacy, Turner pinpointed the core issue in the Reconstruction era: the rights white people had were also now available to Black people. Many Southern white people rejected this idea entirely. On September 3, 1868, along with other elected Black lawmakers, Turner addressed the legislature, demanding that they not be stripped of their elected offices:

> If you deny my right—the right of my constituents to have representa-
> tion here—because it is a "privilege," then, sir, I will show you that I have
> as many privileges as the whitest man on this floor. If I am not permit-

ted to occupy a seat here, for the purpose of representing my constituents, I want to know how white men can be permitted to do so. How can a white man represent a colored constituency, if a colored man cannot do it? The great argument is: "Oh, we have inherited" this, that and the other. Now, I want gentlemen to come down to cool, common sense. Is the created greater than the Creator? Is man greater than God? It is very strange, if a white man can occupy on this floor a seat created by colored votes, and a black man cannot do it.[26]

The speech aroused the ire of the Ku Klux Klan and other white supremacists. A statement in the Columbus *Weekly Sun,* a local newspaper, declared that "we should be neither seized with anger or regret" if Turner were to be lynched.[27] He survived and Congress intervened, compelling the Georgia state legislature to seat the elected Black lawmakers, including Turner. But over the next nine years, Reconstruction would begin to crumble as white politicians, law enforcement, and Christians banded together to push back violently against the autonomy of Black people in the South.

During this period, known as Redemption, starting in the 1870s, white men embraced a completely different religious rationale to methodically erase the gains of Reconstruction. The white "Redeemers" who overturned Reconstruction claimed they were driven by divine right to bring God's order back to the South. According to the historian Daniel Stowell, Redeemers imagined that, like Jesus, they could "redeem" the South with blood sacrifice and rescue their states from the captivity of Northern and African American political power.[28] In the words of Carole Emberton in her book *Beyond Redemption:* "Disparate movements and agendas simultaneously sought redemption *from* violence and also *through* violence."[29] Black families and communities throughout the South, as well as many white people who supported them, were terrorized by waves of ferocious brutality that started almost as soon as the Civil War ended. Frequently, these attacks targeted Black churches.

One episode took place in Memphis in 1866, when the city's police department, along with a mob of white men, attacked Black neighborhoods and contraband camps of formerly enslaved people. The white mob burned down four Black churches, destroyed twelve schools, killed forty-six African Americans, and raped five women.[30]

In the wake of this violence and with a newfound understanding of the futility of working within the system, Turner evolved in new directions. Discouraged by his experience in politics, he became a bishop in the A.M.E. Church, and a more radical voice. He had always advocated an accommodationist relationship with white people; now he began to preach a version of Black nationalism: the belief that Black people should have their own autonomy, even their own country. He became a proponent of the Back to Africa movement, and believed that slavery had existed in order to expose Africans to Christianity. He argued that Black people had "needed to come in contact with Christian civilization and by intercourse with the powerful white race," so that they could "fit themselves to go back to their own land and make of that land what the white man had made of Europe and America."[31] Turner would eventually plant churches in Liberia, Sierra Leone, and South Africa. He believed that Christianity would make Africa a great continent if it was brought there by free African Americans in the form of the A.M.E. Church, which had already done so much to advance the cause of Black liberation in the United States.

The traditions arising out of Black nineteenth-century churches and leadership included social uplift, liberation, pragmatism, and Black nationalism. All of these and more would prove necessary for Black citizens to survive the oppressive laws, terroristic violence, and grinding deprivation of the Jim Crow era. During this period, the church continued to serve as a structure that protected Black Americans, supported them, and shielded them from the wrath of white people who refused to see them as equals. But as time went on, it went beyond being a place of refuge and evolved into the primary site of a revolutionary movement. Buttressed by groups like the NAACP, the National Urban League, and the National Association of Colored Women's Clubs, the church was the home base of the civil rights movement in the 1950s. It was one of the few places where Black people could meet safely, and for leaders of the movement, it offered a connection to prominent people in the community who could provide finances and lodging.

When police arrested Rosa Parks on December 1, 1955, for not giving up her seat on the bus, the Black community in Montgomery was ready; they had been planning this act of civil disobedience. A group of local ministers and community leaders met at the Dexter Avenue Baptist Church to prepare a boycott of the city's buses. They called themselves the Montgomery Improvement Association and elected as the organization's leader the new pastor of the church, a twenty-six-year-old graduate of Boston University's doctoral program in systematic theology named Martin Luther King, Jr. For King, the prophetic confrontation began with the bus boycott, a protest sustained by weekly meetings at the city's churches, where activists would organize car-pools and facilitate support from other church groups around the country.

The Montgomery bus boycott highlighted King's rhetorical skill, as well as his message of nonviolent action. It lasted for just over a year, during which King was arrested and his home firebombed. Speaking after the bombing, King urged his followers to "meet violence with nonviolence." Though his message had been honed by his undergraduate mentor Benjamin Mays, the president of Morehouse College, whose study of Gandhian nonviolence influ-enced King's doctoral work at Boston University, it was also informed by Christian theology:

Remember the words of Jesus: "He who lives by the sword will perish by the sword." We must love our white brothers, no matter what they do to us. We must make them know that we love them. Jesus still cries out in words that echo across the centuries: "Love your enemies; bless them that curse you; pray for them that despitefully use you." This is what we must live by. We must meet hate with love. Remember, if I am stopped, this movement will not stop, because God is with the movement. Go home with this glowing faith and this radiant assurance.[32]

The movement attracted young divinity school scholars like James Law-son, a student at Vanderbilt Divinity School, who organized the Nashville sit-ins in 1960, and John Lewis and C. T. Vivian, both divinity students at American Baptist Theological Seminary in Nashville, as well as college students like Diane Nash, who was at Fisk University. The church sat at the center of their activism, as a locus of worship and as a community and organizing space for political and social engagement. Numerous actions of this period were born in church basements, meeting rooms, and pews, including the Albany Move-ment, a desegregation effort in Georgia; the 1961 Freedom Rides; and the Birmingham campaign.

But not all religious leaders agreed on the way forward. King and other ministers who were active in the movement clashed with Joseph Jackson, the longtime leader of the National Baptist Convention (NBC), who was more moderate and resisted getting the convention more involved in civil rights. As a result, in 1961, King and other ministers would split away from the NBC to form the Progressive National Baptist Convention.

Malcolm X, the Nation of Islam, and the rise of Black Power presented a more serious challenge to the Black church's vision of the path toward free-

dom. Malcolm X not only ridiculed the philosophy of nonviolence and disparaged the desire for integration; he rejected Christianity as "the white man's
religion" and was a vocal detractor of King. In an interview with Eleanor
Fischer in 1961, he explained his denunciation of King's philosophy:

> I think any black man who teaches black people to turn the other cheek
> and suffer peacefully after they have been turning the other cheek and
> suffering peacefully for 400 years in a land of bondage under the most
> cruel, inhuman, and wicked slavemaster that any people have been
> under, he is doing those people an injustice, and he's a traitor to his own
> people.[33]

Malcolm X's articulation of Black nationalism created a growing problem
for King and the Christian leadership of the civil rights movement. For generations, the church had been the primary source of Black resistance to white
racism and oppression, but Black nationalism unsettled the church's centrality in this struggle. It provided an alternate, competing space that affirmed
Black life while critiquing white supremacy.

The Black Power movement would intensify this dilemma for the Black
church. The term "Black Power" was first used in the context of political activism by Stokely Carmichael, a leader of the Student Nonviolent Coordinating
Committee (SNCC).[34] By the mid-1960s, the country was boiling with urban
rebellions and police reprisals. Like many activists, Carmichael had begun to
feel frustrated with the slow progress of the nonviolent movement, which
seemed increasingly out of step with the times. In 1965, during the Watts Rebellion, thirty-four people had been killed in clashes between the city's Black
residents and law enforcement. The following year, Carmichael traveled to
Mississippi to take part in a rally for James Meredith, the Black student who
had integrated the University of Mississippi and had recently been shot and
wounded during his one-man protest, the March Against Fear.[35] Carmichael
and some other SNCC members had been discussing introducing the phrase
"Black Power" during the rally. After Carmichael was arrested and then released, he took the stage and addressed the assembled protesters. "We've
been saying 'freedom' for six years," he said. "What we are going to start saying now is 'Black Power.'"[36]

This rapidly became a mantra for the younger generation. Black Power was a compelling vision of Black self-determination, and a clear repudiation of King's emphasis on nonviolence and integration. "It is a call for Black people in this country to unite," Carmichael explained, "to recognize their heritage, to build a sense of community. It is a call for Black people to define their own goals, to lead their own organizations." It was also far more confrontational: "When you talk of Black Power," Carmichael said, "you talk of building a movement that will smash everything Western civilization has created."[37]

King was initially wary of the idea, commenting in public that "the slogan was an unwise choice." To his staff, he described Black Power as "a cry of pain. It is in fact a reaction to the failure of White Power to deliver promises and to do it in a hurry."[38] But he could not avoid the predicament Black Power created for his movement. Meanwhile, for white churches, Black Power raised a different concern: that perhaps the nonviolence of the civil rights movement would give way to something more aggressive. Alarmed, some white religious leaders criticized the Black Power movement for preaching hatred of white people.

In July 1966, the National Council of Churches, an ecumenical body of Black and white Christian churches formed in 1950, met to discuss the turmoil. At the conference, a group of Black pastors within the NCC came together to form an ad hoc committee that would become, later that year, the National Conference of Negro Churchmen. They were faced with complex fractures within the larger organization. On the one hand, they were disturbed by white clergy members who were up in arms about Black Power; on the other, they were also frustrated by the inability of King's Southern Christian Leadership Conference to respond effectively to the violence of the urban rebellions. Meanwhile SNCC, under the leadership of Carmichael, had fully embraced the Black Power movement, and Carmichael's stature was rising. The Black pastors who came together at the NCC that year sought to navigate the tension between Black Power and the Christian tradition. On July 31, 1966, following the conference, the group took out a full-page ad in *The New York Times*. Their statement began:

We, an informal group of Negro churchmen in America, are deeply disturbed about the crisis brought upon our country by historic distortions of important human realities in the controversy about "black power." What we see shining through the variety of rhetoric is not anything new but the same old problem of power and race which has faced our beloved country since 1619.

We realize that neither the term "power" nor the term "Christian conscience" is an easy matter to talk about, especially in the context of race relations in America. The fundamental distortion facing us in the controversy about "black power" is rooted in a gross imbalance of power and conscience between Negroes and white Americans.[39]

The statement challenged the power imbalance between white men and Black men, but it also addressed how the Black church had been "created as a result of the refusal to submit to the indignities of a false kind of 'integration' in which all power was in the hands of white people."[40] Laying out the reasons why Black Power was important in the moment of struggle, the ministers declared that "America is our beloved homeland. But, America is not God."[41] As in the sermon from Reverend Wright that caused trouble for Obama, the clergymen's statement asserted that America is not to be equated with God, and that America can be culpable for the injustices done to Black people throughout the nation's history.

The statement was a direct influence on a young Black theologian named James Cone. It highlighted the tension between the church's traditional role as the home base of Black resistance and the rising Black Power movement and set the stage for Cone's theology, which would find a way to integrate the two approaches. Cone recalled, "I shouted for joy when I read that statement because it showed that prophetic voices were still present in the Black Church."[42] For Cone, a newly minted PhD from Northwestern University, the statement spoke to his own disappointments with the civil rights movement as well as his growing anger about the failures of white Christians to understand the systemic racism and injustices in America.

Cone was struggling to bring together the theological, ethical, and social implications of the Black church's centuries-long struggle for justice and civil rights at a moment in which that tradition had been plunged into crisis. The uncompromising moral vision of the Black Power movement offered a persuasive answer to a series of questions the Black church was having trouble addressing. As Cone put it, "The black church was thus faced with a theological dilemma: either reject Black Power as a contradiction of Christian love (and thereby join the white church in its condemnation of Black Power advocates as un-American or unchristian), or accept Black Power as the sociopolitical truth of the gospel."[43] Cone's resolution of this dilemma was Black theology.

He presented the idea in his first book, *Black Theology and Black Power,* published in 1969, just a year after King was assassinated in Memphis. "While the gospel itself does not change," he wrote, "every generation is confronted with new problems, and the gospel must be brought to bear on them."[44] Cone sought to reclaim the gospel from a tradition he saw as having become too accepting of "the evils of racism." Black Power, he declared, was not some "heretical idea" but, rather, "Christ's central message to twentieth-century America. And unless the empirical denominational church makes a determined effort to recapture the man Jesus through a total identification with the suffering poor as expressed in Black Power, that church will become exactly what Christ is not."[45] Cone's argument was that God is principally concerned with the suffering of the poor and the oppressed, beginning with the Israelites in Egypt; in America, the poor and the oppressed were Black—therefore, the salvation of Black Americans had to be the central preoccupation of the church.

Cone's vision not only recognized the struggles of Black people as the "point of departure" for a new theology but also called to account the manner in which white churches had been instrumental in upholding the structures of racism. "It seems that the white church is not God's redemptive agent," he wrote, "but, rather, an agent of the old society. Most church fellowships are more concerned about drinking or new buildings or Sunday closing than about children who die of rat bites or men who are killed because they want to be treated like men."[46] It was a scathing indictment of white racism, and it brought together the call for justice that King and others in the civil rights movement had made with Black Power's call for Black agency and self-determination.

Black Theology and Black Power was published three months before another statement from the group of pastors who had come together at the 1966 NCC. They now called themselves the National Conference of Black Churchmen, and their statement opened with a section entitled "Why Black Theology?" The group articulated how Cone's liberatory vision for the Black church, influenced by the rise of Black Power, was rooted in its long history of fighting to protect and redeem Black Americans. "The black church has not only nurtured black people but enabled them to survive brutalities that ought not to have been inflicted on any community of men," they wrote. "Black Theology is the product of black Christian experience and reflection. It comes out of the past. It is strong in the present. And we believe it to be redemptive for the future."[47]

The following year Cone published his second book, *A Black Theology of Liberation.* The book would make him a major expositor of Black liberation theology. It was a heady time for liberation theologies. The Dominican priest

Gustavo Gutiérrez published his book on Catholic liberation theology in 1971. In both the Protestant and the Catholic worlds, theological emphasis on liberation would become a major theme. Much of this emphasis was due to the influence of the civil rights movement in the United States and the central role of the Black church in that movement. Liberation theology in any national context, as Cone says, is an "interpretation of the Christian gospel from the experience and perspectives and lives of people who are at the bottom in society—the lowest economic and racial groups."[48]

Cone became a professor at Union Theological Seminary in New York City, the former academic home to Reinhold Niebuhr and Paul Tillich, major Protestant theologians of the twentieth century. Training students for both the clergy and the academy, Cone's teaching and advocacy would span more than thirty years, and were a major influence on people like Reverend Wright. Cone's thinking influenced the political world too, perhaps most directly through one of his students, Senator Raphael Warnock of Georgia. Warnock, who was born into a Black Pentecostal family, followed his father into the ministry. His dissertation with Cone turned into a book, *The Divided Mind of the Black Church: Theology, Piety, and Public Witness,* which deals with the tension in the Black church between piety and social justice and the public response to that conflict. For Warnock, the Black church has exemplified both radical and unradical tendencies. It has been at once the most prominent instrument of liberation within the African American community and the foremost conservative custodian of an uncritical evangelical piety that undermines the aims of liberation.[49]

Today, Warnock stands as a bridge between the Black church, past, present, and future, and political action. What he learned from Cone is not simply what the theology of Black liberation is but how to be socially active and apply that to his ministry. Warnock's first pastorship was at Douglas Memorial Community Church in Baltimore; then in 2005, he was appointed senior pastor of Ebenezer Baptist Church, King's family church in Atlanta. His career since then has exemplified the civil rights work and prophetic tradition that King embodied, along with the spirit of Cone's Black liberation theology. Warnock was arrested in the U.S. Capitol building in 2017 for leading a prayer in the rotunda protesting the healthcare cuts in then-president Trump's budget. Even before that, he was socially active, taking an HIV test in front of his congregation to affirm testing in the Black community. His election to the U.S. Senate in 2020 made him the first African American senator from Georgia, the same state that had refused to seat Henry McNeal Turner after he was elected to the legislature in 1868.

Warnock's race for that Senate seat pitted him against Kelly Loeffler, who campaigned against him by distorting a sermon he preached in 2011 in which he said, "America, nobody can serve God and the military. You can't serve God and money. You cannot serve God and mammon at the same time. America, choose ye this day who you will serve." The sentiment was straight out of the Bible, Matthew 6:24. But Loeffler highlighted the first sentence, "America, nobody can serve God and the military," and used it to paint Warnock as radical and unsupportive of U.S. troops.[50] It was a technique out of the same playbook used to vilify King, Wright, and other Black preachers who had confronted the broken promises of America. This time, however, it didn't succeed. Warnock won a special election to the U.S. Senate on January 5, 2021, the day before the failed Capitol insurrection.

Loeffler and other Republicans claimed that Warnock's radical liberalism was evident from his commitment to prophetic preaching. But Jonathan Lee Walton, the dean of Wake Forest University School of Divinity, more accurately describes that preaching as stemming from "a deep love for, and thus a deep disappointment in, a country that too often fails to affirm the self-evident truth in our nation's creed, that all people are created equal and endowed by God 'with certain unalienable rights.'"[51]

That deep love accompanied by deep disappointment is what drives the Black church today, and leaders such as Senator Warnock continue to carry forward the tradition of speaking truth to power in the Black church. Others have eschewed the formal Black church tradition and have looked to Black Lives Matter, Color of Change, and other social-justice movements to call America's failings to account. Yet the Black church remains the prophetic voice of condemnation of America's ills. As King so aptly stated in his "I Have a Dream" speech, "America has given the Negro people a bad check, a check which has come back marked 'insufficient funds.'" The Black church, pastors and members alike, is still demanding to cash the check of true democracy and freedom.

September 15, 1963

A group of Ku Klux Klansmen bombs the Sixteenth Street Baptist Church in Birmingham, Alabama, which, like many Black churches, was a center of organizing for the civil rights movement. Four young girls are killed: Addie Mae Collins, Cynthia Wesley, Carole Robertson, and Denise McNair. At least twenty people are injured. Many years later, three of the four conspirators are brought to trial and convicted; the fourth dies before he can be tried.

Youth Sunday

Rita Dove

This morning's already good—summer's
cooling, Addie chattering like a magpie—
but today we are leading the congregation.
Ain't *that* a fine thing! All in white *like angels,*
they'll be sighing when we appear at the pulpit
and proclaim, "Open your hymnals—"
Addie, what's the page number again?
Never mind, it'll be posted. I think. I hope.
Hold still, Carole, or else this sash will never
sit right! There. Now you do mine.
Almost eleven. I'm ready. My, don't we look—
what's that word the reverend used in
last Sunday's sermon? Oh, I got it: *ethereal.*

On "Brevity"

Camille T. Dungy

My daughter's three months old. A nightmare
rocks me awake, and then fourteen words: Brevity.
As in four girls; Sunday dresses: bone, ash, bone, ash, bone.
The end. 1963, but still burning. My darkening girl
lies beside me, her tiny chest barely registering breath.
Had they lived beyond that morning, all the other explosions
shattering Birmingham—even some who called it home
called it Bombingham—three of the girls would be seventy,
the other sixty-seven. Somebody's babies. The sentences I rescue
from that nightmare, I make a poem. Four names,
grayscaled at the bottom of the page:
Addie Mae Collins. Cynthia Wesley. Carole Robertson. Denise McNair.
Revision is a struggle toward truth. In my book I won't keep, The end.
For such terrible brevity—dear Black girls! sweet babies—there's been no end.

Ruby Washington, Greenville, Mississippi, mid-twentieth century HENRY CLAY ANDERSON

CHAPTER 14

Music

WESLEY MORRIS

The week in September 1963 that Addie Mae Collins, Cynthia Wesley, Carole Robertson, and Denise McNair perished in the bombing of Birmingham's Sixteenth Street Baptist Church, the fourth-biggest song in America concerned a euphoria those four little girls were robbed of ever experiencing. "Heat Wave," by Martha and the Vandellas, was a massive hit.[1] Boy loves girl, girl has nervous breakdown: "Has high blood pressure got a hold on me?" Martha sings. "Or is this the way love's supposed to be?"[2]

Do you dance? Do you call a doctor?

The song hailed from Hitsville U.S.A., at 2648 West Grand Boulevard, the modest Detroit headquarters of Motown Records, which might have seemed ill-equipped for, and perhaps incongruous with, the struggles for civil rights taking place seven hundred miles to the south.[3] Motown's songwriters crafted little romances perched between relief and despair: "I got him back in my arms again"; "Don't want to kiss you, but I need to"; "I bet you're wonderin' how I knew, 'bout your plans to make me blue." Politics were scarce, as were allusions to the violence and dehumanization that were regular aspects of life for Black Americans.

Yet, arriving as it did amid the advent of the American teenager, Motown's ascent was a crucial dimension of Black American PR. These kids ached and yearned and lost their cool just as intensely as the white high schoolers who were helping send them to the top of the pop charts. They had hormones in common and much more. The music was an earthquake, not only because of its enormous, rhythm-driven sound (big drums, horns, tambourines) but because it shook with the insistence that the people who made it ought to be embraced as irreducibly human.

After all, it wasn't Black music that Motown's founder and chief architect, Berry Gordy, had envisioned.[4] He wanted what Louis Armstrong and Duke Ellington and Thelonious Monk wanted: to make *American* music. Jazz artists of previous generations had strived, for years, to redefine the all-purpose "American" label, only to realize that their Blackness had been made incompatible with Americanness. The white inventors of race understood that in order for them to remain triumphant atop the mountain, somebody else had to stay put at its feet. But we're talking about paradoxes here. Conscripting jazz to the category of "Black music" just made white people all the hungrier for it.

Since it had radiated out from New Orleans around the turn of the century, jazz had been feverishly clamored for, casting a spell that lasted for at least five decades: James "Bubber" Miley making his trumpet swoon in Ellington's absurdly sensual "The Mooche" in 1928; Ethel Waters, once among the highest-paid women in entertainment, smiling through the melancholy of "Am I Blue" in 1929; Fats Waller's ooze-and-attack stride piano, eight years later, on "The Joint Is Jumpin'"; Ella Fitzgerald finding herself alongside the drummer and bandleader Chick Webb, perfecting a luscious emotional language whose street name was "scat"; Webb's band battling Count Basie's in a live contest at the Savoy Ballroom in 1938, transforming the music's orchestral sound into an Olympics of kinetic innovation.[5]

In those years, white Americans' principal hunger was for secondhand Blackness. They packed clubs that steered them to whites-only sections or, as was the policy at the Roseland Ballroom until 1924, clubs that denied Black people entry altogether, as patrons and performers.[6] It was deemed safer that way. In fact, why not have white guys play the music too? In the hands of Black musicians—the white presumption went—swing was too sexy, too primitive to be suitable for the droves who stuffed dance halls to Lindy Hop, to Susy-Q, to jitterbug. ("Jungle music" was what white people called Ellington's early work.)[7] Before someone like Armstrong could be deemed jazz's epitome, the country needed a non-Black artist to adore, someone with a name that left little doubt about what was what. That's how Americans wound up with an acute Paul Whiteman obsession—Whiteman, who first played George Gershwin's "Rhapsody in Blue," who sold so many millions of records that the white press crowned him "the King of Jazz."[8] Not because he necessarily wanted the title—since he played segregated clubs, he was prohibited from hiring Black arrangers and Black players—but because, in the late 1920s and early 1930s, a pasteurized jazz suited America's tastes. Pass the culture; hold the people.

But as the country approached the 1960s, maybe white Americans were finally ready for the thing itself. Recordings and television broadcasts were putting more Black artists in more white people's homes. Regality and religion helped heighten their allure. An innovative singer and songwriter like Sam Cooke imagined a pop music that induced hyperventilating yet never dared remove its choral robe. It was lush, impassioned, and nestled in the palatable harmonies of 1940s and 1950s serenades and doo-wop singing. Neither hot jazz nor fiery sermon but a dozen roses, a milkshake with two straws. Cooke's arrangements were a perfect fusion between the sacred and the secular, between robust Blackness and the American songbook's high snuggle era. In the late 1950s and early 1960s, Cooke embodied Black pop singing's seamless transition from wailing choirboy to romantic heat source.

Motown went a step further. The chapel became a power station. Gordy oversaw a full-scale integration of Western, classical orchestral instruments (strings, horns, woodwinds) with the Black musical experience: church on a Sunday morning (rhythm sections, gospel harmonies, hand claps) and juke-joint Saturday nights (rhythm sections, guitars, vigor). Pure yet busy. What resulted was the Motown sound: a whole daggone weekend in three minutes.

Motown songs had titles like "Do You Love Me" and "I Second That Emotion," "Ain't Too Proud to Beg" and "I Hear a Symphony." They bounced and lilted in defiance of the violence Black Americans faced, the heaviness so many of them carried. Those songs and the way the company's stars performed them were declarations of war against the insults of the past and the present. The scratchy piccolo at the start of a Four Tops classic was, in its way, an elegant political act: sorrow as raised fist.

The fact that the label specialized in love songs was crucial to its impact. Love was the void at the center of the country. Laws, policies, and codes both stated and implied that Black people were unsuitable for loving, that they were unsuitable for *life*. Now here was music—popular music, *American* music—that insisted the opposite was true. No one had ever heard anything as religious, yet as rough and impassioned, as a song like "Heat Wave," with those Vandellic harmonizing vocals by Rosalind Ashford and Annette Beard responding to the call of Martha Reeves's urgency.

But perhaps the most crucial aspect of Motown, for all that would come after, is that it was a Black-owned company that made stars of Black people. Gordy founded Motown with the mission of making its artists the most desired and most respected people in the country. He presented his artists with a sense of polish, decorum, and self-possession that would have struck anyone who beheld them on *American Bandstand* or *The Ed Sullivan Show* as wholly unlike the servants and fools that had tended to enliven and degrade American entertainment.[9]

Motown's brand of propriety stood in contrast to the gale force of someone like Tina Turner. Her haymaker singing and tornadic stage presence helped instill rock 'n' roll with its exhilarating, ferocious instability; but she might have been too overwhelming for a country determined, as Turner would later put it herself, to keep doing things "nice and easy." Motown read the room and deployed a different strategy. The company unfurled as glamorous a Blackness as this country has ever mass-produced. Black men in formal suits. Black women in ball gowns. Stables of Black writers, producers, and musicians. Backup singers solving social equations with geometric choreography. This wasn't the first Black-owned recording label. It was, however, the first to assert dominion over white America's ancient, ambivalent appetite for Blackness.

Motown's genius for mechanization ensured that, in its wake, other artists could also leave a meteor's dent in the national consciousness. Gordy built an auto plant around Black expression that neither wrecked it nor watered it down. His company confirmed what African Americans had always known about Black culture: that it was American culture, indeed.

From that point forward, art that emerged in poverty, from want, in despair, art forged in immoral quarantine, would take its place at the center of everything. Art created by visionaries, innovators, and synthesists who had previously existed on the margins of American wealth and power would become the sun around which the culture orbited: Aretha Franklin, Quincy Jones, Jimmy Heath, Jimmy Smith, B. B. King, James Brown, Etta James, Inez and Charlie Foxx, Jimi Hendrix, Gladys Knight and the Pips, Dionne Warwick, Nina Simone, Sly and the Family Stone, Ornette Coleman, Stevie Wonder, Curtis Mayfield, Merry Clayton, Pharoah Sanders, Yusef Lateef, Gamble & Huff, the O'Jays, Maurice White, Philip Bailey, Teddy Pendergrass, Herbie Hancock, Roberta Flack, Alice Coltrane, Minnie Riperton, George Benson, Phoebe Snow, Donny Hathaway, the Isley Brothers, Funkadelic, Charly Pride, Patti LaBelle, Chaka Khan, Nona Hendryx, Carl Anderson, Dee Dee Bridgewater, The 5th Dimension, Betty Davis, Al Green, Nick Ashford, Valerie Simpson, Melba Moore, Nile Rodgers, Larry Levan, Buddy Guy, Lionel Richie, Sylvester, Al Jarreau, Bill Withers, Michael Jackson, David Washington, Cecil Taylor, Natalie Cole, Gwen Guthrie, Donna Summer, Phyllis Hyman, Stanley Clarke, Maze Featuring Frankie Beverly, Bad Brains, Prince, Grandmaster Flash, Millie Jackson, Cherrelle, Patti Austin, Klymaxx, Kurtis Blow, Full Force,

Shirley Caesar, Luther Vandross, Stephanie Mills, Andraé Crouch, Jennifer Holliday, Bettye LaVette, Peabo Bryson, Cheryl Lynn, Fishbone, James Ingram, Anita Baker, Rick James, Eric B. and Rakim, LL Cool J, Jimmy Jam and Terry Lewis, Janet Jackson, the Clark Sisters, MC Lyte, Babyface, Whitney Houston, Wynton Marsalis, KRS-One, Queen Latifah, Salt-N-Pepa, Bobby McFerrin, Jody Watley, Teddy Riley, Tracy Chapman, Lenny Kravitz, Public Enemy, Robert Cray, N.W.A, En Vogue, Terri Lyne Carrington, Gang Starr, Mariah Carey, TLC, Mary J. Blige, Kirk Franklin, RuPaul, Raphael Saadiq, Ann Nesby, Living Colour, A Tribe Called Quest, De La Soul, D'Angelo, Darius Rucker, Aaliyah, Nas, Goodie Mob, Keb' Mo', Cassandra Wilson, OutKast, Wu-Tang Clan, The Notorious B.I.G., Thornetta Davis, the Roots, Swizz Beatz, Erykah Badu, Timbaland, Meshell Ndegeocello, Master P, Jay-Z, Pharrell Williams, Lauryn Hill, Snoop Dogg, Tupac Shakur, Kanye West, Sean Combs, Lil' Kim, Missy Elliott, Audra McDonald, Brian Stokes Mitchell, Alice Smith, Jill Scott, Rhiannon Giddens, India.Arie, Alicia Keys, Beyoncé, Tasha Cobbs Leonard, Janelle Monáe, Jennifer Hudson, Kendrick Lamar, Solange, Santigold, Frank Ocean, John Legend, Keyshia Cole, Jason Moran, Kamasi Washington, Christian Scott aTunde Adjuah, Anderson Paak, Childish Gambino, Esperanza Spalding, Jon Batiste, Leslie Odom, Jr., Daveed Diggs, Robert Randolph, Gary Clark, Jr., Future, Valerie June, Brittany Howard, Saweetie, Megan Thee Stallion, Sudan Archives, Christone "Kingfish" Ingram, Mickey Guyton, Cécile McLorin Salvant, Bartees Strange, Lil Baby, Gunna, SZA, Lizzo.

African Americans make up 13 percent of the population yet account for an incalculable amount of what moves us, and how we move.[10] The last twenty years of *Billboard* year-end charts teem with soul music and hip-hop innovations. Black choreography often starts the dance crazes that sweep TikTok's one hundred million–plus active American users—the staccato juts and thrusts, the dips, swerves, and pivots combined with an assortment of gestural herbs and spices.[11] Decades of jams written, produced, and performed by Black artists sustain parties in places that sustain no actual Black people. This unceasing eruption of ingenuity, invention, intuition, and improvisation constitutes the very core of American culture.

And that's in part because white people won't stop putting it there.

The stars of Motown were the descendants of enslaved laborers, women and men who made music as they toiled. This was, in part, to get through the work itself but also to transcend the culture of the slave condition—the mindset of worthlessness and dispossession.

When enslaved Africans arrived in the American colonies, they brought with them traditions of percussive rhythm that could be made on a drum as easily as with the body. The Christianity that defined colonial life had alternative musical priorities, melody being the most substantial. But, gradually, the dislocated, reluctantly acculturated Africans made modifications. One of these became known as the ring shout, wherein people would dance and chant in a circle.[12] Rhythm merged with harmony, culminating in survival songs chiefly inspired by the Bible's most salient tales. When enslavers made the Bible available, they often removed all of Exodus, with its stories of divine justice, of the Lord delivering Israel from bondage.[13] The enslaved people who were familiar with those stories, firsthand or otherwise, built them into sermons and incorporated them into songs, songs intoned in small prayer houses and formal churches. They sang while they worked, achieving conversance in a book many of them were never allowed to become literate enough to read, a book whose allegories some enslavers deemed too resonant for the fertile imaginations of the enslaved.

Sometimes the songs were created under duress, demanded by overseers who distrusted the silence of field work or who, perhaps, couldn't bear the unnatural sounds of enslavement and required a sweetener. "A silent slave is not liked by masters or overseers," reported Frederick Douglass in the second of his autobiographies, *My Bondage and My Freedom*.[14] But the makers of the music found something deeper in it than an obligation to distract or delight. Writing of his enslaved Maryland boyhood and the hymn "Bound for the Land of Canaan," Douglass conjured the spiritual's wishful volition: "A keen observer might have detected in our repeated singing of 'O Canaan, sweet Canaan, I am bound for the land of Canaan,' something more than a hope of reaching heaven. We meant to reach the *North*, and the North was our Canaan."[15]

Those work songs pleaded for deliverance and were sung in defiance of atrocity. Spirituals, they were called. And they are this country's original folk music, songs sung out of the determination by the enslaved to orient themselves toward some higher vocation and, in Douglass's estimation, toward a more humane land—here or perhaps in a less earthly realm.

The singing was done together, in groups, and, according to the anthropologist and Negro folk laureate Zora Neale Hurston, never the same way twice. "Each singing of the piece is a new creation," she wrote.[16] The action in these songs resisted the simple jotting down of musical notation. Nonetheless, after the Civil War and toward the end of the 1800s, attempts were made to reproduce them on paper and have them published. Interpolations of captive people's music commenced at least as soon as 1867 with the publication of *Slave*

Songs of the United States, a collection of 136 songs transcribed and assembled by the white abolitionists Lucy McKim Garrison, Charles Pickard Ware, and William Francis Allen, who didn't always know what they were getting down.[17]

A chief agent in the formal arranging of the spiritual was the composer, pianist, and soprano Ella Sheppard, a Black woman.[18] Sheppard deeply involved herself in both the preservation of this music and its mindful reproduction in concert venues. She helped direct the Fisk Jubilee Singers, a Black student choral ensemble, which, along with the Hampton Singers, began to perform these songs, including Sheppard's interpretations. During and after Reconstruction, the Jubilees were dispatched on tours all over the country to raise money for newly established Black colleges, singing mostly for white audiences. Their arrangements are the bedrock of the American gospel tradition. The Jubilees' version of "Swing Low, Sweet Chariot" has been recorded scores of times, in countless variations—by the likes of Etta James and the Staple Singers, on the one hand, and Johnny Cash and Merle Haggard, on the other.

These attempts at documentation of the spirituals were translations, interpretations, advancements, and, crucially, proof of survival and a record of creativity. But the music just wasn't the same, in part perhaps because the harrowing conditions that produced it had been abolished. And in part because the new versions were laced with something Hurston knew the music disliked: fuss. The original spirituals weren't fussed over. Spontaneity was their power source. "Its truth dies under training like flowers under hot water," Hurston surmised.[19] These songs were in a language of slaps, pats, stomps, guttural sounds, of *breathing*—sounds that defied any ready anglophone linguistics. Black people weren't creating spirituals for wide appeal, either. These songs weren't meant to be "consumed."

Among all else that spirituals could be, they were essentially communal, a people speaking to each other and reaching for God. Together. Their evanescent, evaporative, one-of-a-kind nature seemed to acknowledge the sobering impermanence of the bonds among their singers. Yet to learn a spiritual, no matter how, is to know it forever. Here today and, God willing, here tomorrow, too.

Among the duties of the enslaved was the enslavers' entertainment. Black people were called upon to fiddle and dance for their white owners and their guests. Musicians were loaned out to other enslavers. Eventually, on their days off, they'd take their instruments into town to play and dance for pennies, sometimes for food. White people took in these songs and dances. They considered it "savage," but that alleged wildness turned them on. A white person could deem Black musicians lowly, subhuman, beyond redemption, while still finding himself helpless to resist their talent. Alas, some of these white people were so captivated that gawking was no longer enough.

Before the Hampton Singers and the Jubilees started performing, nineteenth-century Black music had never reached the masses through Black artists. What the country at large heard was something altogether different. It was the music of Black people as performed by white people, a cartoon of the dances they did and the way they spoke. It wasn't Black music at all but blackface minstrelsy—white men painted pitch-black doing dopey (but not unskilled) dances and singing comic songs as they imagined Black people might.

Until the 1830s, American stages had been fat with imported European culture—Shakespeare, operas, waltzes. What was there for the common man to enjoy? Blackface minstrelsy was it: the birth of American popular culture. Minstrelsy's peak stretched from the 1840s to the 1870s, years when the country was at its most violently and legislatively polarized about slavery—years that included the ferocious rhetorical ascent of Douglass, John Brown's botched instigation of a Black insurrection at Harpers Ferry, the Civil War, the assassination of Abraham Lincoln, and Reconstruction. What minstrelsy offered the country during this period was an entertainment of talent, ribaldry, and polemics. But it also lent racism a stage upon which existential fear could become jubilation, and contempt could become fantasy.

The white person most frequently identified as the father of the art form is Thomas Dartmouth Rice, a New Yorker who performed as T. D. Rice and, in acclaim, was lusted after as "Daddy" Rice, "the negro, par excellence."[20] Rice was a minstrel, which by the 1830s, when his stardom was at its most refulgent, meant he painted his face with burned cork in grotesque approximation of the enslaved Black people he was imitating.

In 1828, Rice had been a nobody actor in his early twenties, touring with a theater company in Cincinnati (or Louisville; historians don't know for sure) when, one version of the story goes, he saw a decrepit, possibly disfigured old Black man singing while grooming a horse on the property of a white man whose last name was Crow. On went the light bulb. Rice took in the tune and the movements but failed, it seems, to take down the old man's name. So in his song, the horse groomer became who Rice needed him to be. "Weel about and turn about jus so," went his tune, "ebery time I weel about, I jump Jim Crow." And just like that, this white man had invented the character who would become the mascot for two centuries of legalized racism.

That night, Rice made himself up to look like the old Black man—or something like him, because for his getup, Rice most likely concocted skin blacker than any actual Black person's; he invented a gibberish dialect meant to imply Black speech; and he turned the old man's melody and hobbled movements into a song-and-dance routine that no white audience had ever experienced before. What they saw caused a sensation. The crowd demanded twenty encores.

Rice had a hit on his hands. He repeated the act again, night after night, for audiences so profoundly jolted that he was frequently mobbed *during* performances. Across the Ohio River, a short distance from all that adulation, was Boone County, Kentucky, which was largely populated by enslaved Africans. As they were being worked, sometimes to death, white people, desperate with anticipation, were paying to see a terrible distortion of the enslaved depicted at play.

Other white performers came and conquered, particularly the Virginia Minstrels, who exploded in 1843, burned brightly, and then, after only months, burned out.[21] The circus impresario P. T. Barnum caught the fever, making a habit of booking minstrel troupes for his American Museum; when he was short on performers, he blacked up himself.[22] By the 1840s, minstrel acts were taking over concert halls, doing long residencies at some of the largest theaters in Boston, New York, and Philadelphia.

A blackface minstrel would sing, dance, play music, give speeches, and cut up for white audiences, almost exclusively in the North, at least initially. Blackface was used for mock operas and political monologues (they called them stump speeches), skits, gender parodies, and dances. Its stars were the nineteenth-century versions of Elvis, the Beatles, 'N Sync.[23]

It was, on the one hand, harmless fun: men in silly clothes and garish makeup inventing a kind of sketch-comedy variety show. But the audience's prolonged exposure to these images normalized their intended hideousness. White performers jostled with each other to lay claim to being the "real thing," the real "Black" thing. Night after night, for six solid decades at least, audience upon audience looked on gleefully, and the false ideas being told about Black people took on lives of their own.

An art form populated often entirely by these horrid counterfeits thrilled the white people who paid to see them do skits about bickering Black couples and songs like "Uncle Gabriel," about a coon hunt. The Virginia Minstrels did a version to great acclaim. Sometimes the fourth verse went like this:

De niggers dey come all around, and kick up a debil of a splutter
Dey eat de coon and clar de ground, to dance de chicken flutter

Dey dance all night till de broke of day, to a tune on de old banjo
And den dey all did gwan away, before de chicken crow.[24]

During minstrelsy's heyday, white songwriters like Stephen Foster composed the tunes the minstrels sang, tunes we continue to sing more than a century later, like "Oh! Susanna," "Dixie," "Camptown Races," "Swanee River," and "My Old Kentucky Home, Good Night!" Edwin Pearce Christy's group, Christy's Minstrels, formed a band—banjo, fiddle, bone castanets, tambourine—whose combination of instruments laid the groundwork for American popular music, from bluegrass to Motown. Some of these instruments had come from Africa; among the enslaved, the banjo's body would have been a desiccated gourd. In *Doo-dah!,* his book on Foster's work and life, Ken Emerson writes that the fiddle and banjo were paired for the melody, while the bones "chattered" and the tambourine "thumped and jingled a beat that is still heard 'round the world."[25] This was the root of the American rock band.

The first wave of minstrels had never meaningfully been South. In their shows, the tunes they played were based on Irish melodies and used Western choral harmonies, not the proto-gospel call-and-response spirituals that were the real Real Thing. They tethered Black people and Black life to white musical structures—like, say, the polka. The mix that would define the young nation was already well underway: Europe plus slavery plus the circus times harmony, comedy, and drama equals Americana.

And the muses for their songs were people they had seldom ever encountered, whose enslavement they rarely opposed and instead sentimentalized. Foster's beloved minstrel-show staple "Old Uncle Ned," for instance, warmly if disrespectfully eulogizes the enslaved the way you might a salaried worker—or an actual uncle:

Den lay down de shubble and de hoe
Hang up de fiddle and de bow:
No more hard work for poor Old Ned
He's gone whar de good Niggas go
No more hard work for poor Old Ned
He's gone whar de good Niggas go.[26]

Such an affectionate showcase for poor old (enslaved, soon-to-be-deceased) Uncle Ned was as essential as "air," in the white travel writer, poet, and literary critic Bayard Taylor's assessment, included in his 1850 book *Eldorado: Or, Ad-*

ventures in the Path of Empire. For him, minstrelsy's songs and their attitudes were "true expressions of the more popular side of the national character," a force that follows "the American in all its emigrations, colonizations and conquests, as certainly as the Fourth of July and Thanksgiving Day."[27] It's the rare observation that dared connect the music and its performance to the country's communal rituals. Taylor wasn't denouncing minstrelsy, or slavery. He was merely predicting that the art form's impact would last as long as fireworks and turkey.

One accelerant was Harriet Beecher Stowe's novel *Uncle Tom's Cabin.*[28] The book's florid anti-slavery pleas jolted the nation and loaned minstrelsy a new urgency. Before the book's publication in 1852, blackface minstrels were filler between acts of a play. The average minstrel production featured a semicircle of blackface musicians that ringed an emcee who oversaw the evening's action. There was no one story, no single theme. *Uncle Tom's Cabin* turned the variety show into its own sort of theater. Some producers made straight adaptations that transported some of the novel's most significant characters— noble, enslaved Tom; angelically blond Little Eva; Tom's evil owner Simon Legree—to the stage with little change to Stowe's fervent abolitionism. But many others couldn't tolerate Stowe; in their eyes, the book was blasphemous. They used her denunciation of slavery in *Uncle Tom's Cabin* to create minstrel shows that denounced *her.* Sure enough, among the leading men was T. D. Rice, who, it's said, did a splendid blackface Tom.[29]

Minstrel productions of Stowe's book went on until the end of the Civil War in 1865, doubling as a proxy for the debates raging throughout the country about the institution of slavery itself. The Tom shows were enormously popular and so ubiquitous that they were more commonly known as "U.T.C.s."[30] In 1862, when Abraham Lincoln reportedly (and almost certainly apocryphally) addressed Stowe as "the little woman who wrote the book that started this great war," he would've been talking as much about the minstrel show as her novel.[31] But the U.T.C.s' popularity overrode the reckoning Stowe's imperfectly righteous novel demanded. The minstrel show and its music let the audience choose when to have a heart: they could weep for overworked Uncle Ned as surely as they could ignore or even celebrate his lashed back or his body as it swung from a tree.

Paradoxically, perversely, minstrelsy's grotesquerie deluded white audiences into feeling better about themselves. It induced a bearable cognitive dissonance that outlasted enslavement. The caricatures of Black people as extravagantly lazy, licentious, vulgar, disheveled, and abject always drew a comforting contrast with a white person's sense of honor and civility, with a white person's simply being white. *No matter how bad things might be for us, at least we're not them.*

If blackface minstrelsy ensorcelled white America, it also saddled many a Black performer with a dilemma. By the late 1860s and early 1870s, minstrelsy had become too big for any American performer to escape. In so many ways, it *was* the culture. If a Black performer wanted to be seen or heard, chances were good that he'd have to pretend to be a white person masquerading as a Black person.

There were certainly no substantial paying Black audiences. A Black minstrel worked in front of white audiences, in white concert halls, on white traveling shows. He would have had no choice but to try to figure out what white audiences wanted. As long as blackface was the country's cultural juggernaut, who would pay money to see Negroes in their own skin?

Before the Civil War, there *were* rare occasions when Black artists found a way to perform as themselves. There was, for instance, Elizabeth Taylor Greenfield, an accomplished soprano who performed for all-white audiences in the United States and Europe, singing the gamut from Handel to Foster. Her refulgence baffled audiences accustomed to minstrelsy's inelegance. The dexterous cornetist, fiddler, and pioneering bandleader Frank Johnson, who remains all but unknown, was one of the most acclaimed Black musicians of the nineteenth century.[32] He helped stage the country's first integrated concerts and, in the middle of 1843, along with his all-Black male troupe, endured a stoning in Allegheny City, Pennsylvania, by local white thugs. There was the fiddler Old Corn Meal, who began as a popular street vendor and wound up, in 1837, as the first Black man to perform as himself on a white New Orleans stage.[33] His stuff was copied by George Nichols, a white man who took up blackface after a start in plain old clowning and—surprise, surprise—became much more famous than the Black man whose act he swiped.[34] But for the most part, there was no reliable way, in the antebellum era, for Black entertainers to perform on a stage without the trademark makeup.

When Black performers were hired, things could become complicated. Once, P. T. Barnum needed a replacement for John Diamond, his star white minstrel. In a New York City dance hall, Barnum found a boy who, it was said at the time, could outdo Diamond (and Diamond was reportedly *good*). The boy was genuinely Black, news that would have rendered him an outrageous blight on a white consumer's narrow imagination. As Thomas Low Nichols would write in his 1864 compendium *Forty Years of American Life,* "There was not an audience in America that would not have resented, in a very energetic fashion, the insult of being asked to look at the dancing of a real negro." So Barnum "greased the little nigger's face and rubbed it over with a new blacking of burned cork, painted his thick lips vermilion, put on a woolly wig over his tight curled locks and brought him out as, 'the champion nigger-dancer of the world.' "[35] This child might have been William Henry Lane, whose stage name was Master Juba. Lane was persuasive enough that Barnum could pass him off as a white person in blackface. He ceased being a real Black boy in order to become Barnum's minstrel Pinocchio.[36]

And so was born the upside-down, inside-out phenomenon of Black blackface minstrelsy, in which Black performers corked themselves up—with a straight face or a wink, depending upon the onlooker. Custom obligated them to fulfill an audience's expectations, expectations that white performers had established. A Black minstrel was impersonating the impersonation of himself. According to Henry T. Sampson's book *Blacks in Blackface,* there were no sets or effects, so the Black blackface minstrel show was "a developer of ability because the artist was placed on his own and was not aided by scenery and stage effects to get laughter."[37] For the Black blackface minstrel, mastery entailed both an awareness of a white audience's preferences and the psychological struggle to keep one's own Blackness, not to mention one's own humanity, intact. A Black blackface minstrel had to learn a white minstrel's routine in order to both copy and, perhaps, subvert it.

These were unhappy innovations, and they've maintained a tight grip on American culture, on white perceptions of Blackness, on the psyches of Black people, whether they're on a stage or gazing up at one. The crime of blackface minstrelsy was the number it did on Black people's expectations of themselves. To this day, just a whiff of minstrelsy can so disease a Black person that they think they see it everywhere, in any performance. That's the psychic residue of the minstrel impersonation taking its toll, leaving you riven by distrust. You never quite know whether the Blackness being presented to an audience is true or a performance. Even the most wondrous Black self-expression risks contamination when white people adore it.

That taint of minstrelsy dogged Louis Armstrong after the late 1940s, Nat King Cole in the 1950s, Sammy Davis, Jr., from the 1950s until his death in 1990—all were deemed sellouts, Uncle Toms, minstrels. That same distrust was on full display that night in 1989 when an auditorium full of Black people jeered Whitney Houston at the Soul Train Awards for, essentially, sounding too estranged from Blackness. A ballad like "Where Do Broken Hearts Go" utilizes full-throated funklessness to express the blues. Haters didn't hear Houston going to church; they heard Lawrence Welk. ("Whiteney" is what the skeptics called her.)[38] Those boos at the Soul Train Awards captured exasperation with the long history of white puppetry and suspected that its strings were now pulling on her. The jeers were paranoia expressed as disapproval.

In the antebellum years, the only way for Black people to perform on a stage for a white audience as the Black people they actually were was as orators. Frederick Douglass was the most incandescent and most famed orator of that era. But his peers included, for starters, William C. Nell, Frances Ellen Watkins Harper, Charles Lenox Remond, and Henry Highland Garnet, whose most famous address, often referred to as "The Call to Rebellion," which he delivered at the 1843 National Colored Convention in Buffalo, urged enslaved Americans to revolt. Abolitionist barn burners tingled spines, inflamed hearts, blew minds. Oration served as absolute anti-minstrelsy—Black people summoning galvanic vocal performances in their own skin *for a cause*. Here was a righteous alternative to the insults of blackface. Here was another, altogether more aspirational standard of Black expression. It was moral. It was holy. It was artful—mellifluous speeches, with suspense, structure, repetition, and judgment delivered to white people and free Black people at meetinghouses and enslaved Black people in their places of worship.

Black orators rejected whatever it was that minstrelsy had convinced the country Black people were, and they did so within institutions that were Black-built and Black-maintained. They often strove for betterment, for progress, for uplift, for respect, praising God for helping lead the people out of the valley toward the freedom that drove all that oration in the first place. Comportment was important, from the age of the colored conventions to the civil rights era. That quest for respectability was actually a battle for rights, and in the 1960s the battle was being broadcast into American homes, *white* American homes. It made all the sense in the world that holy men and women did the leading, that the movement's greatest musical avatars were the gospel star Mahalia Jackson and Marian Anderson, an artistic descendant of Elizabeth Taylor Greenfield and the country's preeminent Black opera singer at the time.

But so much classiness, churchiness, and rhetorical brilliance, whether it belonged to Frances Ellen Watkins Harper or Martin Luther King, Jr., also made certain Black people nervous about performances of self-expression beyond the church. Anytime a Black gospel star—Sam Cooke, say, or Aretha Franklin—"went pop," Black congregants suspected that a white producer had gotten his wings. "Going pop" represented one perceived transgression of the idealized embodiment of Blackness offered by reverends and preachers and politicians.

In and of itself, a movement demands respectability. The demand for equality necessitates the *appearance* of seeming equal and, therefore, worthy of respect. This, in part, is how a century's worth of gains were achieved: through the refulgent, relentless, strategic display of worthiness. But there's respectability that empowers and respectability that imprisons. And the imprisoning sort remains a bane for Black America. Its people were fully aware of the abysmal expectations minstrelsy had established: a roulette of contempt, shame, rage, self-consciousness, appeasement. The art form's racism has proved poisonous to a race's collective self-esteem. A nineteenth century full of white people's artistic mockery buried land mines that lasted well into the twentieth century. Does every Black performer who seems to evoke minstrelsy warrant comparison to a minstrel? Is there any way for a Black performer to achieve national acclaim, in a country with a majority-white population, without incurring charges of selling out?

How deeply do those accusations stain, haunt, stifle the accused? Everybody from the blackface comedian Bert Williams and the dancer Bill "Bojangles" Robinson to the rappers Flavor Flav and Kanye West; to O. J. Simpson, during his spokesman stints and acting days; to the entertainer Wayne Brady; to Clarence Thomas, Alan Keyes, Herman Cain in political spheres; to rock-oriented musicians like Tina Turner and Lenny Kravitz; to Diana Ross and Oprah Winfrey—they've all bestirred worry and provoked embarrassment among Black folks. Is *their* Blackness an act? Is the act under white control? Is their Blackness detectable or sufficiently, what, soulful?

The most respectable acts, even when they were Black performers on a Black label, could find themselves accused of minstrelsy. Yes, for some Black people, even Berry Gordy's piloting all those flights to the top of *Billboard*'s Hot 100 singles chart seemed like traveling too close to the sun. "Under Mr. Gordy's strict, hands-on direction," James Brown wrote in his autobiography, "the Motown show and catalogue were shaped around pop, and their acts were made to strut like minstrels."[39] That accursed art form is still misshaping perceptions, so that not every victory gets to feel like a win.

Motown wanted, in its way, to obliterate this neurotic prison, to adjust the scope of the Black self-image. The company's pageant of coordinated crispness was as resolutely *anti*-minstrelsy as the tradition of Black oratory. White people were forced to behold men and women looking as divine as they sounded. The music captured Black America's hearts and opened white America's minds, at the precise moment when that openness seemed vital for the country's very sanity. Today, what Gordy pulled off tends to be reclassified as stodgy or uncool, closer to Brown's assessment that it's not simply evoking an ugly past but exploiting it. Not an unreasonable conclusion in the twenty-first century, during the reign of Drake and Megan Thee Stallion, of a dozen different Lils. Yet Motown remains an unmovable landmark. This, the company has proven, is how things should have been all along, with Black people captaining their artistic and commercial destinies, singing music they composed, cashing checks their music brought in. Their songs understood and appreciated, just as Gordy had dreamt, the sound of America.

This country clings to its institutional orthodoxies about what exactly "American" means when it comes to Black musicians. All seems well—Black artists continue to be widely listened to and lauded (and imitated). Yet trouble simmers below the surface. We've been rid of blackface minstrelsy for more than a century—well, we've had much less of it; let's put it that way. But its tastes and insinuations, its gamesmanship and manipulations are still with us, coursing through institutions, still threatening to bring the house down, still stuffing Black artists in Black boxes.

The dominance Gordy carved out, for instance, is what an artist like Tyler, the Creator wished for himself when he took a moment to ruminate after winning a Grammy in one of the rap categories in 2020. "I'm just like, why can't we be in pop?" he said backstage. "Half of me feels like the rap nomination was just a backhanded compliment."[40] The following year, Beyoncé became the woman with the most Grammys (twenty-eight); the majority of her wins, however, were in a rap or R&B category, and only one was for Song, Record, or Album of the Year.[41] Maybe this would matter less if rap and R&B were marginal elements of the American sound. Instead, they're the music those elite pop Grammys wind up honoring. It's just that, of late, the recipients of that industrial hardware have tended to be other than Black. In 2017, the recording academy that awards the statues handed Album of the Year to Adele, a white Brit who practices a polished kind of adult-contemporary soul music; and the following year the award went to Bruno Mars, an American of Filipino and Puerto Rican descent, whose project partially entails simply dousing funk and R&B with expensive-sounding nostalgia. It's been almost two hundred years since T. D. Rice jumped Jim Crow, but minstrelsy's priorities remain the country's preference.

Americans have made a political investment in a myth of racial separateness, the idea that art forms can be either "white" or "Black" in character, when aspects of many are at least both. Our original art form arose from our original sin, and some white people have always been worried that the primacy of Black music would be a kind of karmic punishment for that sin.

Umbrage is what fueled the explosion, in 2019, of "Old Town Road," a re-mixed duet between a newbie from Atlanta who goes by Lil Nas X and the former honky-tonk heartthrob Billy Ray Cyrus. The song wedded trap music to country, a mash-up the world received as novel when, really, it was a return to everybody's roots. One reason the Black bandleader Frank Johnson isn't better known might be that the styles of music he perfected seem awfully close to what you might hear at a square dance or a hoedown, music that would come to seem synonymous with white culture. Synonymous enough that, in the 1920s, during jazz's ascent, Henry Ford urged Americans to rally around the purported whiteness of the square dance; enough that more than two hundred years after Johnson's birth, we're only lately raising a critical eyebrow at country music's assertion of white purity.[42]

It's true that the proliferation of Black culture across the planet—the proliferation, in so many senses, of being Black—constitutes a magnificent joke on American racism. Yet that popularity hasn't strayed far from that covetous encounter between T. D. Rice and the Black man he watched groom that horse. Something about white America's desire for Blackness warps and perverts its source, lampoons and cheapens it even in adoration. Loving Black culture has never demanded a corresponding love of Black people. And loving Black culture has tended to result in loving the life out of it.

But not always. The ongoing disputes over whose stuff is whose obscures a more important irony: music has midwifed the only true integration this country has known. Minstrelsy's nonconsensual impersonations hog the headlines because it was the start of American popular culture as we still know it. But the history of American music also effervesces with work made by white people *alongside* Black people. It's rich with white artists who worked in Black traditions with admiration and respect, and features the occasional Black artist who, understanding the preference in certain corners of the marketplace for sanitized editions of their songs, counted the money as white artists rode Black music up the charts. Bobby and Shirley Womack's "It's All Over Now" wasn't a big hit until the Rolling Stones made it one in 1964; Womack complained until he got his first royalty check.[43]

Different generations of jazz artists have insisted that race doesn't matter, that the music doesn't care what color you are. That's an American romance. But in jazz it's sometimes a kind of truth in action, provable by the hazards certain acts, like Dave Brubeck's quartet, endured to play (and stay) integrated.

The record producer and concert promoter Norman Granz worked with integrated bands, insisted on equal pay, and would sooner cancel a show than have his artists play for segregated houses.[44] And the risk has often *sounded* worth it.

The historian Ann Douglas writes in *Terrible Honesty,* her history of popular culture in the 1920s, that "American entertainment, whatever the state of American society, has always been integrated, if only by theft and parody."[45] What we've been dealing with ever since is more than a catchall word like "appropriation" can approximate. The truth is more bounteous and more spiritual than that, more confused.

That confusion resides in the notorious tales of Michael Jackson taking from James Brown and Sammy Davis, Jr., over here and Fred Astaire and Freddie Mercury over there; in the arena-ready rock 'n' roll feel that Run DMC and the producer Rick Rubin arrived at together. It's there in the wink-wink costume funk of Beck's 1999 *Midnite Vultures,* an album whose kicky nonsense circles back to the popular culture of 150 years earlier. It's in the melismatic hair flips of Ariana Grande. It's in what we once called "blue-eyed soul," though I've never known what to do with that term, which euphemistically, almost jokingly labels even its most convincing practitioners—the Bee Gees, Michael McDonald, Bobby Caldwell, Hall & Oates, Teena Marie, Annie Lennox, Simply Red, George Michael, Taylor Dayne, Lisa Stansfield, Joss Stone, Robin Thicke—as diet Black music. The term might be out to mock or judge or offset, but it points to a crucial distinction between what's appreciative and what's appropriative. Flaws and all, these are non-Black artists committed to Black music, often working alongside Black musicians—which is to say, with Black musicians' consent.

That kind of collaboration can't change what took place a century or two before. It can't change the sins of the twentieth century. It remains outrageously true, for instance, that once Black musicians like Howlin' Wolf, Sister Rosetta Tharpe, Fats Domino, Chuck Berry, Little Richard, and Ike & Tina Turner built rock 'n' roll, white kids pounced and gentrified. Hip-hop and R&B have proved harder to colonize. This music remains at the creative and commercial center of American popular music—a fact that might further underscore how superfluous Black people can seem in everybody's attempt at Blackness. Yet hip-hop's rapid adaptability also proves how little territory Black people are willing to cede, how they continue to expand the landscape, how there has always been something in Black music that's viscerally attractive yet distinctly elusive, a depth of feeling that the field songs and spirituals instilled, perhaps eternally. The undying attraction to that feeling also gets at something thrillingly crucial about the music and its people, what so much of the sound is staked upon: humanity.

It also gets at what's remained elusive to certain white interlopers. Black music brims with call-and-response, layers of syncopation, and this rougher element called "noise," derived from unique sounds that arise from the particular hue and timbre of an instrument. Little Richard's *woos* and knuckled keyboard zooms. The breathless flutter of Charlie Parker's saxophone. Patti LaBelle's emotional police siren. DMX's scorched-earth bark. The misty wonder of Alberta Hunter and the wondrous hurt of Billie Holiday. The visceral stank of Etta James. The land-mine phrasing of Aretha Franklin. The pulpit ferocity of live-in-concert Whitney Houston. Prince committing arson with an electric guitar.

What you're hearing in what we call Black music is a miracle of sound, an experience that, like the spirituals, can really happen only off the page—not just melisma, glissandi, the rasp of a sax, break beats, or sampling but the mood or inspiration from which those moments arise. Writing down the asides and ad-libs and overdubs and yelps and wails, the extended solos, the mumbled running together of rhymes seems, if you think about it, like a fool's errand, the flowers wilting under hot water that Zora Neale Hurston was talking about. It's not that Black music isn't written. It certainly is. But so much of its glory can't be captured in recorded notes alone. That results from spontaneity. It resides between the notes, in personalities, in grunts, sighs, gestures, timbre, inflections, phrasing. You wouldn't be trying to capture the arrangement of notes, per se. You'd be trying to capture the uncatchable: the spirit.

And that's because what is original to Black American music is a mode by which singers and musicians could be completely free, free in the only way that would have been possible under enslavement: through art, through music. It was music no one "composed" (in part because enslaved people were denied literacy), music born of feeling, of play, of exhaustion, of uncertainty, of anguish. Of existential introspection. It was music whose depth could elude its own makers. Frederick Douglass writes in one of his personal histories, *Narrative of the Life of Frederick Douglass*, about listening to the singing of the enslaved:

> They would sometimes sing the most pathetic sentiment in the most rapturous tone, and the most rapturous sentiment in the most pathetic tone. . . . Especially would they do this when leaving home. They would then sing most exultingly the following words:—

"I am going away to the Great House Farm!
O, yea! O, yea! O!"

This they would sing, as a chorus, to words which to many would seem unmeaning jargon, but which, nevertheless, were full of meaning to themselves. I have sometimes thought that the mere hearing of those songs would do more to impress some minds with the horrible character of Slavery, than the reading of whole volumes of philosophy on the subject could do.[46]

Douglass understood their singing as a testament to a particular kind of pain, and to a unique form of perseverance and self-inquiry. *Why us? And how much longer? And what more?* But also—with respect to both physical and spiritual deliverance—*when?* The music testifies to a perilous condition as much as it offers hope that, somehow, it will end.

This is to say that when we're talking about Black music, we're talking about what the borrowers and collaborators don't want to or simply can't lift—centuries of weight, of atrocity we've never sufficiently worked through, the treasure you know is beyond theft because it's too real, too rich, too heavy to steal.

Doesn't the temptation to take from Blackness make sense, then? Here is the music of a people who have survived, who not only won't stop but also can't *be* stopped. Music by a people whose major innovations—jazz, rock 'n' roll, funk, hip-hop—have been about progress, about the future, about getting as far away from nostalgia as time will allow, music that's thought deeply about the allure of outer space and robotics, music whose promise and possibility, whose rawness, humor, and carnality call out to everybody: to other Black people; to kids in working-class England, middle-class Indonesia, and the *cités* of Paris; to teenagers in Seoul, Mexico City, and Bogotá. If freedom's ringing, who on earth wouldn't want to rock that bell?

August 6, 1965

President Lyndon Johnson signs into law the Voting Rights Act (VRA). The VRA protects rights granted in the Fifteenth Amendment, which states, "The right of citizens of the United States to vote shall not be denied or abridged by the United States or by any State on account of race, color, or previous condition of servitude." Yet despite the amendment's ratification in 1870, many Southern states had used intimidation, legal challenges, and outright violence for decades to stop Black Americans from voting. The VRA outlaws these practices.

Quotidian

Natasha Trethewey

Other rights, even the most basic, are illusory if the right to vote is undermined.

—Justice Hugo Black, 1964

Sometimes she wrote about the weather—
how hot it was, or yet another lightning storm
gone as quick as it came. In the catalog
of her days: a dress she was sewing, car trouble,
payday, laced with declarations of love
to the man who would become my father—
her body bright with desire, a threshold
I would soon cross into being. Two years
before *Loving* will make their love
legal, my mother writes about marrying
despite an unjust law; and because it is 1965,
Mississippi in turmoil, she writes about a cross
burned at the church next door, interracial
outings at the beach, and being followed
by police—all of it side by side in her letters'
tidy script. Reading them, I can't help thinking
how ordinary it seems, injustice—mundane
as a trip to the store for bread. And I know
this is about what has always existed,
side by side, in this country. That summer,

my grandmother brought *The Movement*
home. *It tells the story in pictures, and it is*
beautiful, my mother wrote, adding, *I think*
you know the way I am using the word.
On the cover: a Black protester, caught
in a cop's chokehold, his mouth open to shout
or gasp for air. Inside, pictures I could not bear
to look at as a child: a man tied to a scaffold,
his body burned blacker, the fire still smoldering
beneath him; two boys hanged from a tree
above the smiling white faces of the revelers
turned back toward the camera: a young couple
holding hands, ordinary as any night out
on a date. Now I think of my mother, in love
and writing love letters, cataloging her days,
those terrible/beautiful pictures on the table
next to the crocheted lace doily and crystal bowl
my grandmother kept for candy: butterscotch
in cellophane wrappers, bright and shiny as gold.
It is July 20, 1965, two months before my parents
will break the law to be married, and my mother,
who's just turned twenty-one, signs off—her rights
basic as any other citizen's—*Have to run,* she wrote.
Got to get downtown to register to vote.

October 15, 1966

In response to police brutality against African Americans, Merritt College students Huey Newton and Bobby Seale create the Black Panther Party for Self-Defense in Oakland, California, which monitors the actions of local law enforcement with armed citizen patrols. The organization, which J. Edgar Hoover's FBI names as an enemy of the government, holds that ending the economic exploitation of Black people is central to achieving racial equity. It also operates free breakfast programs, medical clinics, and other community service programs.

The Panther Is a Virtual Animal

Joshua Bennett

With a line from Tavia Nyong'o

Anything that wants to be can be a panther. The black lion
or ocelot, the black cheetah or cornrowed uptown girl sprinting
up her neighborhood block just like one, in dogged pursuit
of the future world. In this frame, I imagine Huey and Bobby
as boys in the sense of gender and genre alike, an unbroken
line reading: *my life is an armor for the other.* Before black berets
or free breakfasts, then, there is friendship. Before gun laws
shifting in the wake of organized strength, leather jackets
shimmering like gypsum in the Northern California twilight—
or else magazine covers running the world over, compelling
everyday ordinary people across the spectrum of context
or color to sing *who wants to be a panther ought to be he can be it*
—there is love. The panther is a virtual animal. The panther
strikes only when it has been assailed. The panther is a human
vision, interminable refusal, our common call to adore ourselves
as what we are and live and die on terms we fashioned from the earth
like this. Our precious metal metonym. Our style of fire and stone.

Lydia Monroe, Chicago, March 1942   JACK DELANO, LIBRARY OF CONGRESS

CHAPTER 15

Healthcare

———

JENEEN INTERLANDI

It was the signature policy proposal of the nation's first Black president, a sweeping overhaul of the healthcare system that broke a decades-long stalemate and brought health coverage to nearly twenty million previously uninsured adults. "It has now been nearly a century since Theodore Roosevelt first called for healthcare reform," President Barack Obama told Congress in the fall of 2009. "Our collective failure to meet this challenge, year after year, decade after decade, has led us to a breaking point." When the Affordable Care Act (ACA)—Obamacare, as it quickly became known—was signed into law, Vice President Joe Biden was heard leaning over to Obama and whispering, "This is a big fucking deal."[1]

Bigger, perhaps, than Biden even knew.

In the decade that followed, Obamacare became a touchstone for both sides of a political debate that swung numerous state and national elections. Republican promises to "repeal and replace" the law, and Democratic vows to save and strengthen it, have echoed down through just about every national election since the original bill was signed into law. On the surface, these were fights over how to fix the nation's exorbitantly priced and deeply inequitable healthcare system. But as charges of socialism and fearmongering over death panels soon revealed, deeper anxieties were also at work.

The United States is the only high-income nation that does not guarantee some form of healthcare to all of its citizens. Medicine here is a commodity, and access to it depends on a suite of factors, including age, income level, employment status, geographic region, and—to an alarming and undeniable extent—race. African and Latino Americans have the highest uninsured rates in the country and, as a result, shoulder a disproportionate burden of the health system's failings: they are more likely to die during pregnancy or from cancers that are treatable when caught early, and more likely to suffer the worst outcomes associated with chronic medical conditions like diabetes.

But while the picture is particularly bad for people of color, they are hardly the only ones suffering from the healthcare system's failings. In fact, America has the lowest life expectancy, the highest incidence of chronic disease, and the highest rate of avoidable hospitalizations and avoidable deaths when compared to other high-income countries, despite spending more money on healthcare by far.[2]

The ACA managed to put a measurable dent in at least some of these grim statistics. But its successes have been uneven and precarious. Republican-led states have spent years resisting the law however they could, including through relentless legal challenges and misinformation campaigns. Twelve states (most of them in the former Confederacy) refused to participate in the ACA's central provision: an expansion of Medicaid, the federal program that provides health coverage to low-income Americans. And in at least twelve other states, Republican lawmakers have tried to restrict access to that program through cumbersome work requirements.

This struggle—between using state resources to provide citizens with healthcare and withholding those resources from people deemed unworthy of support—has become one of the biggest conflicts in contemporary politics, not to mention an incredibly consequential debate for the future of the country's health and well-being. But it's not new. It began during Reconstruction, with four million newly emancipated African Americans.

In the aftermath of the Civil War, the nation faced a full-blown humanitarian disaster. Freed people did not have enough food, clothing, shelter, or medical care. They were plagued by dysentery, cholera, and a bleak roster of other diseases. And they had no reliable help for addressing these problems. Hospitals were few and far between at that time, and most of them were either overwhelmed by the needs of white citizens—to whom hospital administrators granted priority—or unwilling to admit formerly enslaved people under any circumstances, or both. As a result, the death toll of Black people surpassed that of white people by an overwhelming and consistent margin. As the historian Jim Downs details in his 2012 book *Sick from Freedom,* the newly emancipated died in such high numbers that in some communities their bodies littered the streets.

Smallpox was one of several killers that hopscotched across the South during this period. It invaded the makeshift "contraband camps" where Black Americans had taken refuge during the war but left the surrounding mostly white communities comparatively unscathed. The pattern of affliction was no mystery: in the late 1860s, scientists had yet to discover viruses, but they knew that poor nutrition made people more susceptible to illness and that poor sanitation contributed to the spread of disease. They also knew that quarantine and vaccination could help quell outbreaks; they had used those tools to prevent the very same diseases from ravaging the Union army.[3]

In one of their first attempts to claim the rights of citizenship, at least some freed people asked that the same methods be employed in their own burgeoning communities. As Downs notes, one group of newly emancipated men asked for humane quarantine facilities to be erected; others asked for latrines to be moved away from tents in refugee camps. But rather than help these communities, Downs writes, medical authorities often blamed them for causing diseases to spread.[4]

Some of these debates took place in the context of the Freedmen's Bureau. Congress had established the bureau in 1865 as a federal entity meant to oversee the transition from slavery to freedom, including helping the newly emancipated become a paid workforce at the close of the war and ensuring that they were treated equally in judicial procedures. But elected officials were deeply divided over what this bureau's responsibilities should be, or whether it should even exist at all, and some of the disputes concerned healthcare. Some lawmakers, including a contingent of Radical Republicans, believed it was the government's duty to provide medical assistance and other aid to freed people. Opponents of the bureau, including President Andrew Johnson and most Democratic members of Congress, argued that such assistance would only breed dependence, which would keep freed people from returning to the plantations, where their labor was still needed. Black people were idle and depraved by nature, they said. And when it came to Black infirmity, hard work was a better salve than any medicine.[5]

Nevertheless, in 1865, the bureau's commissioner, General O. O. Howard, inaugurated its Medical Division, which, in turn, worked to establish a system of hospitals for the formerly enslaved across the postwar South.[6] The program was unprecedented—the first federally funded healthcare system ever created in the United States—but its goals were never entirely humanitarian. The bureau director put in charge of the program aimed to provide just enough care to just enough freed people to maintain the plantation labor force. And from the start, the program's efforts were mired in anxiety over Black dependency. Officials deployed a mere 120 or so doctors across the war-torn South, then ignored those doctors' pleas for personnel and equipment. They erected more than forty hospitals, often in response to specific medical emergencies in specific jurisdictions, but shuttered most of them long before those emergencies had been resolved or the freed people's medical needs addressed. These contradictions reached their apotheosis in the fall of 1866, when white doctors in Charlotte, North Carolina, discovered smallpox in their city's only hospital for freed people. Terrified, and with no other means of preventing the disease from spreading, they did the only thing they could think of: they burned their own hospital to the ground.[7]

As the smallpox epidemic persisted, and the death toll continued to rise, those who opposed providing any assistance to freed people developed a new and darker argument: Black people were so ill-suited to freedom that the entire race was going extinct, and the best lawmakers could do was let nature take its course. "No charitable black scheme can wash out the color of the Negro, change his inferior nature or save him from his inevitable fate," Ohio Democratic congressman Samuel Cox said in 1865 on the floor of the House of Representatives.[8] Several newspapers agreed, including *The New York Times*, which wrote that the "mortality of the negroes" continued to be very great and that "dirt, debauchery, idleness are the cases of this inordinate mortality."[9]

One of the most eloquent rejoinders to this theory of Black extinction came from Rebecca Lee Crumpler, the nation's first Black female doctor. Crumpler was born free and trained and practiced in Boston. But at the close of the war, she joined the Freedmen's Bureau and worked in the freed people's communities of Virginia. In 1883, she published one of the first treatises by a Black writer on the burden of disease among Black communities. Her book, which addressed Black women specifically, was intended to serve as a call and a guide for the newly emancipated—a message that they could and would survive, even amid so much hatred and neglect. But Crumpler might as well have been speaking to Congressman Cox directly when she wrote that the nation's lawmakers "seem to forget that there is a *cause* for every ailment, and that it may be in their power to remove it."[10] Those causes were external, she explained, not innate.

Crumpler died in 1895, but her spirit lived on in an organization founded that same year, the National Medical Association (NMA), a pioneering organization of Black doctors. Its first president, Robert F. Boyd, had been born into slavery. Through annual conferences and its own medical journal, the NMA became the leading voice on issues surrounding the health and medical treatment of Black people and other disadvantaged groups. As the founding editor of the organization's journal wrote, the NMA was "conceived in no spirit of racial exclusiveness, fostering no ethnic antagonism, but born of the exigencies of the American environment."[11] And one of the best ways to improve health outcomes, the NMA understood, was through increased access to healthcare. At the start of the twentieth century, the group began to argue for nationalized medicine.

This argument, of course, went nowhere. In the decades following Reconstruction, the former slave states came to wield enormous congressional power through a voting bloc that was uniformly segregationist and overwhelmingly Democratic. During the 1930s, Southern congressmen headed many of the key committees in Congress. They used this power to ensure that New Deal measures did not threaten the nation's racial stratification. For example, as the Columbia University historian Ira Katznelson and others have documented, it was largely at the behest of Southern Democrats that farm and domestic workers—who made up more than half the nation's workforce at the time, and an even higher percentage of the Black workforce—were excluded from New Deal policies, including the Social Security Act; the Wagner Act, which ensured the right of workers to collective bargaining; and the Fair Labor Standards Act, which set a minimum wage and established the eight-hour workday. The same voting bloc ensured that states controlled crucial programs like Aid to Dependent Children and the 1944 Servicemen's Readjustment Act, better known as the GI Bill. In the South, especially, state leaders then excluded Black Americans from these programs through a variety of dubious mechanisms, including by creating onerous and subjective tests for determining need.[12]

Southern Democrats also secured local control of other federal healthcare programs under the mantra of "states' rights." In 1945, when President Truman called on Congress to expand the nation's hospital system as part of a larger healthcare plan, they obtained key concessions that excluded Black Americans both explicitly and implicitly and would shape the American medical landscape for decades to come. The Hill-Burton Act provided federal grants for hospital construction to communities in need and gave funding priority to rural areas, many of which were in the South and predominantly Black. But the law also put state leaders in charge of disbursing those funds and did not make any rule against segregating the new facilities. As a result, white communities were prioritized, and Black Americans in the rural South were left in the worst of circumstances: living in the least-resourced part of the country, and deliberately excluded from the exact program meant to fix that problem.[13]

Employer-based health insurance, which took off in the wake of World War II, put yet another hurdle between African Americans and equitable healthcare. "They were denied most of the jobs that offered coverage," says David Barton Smith, an emeritus historian of healthcare policy at Temple University. "And even when some of them got health insurance, as the Pullman porters did, they couldn't make use of white facilities." White doctors helped widen the gap even further: professional societies like the American Medical Association (AMA) allowed Black doctors to be excluded, medical schools barred Black students, and most hospitals and health clinics segregated Black patients. The cumulative effect of these and other privations was to leave Black Americans with statistically shorter, sicker lives than their white counterparts.

But Black communities of the 1930s, '40s, and '50s were no more apt to accept these exclusions than their forebears. Echoing the efforts of Crumpler, Black women began a national community healthcare movement that included fundraising for Black health facilities; campaigns to educate Black communities about nutrition, sanitation, and disease prevention; and programs like National Negro Health Week that drew attention to racial health disparities.[14]

One of the leaders of this effort was the NMA. By the 1950s, after a decades-long debate, its members were pushing aggressively for a federal health-insurance program that would serve all citizens equally—a fight that put them in direct open conflict with their colleagues at the AMA.

The AMA was vehemently opposed to nationalized healthcare. Its members had already defeated two such proposals in the late 1930s and '40s, with a vitriolic campaign whose slogans still reverberate today: they called the idea socialist and un-American and warned of government intervention in the doctor-patient relationship. In the early 1960s, when proponents of a national health plan introduced Medicare, the AMA quickly and aggressively revived those same arguments, and doctors' wives organized "coffee meetings," where they persuaded friends to write letters opposing the program. Their effort, dubbed Operation Coffee Cup, secured an endorsement from Ronald Reagan, who in 1961 recorded an album with a gravelly voiced speech warning that Medicare would lead to "statism or socialism."

But this time, the NMA delivered a countermessage of its own: healthcare was a basic human right, inextricably bound to racial equality. "Man is such a slow learner," NMA president William Montague Cobb said of the fight. "But let us recognize our mistakes and remedy them, without having to repeat the historical process again and again and again."[15]

Together, Medicare and Medicaid helped bring hospital segregation to a circuitous but definitive end: the 1964 Civil Rights Act outlawed segregation for any entity receiving federal funds, and Medicare and Medicaid soon placed every hospital in the country in that category. The programs also secured reliable healthcare for whole swaths of the population—namely, low-income and elderly Americans—for the first time.[16] As has happened so often in our history, Black struggles for equality resulted in greater rights for all Americans. In its fight to secure healthcare for Black Americans, the NMA helped to dramatically improve access for citizens across the racial and socio-economic spectrum.

Many forces have prevented the United States from achieving universal healthcare, including a failure to properly regulate the trillion-dollar health-care industry and a near-total unwillingness to grapple with the ethics of for-profit medicine. But the role of racism and the legacy of slavery cannot be denied. The same arguments—about dependency and socialized medicine, equity and human rights—that thwarted the Freedmen's Bureau Medical Division in Crumpler's time and blocked universal healthcare during Cobb's time have echoed down to the present day.

People of color continue to suffer most from the failure to resolve these arguments; Black and Latino Americans still have the highest uninsured rates in the country and still shoulder a disproportionate share of the nation's poor health outcomes. But they are not alone. After all the debates and elections and bills and lawsuits, millions of Americans—of every race, ethnicity, and political persuasion—still don't have health insurance of any kind, and millions more are still forced to ration crucial medications, or to forgo critical procedures, or to choose in some other way between receiving healthcare and meeting other essential needs.

In the end, everyone is harmed.

June 8, 1972

During her historic campaign as the first Black woman to run for president, Shirley Chisholm visits George Wallace, one of her opponents for the nomination, in the hospital, where he is recovering from an assassination attempt. Both Chisholm, whose campaign slogan is "Unbought and Unbossed," and Wallace, the former governor of Alabama and a staunch segregationist, will lose the nomination to George McGovern, who, in turn, will be defeated in the general election by Richard Nixon.

Unbought, Unbossed, Unbothered

Nafissa Thompson-Spires

I'll admit that I was pretty mad at Congresswoman Chisholm for a minute, visiting a peckerwood like George "Segregation Now, Segregation Tomorrow, and Segregation Forever" Wallace in the hospital just because he got shot. Like worse things haven't been happening to our people forever. Like they didn't kill Kennedy and King right in our faces and then make one of us clean up the blood. Like my little cousin didn't get arrested and roughed up by the Klan to the point of ending his athletic career just for staying out too late on the south side of Fontucky, one of SoCal's many sundown towns, without his school ID. And people think the racism is so much easier in California than in the South, nonexistent even, when really it's like the difference between the cold and the flu: both take you out of work, are contagious, and have you coughing or throwing up, wondering what you did wrong to earn all this suffering.

For several days, I stopped campaigning for Ms. Chisholm, but some little flickering in my chest told me the cause was too big for pettiness. And that's what she tried to show us, real Christian leadership. If it were up to me, I'd have spit in Wallace's wounds and then his eye, but they wanted to keep us distracted with anger. I started teaching myself to contort my rage into more valuable shapes; it doesn't disappear that way, just works for you instead of against you. I could throw faster the more I tapped into it, spirals no one could intercept. So you could say athletics kept me out of trouble, but really it was my secret weaponized anger, used for good, that saved me and helped me potentially save a lot of others.

We couldn't even vote in that election, me and my classmates, except Ronald, who'd been held back twice, and if they hadn't loosened the literacy requirement, he wouldn't have gotten to vote either. I was sixteen and still living with my grandfolks, finally settling into the truth that my mama didn't love me quite enough to bring me home, my dad was probably never coming back for me, and if he did, what'd be the point? I'd be in college by then, and who needs a mama or a dad to pay for it when Chaffey is free and my football and Rotary Club scholarships would cover the books. In North Fontana, past the segregation line, the enthusiasm for Chisholm and the election was pretty clear, but on the other side of the line, we had a lot of those whites who smile in your face and tell you how tall or strong you look and where you from, boy? Football, really? I think I saw you in the North Fontana versus Redlands game. But suppose you don't play sports. Then you have a problem talking to any of those Wallace-Nixon loving fools.

It seemed best not to try to convert the whites but to instead focus on registering voters, especially older ones on our side of town, many of whom, including Gran and PawPaw, couldn't have passed even a basic literacy test. Those folks, we paired with a capable high school student who'd not only help them to the polls but push the buttons for them. I'd been doing that for my grandparents each election since I was eight, but never with any enthusiasm until this one. I mean, here was a Black woman telling a white congressman that if he minded her making equal pay to him so much, then he should "vanish when you see me." Sometimes me and my boys just randomly yell, "Forty-two five," Chisholm's salary, the kind of salary we hope to make someday but also as an inside joke when some white at Baker's looks at us like they might have owned us, if only. "Forty-two five, nigga, forty-two five," like it's the code for a football play. It's just as exhilarating as getting folks registered to vote Chisholm. (The old ones are happy to have a visitor once they let go of their suspicion; then they offer us baked goods.)

I'm not sure I believe in a savior, certainly not a white one, but what if salvation came in the form of a Black woman bold enough to say she's "Unbought and Unbossed"? I fear her assassination every day, but if anyone can raise themselves from the dead, it's gotta be us Black folks. We've already done it so many times, we're the walking dead, carrying all kinds of ancestors and uglier ghosts. That's why they called us spooks, because the whites could see in us something that if only we could fully tap into, it would blow this whole joint up and end white supremacy on this continent and everywhere else in the world.

Right now, though, I have my sights set on getting out the vote in Fontucky, avoiding any trouble that could derail my plans. The way I see it, between escorting Gran and PawPaw, escorting strangers, and getting others to vote, it doesn't matter that I can't officially do it myself. I've voted dozens of times over for Ms. Chisholm, and so have a bunch of us underage students. So even if Fontucky never becomes an integrated Fontana and the Klan stays just as loud across the town line, as long as I make it to college and Ms. Chisholm wins, I, too, can say I'm unbought, unbossed, and, I'll add, unbothered.

September 12, 1974

Following a state court ruling over the summer that found a pattern of de facto segregation in Boston's public schools, the city implements a busing plan on the first day of school. It is met with fierce resistance by local white residents. Throughout the fall, and in years to come, white protesters violently harass buses carrying Black schoolchildren; over the next decade, many white families in Boston, and in other urban areas around the country where deseg-regation busing is used, move to predominantly white suburbs rather than send their children to integrated schools.

Crazy When You Smile

Patricia Smith

I'd never seen them up this close before
or ever known the awkward reckoning
of our collapsing distance. Hatred of
the what I am blooms wreckage on their skin,
their arms and faces blare in crimson while
they wave their placards with my breath
misspelled. I never thought that I would find
myself the object of foreboding thick
enough to make a white man bare his teeth,
all Lucky Struck and rotting, just to hiss
a tightening noose in my direction, or
to spot a mother in a boxy robe
of dimming flowers, hair all done up high
and gelled and wrapped 'round Velcro rollers.
She sidearms rocks to hit the window by
my head—and I refuse to flinch. She calls
me *monkey* and I smile at her beyond
and through the spidered cracking of the glass.

It really drives them crazy when you smile,
my father said this morning, while I scrubbed
my pimpled cheeks and picked my badass 'fro
to sky. *Don't let on that you're mad or scared.*
I can't say that I really understood
the strategy of being less of myself—

pretending deafness, unremembering
my fists. I know what he was thinking of—
those students long ago in counter seats
at Woolworth's, stunned while leering white boys
drenched their heads with flour, ketchup, mustard, spit—
perhaps there was a lesson to be learned.
But this is Boston, ten whole years from then,
and maybe I don't want to be a martyr
because to me it looks like nothing much
has changed. I'm stiff in my seat on this bus
while seething white folks scan the ground for stones,
for shards of glass, for ways to break the skin
that vexes them. I know that this is not the South,
and yet it is. I know God said they know
not what they do—but yeah, they do. I know
that I am not a fool, and yet I feel
like one—the coon they expect to see—
smiling and swallowing. Smiling. Swallowing.

And everyone still sitting on the bus
is silent—fascinated by the spew
of phlegm and venom smearing windows,
the way no matter how they sing our names
it sounds like *nigger—nigger* screeched so wide,
so thousand times and so on-key. I know
that when they let me go, I just might wear
that new name home to show my father.

A man named Lean, Atlanta, 2018 *LEAN*, BY JORGE SIGALA

CHAPTER 16

Traffic

KEVIN M. KRUSE

Atlanta has some of the worst traffic in the United States. Drivers there average two hours each week mired in gridlock, hung up at countless spots, from the constantly clogged State Route 400 to a complicated cluster of overpasses at the Tom Moreland Interchange, better known as "Spaghetti Junction." The Downtown Connector—a megahighway that varies between twelve and fourteen lanes and, in theory, connects the city's north to its south—regularly has three-mile-long traffic jams that last four hours or more. Commuters might assume they're stuck there because some city planner made a mistake, but the heavy congestion actually stems from a great success. In Atlanta, as in dozens of cities across America, daily congestion is a direct consequence of a campaign to segregate the races that unfolded over a century and a half.

For much of the nation's history, the campaign to keep African Americans "in their place" socially and politically manifested itself in an effort to keep them quite literally in one place or another. Before the Civil War, white enslavers kept Black people close at hand, in slave quarters where they could be closely monitored, in order to coerce their labor and guard against revolts. But with the abolition of slavery, the spatial relationship was reversed. Once they had no need to maintain constant watch over African Americans, white people wanted them out of sight. Public and private forces—city planners, local and state elected officials, federal housing program administrators, mortgage bankers, and real estate brokers—worked together to push African Americans into ghettos. The segregation we know today became the rule.[1]

At first the rule was overt, with Southern cities like Baltimore and Louisville enacting laws that mandated residential racial segregation.[2] Such laws were eventually invalidated by the Supreme Court, but later measures achieved the same effect by more subtle means. During the New Deal, federal agencies like the Home Owners' Loan Corporation and the Federal Housing Administration encouraged redlining practices that explicitly marked minority neighborhoods as risky investments and, therefore, discouraged bank loans, mortgages, and insurance there.[3] Other policies simply targeted Black communities for isolation and demolition. The postwar programs for urban renewal, for instance, destroyed Black neighborhoods and displaced their residents with such regularity that African Americans came to believe, in James Baldwin's memorable line, that "urban renewal" meant "Negro removal."[4]

This intertwined history of infrastructure and racial inequality extended into the 1950s and '60s with the creation of the interstate highway system. The federal government shouldered nine-tenths of the cost of the new interstate highways, but local officials often had a say in selecting the path. As in most American cities in the decades after the Second World War, the new highways in Atlanta—local expressways at first, then interstates—steered along routes that invariably ran right through the neighborhoods of racial minorities. Planners often argued that they targeted the most "blighted" regions for bulldozing, and the poor residents there simply happened to be African American.[5]

But wealthy Black enclaves were targeted as well. Auburn Avenue, which once housed so many Black-owned businesses that *Fortune* magazine called it "the richest Negro street in the world," was devastated by the creation of the Downtown Connector.[6] "Sweet Auburn," the home to prominent institutions like Martin Luther King, Jr.'s Ebenezer Baptist Church, had long stood as the core of Black Atlanta, but the intrusions of the interstate proved to be a "death-blow," in the words of one local.[7] The original plans for the Downtown Connector plotted a path directly through the headquarters of the Atlanta Life Insurance Company, the crown jewel of the city's Black business community. The objections of Black leaders succeeded in shifting the route a few blocks east, but the highway still tore through Auburn Avenue, displacing residents and destroying businesses.[8]

This common practice of steering new interstates through minority neighborhoods—rich and poor alike—was repeated across the South in cities like Charlotte, Houston, Jacksonville, Miami, Montgomery, Nashville, New Orleans, Richmond, and Tampa. But it was not simply a Southern phenomenon. Countless metropolitan areas throughout the country saw similar patterns, including Chicago, Cincinnati, Denver, Detroit, Indianapolis, Los Angeles, Milwaukee, Pittsburgh, St. Louis, Syracuse, and Washington. Activists in the capital decried the practice of "white men's roads through Black men's bedrooms," but the phenomenon nevertheless proliferated across the entire nation.[9]

While Interstates were regularly used to destroy Black neighborhoods, they were also used to keep Black and white neighborhoods apart. Today, major roads and highways serve as stark dividing lines between Black and white sections in cities like Buffalo, Hartford, Kansas City, Milwaukee, Pittsburgh, and St. Louis. In Atlanta, the intent to segregate was crystal clear. Interstate 20, the east-west corridor that connects with I-75 and I-85 in Atlanta's center, was deliberately plotted along a winding route in the late 1950s to serve, in the words of Mayor Bill Hartsfield, as "the boundary between the white and Negro communities" on the west side of town. Black neighborhoods, he hoped, would be hemmed in on one side of the new expressway, while white neighborhoods on the other side of it would be protected. Racial residential patterns have long since changed, of course, but the awkward path of I-20 remains in place.[10]

By razing impoverished areas downtown and segregating the races in the western section, Atlanta's leaders hoped to keep downtown and its surroundings a desirable destination for middle-class white people looking to shop and spend. Articulating a civic vision of racial peace and economic progress, Hartsfield bragged that Atlanta was "The City Too Busy to Hate." But urban renewal ultimately failed to keep white residents inside the city. Downtown redevelopment, as was often the case, proved to be more disruptive in its means and less impressive in its ends than city planners had promised. Rather than wait for the central city to be "renewed," many white people decided to move themselves to suburbs that were already new and, with the arrival of the interstate highways, were now affordable and accessible. During the 1960s, roughly sixty thousand white people left the city, with many of them relocating to the suburbs along the northern rim. When another hundred thousand left in the 1970s, a local joke had it that Atlanta had become "The City Too Busy Moving to Hate."[11]

As the new suburbs ballooned in size, traffic along the poorly placed highways became worse and worse. The obvious solution was mass transit—buses, light rail, and trains that would more efficiently link the suburbs and the city—but that, too, faced opposition, largely for racial reasons. The white suburbanites had purposefully left African Americans behind in the central city and worried that mass transit would bring them back.

Accordingly, suburbanites waged a sustained campaign against the Metropolitan Atlanta Rapid Transit Authority (MARTA) from its inception. In a 1965 vote, residents of nearly all-white Cobb County resoundingly rejected extending the system to their neighborhoods. In 1971, Gwinnett and Clayton Counties, which were then also overwhelmingly white, followed suit, voting down a proposal to join MARTA by nearly 4-to-1 margins, and keeping MARTA out became the default position of many local politicians. Emmett Burton, a Cobb County commissioner, won praise for promising to "stock the Chattahoochee with piranha" if that's what it would take to hold MARTA off.[12]

By the 1980s, arguments against MARTA by local politicians were less overtly racialized, but public sentiment remained unchanged. White racists joked that MARTA, with its heavily Black and entirely urban ridership, stood for "Moving Africans Rapidly Through Atlanta."[13] David Chesnut, the white chairman of MARTA, insisted in 1987 that suburban opposition to extending the mass transit system beyond the urban core had been "90 percent a racial issue." Because of that resistance, MARTA became a city-only service that did little to relieve commuter traffic. After Gwinnett County voted the system down again in 1990, a former Republican legislator marveled at the arguments given by opponents. "They will come up with twelve different ways of saying they are not racist in public," he told a reporter. "But you get them alone, behind a closed door, and you see this old blatant racism that we have had here for quite some time."[14]

As these white suburbs seceded from the city and sealed themselves off, they witnessed a tremendous population surge. During the 1980s, roughly 86 percent of Atlanta's metropolitan growth occurred in the suburban ring, especially along its northern rim—Cobb County to the northwest, Gwinnett County to the northeast, and, between them, a small sliver of Fulton County outside the city limits. Of the ten fastest-growing counties in America during the 1980s, three stood outside Atlanta, and one of them, Cobb, took top honors as the fastest-growing county in the entire nation. By the end of the twentieth century, the suburban counties of Cobb and Gwinnett *each* had more residents than the city.[15] As the suburban population and economy boomed, the lack of metropolitan transportation meant that opportunities there were well beyond many Black Atlantans' reach. "For an unemployed Atlantan without a car," a *New York Times* editorial noted in 1988, "jobs in Cobb and Gwinnett counties might as well be in China." But that, of course, was precisely the point.[16]

Even when the suburbs became more racially diverse, they still remained opposed to MARTA. In 2019, Gwinnett County voted MARTA down for a third time. Proponents had hoped that changes in the county's racial composition, which was becoming less white, might make a difference. But the initiative still failed by an eight-point margin. Officials discovered that some nonwhite suburbanites shared the isolationist instincts of earlier white suburbanites. And even though the overt anti-Black racism that had shaped the suburban boom had subsided, new generations of residents there remained constrained by the built environment that panic had etched into the landscape, and they, too, conformed to its limitations. Some of them openly echoed the earlier arguments. One white property manager in her late fifties told a reporter that she had voted against mass transit because it was used by immigrants, whom she called "illegals." "Why should we pay for it?" she asked. "Why subsidize people who can't manage their money and save up a dime to buy a car?"[17]

In the end, Atlanta's traffic is at a standstill because its attitude about transit is at a standstill, too. Decades after its interstates were set down with an eye to segregation and its rapid transit system was stunted by white flight, the city—like so many other cities across America—remains stalled in the past.

July 17, 1984

The Reverend Jesse Jackson gives a historic speech at the Democratic National Convention in San Francisco, where he describes the need for a "Rainbow Coalition," and insists "we must come together." Jackson, the first Black man to mount a viable campaign for president, wins two primaries before losing the Democratic nomination to Walter Mondale.

Rainbows Aren't Real, Are They?

Kiese Laymon

My older sister, Rae, makes me write five hundred words every night before I go to bed. Tonight, I want to write five gazillion because of this speech by a Black man with big beautiful eyeballs and a big beautiful voice named Jesse Jackson.

While we were working on the Barnett house tonight, Rae kept saying that Jesse's speech was going to do for us what Ronald Reagan's speech did for white folks at the Neshoba County Fair four years ago. Ronald Reagan came to the fair and said some words about "states' rights." Those words made a lot of white folks at the fair happy. Those words made Rae, Mama, Granny, and our whole church so scared we had to leave. When we got in the van, Rae told me that Ronald Reagan came to Mississippi to offer white folks an all-you-can-eat buffet of Black suffering.

I asked Rae if white folks left full. She sucked her teeth and told me to let her metaphors ride.

Dafinas, who worked on the house with us this summer, stayed to watch the speech, too. Dafinas is from Oaxaca, Mexico, and his grandmother was just stolen by police in a raid. I don't know if Rae and Dafinas go together, but they look at each other's hands like they do.

All of us watched Jesse Jackson say the names of people I never heard of at school. He talked about Goodman, Chaney, and Schwerner. He talked about Fannie Lou Hamer, Martin Luther King, and Rabbi Abraham Heschel. He talked about Hispanic Americans, Arab Americans, African Americans. He talked about lesbian and gay Americans having something called equal protection under the law. He talked about powerful coalitions made of rainbows.

When we walked out of the Barnett house, a house we were building, in a white neighborhood where none of us would ever be allowed to live, I watched Dafinas and Rae hug for eight seconds.

On the way home, I asked Rae why she seemed so sad. "Rainbows, they pretty, but they ain't real," she said. "The only thing real down here sometimes feels like suffering. And love."

I told Rae that I liked her more than apple Now and Laters. But if believing in rainbows makes us love better, then rainbows can be just as real as work. And love. And if we really believed, we might be able to bring Dafinas's granny back. And one day, instead of building houses for white folks, in neighborhoods we could never even visit if we weren't working there, we could maybe build beautiful houses with gardens where all our grannies could sit on porches, and safely tell all those good lies that sound true.

"I never seen a black-and-brown rainbow," Rae said.

"Me either," I said.

"But I'll always believe in us."

"I'll be sad when you go to college," I told her. "But mostly, I'll be fine, because I can't stop believing that rainbows are real. How are we ever gonna be free if we only believe the things they tell us are possible?"

"We're not," Rae said, as we got out of the car. "We're just not."

May 13, 1985

Philadelphia police end a standoff with MOVE, a Black liberation group, by dropping a bomb on the rowhouse where members live. MOVE was founded the previous decade by John Africa, born Vincent Leaphart, a Korean War veteran and animal rights activist. The group's members took the surname Africa and agreed to live communally, practice strict vegetarianism, and resist various forms of modern life. The 1985 bombing kills eleven of them, including five children, and, because the fire department lets the resulting fire burn, destroys sixty-one houses and leaves 250 people homeless in the Black neighborhood of Cobbs Creek.

A Surname to Honor Their Mother

Gregory Pardlo

What is it about this group—which never numbered more than a few dozen—
that inspired the U.S. government, at all three levels, to spend hundreds of
thousands of man hours, and millions of dollars, working toward its destruction?

—Richard Kent Evans

Homeschoolers, raw vegan zero-wasters,
social-justice warriors, they moved against puppy mills
and flophouses, against zoos and the avarice that fuels
the System. Responding to a noise complaint in '76,
police quieted the Africas of MOVE with clubs, nightsticks.
The infant Life Africa was crushed under an officer's boot.
He'd been delivered at home, and the commonwealth would
neither certify the birth of Life after death, nor the tears
of a mother named Africa. MOVE kept moving each time,

like a river, their movement was dammed by police, an agency
shamed for its failure to contain them. In '78, a riot-geared wall
encircled the creaky Victorian, MOVE's headquarters, while canvas
hoses fed into cellar windows where the Africas held strong,
and forced them to swim for safety.
Deluge upon deluge. Water, bullets. An officer shot from behind
in the melee sparked no investigation. Instead, the city erased

the old house as if it were a bit of graffiti, and announced—a social
execution—MOVE were now cop-killers.

Those Africas not given life
sentences repaired here to this tidy block of mother-loved
homes on a street named to honor the Osage Nation. Here,
where MOVE took its last stand, and let the living stray
indoors and out, the compound was a hive the city clawed at
and swatted, passions fermenting like compost.

John Africa, in the end, "Body F," sixth of eleven bags of charred
remains sent to the morgue, had wrapped MOVE in the manifesto
they megaphoned all hours ("you can't describe something profane
without using profanity"). Their polemics drowned out the music of ice
    cream trucks.

Until Mother's Day of '85. Police went door to door
to door instructing moms to pack their families into overnight bags.
Without so much as their arms could carry, they left behind Bibles
and tax records, record collections and Commodore 64s. They left bowling
trophies, wedding knives, and archives of *Jet* magazine, family albums
and photos propped on credenzas and on top of their Magnavox TVs.
They left wall-hung pictures of King, Kennedy, and Jesus when, stopping
to gossip and speculate, they filled the street that'd been cleared as if
for a block party. In twenty-four hours, they'd watch the city deliver its gift.
The commissioner's recipe for eviction: M16s, Uzi submachine guns,
sniper rifles, tear gas, approximately ten thousand rounds of .50-caliber
bullets, more than five hundred officers, 640,000 gallons of water, and one
    state police
helicopter to drop two pounds of mining explosives combined with two
    pounds of C-4
on the MOVE family compound's roof.

As flames rose like orchids in a vase, the canvas hoses parched
and let an infernal peace engulf the neighborhood. By sunrise, whole
blocks lay open like egg cartons, buildings reduced to their earth-
works, sirens sounded their jubilee to match the mothers' wailing.
Timbers in rubble like mulch piles smoldered as smoke left shadows
espaliered on walls, and twined staircases aimed at the unblemished sky.

Chris Williams with his children, Harley and Hunter, in Silver Spring, Maryland, 2020
MICHAEL A. MCCOY

CHAPTER 17

Progress

IBRAM X. KENDI

———

"That's what we mean when we say America is exceptional. Not that our nation has been flawless from the start, but that we have shown the capacity to change and make life better for those who follow." So said President Barack Obama in his farewell address in January 2017, just days before Donald Trump took office. And yet, many Americans did not see a "more perfect Union" coming.[1] After all, Trump had been endorsed by a leading Ku Klux Klan newspaper and one of the organization's former leaders, David Duke.[2] He was advised by white nationalists like Steve Bannon. He made a political name for himself questioning Obama's citizenship.[3] Trump campaigned on making America "great again" after the first Black president. He framed Latino immigrants as rapists.[4] For many Americans, Trump was not forging a path forward to "make life better." Instead he represented a racist past they believed the nation had left behind, and his victory a reversal of the gradual racial progress they had been told was the American story.

Obama, himself an avatar of that progress, knew he had to explain this in his address. "Yes, our progress has been uneven," he said. "For every two steps forward, it often feels we take one step back. But the long sweep of America has been defined by forward motion, a constant widening of our founding creed to embrace all and not just some."[5]

Obama was embracing a national mythology in which America was marching forward and righting past wrongs, an epic, righteous journey that had led to his own election eight years earlier. This mantra of steady incremental change has long been a part of the American creed. Politicians of all races and parties convey it constantly. I once believed it. Sure, the country may have begun in slavery, but it fought a war to end it. It passed three new amendments to the Constitution to end slavery and give citizenship to those formerly enslaved, and to grant the men among them the right to vote. And though, in the decades that followed, those rights were violently denied, eventually the nation's institutions acted to ensure them. In 1954, the Supreme Court declared segregated public schools unconstitutional. A decade later, Congress passed and President Lyndon B. Johnson signed the Civil Rights Act of 1964 and the Voting Rights Act of 1965. President Johnson appointed the former NAACP attorney Thurgood Marshall to the U.S. Supreme Court in 1967. Into the 1970s and '80s, the Black middle class started emerging and became more visible in culture, media, and politics. There were figures like Ed Bradley, who became the first Black White House television correspondent in 1976, and Harold Washington, who became the first Black mayor of Chicago in 1983 and inspired Obama's generation. In the 1990s, President Bill Clinton appointed what was at the time the most diverse cabinet in history. At the end of the twentieth century and the turn of the twenty-first, Black women and especially men were visible in politics, sports, entertainment, and mass media—people like Michael Jordan, Carol Moseley Braun, Jesse Jackson, Whitney Houston, Tiger Woods, Denzel Washington, Jay-Z, Spike Lee, Robin Roberts, Halle Berry, and Bryant Gumbel. By 2003, media moguls Oprah Winfrey and Robert L. Johnson had become billionaires. All the success stories of these *individuals* ostensibly demonstrated the forward march of the Black *community*.

With Barack Obama arriving on the stage of American history, community representation transmuted into national embodiment. "I stand here knowing that my story is part of the larger American story, that I owe a debt to all of those who came before me, and that in no other country on earth is my story even possible," Obama said during his breakout keynote speech at the Democratic National Convention in 2004.[6] Four years later, when Obama was elected president, he had come to embody racial progress and the arc of American history itself. Obama did not *make* American history when he won the U.S. presidency on November 4, 2008. He *became* American history—an American history popularly written as the story of incremental and steady racial progress.

"HISTORIC WIN," blared the headline of *The Philadelphia Inquirer* the day after his election in 2008. "Change has come to America."[7] Nearly 70 percent of Americans agreed that his election would improve race relations in the country.[8] To some, it was a watershed moment. "'In answer to the question, Is America past racism against black people,' I say the answer is yes," Columbia University linguist John McWhorter wrote in *Forbes* weeks after Obama's election. "Our proper concern is not whether racism still exists, but whether it remains a serious problem. The election of Obama proved, as nothing else could have, that it no longer does."[9]

But when seen as the defining narrative of American history, this vision of our past as a march of racial progress is ahistorical, mythical, and incomplete. Even as those civil rights victories of the 1950s and '60s were transpiring in the courts and streets, the unemployment rates of Black Americans were rising. These persistently poor socioeconomic conditions—not to mention police violence—led to urban rebellions in 1964, 1965, 1966, and 1967—a year when Martin Luther King, Jr., said, "That dream that I had that day [in 1963] has, at many points, turned into a nightmare."[10]

In 1968, in response to these rebellions, President Johnson and, repeatedly, presidential candidate Richard Nixon called for "law and order." During a post–civil rights period of supposed progress, American society also became obsessed with a destructive fear of Black criminality. The call for law and order gave way to the War on Drugs beginning in the 1970s, and to mass incarceration in the 1980s and '90s. Meanwhile, police violence persisted and new forms of voter suppression became so sophisticated that they contributed to Republican presidential victories in Florida in 2000 and Ohio in 2004.[11] In 2009, the first Black president came into office during the Great Recession, which produced the widest racial wealth gap between Black and white Americans since the government began recording such data.[12]

When the long sweep of American history is cast as a constant widening of equity and justice, it overlooks this parallel constant widening of inequity and injustice. The two forces have existed in tandem, dueling throughout our history. The Northern states gradually emancipated enslaved Black people in the early United States—a step forward for justice—but at the same time these states gradually or immediately stripped freed Black people of their civil or voting rights—a step forward for injustice. In 1807, importation of Africans was prohibited by Congress—a step forward for nonviolence—but this led to a consequent boom in the violent and disruptive domestic trade of enslaved people and the "breeding" and spreading of the enslaved population—a step forward for brutal violence. In 1865, Congress abolished chattel slavery—stepping toward justice—but this immediately led to a series of racist "Black Codes" in Southern states that bound and regulated the movements of freed peoples and shifted the nation toward injustice. In the late 1860s, Radical Republican congressmen abolished these Black Codes, reconstructed Southern states, and extended civil and voting rights to Black men—another step forward for equity—but in another step toward inequity, lynchings and Jim Crow reconstructed white supremacy and rescinded some civil and voting rights by the 1890s.

The singular racial history of the United States is therefore a *dual* racial history of two opposing forces: historical steps toward equity and justice and historical steps toward inequity and injustice. But foregrounded in the telling are the steps toward equity and justice as part of a grand American narrative march of liberty and equality for all.

This popular construct of racial progress does more than conceal and obfuscate; it actually undermines the effort to achieve and maintain equality. You can see this in the majority opinion written by Chief Justice John Roberts in *Shelby County v. Holder* in 2013. In that case, the Supreme Court struck down the federal preclearance section of the Voting Rights Act of 1965, which required certain states and counties with a history of electoral racism to receive federal approval before changing local voting laws or practices. In his majority opinion, Roberts acknowledged that there had been a need for "strong medicine" against racism in 1965 but argued that since then, progress had rendered such policies unnecessary. "There is no denying, however, that the conditions that originally justified these measures no longer characterize voting in the covered jurisdictions," he wrote. "Things have changed dramatically."[13]

In the aftermath of this decision, multiple Republican-dominated states, freed of federal oversight, passed laws that disenfranchised Black people by limiting early voting and same-day registration and instituting voter ID laws that "targeted African American voters with surgical precision," to quote the U.S. Court of Appeals for the Fourth Circuit.[14] Fourteen states had new voter restrictions in time for the 2016 election, including Ohio and Wisconsin. These new voter-suppression policies were crucial to Trump's victory.[15] And following Trump's defeat in 2020, Republican state legislators have introduced more than 350 laws in forty-seven states that would make it harder for Americans, particularly Black Americans, to vote.

Inequality lives, in part, because Americans of every generation have been misled into believing that racial progress is inevitable and ongoing. That racial progress is America's manifest destiny. That racial progress defines the arc of American history since 1619. That "things have changed dramatically." In fact, this has more often been rhetoric than reality, more often myth than history. Saying that the nation can progress racially is a necessary statement of hope. Saying that the nation *has* progressed racially is usually a statement of ideology, one that has been used all too often to obscure the opposite reality of *racist* progress.

And it's been this way since the beginning.

———

The propaganda of racial progress took its initial form in the era of slavery. Proponents of the idea held that slavery was justified by the fact that enslavers had improved the lot of the Africans they were enslaving. In the 1660s, prominent English minister Richard Baxter urged American planters in *A Christian Directory* to "make it your chief end in buying and using slaves, to win them to Christ, and save their Souls."[16] The leading theologian in early colonial America, Cotton Mather, admired Baxter and built on his ideas. "You are better fed & better clothed, & better managed by far, than you would be, if you were your own men," Mather informed enslaved Africans in Boston in the 1696 pamphlet *A Good Master Well Served*. It was one of the first articulations of racial progress in colonial America: American slavery was better than "miserable" African freedom, Mather argued. If they obey their masters, he informed enslaved people, their "souls will be washed 'White in the blood of the lamb.' "[17]

By the time of the American Revolution, the first full-blown abolitionist movement had emerged, influencing a newly emergent anti-slavery rhetoric, even among enslavers like Thomas Jefferson. In 1774, he drafted a powerful freedom manifesto, *A Summary View of the Rights of British America,* in which he accused the British king of holding back the march of racial progress that the colonists wanted. "The abolition of domestic slavery is the great object of desire in those colonies, where it was unhappily introduced in their infant state," Jefferson wrote.[18] Several of the admirers of *A Summary View* printed and circulated it widely, launching Jefferson into national recognition.

Two years later, Jefferson found himself in Philadelphia as a delegate at the Second Continental Congress, drafting the Declaration of Independence. "The history of his present majesty is a history of unremitting injuries and usurpations," Jefferson declared. He then listed every wrong, saving perhaps the worst of the king's abuses for last: the king of Great Britain "has waged" what Jefferson, an enslaver, called a "cruel war against human nature itself, violating its most sacred rights of life and liberty in the persons of a distant people who never offended him, captivating and carrying them into slavery in another hemisphere, or to incur miserable death in their transportation hither." The king had suppressed "every legislative attempt to prohibit or to restrain this execrable commerce."[19]

The delegates ended up cutting this anti-slavery passage in its entirety before finalizing the Declaration of Independence on July 4, 1776. But they could not erase its powerful framing: that the founding fathers were not responsible for slavery but, rather, were ushering in a new age of freedom; that Great

Britain was to blame for the trade in enslaved persons; and that racial progress was on the way through American independence.

In reality, some of the Americans who decried British tyranny were themselves opposed to abolition. In his notes on the proceedings of the Second Continental Congress concerning this early draft of the Declaration of Independence, Jefferson wrote, "[T]he clause . . . reprobating the enslaving the inhabitants of Africa, was struck out in complaisance to South Carolina & Georgia who had never attempted to restrain the importation of slaves, and who on the contrary still wished to continue it. [O]ur Northern brethren also I believe felt a little tender under those censures; for tho' their people have very few slaves themselves yet they had been pretty considerable carriers of them to others."[20] Jefferson tried to justify American inaction on the trade in enslaved persons and on slavery by placing the blame on King George's head, but the burden of culpability rested also on American shoulders in both the North and the South.

Soon, the justification for inaction took a different form. Not long after helping to establish the Methodist Church in America in 1784, Thomas Coke started circulating petitions to abolish slavery. In 1785, he led a delegation of abolitionists to Mount Vernon to convince the future first president of the United States to join their movement. But George Washington declined to sign the petition or publicly support the Methodists' anti-slavery efforts, on the premise that "it would be dangerous to make a frontal attack on a prejudice which is beginning to decrease."[21] Washington—perhaps knowingly and strategically—exonerated himself from taking a political stand against slavery on the grounds that progress was being made. Slavery persisted, and grew, protected by the argument that it was going away.

Still, slavery was a political, moral, and intellectual quandary for the founding fathers, who saw themselves as part of the Age of Enlightenment. They were not so blinded by the myth of racial progress that they failed to understand the contradiction of a republic founded on the principles of freedom and equality in which one-fifth of the population was held in bondage. They were embarrassed enough that they left the words "slavery" and "slave" out of the U.S. Constitution entirely.

The awkwardness of the topic did not hinder the economic institution's growth. In the aftermath of the American Revolution, many Northern states that were less reliant on enslaved labor did pass gradual abolition laws, and some enslavers in the Upper South did free their captives, but most in the South did not. Jefferson himself freed only two enslaved people in his lifetime.[22] Americans in both the North and the South came to see slavery as a necessary evil, the only way to pay off their debts and build the new nation. Cotton gins were invented to speedily remove seeds from cotton fibers, making cotton produced by enslaved labor immensely profitable and leading to an insatiable demand for more land and more labor. Enslavers were marching into the Louisiana Territory, which Jefferson secured from France in 1803. The number of enslaved Africans swelled by 70 percent, from 697,681 in the first federal census of 1790 to 1,191,362 in 1810, and more than tripled over the next fifty years.[23]

As slavery grew, so too did the cries to abolish it. Still, many white people, even those who were anti-slavery, couldn't stomach the idea of Black equality. A solution was found in the idea of colonization: freeing and "civilizing" Black people, then sending them out of the country. The idea had been proposed by Jefferson in his *Notes on the State of Virginia,* published in 1785. This new form of racial progress envisioned the United States as a white ethnostate that avoided what Jefferson argued would be a never-ending race war. Black people should "be brought up" until "the females should be eighteen, and the males twenty-one years of age, when they should be colonized to such place as the circumstances of the times should render most proper." To replace them, the nation should "send vessels . . . to other parts of the world for an equal number of white inhabitants," Jefferson wrote.[24]

Into the antebellum era, a big tent of enslavers and centrist anti-slavery reformers—both inspired by Jefferson—came to see colonization as a way to resist those enslaved persons and free abolitionists pressing for the immediate end of slavery. Enslavers came to favor the idea of colonizing all *free* Black people out of the country—to better control the restive population of enslaved people. The minutes from the founding meeting of the American Colonization Society in 1816 record that Virginia congressman John Randolph argued that colonization would "materially tend to secure" slavery, casting off those free Black people whose presence incited "mischief" and "discontent" among the enslaved.[25] The eighth Speaker of the U.S. House of Representatives, Henry Clay, agreed in his speech at the meeting. The society would ignore the "delicate question" of abolition and only promote the deportation of the free Black population, Clay stated. "Can there be a nobler cause than that which," he argued, "while it proposes to rid our own country of a useless and pernicious, if not a dangerous portion of its population, contemplates the spreading of the arts of civilized life, and the possible redemption from ignorance and barbarism of a benighted quarter of the globe!"[26]

Centrist anti-slavery reformers had similar plans for free Black people and different plans for the enslaved. Free Black people must be trained "for self-government" and then return to their land of "origin," New Jersey clergyman Robert Finley wrote in the colonization movement's pioneering manifesto, *Thoughts on the Colonization of Free Blacks*. For the enslaved, he advocated that they be gradually freed over time—as many were in Northern states when they reached a certain age—and colonized out of the United States. "By this means the evil of slavery will be diminished, and in a way so gradual as to prepare the whites for the happy and progressive change."[27] The manifesto was published in 1816, the year he helped enslavers found the American Colonization Society.

The American Colonization Society grew into the preeminent racial "reform" organization in the United States by the late 1820s. By 1832, every Northern state legislature had passed resolutions endorsing colonization. While many Southern white colonizationists sought to remove free Black people, Northern white colonizationists were typically energized by the scenario of removing all Black people, enslaved and free.

Both viewed colonization as incremental progress. Enslaved or free Africans would be civilized and gradually emancipated and sent back to Africa to civilize "miserable" Africans, thus establishing slavery itself as an instrument of racial progress. As the retired Jefferson put it in a letter to anti-slavery sympathizer John Lynch in 1811, "Having long ago made up my mind on this subject, I have no hesitation in saying [that colonization is] most advantageous for themselves as well as for us." He went on to suggest that the plan would also be advantageous for Africa, a continent lacking the "useful arts." Schooled free Black people, Jefferson argued, would "carry back to" Africa "the seeds of civilization, which might render their sojournment here a blessing in the end to that country."[28]

By the 1790s, the abolitionist movement that had begun during the era of the American Revolution had ebbed. White abolitionists, in reviving the movement in the 1830s and '40s, mostly opposed gradual abolition and colonization. Instead, they pushed for immediate emancipation, while fashioning a new form of racial progress, one focused on individual behavior and acceptance. Some white abolitionists agreed with William Lloyd Garrison, who wholeheartedly believed that Black people had "acquired" and would continue to acquire "the esteem, confidence and patronage of the whites, in proportion to [their] increase in knowledge and moral improvement."[29] Garrison called on Black people to follow this lead and behave in an upstanding manner to make white Americans more comfortable setting their brethren free. In an address before Black Philadelphians in 1831, Garrison said, "If you are temperate, industrious, peaceable and pious; if you return good for evil, and blessing for cursing; you will show to the world, that the slaves can be emancipated without danger: but if you are turbulent, idle and vicious, you will put arguments into the mouths of tyrants, and cover your friends with confusion and shame."

This strategy of *uplift suasion* that focused on policing Black behavior actually reinforced racism and slavery. Garrison implied that it was "turbulent" Black behavior that drove racist reactions among white people who would otherwise hold Black people in "esteem," an inversion of the true cause and effect of racism. Likewise, his encouragement of behavioral uplift sidelined the role of anti-racist activism and resistance at a time when they were needed the most. Indeed, racism and Southern slavery were spreading and becoming more powerful in the 1830s and '40s. But many white and Black abolitionists failed to acknowledge this racist progress. As Garrison said in the Philadelphia speech, "The signs of the times do indeed show forth great and glorious and sudden changes in the condition of the oppressed."[30]

In the summer of 1847, Garrison wrote in *The Liberator* that the "slave power" had declined in the past ten years, leading to a "gradual abatement of the prejudice which we have been deploring."[31] These remarks came in the middle of the Mexican-American War, a battle that began after the United States annexed Texas, and perhaps reflected his anxiety about slavery's western expansion more than his belief in its imminent demise. The war with Mexico helped nationalize the slavery debate, since many white Northerners who might not have personally supported abolition nevertheless worried that the new territories would be controlled by the enslavers' interests, shutting out free white labor and increasing the political power of the Southern slaveholding states over the Northern states. Congressional representatives from the North and the South had been in a contentious battle since 1846 over the Wilmot Proviso, which proposed a ban on slavery in any territories acquired during the war.[32]

As sectional political tensions over slavery's expansion heated up in the halls of Congress, some abolitionists established a new rhetorical ground: slavery and anti-Black racism were one and the same, and if slavery ended, racism would vanish as well. "Complexional caste is tolerated no where, excepting in the immediate vicinage of slavery," Garrison declared in 1847, adding that racism's "utter eradication is not to be expected until that hideous system be overthrown."[33] French scholar Alexis de Tocqueville, who traveled across the United States in the early 1830s, had a different observation. "The prejudice of the race appears stronger in the States which have abolished slavery, than in those where it still exists; and nowhere is it so intolerant as in those States where servitude has never been known," Tocqueville wrote in his classic 1835 treatise, *Democracy in America*.[34]

Garrison accompanied Frederick Douglass on a speaking tour in the Old Northwest (what is now the easternmost portion of the Midwest). En route through Pennsylvania, he came face-to-face with racism outside of the immediate vicinage of slavery. When they arrived in Ohio in August 1847, every single free state in the region had restricted Black people from voting and serving in the militia in the prior half century. During this period, Ohio and Illinois explicitly named whiteness as a prerequisite for jurors; Black jury service in Indiana, Michigan, and the territory that would become the state of Wisconsin was unheard of. By 1851, many Midwestern states had restricted Black people from owning land or contracting for labor by forcing them to provide certificates of freedom and posting bonds to ensure that they would not become dependent. Several states prevented Black people who had recently arrived from residing there altogether.[35]

Abraham Lincoln came of age politically in one of these states. As a young Illinois politician, he held both racist and anti-slavery views. He expressed the former and dulled the latter when it suited him politically.[36] During his senatorial bid against Stephen Douglas in 1858, Lincoln appeased the racist ideas of Illinois voters by announcing, "I am not, nor ever have been, in favor of bringing about in any way the social and political equality of the black and white races—that I am not nor ever have been in favor of making voters or jurors of negroes, nor of qualifying them to hold office, nor to intermarry with white people." In the same speech, Lincoln expressed a belief in "a physical difference between the white and black races" that would "forever forbid the two races living together on terms of social and political equality."[37]

During his presidency, Lincoln opposed the expansion of slavery while also supporting colonization schemes as late as 1862.[38] Lincoln's positions on slavery, colonization, and emancipation shifted with the winds of political and military expediency stirred by the Civil War. But when it became a military necessity to save the Union, Lincoln issued and signed the Emancipation Proclamation. While the proclamation opened the door to enrolling around 180,000 Black soldiers in the Union army, it ended up freeing fewer than 200,000 Black people on the day it was signed. Nearly 500,000 Black people in border states; approximately 300,000 Black people in Union-occupied Confederate areas, including the entire state of Tennessee and portions of Virginia and Louisiana; and more than 3,000,000 people in Confederate territories remained enslaved.³⁹ It was incumbent upon those enslaved Black people to emancipate themselves. And that is precisely what they did, running away from enslavers to Union lines; many of them joined the Union army, turning the tide of the war.

Nevertheless, in the next two years, Lincoln sat for journalists, artists, and photographers seeking to sculpt him into history as the Great Emancipator. Painter Francis Bicknell Carpenter spent six months at the White House in 1864 to visually re-create the moment when Lincoln ended slavery; *First Reading of the Emancipation Proclamation of President Lincoln* was intended to "commemorate this new epoch in the history of Liberty," Bicknell wrote.⁴⁰ Some people who witnessed the construction of Lincoln as the Great Emancipator realized that racial-progress mythology was being used to cleanse white people of their guilt and responsibility. "The negro has saved himself," Ralph Waldo Emerson observed around this time, "and the white man very patronizingly says, I have saved you."⁴¹ White people—embodied in the enslaver—enslaved Black people. And then white people—embodied in Lincoln—freed Black people. In the end, it was white people who righted the wrong of slavery.

This formulation stemmed not from an accurate reading of events but from the myth of racial progress. Upon this myth, each successive generation of white Americans is let off the hook for the legacy of slavery. Politicians and the public alike can claim that this sin remains a part of the past, that the country has rid itself of the stain, and that there is no need for antiracist remedies like reparations.

Radical Reconstruction did bring about actual racial progress. The Thirteenth, Fourteenth, and Fifteenth Amendments—ending chattel slavery, granting Black people citizenship, and providing Black men the ability to vote—were passed. Southern constitutional conventions from 1867 to 1869 included Black delegates—about half of whom had been born in slavery—and white and Black elected officials introduced many Southern states' first publicly funded education systems, penitentiaries, orphanages, and asylums for the mentally ill; expanded women's rights and guaranteed rights to Black people; and reorganized local governments.⁴²

And yet, as Eric Foner showed in his classic study of the period, *Reconstruction: America's Unfinished Revolution,* these advances furnished a ready excuse for why more could not be done to achieve true equity and justice for all. The white leaders who advocated for Black men's right to vote absolved themselves of a continued commitment to overturning lingering racist policies and practices by reasoning that Black men could now save themselves and their families through the ballot box. For their own benefit, newly emancipated Black people "should not continue to be kept wards of the nation," said reformer Thomas Wentworth Higginson, who had commanded Black soldiers in the Civil War. Or as congressional representative and future president James A. Garfield put it, "The Fifteenth Amendment confers upon the African race the care of its own destiny. It places their fortunes in their own hands." These sentiments were widespread despite the fact that the formerly enslaved escaped their bondage with absolutely nothing. An Illinois newspaper proclaimed, "The negro is now a voter and a citizen. Let him hereafter take his chances in the battle of life."[43] From this point forward, white Americans were ready to blame Black behavior, and not racism and the deprivations of 250 years of enslavement, for persisting racial inequities.

Meanwhile, under the cover of this narrative of racial progress, racism was advancing. Fierce resistance to Black economic freedom, civil rights, and political power held countless Black Americans in a second slavery, with few rights and powers. Violence from white terrorist groups like the new Ku Klux Klan and the Red Shirts allowed white supremacists to regain power in the early 1870s, while the Panic of 1873 drove many Black Southerners into debt servitude.[44]

In 1875, Congress passed the Civil Rights Act, which prohibited racist discrimination in public places and public facilities, including those that provided transportation or food. But the following year, when nine million people, or one-fifth of the U.S. population, attended the centennial of Jefferson's Declaration of Independence in Philadelphia, celebrated as a monument to that "palladium of our nation's liberties," another series of Black Codes was already restricting the rights of Black people to work and live in Southern states.[45]

Finally, with the Compromise of 1877, Reconstruction was brought to a close, the last federal troops were withdrawn from the South, and Jim Crow was born. As the nation celebrated a postwar unity, Southerners started hailing the *New* South. America was ostensibly marching forward, and if Black people were not keeping up, it was their own fault. In 1883, the Supreme Court used the language of progress to strike down the Civil Rights Act of 1875, opening the legal door to a raft of new Jim Crow laws. "When a man has emerged from slavery and by the aid of beneficent legislation has shaken off the inseparable concomitants of that state," Justice Joseph P. Bradley concluded, writing for the majority, "there must be some stage in the progress of his elevation when he takes the rank of a mere citizen, and ceases to be the special favorite of the laws." The Court twisted the litigants' requests to be treated equitably into a request to be "the special favorite" of the laws. *The New York Times* applauded the Court's "undoing" of Congress's work."[46]

Nearly seventy years later, after the Second World War, the United States emerged as a global superpower, having founded the United Nations and formulated economic plans to protect European nations from staggering war debts. However, the United States and the Soviet Union soon took up arms in a war for influence in decolonizing countries in Latin America, Asia, Africa, and the Middle East. Jim Crow segregation in the United States had been a topic of political discourse in the USSR since the late 1920s, and Black Americans' experiences of racist policies and violence had been featured in the Soviet press to argue for the superiority of communism over capitalism and to charge the United States with hypocrisy for claiming to be the exemplar of global freedom. Racism experienced by Black Americans took on new significance during the Cold War.[47] The U.S. government tried to reconcile the nation's new image as a global beacon of morality and democracy with worldwide press coverage of its pervasive racism.[48] In 1947, the Truman administration issued *To Secure These Rights: The Report of the President's Committee on Civil Rights,* one of the most powerful indictments of racism ever to come from the U.S. government—a sign of progress in the midst of racism. But that same year, the NAACP offered the ninety-four-page *An Appeal to the World: A Statement on the Denial of Human Rights to Minorities in the Case of Citizens of Negro Descent in the United States of America and an Appeal to the United Nations for Redress.* And in 1951, the Civil Rights Congress delivered a petition, *We Charge Genocide,* to a meeting of the United Nations Commission on Human Rights in Paris. The petition documented 152 killings (or lynchings) and 344 other genocidal crimes against African Americans from 1945 to 1951.

American officials grew increasingly concerned that a public projection of racism against its own citizens would cause the United States to lose the support of people of color abroad—especially in those decolonizing African and Asian countries—while increasing their support for joining forces with the USSR. Scurrying into damage control, what is now the United States Information Agency (USIA) produced and circulated around the world a document titled *The Negro in American Life*.[49] "There began in the United States a theory of racial inferiority which became a key tenet in support of slavery and, later, of economic and social discrimination," the pamphlet stated in 1950 or 1951. "It is against this background that the progress which the Negro has made and the steps still needed for the full solutions of his problems must be measured."[50] *The Negro in American Life* ended up advancing the same narrative that Americans do today: a celebration of racial progress. In the context of the Cold War, the government used racial progress rhetoric to prop up the United States as the world's leading democracy.

While *The Negro in American Life* did not want decolonizing nations to see the racist present, Black Americans lived it. Around this time, the majority of white Americans seemed to favor laws and policies that promoted segregated housing.[51] In 1946, only 28 percent of Southerners and 54 percent of Northerners with a high school diploma believed that Black Americans should be entitled to equal job opportunities. Degrees of support correlated to education level, with just 20 percent of Southerners and 46 percent of Northerners with a grade school education in support.[52] In a 1950 Roper Center survey on public school integration, only 41 percent of respondents said that "children of all races and color[s] should be allowed to go to the same schools together everywhere in the country."[53] But still, the USIA pamphlet stated that at the turn of the century, "the majority of whites, northern as well as southern, were unabashed in their estimate of the Negro as an inferior. . . . Today, there is scarcely a community where that concept has not been drastically modified."[54]

Like their predecessors, the writers of this pamphlet situated the past, not the present—or in some cases, the status of individual Black elites, not the masses—as defining the standards of measurements for progress. Over the past fifty years, progress for "the Negro" had occurred in all areas "at a tremendous pace," according to *The Negro in American Life*. The pamphlet disclosed the existence of "large landowners," of "wealthy businessmen," of professionals, of tremendous advances in literacy rates and college enrollments. "Much remains to be done," because the average income of white Americans was still "substantially better than that of Negroes," the pamphlet stated. But the "gap is closing."[55]

The racial-progress story becomes quite familiar from there. In 1954, with *Brown v. Board of Education*, the U.S. Supreme Court ruled that segregated public schools were unconstitutional. *Racial progress*. The Montgomery bus boycott began a movement for desegregation across the South in 1955. *Racial progress*. President Dwight D. Eisenhower sent federal troops to escort the Little Rock Nine in 1957. *Racial progress*. The lunch-counter sit-ins by Black college students in 1960 led to the desegregation of Southern businesses. *Racial progress*. Freedom Riders helped desegregate bus terminals in 1961. *Racial progress*. The March on Washington and the dream of Martin Luther King, Jr., made nationwide news in 1963. *Racial progress*. The Civil Rights Act of 1964 was passed. *Racial progress*.

But what is left out of this story is that this Second Reconstruction was needed because the First Reconstruction, after the Civil War ended in 1865, failed to bring into being and sustain an equitable nation—an effort undermined by the propaganda of racial progress. What is left out of the story of our time is that a Third Reconstruction is needed because the Second Reconstruction failed to actualize King's dream, again undermined by the racial-progress propaganda.

On June 4, 1965, President Lyndon B. Johnson gave the commencement address at Howard University. "It is a tribute to America that, once aroused, the courts and the Congress, the President and most of the people, have been the allies of progress," he said.[56] But he also showed why decades of racial progress rhetoric had been shortsighted. Progress has primarily come for "a growing middle class minority," while for poor Black people "the walls are rising and the gulf is widening," Johnson pointed out. "Thirty-five years ago the rate of unemployment for Negroes and whites was about the same," he noted. "Tonight the Negro rate is twice as high." In recent decades, Johnson added, income disparities, disparities in poverty rates, disparities in infant mortality, and urban segregation were all increasing.[57]

Still, Johnson's racial-progress message lived on in history, and his warnings died in the fires of the late 1960s. After he signed the Voting Rights Act into law on August 6, 1965, the USIA again made sure that the Cold-Warring world digested it as a sign of progress. In 1965, agents composed and circulated *For the Dignity of Man: America's Civil Rights Program*. Progress had arrived, the pamphlet stated. And now racism had been mostly confined to "individuals and some states and local governments." It conveyed to the world a middle-class, interracial, harmonious United States, a country most Black Americans would have hardly recognized.[58]

One year earlier, Malcolm X had stood before a meeting of the Congress of Racial Equality (CORE) at a Methodist church in Cleveland. "How can you thank a man for giving you what's already yours?" he asked, speaking of the Civil Rights Act, which was making its way through Congress at the time. "You haven't even made progress, if what's being given to you, you should have had already. That's not progress."[59] Malcolm X and others remained skeptical of all the progress rhetoric.

To skeptical African Americans it was not surprising when, five days after the passage of the Voting Rights Act, police brutality set off the six-day Watts Rebellion against racism, one of the most destructive urban rebellions in U.S. history. President Johnson was stunned. "After all we've accomplished. How can it be?" he asked a top aide.[60] And then came more than one hundred urban rebellions in the summer of 1967, and Black people demanding more than civil and voting rights. Ruled by white minorities in majority Black counties, neighborhoods, and cities, Black people demanded democracy. They demanded political power—Black Power! But Johnson spoke for many white Americans when he responded to the uprisings in his State of the Union address on January 17, 1968, by stating, to bipartisan applause, that "the American people have had enough of rising crime and lawlessness."[61]

Just six weeks later, the commission Johnson had established the previous summer to study the causes of the urban rebellions issued its report. According to the eleven-member Kerner Commission, the main issue was not crime and lawlessness but white racism. "Our nation is moving towards two societies," the report proclaimed, in its most famous passage, "one black, one white—separate and unequal."[62] To arrest this alarming development, the commission recommended the creation of higher-paying, higher-status jobs for Black people; a federal open-occupancy law that would prohibit racist discrimination against prospective Black renters or home buyers; and an increase in political representation in local governments for poor Black communities.

But in the afterglow of the Civil Rights Act and the Voting Rights Act, as the United States proclaimed racial progress to the world and to itself, Johnson ignored most of the commission's recommendations. The Second Reconstruction's last victory was the Civil Rights Act of 1968, which targeted racism in housing.[63] "We have come some of the way, not near all of it," Johnson remarked on its passage in the aftermath of King's assassination. "There is much yet to do."[64] This iteration of the racial-progress refrain, which can be traced back to the Cold War pamphlet *The Negro in American Life,* focuses our attention on how the United States has come a long way (the past) and how America has a long way to go (the future). This past/future logic has compelled generation after generation to overlook the present—indeed, the presence of racism.

In the 1970s, newly emergent "conservatives," as they self-identified, broke from the liberal past/future refrain that the nation still had a ways to go. They pointed to the legislative gains of the preceding decades to claim that the nation had arrived; Black people in the here and now were no longer facing racism. Conservatives framed supporters of affirmative action as "hard-core racists of reverse discrimination" against white people, as Yale Law professor Robert Bork claimed in 1978.[65] Such arguments echoed the Supreme Court ruling in 1883 that found the Civil Rights Act of 1875 unconstitutional, gutting the anti-racist protections of the Reconstruction amendments on the grounds that Black Americans should not be treated as "the special favorite." Like enslavers and centrist anti-slavery Americans agreeing on the need to colonize free Black people (but disagreeing on colonizing the enslaved), leading white Republicans and Democrats agreed that substantial progress had been made (and disagreed only about whether racism was over).

During the presidential debate on October 28, 1980, between incumbent Jimmy Carter and Ronald Reagan, an audience member highlighted the racist policies that "nonwhite" Americans faced in schools, jobs, and housing. Reagan replied that he was "eternally optimistic" about race relations and expressed his belief "that we've made great progress from the days when I was young and when this country didn't even know it had a racial problem." Carter acknowledged that the United States "still had a long way to go" but highlighted the "good [racial] progress" promoted through Democratic policies involving "unemployment compensation, the minimum wage, welfare, [and] national health insurance."[66]

By the 1990s, the gulf between the rhetoric of racial progress and the reality for millions of Black Americans had grown wider, as the former became more and more triumphant. In 1995, four years after the LAPD brutally beat Rodney King, Dinesh D'Souza, a former Reagan aide, published a book titled *The End of Racism*. This was the year of the O. J. Simpson trial, with its racially polarizing verdict and revelations of racist LAPD behavior, and the beginning of the apex of Black incarceration rates during the War on Drugs, after Bill Clinton signed the devastatingly punitive 1994 crime bill. Two years later, in their 1997 blockbuster *America in Black and White*, Manhattan Institute fellow Abigail Thernstrom and her husband, Harvard historian Stephan Thernstrom, argued that "few whites are now racists" and that what dominates current race relations is "black anger" and "white surrender."[67]

By the century's end, the term "color-blind" was often being used by politicians and thinkers to describe the correct way to think about race, since so much progress had been achieved and apparently all Americans were already being treated equally. "Color-blind" white people were telling Black Americans to stop playing "the race card."[68] Black cultures and behaviors were once again being blamed for racial disparities and inequity, while anti-Black racism was exonerated on the altar of racial progress.

On January 10, 2000, the Harvard University sociologist Orlando Patterson guaranteed that by 2050 the United States "will have problems aplenty. But no racial problem whatsoever."[69] Supreme Court Justice Sandra Day O'Connor cut that time period in half in a 2003 case upholding some forms of affirmative action in university admissions. "We expect that 25 years from now," she wrote, "the use of racial preferences will no longer be necessary to further the interest approved today."[70]

The election of Obama in 2008 became the final proof to some that the United States had achieved the ultimate victory of racial progress, the end of racism. This message was offered as much to Black Americans as to non-Black Americans. In a post-election piece published in the *Los Angeles Times,* Hoover Institution fellow Shelby Steele asked, "Doesn't a black in the Oval Office put the lie to both black inferiority and white racism? Doesn't it imply a 'post-racial' America?"[71] In 2008, the General Social Survey asked whether Black Americans "have worse jobs, income, and housing than White people . . . mainly due to discrimination." Only 35 percent of Americans answered "yes," the fourth-lowest anti-racist response in three decades of polling.[72] During his second term, on the occasion of the fiftieth anniversary of the March on Washington in 2013, President Obama stood on the steps of the Lincoln Memorial. He declared, "The arc of the universe may bend toward justice, but it doesn't bend on its own."[73]

Obama was referring to a phrase from Martin Luther King, Jr.'s 1956 speech after the Montgomery bus boycott: "The arc of the moral universe, although long, is bending toward justice."[74] King himself had paraphrased the words of Theodore Parker, a Unitarian minister and abolitionist, who before the Civil War had believed emancipation was coming. "I do not pretend," Parker wrote, "to understand the moral universe; the arc is a long one, my eye reaches but little ways; I cannot calculate the curve and complete the figure by the experience of sight; I can divine it by conscience. And from what I see I am sure it bends towards justice."[75]

President Obama often paraphrased the quote in speeches. He even had the phrase woven into the rug in the Oval Office.[76] In his farewell address in Chicago in 2017, President Obama told Americans that "we're not where we need to be." But he assured the nation, "The long sweep of America has been defined by forward motion, a constant widening of our founding creed to embrace all, and not just some."[77]

The arc of the moral universe is indeed long, and as Obama observed, it doesn't bend on its own. The people bend it toward justice or injustice, toward equity or inequity. The long sweep of America has been defined by two forward motions: one force widening the embrace of Black Americans and another force maintaining or widening their exclusion. The duel between these two forces represents the duel at the heart of America's racial history. The myth of singular racial progress veils this conflict—and it veils the snowballing racism behind Black people today still weathering the highest unemployment and incarceration rates and the lowest life expectancy and median wealth compared to other racial groups. Until Americans replace mythology with history, until Americans unveil and halt the progression of racism, an arc of the American universe will keep bending toward injustice.

August 29, 2005

Hurricane Katrina makes landfall, becoming one of the deadliest hurricanes to hit the United States in almost a century. In the days to follow, as many as eighteen hundred people die and around one hundred thousand are stranded, mostly in poor Black neighborhoods in New Orleans that are disproportionately susceptible to flooding. Some thirty thousand evacuees, most of them Black, take refuge in a makeshift shelter at the Louisiana Superdome. The chaotic, desperate scene that unfolds there becomes a symbol of rampant racial inequality.

At the Superdome After the Storm Has Passed

Clint Smith

A helicopter hovers overhead like a black cloud of smoke,
its blades dismembering the pewter sky. Men in uniform
stand outside with guns nested under their arms & the hot,

wet air of August licking their weary faces. Two women
push a homemade raft through warm, brown water that rises
up & hugs their chests. There is an old man inside the raft

who was once a stranger to them, when such a word meant
something other than *please help me*. Inside, children are running
across the emerald turf jumping through rings of light that

spill from the sky onto the field. Their small bodies sprinting
between the archipelago of sprawled cots. There is a mother
who sits high in the seats of the stadium rocking her baby

back & forth, her voice cocooning the child in a shell of song.
Before desperation descended under the rounded roof, before
the stench swept across the air like a heavy fog, before the

lights went out & the buses arrived, before the cameras came
inside & showed the failure of an indifferent nation, there were
families inside though there were some who failed to call them

families. There were children inside though there were some who
gave them a more callous name. There were people inside though
there were some who only saw a parade of disembodied shadows.

November 4, 2008

Barack Obama defeats John McCain, becoming the first Black president of the United States.

Mother and Son

Jason Reynolds

It started early. Maybe six in the morning. We'd each drunk a half cup of coffee but there was surely no time to finish because we had to go. My mother put on her hair and lipstick, gold earrings and perfume. But no heels. Not even short ones. Not on this day. She knew we'd be standing. We left the house, the crisp air of November greeting us, and walked the half mile in the autumn orange toward Potomac High School. But halfway there—maybe not even halfway—we met the end of the line.

"All y'all waiting to vote?" my mother asked a young woman, the anchor before us. The woman nodded.

For weeks, the whole neighborhood had been buzzing. The gas stations and barbershops, the mail carriers and preachers. Everyone gabbing about Barack Obama. And we all had shown up as if he'd be waiting for us at the school. As if he'd be the one handing out the confirmation stickers. As if we were voting for a family member, and this was an overdue reunion. Kids were everywhere, some running around playing, others sitting high on the shoulders of young fathers. Elders, like my mother, inching forward with canes and walkers, unwavering smiles smeared across their faces. Dr. Henderson, a neighborhood legend, was there doling out his signature three-fingered handshake (he'd lost two fingers in a lawn mower accident, a story he loved to tell kids). The knuckleheads were there. The nerds were there. The nosy neighbors and never-talk-to-nobodies, all there. Together. Music. Dancing. Jokes. Snacks. There was order, inch by inch. Respect, person to person. And a palpable pride that seemed to tilt the chins of thousands of Black people toward hope.

It took hours. My mother and I got home in the middle of the day, and sat at the kitchen table to confer. I pulled out a small recorder I'd purchased just for this occasion.

"I can't believe I just did that," my mother said. "I voted for a Black man who might *actually* win." She turned the TV on.

"He'll win." I pushed Record.

"Baby, I've been alive a long time. And I know more about America than you ever will. They'll do anything to discredit us. Say we're not human until they can't anymore, then they'll say we're not American. Say we're not smart, and if we are, then they'll say we're too arrogant. So if there's one thing never guaranteed to us here, it's victory."

While we finished our coffee, I asked her questions about how this felt after having been a child in South Carolina in the fifties—she mentioned her memories of Emmett Till's murder—and coming of age in Washington, D.C., and she recounted being at the March on Washington. "But this," she said, flipping through the channels before landing on the news, "this is different."

It was late. Close to midnight. It had been a long day of standing, then sitting, and now my mother was lying in bed. And instead of spending this moment in a bar with friends, I lay next to her, my arms wrapped around her torso like a chrysalis while watching her transform. And like an apparition, the first Black president took the stage, along with his Black wife and two Black daughters. I could feel my mother's blood. Pressed my ear to her neck and could hear her heart. Breath caught in her throat and she broke open and wept the tears of the family members I'd never know, and for the ones yet to come. But her heart seemed to do an opposite thing. It seemed to slow. To beat in rest. A peaceful thump in my ear. A metronome of new potential. And no matter how short-lived it would all be, I knew, without a doubt, it was a sound I'd need to remember.

Portrait of a family, c. 1885

CHAPTER 18

Justice

NIKOLE HANNAH-JONES

Origin stories function, to a degree, as myths designed to create a shared sense of history and purpose. Nations simplify these narratives in order to unify and glorify, and these origin stories serve to illuminate how a society wants to see itself—and how it doesn't. The origin story of the United States that we tell ourselves through textbooks and films, monuments and museums, public speeches and public histories, the one that most defines our national identity, portrays an intrepid, freedom-loving people who rebelled against an oppressive monarchy, won their independence, tamed the West, advanced an exceptional nation based on the radical ideals of self-governance and equality, and heroically fought a civil war to end slavery and preserve that nation. This mythology has positioned almost exclusively white Americans as the architects and champions of democracy. And because of this, some have believed that white people should disproportionately reap the benefits of this democracy.

But as this book has shown, a truer origin story requires us to place Black Americans prominently in the role of democracy's defenders and perfecters. It is Black Americans who have struggled and fought, when many white Americans were willing to abandon the charge that "all men are created equal," to make those words real. It is Black Americans who have consistently made the case, even when they were utterly disenfranchised and forced out of the political process, that *all* citizens deserve equal access to the benefits of a country founded on a government of the people, by the people, and for the people.

The efforts of Black Americans to seek freedom through resistance and rebellion against violations of their rights have always been one of this nation's defining traditions. But the country has rarely seen it that way, because for Black Americans, the freedom struggle has been a centuries-long fight against their own fellow Americans and against the very government intended to uphold the rights of its citizens. Though we are seldom taught this fact, time after time throughout our history, the most ardent, courageous, and consistent freedom fighters *within* this country have been Black Americans.

We see it in the 1739 Stono Rebellion, when about twenty Black men in South Carolina launched the largest revolt of enslaved people in the British mainland colonies before the American Revolution.[1]

We see it in Gabriel, who in 1800 conspired to lead an insurrection of the enslaved against their white enslavers, and whose failed plot included a plan to claim the rhetoric of white revolutionaries by purchasing "a piece of silk" for a flag on which to write the motto "Death or Liberty."[2]

We see it in David Walker, a free Black man who published his *Appeal to the Coloured Citizens of the World* in 1829, calling on enslaved people to rise up and liberate themselves, as white Americans had done, through violence if necessary. He wrote, "I speak Americans for your good. We must and shall be free I say, in spite of you. You may do your best to keep us in wretchedness and misery, to enrich you and your children, but God will deliver us from under you. And wo, wo, will be to you if we have to obtain our freedom by fighting." These words demanding freedom proved so powerful that white Southerners banned the pamphlet; Walker was found dead a few months later.[3]

We see it in Ida B. Wells, who with her fiery pen condemned lynching and violent and legal efforts by white Southerners to deny newly freed Black Americans the vote, writing, "The reproach and disgrace of the twentieth century is that the whole of the American people have permitted a part, to nullify this glorious achievement, and make the fourteenth and fifteenth amendments to the Constitution playthings, a mockery and a byword; an absolute dead letter in the Constitution of the United States. . . . With no sacredness of the ballot there can be no sacredness of human life itself. For if the strong can take the weak man's ballot, when it suits his purpose to do so, he will take his life also."[4]

We see it in Fannie Lou Hamer, a Black woman in Mississippi, the most oppressive apartheid state in America, thrown off her land and beaten repeatedly for demanding the right to vote, who in 1964 said, "Is this America, the land of the free and the home of the brave, where we have to sleep with our telephones off of the hooks because our lives be threatened daily, because we want to live as decent human beings, in America?"[5]

We see it in LaTosha Brown, who co-founded Black Voters Matter and spent 2020 successfully organizing Black voters across the South against voter-suppression efforts in order to try to rescue this democracy, saying, "The Constitution says we the people and that the power is supposed to go to the people. . . . How do we really deal with racism and sexism and all those other things that keep us from tapping into the brilliance and the power of the people that are in this country and how do we form this more perfect union [so] that literally we can get life, liberty, and the pursuit of happiness?"[6]

In this centuries-long tradition of protest there have been hundreds of uprisings in segregated Black communities. In the last century, some have produced substantive change. After the assassination of Reverend Martin Luther King, Jr., in 1968, rebellions erupted in more than one hundred cities, and fear that the country teetered on the brink of civil war broke the congressional deadlock over the Fair Housing Act.[7] The bill, which prohibited housing discrimination on the basis of race, gender, or religion, among other categories, made it illegal to deny people housing simply because they descended from those who had been enslaved. Though King had fought hard for the bill, white congressional representatives from the North had joined with representatives from the South to block its passage. Many considered the proposed law the "Northern" civil rights bill, because racial segregation in the North had largely been accomplished through housing discrimination. Seven days after King's death, President Lyndon B. Johnson signed the act into law from the smoldering capital, which remained under the protection of the National Guard.[8]

Just weeks before King's assassination, Johnson's Kerner Commission, which he had created to study the root causes of the many Black rebellions that had swept through Detroit, Newark, and cities across the nation in the mid-1960s, had issued its report, which recommended a national effort to dismantle segregation and structural racism across American institutions. It was shelved by the president, like so many similar reports, and instead white Americans voted in a "law and order" president, Richard Nixon.

This sort of backlash has been the typical response to Black resistance. The following decades brought increased police militarization, more law enforcement spending, and mass incarceration of Black Americans. And despite continued protests, organizing, and uprisings in Black communities in response to police or vigilante white violence, those movements seldom prodded enough non-Black people—or, more important, enough politicians—into pushing for and enacting substantial change.

In 2020, something changed. The collective witnessing of what must be described without hyperbole as a modern-day lynching by an agent of the state propelled a global protest that would become the largest movement for civil rights in American history. Even as the nature of George Floyd's death shocked us—a white law enforcement officer taking part in the extrajudicial killing of a Black person, nonchalantly pressing the life out of him in plain view of more than a dozen onlookers—it also reminded us that we had not banished this barbaric part of our history.

Yet unlike so many times in the past, in which Black people mostly marched and protested alone to demand recognition of their full humanity and citizenship, in 2020, a multiracial and multigenerational protest army braved a pandemic and took to the streets. The protesters gathered in all fifty states in places big and small, from heavily Black big cities to small, almost entirely white towns.

At first the changes wrought by those protests seemed to come shockingly swift. The weeks of demonstrations finally moved lawmakers in some places to ban chokeholds by police officers, to consider stripping law enforcement of the qualified immunity that has made it almost impossible to hold responsible officers who kill, and to discuss shifting significant parts of ballooning police budgets into funding for social services. Soon the outrage over police violence morphed into something broader. Protesters who understood that police officers are simply the enforcement mechanism of a vastly unequal society maintained by historic and systemic racism took a stand against monuments to enslavers and bigots from Virginia to Philadelphia to Minneapolis and New Mexico, defacing or snatching down statues and pushing local and state politicians to locate the moral courage to realize that they indeed did have the power to purge from public spaces icons to white supremacy.

A rainbow coalition of white, Black, Latino, Asian, and Indigenous voters swept Trump out of office and helped Democrats retake the U.S. Senate, while also electing Kamala Harris as the first Black, the first Asian, and the first female vice president in the history of this country. Those voters also managed to push Joe Biden, a man whose decades-long political career epitomized the moderate Democrat, to the left, and from the first days of his presidency he incorporated racial justice into his rhetoric.

George Floyd, a father, a brother, a regular man who just wanted to live a life free of struggle, did not choose to be a martyr to racial justice. This nation had no right to choose that for him. Yet his death helped spawn an awareness of racial suffering and a willingness to excavate how this nation's racist past deforms our present that I had never before seen in my lifetime.

But those heady days of promise soon gave way to the grim reality that the racist systems that have undergirded our society for four hundred years do not collapse after a few months of protest. The number of voters supporting Trump, a white nationalist president, *increased* when he ran for a second term.[9] And when Trump lost, his supporters led an insurrection in the nation's

Capitol, seeking, just as white mobs had done repeatedly during Reconstruction, to overturn and delegitimize an election won by a multiracial coalition of voters. Then, in response to well-organized Black, Latino, and Indigenous voters helping turn heavily Republican states such as Georgia and Arizona blue, Republicans began a coordinated effort to introduce and pass hundreds of bills that would make it harder for millions of Americans to vote.[10] Some have called these efforts—which came not even a year after the death of the civil rights icon John Lewis, who in the 1960s nearly lost his life to secure voting rights for Black Americans—the worst attacks on voting in more than fifty years. And just as a jury found Derek Chauvin guilty on all three counts against him, including two of murder—the rarest of outcomes—news broke of another police killing, and another, and another.

It is unclear what substantial and transformative change will come from the reckoning that began in 2020 or, distressingly, if whatever changes occur will lead to more freedom and equality or less. But by reading to the end of this book, you have gained a sense of the stark reality we must confront: even if we pass wide-ranging policing and voting reforms, on their own, these cannot bring justice to America. Resolving the policing issue would save precious Black lives and help preserve the dignity Black Americans still must fight for. It would make Black Americans safer and dismantle a tool of social control with a lineage that stretches back to slavery. But it would leave wholly intact the primary culprit of Black suffering today. If we seek to truly make this a transformative moment, if we are indeed serious about creating a more just society, we must go much further than that. We must get to the root of it.

Fifty years after the bloody and brutally repressed protests and freedom struggles of Black Americans brought about the end of legal discrimination in this country, so much of what makes Black lives hard, what takes Black lives earlier, what causes Black Americans to be vulnerable to the type of surveillance and policing that killed Breonna Taylor and George Floyd, what steals opportunities is the lack of wealth that has been a defining feature of Black life since the end of slavery.

Wealth, not simply securing equal rights, is the means to security in America. Wealth—assets and investments minus debt—is what enables you to buy a home in a safer neighborhood with better amenities and better-funded schools. It is what enables you to send your children to college without saddling them with tens of thousands of dollars of debt and what provides money for a down payment on a house. It is what prevents family emergencies or unexpected job losses from turning into catastrophes that leave you homeless and destitute. It is what ensures what every parent wants: that your children will have fewer struggles than you did. Wealth is security and peace of mind. It's not incidental that wealthier people are healthier and live longer. Wealth is, as a 2019 Yale study titled "The Misperception of Racial Economic Inequality" states, "the most consequential index of economic well-being" for most Americans.[11] But wealth is not something most people create solely by themselves; it is accumulated across generations.

While unchecked discrimination still plays a significant role in circumscribing opportunities for Black Americans, it is white Americans' centuries-long economic head start that most effectively maintains racial caste today. As soon as laws began to ban racial discrimination against Black Americans, white Americans created so-called race-neutral means of maintaining political and economic power. In a country where Black people have been kept disproportionately poor and prevented from building wealth, rules and policies involving money can be nearly as effective for maintaining the color line as legal segregation and disenfranchisement. For example, in the late 1800s, soon after the Fifteenth Amendment granted Black men the right to vote, white politicians in many states, understanding that recently freed Black Americans were of course impoverished, implemented poll taxes.[12] And so, when the civil rights movement made explicit discrimination illegal, White Americans understood that they did not have to maintain laws forcing segregated housing and schools if, using their intergenerational wealth and higher incomes, they could simply buy their way into expensive enclaves with exclusive public schools that are out of the price range of most Black Americans.

This has worked with impressive efficiency. Today Black Americans remain the most segregated group of people in America and are five times as likely as white Americans to live in high-poverty neighborhoods.[13] Not even high earnings inoculate Black people against racialized disadvantage. Black families earning $75,000 or more a year live in poorer neighborhoods than white Americans earning less than $40,000 a year, according to research by John Logan, a Brown University sociologist.[14] Another study, by the Stanford sociologist Sean Reardon and his colleagues, shows that the average Black family earning $100,000 a year lives in a neighborhood with an average annual income of $54,000.[15] Black Americans with high incomes are still Black: they face discrimination across American life. But it is because their families have not been able to build wealth that they are often unable to come up with a down payment to buy in more affluent neighborhoods, while white Americans with lower incomes often use familial wealth to do so.

The difference between the lived experience of Black Americans and white Americans when it comes to wealth—along the entire spectrum of income from the poorest to the richest—can be described as nothing other than a chasm. According to research published in 2020 by scholars at Duke University and Northwestern University, the average Black family with children holds just one cent of wealth for every dollar held by the average white family with children.[16]

As President Lyndon Johnson, architect of the Great Society, explained in a 1965 speech titled "To Fulfill These Rights": "Negro poverty is not white poverty. . . . These differences are not racial differences. They are solely and simply the consequence of ancient brutality, past injustice and present prejudice. They are anguishing to observe. For the Negro they are a constant reminder of oppression. For the white they are a constant reminder of guilt. But they must be faced, and they must be dealt with, and they must be overcome; if we are ever to reach the time when the only difference between Negroes and whites is the color of their skin."[17]

We sometimes forget—and I would argue it is an intentional forgetting—that the racism we are fighting today was originally conjured to justify working unfree Black people, often until death, to generate extravagant riches for European colonial powers, the white planter class, and all the ancillary white people, from Midwestern farmers to bankers to sailors to textile workers, who earned their living and built their wealth from that free Black labor and the products that labor produced. The prosperity of this country is inextricably linked with the forced labor of the ancestors of more than 30 million Black Americans, just as it is linked to the stolen land of the country's Indigenous people. Though our high school history books seldom make this plain, slavery and the hundred-year period of racial apartheid and racial terrorism known as Jim Crow were, above all else, systems of economic exploitation. To borrow a phrase from Ta-Nehisi Coates, racism is the child of economic profiteering, not the father.[18]

Innumerable legal efforts to strip Black people of their humanity existed to justify the extraction of profit. Beginning in the 1660s, white officials ensured that all children born to enslaved women would also be enslaved for life and would belong not to their mothers but to the white men who owned their mothers. These officials passed laws dictating that the child's status would follow that of the mother, not the father, upending European norms and guaranteeing that the children of enslaved women who were raped or sexually coerced by white men would be born enslaved—not free, as they would be if their status followed their father's.[19] It meant that profit for white people could be made from Black women's wombs. Laws determining that enslaved people, just like animals, had no recognized kinship ties ensured that human beings could be bought and sold at will to pay debts, buy more acres, or save storied universities like Georgetown from closing.[20] Laws barred enslaved people from making wills or owning property, distinguishing Black people in America from every other group on these shores and assuring that nearly everything of value Black people managed to accrue would add to the wealth of those who enslaved them. At the time of the Civil War, the value of the enslaved human beings held as property added up to more than all of this nation's railroads and factories combined.[21] And yet, enslaved people saw not a dime of this wealth. They owned nothing and were owed nothing from all that had been built from their toil.

Freed people, during and after slavery, tried to compel the government to provide restitution for slavery, to provide at the very least a pension for those who, along with generations of their ancestors, had spent their entire lives toiling for no pay. They filed lawsuits. They organized to lobby politicians. And every effort failed.

The closest the country ever came to delivering on reparations was in the immediate aftermath of slavery's demise, during a moment that offered this nation the chance for redemption. Out of the ashes of sectarian strife, we could have birthed a new country, one that recognized the humanity and natural rights of those who had helped forge this nation, one that attempted to atone and provide redress for the unspeakable atrocities committed against Black people in the name of profit. We could have finally, one hundred years after the American Revolution, embraced its founding ideals.

And, oh so briefly, during the period known as Reconstruction, we moved toward that goal. The historian Eric Foner refers to these twelve years after the Civil War as this nation's second founding, because it is here that America began to redeem the grave sin of slavery.[22] Congress passed amendments abolishing human bondage, enshrining equal protection before the law in the Constitution, and guaranteeing Black men the right to vote. This nation witnessed its first period of biracial governance as the formerly enslaved were elected to public offices at all levels of government. Millions of Black people, liberated with not a cent to their names, desperately wanted property so they could work, support themselves, and be left alone. They understood that land in this country has always meant wealth and, more important, independence. Black people implored federal officials to grant the land confiscated from enslavers who had taken up arms against their own country to those who had worked it for generations. They were asking, as the historian Robin D. G. Kelley puts it, to "inherit the earth they had turned into wealth for idle white people."[23]

And for a fleeting moment, a few white men listened to the pleas of Black people who had fought for the Union and helped deliver its victory. In January 1865, as the Civil War raged toward its final battle, twenty Black leaders, most of whom were ministers who had been born into slavery, gathered in Savannah, Georgia, for a meeting with Secretary of War Edwin Stanton and Union general William Tecumseh Sherman. During his famed "March to the Sea" through Georgia a couple of months earlier, Sherman had largely treated as a nuisance the estimated ten thousand poor and desperate people who'd abandoned their enslavers and begun to follow behind his troops. Many who ran to the Union lines seeking freedom and protection had instead died of starvation and sickness. But a turning point came after a Union brigadier general serving under Sherman ordered his troops to remove a pontoon bridge from Ebenezer Creek before the Black refugees trailing his unit could cross. Confederate scouts began shooting at the refugees and many ran into the icy river and drowned. Others were killed in the stampede and some were likely shot to death. The Confederates re-enslaved those who did not manage to make it across the creek.[24] The tragedy evoked widespread outrage and condemnation in the North, and alarmed the administration in Washington. In response, Stanton traveled to Savannah and called a meeting between Sherman and the Black leaders to pose what at the time was a radical question for white Americans to ask Black ones: "What do you want for your own people?"[25]

The Black delegation's leader, Reverend Garrison Frazier, a sixty-seven-year-old man who had spent fifty-nine years in bondage before purchasing his wife's and his own freedom eight years earlier, asked for the same thing most white Americans wanted. "Slavery is, receiving by irresistible power the work of another man, and not by his consent. The freedom, as I understand it, promised by the [Emancipation] proclamation, is taking us from under the yoke of bondage, and placing us where we could reap the fruit of our own labor, take care of ourselves and assist the Government in maintaining our freedom." The key to that, Frazier said, was land. "The way we can best take care of ourselves is to have land, and turn it and till it by our own labor—that is, by the labor of the women and children and old men; and we can soon maintain ourselves and have something to spare. . . . We want to be placed on land until we are able to buy it and make it our own."[26]

Remarkably, with millions of Black Americans just weeks past being released from generational slavery, they did not seek a government "handout"—even though getting land that they'd worked in order to produce wealth for others could hardly be considered one. They simply asked for land to work until they could earn enough money to purchase it.

Four days later, Sherman issued Special Field Order 15, providing for the distribution of hundreds of thousands of acres of former Confederate land in forty-acre tracts to newly freed people along coastal South Carolina, Georgia, and Florida. This became known as "forty acres and a mule." "Sherman was neither a humanitarian reformer nor a man with any particular concern for Blacks," Eric Foner writes in his groundbreaking book *Reconstruction: America's Unfinished Revolution.* "Instead of seeing Field Order 15 as a blueprint for the transformation of Southern society, he viewed it mainly as a way of relieving the immediate pressure caused by the large number of impoverished Blacks following his army."[27] And yet, Foner writes, the "prospect beckoned of a transformation of Southern society more radical even than the end of slavery."[28] One of the ministers at that meeting, Ulysses L. Houston, organized one thousand Black residents and claimed land in Skidaway Island, Georgia, where they founded a self-governing Black community. Some forty thousand freedpeople staked their claim to four hundred thousand acres of "Sherman land" in a region, Foner writes, "that had spawned one of the wealthiest segments of the planter class."[29]

President Abraham Lincoln, in his second inaugural address, on April 10, 1865, given the day after the final major battle of the Civil War, asked his fellow Americans to consider what the nation owed the enslaved. Speaking of the Union and the Confederacy, Lincoln said, "Neither party expected for the war, the magnitude, or the duration, which it has already attained. Neither anticipated that the cause of the conflict might cease with, or even before, the conflict itself should cease. Each looked for an easier triumph, and a result less fundamental and astounding." Yet, he continued, "if God wills that it continue, until all the wealth piled by the bond-man's two hundred and fifty years of unrequited toil shall be sunk, and until every drop of blood drawn with the lash, shall be paid by another drawn with the sword, as was said three thousand years ago, so still it must be said 'the judgments of the Lord, are true and righteous altogether.' "[30]

Just four days later, an assassin shot Lincoln, who died the next day. Andrew Johnson, the racist, pro-Southern vice president who took over, immediately reneged upon this promise of forty acres, overturning Sherman's order. Many white Americans felt that Black Americans should be grateful for their freedom, that the bloody Civil War had absolved them of any debt. The government confiscated the land from the few formerly enslaved families who had started to eke out a life away from the white whip and gave it back to the traitors. And with that, the only real effort this nation ever made to compensate Black Americans for 250 years of chattel slavery ended.

We still live with the legacy of this choice. As the scholar Henry Louis Gates writes, "Try to imagine how profoundly different the history of race relations in the United States would have been had this policy been implemented and enforced; had the former slaves actually had access to the ownership of land, of property; if they had had a chance to be self-sufficient economically, to build, accrue and pass on *wealth*. After all, one of the principal promises of America was the possibility of average people being able to own *land,* and all that such ownership entailed."[31]

But the formerly enslaved did not give up, and neither have their descendants. During Reconstruction, Black men serving in the U.S. Congress for the first time in history pushed for reparations in the form of federal aid for Black schools.[32] By the late 1800s, Reconstruction had been abandoned and violently concluded and many formerly enslaved people, their bodies debilitated by decades of punishing manual labor for the enrichment of others, by poor nutrition, and by lack of healthcare, were struggling in poverty, often without even enough money to bury their dead. A woman named Callie House, herself born into slavery, widowed in adulthood, and working as a washerwoman in Tennessee, began organizing freedpeople in the early 1900s under the National Ex-Slave Mutual Relief, Bounty and Pension Association.[33] Through this grassroots association, House organized tens of thousands of formerly enslaved people to push Congress to pass a bill to provide "slave pensions," just as the federal government paid pensions to Union soldiers.

After years of organizing failed to pay off with Congress, in 1915, House took an extraordinary step for a Black, formerly enslaved woman living in the Jim Crow South: she retained Cornelius Jones, one of a tiny number of Black lawyers practicing in Washington, D.C., and sued the federal government for reparations.[34] In the suit, Jones argued that the U.S. Treasury owed Black Americans $68,073,388.99 for the taxes it had collected between 1862 and 1868 on the cotton enslaved people had grown. The federal government had identified the cotton and could trace it, and the suit argued that this tax money should be paid in the form of pensions for those who against their will had grown, picked, and processed it.[35]

The audacity of a Black woman demanding payment for her stolen labor and the stolen labor of millions of others, even if it would come directly from proceeds of the cotton they'd picked, brought down the full wrath of one of the most powerful governments in the world. The Treasury Department, under President Woodrow Wilson, first issued a press release insisting the United States owed nothing and that formerly enslaved people, if they had a claim at all, should seek reparations from "their masters."[36] A federal court then rejected the claim, citing government immunity—which says that the government must consent to being sued—and the U.S. Supreme Court upheld the decision.

Not content with crushing the lawsuit, the government went after both Jones and House, accusing them of mail fraud for soliciting funds from formerly enslaved people to help the effort with promises that reparations were coming. The same government that refused to give freedpeople a dime of financial assistance for their enslavement accused those trying to get them aid of "going through the country collecting hard-earned money from poor negroes."[37] Newspaper coverage perpetuated the basest stereotypes of people who'd spent a significant part of their lives working for free for the benefit of white people: "The members of the race have been prone from time immemorial to strive to get something for nothing," an article in the Memphis *Commercial Appeal* announced.[38] The federal government never produced any real evidence that showed that House had defrauded anyone, according to the historian Mary Frances Berry in her book *My Face Is Black Is True,* but it did not matter. Jones, a respected and well-connected civil rights attorney, was not convicted. House, a poor Black woman, was convicted then and sentenced to prison, where she served a year. "Mrs. House lacked Jones's status of black male respectability," Berry writes. "Mrs. House was just a black woman with the audacity—and no money—to stand firmly on claims of citizenship rights for herself and freedmen and -women."[39]

Black Americans would never give up their quest for reparations—for restitution and repayment for the centuries of stolen labor and robbed opportunities. The Black nationalist Marcus Garvey would call for reparations in the 1910s and for Black Americans to leave this country and resettle in a Black one. Like Callie House, Garvey found himself targeted by the federal government for mail fraud. He was imprisoned and then deported.[40] In the 1950s, the activist "Queen Mother" Audley Moore launched a movement for reparations, appealing to the United Nations in 1957 and 1959. In 1968, activists formed the Republic of New Afrika, which claimed that since the United States had reneged on its promise of forty acres, Black Americans should be given territory in the Southeastern United States to form their own Black nation.[41] Malcolm X called for reparations in 1963.[42] In 1987, Adjoa Aiyetoro and Imari Obadele helped found the National Coalition for Reparations in America, known as N'COBRA.[43] And in 2021, the last three survivors of the Tulsa Race Massacre, all centenarians, testified in Congress in support of a reparations bill for the survivors and their descendants, one hundred years after the slaughter that destroyed the prosperous Black neighborhood of Greenwood and killed hundreds,[44] and some twenty years after a state commission recommended reparations that were never given.[45]

None of these efforts succeeded. To this day, the only Americans who have ever received government restitution for slavery were white enslavers in Washington, D.C., whom the federal government compensated after the Civil War for their loss of human property.

We are often taught in school that Lincoln "freed the slaves," but we are not prodded to contemplate what it means to achieve freedom without a home to live in, without food to eat, a bed to sleep on, clothes for your children, or money to buy any of it. Narratives collected from formerly enslaved people for the 1930s Federal Writers' Project reveal the horrors of massive starvation, of "liberated" Black people seeking shelter in burned-out buildings and scrounging for food in decaying fields before eventually succumbing to the heartbreak of returning to bend over in the fields of their former enslavers, as sharecroppers, just so they would not die.[46] "With the advent of emancipation," writes the historian Keri Leigh Merritt, "Blacks became the only race in the U.S. ever to start out, as an entire people, with close to zero capital."[47]

In 1881, Frederick Douglass, surveying the utter privation in which the federal government left the formerly enslaved, wrote: "When the Hebrews were emancipated, they were told to take spoil from the Egyptians. When the serfs of Russia were emancipated, they were given three acres of ground upon which they could live and make a living. But not so when our slaves were emancipated. They were sent away empty-handed, without money, without friends and without a foot of land to stand upon. Old and young, sick and well, were turned loose to the open sky, naked to their enemies."[48]

But even as the federal government decided that Black people were undeserving of any restitution, it was bestowing millions of acres in the West on white Americans under the Homestead Act, while also enticing white foreigners to immigrate with the offer of free land. From 1868 to 1934, the federal government gave away 246 million acres in 160-acre tracts, nearly 10 percent of all the land in the nation, to more than 1.5 million white families, native-born and foreign. Some 46 million American adults today, about 20 percent of all American adults, are descended from those homesteaders, according to research by the social scientist Trina Williams Shanks.[49] "If that many white

Americans can trace their legacy of wealth and property ownership to a single entitlement program," Merritt writes, "then the perpetuation of Black poverty must also be linked to national policy."[50]

The federal government turned its back on its financial obligations to four million newly liberated people, and then it left them without protection as well, as white rule was reinstated across the South starting in the 1870s. Federal troops pulled out of the former Confederacy, and white Southerners overthrew biracial governance using violence, coups, and election fraud.

The campaigns of white terror that marked the period after Reconstruction, known as Redemption, once again guaranteed an exploitable, dependent labor force for the white South. Most Black Southerners had no desire to work on the same forced-labor camps where they had just been enslaved. But white Southerners passed state laws that made it a crime if they didn't sign labor contracts with white landowners or if they changed employers without permission or sold cotton after sunset. As punishment for these "crimes," Black people were arrested and then forcibly leased out to companies and individuals. While white Northerners largely turned a blind eye, white Southerners compelled Black people back into quasi-slavery through sharecropping and convict leasing. This arrangement ensured that once-devastated towns like my father's hometown, Greenwood, Mississippi, could again call themselves the cotton capitals of the world, and companies like United States Steel secured a steady supply of unfree Black laborers who could be worked to death, in what Douglas A. Blackmon calls "slavery by another name."[51]

Yet Black Americans persisted, and despite the odds, some managed to acquire land, start businesses, and build schools for their children. But it was the most prosperous Black people and communities that elicited the most vicious responses. White people regularly deployed lynchings, massacres, and generalized racial terrorism against Black people who bought land, founded schools, built thriving communities, tried to organize sharecroppers' unions, or opened their own businesses, depriving white owners of economic monopolies and the opportunity to cheat Black buyers.

According to a 2020 report by the Equal Justice Initiative, white Americans lynched at least 6,500 Black people from the end of the Civil War to 1950, an average of three every two weeks for eight and a half decades.[52] (Since 2015, law enforcement has killed, on average, nearly five Black people a week.[53])

The scale of the destruction during the 1900s is incalculable. Black farms were stolen, shops burned to the ground. White mobs from Florida to North Carolina to Louisiana to Arkansas razed entire prosperous Black neighborhoods and communities. In Tulsa's Greenwood neighborhood, a district so successful that it became known as Black Wall Street, gangs of white men, armed with guns supplied by public officials, wreaked permanent economic destruction. They burned more than twelve hundred homes and businesses, including a department store, a library, and a hospital, and killed hundreds. These people, it is now believed, were buried in mass graves.[54] Today Greenwood, like so many once-prosperous Black areas, remains severely economically depressed.

Even Black Americans who did not experience theft and violence were continually deprived of the ability to build wealth. They were denied entry into labor unions and turned away from union jobs that ensured middle-class wages.[55] In both the North and the South, racist hiring laws and policies forced them into service jobs even when they held college degrees. Communities legally relegated them into segregated, substandard neighborhoods and segregated, substandard schools that made it impossible for them to compete economically even had they not faced rampant discrimination in the job market. In the South, for most of the period between the Civil War and the 1960s, nearly all of the Black people who wanted to earn professional degrees—law, medical, and master's degrees—had to leave the region to do so, even as white immigrants attended state colleges in the former Confederacy that Black American tax dollars helped pay for.[56]

As part of the New Deal programs, the federal government created redlining maps, marking neighborhoods where Black people lived in red ink to denote that they were uninsurable for federally backed mortgages. As a result, 98 percent of the loans the Federal Housing Administration insured from 1934 to 1962 went to white Americans, locking nearly all Black Americans out of the government program credited with building the modern (white) middle class.[57] "At the very moment when a wide array of public policies was providing most white Americans with valuable tools to advance their social welfare—insure their old age, get good jobs, acquire economic security, build assets, and gain middle-class status—most black Americans were left behind or left out," the historian Ira Katznelson writes in his book *When Affirmative Action Was White*. "The federal government . . . functioned as a commanding instrument of white privilege."[58]

In other words, while Black Americans were being systematically, generationally deprived of the ability to build wealth, and while some of them were also being robbed of the little they had managed to gain, white Americans were not only free to earn money and accumulate wealth with exclusive access to the best jobs, best schools, and best credit terms but were also getting substantial government help in doing so.

The civil rights movement ostensibly ended white advantage by law. And in the gauzy way many white Americans tend to view history, particularly the history of racial inequality, the end of legal discrimination, after 350 years, is all that was required to vanquish this dark history and its effects. Changing the laws, too many Americans have believed, marked the end of the obligation. But the civil rights laws passed in the 1960s merely guaranteed Black people the rights they should have always had. These laws dictated that from that day forward, the government would no longer sanction legal or explicit racial discrimination. But they did not correct the harm nor restore what was taken.

Brown v. Board of Education did not end segregated and unequal schools; it just ended segregation under the law. It took court orders and, at times, federal troops to produce any real integration. Nevertheless, more than six decades after the nation's highest court proclaimed school segregation unconstitutional, Black children remain as segregated from white kids as they were in the early 1970s.[59] There has never been a point in American history when even half of the Black children in this country have attended a majority-white school.

Making school segregation illegal did nothing to repay Black families for the theft of their educations or make up for the loss to generations of Black Americans, many of them still living, who could never go to college because white officials believed that only white students needed a high school education and so refused to operate high schools for Black children. As late as the 1930s, most communities in the South, where the vast majority of Black Americans lived, failed to provide a single public high school for Black children, according to *The Education of Blacks in the South, 1860–1935*, by the historian James D. Anderson.[60] Heavily Black Richmond County in Georgia, for instance, did not provide a four-year Black high school from 1897 to 1945.

The Fair Housing Act, passed in 1968, prohibited discrimination in housing, but it did not reset real estate values so that homes in redlined Black neighborhoods, whose prices had been artificially deflated by government policy, would be valued the same as identical homes in white neighborhoods, whose worth had been artificially inflated. It did not provide restitution for generations of Black homeowners forced into predatory loans because they had been locked out of the prime credit market. It did not repay every Black soldier who returned from World War II to find that he could not use his GI Bill benefits to buy a home for his family in any of the new whites-only suburbs subsidized by the same government he'd fought for. It did not break up the still entrenched housing segregation that had taken decades of government and private policy to create. Lay those redlining maps over almost any city in America with a significant Black population and you will see that the government-sanctioned segregation patterns remain stubbornly intact and that those same communities bore the brunt of the predatory lending and foreclosure crisis of the late 2000s that stole years of Black homeownership and wealth gains.[61]

Making employment discrimination illegal did not come with a check for Black Americans to compensate for all the high-paying jobs they were legally barred from, for the promotions they never got solely because of their race, for the income and opportunities lost to the centuries of discrimination. Nor did these laws end ongoing discrimination, just as speed limits without enforcement fail to stop people from driving too fast. These laws opened up opportunities for limited numbers of Black Americans while largely leaving centuries of meticulously orchestrated inequities soundly in place, but now with the sheen of color-blind magnanimity.

The inclination to bandage over and move on is a definitive American feature when it comes to anti-Black racism and its social and material effects. The 2019 Yale University study describes this phenomenon this way: "A firm belief in our nation's commitment to racial egalitarianism is part of the collective consciousness of the United States of America. . . . We have a strong and persistent belief that our national disgrace of racial oppression has been overcome, albeit through struggle, and that racial equality has largely been achieved."[62] The authors point out how many white Americans love to play up moments of racial progress like the Emancipation Proclamation, *Brown v. Board of Education,* and the election of Barack Obama, while playing down or ignoring lynching, racial apartheid, and the 1985 government bombing of a Black neighborhood in Philadelphia.[63] "When it comes to race relations in the United States," the study said, "most Americans hold an unyielding belief in a specific, optimistic narrative regarding racial progress that is robust to counterexamples: that society has come a very long way already and is moving rapidly and perhaps naturally toward full racial equality."[64]

This remarkable imperviousness to facts when it comes to white advantage and architected Black disadvantage is what emboldens some white Americans to quote the passage from Martin Luther King's 1963 "I Have a Dream" speech about being judged by the content of your character and not by the color of your skin. It's often used as a cudgel against calls for race-specific remedies for Black Americans—while ignoring the part of that same speech where King says Black people have marched on the capital to cash "a check which has come back marked 'insufficient funds.' "[65]

King was evoked continuously during the 2020 season of protests, sometimes to defend those who looted and torched buildings, sometimes to condemn them. But during that time of foment and its ongoing aftermath, we've witnessed an astounding silence around his most radical demands. The seldom-quoted King is the one who said that the true battle for equality, the actualization of justice, required economic repair.

In 1967, King gave a speech in Atlanta to the Hungry Club Forum, a secret gathering of civil rights leaders and white politicians. He had watched Northern cities explode even as his movement successfully pushed for the passage of the 1964 Civil Rights Act and the 1965 Voting Rights Act and he saw the limitations of a movement that sought just to secure legal rights. King told the forum:

> For well now twelve years, the struggle was basically a struggle to end legal segregation. In a sense it was a struggle for decency. It was a struggle to get rid of all of the humiliation and the syndrome of depravation surrounding the system of legal segregation. And I need not remind you that those were glorious days. . . . It is now a struggle for genuine equality on all levels, and this will be a much more difficult struggle. You see, the gains in the first period, or the first era of struggle, were obtained from the power structure at bargain rates; it didn't cost the nation anything to integrate lunch counters. It didn't cost the nation anything to integrate hotels and motels. It didn't cost the nation a penny to guarantee the right to vote. Now we are in a period where it will cost the nation billions of dollars to get rid of poverty, to get rid of slums, to make quality integrated education a reality. This is where we are now. Now we're going to lose some friends in this period. The allies who were with us in Selma will not all stay with us during this period. We've got to understand what is happening. Now they often call this the white backlash. . . . It's just a new name for an old phenomenon. The fact is that there has never been any single, solid, determined commitment on the part of the vast majority of white Americans to genuine equality for Negroes.[66]

A year later, in March 1968, King spoke to striking, impoverished Black sanitation workers in Memphis, "Now our struggle is for genuine equality, which means economic equality," he told the crowd. "For we know that it isn't enough to integrate lunch counters. What does it profit a man to be able to eat at an integrated lunch counter if he doesn't earn enough money to buy a hamburger and a cup of coffee?"[67] A month later, a white man assassinated King.

Decades after the end of the civil rights movement, which resulted in a nation where—for the first time since 1619—it was not legal to treat Black people differently than white ones, perhaps the starkest indication of our societal failures is that racial income disparities today look no different than they did the decade before King's March on Washington. According to a study published in September 2020 by the economists Moritz Kuhn, Moritz Schularick, and Ulrike Steins in the *Journal of Political Economy,* Black median household income in 1950 was about half that of white Americans, and today it remains so. More critical, the racial wealth gap is in relative terms about the same as it was in the 1950s as well. The typical Black household today is poorer than 80 percent of white households. "No progress has been made over the past 70 years in reducing income and wealth inequalities between Black and white households," according to the study.[68]

And yet most Americans remain in an almost pathological denial about the depth of Black financial struggle. That 2019 Yale University study, discussed in "The Misperception of Racial Economic Inequality," found that most Americans believe that Black households hold $90 in wealth for every $100 held by white households. The actual amount is $10. About 97 percent of the study participants overestimated Black-white wealth equality, and most assumed that highly educated, high-income Black households were the most likely to achieve economic parity with white counterparts. That is also wrong. The magnitude of the wealth gap only widens as Black people earn more income.[69]

"These data suggest that Americans are largely unaware of the striking persistence of racial economic inequality in the United States," the study's authors write. Americans, they note, tend to explain away or justify persistent racial inequality by ignoring the "tailwinds that have contributed to their economic success while justifying inequalities of wealth and poverty by invoking the role of individuals' traits and skills as explanations for these disparities."[70] They use the exceptional examples of very successful Black people to prove that systemic racism does not hold Black Americans back and point to the large numbers of impoverished Black people as evidence that Black people are largely responsible for their own struggles. In 2018, Duke University's Samuel DuBois Cook Center on Social Equity and the Insight Center for Community Economic Development published *What We Get Wrong About Closing the Racial Wealth Gap.* This report examined the common misperceptions about the causes of the racial wealth gap and presented data and social-science research that refutes all of them.[71]

The Duke study shows that the racial wealth gap is not about poverty. Poor white families earning less than $27,000 a year hold nearly the same amount of wealth as Black families earning between $48,000 and $76,000 annually.[72] It's not because of Black spending habits. Black Americans have lower incomes overall but save at a slightly higher rate than white Americans with similar incomes. It's not that Black people need to value education more. Black parents, when correlated by household type and socioeconomic status, actually offer more financial support for their children's higher education than white parents do, according to the study.[73] And some studies have shown that Black youths, when compared with white youths whose parents have similar incomes and education levels, are actually more likely to go to college and earn additional credentials.[74] But what's probably most astounding to many Americans is that college simply does not pay off for Black Americans the way it does for other groups. Black college graduates are about as likely to be unemployed as white Americans with a high school diploma, and Black Americans with a college education hold less wealth than white Americans who have not even completed high school. Further, because Black families hold almost no wealth to begin with, Black students are the most likely to borrow money to pay for college and then to borrow more money in total. That debt, in turn, means that Black students cannot start saving immediately upon graduation, the way their less-debt-burdened peers can.[75]

It's not a lack of homeownership. While it's true that Black Americans have the lowest homeownership rates in the nation, simply owning a home does not have the same asset value as it does for white Americans. Black Americans get higher mortgage rates even with equal credit worthiness, and homes in Black neighborhoods do not appreciate at the same rate as those in white areas, because housing prices are still driven by the racial makeup of communities.[76] As the Duke University economist William Darity, Jr., the study's lead author, points out, the ability to purchase a home in the first place is seldom a result of just the hard work and frugality of the buyer: "It's actually parental and grandparental wealth that facilitates the acquisition of a home."[77]

It's not because a majority of Black families are led by a single mother. White single women with children hold the same amount of wealth as single Black women with no children, and the typical white single parent has twice the wealth of the typical two-parent Black family.

To summarize, none of the actions we are told Black people must take if they want to "lift themselves" out of poverty and gain financial stability—not marrying, not getting an education, not saving more, not owning a home—can mitigate four hundred years of racialized plundering. Wealth begets wealth, and white Americans have had centuries of government assistance to accumulate wealth, while the government has for the vast history of this country worked against Black Americans' efforts to do the same.

"The cause of the gap must be found in the structural characteristics of the American economy, heavily infused at every point with both an inheritance of racism and the ongoing authority of white supremacy," the authors of the Duke study write. "There are no actions that Black Americans can take unilaterally that will have much of an effect on reducing the wealth gap."[78] For the gap to be closed, America must undergo a vast social transformation produced by the adoption of bold national policies.

At the center of those policies must be reparations. "The process of creating the racial wealth chasm begins with the failure to provide the formerly enslaved with the forty acres they were promised," Darity told me. "So the restitution has never been given, and it's a hundred and fifty-five years overdue."[79]

Darity has been studying and advocating for reparations for thirty years, and in 2020 he and his partner, A. Kirsten Mullen, published *From Here to Equality: Reparations for Black Americans in the Twenty-first Century*. Both history and road map, the book answers many questions about who should receive reparations and how a program would work. I will not spend much time on that here, except to make these few points: Reparations are not about punishing white Americans, and white Americans are not the ones who would pay for them. It does not matter if your ancestors engaged in slavery or if you just immigrated here two weeks ago. Reparations amount to a societal obligation in a nation where our Constitution sanctioned slavery, Congress passed laws protecting it, and our federal government initiated, condoned, and practiced legal racial segregation and discrimination against Black Americans until half a century ago. And so it is the federal government that would pay.

Nor is it impossible to figure out who is eligible. Reparations would go to any person who has documentation that he or she identified as a Black person for at least ten years before the beginning of any reparations process and can trace at least one ancestor back to American slavery. Reparations should provide a commitment to vigorously enforce existing civil rights prohibitions against housing, educational, and employment discrimination, as well as including targeted investments in Black communities segregated through government policy and the segregated, high-poverty schools that serve a disproportionate number of Black children. But critically, reparations must include individual cash payments to descendants of the enslaved in order to close the wealth gap. We must stop thinking of restitution for slavery as a zero-sum game. As this book has shown, the legacy of 1619 has harmed all Americans, and we are all suffering for it to some degree. In addition to reparations, our wealthy nation is morally obligated to do more for all Americans who struggle by adopting such things as a livable wage; universal healthcare, childcare, and college; and student loan debt relief. We can acknowledge our need to better support all of our citizens, and also the particular debt owed Black Americans.

The technical details, frankly, are the easier part. The real obstacle, the obstacle we have never overcome, is garnering the political will—convincing enough Americans that the centuries-long forced economic disadvantage of Black Americans should be remedied, that restitution is owed to people who have never had an equal chance to take advantage of the bounty they played such a significant part in creating.

This country can be remarkably generous. Each year Congress allocates money—in 2020, $5 million—to help support Holocaust survivors living in America.[80] In backing the funding measure in 2018, Representative Richard E. Neal, a Democrat from Massachusetts, said that this country has a "responsibility to support the surviving men and women of the Holocaust and their families."[81] And he is right. It is the moral thing to do. This country has also paid reparations to Japanese American victims of internment during World War II and to some Native American nations. And yet Congress has refused for three decades to pass H.R. 40, a bill introduced shortly after Congress approved reparations for Japanese Americans, which seeks to simply study the issue of reparations for descendants of American slavery. Its drafter, Representative John Conyers, Jr., a Michigan Democrat and the descendant of enslaved Americans, died in 2019—during the four hundredth anniversary of the arrival of the first Africans enslaved in Virginia—without the bill ever making it out of committee. It finally did so in early 2021.[82]

There are living victims of racial apartheid and terrorism born in *this* country, including civil rights activists who lost their homes and jobs fighting to make this country a democracy, who have never received any sort of restitution for what they endured. Soon, like their enslaved ancestors, they will all be dead, and then we'll hear the worn excuse that this country owes no reparations because none of the victims are still alive. Darity and Mullen call this the "delay until death" tactic.[83] Procrastination, they say, does not erase what is owed.

It is time, it is long past time, for reparations.

In the year 1903, perhaps the low point of the Great Nadir when Black Americans were being consumed by the violent retraction of their newly gained citizenship rights, the scholar W.E.B. Du Bois published one of this nation's most important literary works. It is called *The Souls of Black Folk*, though a more accurate title for the seminal text might have been *The Soul of America*. A synergy of sociology, history, and literary prose, the book excavates the central tension in American life—the color line—while also reinforcing the unparalleled and largely erased place that Black Americans hold in the American story. In the opening paragraph of the opening chapter, Du Bois begins with a searing question: "Between me and the other world, there is ever an unasked question . . . How does it feel to be a problem?"[84] And in the final pages of the final chapter, Du Bois answers with a rousing declaration that Black people are not this nation's problem, but its heart.

> Your country? How came it yours? Before the Pilgrims landed we were here. Here we have brought our three gifts and mingled them with yours: a gift of story and song—soft, stirring melody in an ill-harmonized and unmelodious land; the gift of sweat and brawn to beat back the wilderness, conquer the soil, and lay the foundations of this vast economic empire two hundred years earlier than your weak hands could have done it; the third, a gift of the Spirit. Around us the history of the land has centered for thrice a hundred years; out of the nation's heart we have called all that was best to throttle and subdue all that was worst; fire and blood, prayer and sacrifice, have billowed over this people, and they have found peace only in the altars of the God of Right. Nor has our gift of the Spirit been merely passive. Actively we have woven ourselves with the very warp and woof of this nation,—we fought their battles, shared their sorrow, mingled our blood with theirs, and generation after generation have pleaded with a headstrong, careless people to despise not Justice, Mercy, and Truth, lest the nation be smitten with a curse. Our song, our toil, our cheer, and warning have been given to this nation in blood-brotherhood. Are not these gifts worth the giving? Is not this work and striving? Would America have been America without her Negro people?[85]

This is our national truth: America would not be America without the wealth from Black labor, without Black striving, Black ingenuity, Black resistance. So much of the music, the food, the language, the art, the scientific advances, the athletic renown, the fashion, the guarantees of civil rights, the oratory and intellectual inspiration that we export to the world, that draws the world to us, comes forth from Black Americans, from the people born on the water. That is Black Americans' legacy to this nation.

The legacy of this nation to Black Americans has consisted of immorally high rates of poverty, incarceration, and death and the lowest rates of land and home ownership, employment, school funding, and wealth. All of this reveals that Black Americans, along with Indigenous people—the two groups forced to be part of this nation—remain the most neglected beneficiaries of the America that would not exist without us. This unacknowledged debt, all of it, is still accruing. And it will continue to accrue until we as a society decide to tolerate it no longer.

Black Americans helped build the economic foundation that has made the United States a global power, but, as the first chapter of this book shows, they have also played an unparalleled and *uncompensated* role in building our democracy itself. For generations, U.S. soldiers whose stated mission was to spread freedom abroad have received pensions, federal grants, healthcare, and burial assistance. But the Black foot soldiers who fought over many generations to spread freedom *here* received no measure of compensation, even as that fight cost them their homes, their land, their educations, their employment, and, too often, their lives. And yet Black Americans fight to make this nation a democracy still.

We cannot change the hypocrisy upon which we were founded. We cannot change all the times in the past when this nation had the opportunity to do the right thing and chose to return to its basest inclinations. We cannot make up for all of the lives lost and dreams snatched, for all the suffering endured. But we can atone for it. We can acknowledge the crime. And we can do something to try to set things right, to ease the hardship and hurt of so many of our fellow Americans. It is one thing to say you do not support reparations because you did not know the history, that you did not understand how things done long ago helped create the conditions in which millions of Black Americans live today. But you now have reached the end of this book, and nationalized amnesia can no longer provide the excuse. None of us can be held responsible for the wrongs of our ancestors. But if today we choose not to do the right and necessary thing, *that* burden we own.

It is time for this country to pay the debt it began incurring four hundred years ago, when it first decided that human beings could be purchased and held in bondage. What happened in 1619, the tragic origin story unveiled throughout this book, set in motion the defining struggle of American life, between freedom and oppression, equality and racism, between the lofty ideals of democracy and the fight to make them real. We must confront this four-hundred-year war between these opposing forces, and then we must make a choice about which America we want to build for tomorrow. The time for slogans and symbolism and inconsequential actions has long passed. Citizens inherit not just the glory of their nation but its wrongs, too. A truly great country does not ignore or excuse its sins. It confronts them, and then works to make them right.

If we are to be redeemed, we must do what is just: we must, finally, live up to the magnificent ideals upon which we were founded.

May 2020

In response to the murder of George Floyd by a Minneapolis police officer, a global protest movement erupts, with demonstrations across the United States and around the world that last for months.

Progress Report

Sonia Sanchez

In this country
where history and herstory stretches
in aristocratic silence,
our Black, white, brown activists
have come at the beginning
of the twenty-first century carrying
the quiet urgency of a star.
And the country is not the same.

    i say, who are these people singing down
    the lids of cities with color?

    i say, i say, who are these people always
    punctual with their eyes, their hearts, their hands?

    i say, i say, i say, who are these
    singers who resurrect summer
language on our winter landscape?
They remind each other
of what Fanon said: *what is needed is to hold*
one's self like a sliver to the heart of the world, to
interrupt if necessary the rhythm of the world, to
upset if necessary the chain of command but . . .
to stand up to the world: I do battle for the

creation of a human world that is a world of
reciprocal recognition.

What does honor taste like?
Does honor have a long memory?
What is the color of honor?

> José Martí wrote: *in the world there must*
> *be a certain degree of honor just as there must be*
> *a certain amount of light. When there are many men*
> *without honor, there will always be some others who*
> *bear in themselves the honor of many men.*

i turn the corner
of these honor-driven activists
find memory beneath their doors
taste the blessings of their midwifery
their miracle songs giving birth
to un-ghosted wounds
their words coming to us
glittering like silver stars,
and I catch them in mid-flight,
swallow them whole.

> i say, behold our sisters and our brothers
> questioning the flesh of national monuments
> peeling them down to a waste of bones.

> i say, behold our sisters and our brothers
> shaking dew from their eyes, as they remember
> Brother Floyd's last words:

> *i can't breathe, i can't breathe, i can't breathe . . .*

And we greet him,
his body submerged with no air
and we anoint his eyes
with ancestral light

and we all breathe . . .

ACKNOWLEDGMENTS

This book grew out of the original version of the 1619 Project, which was published in *The New York Times Magazine* in August 2019. That version comprised two publications: a special issue of the magazine containing ten nonfiction essays, one photo portfolio, and sixteen works of creative writing, and a special broadsheet section of the newspaper depicting a visual history of slavery.

We are grateful to the numerous members of the magazine's staff who contributed to those two publications. The magazine's editors, including Nitsuh Abebe, Jeannie Choi, Sheila Glaser, Claire Gutierrez, Charles Homans, Mark Jannot, Jessica Lustig, Luke Mitchell, Dean Robinson, Willy Staley, Bill Wasik, and Sasha Weiss, embraced Nikole's original concept and ran with it, helping to develop and hone the writing and thinking in the special issue, which was copyedited by Harvey Dickson, Dan Fromson, Rob Hoerburger, Missy Prebula, and Andrew Willett. Creative director Gail Bichler and art director Ben Grandgenett together devised the look and feel of the issue, many design elements of which remain in use in this book. We are grateful for their efforts, and those of designers Claudia Rubín and Rachel Willey and illustrators Michael Paul Britto, Diana Ejaita, and Jon Key. We are especially indebted to the artist Adam Pendleton, who created an original work to accompany the opening essay.

The photography in the issue, including Dannielle Bowman's cover photograph showing a portion of the harbor where the *White Lion* first appeared, was commissioned, researched, and edited by the magazine's photo desk, run by director of photography Kathy Ryan and deputy director of photography Jessica Dimson, and including David Carthas, Kristen Geisler, Amy Kellner, Pia Peterson, and Jessica Tang. Additional photos in that issue were taken by

Djeneba Aduayom, Humza Deas, Lyle Ashton Harris, Zora J Murff, Brian Ul-rich, and D'Angelo Lovell Williams.

The dedicated individuals on the magazine's research desk fact-checked the issue. We are grateful to our head of research, Nandi Rodrigo, and her crew: Riley Blanton, Julia Bozzone, Alex Carp, David Ferguson, Jamie Fisher, Tim Hodler, Robert Liguori, Renee Michael, Lia Miller, Christian Smith, Ste-ven Stern, and Bill Vourvoulias. In addition, the magazine's digital team, over-seen by Blake Wilson and including designer Kate LaRue, as well as Iva Dixit and Kyle Ligman, created a memorable online experience; its production de-partment, led by Anick Pleven, and including Hilary Shanahan and Ilona Fa-bian, managed the print experience. Erika Sommer organized many aspects of the editorial process, in particular a special printing and distribution effort. Pierre-Antoine Louis, Wadzanai Mhute, Jake Nevins, and Astha Rajvanshi also contributed in significant ways.

A separate but overlapping editorial team worked on the broadsheet sec-tion, which was overseen by Caitlin Roper and designed by Deb Bishop. We wish to acknowledge the work on this section of Mary Elliott, a historian and curator at the Smithsonian's National Museum of African American History and Culture (NMAAHC); *New York Times* reporters Jazmine Hughes and Ni-kita Stewart; and editor Claire Gutierrez. The editorial team that supported them included Molly Bennet, Cynthia Cotts, Maddy Crowell, Erica Deeman, Jessica Dimson, Lu Fong, Dan Fromson, Najeebah al-Ghadban, Rudy Lee, Le-ticia Sarmento, Hilary Shanahan, and Jessica Tang, as well as Ayla Amon and Candace Oubre from the NMAAHC.

That section was produced in partnership with the NMAAHC, then under the direction of Lonnie Bunch, who is now the fourteenth secretary of the Smithsonian Institution. Two months after publication, the museum wel-comed us for a 1619 Project symposium that helped spur further conversa-tions. We are indebted to Secretary Bunch and Mary Elliott, as well as numerous other members of the Smithsonian and the NMAAHC, including Kinshasha Holman Conwill, Spencer Crew, Shrita Penn Hernandez, Julissa Marenco, and Fleur Paysour.

Many scholars of American history contributed to the original version of the project. Some helped us brainstorm ideas; others gave us input about how to refine and improve some of the project's central concepts; still others of-fered their counsel for how to grow and deepen the project after it was pub-lished. We are grateful to the following scholars for their support of the original version of the project: Danielle Allen, Edward E. Baptist, Christopher L. Brown, Greg Carr, Jelani Cobb, William A. Darity, Jr., Eric Foner, Henry Louis Gates, Jr., Annette Gordon-Reed, Eliga H. Gould, Nicholas Guyatt, Woody Holton, Gerald Horne, Kelli Jones, Martha S. Jones, Kay Wright Lewis, Nell Irvin Painter, Andre M. Perry, Jack N. Rakove, Jason Stanley, James Brewer Stewart, Jeffrey C. Stewart, Alan Taylor, Keeanga-Yamahtta Taylor, David Waldstreicher, and Karin Wulf.

The historian Anne C. Bailey wrote a short feature for the original magazine issue about an auction of enslaved people. In the February 16, 2020, issue of the magazine, she expanded on that work, researching and writing the text for a photo portfolio that documented a number of other sites, some previously unknown, where auctions of enslaved people were held. We are grateful to Anne Bailey for all she has done to support and contribute to the project.

Following the publication of the special issue of the magazine, the *New York Times* audio team created the podcast *1619*. That series was led by Annie Brown, Adizah Eghan, and Kelly Prime; it also included Larissa Anderson, Daoud Anthony, Lisa Chow, Wendy Dorr, Brad Fisher, Andy Mills, Dan Powell, Stella Tan, and Lisa Tobin. Their powerful work expanded on the original magazine issue and brought the project to millions of listeners.

Our partners at the Pulitzer Center converted the magazine issue and special section into a set of lesson plans that have been put to use in all fifty states by teachers interested in supplementing their standard social studies and history courses in K–12 and university classrooms. The writing that students have done in these classrooms has been some of the most cherished responses we have received to the project. We are grateful to the director of the Pulitzer Center, Jon Sawyer, a stalwart friend and partner who has worked with great vision to expand this educational mission, which in 2021 grew to include a law school initiative created in partnership with the Howard University School of Law and the University of Miami School of Law. In addition to Jon, everyone on the staff at the Pulitzer Center has contributed to this effort, especially Fareed Mostoufi, Ann Peters, Mark Schulte, and Donnalie Jamnah. Their hard work has helped the project continue to have an impact long after its initial publication.

The project has sparked numerous debates about American history, not only in classrooms but also on the campaign trail, in school board meetings, on Facebook groups, and in the halls of Congress. So we are doubly grateful for the institutional support we received from A. G. Sulzberger, publisher of *The New York Times;* Meredith Kopit Levien, the newspaper's CEO; and Dean Baquet, our fearless newsroom leader. We count ourselves lucky to have brought this project forth during their tenures. As the paper's executive editor, Dean is our ultimate boss, and we will always be grateful for his steadfast leadership and kindness.

A.G., Meredith, and Dean are only three of the many people at *The New York Times* whose support has made the 1619 Project possible. We also wish to express our gratitude to Julian Ahye, R. C. Archibold, Mel Boothe, Karen Brown, Jordan Cohen, Mike Connors, Phil Corbett, Sam Dolnick, Monica Drake, Blair Ecton, Karen Farina, Sara Fitts, Laura Forde, Alix Forstenzer, Holly Harnisch, Joe Kahn, Maggie Kiselick, Glenn Kramon, Cliff Levy, Lauren McCarthy, Marilyn McCauley, Eileen Murphy, Matt Purdy, Danielle Rhoades Ha, David Rubin, Julie Sauro, Brenna King Schleifer, Todd Socia, Brent Staples, Annie Tressler, Valery Upson, Morgan Ward, Amy Weisenbach, Keiona Williamson, and Hannah Wulkan.

In the New York Times Books division, Caroline Que helped us figure out the best path to take as we sought to turn the 1619 Project into a series of books, of which this is the first. We are thankful for her efforts, and those of Erika Sommer and Anika Burgess, who played critical organizational roles.

We are deeply grateful to Alia Hanna Habib, our extraordinary book agent, who guided us through every step of this process and whose faith, vision, and unending support made the work possible. Alia has been a fierce promoter and defender of the project from the beginning, and we are lucky to have her in our corner.

The process of turning the original magazine issue into this book began in late 2019 and has taken almost two years. More than anyone else, the people responsible for that accomplishment are the writers whose essays, poems, and fiction are found in these pages. We are enormously grateful for the work they shared with us. Those who are new to the project brought fresh energy that enlarged and sharpened our vision. To those whose work appeared in the original magazine, we will always feel a particular sense of gratitude. They gave the project its start, and our admiration for them has been deepened by the dedication they have shown in revising and expanding on their original compositions.

In preparing this book, we sought the counsel of numerous historians as peer reviewers. All of the essays were reviewed in their entirety by scholars with subject-area expertise. Their notes, suggestions, and big-picture feedback strengthened the book, and we are grateful for their time and expertise. We wish to acknowledge the contributions of the following peer reviewers: Daina Ramey Berry, David Blight, Daphne Brooks, William Darity, Marlene Daut, James Downs, Mary Elliott, Eric Foner, Eddie Glaude, Kali Gross, Nicholas Guyatt, Evelynn Hammonds, Kellie Carter Jackson, Walter Johnson, Martha Jones, Peniel Joseph, Rowena McClinton, Caitlin Rosenthal, Walter Rucker, Claudio Saunt, Calvin Schermerhorn, Manisha Sinha, Thomas Sugrue, Alan Taylor, David Waldstreicher, and Judith Weisenfeld. The input we received from these distinguished scholars was a critical stage of the book's development process. Martha Jones, in particular, has gone above and beyond in her support and helpful advice.

We are especially indebted to Eric Foner, who has been a key source of information, insight, guidance, and support since the project's early days. His teaching has informed the project in many ways (not the least of which is that several of its contributors and peer reviewers are his former students). He gave us critical feedback on all aspects of the book that relate to Reconstruction, a period his scholarship has illuminated perhaps more than any other living historian's.

In addition to those historians and scholars consulted during the peer review process, our fact-checkers drew upon the expertise of many others. In particular, we wish to recognize Douglas A. Blackmon, Lundy Braun, Elizabeth Hinton, Woody Holton, Philip Misevich, Ashley Nellis, Greg O'Malley, Seth Rockman, and Wendy Sawyer. We are grateful to all of the scholars who read the book and gave us suggestions for improving it. Any errors that remain are ours, not theirs.

Care and thoughtfulness also went into selecting the portrait photography that appears in this book. For that we are grateful to our collaborator Kimberly Annece Henderson, whose deep knowledge of African American archival photography was a gift.

We were fortunate to have a true design pro pulling all of these disparate elements together. Many thanks are due to Bobby Martin of Champions Design for his expertise, steady hands, smart ideas, and considerable grace under deadline pressure.

Late in the game, on a tight schedule, Adam McNeil compiled, vetted, and formatted the endnotes, and we are grateful for his efforts.

All of this was made possible by the wisdom, vision, and patience of an extraordinary editor and publisher, Christopher Jackson, who began speaking to us about turning the project into a book the week after it was published. We could not have done so without his deft guidance. Chris's incisive notes sharpened the essays, and his support and understanding during a long and challenging process made the job less daunting. We are lucky to have found an editor and publisher who presided over the creation of this book with benevolence, graciousness, and calm.

Chris also assembled a remarkable team at his imprint, One World, and from the Penguin Random House staff, to help usher this book into print. That team includes Avideh Bashirrad, Mika Kasuga, and Sun Robinson-Smith on the editorial side, and the production team of Liz Carbonell, Jane Farnol, Sarah Feightner, Alice Gribbin, Loren Noveck, Simon Sullivan, and Bonnie Thompson, who managed copy and design. We are grateful as well to Carla Bruce, Susan Corcoran, Andrea Pura, and Rachel Rokicki in publicity; Jennifer Childs, Elizabeth Fabian, Michael Gentile, Lulu Martinez, Allan Spencer, Travis Temple, Alan Walker, Daniel Wikey, Kaiulani Williams, and Kaz Woods in marketing; and Cynthia Lasky, Ruth Liebmann, and Allyson Pearl in sales. Lastly we are indebted to Greg Mollica and Michael Morris for their work on the cover design. It takes many people to launch a book like this, and we appreciate all of them.

Though most of the members of the staff of *The New York Times Magazine* did not work directly on this book, without their support and understanding we would never have been able to give it the focus it required. Some members of the staff also contributed directly to these pages. Gail Bichler's guidance helped us arrive at the final design. Sasha Weiss edited the chapter on the history of American music. And the entire book was fact-checked by the magazine's researchers. Once again, their work on this book was indispensable. We are indebted to Riley Blanton, Julia Bozzone, Jennifer Conrad, Mark de Silva, Jamie Fisher, Lu Fong, Sameen Gauhar, Timothy Hodler, Robert Liguori, Lia Miller, Jordan Reed, Christian Smith, Steven Stern, and Bill Vourvoulias for their careful attention to the essays, fiction, and poetry in the book. Their diligence did more than catch errors; it deepened and improved the work. Thanks, as well, to Nandi Rodrigo and David McCraw, who gave important legal advice.

Special recognition is due to Alexander Samaha, an assistant editor at the magazine, who wore so many hats it is difficult to count them all. Without his dedication and masterful organizational skills, our efforts would surely have run aground.

We feel more gratitude than can be expressed for our families, whose patience was sometimes tried by the many twists and turns of this long process, but whose support and dedication were never ever found wanting. Mary, Leo, and Josiah; Sam, Wyatt, and June; Sam, Anya, Katya, and Silas; Faraji and Najya—thank you all for your love and understanding.

When the special issue of the magazine was first published, in the summer of 2019, on the four hundredth anniversary of the beginning of American slavery, we decided we would call this effort a "project" because we wanted to emphasize that its work would be ongoing and would not culminate with any single publication. What has made that true is the enthusiasm of the many readers, listeners, teachers, students, and supporters whose engagement has sustained the project and brought it to this point. We are grateful for your response, and we trust you will help us continue this work long into the future.

—Nikole Hannah-Jones, Caitlin Roper, Ilena Silverman, and Jake Silverstein

Nikole's Acknowledgments

How does one even begin to write an acknowledgment for a project that has been in some ways a decades-long endeavor, that has completely consumed and subsumed my life for more than two years, that could not exist without the input, support, encouragement, affirmation, empathy, and strength so freely, consistently, and graciously offered by so many? I write this as a way of saying that the task is impossible. I have been touched and lifted up and inspired by so many. If you are not mentioned here, it is a failing of the mind and not of the heart.

As a group, the 1619 Project editors have tried to acknowledge and express gratitude to the many, many people who made this work possible. Here I want to add some thanks that are personal to me.

First, I have to thank my partners Jake Silverstein, Ilena Silverman, and Caitlin Roper. From the moment I first pitched this project, you all embraced the idea with passion and a sense of purpose. The respect, care, and sense of mission that you have shown for this work is something I will never forget. Without your myriad talents, your vision and belief, and the countless hours we spent to make sure we did this work justice, the 1619 Project simply would not be. Your unwavering commitment to telling these stories the right way is something I will cherish. We began this journey as colleagues, but we arrive here as dear friends.

I am grateful to a brilliant, warm, and encouraging educator named Ray Dial. Mr. Dial, you introduced a sassy, curious young girl to an entire world of knowledge, and sowed the seeds for all that would come after. You fed my intellect, encouraged my skepticism, and taught me it is okay to push the boundaries of others' expectations of you. I wish that every student could have a Mr. Dial in her life. Thank you.

Alia Habib, the moment we met, it was clear that you were the one—you are brilliant, confident, real, and a fiercely loyal advocate for your writers.

Thank you for understanding me, for fighting for me, and for helping usher this work into the world.

And to Chris Jackson, I knew from the beginning only you could edit this book. Your mind, skill, and dedication to centering our stories are unmatched. Thank you for your faith, and I promise I will eventually give you that other book I owe you!

I am thankful for the constellation of writers and scholars—too many to name—whose work has inspired and influenced my own and who have publicly and privately supported me and this work even when it was not politically comfortable to do so. This was especially true of Black women scholars and writers, whose constant words of encouragement and affirmation on my hardest days were the only reason I got out of bed. Especially, I'd like to thank Carol Anderson, Keisha N. Blain, Kimberlé Crenshaw, Tiffany Cross, Melissa Harris-Perry, Karla FC Holloway, Sherrilyn Ifill, Kellie Jones, Robin Mitchell, Soledad O'Brien, Joy-Ann Reid, and Deb Willis. And Martha S. Jones, I can never repay the debt I owe. You are truly the vanguard and the type of woman every woman deserves to have in her corner.

To Yamiche Alcindor, LaSharah S. Bunting, Mary Elliott, Erica L. Green, Errin Haines, Joy Harrington, Andrea Jordan, Shanitha McAfee, Kim Melton, Natalie Moore, Melissa Navas, Nikita Stewart, Sheritta Stokes, Chabre Vickers, Keiona Williams, Lauren Williams, and Jenna Wortham, I would do battle with you and for you any and every day, just as you would for me. You are dazzling lights and among the strongest women I know. I will never forget how you helped get me through, built me up, and straightened my back again and again.

Reginald Dwayne Betts, Jelani Cobb, Trymaine Lee, Wesley Lowery, Wesley Morris, Ron Nixon, and my mentors Kevin Merida, Brent Staples, Will Sutton, and DeWayne Wickham, your support and your counsel have been invaluable in my life. To Ben and Shonique Greene, thank you for your friendship.

To every friend and stranger who has sent emails, cards, flowers, bourbon, since this project first published, you sustained me and I will never forget these kindnesses.

To Ta-Nehisi, my brother, what can I say? No one who is not related to me is as real with me as you are. I keep that note you sent me during one of my lowest moments, and I promise to try to live up to the charge. Grateful to be a sword among lions with you.

To Pierre-Antoine Louis, it's not often that a woman in her forties finds a new best friend, but I think we knew each other in another life. Thank you for the listening ear during the tough times, and the joy during the best. I would not survive any of this without you.

DaVonne Darby, you have kept me sane, you have kept me kind, and I do not know how I got so lucky to find that gem from Detroit, but I am grateful every day.

To the Hillmans—Eric, Tiara, Sam, Scarlett, and Charlie—you have looked out for me, you have looked out for my family through all the long hours, the stress, the highs and the lows of birthing this project. You all are closer to family than friends. Thank you.

To my sister-cousin Chimere, your daily texts, just to make sure I was still breathing, just to make sure I was taking care of myself, just to tell me how proud you are of me, are something for which I will always be grateful and will always cherish. To my sisters, Traci Hannah-Cauchi and Michele Hannah de Gutierrez, and my nieces Shabbrea, Briana, and Temiah Tooson, I love you. To the other half of my family, the Lewises and Joneses, thank you for making me your daughter and your sister and for the constant love and support.

To Sister Sonia Sanchez, I do not think it is possible for you to understand what it meant to me when you told me that even though the greatest Black writers of your generation, who wrote Black works about Black people for Black people, never earned the Pulitzer, because I had won it for the 1619 Project your sacrifices had not been in vain. Nothing I have achieved, no word I have written, would be possible without you all. You deserved better from our country, but we, your people, see you and we honor you.

Ida B. Wells-Barnett, you gave me the template, providing a fearless example of what I myself one day would try to be. I pray my legacy honors you.

To my mom, Cheryl Novotny Hannah, no daughter could ever ask for a better champion, a more kind and nurturing influence. There has never been a time when I needed you that you have not been there. There has not been a single dream of mine that you did not support. I inherited my empathy and determination to make this a more just world from you. I am so grateful to be your child.

To my dad, Milton Hannah, I know you died thinking your life had not been much—you said these words to me. But even though you did not live to see this day, you planted the seeds. Your story has helped millions of Americans to see this country for what it is and to understand Black Americans as the greatest force for freedom in this land. You have accomplished things you could not have imagined. I am so proud that your face is the first face every person who purchases this book will see.

To Faraji, my partner, my friend, my proudest advocate, and my most ardent defender. You have been here since I was working two jobs and wondering if I'd ever live up to my own expectations. You have picked me up, cussed me out when I deserved it, put up with my moods when you didn't deserve it, taken up the slack when I was working long hours or on the road, and, most of all, loved me unconditionally. I could not have done this without you. Thank you for always, always being there.

Najya, you are and shall remain my greatest achievement. I know it has not been easy for you to have to share me so often, to pass all those nights where I have not been there to tuck you in. I hope you know how your hugs make everything in my world feel right and how your spirit affirms every day why I do what I do. Keep that heart, keep that sense of justice, keep that powerful sense of self. You are the embodiment not only of my wildest dreams, but of our ancestors as well. Momma loves you so much.

I want to express my gratitude to every person who has supported the 1619 Project since we first published in August 2019. I will always cherish the videos and photos and posts you have shared, the emails and notes you have sent me, the conversations we took part in together as we gathered all over the country to discuss this work. I am particularly grateful to the fearless educators who are determined to teach this, and our history, more truthfully even as they face prohibitions from state legislatures, and to those who have organized against these laws all across the country. You all have affirmed why this project exists.

And last, I want to thank the ancestors and the more than 30 million descendants of American slavery. I never forget who this work is for and to whom I belong. We must always hold our heads up high because we come from, and we are, a great people.

I am just a girl from Waterloo who saw more for my life than this world could imagine. Over the course of the last two years, I have experienced the most exhilarating highs and some of the most painful lows, but I have never wavered from the certainty that this is the work I have been called to do. It is my greatest honor. I am not perfect, but I have strived to do this work justice and with integrity. I close with the fuller context of the words you read in the preface, words of Frederick Douglass, our nation's North Star and mine:

"As far as this volume can reach that point I have now brought my readers to the end of my story. What may remain of life to me, through what experiences I may pass, what heights I may attain, into what depths I may fall, what good or ill may come to me, or proceed from me in this breathing world where all is change and uncertainty and largely at the mercy of powers over which the individual man has no absolute control; all this, if thought worthy and useful, will probably be told by others when I have passed from the busy stage of life. The story of the master never wanted for narrators. The masters, to tell their story, had at call all the talent and genius that wealth and influence could command. They have had their full day in court. Literature, theology, philosophy, law and learning have come willingly to their service, and, if condemned, they have not been condemned unheard." As Douglass said, "My part has been to tell the story of the slave."

NOTES

Preface: Origins

1. Lerone Bennett, Jr., *Before the Mayflower: 1619–1962* (New York: Penguin Books, 1968), 28–29.
2. "Executive Summary," *Teaching Hard History*, Southern Poverty Law Center, January 31, 2018, www.splcenter.org/20180131/teaching-hard-history.
3. Yanan Wong, "'Workers' or Slaves? Textbook Maker Backtracks After Mother's Online Complaint," *Washington Post*, October 5, 2015, www.washingtonpost.com/news/morning-mix/wp/2015/10/05/immigrant-workers-or-slaves-textbook-maker-backtracks-after-mothers-online-complaint/.
4. "Executive Summary," *Teaching Hard History*.
5. Texas Administrative Code, Rule §113.16, Social Studies, Grade 5, Adopted 2018, texreg.sos.state.tx.us/public/readtac$ext.TacPage?sl=T&app=9&p_dir=F&p_rloc=196530&p_tloc=14782&p_ploc=1&pg=3&p_tac=&ti=19&pt=2&ch=113&rl=15; tea.texas.gov/sites/default/files/2019_2020%20Gr8%20SS_Curriculum%20Framework FORWEB.pdf.
6. "Texas 8th-Graders Asked to List Positives of Slavery," Associated Press, April 21, 2018, apnews.com/article/95a731ccf60341c49d3db65c07fc1bed.
7. Emily Guskin, Scott Clement, and Joe Heim, "Americans Show Spotty Knowledge About the History of Slavery but Acknowledge Its Enduring Effects," *Washington Post*, August 28, 2019, www.washingtonpost.com/education/2019/08/28/americans-show-spotty-knowledge-about-history-slavery-acknowledge-its-enduring-effects/.
8. Hasan Kwame Jeffries, "Preface," *Teaching Hard History*, www.splcenter.org/20180131/teaching-hard-history.
9. "How Slavery Is Taught Today," *Teaching Hard History*, www.splcenter.org/20180131/teaching-hard-history.
10. Ira Berlin, "Coming to Terms with Slavery in Twenty-first-Century America," in *Slavery and Public History: The Tough Stuff of American Memory*, ed. James Oliver Horton and Lois E. Horton (New York: New Press, 2006), 4.
11. Author interview with Jelani Cobb.
12. Guskin, Clement, and Heim, "Americans Show Spotty Knowledge."
13. Nikita Stewart, "The 1619 Project," *New York Times Magazine*, August 19, 2019, www.nytimes.com/interactive/2019/08/19/magazine/slavery-american-schools.html.
14. Hasan Kwame Jeffries, "The Courage to Teach Hard History," Learning for Justice, February 1, 2018, www.learningforjustice.org/magazine/the-courage-to-teach-hard-history.

15. Nadar Issa, "How CPS Students Are Learning About Black History and White Supremacy—and How That's Helping Them Understand George Floyd," *Chicago Sun-Times*, June 5, 2020, chicago.suntimes.com/education/2020/6/5/21279788/1619-project-cps-chicago-public-schools-black-history-white-supremacy-george-floyd-civil-rights.

16. The sentence, which has been slightly revised in the context of the new material, can be found on page 16 of this book.

17. "From the Editor's Desk: 1619 and All That," *American Historical Review* 125, no. 1 (February 2020): xv–xxi, doi.org/10.1093/ahr/rhaa041.

18. Mary Ellen Hicks, Twitter, May 24, 2021, twitter.com/DrMaryHicks/status/1396843472930357251.

19. Allen C. Guelzo, "Preaching a Conspiracy Theory," *City Journal*, December 8, 2019, www.city-journal.org/1619-project-conspiracy-theory.

20. Saving American History Act of 2020, S. 4292, 116th Cong., 2nd Session (July 23, 2020), www.cotton.senate.gov/imo/media/doc/200723%20Saving%20American%20History%20Act.pdf.

21. "President's Advisory 1776 Commission," *Federal Register*, January 12, 2021, www.federalregister.gov/documents/2021/01/12/2021-00525/presidents-advisory-1776-commission.

22. American Historical Association, "AHA Condemns Report of Advisory 1776 Commission (January 2021)," January 20, 2021, www.historians.org/news-and-advocacy/aha-advocacy/aha-statement-condemning-report-of-advisory-1776-commission-(january-2021).

23. Michael D. Shear, "On Day 1, Biden Moves to Undo Trump's Legacy," *New York Times*, March 5, 2021, www.nytimes.com/2021/01/20/us/politics/biden-executive-action.html.

24. www.chalkbeat.org/22525983/map-critical-race-theory-legislation-teaching-racism.

25. Texas Legislature, A Bill to Be Entitled: An Act Relating to the Establishment and Duties of the Texas 1836 Project, H.B. 2497, capitol.texas.gov/tlodocs/87R/billtext/pdf/HB02497I.pdf#navpanes=0.

26. Peter H. Wood, "Slave Labor Camps in Early America: Overcoming Denial and Discovering the Gulag," in *Inequality in Early America*, ed. Carla Gardina Pestana and Sharon V. Salinger (1999; repr., Hanover, N.H.: University Press of New England, 2015), 222.

27. Frederick Douglass, *The Life and Times of Frederick Douglass* (Boston: De Wolfe, Fiske, 1892), 581.

28. One essay was written jointly by a historian and a former law professor.

29. Michael A. McDonnell, Clare Corbould, Frances M. Clarke, and W. Fitzhugh Brundage, eds., *Remembering the Revolution: Memory, History, and Nation Making from Independence to the Civil War* (Amherst: University of Massachusetts Press, 2013), 3.

30. Gary B. Nash, "For Whom Will the Liberty Bell Toll? From Controversy to Cooperation," in Horton and Horton, *Slavery and Public History*, 82.

31. McDonnell, Corbould, Clarke, and Brundage, *Remembering the Revolution*, 13.

32. Author interview with Woody Holton.

33. Ana Lucia Araujo, *Slavery in the Age of Memory: Engaging the Past* (New York: Bloomsbury, 2020), 184.

34. Michel-Rolph Trouillot, *Silencing the Past: Power and the Production of History* (Boston: Beacon, 1995), xxiii.

35. David W. Blight, *Race and Reunion: The Civil War in American Memory* (Cambridge, Mass.: Harvard University Press, 2001), 9.

36. Nikole Hannah-Jones, "The Resegregation of Jefferson County," *New York Times Magazine*, September 6, 2017, www.nytimes.com/2017/09/06/magazine/the-resegregation-of-jefferson-county.html.

37. Frederick Douglass, *Oration Delivered in Corinthian Hall, Rochester* (Rochester, N.Y.: Lee, Mann, 1852), 20.

38. John R. McKivigan, Julie Husband, and Heather L. Kaufman, eds., *The Speeches of Frederick Douglass: A Critical Edition* (New Haven, Conn.: Yale University Press, 2018), 205.

39. W.E.B. Du Bois, *Black Folk Then and Now: An Essay in the History and Sociology of the Negro Race* (New York: Henry Holt and Company, 1939), vii.

Chapter 1: Democracy

1. Campbell Gibson and Kay Jung, "Historical Census Statistics on Population Totals by Race, 1790 to 1990, and by Hispanic Origin, 1970 to 1990, for the United States, Regions, Divisions, and States," Working Paper No. 56 (2002), www.census.gov/content/dam/Census/library/working-papers/2002/demo/POP-twps0056.pdf.

2. NAACP, "History of Lynching in America," naacp.org/find-resources/history-explained/history-lynching-america.

3. The Equal Justice Initiative, "Lynching in America: Confronting the Legacy of Racial Terror," 2017, lynchinginamerica.eji.org/report/.

4. Beth Austin, "1619: Virginia's First Africans," Hampton History Museum, hampton.gov/DocumentCenter/View/24075/1619-Virginias-First-Africans?bidId=.

5. SlaveVoyages, "Trans-Atlantic Slave Trade—Estimates," www.slavevoyages.org/assessment/estimates.

6. Ibid.

7. Ibid.

8. "The Fight over Inoculation During the 1721 Boston Smallpox Epidemic," Science in the News, Graduate School of Arts of Sciences, Harvard University, sitn.hms.harvard.edu/flash/special-edition-on-infectious-disease/2014/the-fight-over-inoculation-during-the-1721-boston-smallpox-epidemic/.

9. Edward E. Baptist, *The Half Has Never Been Told: Slavery and the Making of American Capitalism* (New York: Basic Books, 2014), 114. (Baptist cites data from *Cotton and the Growth of the American Economy*, a 1967 book by the economic historian Stuart Bruchey that makes this case.)

10. Edward Lawler, Jr., "President's House Slavery: By the Numbers," www.ushistory.org/presidentshouse/slaves/numbers.php.

11. Architect of the Capitol, "Philip Reid and the Statue of Freedom," www.aoc.gov/explore-capitol-campus/art/statue-freedom/philip-reid.

12. Tracing Center, "James DeWolf," tracingcenter.org/resources/background/james-dewolf/.

13. Anne Farrow, Joel Lang, and Jenifer Frank, *Complicity: How the North Promoted, Prolonged, and Profited from Slavery* (New York: Ballantine Books, 2006), 4.

14. Eli Ginzberg, *The Troublesome Presence: American Democracy and the Negro* (New York: Free Press of Glencoe, 1964), 44.

15. National Park Service, "Declaration House: Independence National Historical Park, Pennsylvania," www.nps.gov/inde/learn/historyculture/places-declarationhouse.html.

16. "Robert Hemmings," Thomas Jefferson Encyclopedia, www.monticello.org/site/research-and-collections/robert-hemings.

17. Annette Gordon-Reed, *The Hemingses of Monticello: An American Family* (New York: Norton, 2008), 131–32.

18. Smithsonian National Museum of African American History and Culture, "Africans in British North America," www.monticello.org/slavery/paradox-of-liberty/african-slavery-in-colonial-british-north-america/africans-in-british-north-america.

19. William Goodell, *The American Slave Code in Theory and Practice: Its Distinctive Features Shown by Its Statutes, Judicial Decisions, and Illustrative Facts* (New York: American and Foreign Anti-Slavery Society, 1853), 105.

20. Peter A. Dorsey, *Common Bondage: Slavery as Metaphor in Revolutionary America* (Knoxville: University of Tennessee Press, 2009), xi.

21. Ibid.

22. Patricia Bradley, *Slavery, Propaganda, and the American Revolution* (Jackson: University of Mississippi Press, 1999), xx–xxi.

23. George Washington to Bryan Fairfax, August 24, 1774, Founders Online, founders.archives .gov/GEWN-02-10-02-0097.

24. Bradley, *Slavery, Propaganda, and the American Revolution*, 24.

25. Author interview with Woody Holton, April 30, 2021.

26. Woody Holton, *Forced Founders: Indians, Debtors, Slaves, and the Making of the American Revolution in Virginia* (Chapel Hill: University of North Carolina Press, 1999), 145.

27. Ibid., 133–36.

28. Lord Dunmore's Proclamation, November 7, 1775, www.gilderlehrman.org/history-resources/ spotlight-primary-source/lord-dunmores-proclamation-1775#.

29. Holton, *Forced Founders*, 158.

30. Alan Taylor, *The Internal Enemy: Slavery and War in Virginia, 1772–1832* (New York: Norton, 2013), 21.

31. Holton, *Forced Founders*, 140–41.

32. Author interview with Woody Holton.

33. Gerald Horne, *The Counter-Revolution of 1776: Slave Resistance and the Origins of the United States of America* (New York: New York University Press, 2014), 224.

34. Samuel Johnson, *Taxation No Tyranny: An Answer to the Resolutions and Address of the American Congress* (London: T. Cadell, 1775), 89.

35. Sidney Kaplan, "The 'Domestic Insurrections' of the Declaration of Independence," *Journal of Negro History* 61, no. 3 (1976): 243.

36. Holton, *Forced Founders*, 158.

37. Michael E. Groth, "Black Loyalists and African American Allegiance in the Mid-Hudson Valley," in *The Other Loyalists: People, Royalism, and the Revolution in the Middle Colonies, 1763–1787*, ed. Joseph S. Tiedmann, Eugene R. Fingerhut, and Robert W. Venables (Albany: SUNY Press, 2009), 82.

38. James Oliver Horton and Lois E. Horton, *Slavery and Public History: The Tough Stuff of American History* (Chapel Hill: University of North Carolina Press, 2009), 36.

39. "Interview with Ira Berlin," *Race: The Power of an Illusion*, PBS, 2003, www.pbs.org/race/000 _About/002_04-background-02-08.htm.

40. Those five slave societies are ancient Rome, ancient Greece, Brazil, all of the Caribbean during the eighteenth and nineteenth centuries, and the American South.

41. David Blight, "The Civil War and Reconstruction Era, 1845–1877: Lecture 3 Transcript," openmedia.yale.edu/projects/iphone/departments/hist/hist119/transcript03.html.

42. "The Story We Tell," *Race: The Power of an Illusion*, California Newsreel, newsreel.org/ transcripts/race2.htm.

43. Edmund S. Morgan, *American Slavery, American Freedom* (New York: Norton, 1975), 381.

44. David Waldstreicher, *Slavery's Constitution: From Revolution to Ratification* (New York: Hill and Wang, 2009), 3–9.

45. Nathaniel Breading, Edmund Randolph, and Samuel Bryan, *Observations on the Proposed Constitution for the United States of America, Clearly Shewing It to Be a Complete System of Aristocracy and Tyranny, and Destructive of the Rights and Liberties of the People*, Evans Early American Imprint Collection, University of Michigan, 81, quod.lib.umich.edu/e/evans/n16599.00 01.001?rgn=main;view=fulltext.

46. Nicholas Buccola, ed., *The Essential Douglass: Selected Writings and Speeches* (New York: Hackett, 2016), 41.
47. Ibid., 39, 69.
48. "Jeff. Davis' Inaugural Address," *New York Times*, February 26, 1862, www.nytimes.com/1862/02/26/archives/jeff-davis-inaugural-address-acknowledgment-of-rebel-defeats-the.html.
49. "Remember Haiti," John Carter Brown Library, www.brown.edu/Facilities/John_Carter_Brown_Library/exhibitions/remember_haiti/economy.php.
50. The Haitian Revolution led to the Louisiana Purchase, which expanded slavery in the United States. "The United States and the Haitian Revolution, 1791–1804," Office of the Historian, Foreign Service Institute, United States Department of State, history.state.gov/milestones/1784-1800/haitian-rev.
51. Thomas Jefferson to John Wayles Eppes, June 30, 1820, The Jefferson Monticello, tjrs.monticello.org/letter/380.
52. Taylor, *Internal Enemy*, 51.
53. Taylor, *Internal Enemy*, 30.
54. David Brion Davis, *Inhuman Bondage: The Rise and Fall of Slavery in the New World* (New York: Oxford University Press, 2006), 6.
55. Robert J. Cottrol, Raymond T. Diamond, and Leland B. Ware, *Brown v. Board of Education: Caste, Culture, and the Constitution* (Lawrence: University Press of Kansas), 3.
56. United States Supreme Court, Roger Brooke Taney, John H. Van Evrie, and Samuel A. Cartwright, *The Dred Scott Decision: Opinion of Chief Justice Taney* (New York: Van Evrie, Horton, 1860), 27, www.loc.gov/item/17001543/.
57. Kate Masur, "The African American Delegation to Abraham Lincoln: A Reappraisal," *Civil War History* 56, no. 2 (June 2010): 117–18.
58. Abraham Lincoln's first debate with Stephen Douglas, August 21, 1858, housedivided.dickinson.edu/sites/lincoln/first-debate-with-douglas-august-21-1858/.
59. Michael Vorenberg, "Abraham Lincoln and the Politics of Black Colonization," *Journal of the Abraham Lincoln Association* 14, no. 2 (Summer 1993): 22–45, quod.lib.umich.edu/j/jala/2629860.0014.204/--abraham-lincoln-and-the-politics-of-black-colonization?rgn=main;view=fulltext.
60. Abraham Lincoln, "Address on Colonization to a Deputation of Negroes," *Collected Works of Abraham Lincoln*, vol. 5, University of Michigan Digital Library Production Services, 372–75, quod.lib.umich.edu/l/lincoln/lincoln5/1:812?rgn=div1;view=fulltext.
61. Ibid.
62. Even those Black men who were in support of colonization were angered by his condescension in this meeting.
63. Lincoln, "Address on Colonization to a Deputation of Negroes."
64. Dora L. Costa, "Pensions and Retirement Among Black Union Army Veterans," *Journal of Economic History* 70, no. 3 (September 2010): 22, www.ncbi.nlm.nih.gov/pmc/articles/PMC3004158/pdf/nihms-200553.pdf.
65. "Black Soldiers in the U.S. Military During the Civil War," National Archives, www.archives.gov/education/lessons/blacks-civil-war; Eric Foner, *The Second Founding: How the Civil War and Reconstruction Remade the Constitution* (New York: Norton, 2019), 44; Martha S. Jones, *Vanguard: How Black Women Broke Barriers, Won the Vote, and Insisted on Equality for All* (New York: Basic Books, 2020), 98.
66. Thavolia Glymph, "'Between Slavery and Freedom': Rethinking the Slaves' War" (conference presentation, The Future of the African Past, Washington, D.C., May 19–21, 2016).
67. "Timeline of Frederick Douglass and Family," www.math.buffalo.edu/~sww/0history/hwny

-douglass-family.html; "Frederick Douglass and Abraham Lincoln," www.whitehouse history.org/frederick-douglass-and-abraham-lincoln.

68. Buccola, *Essential Douglass*, 242–43.

69. Author interview with Christopher Bonner, March 18, 2021.

70. "The African American Mosaic: Abolition," Library of Congress, www.loc.gov/exhibits/african/afam005.html.

71. W.E.B. Du Bois, *The Souls of Black Folk: Essays and Sketches* (Chicago: A. C. McClung, 1903), 5.

72. Martin R. Delany, "Our Elevation in the United States," 1852, *Teaching American History*, teachingamericanhistory.org/library/document/our-elevation-in-the-united-states/.

73. Foner, *Second Founding*, 51.

74. Ibid., 56.

75. Civil Rights Act of 1866, An Act to Protect All Persons in the United States in Their Civil Rights, and Furnish the Means of Their Vindication, loveman.sdsu.edu/docs/1866FirstCivil RightsAct.pdf.

76. Foner, *Second Founding*, 56.

77. History.com Editors, "Black Leaders During Reconstruction," History, June 24, 2010, www .history.com/topics/american-civil-war/black-leaders-during-reconstruction.

78. "Building the Black Community: The School," America's Reconstruction: People and Politics After the Civil War, www.digitalhistory.uh.edu/exhibits/reconstruction/section2/section2 _school.html.

79. James Anderson, *The Education of Blacks in the South, 1860–1935* (Chapel Hill: University of North Carolina Press, 1988), 18.

80. University of South Carolina Reconstruction Records, delphi.tcl.sc.edu/library/digital/collections/reconstruct.html.

81. Davis, *Inhuman Bondage*, 226.

82. Waters McIntosh, *Slave Narratives: A Folk History of Slavery in the United States from Interviews with Former Slaves*, vol. 2 (Washington, D.C.: Federal Writers' Project of the Works Progress Administration for the State of Arkansas, 1941).

83. Deposition of Isaac Woodard, Jr., April 23, 1946, faculty.uscupstate.edu/amyers/deposition .html.

84. Alex Ross, "How American Racism Influenced Hitler," *New Yorker,* April 23, 2018, www .newyorker.com/magazine/2018/04/30/how-american-racism-influenced-hitler.

85. "A Brief History of Jim Crow," Constitutional Rights Foundation, www.crf-usa.org/black -history-month/a-brief-history-of-jim-crow; "What Was Jim Crow," Jim Crow Museum of Racist Memorabilia, Ferris State University, www.ferris.edu/jimcrow/what.htm; Pauli Murray, ed., *States' Laws on Race and Color* (Athens: University of Georgia Press, 1997), 15–18.

86. Chad Williams, *Torchbearers of Democracy: African American Soldiers in the World War I Era* (Chapel Hill: University of North Carolina Press, 2010), 31.

87. "Double V Campaign," *Pittsburgh Courier,* February 7, 1942; "The Courier's Double 'V' for a Double Victory Campaign Gets Country-Wide Support," *Pittsburgh Courier,* February 14, 1942.

88. "The Civil Rights Act of 1875: February 04, 1875," History, Arts, & Archives, United States House of Representatives, history.house.gov/Historical-Highlights/1851-1900/The-Civil-Rights -Act-of-1875/.

89. www.americanprogress.org/issues/economy/news/2020/09/28/490702/persistent-black -white-unemployment-gap-built-labor-market; www.pewresearch.org/fact-tank/2018/05/ 24/republicans-turn-more-negative-toward-refugees-as-number-admitted-to-u-s-plummets/; www.pewresearch.org/politics/2021/06/02/most-americans-favor-the-death-penalty-despite -concerns-about-its-administration/; www.pewresearch.org/fact-tank/2021/04/22/most-ameri cans-support-a-15-federal-minimum-wage/.

90. Joe R. Feagin, *How Blacks Built America: Labor, Culture, Freedom, and Democracy* (Oxford: Taylor & Francis, 2015), 125.
91. Bracey's quote is taken from Feagin's *How Blacks Built America,* 12.
92. Sidney Mintz and Richard Price, *The Birth of African American Culture: An Anthropological Perspective* (Boston: Beacon, 1975), 20.
93. Ibid., 51.
94. Langston Hughes, "I Too," www.poetryfoundation.org/poems/47558/i-too.

Chapter 2: Race

1. Arlington County, Virginia Marriage License Registry, www.robinhoodesq.com/docs/marriage/documents/va/1_Arlington_Races.pdf.
2. Author interview with Ashley Ramkishun, January 29, 2021.
3. John Eligon, "Quadroon? Moor? Virginia Sued for Making Those Who Wed Say What They Are," *New York Times,* September 8, 2019, www.nytimes.com/2019/09/08/us/virginia-marriage-race.html; Hannah Natanson, "Virginia Couples No Longer Have to Disclose Race on Marriage License Applications, State Attorney General Says," *Washington Post,* September 14, 2019, www.washingtonpost.com/local/social-issues/virginia-couples-no-longer-have-to-disclose-race-on-marriage-license-applications-state-attorney-general-says/2019/09/14/4f40d578-d6fb-11e9-9610-fb56c5522e1c_story.html.
4. *Sophie Rogers v. Virginia State Registrar,* Order, E.D. Va. Civil Action No. 1:19-cv-01149 (RDA/IDD) (October 11, 2019), www.robinhoodesq.com/docs/marriage/documents/va/49-O-Granting PIMSJ.pdf.
5. An Act to Preserve Racial Integrity, March 1924, www.robinhoodesq.com/docs/marriage/documents/va/5_Plecker_Report_and_Racial_Integrity_Act.pdf.
6. *Loving v. Virginia,* 388 U.S. 1, 11 (1967), www.oyez.org/cases/1966/395.
7. Gandalf Nicholas and Allison L. Skinner, "Constructing Race: How People Categorize Others and Themselves in Racial Terms," in *Handbook of Categorization in Cognitive Science,* ed. Henri Cohen and Claire Lefebvre, 2nd ed. (Amsterdam: Elsevier Science, 2017), 607, 612.
8. Destiny Peery, "Race at the Boundaries: Toward a Better Understanding of the Construction of Race Through the Study of Racial Categorization of Ambiguous Targets" (PhD diss., Northwestern University, 2012); Destiny Peery and Galen V. Bodenhausen, "Black + White = Black: Hypodescent in Reflexive Categorization of Racially Ambiguous Faces," *Psychological Science* 19, no. 10 (2008): 973–77.
9. Osagie K. Obasogie, *Blinded by Sight: Seeing Race Through the Eyes of the Blind* (Stanford, Calif.: Stanford Law Books, 2014), 9.
10. Paul A. Lombardo, "Miscegenation, Eugenics, and Racism: Historical Footnotes to *Loving v. Virginia,*" *U.C. Davis Law Review* 21, no. 421 (1987–88): 424–25 and throughout.
11. *Loving v. Virginia.*
12. Gunnar Myrdal, "Racial Beliefs in America," in *Theories of Race and Racism: A Reader,* ed. Les Back and John Solomos (London: Routledge, 2000), 87; Paul Finkelman, "Slavery, Law Of," Oxford African American Studies Center, December 1, 2006, oxfordaasc.com/view/10.1093/acref/9780195301731.001.0001/acref-9780195301731-e-51101.
13. Dorothy Roberts, *Fatal Invention: How Science, Politics, and Big Business Re-create Race in the Twenty-first Century* (New York: New Press, 2011), 8; Nell Irvin Painter, *The History of White People* (New York: Norton, 2011), 42.
14. Kevin Mumford, "After Hugh: Statutory Race Segregation in Colonial America, 1630–1725," *The American Journal of Legal History* 43, no. 3 (1999): 280.

15. Howard Bodenhorn, "The Mulatto Advantage: The Biological Consequences of Complexion in Rural Antebellum Virginia," *Journal of Interdisciplinary History* 33, no. 1 (2002): 24.

16. "Negro womens children to serve according to the condition of the mother" (1662), *Encyclopedia Virginia* (2020), encyclopediavirginia.org/entries/negro-womens-children-to-serve-according-to-the-condition-of-the-mother-1662/.

17. Jeffrey J. Pokorak, "Rape as a Badge of Slavery: The Legal History of, and Remedies for, Prosecutorial Race-of-Victim Charging Disparities," *Nevada Law Journal* 7, no. 1 (2006): 8–9.

18. Quoted in Estelle B. Freedman, *Redefining Rape* (Cambridge, Mass.: Harvard University Press, 2013), 29.

19. Daina Ramey Berry and Kali Nicole Gross, *A Black Women's History of the United States* (Boston: Beacon, 2020), 34.

20. Peter Wallenstein, "Race, Marriage, and the Law of Freedom: Alabama and Virginia, 1860s–1960: Personal Liberty and Private Law," *Chicago-Kent Law Review* 70, no. 371 (1994): 390, scholarship.kentlaw.iit.edu/cgi/viewcontent.cgi?article=2967&context=cklawreview.

21. Ibid., 392.

22. Ariela Gross and Alejandro de la Fuente, "Slaves, Free Blacks, and Race in the Legal Regimes of Cuba, Louisiana, and Virginia: A Comparison," *North Carolina Law Review* 91 (2013): 1699 and 1722, note 128, scholarship.law.unc.edu/cgi/viewcontent.cgi?article=4624&context=nclr&httpsredir=1&referer=.

23. Mary Sarah Bilder, "The Struggle over Immigration: Indentured Servants, Slaves, and Articles of Commerce," *Missouri Law Review* 61, no. 743 (1996): 759; William Waller Hening, ed., *The Statutes at Large; Being a Collection of All the Laws of Virginia, from the First Session of the Legislature, in the Year 1619* (New York: R. & W. & G. Bartow, 1819–23), specifically the passages at October 1705, "An Act Concerning Servants and Slaves," www.houseofrussell.com/legalhistory/alh/docs/virginiaslaverystatutes.html.

24. A. Leon Higginbotham, Jr., and Anne F. Jacobs, "The Law Only as an Enemy: The Legitimization of Racial Powerlessness Through the Colonial and Antebellum Criminal Laws of Virginia," *North Carolina Law Review* 70, no. 969 (1992): 1027–28, core.ac.uk/download/pdf/151514234.pdf.

25. Ibid., 1027.

26. Gross and de la Fuente, "Slaves, Free Blacks, and Race," 1730; Higginbotham and Jacobs, "The Law Only as an Enemy," 994.

27. Saidiya V. Hartman, *Scenes of Subjection: Terror, Slavery, and Self-Making in Nineteenth-Century America* (New York: Oxford University Press, 1997), 79–80.

28. Annette Gordon-Reed, "Sally Hemings," in *Four Hundred Souls: A Community History of African America, 1619–2019,* ed. Ibram X. Kendi and Keisha N. Blain, (New York: One World, 2021), 158–61.

29. *George v. State,* 37 Miss. 316, 317 (1859).

30. Jill Elaine Hasday, "Contest and Consent: A Legal History of Marital Rape," *California Law Review* 88, no. 1373 (2000): 1375–76, 1392.

31. Freedman, *Redefining Rape,* 15, 27; Deborah Gray White, *Ar'n't I a Woman?: Female Slaves in the Plantation South* (New York: Norton, 1999), 28–29.

32. White, *Ar'n't I a Woman?,* 28–29; Sharon Block, *Rape and Sexual Power in Early America* (Chapel Hill: University of North Carolina Press/Omohundro Institute of Early American History and Culture, 2006), 178.

33. Thelma Jennings, " 'Us Colored Women Had to Go Through A Plenty': Sexual Exploitation of African-American Slave Women," *Journal of Women's History* 1, no. 3 (1990): 60–61.

34. Rachel A. Feinstein, *When Rape Was Legal: The Untold History of Sexual Violence During Slavery* (New York: Routledge, 2019), 2.

35. Christine Kenneally, "Large DNA Study Traces Violent History of American Slavery," *New York Times,* July 23, 2020, nytimes.com/2020/07/23/science/23andme-african-ancestry.html; Steven J. Micheletti, Kaisa Bryc, Samantha G. Ancona Esselmann, William A. Freyman, Meghan E. Moreno, G. David Poznik, Anjali J. Shastri, and 23andMe Research Team, "Genetic Consequences of the Transatlantic Slave Trade in the Americas," *American Journal of Human Genetics* 107, no. 2 (2020): 265–77.

36. Freedman, *Redefining Rape,* 29.

37. Feinstein, *When Rape Was Legal,* 1.

38. Wilma King, " 'Prematurely Knowing of Evil Things': The Sexual Abuse of African American Girls and Young Women in Slavery and Freedom," *Journal of African American History* 99, no. 3 (2014): 179; Berry and Gross, *Black Women's History of the United States,* 82–83.

39. Stephanie M. H. Camp, "Early European Views of African Bodies: Beauty," in *Sexuality and Slavery: Reclaiming Intimate Histories in the Americas,* ed. Daina Ramey Berry and Leslie M. Harris (Athens: University of Georgia Press, 2018); Winthrop D. Jordan, *White Over Black: American Attitudes Toward The Negro, 1550–1812* (Chapel Hill: University of North Carolina Press, 1968), 32–40, 151.

40. White, *Ar'n't I a Woman,* 30.

41. Ibid., 37.

42. Freedman, *Redefining Rape,* 28.

43. Philip Alexander Bruce, *The Plantation Negro as a Freeman: Observations on His Character, Condition, and Prospects in Virginia* (New York: G.P. Putnam's Sons, 1889), 11.

44. Gregory N. Price, William Darity, Jr., and Rhonda V. Sharpe, "Did North Carolina Economically Breed-Out Blacks During Its Historical Eugenic Sterilization Campaign?," *American Review of Political Economy* 15, no. 1 (2020), arpejournal.com/article/id/167.

45. Southern Poverty Law Center, Landmark Case: *Relf v. Weinberger,* Sterilization Abuse, www .splcenter.org/seeking-justice/case-docket/relf-v-weinberger.

46. *Relf v. Weinberger,* 372 F. Supp. 1196, 1199 (D.D.C. 1974), law.justia.com/cases/federal/district -courts/FSupp/372/1196/1421341/.

47. Elizabeth Hinton, *From the War on Poverty to the War on Crime: The Making of Mass Incarceration in America* (Cambridge, Mass.: Harvard University Press 2016), 2–3.

48. Dorothy Roberts, *Killing the Black Body: Race, Reproduction, and the Meaning of Liberty* (New York: Vintage, 1999), 153–62; Susan Okie, "The Epidemic That Wasn't," *New York Times,* January 26, 2009, www.nytimes.com/2009/01/27/health/27coca.html?_r=1; Jessie Daniels, Julie C. Netherland, and Alyssa Patricia Lyons, "White Women, U.S. Popular Culture, and Narratives of Addiction," *Contemporary Drug Problems* 45, no. 3 (2018): 329–346, 242–243, journals .sagepub.com/doi/10.1177/0091450918766914.

49. Susan FitzGerald, " 'Crack Baby' Study Ends with Unexpected but Clear Result," *Philadelphia Inquirer,* July 21, 2013, www.inquirer.com/philly/health/20130721_Crack_baby_study_ends _with_unexpected_but_clear_result.html.

50. Joanna Walters, "An 11-Year-Old Reported Being Raped Twice, Wound Up with a Conviction," *Washington Post Magazine,* March 12, 2015, washingtonpost.com/lifestyle/magazine/ a-seven-year-search-for-justice/2015/03/12/b1cccb30-abe9-11e4-abe8-e1ef60ca26de_story .html; Amanda Marcotte, "Cops on an 11-Year-Old Who Says She Was Raped: 'Child's Promiscuous Behavior Caused This,'" *Slate,* March 16, 2015, slate.com/human-interest/2015/03/ danielle-hicks-best-says-she-was-raped-when-she-was-11-but-cops-say-all-sex-was-consen sual.html.

51. Rebecca Epstein, Jamilia J. Blake, and Thalia González, "Girlhood Interrupted: The Erasure of Black Girls' Childhood," Center on Poverty and Inequality, Georgetown Law Center (2015), 4.

52. King, "Prematurely Knowing of Evil Things," 188.

53. Pokorak, "Rape as a Badge of Slavery," 36–38.

54. Cassia Spohn and David Holleran, "Prosecuting Sexual Assault: A Comparison of Charging Decisions in Sexual Assault Cases Involving Strangers, Acquaintances, and Intimate Partners," *Justice Quarterly* 18, no. 3 (2001): 671.

55. Blackburn Center, "The Barriers That May Prevent Black Women from Reporting Sexual Assault," February 19, 2020, www.blackburncenter.org/post/2020/02/19/the-barriers-that-may -prevent-black-women-from-reporting-sexual-assault.

56. Andrea J. Ritchie, *Invisible No More: Police Violence Against Black Women and Women of Color* (Boston: Beacon, 2017), 185.

57. Ibid., 104–26; African American Policy Forum, *Say Her Name: Resisting Police Brutality Against Black Women* (New York: African American Policy Forum, Center for Intersectionality and Social Policy Studies, 2015); Michelle S. Jacobs, "The Violent State: Black Women's Invisible Struggle Against Police Violence," *William & Mary Journal of Women and the Law* 24 (2017): 69–74.

58. Jessica Lussenhop, "Daniel Holtzclaw Trial: Standing with 'Imperfect' Accusers," *BBC News Magazine,* November 13, 2015, https://www.bbc.com/news/magazine-34791191; Sarah Kaplan, "A Serial Rapist Cop's 'Mistake': Assaulting the Grandmother Who Finally Reported Him," *Washington Post,* December 11, 2015, www.washingtonpost.com/news/morning-mix/ wp/2015/12/11/daniel-holtzclaws-mistake-assaulting-the-grandmother-who-finally -reported-him/.

59. Ritchie, *Invisible No More,* 107.

60. Ibid., 106; Richard L. Eldredge, "Jannie Ligons, Who Helped Bring Former Police Officer Daniel Holtzclaw to Justice, Is Honored in Atlanta this Weekend," *Atlanta,* April 1, 2016, www.atlantamagazine.com/news-culture-articles/jannie-ligons-helped-bring-former -police-officer-daniel-holtzclaw-justice-honored-atlanta-weekend/.

61. Matt Sedensky and Nomaan Merchant, "AP: Hundreds of Officers Lose Licenses over Sex Misconduct," Associated Press, November 1, 2015, apnews.com/article/5a66f08987f445d9b a9253ba3d706691.

62. Roberts, *Killing the Black Body,* 45–55; Stephanie M. H. Camp, *Closer to Freedom: Enslaved Women and Everyday Resistance in the Plantation South* (Chapel Hill: University of North Carolina Press, 2004); Jennifer L. Morgan, *Laboring Women: Reproduction and Gender in New World Slavery* (Philadelphia: University of Pennsylvania Press, 2004).

63. Jenn Stanley, "Loretta Ross on the Dalkon Shield Disaster," *Choiceless: The Backstory,* rewire newsgroup.com/wp-content/uploads/2017/06/CHOICELESS-The-Backstory-Loretta-Ross -on-the-Dalkon-Shield-Disaster.pdf; "The Power of Women's Voices: Loretta Ross," Sophia Smith Collection, Smith College Libraries, www.smith.edu/libraries/libs/ssc/pwv/pwv-ross .html.

64. Rebecca Farmer, "Spotlight: Loretta Ross—Three Decades of Advocating for the Health and Rights of Women of Color," Breast Cancer Action, *The Source* 93 (October–November 2006), bcaction.org/2006/10/21/spotlight-loretta-ross-three-decades-of-advocating-for-the-health -and-rights-of-women-of-color/.

65. Combahee River Collective, *The Combahee River Collective Statement* (1977), www.blackpast .org/african-american-history/combahee-river-collective-statement-1977/.

66. Alexis Okeowo, "Fighting for Abortion Access in the South," *New Yorker,* October 7, 2019, www.newyorker.com/magazine/2019/10/14/fighting-for-abortion-access-in-the-south; Zakiya Luna, *Reproductive Rights as Human Rights: Women of Color and the Fight for Reproductive Justice* (New York: New York University Press, 2020), 3–22. Loretta Ross has co-authored

three books on reproductive justice: Loretta J. Ross and Rickie Solinger, *Reproductive Justice: An Introduction* (Oakland: University of California Press, 2017); Loretta Ross, Lynn Roberts, Erika Derkas, Whitney Peoples, and Pamela Bridgewater, *Radical Reproductive Justice: Foundation, Theory, Practice, Critique* (New York: Feminist Press at CUNY, 2017); and Jael Silliman, Marlene Gerber Fried, Loretta Ross, and Elena R. Gutiérrez, *Undivided Rights: Women of Color Organizing for Reproductive Justice,* 2nd ed. (Chicago: Haymarket, 2016).

67. Ciarra Davison, "Q&A: Reproductive Justice Champion Loretta Ross on Resistance and Redefining Our Fight," *Ms.,* September 25, 2017, msmagazine.com/2017/09/25/qa-reproductive -justice-champion-loretta-ross-resistance-redefining-fight/.

68. Eesha Pandit, "Live from SisterSong: Let's Talk About Sex!," Rewire News Group, June 1, 2007, rewirenewsgroup.com/article/2007/06/01/live-from-sistersong-let-s-talk-about-sex/; Thao Nguyen, "Let's Talk About Sex: SisterSong's Reproductive Justice Conference," National Women's Law Center, July 15, 2011, nwlc.org/blog/let's-talk-about-sex-sistersong's -reproductive-justice-conference/; Francesca Witcher, "My Sistas Have Spoken! Now It's Time to Act: The 2011 SisterSong 'Let's Talk About Sex' Conference," Feminist Campus, July 21, 2011, feministcampus.org/my-sistas-have-spoken-now-its-time-to-act-the-2011-sister -song-lets-talk-about-sex-conference/.

Chapter 3: Sugar

1. Ibrahima Seck, *Bouki Fait Gombo: A History of the Slave Community of Habitation Haydel (Whitney Plantation) Louisiana, 1750–1860* (New Orleans: University of New Orleans Press, 2014), 19–20.

2. USDA Economic Research Service, Food Availability (Per Capita) Data System, www.ers .usda.gov/data-products/food-availability-per-capita-data-system/. See the data set "Sugar and Sweeteners (added)" in the Loss-Adjusted Food Availability section.

3. Cheryl D. Fryar, Margaret D. Carroll, and Joseph Afful, "Prevalence of Overweight, Obesity, and Severe Obesity Among Adults Aged 20 and Over: United States, 1960–1962 Through 2017–2018," National Center for Health Statistics, Table 1, www.cdc.gov/nchs/data/hestat/ obesity-adult-17-18/obesity-adult.htm#table1.

4. "National Diabetes Statistics Report, 2020: Estimates of Diabetes and Its Burden in the United States," 16, www.cdc.gov/diabetes/pdfs/data/statistics/national-diabetes-statistics -report.pdf.

5. Sidney Mintz, *Sweetness and Power: The Place of Sugar in Modern History* (New York: Penguin, 1986), 23–25.

6. Marc Aronson and Marina Budhos, *Sugar Changed the World: A Story of Magic, Spice, Slavery, Freedom, and Science* (Boston: Clarion, 2010), 35.

7. David A. Love, "1669–1674: The Royal African Company," in *Four Hundred Souls: A Community History of African America, 1619–2019,* ed. Ibram X. Kendi and Keisha N. Blain (New York: One World, 2021), 49; Sarah Pruitt, "What Was the Royal African Company," *History,* August 22, 2018, www.history.com/news/what-was-the-royal-african-company.

8. Eric Williams, *Capitalism and Slavery* (1944; repr., Chapel Hill: University of North Carolina Press, 1994), 65.

9. James Rawley and Stephen D. Behrendt, *The Transatlantic Slave Trade: A History,* rev. ed. (Lincoln: University of Nebraska Press, 2005), 212–13.

10. Ibid., 143.

11. Williams, *Capitalism and Slavery,* 61.

12. Mintz, *Sweetness and Power,* 148.

13. Love, "1669–1674: The Royal African Company," 47.

14. Sowande' Mustakeem, *Slavery at Sea: Terror, Sex, and Sickness in the Middle Passage* (Champaign: University of Illinois Press, 2016), 48.

15. James T. Campbell, *Middle Passages: African American Journeys to Africa, 1787–2005* (New York: Penguin Books, 2007), 10.

16. Rawley and Behrendt, *Transatlantic Slave Trade,* 233–34.

17. Mustakeem, *Slavery at Sea,* 63.

18. Ibid.

19. Rawley and Behrendt, *Transatlantic Slave Trade,* 233–34.

20. Ibid., 291.

21. Ibid., 136.

22. Mustakeem, *Slavery at Sea,* 74, 77–78.

23. Ibid., 114–16.

24. Ibid., 105.

25. Ibid., 106.

26. Ibid., 76.

27. Ibid., 141–43.

28. Rawley and Behrendt, *Transatlantic Slave Trade,* 226.

29. Mustakeem, *Slavery at Sea,* 200.

30. Ibid., 209–26.

31. Ibid., 42.

32. Rawley and Behrendt, *Transatlantic Slave Trade,* 309.

33. Ibid., 297.

34. Williams, *Capitalism and Slavery,* 78–80.

35. Rawley and Behrendt, *Transatlantic Slave Trade,* 297.

36. Williams, *Capitalism and Slavery,* 78.

37. Rawley and Behrendt, *Transatlantic Slave Trade,* 305.

38. Aronson and Budhos, *Sugar Changed the World,* 73.

39. Ibid., 307.

40. Matthew Pratt Guterl, *American Mediterranean: Southern Slaveholders in the Age of Emancipation* (Cambridge, Mass.: Harvard University Press, 2008).

41. Jean-Pierre Leglaunec, "Slave Migrations in Spanish and Early American Louisiana: Sources and New Estimates," *Journal of the Louisiana Historical Association* (Spring 2005): 209.

42. Seck, *Bouki Fait Gombo,* 10.

43. Ibid., 1.

44. Ibid., 80–81.

45. Richard Follett, *The Sugar Masters: Planters and Slaves in Louisiana's Cane World, 1820–1860* (Baton Rouge: Louisiana State University Press, 2007), 4.

46. "The Sugar Interests—No. 2," *De Bow's Review,* April 1857, 435; Follett, *Sugar Masters,* 22.

47. John C. Rodrigue, *Reconstruction in Cane Fields: From Slavery to Free Labor in Louisiana's Sugar Parishes, 1862–1882* (Baton Rouge: Louisiana State University Press, 2001), 320.

48. Solomon Northup, *Twelve Years a Slave: Narrative of Solomon Northup, a Citizen of New-York, Kidnapped in Washington City in 1841, and Rescued in 1853, from a Cotton Plantation near the Red River in Louisiana,* ed. David Wilson (Auburn, N.Y.: Derby and Miller, 1853), 211–12.

49. Ibid., 195.

50. Quotation taken from Follett's *Sugar Masters,* 175.

51. Michael Tadman, "The Demographic Cost of Sugar: Debates on Slave Societies and Natural Increase in the Americas," *American Historical Review* 105 (December 2000), 1534.

52. Ibid., 1554.

53. Author interview with Ashley Rogers, June 13, 2019.

54. Rodrigue, *Reconstruction in Cane Fields,* 96.

55. W.E.B. Du Bois, *Black Reconstruction in America, 1860–1880* (1935; repr., New York: Free Press, 1992), 30.

56. Follett, *Sugar Masters,* 234.

57. Rebecca J. Scott, "Defining the Boundaries of Freedom in the World of Cane: Cuba, Brazil, and Louisiana After Emancipation," *American Historical Review* 99 (February 1994): 78.

58. Kelly M. Bower, Roland J. Thorpe, Jr., Charles Rohde, and Darrel J. Gaskin, "The Intersection of Neighborhood Racial Segregation, Poverty, and Urbanicity and Its Impact on Food Store Availability in the United States," *Preventative Medicine,* October 23, 2013, 34.

59. Michael Miller, Gerad Middendorf, and Spencer D. Wood, "Food Availability in the Heartland: Exploring the Effects of Neighborhood Racial and Income Composition," *Rural Sociology* 80, no. 3 (2015): 357.

60. Cheryl D. Fryar, Margaret D. Carroll, Namanjeet Ahluwalia, and Cynthia L. Ogden, "Fast Food Intake Among Children and Adolescents in the United States, 2015–2018," NCHS Data Brief, No. 375, August 2020, www.cdc.gov/nchs/data/databriefs/db375-h.pdf; Cheryl D. Fryar, Jeffrey P. Hughes, Kirsten A. Herrick, and Namanjeet Ahluwalia, "Fast Food Consumption Among Adults in the United States, 2013–2016," NCHS Data Brief, No. 322, October 2018, www.cdc.gov/nchs/data/databriefs/db322-h.pdf.

61. Shamard Charles, "Junk Food Ads Disproportionately Target Black and Hispanic Kids, Study Finds," NBC Health, January 16, 2019, www.nbcnews.com/health/health-news/junk-food-ads-disproportionately-target-black-hispanic-kids-study-finds-n959111.

Chapter 4: Fear

1. Eric Levenson, "Former Officer Knelt on George Floyd for 9 Minutes and 29 Seconds—Not the Infamous 8:46," CNN, March 30, 2021, www.cnn.com/2021/03/29/us/george-floyd-timing-929-846/index.html; Nicholas Bogel-Burroughs, "Prosecutors Say Derek Chauvin Knelt on George Floyd for 9 Minutes 29 Seconds, Longer Than Initially Reported," *New York Times,* March 30, 2021, www.nytimes.com/2021/03/30/us/derek-chauvin-george-floyd-kneel-9-minutes-29-seconds.html.

2. Michelle L. Norris, "How Amy Cooper and George Floyd Represent Two Versions of Racism That Black Americans Face Every Day," *Washington Post,* May 28, 2020, www.washingtonpost.com/opinions/2020/05/28/how-amy-cooper-george-floyd-represent-two-versions-racism-that-black-americans-face-every-day/.

3. Roudabeh Kishi and Sam Jones, "Demonstrations & Political Violence in America: New Data for Summer 2020," US Crisis Monitor, September 3, 2020, acleddata.com/2020/09/03/demonstrations-political-violence-in-america-new-data-for-summer-2020/; Harmeet Kaur, "About 93% of Racial Justice Protests in the US Have Been Peaceful, a New Report Finds," CNN, September 4, 2020, www.cnn.com/2020/09/04/us/blm-protests-peaceful-report-trnd/index.html; Lois Beckett, "Nearly All Black Lives Matter Protests Are Peaceful Despite Trump Narrative, Report Finds," *Guardian,* September 5, 2020, www.theguardian.com/world/2020/sep/05/nearly-all-black-lives-matter-protests-are-peaceful-despite-trump-narrative-report-finds.

4. Mike Baker, Thomas Fuller, and Sergio Olmos, "Federal Agents Push into Portland Streets, Stretching Limits of Their Authority," *New York Times,* July 25, 2020, www.nytimes.com/2020/07/25/us/portland-federal-legal-jurisdiction-courts.html; "Portland Protests: Federal Forces Ready for Phased Pullout," BBC News, July 30, 2020, www.bbc.com/news/world-us-canada-53589275; Chris McGreal, "Federal Agents Show Stronger Force at Portland Pro-

tests Despite Order to Withdraw," *Guardian,* July 30, 2020, www.theguardian.com/us-news/
2020/jul/30/federal-agents-portland-oregon-trump-troops; "Portland Clashes: Fatal Shooting as Rival Groups Protest," BBC News, August 30, 2020, www.bbc.com/news/world-us
-canada-53963625.

5. Eric Litke, "Fact Check: Police Gave Kyle Rittenhouse Water and Thanked Him Before
Shooting," *USA Today,* August 29, 2020, www.usatoday.com/story/news/factcheck/2020/
08/29/fact-check-video-police-thanked-kyle-rittenhouse-gave-him-water/5661804002/.

6. Howard Altman, "National Guard Civil Unrest Update: More Than 17,000 Troops in 23
States and DC Activated," *Military Times,* June 1, 2020, www.militarytimes.com/news/your
-military/2020/06/01/national-guard-civil-unrest-update-more-than-17000-troops-in-23
-states-and-dc-activated/.

7. James Baldwin, interview by Dick Cavett, *The Dick Cavett Show,* May 16, 1969, www.youtube
.com/watch?v=WWwOi17WHpE.

8. "Declaration of Independence," National Archives, www.archives.gov/founding-docs/
declaration.

9. Thomas Jefferson, *Notes on the State of Virginia, Query XVIII: Manners,* Teaching American
History, 1781, teachingamericanhistory.org/library/document/notes-on-the-state-of-virginia
-query-xviii-manners/.

10. Thomas Jefferson to John Holmes, April 22, 1820, Thomas Jefferson Papers, Library of Congress, www.loc.gov/exhibits/jefferson/159.html.

11. Thomas Cooper and David J. McCord, eds., *The Statutes at Large of South Carolina,* vol. 1
(Columbia, S.C.: A. S. Johnston, 1836), 22; Philip L. Reichel, "Southern Slave Patrols as a
Transitional Police Type," *American Journal of Police* 7, no. 2 (1988): 57.

12. William Waller Hening, ed., *The Statutes at Large; Being a Collection of All the Laws of Virginia,
from the First Session of the Legislature, in the Year 1619* (New York: R. & W. & G. Bartow, 1819–23),
2:481–82; Alejandro de la Fuente and Ariela J. Gross, *Becoming Free, Becoming Black: Race,
Freedom, and Law in Cuba, Virginia, and Louisiana* (Cambridge: Cambridge University Press,
2020), 27, 338, 341.

13. Hening, *Statutes at Large,* 1:270; Sally E. Hadden, *Slave Patrols: Law and Violence in Virginia
and the Carolinas* (Cambridge, Mass.: Harvard University Press, 2001), 18.

14. H. M. Henry, "The Police Control of the Slave in South Carolina," (PhD diss., Vanderbilt
University, 1914), 148; Thomas D. Morris, *Southern Slavery and the Law, 1619–1860* (Chapel
Hill: University of North Carolina Press, 1996), 341.

15. Hening, *Statutes at Large,* 3:86–87, 447.

16. Jason T. Sharples, *The World That Fear Made: Slave Revolts and Conspiracy Scares in Early
America* (Philadelphia: University of Pennsylvania Press, 2020), 255–57.

17. Leslie Harris, *In the Shadow of Slavery: African Americans in New York City, 1626–1863* (Chi-
cago: University of Chicago Press, 2003), 34–40; Walter C. Rucker, *The River Flows On: Black
Resistance, Culture, and Identity Formation in Early America* (Baton Rouge: Louisiana State
University Press, 2006), 27.

18. Hadden, *Slave Patrols,* 3–4.

19. Peter Wood, *Black Majority: Negroes in Colonial South Carolina from 1670 Through the Stono
Rebellion* (New York: Norton, 1974), 4.

20. Hadden, *Slave Patrols,* 3.

21. Ibid., 19–20.

22. Henry, "Police Control of the Slave in South Carolina," 32–33.

23. Hadden, *Slave Patrols,* 21–24.

24. Ibid., 4, 38–40, 106–8, 117, 123.

25. Wood, *Black Majority,* 315–20; Rucker, *The River Flows On,* 100–101.

26. An Act for the Better Ordering and Governing Negroes and Other Slaves in This Province (1740), digital.scetv.org/teachingAmerhistory/pdfs/Transciptionof1740SlaveCodes.pdf; Cooper and McCord, *Statutes at Large of South Carolina*, 7:397.

27. Harris, *In the Shadow of Slavery*, 33; Rucker, *The River Flows On*, 25; Jill Lepore, "The Invention of the Police," *New Yorker*, July 13, 2020, newyorker.com/magazine/2020/07/20/the-invention-of-the-police.

28. Elizabeth Stordeur Pryor, *Colored Travelers: Mobility and the Fight for Citizenship Before the Civil War* (Chapel Hill: University of North Carolina Press, 2016), 47.

29. Laurent Dubois, *Avengers of the New World: The Story of the Haitian Revolution* (Cambridge, Mass.: Belknap Press of Harvard University Press, 2004), 45–47.

30. Dubois, *Avengers of the New World*, 37–40, 45.

31. Ibid., 94–95, 100, 113.

32. Charles Pinckney to George Washington, September 20, 1791, founders.archives.gov/documents/Washington/05-08-02-0379.

33. George Washington to John Vaughan, December 27, 1791, founders.archives.gov/documents/Washington/05-09-02-0212; Gerald Horne, "The Haitian Revolution and the Central Question of African American History" *Journal of African American History* 100, no. 1 (2015): 26.

34. Thomas Jefferson to David Humphreys, November 29, 1791, founders.archives.gov/documents/Jefferson/01-22-02-0316; Alexander Hamilton to Jean Baptiste de Ternant, September 21, 1791, founders.archives.gov/documents/Hamilton/01-09-02-0181.

35. Horne, "Haitian Revolution," 30.

36. Gordon S. Brown, *Toussaint's Clause: The Founding Fathers and the Haitian Revolution* (Jackson: University of Mississippi Press, 2005), 99–100.

37. Hadden, *Slave Patrols*, 148–49.

38. An Act Respecting Fugitives from Justice, and Persons Escaping from the Service of Their Masters, 2nd Cong., 2nd Sess (1793), tile.loc.gov/storage-services/service/ll/llsl//llsl-c2/llsl-c2.pdf; Andrew Delbanco, *The War Before the War: Fugitive Slaves and the Struggle for America's Soul from the Revolution to the Civil War* (New York: Penguin Books, 2019), 20–21.

39. Dubois, *Avengers of the New World*, 169–70, 184–93.

40. For more on rebellions in the Atlantic world following the Haitian Revolution, see Gerald Horne, *Confronting Black Jacobins: The United States, the Haitian Revolution, and the Origins of the Dominican Republic* (New York: Monthly Review Press, 2015).

41. Arthur Campbell to Thomas Jefferson, September 30, 1797, founders.archives.gov/documents/Jefferson/01-29-02-0426.

42. Henry Tazewell to Thomas Jefferson, July 5, 1798, founders.archives.gov/documents/Jefferson/01-30-02-0320.

43. Timothy Pickering to John Adams, June 7, 1799, founders.archives.gov/documents/Adams/99-02-02-3608.

44. Douglas R. Egerton, "Gabriel's Conspiracy and the Election of 1800," *Journal of Southern History* 56, no. 2 (May 1990): 196–97, Rucker, *The River Flows On*, 140.

45. James Monroe to Thomas Jefferson, September 15, 1800, founders.archives.gov/documents/Jefferson/01-32-02-0094.

46. Hadden, *Slave Patrols*, 149–50.

47. Douglas R. Egerton, *Gabriel's Rebellion: The Virginia Slave Conspiracies of 1800 and 1802* (Chapel Hill: University of North Carolina Press, 1993), 157–59; Rucker, *The River Flows On*, 140.

48. Julia Gaffield, ed., *The Haitian Declaration of Independence: Creation, Context, and Legacy* (Charlottesville: University of Virginia Press, 2016), 5.

49. Ibid., 245–46.

50. Dubois, *Avengers of the New World*, 21.

51. Michel-Rolph Trouillot, *Silencing the Past: Power and the Production of History* (Boston: Beacon, 1995), 82.

52. Junius Rodriguez, "Rebellion on the River Road: The Ideology and Influence of Louisiana's German Coast Slave Insurrection of 1811," in John R. McKivigan and Stanley Harrold, *Antislavery Violence: Sectional, Racial, and Cultural Conflict in Antebellum America* (Knoxville: University of Tennessee Press, 1999), 69–70.

53. James O'Neil Spady, "Power and Confession: On the Credibility of the Earliest Reports of the Denmark Vesey Slave Conspiracy," *William and Mary Quarterly* 68, no. 2 (2011): 287–304. For more on the debate over the veracity of the Vesey conspiracy, see Michael P. Johnson, "Denmark Vesey and His Co-Conspirators," *William and Mary Quarterly* 58, no. 4 (2001), 915–76.

54. Samuel Wood to Thomas Jefferson, March 3, 1821, founders.archives.gov/documents/Jefferson/98-01-02-1878.

55. Thomas R. Gray, *The Confessions of Nat Turner, the Leader of the Late Insurrection in Southampton, Va.* (Baltimore: Thomas R. Gray, 1831), docsouth.unc.edu/neh/turner/turner.html; Rucker, *The River Flows On*, 193–98.

56. Patrick H. Breen, *The Land Shall Be Deluged in Blood: A New History of the Nat Turner Revolt* (New York: Oxford University Press, 2015), 98.

57. Herbert Aptheker, *American Negro Slave Revolts* (New York: International Publishers, 1943), 300–301.

58. Gray, *Confessions of Nat Turner*.

59. Hadden, *Slave Patrols*, 146.

60. Laurence Ralph, "The Logic of the Slave Patrol: The Fantasy of Black Predatory Violence and the Use of Force by the Police," *Palgrave Communications* 5, no. 130 (2019): 3.

61. Hadden, *Slave Patrols*, 51–53, 60.

62. Marlese Durr, "What Is the Difference Between Slave Patrols and Modern Day Policing? Institutional Violence in a Community of Color," *Critical Sociology* 41, no. 6 (2015): 875.

63. William Goodell, *American Slave Code in Theory and Practice: Distinctive Features, Its Statutes, Judicial Decisions, Illustrative Facts* (New York: American Anti-Slavery Society, 1853), 357.

64. Steven Deyle, *Carry Me Back: The Domestic Slave Trade in American Life* (New York: Oxford University Press, 2005), 60.

65. Gene Demby and Natalie Escobar, "From Negro Militias to Black Armament," *Code Switch* (podcast), December 22, 2020, www.npr.org/sections/codeswitch/2020/12/22/949169826/from-negro-militias-to-black-armament.

66. Carol Anderson, *White Rage: The Unspoken Truth of Our Racial Divide* (New York: Bloomsbury, 2016), 3.

67. William Cohen, *At Freedom's Edge: Black Mobility and the Southern White Quest for Racial Control* (Baton Rouge: Louisiana State University Press, 1991), 28.

68. W.E.B. Du Bois, "Reconstruction and Its Benefits," *American Historical Review* 15, no. 4 (1910): 784.

69. Anderson, *White Rage*, chapter 1.

70. Caleb Crain, "What a White-Supremacist Coup Looks Like," *New Yorker*, April 20, 2020, www.newyorker.com/magazine/2020/04/27/what-a-white-supremacist-coup-looks-like; Jacob Shelton, "The White Declaration of Independence: When White Supremacists Overthrew the Democratically Elected Government of Wilmington, North Carolina," *History Daily*, July 3, 2020, historydaily.org/white-declaration-independence-wilmington-massacre-1898.

71. Hadden, *Slave Patrols*, 4, 209–12, 219.

72. *Lynching in America: Confronting the Legacy of Racial Terror*, 3rd ed. (Montgomery, Ala.: Equal Justice Initiative, 2017), lynchinginamerica.eji.org/report/.

73. See Harper Barnes, *Never Been a Time: The 1917 Race Riot That Sparked the Civil Rights Movement* (New York: Walker & Company, 2008); Allison Keyes, "The East St. Louis Race Riot Left Dozens Dead, Devastating a Community on the Rise," *Smithsonian Magazine*, June 30, 2017, www.smithsonianmag.com/smithsonian-institution/east-st-louis-race-riot-left-dozens-dead-devastating-community-on-the-rise-180963885/.

74. "Report on Tulsa Race Riot of 1921," archive.org/details/ReportOnTulsaRaceRiotOf1921.

75. Anderson, *White Rage*, 15.

76. Senate Select Committee to Study Governmental Operations with Respect to Intelligence Activities, "Supplementary Detailed Staff Reports on Intelligence Activities and the Rights of Americans" (Washington, D.C.: U.S. Government Printing Office, 1976), 3, www.intelligence.senate.gov/sites/default/files/94755_III.pdf.

77. Ibid.

78. J. Edgar Hoover, "The FBI Sets Goals for COINTELPRO," SHEC: Resources for Teachers, shec.ashp.cuny.edu/items/show/814, accessed November 20, 2020; For more on COINTELPRO and the FBI, see Kenneth O'Reilly, *Racial Matters: The FBI's Secret File on Black America, 1960–1972* (New York: Free Press, 1991); Ward Churchill and Jim Vander Wall, *The COINTELPRO Papers: Documents from the FBI's Secret Wars Against Dissent in the United States* (New York: South End Press, 2001); Curtis Austin, *Up Against the Wall: Violence in the Making and Unmaking of the Black Panther Party* (Fayetteville: University of Arkansas Press, 2008); Tim Weiner, *Enemies: A History of the FBI* (New York: Penguin, 2013).

79. For a comprehensive study of the role of government in creating and perpetuating racial segregation in the North and South, see Richard Rothstein, *The Color of Law: The Forgotten History of How Our Government Segregated America* (New York: Liveright, 2017).

80. Brooke Ross, "MLK 50 Years Later," *New York Times Upfront*, January 29, 2018, upfront.scholastic.com/issues/2017-18/012918/mlk-50-years-later.html#1210L.

81. Peter Levy, *The Great Uprising: Race Riots in Urban America During the 1960s* (Cambridge: Cambridge University Press, 2018).

82. "McKissick Says Nonviolence Has Become Dead Philosophy," *New York Times*, April 5, 1968, timesmachine.nytimes.com/timesmachine/1968/04/05/90666317.html.

83. Ibid.

84. Elizabeth Hinton, *America on Fire: The Untold History of Police Violence and Black Rebellion Since the 1960s* (New York: Norton, 2021), introduction.

85. Ibid., 2–3.

86. Ibid., 5–6.

87. "Our Nation Is Moving Toward Two Societies, One Black, One White—Separate and Unequal": Excerpts from the Kerner Commission's report, historymatters.gmu.edu/d/6545/. For a comprehensive account of how the government created segregation and ghettos in the North and the South, see Rothstein, *The Color of Law*.

88. Richard Nixon, "If Mob Rule Takes Hold in U.S.," *U.S. News and World Report*, August 15, 1966, 64.

89. Katherine Beckett, *Making Crime Pay: Law and Order in Contemporary Politics* (New York: Oxford University Press, 1997), 32; Marc Mauer, "Two-Tiered Justice: Race, Class and Crime Policy," in *The Integration Debate: Competing Futures for American Cities*, ed. Chester Hartman and Gregory Squires (New York: Routledge, 2005), 171; Vesla Weaver, "Frontlash: Race and the Development of Punitive Crime Policy," *Studies in American Political Development* 21 (Fall 2007): 242.

90. Kyle Longley, "Our Leaders Can Look to Lyndon Johnson to See How to Minimize Damage Today," *Washington Post*, May 31, 2020, www.washingtonpost.com/outlook/2020/05/31/our-leaders-can-look-lyndon-johnson-see-how-minimize-damage-today/; Josh Israel, "How

Lyndon Johnson Responded to Baltimore's Last Riots," Think Progress, April 28, 2015, archive.thinkprogress.org/how-lyndon-johnson-responded-to-baltimores-last-riots -f3c0378909c/.

91. Lyndon B. Johnson, "July 27, 1967: Speech to the Nation on Civil Disorders," millercenter.91/ the-presidency/presidential-speeches/july-27-1967-speech-nation-civil-disorders.

92. See Hinton, *America on Fire*, 15. See also Gareth Davies, *From Opportunity to Entitlement: The Transformation and Decline of Great Society Liberalism* (Lawrence: University Press of Kansas, 1999), 191; Otto Kerner et al., *Report of the National Advisory Commission on Civil Disorders* (Washington, D.C.: U.S. Government Printing Office, 1968), 160.

93. See, e.g., Elizabeth Hinton, *From the War on Poverty to the War on Crime: The Making of Mass Incarceration in America* (Cambridge, Mass: Harvard University Press, 2017), and Radley Balko, *Rise of the Warrior Cop: The Militarization of America's Police Forces* (New York: Public-Affairs, 2014).

94. Heather Long and Andrew Van Dam, "The Black-White Economic Divide Is as Wide as It Was in 1968," *Washington Post*, June 4, 2020, www.washingtonpost.com/business/2020/ 06/04/economic-divide-black-households/; see also "Trends in U.S. Corrections," The Sentencing Project, www.sentencingproject.org/wp-content/uploads/2021/07/Trends-in-US -Corrections.pdf.

95. Elizabeth Hinton, Julilly Kohler-Hausmann, and Vesla M. Weaver, "Did Blacks Really Endorse the 1994 Crime Bill?," *New York Times*, April 13, 2016, www.nytimes.com/2016/04/13/ opinion/did-blacks-really-endorse-the-1994-crime-bill.html.

96. See Lawrence Glickman, "How White Backlash Controls American Progress," *Atlantic*, May 21, 2020, www.theatlantic.com/ideas/archive/2020/05/white-backlash-nothing-new/ 611914/; Michael Kimmel, *Angry White Men: American Masculinity at the End of an Era* (New York: Bold Type, 2017); and Carl McClendon, "The 'Angry White Men,'" *Tampa Bay Times*, October 8, 2005, www.tampabay.com/archive/1994/11/20/the-angry-white-men/.

97. Char Adams, "Here's How White Nationalism Moved from the Fringes to the Mainstream," Research, Innovation, and Creativity at CUNY, October 5, 2020, sum.cuny.edu/white -supremacy-center-american-politics-hunter/.

Chapter 5: Dispossession

1. Daniel J. Tortora, *Carolina in Crisis: Cherokees, Colonists, and Slaves in the American Southeast, 1756–1763* (Chapel Hill: University of North Carolina Press, 2015), 117, 138, 169, 189, 190.

2. Some Native nations split their decisions about how to side in America's Revolutionary War, with differing views leading to internal conflict and dual military allegiances. While many groups sided with the British, some nations and subgroups sided with the Americans.

3. Rod Andrew, Jr., *The Life and Times of General Andrew Pickens: Revolutionary War Hero, American Founder* (Chapel Hill: University of North Carolina Press, 2017), Kindle loc. 269, 270, 355, 364, 3693, 3873, 3878. For more on the Hopewell Plantation and the history of slavery and Native residency on the Clemson University campus, see www.clemson.edu/about/history/ properties/hopewell/. Andrew Pickens, Sr., was uncle to John C. Calhoun by way of his marriage to Rebecca "Becky" Calhoun. The Calhoun plantation, which became the grounds of Clemson University, was called Fort Hill. Andrew, *Life and Times*, Kindle loc. 260, 270, 697, 6248. See also Rhondda Robinson Thomas, "Meeting the Challenge of Honoring Clemson University's Invisible Black Founders," *Public Historian* 42, no. 4 (2020): 41–55; "Call My Name: African Americans in Clemson University History": spark.adobe.com/page/wQoPG/; Decolonize Clemson University: www.decolonizecu.org/.

4. Merritt B. Pound, *Benjamin Hawkins: Indian Agent* (Athens: University of Georgia Press, 1951), 37–39, 42, 43.

5. Ibid., 46.

6. Quoted in Colin G. Calloway, *The Indian World of George Washington* (New York: Oxford University Press, 2008), 307; Pound, *Benjamin Hawkins*, 47.

7. Colin G. Calloway, *The American Revolution in Indian Country: Crisis and Diversity in Native American Communities* (New York: Cambridge University Press, 1995), 50; Andrew, *Life and Times*, Kindle loc. 77, 206, 217, 324, 334; detailed descriptions of attacks on Cherokee villages: 3473, 3496, 3568, 3579, 3600, 3611, 3621.

8. "1785 Treaty of Hopewell," *Cherokee Phoenix*, www.cherokeephoenix.org/news/1785-treaty-of -hopewell/article_321e6d88-2afd-5152-b0ea-d8238641ebaf.html; Pound, *Benjamin Hawkins*, 47; Theda Perdue, *Slavery and the Evolution of Cherokee Society, 1540–1866* (Knoxville: University of Tennessee Press, 1979), 39–40.

9. "1785 Treaty of Hopewell."

10. Andrew, *Life and Times*, loc. 4449, 4473; Calloway, *Indian World of George Washington*, 507 note 4. The Creeks declined to come to Hopewell, but in 1790 they contracted the Treaty of New York with the United States, which had a similar outcome.

11. Pound, *Benjamin Hawkins*, 47; "1785 Treaty of Hopewell"; Theda Perdue and Michael D. Green, *The Columbia Guide to American Indians of the Southeast* (New York: Columbia University Press, 2001), 176. States bordering the Cherokee Nation were unhappy with this outcome. Representatives from North Carolina and Georgia who were also present for the negotiations criticized the imposition of top-down boundaries and trade regulation as federal overreach.

12. Descendants of Freedmen Virtual Conference, 2020; Nicholas Kristof, "The Top U.S. Coronavirus Hot Spots Are All Indian Lands," *New York Times*, May 30, 2020, www.nytimes .com/2020/05/30/opinion/sunday/coronavirus-native-americans.html; Mary Smith, "Covid-19 in Native American Communities: A Quiet Crisis That Has Become an Ear-Deafening Emergency," Medium.com, June 2, 2020, marysmith828-63980.medium.com/covid-19-in-native -american-communities-a-quiet-crisis-that-has-become-an-ear-deafening-emergency -51da2ef67253; Katrina Phillips, "Longtime Police Brutality Drove American Indians to Join the George Floyd Protests," *Washington Post*, June 6, 2020, www.washingtonpost.com/ outlook/2020/06/06/longtime-police-brutality-drove-american-indians-join-george-floyd -protests/.

13. Jeffrey Ostler, "The Shameful Final Grievance of the Declaration of Independence," *Atlantic*, February 8, 2020, theatlantic.com/ideas/archive/2020/02/americas-twofold-original-sin/ 606163/; Matthew L. M. Fletcher, *The Ghost Road: Anishinaabe Responses to Indian Hating* (Wheat Ridge, Colo.: Fulcrum, 2020), 18. Fletcher, a legal historian, suggests further that in addition to providing colonists with the means to defend themselves against potential British attack and the means to prevent slave rebellions, the Second Amendment of the Constitution was devised to forestall Indigenous revolts, 19.

14. Calloway, *Indian World of George Washington*, 14.

15. David E. Wilkins, *American Indian Sovereignty and the U.S. Supreme Court: The Masking of Justice* (Austin: University of Texas Press, 97), 20–21; Sidney L. Harring, *Crow Dog's Case: American Indian Sovereignty, Tribal Law, and United States Law in the Nineteenth Century* (New York: Cambridge University Press, 1994), 6–7, 20, 27–33.

16. Robin A. Beck, Jr., "Catawba Coalescence and the Shattering of the Carolina Piedmont, 1540–1675," in *Mapping the Mississippian Shatter Zone: The Colonial Indian Slave Trade and Regional Instability in the American South*, ed. Robbie Ethridge and Sheri M. Shuck-Hall (Lincoln: University of Nebraska Press, 2009), 116–21, 135–37; Chester B. Depratter, "The Chief-

dom of Cofitachequi," in *The Forgotten Centuries: Indians and Europeans in the American South, 1521–1704*, ed. Charles Hudson and Carmen Chaves Tesser (Athens: University of Georgia Press, 1994), 199–201. The historian Christina Snyder notes that the Lady of Cofitachequi "brought several 'slave women' to carry her things when she was kidnapped by de Soto." Christina Snyder, *Slavery in Indian Country: The Changing Face of Captivity in Early America* (Cambridge, Mass.: Harvard University Press, 2010), 38. The poet Qwo-Li Driskill offers an alternative interpretation of the Lady of Cofitachequi's story in which they render her as a "queer" figure with unrecognized power in southeastern Indigenous history. Qwo-Li Driskill, *Asegi Stories: Cherokee Queer and Two-Spirit Memory* (Phoenix: University of Arizona Press, 2016), Kindle loc. 954, 1267–1531.

17. Depratter, "The Chiefdom," 205; Beck, "Catawba Coalescence," 137; Robbie Ethridge, *From Chicaza to Chickasaw: The European Invasion and the Transformation of the Mississippian World, 1540–1715* (Chapel Hill: University of North Carolina Press, 2010), 4.

18. Alan Gallay, *The Indian Slave Trade: The Rise of the English Empire in the American South, 1670–1717* (New Haven, Conn.: Yale University Press, 2002), 299; Jack D. Forbes, *Africans and Native Americans: The Language of Race and the Evolution of Red-Black Peoples* (Champaign: University of Illinois Press, 1993), 47, 64.

19. Forbes, *Africans and Native Americans*, 54, 55, 56, 60, 63; Wendy Warren, *New England Bound: Slavery and Colonization in Early America* (New York: Liveright, 2016), 6, 7, 34, 36.

20. Specific examples of these relationships have been documented extensively in New England and to some extent in the South. However, there were certainly more of these unions than can be documented through written records. See, for example, Daniel Mandell, "The Saga of Sarah Muckamugg: Indian and African American Intermarriage in Colonial New England," in *Sex, Love, Race: Crossing Boundaries in North American History*, ed. Martha Hodes (New York: New York University Press, 1999); Daniel R. Mandell, *Tribe, Race, History: Native Americans in Southern New England, 1780–1880* (Baltimore: Johns Hopkins University Press, 2008); Peter H. Wood, *Black Majority: Negroes in Colonial South Carolina from 1670 Through the Stono Rebellion* (New York: Norton, 1974), 114–15; J. Leitch Wright, Jr., *The Only Land They Knew: The Tragic Story of the American Indians in the Old South* (New York: Free Press, 1981), 148.

21. Tiya Miles, "Taking Leave, Making Lives: Creative Quests for Freedom in Early Black and Native America," in *IndiVisible: African-Native American Lives in the Americas*, ed. Gabrielle Tayac (Washington, D.C.: Smithsonian Institution, 2009), 140–45; Jonathan Brennan, "Introduction," in *When Brer Rabbit Meets Coyote: African-Native American Literature*, ed. Jonathan Brennan (Champaign: University of Illinois Press, 2003), 7–10, 17–21; L. Daniel Mouer et al., "Colonoware Pottery, Chesapeake Pipes, and 'Uncritical Assumptions,'" in *"I, Too, Am America": Archaeological Studies of African-American Life*, ed. Theresa A. Singleton (Charlottesville: University of Virginia Press, 1999): 83–115, 113. Colonoware pottery has European influences as well, especially regarding "vessel forms" (84). Wright, *The Only Land*, 263–267; Wood, *Black Majority*, 121, 122, 124.

22. Claudio Saunt, *A New Order of Things: Property, Power, and the Transformation of the Creek Indians, 1733–1816* (New York: Cambridge University Press, 1999), 52–53; Claudio Saunt, *Unworthy Republic: The Dispossession of Native Americans and the Road to Indian Territory* (New York: Norton, 2020), 244–45. I am grateful to Claudio Saunt for his invaluable feedback on this essay. See also Sylviane A. Diouf, *Slavery's Exiles: The Story of the American Maroons* (New York: New York University Press, 2014), 22–24; Kathryn E. Holland Braund, "The Creek Indians, Blacks, and Slavery," *Journal of Southern History* 57, no. 4 (November 1991): 601–36, 606; Perdue, *Slavery and the Evolution of Cherokee Society*, 40–41. On the Seminole Wars see, for example, Deborah A. Rosen, *Border Law: The First Seminole War and American Nationhood*

(Cambridge, Mass.: Harvard University Press, 2015), and Bruce Edward Twyman, *The Black Seminole Legacy and North American Politics, 1693–1845* (Washington, D.C.: Howard University Press, 2000).

23. James H. Merrell, "The Racial Education of the Catawba Indians," *Journal of Southern History* 50 (1984): 363–84, 370; Snyder, *Slavery in Indian Country*, 6, 21–22, 26–27.

24. For Little Turkey, see Perdue, *Slavery and the Evolution of Cherokee Society*, 48. Brown quoted in William G. McLoughlin, *Cherokee Renascence in the New Republic* (Princeton, N.J.: Princeton University Press, 1992), 55.

25. McLoughlin, *Cherokee Renascence*, 34.

26. Calloway, *Indian World of George Washington*, 340–41.

27. "Treaty with the Cherokee: 1791," The Avalon Project, Yale Law School, avalon.law.yale.edu/18th_century/chr1791.asp.

28. Quoted in Jack D. L. Holmes, "Benjamin Hawkins and United States Attempts to Teach Farming to Southeastern Indians," *Agricultural History* 60, no. 2 (Spring 1986): 216–32, 224. Calloway, *Indian World of George Washington*, 8.

29. Perdue and Green, *Columbia Guide to American Indians of the Southeast*, 75–79; quotes: 77. On the emphasis on the plow and cotton, see Saunt, *New Order of Things*, 155–57.

30. Quoted in McLoughlin, *Cherokee Renascence*, 36.

31. The federal plan for civilization was articulated in the Treaty of Holston of 1791 (with the Cherokees), in George Washington's message to Congress in 1791, and in the revised Trade and Intercourse Act of 1793. Calloway, *Indian World of George Washington*, 340–41; Perdue, *Slavery and the Evolution of Cherokee Society*, 53–55; McLoughlin, *Cherokee Renascence*, 34–37; Angela Pulley Hudson, *Creek Paths and Federal Roads: Indians, Settlers, and Slaves and the Making of the American South* (Chapel Hill: University of North Carolina Press, 2010), 34–35.

32. Claudio Saunt, *Black, White, and Indian: Race and the Unmaking of an American Family* (New York: Oxford University Press, 2005), 18; Robbie Ethridge, *Creek Country: The Creek Indians and Their World* (Chapel Hill: University of North Carolina Press, 2003), 155; Saunt, *New Order of Things*, 117–18; Merrell, "Racial Education," 382.

33. Perdue, *Slavery and the Evolution of Cherokee Society*, 53–55; Tiya Miles, *Ties That Bind: The Story of an Afro-Cherokee Family in Slavery and Freedom*, 2nd ed. (Oakland: University of California Press, 2015), 35–36. For an analysis of Hawkins's visits with Cherokee women, see Theda Perdue, *Cherokee Women: Gender and Culture Change, 1700–1835* (Lincoln: University of Nebraska Press, 1999), 115–18. For an analysis of Hawkins's attempt to change Creek gender roles, see Saunt, *New Order of Things*, 139, 155.

34. Benjamin Hawkins, "A Sketch of the Creek Country in the Years 1798 and 1799," in *Letters, Journals, and Writings of Benjamin Hawkins*, vol. 1, *1796–1801*, ed. C. L. Grant (Savannah, Ga.: Beehive, 1980), 298. Quoted in Daniel F. Littlefield, *Africans and Creeks: From the Colonial Period to the Civil War* (Westport, Conn.: Greenwood, 1979), 36.

35. See, for example, Barbara Krauthamer, *Black Slaves, Indian Masters: Slavery, Emancipation and Citizenship in the Native American South* (Chapel Hill: University of North Carolina Press, 2013), and Gary Zellar, *African Creeks: Estelvste and the Creek Nation* (Norman: University of Oklahoma Press, 2007). See also Celia Naylor, *African Cherokees in Indian Territory, from Chattel to Citizens* (Chapel Hill: University of North Carolina Press, 2009).

36. Michael F. Doran, "Negro Slaves of the Five Civilized Tribes," *Annals of the Association of American Geographers* 68 (September 1978): 335–50, 346, table 2; and Michael F. Doran, "Population Statistics of Nineteenth-Century Indian Territory," *Chronicles of Oklahoma* 53 (Winter 1975–76): 492–515, 501, table 3.

37. Donald L. Shadburn, *Unhallowed Intrusion: A History of Cherokee Families in Forsyth County, Georgia* (Cumming, Ga.: Cottonpatch, 1993), 30; Tiya Miles, *The House on Diamond Hill: A*

Cherokee Plantation Story (Chapel Hill: University of North Carolina Press, 2010), 56–57, 79. For more on the Vann plantation as described by the resident missionaries, see Rowena McClinton, ed., *The Moravian Springplace Mission to the Cherokees* (Lincoln: University of Nebraska Press, 2010). I am grateful to Rowena McClinton for her invaluable feedback on this essay.

38. Specific information about Vann's second home, built in 1804–5, does not exist. The building may have resembled the large log home with multiple glass windows built around 1797 and occupied by Cherokee leader John Ross in present-day Tennessee. "Scholars Track History of John Ross House," *Chattanooga Times Free Press*, March 4, 2007.

39. Miles, *House on Diamond Hill*, 166–70; Tiya Miles, "Showplace of the Cherokee Nation: Race and the Making of a Southern House Museum," *Public Historian* 33, no. 4 (November 2011): 11–34.

40. "First Inaugural Address of Andrew Jackson," March 4, 1829, The Avalon Project, Yale Law School, avalon.law.yale.edu/19th_century/jackson1.asp.

41. Andrew Jackson, "State of the Union Address," December 6, 1830, in Theda Perdue and Michael D. Green, eds., *The Cherokee Removal: A Brief History with Documents*, 2nd ed. (Boston: Bedford / St. Martin's, 2005), 119–20.

42. Ibid., 120.

43. Ibid.

44. *Southern Recorder*, 1827, quoted in Saunt, *Unworthy Republic*, 40, 95.

45. Details about land exchanges would be worked out in new treaties with each nation enacted for that purpose. "An Act to Provide for an Exchange of Lands with the Indians, Residing in Any of the States or Territories, and for Their Removal West of the River Mississippi," Indian Removal Act, Primary Documents in American History, Library of Congress, guides.loc.gov/indian-removal-act/digital-collections. Scan of original: memory.loc.gov/cgi-bin/ampage?collId=llsl&fileName=004/llsl004.db&recNum=458.

46. McLoughlin, *Cherokee Renascence*, 436–37; H. David Williams, "Gambling Away the Inheritance: The Cherokee Nation and Georgia's Gold and Land Lotteries of 1832–1833," *Georgia Historical Quarterly* 73, no. 3, Special Issue Commemorating the Sesquicentennial of Cherokee Removal, 1838–1839 (Fall 1989): 519–39, especially 519, 521; Saunt, *Unworthy Republic*, 161; Miles, *House on Diamond Hill*, 176–77.

47. Miles, *House on Diamond Hill*, 178–79.

48. Marguerite McFadden, "The Saga of 'Rich Joe' Vann," *Chronicles of Oklahoma* 61, no. 1 (1983): 68–79, especially 68, 73.

49. Quoted in Grant Foreman, *Indian Removal* (1932; repr., Norman: University of Oklahoma Press, 1972), 286.

50. Daniel Butrick, *The Journal of Rev. Daniel S. Butrick, May 19, 1838–April 1, 1839, Monograph One* (1839; repr., Park Hill: Trail of Tears Association Oklahoma Chapter, 1998), 2.

51. James Mooney, *Historical Sketch of the Cherokee* (1879; repr., Washington, D.C.: Smithsonian Institution Press), 124.

52. Russell Thornton, "The Demography of the Trail of Tears Period: A New Estimate of Cherokee Population Losses," in *Cherokee Removal: Before and After*, ed. William Anderson (Athens: University of Georgia Press, 1991), 75–95, 80.

53. Mooney, *Historical Sketch*, 126; Foreman, *Indian Removal*, 302–3; Miles, *Ties That Bind*, 153–55. Patrick Minges asserts that some Blacks outside of Indian country freely chose to emigrate with the Cherokees or other tribes after assessing their situation in the U.S. South; Patrick Minges, "Beneath the Underdog: Race, Religion, and the Trail of Tears," *American Indian Quarterly* 25, no. 3 (2001): 453–79, especially 467.

54. Perdue, *Slavery and the Evolution of Cherokee Society*, 71.

55. Butrick, *Journal of Rev. Daniel S. Butrick,* 32–33, 54, 61, 58.

56. The Cherokee demographer Russell Thornton places these death rates at approximately four thousand and ten thousand, respectively; Thornton, "Demography of the Trail of Tears Period," 91. However, Claudio Saunt cites the numbers stated in this essay, working from a correction made by Cherokee tribal historian and tribal council member Jack D. Baker of Thornton's original reading of a census. Saunt, *Unworthy Republic,* 372, note 44.

57. Mary Hershberger, "Mobilizing Women, Anticipating Abolition: The Struggle Against Indian Removal in the 1830s," *Journal of American History* 86, no. 1 (June 1999): 15–40, especially 15, www.historycooperative.org/journals/jah/86.1/hershberger.html.

58. David S. Heidler and Jeanne T. Heidler, *Indian Removal: A Norton Casebook* (New York: Norton, 2007), 30.

59. Saunt, *Unworthy Republic,* xiii, 43, 320.

60. Descendants of Freedmen of the Five Civilized Tribes Association, "About Us," freedmen 5tribes.com.

61. For a new treatment of the politics of the Civil War in Indian Territory, see Fay A. Yarbrough, *Choctaw Confederates: The American Civil War in Indian Country* (Chapel Hill: University of North Carolina Press, forthcoming 2021).

62. See Annie Heloise Abel, *The American Indian as Slaveholder and Secessionist* (Lincoln: University of Nebraska Press, 1992), 215, 225. See also Annie Heloise Abel, *The American Indian in the Civil War, 1862–1865* (Lincoln: University of Nebraska Press, 1992); Yarbrough, *Choctaw Confederates;* and Alaina E. Roberts, *I've Been Here All the While: Black Freedom on Native Land* (Philadelphia: University of Pennsylvania Press).

63. This estimated figure is 8,300 Blacks enslaved by Native Americans in the year 1860, just before the Civil War broke out. It is derived from Doran, "Population Statistics of Nineteenth-Century Indian Territory," 501, table 3. Quintard Taylor gives this number as 7,000, also citing Doran's chart as a source; Quintard Taylor, *In Search of the Racial Frontier: African Americans in the American West, 1528–1990* (New York: Norton, 1999), Kindle loc. 675.

64. Howard Wayne Morgan and Anne Hodges Morgan, *Oklahoma: A Bicentennial History* (New York: Norton, 1977), 91; Muriel Wright, *Our Oklahoma* (Guthrie, Okla.: Cooperative Publishing, 1939), 279; Max Nichols, "'Marriage' Merges Two Territories: Symbolic Ceremony Part of Statehood Day," *Oklahoman,* October 27, 2002, www.oklahoman.com/article/2812746/marriage-merges-two-territories-symbolic-ceremony-part-of-statehood-day; *Journal of the Proceedings of the Senate of the First Legislature of the State of Oklahoma, 1907–1908* (Muskogee, Okla.. Muskogee Printing, 1909), oksenate.gov/sites/default/files/journals/sj1907v1.pdf; Taylor, *In Search of the Racial Frontier,* Kindle loc. 2546; "Senate Bill One," *Encyclopedia of Oklahoma History and Culture,* www.okhistory.org/publications/enc/entry.php?entry=SE017; "Segregation," *Encyclopedia of Oklahoma History and Culture,* www.okhistory.org/publications/enc/entry.php?entryname=SEGREGATION.

65. For more on Vann, see Marilyn Vann, "Oklahoma Universal Human Rights Alliance," okhumanrights.org/awards/recipients/2018-awards/name/marilyn-vann/. For examples of these mixed-race Native/Black and free/unfree families, see Saunt, *Black, White, and Indian;* Miles, *Ties That Bind;* Miles, *House on Diamond Hill;* Christina Snyder, *Great Crossings: Indians, Settlers, and Slaves in the Age of Jackson* (New York: Oxford University Press, 2017); Fay Yarbrough, *Race and the Cherokee Nation: Sovereignty in the Nineteenth Century* (Philadelphia: University of Pennsylvania Press, 2008); and Theda Perdue, *"Mixed Blood" Indians: Racial Construction in the Early South* (Athens: University of Georgia Press, 2003).

66. *The Cherokee Nation v. Raymond Nash, et al., and Marilyn Vann, et al., and Ryan Zinke, Secretary of the Interior, and the United States Department of the Interior,* August 30, 2017. For more on these legal cases, see Circe Sturm, "Race, Sovereignty, and Civil Rights: Understanding the

Cherokee Freedmen Controversy," *Cultural Anthropology* 2, no. 3 (2010): 575–98; Lolita Buckner Inniss, "Cherokee Freedmen and the Color of Belonging," *Columbia Journal of Race and Law* 5, no. 2 (2015): 101–18; Tiya Miles, "'Free Citizens of This Nation': Cherokee Slavery, Descendants of Freedpeople, and Possibilities for Repair," in *Time for Reparation,* ed. Jacqueline Bhabha (Philadelphia: University of Pennsylvania Press, forthcoming).

67. The speakers who presented talks, prayers, or songs at this conference were, in order of their appearance on the program: Vanessa Adams Harris, Marilyn Vann, Leetta Osborne-Sampson, Willard Linzy, Regina Goodwin, Phil Armstrong, Chuck Hoskin, John W. Franklin, Luke Barteaux, John Parris, Branton Grissum, Keith Daniels, Joe Deere, Kristi Williams, Randy Krehbiel, Art. T. Burton, Hannibal Johnson, Angela Walton-Raji, Eli Grayson, David Cornsilk, and Reuben Gran. Descendants of Freedmen of the Five Civilized Tribes Association Virtual Conference, November 7, 2020, Program Schedule.

68. Descendants of Freedmen Virtual Conference, 2020.

69. Cherríe L. Moraga, foreword to *This Bridge Called My Back: Writings by Radical Women of Color,* ed. Cherríe L. Moraga and Gloria E. Anzaldúa (1981; repr., Saline, Mich.: Third Woman, 2002), xv–xxxiii, xvi.

70. Nick Estes, *Our History Is the Future: Standing Rock Versus the Dakota Access Pipeline, and the Long Tradition of Indigenous Resistance* (London: Verso, 2019), 1–7. For a sense of the racial tensions that emerged at Standing Rock, see Chris Finley, "Building Maroon Intellectual Communities," in *Otherwise Worlds: Against Settler Colonialism and Anti-Blackness,* ed. Tiffany Lethabo King, Jenell Navarro, and Andrea Smith (Durham, N.C.: Duke University Press, 2020). I became vaguely aware of tensions among the demonstrators when I was asked to write a paper for the Majority Coalition for the Black Lives Matter Movement on Black and Native histories that might aid in the activists' mutual understanding. I took up the work as a collaborative classroom-based project, and I submitted it to the coalition and posted it to my website: tiyamiles.com/working-paper-on-black-and-native-historical-intersections/.

71. For an insightful and candid discussion of the tensions that still exist between Native and Black people, as well as in Black studies and Native American studies, and the hope to overcome them, see Tiffany Lethabo King, *The Black Shoals: Offshore Formations of Black and Native Studies* (Durham, N.C.: Duke University Press, 2019), especially 36–42.

Chapter 6: Capitalism

1. Carolyn Y. Johnson, "Doctors, Hospitals Condemn Out-Of-Control Drug Prices as Senate Investigation Begins," *Washington Post,* December 9, 2015, www.washingtonpost.com/news/wonk/wp/2015/12/09/doctors-hospitals-condemn-out-of-control-drug-prices-as-senate-investigation-begins/.

2. Rene Rodriguez, "Miami Condo King Jorge Pérez on Gentrification, Liberty Square and Federal Investigations," *Miami Herald,* August 6, 2018, www.miamiherald.com/news/business/real-estate-news/article215913130.html; Eric Olin Wright and Joel Rogers, *American Society: How It Really Works,* 2nd ed. (New York: Norton, 2015), 228–31.

3. "Social Expenditure—Aggregated Data," OECD Social Expenditure Database (SOCX), stats.oecd.org/Index.aspx?datasetcode=SOCX_AGG; Christopher Ingraham, "The Richest 1 Percent Now Owns More of the Country's Wealth Than at Any Time in the Past 50 Years," *Washington Post,* December 6, 2017, www.washingtonpost.com/news/wonk/wp/2017/12/06/the-richest-1-percent-now-owns-more-of-the-countrys-wealth-than-at-any-time-in-the-past-50-years/.

4. OECD and J. Visser, ICTWSS database, "Institutional Characteristics of Trade Unions, Wage Setting, State Intervention and Social Pacts, 1960–2010," version 3.

5. Walter Johnson, *River of Dark Dreams: Slavery and Empire in the Cotton Kingdom* (Cambridge, Mass.: Harvard University Press, 2013), 5.

6. Edward E. Baptist, *The Half Has Never Been Told: Slavery and the Making of American Capitalism* (New York: Basic Books, 2014), 254–55.

7. Sven Beckert and Seth Rockman, eds., *Slavery's Capitalism: A New History of American Economic Development* (Philadelphia: University of Pennsylvania Press, 2016), 3.

8. Peter Lindert and Jeffrey Williamson, *Unequal Gains: American Growth and Inequality Since 1700* (Princeton, N.J.: Princeton University Press, 2016), 33–43, 68.

9. Mark Graber, *Dred Scott and the Problem of Constitutional Evil* (New York: Cambridge University Press, 2006), 106; Paul Starr, *Entrenchment: Wealth, Power, and the Constitution of Democratic Societies* (New Haven, Conn.: Yale University Press, 2019), 71; Lindert and Williamson, *Unequal Gains,* 93.

10. Erica Armstrong Dunbar, *Never Caught: The Washingtons' Relentless Pursuit of Their Runaway Slave, Ona Judge* (New York: Simon & Schuster, 2017); Paul Finkelman, *Slavery and the Founders: Race and Liberty in the Age of Jefferson,* 3rd ed. (New York: Routledge, 2015) ix, 10, 14, 20; Staughton Lynd, *Class Conflict, Slavery, and the United States Constitution* (1967; repr., New York: Cambridge University Press, 2009), 19, 162–63; Starr, *Entrenchment,* 67.

11. Why did the North go for this? Because those New Englanders naïvely predicted, on the one hand, that slavery was on the wane, but they also believed, on the other, that the South simply would not ratify the Constitution without concessions protecting the peculiar institution. And so "not for the last time," as the historical sociologist Paul Starr has written, "the interests of Black people were sacrificed in the name of compromise and national unity." Graber, *Dred Scott and the Problem of Constitutional Evil,* 5; Paul Finkelman, *Supreme Injustice: Slavery in the Nation's Highest Court* (Cambridge, Mass.: Harvard University Press, 2018), 12–15, 17, 291; Finkelman, *Slavery and the Founders,* 11, 14; Starr, *Entrenchment,* 72.

12. Graber, *Dred Scott and the Problem of Constitutional Evil,* 92, 104; Finkelman, *Supreme Injustice,* 19.

13. Alfred Stepan and Juan Linz, "Comparative Perspectives on Inequality and the Quality of Democracy in the United States," *Perspective on Politics* 9 (2011): 841–56; 845, table 1.

14. Robin Einhorn, "Slavery and the Politics of Taxation in the Early United States," *Studies in American Political Development* 14 (2000): 156–83; Finkelman, *Supreme Injustice,* 13.

15. Ibid.

16. Esteban Ortiz-Ospina and Max Roser, "Taxation," Our World in Data (2016), ourworldindata.org/taxation. See also Peter Flora et al., *State, Economy and Society in Western Europe, 1815–1975* (Frankfurt: Campus Verlag, 1983).

17. Matthew Gardner, Steve Wamhoff, Mary Martellotta, and Lorena Roque, *Corporate Tax Avoidance Remains Rampant Under New Tax Law* (Washington, D.C.: Institute on Taxation and Economic Policy, 2019).

18. Robin Einhorn, "Slavery," *Enterprise and Society* 9 (2009): 491–506, especially 500; Finkelman, *Slavery and the Founders,* x; Graber, *Dred Scott and the Problem of Constitutional Evil,* 12; Lynd, *Class Conflict, Slavery,* 154.

19. Einhorn, "Slavery," 499; Robin Einhorn, *American Taxation, American Slavery* (Chicago: University of Chicago Press, 2006), 218; Finkelman, *Slavery and the Founders,* 7–8; Lynd, *Class Conflict, Slavery,* 159.

20. Einhorn, *American Taxation, American Slavery,* 245–46, 249–50; Finkelman, *Supreme Injustice,* 60–63, 221–22.

21. Einhorn, "Slavery," 492; Graber, *Dred Scott and the Problem of Constitutional Evil*, 18–20.

22. William Parker, "The Magic of Property," *Agricultural History* 54 (1980): 477–89; Stephanie E. Jones-Rogers, *They Were Her Property* (New Haven, Conn.: Yale University Press, 2019); Stephanie E. Jones-Rogers, "White Women and the Economy of Slavery," *Not Even Past*, February 1, 2019, notevenpast.org/white-women-and-the-economy-of-slavery/. On "fictitious commodities" that "subordinate the substance of society itself into the laws of the market," see Karl Polanyi, *The Great Transformation: The Political and Economic Origins of Our Time* (1944; repr., Boston: Beacon, 2001), 75.

23. Katie Thoennes, "Frankenstein Incorporated: The Rise of Corporate Power and Personhood in the United States," *Hamline Law Review* 28 (204): 204–36, especially 207. See also Leo Strine, Jr., "Corporate Power Ratchet: The Courts' Role in Eroding We the People's Ability to Constrain Our Corporate Creations," *Harvard Civil Rights–Civil Liberties Law Review* 51 (2016): 423–80.

24. Einhorn, "Slavery," 492; Starr, *Entrenchment*, 103. See also Charles Wallace Collins, *The Fourteenth Amendment and the States* (Boston: Little, Brown, 1912); Edward Corwin, *The Doctrine of Judicial Review: Its Legal and Historical Basis and Other Essays* (1914; repr., New York: Routledge, 2017); Joseph Losos, "The Impact of the Fourteenth Amendment upon Private Law," *Saint Louis University Law Journal* 6 (1961): 368–79; Sarah Pruitt, "How the 14th Amendment Made Corporations into People," *History Studies*, June 15, 2018.

25. Graber, *Dred Scott and the Problem of Constitutional Evil*, 15; Pruitt, "How the 14th Amendment Made Corporations into People"; Wendy Hansen, Michael Rocca, and Brittany Ortiz, "The Effects of Citizens United on Corporate Spending in the 2012 Presidential Election," *Journal of Politics* 77 (2015): 535–45.

26. Baptist, *The Half Has Never Been Told*, 131.

27. Ibid., 118–19.

28. Solomon Northup, *Twelve Years a Slave: Narrative of Solomon Northup, a Citizen of New-York, Kidnapped in Washington City in 1841, and Rescued in 1853, from a Cotton Plantation near the Red River in Louisiana*, ed. David Wilson (Auburn, N.Y.: Derby and Miller, 1853), 167.

29. Beckert and Rockman, *Slavery's Capitalism*, 13.

30. Baptist, *The Half Has Never Been Told*, 258.

31. Johnson, *River of Dark Dreams*, 154.

32. Ibid., 155.

33. Cotton was not antebellum America's most valuable agricultural commodity (corn was); nor did it account for a large share of the total national product. However, it did yield higher returns than other staple crops and, most important, utterly changed the economic landscape. Sven Beckert, *Empire of Cotton: A Global History* (New York: Knopf, 2014), xvii; Fernand Braudel, *Afterthoughts on Material Civilization and Capitalism* (Baltimore: Johns Hopkins University Press, 1977); Gavin Wright, "Slavery and the Cotton Boom," *Explorations in Economic History* 12 (1975): 439–51.

34. Stanley Engerman and Robert Gallman, "The Emergence of a Market Economy Before 1860," in *A Companion to 19th-Century America*, ed. William Barney (New York: John Wiley, 2001), 121–38, 129; Alan Olmstead and Paul Rhode, "Cotton, Slavery, and the New History of Capitalism," *Explorations in Economic History* 67 (2018): 1–17, 13.

35. Beckert, *Empire of Cotton*, 37.

36. Joshua Rothman, *Flush Times and Fever Dreams: A Story of Capitalism and Slavery in the Age of Jackson* (Athens: University of Georgia Press, 2012), 3, 7.

37. Eric Kimball, "'What Have We to Do with Slavery?': New Englanders and the Slave Economies of the West Indies," in Beckert and Rothman, *Slavery's Capitalism*, 161.

38. Herman Freudenberger and Jonathan Pritchett, "The Domestic United States Slave Trade: New Evidence," *Journal of Interdisciplinary History* 21 (1991): 447–77, figure 2.
39. Bonnie Martin, "Slavery's Invisible Engine: Mortgaging Human Property," *The Journal of Southern History* 76 (2010): 817–66.
40. Joseph Baldwin, *The Flush Times of Alabama and Mississippi, a Series of Sketches* (New York: D. Appleton & Co., 1854).
41. Baptist, *The Half Has Never Been Told*, 253.
42. Henry Wiencek, *Master of the Mountain: Thomas Jefferson and His Slaves* (New York: Farrar, Straus and Giroux, 2012), 96–98; The Jefferson Monticello, "The Business of Slavery at Monticello," www.monticello.org/thomas-jefferson/jefferson-slavery/the-business-of-slavery-at-monticello.
43. Baptist, *The Half Has Never Been Told*, 85–86.
44. Rothman, *Flush Times and Fever Dreams*, 5, 9, 11.
45. Orlando Patterson, "On Slavery and Slave Formations," *New Left Review* 117 (1979): 31–67, 51.
46. Baptist, *The Half Has Never Been Told*, 269–74.
47. John Clegg, "Capitalism and Slavery," *Critical Historical Studies* 2, no. 2 (2015): 300.
48. Seth Rockman, "What Makes the History of Capitalism Newsworthy?," *Journal of the Early Republic* 34, no. 3 (2014): 456.
49. Clegg, "Capitalism and Slavery," 299–301.
50. Baptist, *The Half Has Never Been Told*, 274, 290; Wright, "Slavery and the Cotton Boom," 446; Gavin Wright, "The Efficiency of Slavery: Another Interpretation," *American Economic Review* 69 (1979): 219–26; Gavin Wright, *Slavery and American Economic Development* (Baton Rouge: Louisiana State University Press, 2006).
51. Rothman, *Flush Times and Fever Dreams*, 6.
52. Adela Luque, Ron Jarmin, and C. J. Krizan, "Owner Characteristics and Firm Performance During the Great Recession" (Working Paper No. 2014-36, Center for Economic Studies, Washington, D.C., 2014); Signe-Mary McKernan, Caroline Ratcliffe, Eugene Steuerle, and Sisi Zhang, "Impact of the Great Recession and Beyond Disparities in Wealth Building by Generation and Race" (Urban Institute Working Paper, Washington, D.C., April 2014).
53. Caitlin Rosenthal, *Accounting for Slavery: Masters and Management* (Cambridge, Mass.: Harvard University Press, 2018), 6, 48.
54. Ibid.
55. Jan Richard Heier, "A Content Comparison of Antebellum Plantation Records and Thomas Affleck's Accounting Principles," *Accounting Historians Journal* 15 (1988): 131 50, 134.
56. Author email exchange with Caitlin Rosenthal, July 12, 2019.
57. Rosenthal, *Accounting for Slavery*, 127; Daina Ramey Berry, *The Price for Their Pound of Flesh: The Value of the Enslaved, from Womb to Grave, in the Building of a Nation* (Boston: Beacon, 2017).
58. James Breeden, ed., *Advice Among Masters: The Ideal in Slave Management in the Old South* (New York: Praeger, 1980), 54.
59. Baptist, *The Half Has Never Been Told*, 121.
60. Rosenthal, *Accounting for Slavery*, 115.
61. Breeden, *Advice Among Masters*, 10.
62. Alan Olmstead and Paul Rhode, "Productivity Growth and the Regional Dynamics of Antebellum Southern Development" (NBER Working Paper No. 16494, October 2010); Alan Olmstead and Paul Rhode, *Creating Abundance: Biological Innovation and American Agricultural Development* (New York: Cambridge University Press, 2008).
63. Rosenthal, *Accounting for Slavery*, 81.

64. Baptist, *The Half Has Never Been Told*, 121, 134.

65. Henry Watson, *Narrative of Henry Watson: A Fugitive Slave* (Boston: Abner Forbes, 1848), 19–20.

66. Northup, *Twelve Years a Slave*, 167–68.

67. John Brown, *Slave Life in Georgia: A Narrative of the Life, Sufferings, and Escape of John Brown, a Fugitive Slave, Now in England* (London: n.p., 1855), 171.

68. Historians and economists have long debated the extent to which slavery gave rise to industrial capitalism. Some have argued that Northern industry was dependent on slavery, while others have made the opposite claim: that slavery was dependent on Northern industry. There is much more consensus about the centrality of slavery to the development of capitalism throughout the nineteenth century. See Clegg, "Capitalism and Slavery," 295–99.

69. John Forsyth, "The North and the South," *De Bow's Review* 17 (October 1854): 365.

70. Beckert, *Empire of Cotton*, 179.

71. Tony Judt, *Socialism in Provence, 1871–1914: A Study in the Origins of the Modern French Left* (Cambridge: Cambridge University Press, 1979); John Saville, *1848: The British State and the Chartist Movement* (Cambridge: Cambridge University Press, 1990).

72. Seymour Martin Lipset, *American Exceptionalism: A Double-Edged Sword* (New York: Norton, 1996), 33, 77; Kim Voss, *The Making of American Exceptionalism* (Ithaca, N.Y.: Cornell University Press, 1993); Werner Sombart, *Why Is There No Socialism in the United States?* (1906; repr., White Plains, N.Y.: International Arts and Sciences Press, 1976).

73. Michael Hanagan, "Response to Sean Wilentz, 'Against Exceptionalism: Consciousness and the American Labor Movement, 1790–1920,'" *International Labor and Working Class History* 26 (1984): 31–36, especially 33; Lane Kenworthy, *Social Democratic Capitalism* (New York: Oxford University Press, 2020).

74. Arthur Alderson and François Nielsen, "Globalization and the Great U-turn: Income Inequality Trends in 16 OECD Countries," *American Journal of Sociology* 107 (2002): 1244–99; Henry Farber, Daniel Herbst, Ilyana Kuziemko, and Suresh Naidu, "Unions and Inequality over the Twentieth Century: New Evidence from Survey Data" (Working Paper 24587, National Bureau of Economic Research, Cambridge, Mass., 2018); Bruce Western and Jake Rosenfeld, "Unions, Norms, and the Rise in U.S. Wage Inequality," *American Sociological Review* 76 (2011): 513–37.

75. Eric Foner, *The Story of American Freedom* (New York: Norton, 1998), 59–60, 65; Eric Foner, *Reconstruction: America's Unfinished Revolution, 1863–1877,* updated ed. (New York: Harper-Perennial, 2014), 110, 404–5, 408; Seth Rockman, *Scraping By: Wage Labor, Slavery, and Survival in Early Baltimore* (Baltimore: Johns Hopkins University Press, 2009), 141, 241; Erica Armstrong Dunbar, *A Fragile Freedom: African American Women and Emancipation in the Antebellum City* (New Haven, Conn.: Yale University Press, 2008), 36.

76. Philip Dray, *There Is Power in a Union: The Epic Story of Labor in America* (New York: Anchor, 2010), 24–25; Joseph Reidy, *From Slavery to Agrarian Capitalism in the Cotton Plantation South: Central Georgia, 1800–1880* (Chapel Hill: University of North Carolina Press, 1992), 54–55; Foner, *Story of American Freedom*, 60, 62.

77. Dray, *There Is Power in a Union*, 53, 66.

78. Joe William Trotter, Jr., *Workers on Arrival: Black Labor in the Making of America* (Oakland: University of California Press, 2019), 53.

79. Ibid., 28; Leslie Harris, *In the Shadow of Slavery: African Americans in New York City, 1626–1863* (Chicago: University of Chicago Press, 2002); Nikki Taylor, *Frontiers of Freedom: Cincinnati's Black Community, 1802–1868* (Athens: Ohio University Press, 2005); W.E.B. Du Bois, *The Philadelphia Negro: A Social Study* (1899; repr., Philadelphia: University of Pennsylvania Press, 1996).

80. Rayford Whittingham Logan, *The Betrayal of the Negro: From Rutherford B. Hayes to Woodrow Wilson* (1954; repr., New York: Collier, 1965), 142.

81. Dray, *There Is Power in a Union*, 184. See also Foner, *Reconstruction*, 479–80.

82. Eric Arnesen, "The Quicksands of Economic Insecurity: African Americans, Strikebreaking, and Labor Activism in the Industrial Era," in *The Black Worker: Race, Labor, and Civil Rights since Emancipation,* ed. Eric Arnesen (Champaign: University of Illinois Press, 2007), 41–71; Trotter, *Workers on Arrival,* 65–66; Dray, *There Is Power in a Union,* 185.

83. W.E.B. Du Bois, *Black Reconstruction in America, 1860–1880* (1935; repr., New York: Free Press, 1998), 700. See also David Roediger and Elizabeth Esch, *The Production of Difference: Race and the Management of Labor in U.S. History* (New York: Oxford University Press, 2012).

84. Reidy, *From Slavery to Agrarian Capitalism,* 222–26, 240–47. On the role of indebtedness and market dependency, see John Clegg, "A Theory of Capitalist Slavery," *Journal of Historical Sociology* 33 (2020): 74–98.

85. Reidy, *From Slavery to Agrarian Capitalism,* 84–85.

86. Stanley Engerman, "Slavery at Different Times and Places," *American Historical Review* 105 (April 2000): 480.

87. Robert Fogel, *Without Consent or Contract: The Rise and Fall of American Slavery* (New York: Norton, 1994), 85; Lee Soltow, *Men and Wealth in the United States, 1850–1870* (New Haven, Conn.: Yale University Press, 1971), 101; Lindert and Williamson, *Unequal Gains,* 116–17.

88. Talitha LeFlouria, *Chained in Silence: Black Women and Convict Labor in the New South* (Chapel Hill: University of North Carolina Press, 2015), 15. See also Dunbar, *A Fragile Freedom.*

89. Alexis de Tocqueville, *Democracy in America*, trans. Henry Reeve (1835; repr., Cambridge: Sever and Francis, 1863), 159, 127.

90. Du Bois, *Black Reconstruction,* 586.

91. Dray, *There Is Power in a Union,* 184, 368–69, 482–83.

92. Emmanuel Saez and Gabriel Zucman, "The Rise of Income and Wealth Inequality in America: Evidence from Distributional Macroeconomic Accounts," *Journal of Economic Perspectives* 34 (2020): 3–26, especially 9.

Chapter 7: Politics

1. "Donald Trump 2020 Election Night Speech Transcript," November 4, 2020, www.rev.com/blog/transcripts/donald-trump-2020-election-night-speech-transcript.

2. "Donald Trump White House Press Conference as Election Counts Continue," November 5, 2020, www.rev.com/blog/transcripts/donald-trump-white-house-press-conference-as-election-counts-continue-transcript-november-5.

3. Salvador Rizzo, "Attorney General Barr's False Claims About Voting by Mail," *Washington Post,* September 4, 2020, www.washingtonpost.com/politics/2020/09/04/attorney-general-barrs-false-claims-about-voting-by-mail/; James Rainey, "'There Is a Voter-Suppression Wing': An Ugly American Tradition Clouds the 2020 Presidential Race," *Los Angeles Times,* October 24, 2020, www.latimes.com/politics/story/2020-10-24/voter-suppression-clouds-2020-vote.

4. Juana Summers, "Trump Push to Invalidate Votes in Heavily Black Cities Alarms Civil Rights Groups," *All Things Considered,* November 24, 2020, www.npr.org/2020/11/24/938187233/trump-push-to-invalidate-votes-in-heavily-black-cities-alarms-civil-rights-group.

5. "Transcript of Trump's Speech at Rally Before US Capital Riot," January 13, 2021, www.usnews.com/news/politics/articles/2021-01-13/transcript-of-trumps-speech-at-rally-before-us-capitol-riot.

6. Edward E. Baptist, *The Half Has Never Been Told: Slavery and the Making of American Capitalism* (New York: Basic Books, 2014), xxi.

7. Manisha Sinha, *The Counterrevolution of Slavery: Politics and Ideology in Antebellum South Carolina* (Chapel Hill: University of North Carolina Press, 2000), 12.

8. Ibid., 20–21.

9. Richard Elder, *Calhoun: American Heretic* (New York: Basic Books, 2021), 335–36.

10. Robert James Turnbull, *The Crisis: Or, Essays on the Usurpations of the Federal Government* (Charleston, S.C.: A. E. Miller, 1827), 137, www.google.com/books/edition/The_Crisis/GlZgAAAAcAAJ?hl=en&gbpv=0.

11. Letter from John C. Calhoun to Littleton Waller Tazewell, August 25, 1827, civilwarcause.com/calhoun/caltaz.html; emphasis added.

12. John Caldwell Calhoun, William Edwin Hemphill, Clyde Norman Wilson, and Robert Lee Meriwether, *The Papers of John C. Calhoun* (Columbia: University of South Carolina Press, 1959), 15:357.

13. Quote taken from Sinha, *Counterrevolution of Slavery*, 22.

14. Richard Kenner Crallé, ed., *The Works of John C. Calhoun: Reports and Public Letters* (New York, Appleton, 1855), 110, www.google.com/books/edition/Reports_and_public_letters/BoxLAAAAYAAJ?hl=en&gbpv=0.

15. Richard Kenner Crallé, ed., *The Works of John C. Calhoun*, Vol. 4 (Wentworth Press, 2016), 46.

16. Elder, *Calhoun*, 388–89.

17. John C. Calhoun, "Slavery a Positive Good," February 6, 1837, Teaching American History, teachingamericanhistory.org/library/document/slavery-a-positive-good/.

18. John C. Calhoun, *Disquisition on Government*, 1840, Teaching American History, teachingamericanhistory.org/library/document/disquisition-on-government/.

19. William F. Buckley, Jr., "Why the South Must Prevail," *National Review*, August 24, 1957, 148–49. Also see Paul Krugman's *The Conscience of a Liberal* (New York: Norton, 2007), 102–3.

20. Barry Goldwater, *The Conscience of a Conservative* (Shepherdsville, Ky.: Victor, 1960), 25, 33, 36. On Goldwater's appeal to white Southern voters, see Angie Maxwell, "What We Get Wrong About the Southern Strategy," *Washington Post*, July 29, 2019, www.washingtonpost.com/outlook/2019/07/26/what-we-get-wrong-about-southern-strategy/.

21. Samuel Francis, "The Education of David Duke," *Chronicles*, February 1992, www.chroniclesmagazine.org/the-education-of-david-duke/.

22. Matt A. Barreto and Christopher S. Parker, *Change They Can't Believe In: The Tea Party and Reactionary Politics in America* (Princeton, N. J.: Princeton University Press, 2013), 35.

23. Theda Skocpol and Vanessa Williamson, *The Tea Party and the Remaking of Republican Conservatism* (New York: Oxford University Press, 2012), 74.

24. Brady Dennis, Alec MacGillis, and Lori Montgomery, "Origins of the Debt Showdown," *Washington Post*, August 3, 2011, www.washingtonpost.com/business/economy/origins-of-the-debt-showdown/2011/08/03/gIQA9uqIzI_story.html.

25. Michael Wines and Alan Blinder, "Federal Appeals Court Strikes Down North Carolina Voter ID Requirement," *New York Times*, July 29, 2016, www.nytimes.com/2016/07/30/us/federal-appeals-court-strikes-down-north-carolina-voter-id-provision.html.

26. Michael Li, "Gerrymandering Meets the Coronavirus in Wisconsin," April 8, 2020, www.brennancenter.org/our-work/analysis-opinion/gerrymandering-meets-coronavirus-wisconsin; "Michigan Republicans Vote to Strip Power from Incoming Democrat," December 6, 2018, www.theguardian.com/us-news/2018/dec/06/republicans-michigan-wisconsin-strip-power-incoming-democrats.

27. "Sen. Fitzgerald: Statement on Extraordinary Session," Wisconsin Politics, www.wispolitics.com/2018/sen-fitzgerald-statement-on-extraordinary-session/; Molly Beck, "A Blue Wave Hit

Statewide Races, but Did Wisconsin GOP Gerrymandering Limit Dem Legislative Inroads?" *Milwaukee Journal Sentinel,* www.jsonline.com/story/news/politics/elections/2018/11/08/wisconsin-election-did-redistricting-limit-dem-inroads-legislature/1919288002/.

28. Nina Totenberg, "Sen. McCain Says Republicans Will Block All Court Nominations If Clinton Wins," October 17, 2016, NPR Politics, www.npr.org/2016/10/17/498328520/sen-mccain-says-republicans-will-block-all-court-nominations-if-clinton-wins.

Chapter 8: Citizenship

1. *Proceedings of the Colored National Convention, Held in Rochester, July 6th, 7th, and 8th, 1853* (Rochester, N.Y.: F. Douglass' Paper, 1853); "National Convention of Colored Men," *Trenton State Gazette,* July 8, 1853. On the Colored Conventions movement, see P. Gabrielle Foreman, Jim Casey, and Sarah Lynn Patterson, eds., *The Colored Conventions Movement: Black Organizing in the Nineteenth Century* (Chapel Hill: University of North Carolina Press, 2021), and Christopher James Bonner, *Remaking the Republic: Black Politics and the Creation of American Citizenship* (Philadelphia: University of Pennsylvania Press, 2020).
2. *Proceedings of the Colored National Convention* (1853); "National Convention of Colored Men."
3. Martha S. Jones, *Birthright Citizens: A History of Race and Rights in Antebellum America* (New York: Cambridge University Press, 2018), 1–15; Manisha Sinha, *The Slave's Cause: A History of Abolition* (New Haven, Conn.: Yale University Press, 2016), 65–98; U.S. Constitution, Amendment XIV, § 2.
4. Declaration of Independence (United States, 1776); Articles of Confederation (1777).
5. "A Request to Selectmen of Dartmouth, April 22, 1781," www.westport-ma.com/sites/g/files/vyhlif1441/f/uploads/27._cuffe_1781_request_for_relief_from_taxation.jpg; Lamont D. Thomas, *Rise to Be a People: A Biography of Paul Cuffe* (Champaign: University of Illinois Press 1986), 9–12; "Petition Signed by John Cuffe and Paul Cuffe Regarding Taxation, December 19, 1870," Collection of the Smithsonian National Museum of African American History and Culture; "A Request to the Select Men of Dartmouth, Massachusetts, April 22, 1781," Paul Cuffe: An African-American and Native-American Heritage Trail, paulcuffe.org/primary-documents/#gallery-1.
6. U.S. Constitution, Article I, § 1; Article II, § 2 and 3; Article III, §2; Article IV, § 2.
7. Gary B. Nash, *Forging Freedom: The Formation of Philadelphia's Black Community, 1720–1840* (Cambridge, Mass.: Harvard University Press, 1988); Erica Armstrong Dunbar, *A Fragile Freedom: African American Women and Emancipation in the Antebellum City* (New Haven, Conn.: Yale University Press, 2008); Julie Winch, *A Gentleman of Color: The Life of James Forten* (New York: Oxford University Press, 2002); Naturalization Act of 1790, 1 Stat. 103.
8. Petition of Absalom Jones, and Others, People of Color, and Freemen Against the Slave Trade to the Coast of Guinea, HR 6A-F4.2, Records of the U.S. House of Representatives, Record Group 233, National Archives Building, Washington, D.C.; Nicholas P. Wood, "A 'Class of Citizens': The Earliest Black Petitioners to Congress and Their Quaker Allies," *William and Mary Quarterly* 74, no. 1 (January 2017): 109–44.
9. Wood, "A 'Class of Citizens.'"
10. William Wirt, "Rights of Free Virginia Negroes," in *Official Opinions of the Attorneys General of the United States, Advising the President and Heads of Departments in Relation to Their Official Duties,* ed. Benjamin F. Hall (Washington, D.C.: Robert Farnham, 1852), 506–9.
11. Jones, *Birthright Citizens,* 26–28.
12. Ibid.; Annals of Congress, 16th Congress, 2nd Session (1821), 985–95.
13. Jones, *Birthright Citizens,* 26–28; Annals of Congress, 17th Congress, 1st Session (1821), 1236–40.
14. Nicholas Guyatt, "'The Outskirts of Our Happiness': Race and the Lure of Colonization in

the Early Republic," *Journal of American History* 95, no. 4 (March 2009): 986–1011; Alex Lovit, "'The Bounds of Habitation': The Geography of the American Colonization Society, 1816–1860" (PhD diss., University of Michigan, 2011).

15. *Constitution of the American Society of Free Persons of Colour . . . Also Proceedings of the Convention with Their Address to the Free Persons of Colour in the United States* (Philadelphia: J. W. Allen, 1830).

16. A Colored Baltimorean, "For the Genius of Universal Emancipation," *Genius of Universal Emancipation*, July 1831.

17. Ibid.

18. See, for example, Leon Litwack and August Meier, eds., *Black Leaders of the Nineteenth Century* (Champaign: University of Illinois Press, 1988), 17. See also Leslie M. Alexander, *African or American? Black Identity and Political Activism in New York City, 1784–1861* (Champaign: University of Illinois Press, 2008), 70–71.

19. *Minutes and Proceedings of the First Annual Convention of the People of Colour, Held by Adjournments in the City of Philadelphia, from the Sixth to the Eleventh of June, Inclusive, 1831* (Philadelphia: Committee of Arrangements, 1831), 4–5.

20. *Reports of the Proceedings and Debates of the Convention of 1821, Assembled for the Purpose of Amending the Constitution of the State of New York* (Albany: E. and E. Hosford, 1821).

21. William A. Blair, "Vagabond Voters and Racial Suffrage in Jacksonian-Era Pennsylvania," *Journal of the Civil War Era* 9, no. 4 (January 2019): 569–87; Nicholas Wood, "'Sacrifice on the Altar of Slavery': Doughface Politics and Black Disenfranchisement in Pennsylvania, 1837–1838," *Journal of the Early Republic* 31, no. 1 (January 2011): 75–106.

22. For more on how Black activists developed notions of belonging, see Foreman, Casey, and Patterson, eds., *The Colored Conventions Movement.*

23. *Minutes of the National Convention of Colored Citizens: Held at Buffalo* (New York: Piercy & Reed, 1843); William J. Richardson, "The Life and Times of Samuel H. Davis: An Anti Slavery Activist," *Afro-Americans in New York Life and History* 33, no. 1 (January 2009): 47–89.

24. *Proceedings of the Colored National Convention, 1853.*

25. Martin Delany, *The Condition, Elevation, Emigration and Destiny of the Colored People of the United States, Politically Considered* (Philadelphia: 1852), 48–49, www.googlecom/books/edition/The_Condition_Elevation_Emigration_and_D/laJqaN7UOgcC?hl=en&gbpv=1&dq=%22We+are+Americans,+having+a+birthright+citizenship%22&pg=PA48&printsec=frontcover.

26. H. Jefferson Powell, "Attorney General Taney and the South Carolina Police Bill." *Green Bag 2D* 5 (2001): 75–100; *Smith v. Turner*, 48 U.S. 283 (1849); "Opinions of the Judges of the Supreme Court of the United States in the Cases of 'Smith v. Turner' and 'Norris v. the City of Boston,'" *Southern Quarterly Review* 16, no. 32 (January 1850): 444–502.

27. *Dred Scott v. Sandford*, 60 U.S. (19 How) 393 (1857), www.law.cornell.edu/supremecourt/text/60/393.

28. Ibid.

29. Jones, *Birthright Citizens*, 1–15.

30. *Scott v. Sandford*, 60 U.S, 508.

31. Ibid., 518.

32. Ibid., 769–70.

33. Ibid.

34. Jones, *Birthright Citizens*, 128–37.

35. Ibid.

36. Frederick Douglass, "Speech on the Dred Scott Decision," May 1857, teachingamericanhistory.org/library/document/speech-on-the-dred-scott-decision-2/.

37. Jones, *Birthright Citizens*, 128–37.

38. Edward Bates, *Opinion of Attorney General Bates on Citizenship* (Washington, D.C.: Government Printing Office, 1863), 3–4.

39. Ibid., 12.

40. Ibid.

41. *Proceedings of the National Convention of Colored Men, Held in the City of Syracuse, N.Y., October 4, 5, 6, and 7, 1864* (By the Convention, 1864), 15.

42. Civil Rights Act of 1866, Public Law 39-26, 14 STAT 27.

43. Andrew Johnson, "Veto Message on Civil Rights Legislation, March 27, 1866," millercenter .org/the-presidency/presidential-speeches/march-27-1866-veto-message-civil-right -legislation; "Transcript, Meeting Between President Andrew Johnson and a Delegation of African-Americans, White House, February 7, 1866," House Divided: The Civil War Research Engine at Dickinson College, hd.housedivided.dickinson.edu/node/45144. For Douglass's reply, see Frederick Douglass, "Reply of the Colored Delegation to the President, February 7, 1866," rbscp.lib.rochester.edu/4391.

44. U.S. Constitution, Amendment XIV; Eric Foner, *The Second Founding: How the Civil War and Reconstruction Remade the Constitution* (New York: Norton, 2019), 55–92; Garrett Epps, *Democracy Reborn: The 14th Amendment and the Fight for Civil Rights in Post–Civil War America* (New York: Holt, 2006).

45. Epps, *Democracy Reborn;* Foner, *Second Founding,* 55–92.

46. Ibid.

47. *Proceedings of the National Convention of the Colored Men of America, Held in Washington, D.C., on January 13, 14, 15, and 16, 1869* (Washington, D.C.: n.p., 1869), 1, udspace.udel.edu/bitstream/ handle/19716/18335/1869DC-National-Washington_Proccedings.pdf?sequence=1&is Allowed=y .

48. Ibid.

49. Ibid.

50. Ibid.

51. Ibid.

52. Foner, *Second Founding,* 93–124.

53. Frederick Douglass, "Composite Nation: A Lecture by Frederick Douglass, in the Parker Fraternity Course, Boston, 1867," folder 1 of 3, 1867, manuscript/mixed material, www.loc .gov/item/mfd.22016/.

54. Foner, *Second Founding.*

55. "Colored Convention: Bishop Turner, of Atlanta, Calls the Meeting to Order in Cincinnati," *Atchison Daily Globe,* November 29, 1893.

Chapter 9: Self-Defense

1. Elie Mystal, "Black People Are Not Even Legally Allowed to Be Afraid of White People," Above the Law, June 22, 2017, abovethelaw.com/2017/06/black-people-are-not-even-legally -allowed-to-be-afraid-of-white-people/; Aungelique Proctor, "Jessie Murray Trial Underway, Jury Selection Continues," Fox 5 Atlanta, June 27, 2017, www.fox5atlanta.com/news/ jessie-murray-trial-underway-jury-selection-continues; Marcus K. Garner, "Former Cop Shot, Killed at Clayton County Bar," *Atlanta Journal-Constitution,* February 18, 2014, www.ajc.com/ news/former-cop-shot-killed-clayton-county-bar/XgDxTu2bnwqCHoQw4cwztL/.

2. Proctor, "Jessie Murray Trial Underway"; "Man Claims Self-Defense in Deadly Bar Fight," WSB-TV, February 19, 2014, www.wsbtv.com/news/local/man-claims-self-defense-deadly -bar-fight/138153080/.

3. Mo Barnes, "Attorney Mawuli Davis on Jessie Murray's Victory and Georgia Stand Your

Ground," *DeAndo* (blog), June 30, 2017, deando.com/attorney-mawuli-davis-on-jessie-murrays-victory-and-georgia-stand-your-ground/.

4. "Georgia Right to Self-defense Act of 2006," H.B. 1061, www.legis.ga.gov/legislation/17350.

5. Katheryn Russell-Brown, "Go Ahead and Shoot—the Law Might Have Your Back: History, Race, Implicit Bias, and Justice in Florida's Stand Your Ground Law," in *Deadly Justice: Trayvon Martin, Race, and the Criminal Justice System*, ed. Devon Johnson, Patricia Y. Warren, and Amy Farrell (New York: New York University Press, 2015), 118–20.

6. *District of Columbia v. Heller*, 544 U.S. 570 (2008), 26, 56, www.supremecourt.gov/opinions/07pdf/07-290.pdf, emphasis in the original; *McDonald v. City of Chicago* 561 U. S. 742 (2010), www.supremecourt.gov/opinions/09pdf/08-1521.pdf.

7. Justin A. Joyce, *Gunslinging Justice: The American Culture of Gun Violence in Westerns and the Law* (Manchester, U.K.: Manchester University Press, 2018), 51, 53, 69; Antonin Scalia concurrence in *Minnesota v. Carter* (569 N. W. 2d 169).

8. David B. Kopel, "Hold Your Fire: Gun Control Won't Stop Rising Violence," *Policy Review* 93, no. 63 (Winter 1993), 58.

9. Joyce Tang, "Enslaved African Rebellions in Virginia," *Journal of Black Studies* 27, no. 5 (May 1997): 601; Transcription from David J. McCord, ed., *The Statutes at Large of South Carolina*, vol. 7, *Containing the Acts Relating to Charleston, Courts, Slaves, and Rivers* (Columbia, S.C.: A. S. Johnston, 1840), 397, digital.scetv.org/teachingAmerhistory/pdfs/Transciptionof1740SlaveCodes.pdf; Sally E. Hadden, *Slave Patrols: Law and Violence in Virginia and the Carolinas* (Cambridge, Mass.: Harvard University Press, 2003), 106, 123; Peter H. Wood, *Black Majority: Negroes in Colonial South Carolina from 1670 Through the Stono Rebellion* (New York: Knopf, 1974), Kindle loc. 6836, 6839–40.

10. *Dred Scott v. Sandford*, 60 U.S. 393 (1856), 60, supreme.justia.com/cases/federal/us/60/393/#tab-opinion-1964281; Carol Anderson, *The Second: Race and Guns in a Fatally Unequal America* (New York: Bloomsbury, 2021), 82.

11. Cited in *District of Columbia v. Heller*, 39.

12. Ibid., emphasis in the original.

13. Nicholas J. Johnson, David B. Kopel, George A. Mocsary, and Michael P. O'Shea, *Firearms Law and the Second Amendment: Regulation, Rights, and Policy* (New York: Wolters Kluwer Law and Business, 2012), 277–78.

14. Adam Weinstein, "The Trayvon Martin Killing, Explained," *Mother Jones*, March 18, 2012, www.motherjones.com/politics/2012/03/what-happened-trayvon-martin-explained/#newvideo; Mike Schneider, "Instructions to the Jury Were at the Forefront of the Zimmerman Verdict," *Business Insider*, July 14, 2013, www.businessinsider.com/instructions-to-the-jury-were-at-the-forefront-of-the-zimmerman-verdict-2013-7.

15. Mystal, "Black People Are Not Even Legally."

16. Jennifer L. Eberhardt, *Biased: Uncovering the Hidden Prejudice That Shapes What We See, Think, and Do* (New York: Viking, 2019), 35, 36, 62.

17. Jennifer L. Eberhardt, Phillip Atiba Goff, V. J. Purdie, and P. G. Davies, "Seeing Black: Race, Crime, and Visual Processing," *Journal of Personality and Social Psychology* 87, no. 6 (2004): 876–93, doi.org/10.1037/0022-3514.87.6.876; Eberhardt, *Biased*, 66.

18. Phillip Atiba Goff, Matthew Christian Jackson, Brooke Allison Lewis Di Leone, Carmen Marie Culotta, and Natalie Ann DiTomasso, "The Essence of Innocence: Consequences of Dehumanizing Black Children," *Journal of Personality and Social Psychology* 106, no. 4 (2014): 526–45, doi.org/10.1037/a0035663.

19. Anthony G. Greenwald, Mark A. Oakes, and Hunter G. Hoffman, "Targets of Discrimination: Effects of Race on Responses to Weapons Holders," *Journal of Experimental Social Psychology* 39 (2003): 399–405, doi.org/10.1016/S0022-1031(03)00020-9.

20. Russell-Brown, "Go Ahead and Shoot," 132–33; U.S. Commission on Civil Rights, *Examining the Race Effects of Stand Your Ground Laws and Related Issues* (Washington, D.C.: U.S. Commission on Civil Rights, 2020), 16.

21. Noel B. Poirier, "A Legacy of Integration: The African American Citizen-Soldier and the Continental Army," *Army History* 56 (Fall 2002): 20; Benjamin Quarles, *The Negro in the American Revolution* (Chapel Hill: University of North Carolina Press, 1961), 53–54, 56.

22. Quarles, *Negro in the American Revolution,* 64; Robert A. Olwell, "'Domestick Enemies': Slavery and Political Independence in South Carolina, May 1775–March 1776," *Journal of Southern History* 55, no. 1 (February 1989): 32, 35.

23. John Buchanan, *The Road to Charleston: Nathanael Greene and the American Revolution* (Charlottesville: University of Virginia Press, 2019), Kindle loc. 6337.

24. Poirier, "A Legacy of Integration," 18, 22; Robert G. Parkinson, *The Common Cause: Creating Race and Nation in the American Revolution* (Chapel Hill: University of North Carolina Press, 2016), Kindle loc. 9865–66, 9890–9901.

25. James T. Kloppenberg, *Toward Democracy: The Struggle for Self-Rule in European and American Thought* (New York: Oxford University Press, 2016), 407.

26. Stephanie E. Smallwood, *Saltwater Slavery: A Middle Passage from Africa to American Diaspora* (Cambridge, Mass.: Harvard University Press, 2007) Kindle loc. 387, 392, 395, 398; Michael J. Klarman, *The Framers' Coup: The Making of the United States Constitution* (New York: Oxford University Press, 2016), 268; James Madison, Edward J. Larson, and Michael P. Winship, *The Constitutional Convention* (New York: Modern Library, 2011), Kindle loc. 2706.

27. Andrew Delbanco, *The War Before the War: Fugitive Slaves and the Struggle for America's Soul from the Revolution to the Civil War* (New York: Penguin Books, 2019), 48–49; Pauline Maier, *Ratification: The People Debate the Constitution, 1787-1788* (New York: Simon & Schuster, 2010), 284.

28. Don Higginbotham, "The Federalized Militia Debate: A Neglected Aspect of Second Amendment Scholarship," *William and Mary Quarterly* 55, no. 1 (January 1998): 40.

29. David Waldstreicher, *Slavery's Constitution: From Revolution to Ratification* (New York: Hill and Wang, 2009), 99–100; Higginbotham, "Federalized Militia Debate," 47–48.

30. The Constitution Annotated, constitution.congress.gov/browse/article-1/section-8/.

31. Maier, *Ratification,* 283.

32. Anderson, *The Second,* 28; Waldstreicher, *Slavery's Constitution,* 120; Klarman, *Framers' Coup,* 294; Paul Finkelman, *Beyond Confederation: Origins of the Constitution and American National Identity* (Chapel Hill: University of North Carolina Press, Omohundro Institute of Early American History, 1987), 212.

33. Kenneth R. Bowling, "'A Tub to the Whale': The Founding Fathers and Adoption of the Federal Bill of Rights," *Journal of the Early Republic* 8, no. 3 (Autumn 1988): 226–27.

34. Maier, *Ratification,* 216.

35. Waldstreicher, *Slavery's Constitution,* 144.

36. Michael Waldman, *The Second Amendment: A Biography* (New York: Simon & Schuster, 2014), 38.

37. Ibid., 37.

38. Ibid., 39.

39. Maier, *Ratification,* 307, 308; Virginia Declaration of Rights, June 12, 1776, Section 13, www.archives.gov/founding-docs/virginia-declaration-of-rights.

40. Maier, *Ratification,* 316.

41. Higginbotham, "Federalized Militia Debate," 48.

42. Bowling, "'A Tub to the Whale,'" 224.

43. Joseph J. Ellis, *The Quartet: Orchestrating the Second American Revolution, 1783-1789* (New York: Vintage, 2016), 206.

44. Carl T. Bogus, "The Hidden History of the Second Amendment," *U.C. Davis Law Review* 31 (1998): 350.
45. Ibid., 368.
46. Herbert Aptheker, "American Negro Slave Revolts," *Science and Society* 1, no. 4 (Summer 1937): 531.
47. Robert J. Cottrol and Raymond T. Diamond, "The Second Amendment: Toward an Afro-Americanist Reconsideration," *Georgetown Law Journal* 80 (1991): 336–37.
48. Michael L. Nicholls, "'Holy Insurrection': Spinning the News of Gabriel's Conspiracy," *Journal of Southern History* 78, no. 1 (February 2012): 50.
49. Jack P. Greene, "The Background of the Articles of Confederation," *Publius* 12, no. 4 (Autumn 1982): 16, 20.
50. Kellie Carter Jackson, *Force and Freedom: Black Abolitionists and the Politics of Violence* (Philadelphia: University of Pennsylvania Press, 2019), Kindle loc. 990; Lucy Maddox, *The Parker Sisters: A Border Kidnapping* (Philadelphia: Temple University Press, 2016), 25.
51. Maddox, *Parker Sisters*, 31–32; Jackson, *Force and Freedom*, loc. 1047.
52. Jackson, *Force and Freedom*, loc. 1074.
53. James J. Robbins, *Report of the Trial of Castner Hanway for Treason, in the Resistance of the Execution of the Fugitive Slave Law of September, 1850* (Philadelphia: King & Baird, 1852), found in "Christiana Treason Trial (1851)," Digital Bookshelf: Records and Court Cases, www .housedivided.dickinson.edu/ugrr/case_1851.htm; Jackson, *Force and Freedom*, loc. 1071, 1085, 1090.
54. Nicholas Johnson, *Negroes and the Gun: The Black Tradition of Arms* (Amherst, N.Y.: Prometheus, 2014), 64–65; Robbins, *Report of the Trial*.
55. Maddox, *Parker Sisters*, 86.
56. Ibid., 109–11.
57. Ibid., 161.
58. "Kidnapping—Death of Miller—Escape of George Williams—Release of All Christiana Prisoners," *Frederick Douglass' Paper*, February 19, 1852, tile.loc.gov/storage-services/service/ sgp/sgpbatches/batch_dlc_coneflower_ver01/data/sn84026366/0041755726A/1852021901/ 0001.pdf.
59. Maddox, *Parker Sisters*, 157–63.
60. "Black Soldiers in the U.S. Military During the Civil War," www.archives.gov/education/ lessons/blacks-civil-war.
61. Erica Armstrong Dunbar, *She Came to Slay: The Life and Times of Harriet Tubman* (New York: 37 Ink / Simon & Schuster, 2019), 91–93.
62. Kopel, "Hold Your Fire."
63. Anderson, *The Second*, 85–86.
64. Steven Hahn, *A Nation Under Our Feet: Black Political Struggles in the Rural South from Slavery to the Great Migration* (Cambridge, Mass.: Belknap Press of Harvard University Press, 2003), 267.
65. Johnson, *Negroes and the Gun*, 80–82, 86, 92.
66. Andrew F. Lang, "Republicanism, Race, and Reconstruction: The Ethos of Military Occupation in Civil War America," *Journal of the Civil War Era* 4, no. 4 (December 2014): 572–73, 575–76.
67. Carl Schurz, *Report on the Condition of the South* ([1865?]; repr., n.p.:, 2012), 152.
68. Ibid., 49.
69. Ibid., 152. Emphasis in the original.
70. Ibid., 144.

71. Annette Gordon-Reed, *Andrew Johnson* (New York: Times Books, 2011), 117–18.

72. Ibid., 118.

73. Ron Chernow, *Grant* (New York: Penguin Press, 2017), 841.

74. David Fort Godshalk, *Veiled Visions: The 1906 Atlanta Race Riot and the Reshaping of American Race Relations* (Chapel Hill: University of North Carolina Press, 2005), 102, 103, 104.

75. Cameron McWhirter, *Red Summer: The Summer of 1919 and the Awakening of Black America* (New York: Holt, 2011), 13.

76. Robert Whitaker, *On the Laps of Gods: The Red Summer of 1919 and the Struggle for Justice That Remade a Nation* (New York: Crown, 2008), 3, 111–12; Griff Stockley, Brian K. Mitchell, and Guy Lancaster, *Blood in Their Eyes: The Elaine Massacre of 1919* (Fayetteville: University of Arkansas Press, 2020), 12.

77. McWhirter, *Red Summer,* 173–80.

78. Carlee Hoffman and Claire Strom, "A Perfect Storm: The Ocoee Riot of 1920," *Florida Historical Quarterly* 93, no. 1 (Summer 2014): 25; Paul Ortiz, *Emancipation Betrayed: The Hidden History of Black Organizing and White Violence in Florida from Reconstruction to the Bloody Election of 1920* (Berkeley: University of California Press, 2005), 207, 212, 220, 221–28; Desiree Stennett, "Voter Suppression Was Spark That Ignited Ocoee Massacre: A Century Later, Florida's Black Voters Are Still Facing Obstacles," *Orlando Sentinel,* October 22, 2020, www .orlandosentinel.com/news/ocoee-massacre/os-ne-black-voter-suppression-ocoee -20201022-z6kwn5xuafdevlhkvy6g6effui-htmlstory.html.

79. Lela Bond Phillips, *The Lena Baker Story* (Atlanta: Wings, 2001), 25, 71.

80. Ibid., 22–23.

81. Ibid., 26.

82. "Mother of 3 to Die in Ga. Electric Chair," *Chicago Defender,* January 27, 1945.

83. Phillips, *Lena Baker Story,* 96.

84. Donna Jean Murch, *Living for the City: Migration, Education, and the Rise of the Black Panther Party in Oakland, California* (Chapel Hill: University of North Carolina Press, 2010), 38–39; Joshua Bloom and Waldo E. Martin, *Black Against Empire: The History and Politics of the Black Panther Party* (Oakland: University of California Press, 2016), Kindle loc. 1118–40.

85. Jerry Belcher, "It's All Legal: Oakland's Black Panthers Wear Guns, Talk Revolution," *San Francisco Examiner,* April 30, 1967, found in Mulford Act Files, firearmspolicy.org/resources.

86. Adam Winkler, *Gun Fight: The Battle over the Right to Bear Arms in America* (New York: Norton, 2011), 239.

87. Tod Sloan, handwritten notes, n.d., sites.law.duke.edu/secondthoughts/wp-content/uploads/ sites/13/2020/04/Ted-Sloan-Notes-1967-Mulford-Papers.pdf.

88. Don Mulford to Arthur E. de la Barra, June 22, 1967, sites.law.duke.edu/secondthoughts/ wp-content/uploads/sites/13/2020/04/Mulford-Letter-1.pdf.

89. Cynthia Deitle Leonardatos, "California's Attempts to Disarm the Black Panthers," *San Diego Law Review* 36, no. 4 (1999): 973, 992, 994–95.

90. Don Mulford to Ronald Reagan, April 21, 1967, sites.law.duke.edu/secondthoughts/wp -content/uploads/sites/13/2020/04/Mulford-Letter-3.pdf; John A. Nejedly to Ronald Reagan, April 20, 1967, Mulford Act Files, firearmspolicy.org/resources.

91. Jack Lindsey (legislative secretary to Governor Ronald Reagan) to Don Mulford, May 19, 1967, publicfiles.firearmspolicy.org/mulford-act/california-ab1591-1967-mulford-act-bill-file .pdf.

92. William Brink and Louis Harris, *Black and White: A Study of U.S. Racial Attitudes Today* (New York: Simon & Schuster, 1966), 121.

93. Ibid., 123.

94. Ibid., 124.

95. Naomi Murakawa, *The First Civil Right: How Liberals Built Prison America* (New York: Oxford University Press, 2014), 2.

96. Jonathan Simon, *Governing Through Crime: How the War on Crime Transformed American Democracy and Created a Culture of Fear* (New York: Oxford University Press, 2007), 22–23; Peter Baker, "Bush Made Willie Horton an Issue in 1988, and the Racial Scars Are Still Fresh," *New York Times*, December 3, 2018, www.nytimes.com/2018/12/03/us/politics/bush-willie-horton .html.

97. Brink and Harris, *Black and White*, 123–24.

98. Susan D. Greenbaum, *Blaming the Poor: The Long Shadow of the Moynihan Report on Cruel Images About Poverty* (New Brunswick, N.J.: Rutgers University Press, 2015), 91.

99. Caroline E. Light, *Stand Your Ground: A History of America's Love Affair with Lethal Self-Defense* (Boston: Beacon, 2017), 1–11.

100. Charles Krauthammer, "Essay: Toasting Mr. Goetz," *Time*, January 21, 1985, content.time.com/ time/subscriber/article/0,33009,956287,00.html.

101. Joseph Berger, "Goetz Case: Commentary on Nature of Urban Life," *New York Times*, June 18, 1987, www.nytimes.com/1987/06/18/nyregion/analysis-goetz-case-commentary-on-nature-of -urban-life.html.

102. U.S. Commission on Civil Rights, *Examining the Race Effects of Stand Your Ground Laws*, 16.

103. Ibid., 18.

104. Southern Poverty Law Center, "'Stand Your Ground' Kills: How These NRA-Backed Laws Promote Racist Violence," July 2020, 11, splcenter.org/sites/default/files/_stand_your_ground _kills_-_how_these_nra-backed_laws_promote_racist_violence_1.pdf.

Chapter 10: Punishment

1. According to the Bureau of Justice Statistics' report "Historical Statistics on Prisoners in State and Federal Institutions, 1925–86" (www.bjs.gov/content/pub/pdf/hspsfiy25-86.pdf#page=17), there were 176,403 people held in state prisons and 20,038 people held in federal prisons in 1970. And according to the BJS report "Historical Corrections Statistics in the United States, 1850–1984" (Table 4-1, www.bjs.gov/content/pub/pdf/hcsus5084.pdf#page=91), there were 129,189 people held in local jails in 1970. So combined, there were a total of 325,630 people held in prisons and jails in 1970.

2. Casey Kuhn, "The U.S. Spends Billions to Lock People Up, but Very Little to Help Them Once They're Released," PBS NewsHour, April 7, 2021, www.pbs.org/newshour/economy/the -u-s-spends-billions-to-lock-people-up-but-very-little-to-help-them-once-theyre-released; Nazgol Ghandnoosh, "U.S. Prison Population Trends: Massive Buildup and Modest Decline," The Sentencing Project, September 19, 2019, www.sentencingproject.org/publications/u-s -prison-population-trends-massive-buildup-and-modest-decline/; "Criminal Justice Facts," The Sentencing Project, www.sentencingproject.org/criminal-justice-facts/.

3. Ashley Nellis, "No End in Sight: America's Enduring Reliance on Life Imprisonment," The Sentencing Project, February 17, 2021, www.sentencingproject.org/publications/no-end-in -sight-americas-enduring-reliance-on-life-imprisonment/.

4. Ashley Nellis, "Still Life: America's Increasing Use of Life and Long-Term Sentences," The Sentencing Project, 2017, 14, www.sentencingproject.org/wp-content/uploads/2017/05/Still -Life.pdf.

5. Ashley Nellis, "The Lives of Juvenile Lifers: Findings from a National Survey," The Sentencing Project, March 1, 2012, www.sentencingproject.org/publications/the-lives-of-juvenile

-lifers-findings-from-a-national-survey/; "Cruel and Unusual: Sentencing 13- and 14-Year-Old Children to Die in Prison," Equal Justice Initiative, January 2008, eji.org/wp-content/uploads/2019/10/cruel-and-unusual.pdf.

6. Jeffrey Goldberg, "The End of the Line: Rehabilitation and Reform in Angola Penitentiary," *Atlantic,* September 9, 2015, www.theatlantic.com/politics/archive/2015/09/a-look-inside-angola-prison/404377/.

7. "An Act Concerning Negroes & other Slaues [*sic*]," vol. 1, September 1664, Maryland State Archives, aomol.msa.maryland.gov/000001/000001/html/am1--533.html.

8. "Proceedings and Acts of the General Assembly, 1727–1729, with Appendix of Statutes, 1714–1726," vol. 36, July 18, 1729, Maryland State Archives, aomol.msa.maryland.gov/000001/000036/html/am36--321.html.

9. William Rice, ed., *A Digested Index of the Statute Laws of South-Carolina from the Earliest Period to the Year 1836, Inclusive* (Charleston, S.C.: J. S. Burges, 1838), 241.

10. *Becton v. Ferguson* (1853) in *Reports of Cases Argued and Determined in the Supreme Court of Alabama* (St. Paul, Minn.: West Publishing, 1907), 254.

11. *Creswell's Executor v. Walker,* 37 Ala. 229 (1861), cite.case.law/ala/37/229/.

12. Thirteenth Amendment, National Constitution Center, constitutioncenter.org/interactive-constitution/amendment/amendment-xiii.

13. "Farewell Adress [*sic*] of Gov. Perry Gov. Orr's Inaugural Address," *New York Times,* December 8, 1865, 1, www.nytimes.com/1865/12/08/archives/south-carolina-inauguration-of-gov-orr-farewell-adress-of-gov-perry.html.

14. "The Southern 'Black Codes' of 1865–66," Constitutional Rights Foundation, www.crf-usa.org/brown-v-board-50th-anniversary/southern-black-codes.html.

15. "Our Ticket, Our Motto: This Is a White Man's Country; Let White Men Rule,"1868, Schomburg Center for Research in Black Culture, Photographs and Prints Division, New York Public Library, digitalcollections.nypl.org/items/62a9d0e6-4fc9-dbce-e040-e00a18064a66.

16. "Prison Abuses in Mississippi," *Chicago Daily Tribune,* July 11, 1887.

17. Douglas Blackmon, *Slavery by Another Name: The Re-Enslavement of Black Americans from the Civil War to World War II* (New York: Anchor, 2008).

18. David Oshinsky, *Worse Than Slavery: Parchman Farm and the Ordeal of Jim Crow Justice* (New York: Free Press, 1996).

19. "93 Negroes Face Trial Tomorrow," *New York Times,* March 18, 1956, timesmachine.nytimes.com/timesmachine/1956/03/18/90495007.pdf?pdf_redirect=true&ip=0; "Remembering the Montgomery Bus Boycott," UAW, February 22, 2016, uaw.org/remembering-the-montgomery-bus-boycott/.

Chapter 11: Inheritance

1. Melissa Brown, "An Era of Terror: Montgomery Family Remembers Father's Lynching, Legacy," *Montgomery Advertiser,* April 25, 2018, www.montgomeryadvertiser.com/story/news/2018/04/25/equal-justice-initiative-eji-alabama-lynchings-elmore-bolling/524675002/.

2. The Elmore Bolling Foundation, www.bollingfoundation.org/elmore-bolling.html.

3. Ibid.

4. Brown, "An Era of Terror."

5. "Enraged, Jealous Whites Shoot Down Successful Business Man: Believe Dixie Gang Murdered Young Father," *Chicago Defender,* December 20, 1947.

6. "The Reconstruction Amendments," National Constitution Center, constitutioncenter.org/learn/educational-resources/historical-documents/the-reconstruction-amendments.

7. Eric Foner, *A Short History of Reconstruction, 1863–1877* (New York: Harper & Row, 1990), xv.

8. Ibid., 65.

9. Reginald Washington, "The Freedman's Savings and Trust Company and African American Genealogical Research," *Federal Records and African American History* 29, no. 2 (Summer 1997), www.archives.gov/publications/prologue/1997/summer/freedmans-savings-and-trust.html.

10. Foner, *Short History of Reconstruction*, 135.

11. William T. Sherman, "Special Order No. 15," January 16, 1865, 2, William A. Gladstone Afro-American Military Collection, Manuscript Division, Library of Congress, www.loc.gov/exhibits/civil-war-in-america/november-1863-april-1865.html#obj38.

12. Quote taken from "Andrew Johnson: the Most-Criticized President Ever," *Constitution Daily*, July 31, 2019, constitutioncenter.org/blog/marking-the-passing-of-maybe-the-most-criticized-president-ever.

13. "The Freedman's Savings Bank: Good Intentions Were Not Enough; A Noble Experiment Goes Awry," Office of the Comptroller of the Currency, www.occ.treas.gov/about/who-we-are/history/1863-1865/1863-1865-freedmans-savings-bank.html.

14. Foner, *Short History of Reconstruction*, 244–45.

15. LeRae Umfleet, "1898 Wilmington Race Riot Report," Durham: Research Branch, Office of Archives and History, N.C. Dept. of Cultural Resources (2006), 13, digital.ncdcr.gov/digital/collection/p249901coll22/id/5842.

16. "Tulsa Race Riot: A Report by the Oklahoma Commission to Study the Tulsa Race Riot of 1921," February 28, 2001, iv, www.okhistory.org/research/forms/freport.pdf.

17. "Convict Williams of Peonage Murder: Jury, Whose Verdict Carries Life Sentence, Asks for Mercy for Plantation Owner," *New York Times*, April 10, 1921, timesmachine.nytimes.com/timesmachine/1921/04/10/98666726.pdf.

18. Hugh Dorsey, "A Statement from Governor Hugh M. Dorsey as to the Negro in Georgia," 1921, archive.org/details/statementfromgov01geor/page/n9/mode/2up?q=justly+condemn.

19. Ibid., 24.

20. Ibid., 25.

21. Ibid., 25–26.

22. Ibid., 26–27.

23. Ibid., 26.

24. Janelle Jones, "Receiving an Inheritance Helps White Families More Than Black Families," Economic Policy Institute, February 17, 2017, www.epi.org/publication/receiving-an-inheritance-helps-white-families-more-than-black-families/.

25. Lily L. Batchelder, "Leveling the Playing Field Between Inherited Income and Income from Work Through an Inheritance Tax," in *Tackling the Tax Code: Efficient and Equitable Ways to Raise Revenue*, ed. Jay Shambaugh and Ryan Nunn (Washington, D.C.: Brookings Institution, 2020), 47, www.brookings.edu/wp-content/uploads/2020/01/TaxBookforWeb_12320.pdf.

26. Brown, "An Era of Terror."

27. Josephine Bolling McCall, *The Penalty for Success: My Father Was Lynched in Lowndes County, Alabama* (New York: Penguin, 2015).

Chapter 12: Medicine

1. Matthew Wixson, "Anti-Racism and Dr. Susan Moore's Legacy," January 7, 2021, University of Michigan Health Lab Blog, labblog.uofmhealth.org/rounds/anti-racism-and-dr-susan-moores-legacy.

2. John Eligon, "Black Doctor Dies of Covid-19 After Complaining of Racist Treatment," *New York Times,* December 23, 2020, www.nytimes.com/2020/12/23/us/susan-moore-black-doctor -indiana.html.

3. Susan Moore, Facebook, www.facebook.com/susan.moore.33671748/posts/3459157600869878.

4. Eligon, "Black Doctor Dies."

5. "Emergency Department Visits for COVID-19 by Race and Ethnicity—13 States, October–December 2020," www.cdc.gov/mmwr/volumes/70/wr/mm7015e3.htm?s_cid=mm7015e3_w; "Key Updates for Week 50, Ending December 12, 2020," www.cdc.gov/coronavirus/2019 -ncov/covid-data/pdf/covidview-12-18-2020.pdf.

6. "Health Equity Considerations and Racial and Ethnic Minority Groups," Centers for Disease Control and Prevention, April 19, 2021, www.cdc.gov/coronavirus/2019-ncov/community/ health-equity/race-ethnicity.html.

7. Lisa Friedman, "New Research Links Air Pollution to Higher Coronavirus Death Rates," *New York Times* April 7, 2020, www.nytimes.com/2020/04/07/climate/air-pollution-coronavirus -covid.html.

8. Arline T. Geronimus, Margaret Hicken, Danya Keene, and John Bound, "'Weathering' and Age Patterns of Allostatic Load Scores Among Blacks and Whites in the United States," *American Journal of Public Health* 96, no. 5 (2006): 826–33.

9. Ronald Wyatt, "Pain and Ethnicity," *AMA Journal of Ethics* (May 2013): 449–54, journalof ethics.ama-assn.org/article/pain-and-ethnicity/2013-05.

10. Vanessa Northington Gamble, "A Legacy of Distrust: African Americans and Medical Research," *American Journal of Preventive Medicine* 9 (6 Supp., 1993): 35–38, www.columbia.edu/ itc/history/rothman/COL479E3421.pdf.

11. Hamza Shaban, "How Racism Creeps into Medicine," *Atlantic,* August 29, 2014, www .theatlantic.com/health/archive/2014/08/how-racism-creeps-into-medicine/378618/; Michael E. Ruane, "A Brief History of the Enduring Phony Science that Perpetuates White Supremacy," *Washington Post,* April 20, 2019, www.washingtonpost.com/local/a-brief-history-of-the -enduring-phony-science-that-perpetuates-white-supremacy/2019/04/29/20e6aef0-5aeb -11e9-a00e-050dc7b82693_story.html.

12. Kelly M. Hoffman, Sophie Trawalter, Jordan R. Axt, and M. Norman Oliver, "Racial Bias in Pain Assessment," *Proceedings of the National Academy of Sciences,* April 19, 2016, www.pnas .org/content/early/2016/03/30/1516047113.full; Ike Swetlitz, "Some Medical Students Still Think Black Patients Feel Less Pain Than Whites," STAT, April 4, 2016, www.statnews .com/2016/04/04/medical-students-beliefs-race-pain.

13. Infant Mortality Statistics, Division of Reproductive Health, National Center for Chronic Disease Prevention and Health Promotion, www.cdc.gov/reproductivehealth/maternal infanthealth/infantmortality.htm; Population Reference Bureau Analysis of 1990–2019 Final Birth Data, National Center for Health Statistics, datacenter.kidscount.org/data/tables/6038 -total-births-by-race.

14. Tiana Hicklin, "Factors Contributing to Higher Incidence of Diabetes for Black Americans," National Institutes of Health, January 9, 2018, www.nih.gov/news-events/nih-research-matters/ factors-contributing-higher-incidence-diabetes-black-americans; Daniel T. Kackland, "Racial Differences in Hypertension: Implications for High Blood Pressure Management," *American Journal of the Medical Sciences* 348, no. 2 (2014): 135–38. www.ncbi.nlm.nih.gov/pmc/articles/ PMC4108512/.

15. The long list of Black medical and social scientists, historians, and scholars who have attempted to correct these false ideas includes W.E.B. Du Bois, W. Montagu Cobb, V. N. Gamble, S. Reverby, H. Washington, E. Hammonds, and many others.

16. Benjamin Moseley, *A Treatise on Tropical Diseases; and on the Climate of the West-Indies* (London: T. Cadell, 1787), 472–73, archive.org/stream/trropic00mose/trropic00mose_djvu.txt.
17. Thomas Jefferson, *Notes on the State of Virginia* (Philadelphia: Pritchard and Hall, 1787), 189.
18. Ibid., 190–91.
19. Ibid., 191.
20. Samuel Cartwright, "Report on the Diseases and Physical Peculiarities of the Negro Race," *New-Orleans Medical and Surgical Journal* 7 (1851), 691–715, archive.org/details/TheNewOrleansMedicalAndSurgicalJournal/mode/2up?q=Spirometer.
21. Samuel Cartwright, "Philosophy of the Negro Constitution," *New-Orleans Medical and Surgical Journal* 9 (1853): 195–208.
22. Cartwright, "Report on the Diseases and Physical Peculiarities," 707–8.
23. J. Marion Sims, *The Story of My Life* (New York: D. Appleton, 1884), 222–47.
24. John Brown, *Slave Life in Georgia: A Narrative of the Life, Sufferings, and Escape of John Brown, a Fugitive Slave, Now in England* (London: W. M. Watts, 1855), 48.
25. *Memoirs of Georgia: Containing Historical Accounts of the State's Civil, Military, Industrial and Professional Interests, and Personal Sketches of Many of Its People* (N.p.: Southern Historical Association, 1895), 2:148.
26. Gamble, "A Legacy of Distrust," 35–36.
27. "Final Report of the Syphilis Study Legacy Committee—May 20, 1996," www.tuskegee.edu/Content/Uploads/Tuskegee/files/Bioethics/SyphilisStudyCommitteeReport.pdf.
28. "Autopsies," Tuskegee Syphilis Study Administrative Records, 1929–1972, National Archives, catalog.archives.gov/id/650718.
29. "Remarks by the President in Apology for Study Done in Tuskegee," May 16, 1997, clintonwhitehouse4.archives.gov/textonly/New/Remarks/Fri/19970516-898.html.
30. Sarah Zhang, "The Surgeon Who Experimented on Slaves," *Atlantic,* April 18, 2018, www.theatlantic.com/health/archive/2018/04/j-marion-sims/558248/.
31. Lundy Braun, *Breathing Race into the Machine: The Surprising Career of the Spirometer from Plantation to Genetics* (Minneapolis: University of Minnesota Press, 2014), xv–xvi.
32. Hoffman et al., "Racial Bias in Pain Assessment."
33. Dennis M. Murphy, "Statement from IU Health CEO Dennis Murphy on External Review of Dr. Susan Moore's Care," Indiana University Health, May 12, 2021, iuhealth.org/for-media/press-releases/statement-from-iu-health-ceo-dennis-murphy-on-external-review-of-dr-susan-moores-care.
34. Dennis M. Murphy, "Directly Addressing the Issue of Racial Equity in Our Facilities," Indiana University Health, December 24, 2020, iuhealth.org/for-media/press-releases/directly-addressing-the-issue-of-racial-equity-in-our-facilities.

Chapter 13: Church

1. Barack Obama, "A More Perfect Union" (speech, National Constitution Center, Philadelphia, March 18, 2008), constitutioncenter.org/amoreperfectunion/docs/Race_Speech_Transcript.pdf.
2. "Reverend Wright Transcript," ABC News, April 27, 2008, abcnews.go.com/Blotter/story?id=4719157&page=1.
3. Jodi Kantor, "Obama Denounces Statements of His Pastor as 'Inflammatory,'" *New York Times,* March 15, 2008, www.nytimes.com/2008/03/15/us/politics/15wright.html.
4. Barack Obama, "A More Perfect Union."
5. James H. Cone, *Black Theology and Black Power* (1969; repr., New York: Orbis, 1997), 12.

6. For a more in-depth understanding of prohibitions regarding women's preaching, see Anthea Butler, *Women in the Church of God in Christ: Making a Sanctified World* (Chapel Hill: University of North Carolina Press, 2007).

7. Sacvan Bercovitch, *The American Jeremiad* (1978; repr., Madison: University of Wisconsin Press, 2012,), xiii.

8. David Walker, *Walker's Appeal, in Four Articles; Together with a Preamble, to the Coloured Citizens of the World, but in Particular, and Very Expressly, to Those of the United States of America, Written in Boston, State of Massachusetts, September 28, 1829,* 3rd ed., revised (1829; repr., Boston: David Walker, 1830), 83, docsouth.unc.edu/nc/walker/walker.html.

9. Martin Luther King, Jr., "Beyond Vietnam" (speech, Riverside Church, New York City, April 4, 1967), www.crmvet.org/info/mlk_viet.pdf.

10. Lilly Fowler, "Federal Officials Investigating Fire at Church Connected to Michael Brown Family," *St. Louis Post-Dispatch,* November 27, 2014, www.stltoday.com/lifestyles/faith-and -values/federal-officials-investigating-fire-at-church-connected-to-michael-brown-family/ article_e4b41d11-a02d-5956-b396-b67b36302410.html; Wesley Lowery, "The Brown Family's Pastor Tries to Make Sense of the Fire That Gutted His Church," *Washington Post,* November 28, 2014, www.washingtonpost.com/national/the-brown-familys-pastor-tries-to-make -sense-of-fire-that-gutted-his-church/2014/11/28/15520f3e-7711-11e4-a755-e32227229e7b _story.html.

11. Elisha Fieldstadt, "Charleston Church Shooting: Families of Victims Address Dylann Roof at Bond Hearing," NBC News, June 19, 2015, www.nbcnews.com/storyline/charleston-church -shooting/hate-won-t-win-kin-victims-address-church-shooter-dylann-n378641.

12. Scott Neuman, "Emotional Service Held at Charleston Church Days After Shootings," NPR, June 21, 2015, www.npr.org/sections/thetwo-way/2015/06/21/416192033/emotional-services -held-at-charleston-church-days-after-shootings.

13. For more on this, see Albert J. Raboteau, *Slave Religion: The Invisible Institution in the Antebellum South* (Oxford: Oxford University Press, 1978).

14. Judith Weisenfeld, "Religion in African American History," *Oxford Research Encyclopedia of American History,* March 2, 2015, oxfordre.com/americanhistory/view/10.1093/acrefore/ 9780199329175.001.0001/acrefore-9780199329175-e-24.

15. Quoted in Frank E. Grizzard, Jr., and D. Boyd Smith, eds., *Jamestown Colony: A Political, Social, and Cultural History* (Santa Barbara, Calif.: ABC-Clio, 2007), 201.

16. An early example of a Black church was in Savannah, Georgia. See "Savannah's History: First African Baptist Church," www.savannah.com/savannahs-history-first-african-baptist-church/.

17. Richard Allen, *The Life, Experience, and Gospel Labours of the Rt. Rev. Richard Allen to Which Is Annexed the Rise and Progress of the African Methodist Episcopal Church in the United States of America. Containing a Narrative of the Yellow Fever in the Year of Our Lord 1793: With an Address to the People of Colour in the United States* (Philadelphia: Martin & Boden, 1833), 13, docsouth .unc.edu/nch/allen/allen.html.

18. Benjamin Rush, *An Account of the Bilious Remitting Yellow Fever, as It Appeared in Philadelphia, in the Year 1793,* quoted in www.historyofvaccines.org/content/yellow-fever-decimates -philadelphia.

19. Isaac Heston to Abraham Heston, September 19, 1793, journals.psu.edu/pmhb/article/down load/41767/41488.

20. Jacqueline Bacon, "Rhetoric and Identity in Absalom Jones and Richard Allen's *Narrative of the Proceedings of the Black People, During the Late Awful Calamity in Philadelphia,*" *Pennsylvania Magazine of History and Biography* 125, no. 1–2 (January–April, 2001): 61–90, www.jstor .org/stable/20093427?read-now=1&refreqid=excelsior%3A101fb1f5738a1839f870699a6806 64a3&seq-7#page_scan_tab_contents.

21. Ricardo Howell, "Mother Bethel AME Church: Congregation and Community," *The Encyclopedia of Greater Philadelphia,* philadelphiaencyclopedia.org/archive/mother-bethel-ame-church-congregation-and-community-2/.

22. To learn more about Jarena Lee, see *Religious Experiences and Journal of Mrs. Jarena Lee: Giving an Account of Her Call to Preach the Gospel* (Philadelphia: Printed and published for the Author, 1849).

23. Christina Cecilia Davidson, "Black Protestants in a Catholic Land: The AME Church in the Dominican Republic," *New West Indian Guide* 89, no. 3–4 (2015): 258, brill.com/view/journals/nwig/89/3-4/article-p258_2.xml?language=en.

24. Allen, *Life, Experience, and Gospel Labours,* 70.

25. *Constitution of the American Society of Free Persons of Colour, for Improving Their Condition in the United States; for Purchasing Lands; and for the Establishment of a Settlement in Upper Canada: Also, The Proceedings of the Convention with Their Address to Free Persons of Colour in the United States* (Philadelphia: J. W. Allen, 1830), Colored Conventions Project Digital Records, omeka.coloredconventions.org/items/show/70.

26. Henry McNeal Turner, "Speech on the Eligibility of Colored Members to Seats in the Georgia Legislature" (also known as "I Claim the Rights of Man"), September 3, 1868, the Henry McNeal Turner Project, www.thehenrymcnealturnerproject.org/2019/03/speech-on-eligibility-of-colored.html.

27. Stephen W. Angell, *Bishop Turner and African American Religion in the South* (Knoxville: University of Tennessee Press, 1992), 90.

28. Daniel W. Stowell, *Rebuilding Zion: The Religious Reconstruction of the South, 1863–1877* (New York: Oxford University Press, 1998), 51.

29. Carole Emberton. *Beyond Redemption: Race, Violence, and the American South After the Civil War* (Chicago: University of Chicago Press, 2013), 4.

30. Select Comm. on the Memphis Riots, House of Representatives, "Memphis Riots and Massacres," Report No. 101, 30th Cong., 1st Session, in *Reports of Committees: 16th Congress, 1st Session—49th Congress,* 3:1–36.

31. "Henry McNeal Turner, Bishop of the African Methodist Episcopal Church, Author, Editor, Human Rights Advocate and Fervent Proponent of the 'Back to Africa' Movement," Boston University, School of Theology, History of Missiology, www.bu.edu/missiology/missionary-biography/t-u-v/turner-henry-mcneal-1834-1915/.

32. King's words are taken from Gary Dorrien, *Breaking White Supremacy: Martin Luther King Jr. and the Black Social Gospel* (New Haven, Conn.: Yale University Press, 2018), 294.

33. Stephen Nessen, "Remembering Malcolm X: Rare Interviews and Audio," WNYC News, February 4, 2015, www.wnyc.org/story/87636-remembering-malcolm-x-rare-interviews-and-audio/.

34. "Carmichael, Stokeley," The Martin Luther King, Jr. Research and Education Institute, Stanford University, kinginstitute.stanford.edu/encyclopedia/carmichael-stokely.

35. "Meredith, James Howard," The Martin Luther King, Jr. Research and Education Institute, Stanford University, kinginstitute.stanford.edu/encyclopedia/meredith-james-howard.

36. History.com Editors, "Stokely Carmichael," June 10, 2019, www.history.com/topics/black-history/stokely-carmichael.

37. Ibid.

38. "Black Power," The Martin Luther King, Jr. Research and Education Institute, Stanford University, kinginstitute.stanford.edu/encyclopedia/black-power.

39. "Statement by the National Committee of Negro Churchmen, July 31, 1966," in *The Columbia Documentary History of Religion in America Since 1945,* ed. Paul Harvey and Philip Goff (New York: Columbia University Press, 2005), 176–77.

40. Ibid., 178.

41. Ibid.

42. James H. Cone, *My Soul Looks Back* (Nashville: Abingdon, 1982), 44.

43. James H. Cone, "Black Theology and the Black Church: Where Do We Go From Here?," *CrossCurrents* 27, no. 2 (1977): 147.

44. James H. Cone, *Black Theology and Black Power* (New York: Seabury, 1969), 31.

45. Ibid., 1–2.

46. Ibid., 71.

47. "Statement by the National Committee of Black Churchmen, June 13, 1969," in Milton C. Sernett, ed., *African American Religious History: A Documentary Witness* (Durham, N.C.: Duke University Press, 2000), 564.

48. Mark Oppenheimer, "A Campaign Pitch Rekindles the Question: Just What Is Liberation Theology?," *New York Times,* May 25, 2012, www.nytimes.com/2012/05/26/us/a-campaign -pitch-rekindles-questions-about-liberation-theology.html.

49. Raphael G. Warnock, *The Divided Mind of the Black Church: Theology, Piety, and Public Witness* (New York: New York University Press, 2014), 29.

50. Ben Brasch, "Campaign Check: Loeffler Says Warnock Disparages Military," *Atlanta Journal-Constitution,* December 7, 2020, www.ajc.com/politics/senate-watch/campaign-check-loeffler -says-warnock-disparages-military/YPI3JA7R7NBOPDYYKVC4MBH3VQ/.

51. Jonathan Lee Walton, "Raphael Warnock's Georgia Critics Don't Understand Black Churches," *Washington Post,* December 30, 2020, www.washingtonpost.com/outlook/2020/12/30/warnock -georgia-senate-runoff-black-church/.

Chapter 14: Music

1. Howell Raines, "The Birmingham Bombing," *New York Times,* July 24, 1983, www.nytimes .com/1983/07/24/magazine/the-birmingham-bombing.html. Martha and the Vandellas' "Heat Wave" peaked at No. 4 on the *Billboard* Hot 100 on September 21, 1963; see *Billboard,* www .billboard.com/music/martha-reeves-the-vandellas/chart-history/HSI/song/580396.

2. Martha and the Vandellas' "Heat Wave" lyrics, Genius, genius.com/Martha-reeves-and-the -vandellas-love-is-like-a-heat-wave-lyrics.

3. Motown Museum, www.motownmuseum.org/about/.

4. Berry Gordy, www.motownmuseum.org/legacy/berry-gordy/.

5. Waller: James Padilioni, "It's Getting 'Hot' in Here," National Museum of American History, Smithsonian Institution, July 26, 2012, americanhistory.si.edu/blog/2012/07/its-getting-hot -in-here.html. Fitzgerald: Kevin Whitehead, "Ella Fitzgerald's Early Years Collected in a Chick Webb Box Set," *Fresh Air,* NPR, December 11, 2013, www.npr.org/2013/12/11/250200123/ ella-fitzgeralds-early-years-collected-in-a-chick-webb-box-set. Webb and Basie: Padilioni, "It's Getting 'Hot' in Here."

6. Jon Pareles and Lori Holcomb-Holland, "Taxi Dancers to Gaga: Roseland's Life and Death," *New York Times,* March 27, 2014, www.nytimes.com/2014/03/28/arts/music/taxi-dancers-to -gaga-roselands-life-and-death.html.

7. Sandra Burlingame, "Duke Ellington (1899–1974)," Naxos Records (courtesy of JazzStandards .com), www.naxos.com/person/Duke_Ellington_1816/1816.htm.

8. "Rhapsody in Blue," gershwin.com/publications/rhapsody-in-blue/; Alden Whitman, "Paul Whiteman, 'the Jazz King' of the Jazz Age, Is Dead at 77," *New York Times,* December 30, 1967, timesmachine.nytimes.com/timesmachine/1967/12/30/91667756.html?pageNumber=1.

9. Mick Brown, "Berry Gordy: The Man Who Built Motown," *Telegraph,* January 23, 2016, s.telegraph.co.uk/graphics/projects/berry-gordy-motown/index.html.

10. 2020 U.S. Federal Census, www.census.gov/quickfacts/fact/table/US/PST045219.

11. Alex Sherman, "TikTok Reveals Detailed User Numbers for the First Time," CNBC, August 24, 2020, www.cnbc.com/2020/08/24/tiktok-reveals-us-global-user-growth-numbers -for-first-time.html.

12. *McIntosh County Shouters: Gullah-Geechee Ring Shout from Georgia,* Library of Congress, December 2, 2010, www.loc.gov/item/webcast-5109/.

13. Brigit Katz, "Heavily Abridged 'Slave Bible' Removed Passages That Might Encourage Uprisings," *Smithsonian Magazine,* January 4, 2019, www.smithsonianmag.com/smart-news/ heavily-abridged-slave-bible-removed-passages-might-encourage-uprisings-180970989.

14. Frederick Douglass, *My Bondage and My Freedom* (New York: Miller, Orton & Mulligan, 1855), 75, avalon.law.yale.edu/19th_century/douglas01.asp.

15. Ibid., 215.

16. Zora Neale Hurston, "Spirituals and Neo-Spirituals," in *Music in the USA: A Documentary Companion,* ed. Paul Beaudoin and Judith Tick (New York: Oxford University Press, 2008), 507.

17. William Francis Allen, Lucy McKim Garrison, and Charles Pickard Ware, *Slave Songs of the United States* (New York: A. Simpson, 1867), doi.org/10.5479/sil.78680.39088002074508.

18. "Ella Sheppard, Soprano," *American Experience,* PBS, www.pbs.org/wgbh/americanexperience/ features/singers-sheppard/.

19. Hurston, "Spirituals and Neo-Spirituals," 507.

20. Quoted in Josephine Lee, "Authenticity, Mimicry, and Early African American Entertainment." *American Quarterly* 73, no. 1 (2021): 151.

21. "The Celebrated Negro Melodies as Sung by the Virginia Minstrels, Adapted for the Piano Forte by Thos. Comer," New York Public Library Digital Collections, Music Division, New York Public Library, digitalcollections.nypl.org/items/89cd61e5-eb62-ad8d-e040-e00a18060a1c.

22. Jack Hitt, "P. T. Barnum, the Showman and Grifter Who Held up a Funhouse Mirror to America," *Washington Post,* October 18, 2019, www.washingtonpost.com/outlook/pt-barnum -the-showman-and-grifter-who-held-up-a-funhouse-mirror-to-america/2019/10/18/7e3cec88 -d4d3-11e9-9343-40db57cf6abd_story.html.

23. "Blackface Minstrelsy," *American Experience,* PBS, www.pbs.org/wgbh/americanexperience/ features/foster-blackface-minstrelsy/.

24. Sheet music for "Uncle Gabriel" (New York: Firth, Pond, 1848), www.loc.gov/item/sm1848 .441700/.

25. Ken Emerson, *Doo-dah: Stephen Foster and the Rise of American Popular Culture* (New York: Simon & Schuster, 1997), 91.

26. Stephen Collins Foster, Anthony F. Winnemore, and Augustus Clapp, "Old Uncle Ned," (1847), Historic Sheet Music Collection, 846, digitalcommons.conncoll.edu/sheetmusic/846.

27. Bayard Taylor, *Eldorado: Or, Adventures in the Path of Empire: Comprising a Voyage to California, via Panama; Life in San Francisco and Monterey; Pictures of the Gold Region, and Experiences of Mexican Travel,* vol. 2 (New York: G. P. Putnam, 1850), 20, www.loc.gov/item/rc01000822/.

28. "A Moral Battle Cry of Freedom," Harriet Beecher Stowe Center, www.harrietbeecherstowe center.org/harriet-beecher-stowe/uncle-toms-cabin/.

29. "Why African-Americans Loathe 'Uncle Tom,'" *In Character* (special series), NPR, July 30, 2008, www.npr.org/templates/story/story.php?storyId=93059468.

30. Stephen Railton, "45 Tom Show Want Ads: Electronic Edition," Institute for Advanced Technology in the Humanities, University of Virginia, 2005; originally printed in *The Billboard,* Cincinnati, January 14–December 30, 1911, utc.iath.virginia.edu/onstage/revus/osar48awt.html.

31. Randy Dotinga, "The Little Woman Behind a Very Big War," *Christian Science Monitor,*

June 30, 2011, www.csmonitor.com/Books/chapter-and-verse/2011/0630/The-little-woman-behind-a-very-big-war.

32. "Frank (Francis) Johnson, Musician and Teacher Born," African American Registry, aaregistry.org/story/frank-johnson-a-first-for-black-music/.

33. Henry A. Kmen, "Old Corn Meal: A Forgotten Urban Negro Folksinger," *Journal of American Folklore* 75, no. 295 (1962): 30, doi.org/10.2307/537839.

34. Ibid., 32–33.

35. Thomas Low Nichols, *Forty Years of American Life: 1821–1861* (1864; repr., Lanham, Md.: Stackpole, 2017), 337.

36. John Jeremiah Sullivan, "'Shuffle Along' and the Lost History of Black Performance in America," *New York Times Magazine,* March 24, 2016, www.nytimes.com/2016/03/27/magazine/shuffle-along-and-the-painful-history-of-black-performance-in-america.html.

37. Henry T. Sampson, *Blacks in Blackface: A Sourcebook on Early Black Musical Shows* (New York: Scarecrow, 1980), 2.

38. Soraya Nadia McDonald, "America Created Whitney Houston and Then It Destroyed Her; Her Family Created Nippy, Then Did the Same," *Undefeated,* July 5, 2008, theundefeated.com/features/whitney-houston-documentary-review/.

39. James Brown, *I Feel Good: A Memoir of a Life of Soul* (New York: New American Library, 2005), 108.

40. Katie Atkinson, "Tyler, the Creator Calls Out Grammy Categories: 'Urban' Is Just 'A Politically Correct Way to Say the N-Word,'" *Billboard,* January 26, 2020, www.billboard.com/articles/news/awards/8549244/tyler-the-creator-grammys-best-rap-album-win-backstage-comments-categories-urban.

41. "Beyoncé Knowles," Recording Academy Grammy Awards, www.grammy.com/grammys/artists/beyonc%C3%A9-knowles/12474.

42. David L. Lewis, "The Square Dancing Master," *American Heritage* 23, no. 2, February 1972, www.americanheritage.com/square-dancing-master.

43. Gavin Edwards, "Bobby Womack," *Rolling Stone,* June 28, 2014, www.rollingstone.com/music/music-news/bobby-womack-1944-2014-246105/.

44. Nat Hentoff, "The Man Who Used Jazz for Justice," *Washington Post,* May 7, 1994, www.washingtonpost.com/archive/1994/05/07/the-man-who-used-jazz-for-justice/023fdf18-1d01-4f31-ad3b-6a7ed5ea4b9d/.

45. Ann Douglas, *Terrible Honesty: Mongrel Manhattan in the 1920s* (New York: Farrar, Straus and Giroux, 1996), 76.

46. Frederick Douglass, *Narrative of the Life of Frederick Douglass, an American Slave: Written by Himself* (Boston: Anti-Slavery Office, 1845), 13.

Chapter 15: Healthcare

1. "Obama's Health Care Speech to Congress," *New York Times,* September 9, 2009, www.nytimes.com/2009/09/10/us/politics/10obama.text.html.

2. Roosa Tikkanen and Melinda K. Abrams, "U.S. Health Care from a Global Perspective, 2019: Higher Spending, Worse Outcomes?," Commonwealth Fund, January 30, 2020, www.commonwealthfund.org/publications/issue-briefs/2020/jan/us-health-care-global-perspective-2019.

3. Jim Downs, *Sick from Freedom: African-American Illness and Suffering During the Civil War and Reconstruction* (New York: Oxford University Press, 2012), 98.

4. Ibid., 111.

5. Ibid., 93.

6. Ibid., 72.

7. Ibid., 108.

8. Ibid., 61.

9. "Report of the Commission on the Freedmen—Its Suggestions and Recommendations," *New York Times,* January 22, 1866, www.newspapers.com/browse/us/new-york/new-york/the-new-york-times_395/1866/01/22.

10. Rebecca Lee Crumpler, *A Book of Medical Discourse: In Two Parts* (Boston: Cashman, Keaton, 1883), 4.

11. National Medical Association, "Historical Manifesto," www.nmanet.org/page/Mission.

12. Ira Katznelson, *Fear Itself: The New Deal and the Origins of Our Time* (New York: Liveright, 2013), 15, 368.

13. Ibid., 20–22.

14. Sandra Crouse Quinn and Stephen B. Thomas, "The National Negro Health Week, 1915 to 1951: A Descriptive Account," *Minority Health Today* 2, no. 3 (2001): 44.

15. "Episode 4: How the Bad Blood Started," *1619* (podcast), September 13, 2019, www.nytimes.com/2019/09/13/podcasts/1619-slavery-healthcare.html.

16. John Henning Schumann, "A Bygone Era: When Bipartisanship Led to Health Care Transformation," NPR Shots, October 2, 2016, www.npr.org/sections/health-shots/2016/10/02/495775518/a-bygone-era-when-bipartisanship-led-to-health-care-transformation.

Chapter 16: Traffic

1. Howard Rabinowitz, *Race Relations in the Urban South, 1865–1890* (New York: Oxford University Press, 1978); Don H. Doyle, *New Men, New Cities, New South: Atlanta, Nashville, Charleston, Mobile, 1860–1910* (Chapel Hill: University of North Carolina Press, 1990).

2. Roger L. Rice, "Residential Segregation by Law, 1910–1917," *Journal of Southern History* (May 1968): 179–99; Emily Lieb, "The 'Baltimore Idea' and the Cities It Built," *Southern Cultures* (Summer 2019): 104–19.

3. Kenneth T. Jackson, *Crabgrass Frontier: The Suburbanization of the United States* (New York: Oxford University Press, 1985): 190–218; David M. P. Freund, *Colored Property: State Policy and White Racial Politics in Suburban America* (Chicago: University of Chicago Press, 2010); Richard Rothstein, *The Color of Law: A Forgotten History of How Our Government Segregated America* (New York: Liveright, 2018).

4. James Baldwin, Fred L. Standley, and Louis H. Pratt, *Conversations with James Baldwin* (Jackson: University Press of Mississippi, 1989), 42.

5. For exceptional studies of urban renewal, see Samuel Zipp, *Manhattan Projects: The Rise and Fall of Urban Renewal in Cold War New York* (New York: Oxford University Press, 2012), and Lizabeth Cohen, *Saving America's Cities: Ed Logue and the Struggle to Renew Urban America in the Suburban Age* (New York: Farrar, Straus and Giroux, 2019).

6. Tomiko Brown-Nagin, *Courage to Dissent: Atlanta and the Long History of the Civil Rights Movement* (Oxford: Oxford University Press, 2011), 33.

7. Danielle Wiggins, "Remembering Sweet Auburn Before the Expressway: What Nostalgia Reveals About the Limits of Postwar Liberalism," *Metropole,* themetropole.blog/2021/04/14/remembering-sweet-auburn-before-the-expressway-what-nostalgia-reveals-about-the-limits-of-postwar-liberalism/#_edn2.

8. Kevin M. Kruse, *White Flight: Atlanta and the Making of Modern Conservatism* (Princeton, N.J.: Princeton University Press, 2005), 29; Ronald Bayor, *Race and the Shaping of Twentieth-Century Atlanta* (Chapel Hill: University of North Carolina Press, 1996), 74.

9. Alana Semuels, "The Role of Highways in American Poverty," *Atlantic*, March 18, 2016, www .theatlantic.com/business/archive/2016/03/role-of-highways-in-american-poverty/474282/; Johnny Miller, "Roads to Nowhere: How Infrastructure Built on American Inequality," *Guardian*, February 21, 2018, www.theguardian.com/cities/2018/feb/21/roads-nowhere-infra structure-american-inequality; Institution of Government, Florida International University, "The Historical Impacts of Transportation Projects on the Overtown Community" (Miami: Metropolitan Planning Organization of Miami-Dade County, 1998); Ruben L. Anthony, Jr., and Joseph Rodriguez, "Harnessing the Memory of Freeway Displacement in the Cream City," *Metropole*, themetropole.blog/2021/04/12/harnessing-the-memory-of-freeway-displacement-in -the-cream-city/; Ronald G. Shafer, "Efforts Grow to Ease Disruption from Roads Through Urban Areas," *Wall Street Journal*, June 27, 1968.

10. Bayor, *Race and the Shaping of Twentieth-Century Atlanta*, 61–69.

11. Kruse, *White Flight*, 5.

12. Peter Applebome, "A Suburban Eden Where the Right Rules," *New York Times*, August 1, 1994, www.nytimes.com/1994/08/01/us/a-suburban-eden-where-the-right-rules.html.

13. Kruse, *White Flight*, 247–51; David Dale, "Yankees Had Right Idea When They Burned Atlanta," *Atlanta Constitution*, November 18, 1984, www.newspapers.com/image/399301062/.

14. Kruse, *White Flight*, 251.

15. Ibid., 243.

16. "Who Will Speak for the Inner Cities?," *New York Times*, February 7, 1988, www.nytimes .com/1988/02/07/opinion/who-will-speak-for-the-inner-cities.html.

17. Josh Green, "Gwinnett County Rejects MARTA Transit Expansion. Here's the Early Reaction," Curbed Atlanta, March 20, 2019, atlanta.curbed.com/2019/3/20/18274193/gwinnett county-marta-transit-expansion-transportation; Tyler Estep and John Perry, "Gwinnett MARTA Voting Analysis: 5 Takeaways You Need to Know," *Atlanta Journal-Constitution*, April 22, 2019, www.ajc.com/news/local-govt--politics/gwinnett-marta-voting-analysis-take aways-you-need-know/ZemqhaQr9CXqSnEqEouvjM/; Jenny Jarvie, "After Decades of Resistance, Atlanta's Booming Suburbs Face a Historic Vote on Public Transit," *Los Angeles Times*, March 18, 2019, www.latimes.com/nation/la-na-gwinnett-public-transit-race-20190318 -story.html.

Chapter 17: Progress

1. Office of the Press Secretary, "Remarks by the President in Farewell Address," January 10, 2017, obamawhitehouse.archives.gov/the-press-office/2017/01/10/remarks-president-farewell -address.

2. Peter Holley, "KKK's Official Newspaper Supports Donald Trump for President," *Washington Post*, November 2, 2016, www.washingtonpost.com/news/post-politics/wp/2016/11/01/the -kkks-official-newspaper-has-endorsed-donald-trump-for-president/; Josh Hafner, "Former Ku Klux Klan leader declares support for Donald Trump," *USA Today*, February 25, 2016, www.usatoday.com/story/news/politics/onpolitics/2016/02/25/david-duke-trump/ 80953384/.

3. Alana Abramson, "How Donald Trump Perpetuated the 'Birther' Movement for Years," ABC News, September 16, 2016, abcnews.go.com/Politics/donald-trump-perpetuated-birther-move ment-years/story?id=42138176.

4. Michelle Ye Hee Lee, "Donald Trump's False Comments Connecting Mexican Immigrants and Crime," *Washington Post*, July 8, 2015, www.washingtonpost.com/news/fact-checker/wp/ 2015/07/08/donald-trumps-false-comments-connecting-mexican-immigrants-and-crime/.

5. Office of the Press Secretary, "Remarks by the President in Farewell Address."

6. "Barack Obama's Remarks to the Democratic National Convention," *New York Times,* July 27, 2004, www.nytimes.com/2004/07/27/politics/campaign/barack-obamas-remarks-to-the-demo cratic-national.html.

7. *Philadelphia Inquirer,* November 5, 2008, 1.

8. Frank Newport, "Americans See Obama Election as Race Relations Milestone," Gallup, November 7, 2008, news.gallup.com/poll/111817/americans-see-obama-election-race-relations -milestone.aspx.

9. John McWhorter, "Racism in America Is Over," *Forbes,* December 30, 2008, www.forbes .com/2008/12/30/end-of-racism-oped-cx_jm_1230mcwhorter.html?sh=2054128c49f8.

10. "King: My Dream Has 'Turned into a Nightmare,'" NBC News, August 27, 2013, www.nbc news.com/nightly-news/video/king-my-dream-has-turned-into-a-nightmare-41107011940.

11. Dan Keating and John Mintz, "Florida Black Ballots Affected Most in 2000," *Washington Post,* November 13, 2001, www.washingtonpost.com/archive/politics/2001/11/13/florida-black -ballots-affected-most-in-2000/16784e7d-439a-4b96-9653-1b7362312d2a/; Michael Powell and Peter Slevin, "Several Factors Contributed to 'Lost' Voters in Ohio," *Washington Post,* December 15, 2004, www.washingtonpost.com/archive/politics/2004/12/15/several-factors -contributed-to-lost-voters-in-ohio/73aefa72-c8e5-4657-9e85-5ec8b2451202/; James Drew, "Blackwell Defined by '04 Vote, Supporters and Opponents Say," *Blade,* April 23, 2006, web cache.googleusercontent.com/search?q=cache:_yRbYrPslH4J:https://www.toledoblade .com/local/politics/2006/04/23/Blackwell-defined-by-04-vote-supporters-and-opponents -say/stories/200604230043+&cd=18&hl=en&ct=clnk&gl=us.

12. Rakesh Kochhar, Richard Fry, and Paul Taylor, *Twenty-to-One: Wealth Gaps Rise to Record Highs Between Whites, Blacks, and Hispanics,* Pew Research Center, July 26, 2011, www.pew research.org/wp-content/uploads/sites/3/2011/07/SDT-Wealth-Report_7-26-11_FINAL.pdf, 1.

13. *Shelby County v. Holder,* 570 U.S. 529 (2013).

14. Camila Domonoske, "U.S. Appeals Court Strikes Down North Carolina's Voter ID Law," NPR, July 29, 2016, www.npr.org/sections/thetwo-way/2016/07/29/487935700/u-s-appeals -court-strikes-down-north-carolinas-voter-id-law.

15. Brennan Center for Justice, "Election 2016: Restrictive Voting Laws by the Numbers," September 28, 2016, www.brennancenter.org/our-work/research-reports/election-2016-restrictive -voting-laws-numbers#section5.

16. Richard Baxter, *A Christian Directory,* in *The Practical Works of Richard Baxter* (London: George Virtue, 1838), 1:463.

17. Cotton Mather, *A Good Master Well Served: A Brief Discourse on the Necessary Properties & Practices of a Good Servant* (Boston: B. Green and J. Allen, 1696), 53–54.

18. Thomas Jefferson, *A Summary View of the Rights of British America,* 16–17, www.loc.gov/ item/08016823/.

19. "Jefferson's 'Original Rough Draught' of the Declaration of Independence," Library of Congress, www.loc.gov/exhibits/declara/ruffdrft.html.

20. "Extract from Thomas Jefferson's Notes of Proceedings in the Continental Congress," July 2, 1776, Jefferson Quotes & Family Letters, The Jefferson Monticello, tjrs.monticello.org/ letter/54.

21. George Washington quoted in David R. Roediger, *How Race Survived U.S. History: From Settlement and Slavery to the Obama Phenomenon* (New York: Verso, 2019), 46.

22. "Slavery FAQs—Property," www.monticello.org/slavery/slavery-faqs/property/.

23. United States Bureau of the Census, *A Century of Population Growth, 1790–1800* (Washington, D.C.: Government Printing Office, 1909), 132.

24. Thomas Jefferson, *Notes on the State of Virginia* (1785; repr, Philadelphia: Prichard and Hall, 1788), 147.

25. *A View of Exertions Lately Made for the Purpose of Colonizing the Free People of Colour in the United States, in Africa, or Elsewhere* (Washington, D.C.: Jonathan Elliot, 1817), 9.

26. Ibid., 5.

27. Robert Finley, "Thoughts on the Colonization of Free Blacks," *African Repository and Colonial Journal* 9 (1834): 332–34.

28. Thomas Jefferson to John Lynch, January 21, 1811, Founders Online, National Archives, founders.archives.gov/documents/Jefferson/03-03-02-0243.

29. William Lloyd Garrison, *An Address, Delivered Before the Free People of Color, in Philadelphia,* 2nd ed. (Boston: S. Foster, 1831), 5–6.

30. Ibid.

31. William Lloyd Garrison, "American Colorphobia," *Liberator,* June 11, 1847, fair-use.org/the -liberator/1847/06/11/american-colorphobia.

32. Though ultimately unsuccessful, the Wilmot Proviso "thrust the contentious issue of slavery expansion into the center of the national political debate." See Stephen E. Maizlish, *A Strife of Tongues: The Compromise of 1850 and the Ideological Foundations of the American Civil War* (Charlottesville: University of Virginia Press, 2018), 3, 111, 118–19.

33. Garrison, "American Colorphobia."

34. Alexis de Tocqueville, *Democracy in America,* trans. Henry Reeve (1835; repr., Clark, N.J.: Lawbook Exchange, 2003), 339.

35. Jennifer R. Harbour, *Organizing Freedom: Black Emancipation Activism in the Civil War Midwest* (Carbondale: Southern Illinois University Press, 2020), 12–13, 26.

36. Manisha Sinha, "Did He Die an Abolitionist? The Evolution of Abraham Lincoln's Antislavery," *American Political Thought* 4, no. 3 (2015): 439–54.

37. "Mr. Lincoln and Negro Equality," *New York Times,* December 28, 1860, www.nytimes .com/1860/12/28/archives/mr-lincoln-and-negro-equality.html.

38. Ibram X. Kendi, *Stamped from the Beginning: The Definitive History of Racist Ideas in America* (New York: Bold Type Books, 2016), 217–19.

39. Ibid., 221.

40. Francis Bicknell Carpenter, *The Inner Life of Abraham Lincoln: Six Months at the White House* (Riverside, N.Y.: H. O. Houghton, 1867), 11.

41. *The Journals and Miscellaneous Notebooks of Ralph Waldo Emerson,* eds. Ralph H. Orth and Alfred R. Ferguson (Cambridge, Mass.: Harvard University Press, 1970), 9:126.

42. Kendi, *Stamped from the Beginning,* 250.

43. Forrest G. Wood, *Black Scare: The Racist Response to Emancipation and Reconstruction* (Berkeley: University of California Press, 1968), 102; Eric Foner, *Reconstruction: America's Unfinished Revolution, 1863–1877,* updated ed. (New York: HarperPerennial, 2014), 448–49.

44. Kendi, *Stamped from the Beginning,* 254.

45. J. S. Ingram, *The Centennial Exposition, Described and Illustrated, Being a Concise and Graphic Description of This Grand Enterprise, Commemorative of the First Centenary of American Independence* (Philadelphia: Hubbard Brothers, 1876), 52.

46. Joseph Bradley and *New York Times* quoted in Peter H. Irons, *A People's History of the Supreme Court* (New York: Viking, 1999), 214–15.

47. Meredith Lynn Roman, *Opposing Jim Crow: African Americans and the Soviet Indictment of U.S. Racism, 1928–1937* (Lincoln: University of Nebraska Press, 2012), 57–89.

48. Mary L. Dudziak, *Cold War Civil Rights: Race and the Image of American Democracy* (Princeton, N.J.: Princeton University Press, 2002), 49.

49. Dudziak, *Cold War Civil Rights,* 268, note 5, addresses the publication date of *The Negro in American Life.* While the pamphlet is undated, Dudziak uses several pieces of evidence to date the document to 1950 or 1951: the use of 1950 census data and Supreme Court deci-

sions; affiliation with papers from Chester Bowles's first ambassadorship to India, between 1951 and 1953; and the omission of the Supreme Court's decision in *Brown v. Board of Education* in 1954.

50. *The Negro in American Life,* quoted in Dudziak, *Cold War Civil Rights,* 49–54.

51. Mildred A. Schwartz, *Trends in White Attitudes Toward Negroes,* Report No. 119 (Chicago: National Opinion Research Center, 1967), 60, www.norc.org/PDFs/publications/NORCRpt _119.pdf.

52. Ibid., 33.

53. Ibid., 24.

54. *The Negro in American Life,* quoted in Dudziak, *Cold War Civil Rights,* 53.

55. Ibid., 51.

56. Lyndon B. Johnson, Commencement Address at Howard University, June 4, 1965, in *Public Papers of the Presidents of the United States: Lyndon B. Johnson, 1965* (Washington, D.C.: Government Printing Office, 1966), 2:635–36.

57. Ibid., 2:637.

58. U.S. Information Agency, *For the Dignity of Man: America's Civil Rights Program* (undated), folder: United States Information Agency 1965, Papers of Lyndon Baines Johnson, Papers as President, 1963–1969, Confidential File, box 135, LBJ Presidential Library.

59. Malcolm X, "The Ballot or the Bullet," in *Malcolm X Speaks: Selected Speeches and Statements,* ed. George Breitman (New York: Grove, 1990), 31.

60. David C. Carter, *The Music Has Gone Out of the Movement: Civil Rights and the Johnson Administration, 1965–1968* (Chapel Hill: University of North Carolina Press, 2012), 57.

61. Lyndon B. Johnson, Annual Message to the Congress on the State of the Union, January 17, 1968, American Presidency Project, www.presidency.ucsb.edu/documents/annual-message -the-congress-the-state-the-union-29.

62. National Advisory Commission on Civil Disorders, *Report of the National Advisory Commission on Civil Disorders* (Washington, D.C.: U.S. Government Printing Office, 1968), 1.

63. Ibid., 20–21, 14.

64. Lyndon B. Johnson, Remarks upon Signing the Civil Rights Act, April 11, 1968, American Presidency Project, www.presidency.ucsb.edu/documents/remarks-upon-signing-the-civil -rights-act.

65. Robert Bork, "The Unpersuasive Bakke Decision," *Wall Street Journal,* July 21, 1978.

66. "The Carter-Reagan Presidential Debate" transcript, October 28, 1980, The Commission on Presidential Debates, www.debates.org/voter-education/debate-transcripts/october-28-1980 -debate-transcript/.

67. Stephan Thernstrom and Abigail Thernstrom, *America in Black and White: One Nation, Indivisible* (New York: Simon & Schuster, 1997), 500, 494.

68. Peter Collier and David Horowitz, eds., *The Race Card: White Guilt, Black Resentment, and the Assault on Truth and Justice* (Roseville, Calif.: Prima Lifestyle, 1997).

69. Orlando Patterson, "Race Over," *New Republic,* January 10, 2000, 6–8.

70. *Grutter v. Bollinger,* 539 U.S. 306 (2003).

71. Shelby Steele, "Obama's Post-racial Promise," *Los Angeles Times,* November 5, 2008, www .latimes.com/opinion/opinion-la/la-oe-steele5-2008nov05-story.html.

72. To see the General Social Survey, go to gss.norc.org/.

73. Zeke J. Miller, "In Commemorative MLK Speech, President Obama Recalls His Own 2008 Dream," *Time,* August 28, 2013, swampland.time.com/2013/08/28/in-commemorative-mlk -speech-president-obama-recalls-his-own-2008-dream/.

74. Martin Luther King, Jr., "Statement on Ending the Bus Boycott," December 20, 1956, king institute.stanford.edu/king-papers/documents/statement-ending-bus-boycott.

75. *The Collected Works of Theodore Parker,* ed. Frances Power Cobbe, vol 2, *Sermons—Prayers* (London: N. Trübner, 1867), 48.

76. Mychal Denzel Smith, "The Truth About 'The Arc of the Moral Universe,'" *Huffington Post,* January 18, 2018, www.huffpost.com/entry/opinion-smith-obama-king_n_5a5903e0e4b04f3c55a252a4.

77. Office of the Press Secretary, "Remarks by the President in Farewell Address," January 10, 2017.

Chapter 18: Justice

1. Ira Berlin, *Many Thousands Gone: The First Two Centuries of Slavery in North America* (Cambridge, Mass.: Belknap Press of Harvard University Press, 1998), 73.

2. Library of Virginia, "Gabriel's Conspiracy," www.lva.virginia.gov/exhibits/deathliberty/gabriel/index.htm.

3. David Walker, *Walker's Appeal, in Four Articles; Together with a Preamble, to the Coloured Citizens of the World, but in Particular, and Very Expressly, to Those of the United States of America, Written in Boston, State of Massachusetts, September 28, 1829,* 3rd ed., revised (1829; repr., Boston: David Walker, 1830), 10, docsouth.unc.edu/nc/walker/walker.html.

4. Ida B. Wells, "How Enfranchisement Stops Lynchings," *Original Rights Magazine* 1, no. 4 (June 1910): 43–45, www.lib.uchicago.edu/ead/pdf/ibwells-0008-008-05.pdf.

5. Keisha N. Blain, "This Speech Changed the Course of Black Voting Rights in America," *Timeline,* August 23, 2016, timeline.com/hamer-speech-voting-rights-d5f6ddc7470a?gi=c29d360d9ae0.

6. LaTosha Brown, "Ahead of Election Season, LaTosha Brown Discusses Empowering Black Voters," interview by Elizabeth Gabriel, aired January 20, 2020, on KLCC, NPR for Oregonians, www.klcc.org/post/ahead-election-season-latosha-brown-discusses-empowering-black-voters.

7. Erin Blakemore, "Why People Rioted After Martin Luther King, Jr.'s Assassination," History, April 2, 2018, www.history.com/news/mlk-assassination-riots-occupation.

8. DeNeen L. Brown, "The Fair Housing Act Was Languishing in Congress. Then Martin Luther King Jr. Was Killed," *Washington Post,* April 11, 2018, www.washingtonpost.com/news/retropolis/wp/2018/04/11/the-fair-housing-act-was-languishing-in-congress-then-martin-luther-king-jr-was-killed/.

9. Ford Fessenden, Lazaro Gamio, and Rich Harris, "Even in Defeat, Trump Found New Voters Across the U.S.," *New York Times,* November 16, 2020, www.nytimes.com/interactive/2020/11/16/us/politics/election-turnout.html.

10. Alex Samuels, Elena Mejía, and Nathaniel Rakich, "The States Where Efforts to Restrict Voting Are Escalating," FiveThirtyEight, March 29, 2021, fivethirtyeight.com/features/the-states-where-efforts-to-restrict-voting-are-escalating/.

11. Michael W. Kraus, Ivuoma N. Onyeador, Natalie M. Daumeyer, Julian M. Rucker, and Jennifer A. Richeson, "The Misperception of Racial Economic Inequality," *Perspectives on Psychological Science* 14, no. 6 (November 2019): 902.

12. Allison Keyes, "Recalling an Era When the Color of Your Skin Meant You Paid to Vote," *Smithsonian Magazine,* March 18, 2016, www.smithsonianmag.com/smithsonian-institution/recalling-era-when-color-your-skin-meant-you-paid-vote-180958469.

13. National Equity Atlas, "Neighborhood Poverty: All Neighborhoods Should Be Communities of Opportunity," National Equity Atlas, last modified 2021, nationalequityatlas.org/indicators/Neighborhood_poverty.

14. John R. Logan, "Separate and Unequal: The Neighborhood Gap for Blacks, Hispanics and Asians in Metropolitan America," Brown University, 2011, eric.ed.gov/?id=ED471515.

15. Sean F. Reardon, Lindsay Fox, and Joseph Townsend, "Neighborhood Income Composition by Race and Income, 1990–2009," *Annals of the American Academy of Political and Social Science* 660, no. 1 (2015): 92.

16. Christine Percheski and Christina Gibson-Davis, "A Penny on the Dollar: Racial Inequalities in Wealth Among Households with Children," *Socius* (January 2020): 1.

17. Lyndon B. Johnson, "Commencement Address at Howard University: 'To Fulfill These Rights'" (speech, Howard University, Washington, D.C., June 4, 1965), www.presidency.ucsb.edu/documents/commencement-address-howard-university-fulfill-these-rights.

18. Ta-Nehisi Coates, *Between the World and Me* (New York: Spiegel & Grau, 2015), 7.

19. William Waller Hening, ed., *The Statutes at Large; Being a Collection of All the Laws of Virginia, from the First Session of the Legislature, in the Year 1619*, vol. 11 (New York: R. & W. & G. Bartow, 1819–23), 170, 260, 266, 270.

20. Rachel L. Swarns, "272 Slaves Were Sold to Save Georgetown. What Does It Owe Their Descendants?," *New York Times*, April 16, 2016, www.nytimes.com/2016/04/17/us/georgetown-university-search-for-slave-descendants.html.

21. Edward E. Baptist, *The Half Has Never Been Told: Slavery and the Making of American Capitalism* (New York: Basic Books, 2014), 254–55.

22. Eric Foner, *The Second Founding: How the Civil War and Reconstruction Remade the Constitution* (New York: Norton, 2019).

23. Robin D. G. Kelley, *Freedom Dreams: The Black Radical Imagination* (Boston: Beacon, 2002), 115.

24. Noah Andre Trudeau, *Southern Storm: Sherman's March to the Sea* (New York: HarperCollins, 2008), 382–83.

25. Ibid., 519–20.

26. William A. Darity, Jr., and A. Kirsten Mullen, *From Here to Equality: Reparations for Black Americans in the Twenty-first Century* (Chapel Hill: University of North Carolina Press, 2020), 157–58.

27. Eric Foner, *Reconstruction: America's Unfinished Revolution, 1863–1877*, updated ed. (New York: HarperPerennial, 2014), 70.

28. Ibid.

29. Ibid., 71.

30. Abraham Lincoln, "Second Inaugural Address" (speech presented in Washington, D.C., April 10, 1865), Library of Congress, www.loc.gov/resource/mal.4361300/?st=text.

31. Henry Louis Gates, Jr., "The Truth Behind '40 Acres and a Mule,'" PBS, 2014, www.pbs.org/wnet/african-americans-many-rivers-to-cross/history/the-truth-behind-40-acres-and-a-mule/.

32. Mary Frances Berry, *My Face Is Black Is True: Callie House and the Struggle for Ex-Slave Reparations* (New York: Random House, 2005), 39.

33. Ibid., 51.

34. Ibid., 176.

35. Ibid., 178.

36. Ibid., 179.

37. Ibid., 180–83.

38. Ibid., 184.

39. Ibid., 186–87.

40. Ibid., 235.

41. Darity and Mullen, *From Here to Equality*, 13.

42. Malcolm X, "The Race Problem" (speech presented to the African Students Association and the NAACP Campus Chapter, Michigan State University, East Lansing, January 23, 1963), onthebanks.msu.edu/Object/162-565-2359/malcolm-x-speaks-at-michigan-state-university-1963/.

43. N'COBRA, "We Are the National Coalition of Blacks for Reparations in America (N'COBRA)," www.ncobraonline.org/leadership/.

44. DeNeen L. Brown, "Reparations Bill for Tulsa Race Massacre Survivors Introduced in Congress," *Washington Post,* May 21, 2021, www.washingtonpost.com/history/2021/05/21/tulsa -massacre-reparations-bill/.

45. "US: Failed Justice 100 Years After Tulsa Race Massacre," Human Rights Watch, May 21, 2021, www.hrw.org/news/2021/05/21/us-failed-justice-100-years-after-tulsa-race-massacre.

46. Federal Writers' Project, *Born in Slavery: Slave Narratives from the Federal Writers' Project, 1936 to 1938* (Washington, D.C.: Library of Congress, 1941).

47. Keri Leigh Merritt, "Land and the Roots of African-American Poverty," *Aeon,* March 11, 2016, aeon.co/ideas/land-and-the-roots-of-african-american-poverty.

48. Frederick Douglass, *The Life and Times of Frederick Douglass* (Boston: De Wolfe, Fiske, 1892), 613, docsouth.unc.edu/neh/dougl92/dougl92.html.

49. Trina Williams Shanks, "The Homestead Act: A Major Asset-Building Policy in American History," Center for Social Development, Working Paper 00-9 (2000): 8.

50. Merritt, "Land and the Roots of African-American Poverty."

51. Douglas A. Blackmon, *Slavery by Another Name: The Re-Enslavement of Black Americans from the Civil War to World War II* (New York: Anchor, 2008).

52. Equal Justice Initiative, *Reconstruction in America: Racial Violence After the Civil War* (Montgomery, Ala.: Equal Justice Initiative, 2020), eji.org/reports/reconstruction-in-america-overview/.

53. Julie Tate, Jennifer Jenkins, and Steven Rich, "Fatal Force," *Washington Post,* June 18, 2021, www.washingtonpost.com/graphics/investigations/police-shootings-database/.

54. Brent Staples, "The Burning of Black Wall Street, Revisited," *New York Times,* June 19, 2020, www.nytimes.com/2020/06/19/opinion/tulsa-race-riot-massacre-graves.html.

55. University of Maryland Libraries, "A House Divided: African American Workers Struggle Against Segregation," *African-American's Rights* (exhibit), exhibitions.lib.umd.edu/unions/ social/african-americans-rights.

56. Crystal R. Sanders, "Katherine Johnson Should Also Be Remembered for Desegregating Higher Education," *Washington Post,* February 25, 2020, www.washingtonpost.com/outlook/2020/ 02/25/katherine-johnson-should-also-be-remembered-desegregating-higher-education/.

57. George Lipsitz, *The Possessive Investment in Whiteness: How White People Profit from Identity Politics* (Philadelphia: Temple University Press, 1998), 6.

58. Ira Katznelson, *When Affirmative Action Was White: An Untold History of Racial Inequality in Twentieth-Century America* (New York: Norton, 2006), 23, 18.

59. Erica Frankenberg, Jongyeon Ee, Jennifer B. Ayscue, and Gary Orfield, *Harming Our Common Future: America's Segregated Schools 65 Years After Brown* (Los Angeles: Civil Rights Project, May 10, 2019), 7, escholarship.org/uc/item/23j1b9nv.

60. James D. Anderson, *The Education of Blacks in the South, 1860–1935* (Chapel Hill: University of North Carolina Press, 1988).

61. Bruce Mitchell, and Juan Franco, *HOLC "Redlining" Maps: The Persistent Structure of Segregation and Economic Inequality* (Washington, D.C.: NCRC, March 2018), 4–6, ncrc.org/holc/.

62. Kraus et al., "Misperception of Racial Economic Inequality," 900.

63. Ed Pilkington, "The Day Police Bombed a City Street: Can Scars of 1985 MOVE Atrocity Be Healed?" *Guardian,* May 10, 2020, www.theguardian.com/us-news/2020/may/10/move-1985 -bombing-reconciliation-philadelphia.

64. Kraus et al., "Misperception of Racial Economic Inequality," 900.

65. Martin Luther King, Jr., "I Have a Dream" (speech presented at the March on Washington for Jobs and Freedom, Washington, D.C., August 28, 1963), www.npr.org/2010/01/18/ 122701268/i-have-a-dream-speech-in-its-entirety.

66. Martin Luther King, Jr., "The Three Evils" (speech presented at the Hungry Club Forum, Atlanta, Ga., May 10, 1967), www.theatlantic.com/magazine/archive/2018/02/martin-luther-king-hungry-club-forum/552533/.

67. Michael K. Honey, *Going Down Jericho Road: The Memphis Strike, Martin Luther King's Last Campaign* (New York: Norton, 2007), 300.

68. Moritz Kuhn, Moritz Schularick, and Ulrike I. Steins, "Income and Wealth Inequality in America, 1949–2016," *Journal of Political Economy* 128, no. 9 (September 2020): 3469–519.

69. Kraus et al., "Misperception of Racial Economic Inequality," 911–12.

70. Ibid., 907.

71. William Darity, Jr., Darrick Hamilton, Mark Paul, Alan Aja, Anne Price, Antonio Moore, and Caterina Chiopris, *What We Get Wrong About Closing the Racial Wealth Gap* (Durham, N.C.: Duke University, April 2018).

72. Ibid., 9.

73. Ibid., 7.

74. Ibid., 7.

75. Ibid., 6.

76. Ibid., 14.

77. Author interview with William Darity, Jr., New York, June 2020.

78. Darity et al., *What We Get Wrong About Closing the Racial Wealth Gap,* 3–4.

79. Author interview with William Darity, Jr., New York, June 2020.

80. *Congressional Record,* 116th Congress, 1st Session, 1-424 (2019), 19.

81. Richard E. Neal, press release in recognition of Holocaust Remembrance Day, April 12, 2018, neal.house.gov/media-center/press-releases/statement-congressman-richard-neal-holocaust-remembrance-day.

82. Commission to Study and Develop Reparation Proposals for African-Americans Act, H.R. 40, 117th Congress, April 14, 2021, www.congress.gov/bill/117th-congress/house-bill/40/all-info.

83. Darity and Mullen, *From Here to Equality,* 243.

84. W.E.B. Du Bois, *The Souls of Black Folk: Essays and Sketches* (Chicago: A. C. McClurg, 1903), 1–2.

85. Ibid., 253–54.

CONTRIBUTORS

Nikole Hannah-Jones is a staff writer at *The New York Times Magazine* and the Knight Chair in Race and Journalism at Howard University. She is the founder of the Howard University Center for Journalism and Democracy, and the co-founder of the Ida B. Wells Society for Investigative Reporting. She reports on racial injustice and was named a MacArthur Fellow in 2017 for her work on the persistence of racial segregation in the United States, particularly in schools. Her journalism has earned two George Polk Awards, a Peabody, three National Magazine Awards, and the 2020 Pulitzer Prize for Commentary. In 2021, she was elected a member of the American Academy of Arts & Sciences.

Caitlin Roper is the executive producer for scripted projects at *The New York Times*. She was previously the special projects editor for *The New York Times Magazine*, creating *The New York Times for Kids*, among other special sections. Before joining the *Times*, she was an editor at *Wired* and *The Paris Review*.

Ilena Silverman is the features editor of *The New York Times Magazine* and the primary editor for the essays in this book. Over the course of her career, the journalism she edited has won several National Magazine Awards and the Pulitzer Prize.

Jake Silverstein is the editor in chief of *The New York Times Magazine*. He edited the essays in this book as well as the fiction and poetry. During his tenure, the magazine has won eleven National Magazine Awards and two Pulitzer Prizes.

Essays

Leslie Alexander is a professor of history and African American studies at Arizona State University. She is the author of *African or American? Black Identity and Political Activism in New York City, 1784–1861* and *Fear of a Black Republic: How Haitian Independence Inspired the Birth of Black Internationalism* (forthcoming in 2022), for which she was awarded a Ford Foundation Senior Fellowship. Her current research explores the history of policing during the era of slavery.

Michelle Alexander is a civil rights lawyer, a legal scholar, and the author of *The New Jim Crow: Mass Incarceration in the Age of Colorblindness*, which shifted the national discourse on the U.S. criminal justice system. She is a former associate professor of law at Stanford Law School and Ohio State University, and her writing has been featured in *The New York Times, The Washington Post, The Nation,* and other outlets. She is currently a visiting professor of social justice at Union Theological Seminary in New York City.

Carol Anderson is a historian, author, and professor of African American studies at Emory University. Her research focuses on public policy with regards to race, justice, and equality. Her book *The Second: Race and Guns in a Fatally Unequal America* was published in June 2021. She also wrote *White Rage: The Unspoken Truth of Our Racial Divide* and *One Person, No Vote: How Voter Suppression Is Destroying Our Democracy,* which have won several awards and received critical acclaim. She was awarded a Guggenheim Fellowship in 2018.

Jamelle Bouie is a journalist, writer, and political analyst. Currently a columnist for *The New York Times* and an analyst for CBS News, he was previously the chief political correspondent for *Slate* magazine. He writes extensively about national politics, race, and public policy.

Anthea Butler is a professor of religious studies and Africana studies at the University of Pennsylvania. Her research focuses on race, religion, and politics. She received a Luce/ACLS Fellowship in Religion, Journalism and

International Affairs in 2018. A contributor to *MSNBC Daily*, she has written for *The Washington Post*, CNN, and other national outlets.

Matthew Desmond is a professor of sociology at Princeton University and a contributing writer for *The New York Times Magazine*. His work focuses on the intersection of race, poverty, and public policy in the United States. He received a MacArthur Fellowship in 2015 for his work on the American housing crisis and won the 2017 Pulitzer Prize for General Nonfiction for his book *Evicted: Poverty and Profit in the American City*.

Jeneen Interlandi is a staff writer at *The New York Times Magazine* and a member of the *New York Times* editorial board. She primarily covers public health, bioethics, and healthcare policy, and was a Nieman Fellow at Harvard University in 2013.

Martha S. Jones is a professor of history at Johns Hopkins University, where her research examines how Black Americans have shaped U.S. democracy. She is the prize-winning author of *Birthright Citizens: A History of Race and Rights in Antebellum America* and *Vanguard: How Black Women Broke Barriers, Won the Vote, and Insisted on Equality for All*. She has written for *The New York Times*, *The Washington Post*, *The Atlantic*, *Time*, and *Politico*.

Ibram X. Kendi is the Andrew W. Mellon Professor in the Humanities and the director of the Center for Antiracist Research at Boston University. His book *Stamped from the Beginning* won the National Book Award for Nonfiction in 2016. He received a Guggenheim Fellowship in 2019, and both his book *How to Be an Antiracist* and *Four Hundred Souls: A Community History of African America, 1619–2019*, which he coedited, are national bestsellers.

Kevin M. Kruse is a professor of history at Princeton University. He specializes in the political, social, and urban history of twentieth-century America, with a particular interest in conflicts over race, rights, and

religion. His book *White Flight: Atlanta and the Making of Modern Conservatism* won awards from the Southern Historical Association and the American Political Science Association, and he received a Guggenheim Fellowship in 2019.

Trymaine Lee is a journalist and correspondent for MSNBC, where he covers race, violence, and law enforcement in the United States. He is the host of the podcast *Into America* and has reported for *The New York Times*, *HuffPost*, and the New Orleans *Times-Picayune*. He worked on teams that won the Pulitzer Prize for Breaking News Reporting in both 2006 and 2009, and he won an Emmy Award in 2018 for news analysis.

Tiya Miles is a professor of history at Harvard University whose work explores the intersections of African American, Native American, and women's histories. She is the author of three prize-winning histories on early American race relations, including *The Dawn of Detroit: A Chronicle of Slavery and Freedom in the City of the Straits*. She was awarded a MacArthur Fellowship in 2011 for her work on the complex interrelationships between enslaved Africans and the Cherokee people in colonial America.

Wesley Morris is a staff writer at *The New York Times Magazine* and a critic at large for *The New York Times*. He covers culture, film, and music, and is a co-host of the podcast *Still Processing*. He is the only person ever to be awarded the Pulitzer Prize for Criticism twice, winning first in 2012 for his culture writing at *The Boston Globe* and again in 2021 for a set of essays at *The New York Times* exploring the intersection of race and pop culture.

Khalil Gibran Muhammad is a professor of history, race, and public policy at Harvard Kennedy School whose research examines race, the construction of criminality, and the origins of the carceral state in the United States. His book *The Condemnation of Blackness: Race, Crime, and the Making of Modern Urban America* won the 2011 John

Hope Franklin Prize, and his scholarship has appeared widely in national print and broadcast media. He is the former director of the Schomburg Center for Research in Black Culture.

Dorothy Roberts is a professor of law, sociology, and Africana studies at the University of Pennsylvania. Her scholarship and activism are centered on the interplay of gender, race, and class in legal and social-justice issues. The award-winning author of *Killing the Black Body* and *Shattered Bonds,* she is an expert on reproductive justice, bioethics, and child welfare.

Bryan Stevenson is a lawyer, a professor, and the founder of the Equal Justice Initiative (EJI), an organization that fights to eliminate excessive sentencing and wrongful incarcerations. He has argued and won multiple cases in the U.S. Supreme Court and is the author of the critically acclaimed book *Just Mercy: A Story of Justice and Redemption.* Through EJI, he established the Legacy Museum and the National Memorial for Peace and Justice in Montgomery, Alabama, which honors thousands of African Americans lynched in the United States from 1877 to 1950.

Linda Villarosa is a journalist, educator, and contributing writer for *The New York Times Magazine,* where she covers the intersection of health, medicine, and social justice. She is currently a journalist in residence at the Craig Newmark Graduate School of Journalism at CUNY and also teaches journalism and Black studies at the City College of New York in Harlem. She was an executive editor of *Essence* magazine.

Photographs

Kimberly Annece Henderson is a writer and curator based in New York City. Her work centers on genealogy and Black American lineages through photography, historical preservation, and archives. She currently facilitates digital projects for the Schomburg Center for Research in Black Culture and is the creator and curator of @emalineandthem, an archival photo collection on Instagram of everyday Black Americans from the late 1800s and early 1900s.

Literary Timeline

Joshua Bennett is an assistant professor of English and creative writing at Dartmouth College. He is the author of three books of poetry and literary criticism: *The Sobbing School, Owed,* and *Being Property Once Myself.* Bennett's writing has been published in *The Best American Poetry, The New York Times Magazine,* and *The Paris Review.* In 2021, he received a Guggenheim Fellowship and a Whiting Award for poetry and nonfiction.

Reginald Dwayne Betts is currently the poetry editor of *The New York Times Magazine.* He is a lawyer, writer, and poet. Betts is the author of four books and has been published in *The New York Times, Time,* and *The Washington Post.* In 2018, he received a Guggenheim Fellowship, and his collection *Felon: Poems* was the recipient of the 2020 NAACP Image Award for Outstanding Literary Work.

Rita Dove is a poet, essayist, and editor, and the Henry Hoyns Professor of Creative Writing at the University of Virginia. She served as the poet laureate of the United States from 1993 to 1995. Just forty years old at the time of her appointment, she was the youngest person and the first Black poet ever to hold the title. She won the Pulitzer Prize for Poetry in 1987 for her verse-novel *Thomas and Beulah,* was awarded the National Humanities Medal in 1996, and received a 2011 National Medal of Arts.

Camille T. Dungy is a poet, writer, editor, and a University Distinguished Professor in the Department of English at Colorado State University. She is the author of four collections of poetry, most recently *Trophic Cascade;* her poems and essays have appeared in *The Best American Poetry, The Best American*

Travel Writing, Poetry magazine, *The American Poetry Review, VQR, Guernica, The 100 Best African American Poems,* and nearly thirty other anthologies and journals. She was awarded a Guggenheim Fellowship in 2019.

Cornelius Eady is a poet, author, and professor. He has published eight volumes of poetry, among them *Victims of the Latest Dance Craze,* which won the 1985 Lamont Poetry Prize. He is a co-founder of Cave Canem Foundation, an organization that supports Black poets through a summer retreat, regional workshops, anthologies, and more. He was awarded a Guggenheim Fellowship in 1993 and has taught poetry at several institutions, most recently the University of Tennessee, Knoxville, where he holds the John C. Hodges Chair of Excellence.

Eve L. Ewing is a writer and scholar from Chicago. She is the award-winning author of two poetry collections, *Electric Arches* and *1919;* the nonfiction work *Ghosts in the Schoolyard: Racism and School Closings on Chicago's South Side;* and the novel for young readers *Maya and the Robot.* She is a professor at the University of Chicago.

Nikky Finney is a poet and professor of English language and literature at the University of South Carolina. She has written several books, including *Head Off & Split,* which was awarded the 2011 National Book Award for Poetry. Her most recent collection, *Love Child's Hotbed of Occasional Poetry: Poems and Artifacts,* was a finalist for the 2020 Los Angeles Times Book Prize for Poetry. In 2020, she won the Wallace Stevens Award for lifetime achievement from the Academy of American Poets.

Vievee Francis is a poet, author, editor, and associate professor of English and creative writing at Dartmouth College. She has published three collections of poetry: *Blue-Tail Fly, Horse in the Dark,* and *Forest Primeval,* which won the Kingsley Tufts Poetry Award and the 2016 Hurston/Wright Legacy Award for Poetry. She currently serves as an editor for *Callaloo.*

Yaa Gyasi is a novelist, the author of *Homegoing* and *Transcendent Kingdom.* Among other honors, she has received the National Book Critics Circle's John Leonard Prize and the PEN/Hemingway Award for Debut Novel. Born in Ghana and raised in Alabama, she is a graduate of Stanford University and the Iowa Writers' Workshop.

Forrest Hamer is a poet and a psychoanalyst. He is the author of several books of poetry, including *Call & Response,* which won the 1995 Beatrice Hawley Award. Hamer's poems have been published in *The American Poetry Review,* the *Beloit Poetry Journal,* the *Kenyon Review, Callaloo, Zyzzyva,* and other journals. He has taught psychology and social welfare at the University of California, Berkeley.

Terrance Hayes is a poet, author, and educator. He has published seven poetry collections, including *Lighthead,* which won the National Book Award for Poetry in 2010. He is a professor of creative writing at New York University, and his work has appeared in *The New Yorker, The American Poetry Review,* the *Kenyon Review,* and *Poetry* magazine. He received a Guggenheim Fellowship in 2009 and was named a MacArthur Fellow in 2014.

Honorée Fanonne Jeffers is a poet, novelist, essayist, and professor of English at the University of Oklahoma. She has authored five collections of poetry and a novel, *The Love Songs of W.E.B. Du Bois.* Her book *The Age of Phillis,* a reexamination of the life of the American poet Phillis Wheatley Peters based on fifteen years of archival research, was long-listed for the 2020 National Book Award for Poetry and won the 2021 NAACP Image Award for Poetry. She is the recipient of a 2021 USA Fellowship.

Barry Jenkins is a film director, producer, and screenwriter. He directed and co-wrote the film *Moonlight,* which won the 2017 Academy Award for Best Picture. For his work on *Moonlight,* he also received the Academy Award for Best Adapted Screenplay, along with Tarell Alvin McCraney. He wrote and directed a 2018 film adaptation of James

Baldwin's *If Beale Street Could Talk*, and in 2021, he directed a television adaptation of Colson Whitehead's novel *The Underground Railroad*.

Tyehimba Jess is a poet, editor, and assistant professor of English at the College of Staten Island. He has published two books, *leadbelly* and *Olio*, which received the 2017 Pulitzer Prize for Poetry. He is a former poetry and fiction editor at *African American Review*, was awarded the Whiting Award in 2006, and won a 2016 Lannan Literary Award for Poetry. He received a Guggenheim Fellowship in 2018.

Robert Jones, Jr., is a writer, novelist, and activist. He created the blog *Son of Baldwin* in 2008, both as homage to James Baldwin and to engage in critical analysis from a Black queer perspective. His novel *The Prophets* was published in 2021, and he has been featured in *The New York Times, Essence,* and *The Paris Review,* as well as on the Grio and WNYC.

A. Van Jordan is a poet, author, and professor of English language and literature at the University of Michigan. He has published four poetry collections: *Rise, M-A-C-N-O-L-I-A, Quantum Lyrics,* and *The Cineaste*. His work has received numerous honors, including a Whiting Award in Poetry, the Anisfield-Wolf Book Award, a Pushcart Prize, and a Guggenheim Fellowship in 2007. In 2015, he won the Lannan Literary Award for Poetry.

Yusef Komunyakaa is a poet, author, and educator. He has published twenty poetry collections and books, including *Neon Vernacular*, which won the 1994 Pulitzer Prize for Poetry. He served as a chancellor of the Academy of American Poets from 1999 to 2005 and has taught at many institutions, including the University of New Orleans, Indiana University, and Princeton University. He retired in 2021 as Distinguished Senior Poet in New York University's graduate creative writing program.

Kiese Laymon is a writer, novelist, and professor of English and creative writing at the University of Mississippi. He is the author of the novel *Long Division,* a book of essays

called *How to Slowly Kill Yourself and Others in America,* and *Heavy: An American Memoir,* which won the 2019 Andrew Carnegie Medal for Excellence in Nonfiction. His work has been published by many journals, websites, and anthologies, including *The New York Times, Esquire,* ESPN.com, Colorlines, NPR, and *Guernica.*

Jasmine Mans is a poet, author, and artist. She has published two books of poetry: *Chalk Outlines of Snow Angels* and *Black Girl, Call Home*. She creates her work in multiple mediums and is known for her audio, visual, and performance poetry. Mans has worked with the Strivers' Row collective and is the resident poet at the Newark Public Library.

Terry McMillan is a novelist and short story writer. She is the author of nearly a dozen books; her debut novel, *Mama,* won the Doubleday New Voices in Fiction Award in 1986. Many of her novels, including *Waiting to Exhale* and *How Stella Got Her Groove Back,* were made into films that became box office successes. She was awarded an *Essence* Lifetime Achievement Award in 2008.

Lynn Nottage is a playwright, screenwriter, and producer and an associate professor of theater at Columbia University School of the Arts. She won the 2009 Pulitzer Prize for Drama for her play *Ruined,* and then received the Pulitzer again in 2017 for her play *Sweat*. She is the only woman to have won the prize twice. She has received a number of other honors, including a Guggenheim Fellowship in 2005, a MacArthur Fellowship in 2007, and the Steinberg Distinguished Playwright Award in 2010.

ZZ Packer is a writer and educator. She is the author of the story collection *Drinking Coffee Elsewhere;* her fiction has appeared in *The New Yorker, Harper's Magazine, The Guardian, Ploughshares,* and *The Best American Short Stories*. Her nonfiction has appeared in *The New York Times Magazine, The New York Times Book Review,* and *The American Prospect*. She has received numerous honors, including a Whiting Award in Fiction in 1999 and a

Guggenheim Fellowship in 2005. She has taught creative writing at several institutions, including Hunter College, MIT, and San Francisco State University.

Gregory Pardlo is a poet, writer, editor, translator, and educator. He is the author of *Totem, Digest,* and *Air Traffic,* a memoir in essays. He received the Pulitzer Prize for Poetry in 2015 for *Digest* and has been awarded fellowships from the Dorothy and Lewis B. Cullman Center for Scholars and Writers of the New York Public Library, the Guggenheim Foundation, and the New York Foundation for the Arts, among others. He is currently the poetry editor for *VQR* and serves as co-director of the Camden campus of the Institute for the Study of Global Racial Justice at Rutgers University.

Darryl Pinckney is a longtime contributor to *The New York Review of Books.* He is the author of two novels, *High Cotton* and *Black Deutschland,* and three works of nonfiction: *Out There: Mavericks of Black Literature, Blackballed: The Black Vote and U.S. Democracy,* and *Busted in New York and Other Essays.* For more than thirty years, he has collaborated on works for the theater with Robert Wilson. A recipient of Guggenheim and Hodder Fellowships, he has won a Whiting Award and been a recipient of the Harold D. Vursell Memorial Award from the American Academy of Arts and Letters.

Claudia Rankine is a poet, editor, writer, playwright, and professor of poetry at Yale University. She is the author of six collections of poetry, including *Citizen: An American Lyric,* which won the 2014 National Book Critics Circle Award for poetry. Her writing has appeared in *The New York Times Magazine, The New York Times, The Guardian, New York* magazine, and *Vogue,* among other publications. She has received numerous honors, including the Jackson Poetry Prize in 2014, a MacArthur Fellowship in 2016, and a Guggenheim Fellowship in 2017.

Jason Reynolds is a poet, writer, and novelist. He writes primarily for young adults and is the author of more than a dozen books, including *Stamped,* his collaboration with Ibram X. Kendi, and *Look Both Ways,* which was a finalist for the 2019 National Book Award for Young People's Literature. His 2018 book *Long Way Down* received a John Newbery silver honor, a Michael L. Printz Honor award, and a Coretta Scott King Honor award. He currently teaches creative writing at Lesley University.

Sonia Sanchez is a poet, writer, playwright, professor, and activist. She was a leading figure of the Black Arts Movement during the 1960s and '70s. Sanchez is the author of more than a dozen books of poetry, plays, and short stories, as well as works for children. She has lectured at more than five hundred universities and colleges in the United States, and in 1977 she became the first Presidential Fellow at Temple University, where she was a professor of English and women's studies until her retirement in 1999. In 2001, she was awarded the Frost Medal for her lifetime contributions to the canon of American poetry.

Tim Seibles is a poet, author, and educator. He has published several collections of poetry, including *Body Moves, Hurdy-Gurdy, Hammerlock, Buffalo Head Solos, One Turn Around the Sun,* and *Fast Animal,* which won the Theodore Roethke Memorial Poetry Prize. His work has appeared in *Callaloo,* the *Kenyon Review, Ploughshares,* and *Rattle,* and he served as the poet laureate of Virginia from 2016 to 2018. He was a professor of English at Old Dominion University until he retired, in 2019.

Evie Shockley is a poet and scholar. She is the author, most recently, of *semiautomatic,* which won the 2018 Hurston/Wright Legacy Award and was a finalist for the 2018 Pulitzer Prize for Poetry. Her other books include *a half-red sea, the new black,* and *Renegade Poetics: Black Aesthetics and Formal Innovation in African American Poetry.* She was the recipient of the 2019 Lannan Literary Award for Poetry, among other honors. She is a professor of English at Rutgers University–New Brunswick and is the poetry editor at *Contemporary Literature.*

Clint Smith is a poet and writer of nonfiction. A staff writer at *The Atlantic,* he has also published work in *The New Yorker, The New York Times Magazine, The New Republic, Poetry* magazine, and *The Paris Review.* In 2017, his poetry collection *Counting Descent* was a finalist for an NAACP Image Award. His book *How the Word Is Passed: A Reckoning with the History of Slavery Across America* was published in 2021.

Danez Smith is a poet, writer, and performer. They are the author of four books: *Homie, hands on ya knees, [insert] Boy,* and *Don't Call Us Dead,* which was a finalist for the 2017 National Book Award. Their writing has appeared in *Poetry* magazine, *Ploughshares,* the *Beloit Poetry Journal,* and *Kinfolk,* and they are the winner of a Pushcart Prize. They are a co-host of the Poetry Foundation's podcast *VS,* and a founding member of the multigenre, multicultural Dark Noise collective.

Patricia Smith is a poet, writer, playwright, performance artist, and professor of English at the College of Staten Island. She is the author of eight books of poetry, including *Incendiary Art,* which was a finalist for the 2018 Pulitzer Prize for Poetry. Her work has appeared in *The New York Times, The Washington Post, Poetry* magazine, *The Paris Review,* and other outlets. She received a Guggenheim Fellowship in 2014 and is a four-time individual champion of the National Poetry Slam, making her the most successful poet in the competition's history.

Tracy K. Smith is a poet, writer, editor, and professor of English and of African and African American studies at Harvard University. She is the author of five books of poetry: *Such Color: New and Selected Poems, The Body's Question, Duende, Wade in the Water,*

and *Life on Mars,* which won the 2012 Pulitzer Prize for Poetry. Her memoir *Ordinary Light* was a finalist for the National Book Award for Nonfiction. She served as poet laureate of the United States from 2017 to 2019.

Nafissa Thompson-Spires is a poet, writer, and assistant professor of literatures in English at Cornell University. She is the author of the short story collection *Heads of the Colored People,* which won the 2019 PEN Open Book Award, the Hurston/Wright Legacy Award for Fiction, and a Whiting Award in Fiction. It also was long-listed for the National Book Award in 2018. Her work has appeared in *The Paris Review*'s *Daily, Dissent, The Root, StoryQuarterly, Lunch Ticket,* and other publications.

Natasha Trethewey is a poet, writer, and professor of English at Northwestern University. She is the author of several books, including *Native Guard,* which received the Pulitzer Prize for Poetry in 2007. She has served as the poet laureate of Mississippi and was appointed poet laureate of the United States, serving from 2012 to 2014. She received a Guggenheim Fellowship in 2003 and was awarded the Rebekah Johnson Bobbitt National Prize for Poetry from the Library of Congress in 2020.

Jesmyn Ward is a writer, editor, novelist, and professor of English at Tulane University, where she teaches creative writing. She is the author of *Where the Line Bleeds; Men We Reaped: A Memoir; Salvage the Bones,* which won the National Book Award for Fiction in 2011; and *Sing, Unburied, Sing,* which won the National Book Award for Fiction in 2017. She is the only woman and only Black person to have won the award twice. She is also the editor of the anthology *The Fire This Time* and received a MacArthur Fellowship in 2017.

CREDITS

Page 3: "The White Lion" by Claudia Rankine © 2020 by Claudia Rankine

Page 39: "Daughters of Azimuth" by Nikky Finney © 2020 by Nikky Finney

Page 43: "Loving Me" by Vievee Francis © 2020 by Vievee Francis

Page 45: "Race" by Dorothy Roberts © 2020 by Dorothy Roberts

Page 63: "Conjured" by Honorée Fanonne Jeffers © 2020 by Honorée Fanonne Jeffers

Page 67: "A Ghazalled Sentence After 'My People . . . Hold On' by Eddie Kendricks and the Negro Act of 1740" by Terrance Hayes © 2020 by Terrance Hayes

Page 71: "Sugar" by Khalil Gibran Muhammad © 2019, 2021 by Khalil Gibran Muhammad

Page 89: "First to Rise" by Yusef Komunyakaa © 2019 by Yusef Komunyakaa

Page 93: "proof [dear Phillis]" by Eve L. Ewing © 2019 by Eve L. Ewing

Page 97: "Fear" by Leslie M. Alexander and Michelle Alexander © 2020 by Leslie M. Alexander and Michelle Alexander

Page 125: "Freedom Is Not for Myself Alone" by Robert Jones, Jr. © 2021 by Robert Jones, Jr.

Page 129: "Other Persons" by Reginald Dwayne Betts © 2020 by Reginald Dwayne Betts

Page 135: "Dispossession" by Tiya Miles © 2020 by Tiya Miles

Page 157: "Trouble the Water" by Barry Jenkins © 2019 by Barry Jenkins

Page 161: "Sold South" by Jesmyn Ward © 2019 by Jesmyn Ward

Page 165: "Capitalism" by Matthew Desmond © 2019, 2021 by Matthew Desmond

Page 187: "Fort Mose" by Tyehimba Jess © 2019 by Tyehimba Jess

Page 191: "Before His Execution" by Tim Seibles © 2020 by Tim Seibles

Page 211: "We as People" by Cornelius Eady © 2021 by Cornelius Eady

Page 215: "A Letter to Harriet Hayden" by Lynn Nottage © 2019 by Lynn Nottage

Page 219: "Citizenship" by Martha S. Jones © 2020 by Martha S. Jones

Page 239: "The Camp" by Darryl Pinckney © 2019 by Darryl Pinckney

Page 245: "An Absolute Massacre" by ZZ Packer © 2019 by ZZ Packer

Page 249: "Self-Defense" by Carol Anderson © 2020 by Carol Anderson

Page 269: "Like to the Rushing of a Mighty Wind" by Tracy K. Smith © 2020 by Tracy K. Smith

Page 273: "no car for colored [ ] ladies (or, miss wells goes off [on] the rails)" by Evie Shockley © 2020 by Evie Shockley

Page 275: "Punishment" by Bryan Stevenson © 2019, 2021 by Bryan Stevenson

Page 285: "Race Riot" by Forrest Hamer © 2020 by Forrest Hamer

Page 289: "Greenwood" by Jasmine Mans © 2020 by Jasmine Mans

Page 293: "Inheritance" by Trymaine Lee © 2019, 2020 by Trymaine Lee

Page 307: "The New Negro" by A. Van Jordan © 2020 by A. Van Jordan

Page 311: "Bad Blood" by Yaa Gyasi © 2019 by Yaa Gyasi

Page 325: "1955" by Danez Smith © 2021 by "Danez Smith"

Page 329: "From Behind the Counter" by Terry McMillan © 2021 by Terry McMillan

Page 335: "Church" by Anthea Butler © 2020 by Anthea Butler

Page 355: "Youth Sunday" by Rita Dove © 2019 by Rita Dove

Page 356: "On ''Brevity'''" by Camille T. Dungy © 2019 by Camille T. Dungy

Page 381: "Quotidian" by Natasha Trethewey © 2020 by Natasha Trethewey

Page 385: "The Panther Is a Virtual Animal" by Joshua Bennett © 2019 by Joshua Bennett

Page 397: "Unbought, Unbossed, and Unbothered" by Nafissa Thompson-Spires © 2020 by Nafissa Thompson-Spires

Page 401: "Crazy When You Smile" by Patricia Smith © 2021 by Patricia Smith

CREDITS

Page 405: "Traffic" by Kevin M. Kruse © 2019, 2021 by Kevin M. Kruse
Page 413: "Rainbows Aren't Real, Are They?" by Kiese Laymon © 2019 by Kiese Laymon
Page 417: "A Surname to Honor Their Mother" by Gregory Pardlo © 2021 by Gregory Pardlo
Page 421: "Progress" by Ibram X. Kendi © 2020 by Ibram X. Kendi
Page 443: "At the Superdome After the Storm Has Passed" by Clint Smith © 2019 by Clint Smith
Page 447: "Mother and Son" by Jason Reynolds © 2020 by Jason Reynolds
Page 479: "Progress Report" by Sonia Sanchez © 2020 by Sonia Sanchez

Photo Credits

Democracy (page 6): Courtesy of Nikole Hannah-Jones

Race (page 44): Randolph Linsly Simpson African-American Collection. Yale Collection of American Literature, Beinecke Rare Book and Manuscript Library

Sugar (page 70): Mario Tama/Getty Images

Fear (page 96): Jamel Shabazz

Dispossession (page 134): Wisconsin Historical Society, WHS-60687

Capitalism (page 164): Holsinger Studio Collection, Albert and Shirley Small Special Collections Library, University of Virginia

Politics (page 194): Division of Work and Industry, National Museum of American History, Smithsonian Institution

Citizenship (page 218): Eli Reed/Magnum Photos

Self-Defense (page 248): Library of Congress, Prints and Photographs Division, Alfred Bendiner Memorial Collection, LC-DIG-ppmsca-11524

Punishment (page 274): Library of Congress, Prints and Photographs Division, Alfred Bendiner Memorial Collection, LC-DIG-ppmsca-11196

Inheritance (page 292): Courtesy of Josephine Bolling McCall

Medicine (page 314): Maya Iman

Church (page 334): Ming Smith

Music (page 358): Collection of the Smithsonian National Museum of African American History and Culture, © Smithsonian National Museum of African American History and Culture, 2007.1.69.6.8.D.

Healthcare (page 386): Library of Congress, Prints & Photographs Division, FSA/OWI Collection, LC-USW38- 000316-D

Traffic (page 404): Jorge Sigala

Progress (page 420): Michael A. McCoy

Justice (page 450): Randolph Linsly Simpson African-American Collection. Yale Collection of American Literature, Beinecke Rare Book and Manuscript Library

INDEX